Fauquier County [Virginia] Tombstone Inscriptions

Volumes 1 and 2

Nancy Baird
Carol Jordan
and Joseph Scherer

Heritage Books, Inc.

Published 2000 by

HERITAGE BOOKS, INC.
1540E Pointer Ridge Place
Bowie, Maryland 20716
1-800-398-7709
www.heritagebooks.com

ISBN 0-7884-1626-X

PREFACE

When John Jennings was Director of the Virginia Historical Society, he wrote an article for their magazine on his concerns about the disappearance of cemeteries. He would like to see all the tombstone inscriptions in the state recorded before they vanished. I knew that here in Fauquier County livestock were a destroyer of cemetery walls and markers. Some farmers and developers likewise bulldoze them away for their own convenience. Therefore, I decided to undertake the mammoth project. By 1970, I had covered 261 cemeteries and published my findings. Since then I had met Carol Jordan, who had done similar work in the Centreville area. We resurveyed all of the larger cemeteries, adding the new inscriptions of the past twenty years and making corrections to the old ones. In the meantime, we learned of over two hundred more cemeteries, expanding this work to two volumes. There are probably others that may never be found.

Our research started in the northern end of Fauquier County and we generally worked our way south. We would usually enter the cemetery, start on the first row of tombstones, work across it, turn and work back on the second row, turn and go across the third row, etc. This is the order in which the names appear in this work. Our tools were clipboards, chalk, and notebooks of both paper and electronic variety. I tried to record the data within a day or two of the research while fresh in my mind, at first on a typewriter for the initial 1970 publication, and then on a computer in later volumes. If something looked wrong I would recheck the next time we were in the area of that cemetery. Filmmaker Tom Davenport of Delaplane, Virginia, produced a "how to" film in which we demonstrated our techniques for organizations such as the DAR, who wish to do similar research.

The inscriptions in these volumes are just as they appear on the tombstone. Where an inscription is difficult to decipher, we have bracketed it. Data not included on the inscription, but given us that would be helpful is also included in brackets. DAR *(Daughters of the American Revolution)*, SAR *(Sons of the American Revolution)*, UDC *(United Daughters of the Confederacy)*, American Legion markers, and Confederate States of America iron crosses are noted after the inscription. Funeral home marked graves have *"fhm"* in parentheses after the inscription. Many of the inscriptions date back to the early 18th century, the earliest date of death being 1724.

Some inscriptions border on the humorous. The cause of death recorded on the tombstone of one Confederate soldier who seems to have had a fatal sweet tooth leaves one wondering just how much he consumed. It reads "a soldier who ate too much honey and died."

Where there are only fieldstone markers, but we have been able to find out names of persons thus marked, we have noted their name, as this saves the genealogist from looking for a non-existing inscription. With each cemetery we give directions to its location based on the Virginia Highway Department Map of Fauquier. We have given the distinctive features of the cemetery to help others more easily locate it. Cemeteries that exclusively hold the remains of black families are so designated in the name of the cemetery.

A special list has been included in Volume 2 of known Civil War soldiers buried in Fauquier County cemeteries. This list was compiled by Carol Jordan using many different sources. Lists of Revolutionary War soldiers buried in Fauquier County cemeteries and Civil War soldiers buried at the Confederate Memorial Wall in Warrenton Cemetery are also included in Volume 2. We are very grateful to Robert E. Smith, of Carpenterville, Illinois, for the latter. While unsuccessfully researching the medical records of Warrenton Civil War hospitals for his great great-grandfather he discovered the names of the previously unknown soldiers buried at Warrenton Cemetery's Confederate Memorial.

We were assisted in locating graves by military histories of the local units such as *6th Virginia Cavalry* by Michael Musick, the *WPA Cemetery Records, Fauquier, Virginia 1759–1959* by Emily Ramey and John K. Gott, *Years of Anguish* by Emily G. Ramey and John K. Gott, and county maps such as Eugene Scheels' *Map of Fauquier County.*

As a whole, people were helpful in guiding me to cemeteries and in many cases went with me. Some collected the data for me on their cemeteries, when I lived a great distance from them or, like Arthur Grove, who became so interested that after I thought I had finished their area, he found and copied others. I am particularly indebted for their assistance to:

Rev. Charles Allen
Mr. and Mrs. Bryan Ashby
Alvin V. Baird. Jr.
Earl Baltimore
Mrs. Jean Smith Barnes
Mr. Bud Beane
Mrs. Alice Virginia Maddux Bennett
Mr. Harold Berry
Mr. & Mrs. Henry Bierne
Mr. Edward Blanchard
Mrs. Minnie Hall Grant Bolden
Mr. W. W. Bowen
Mrs. Iris Brown
Misses Marthalee & Joanne Browning
Mr. H. Thomas Browning
Mr. W. E. Butler
Miss Alice E. Carter
Mrs. Virginia Jeffries Coles
Ed Cooper
Mrs. Dan Cox
Mrs. Blanche Day
Daniel H. de Butts
Mrs. Gladys Downing Duvall
Mr. Ellsworth Edwards
Mr. Kenneth Eldridge
Mr. Roger Elgin
Miss Clarissa Fleming
James N. Fletcher, Jr.
Mrs. Marvin Grant Gold
Mr. John K. Gott
Mrs. Francis Greene
Preston Greene
Mr. Arthur Grove
Mr. Lloyd Grove
Mr. Walter Grove
Chester Hall
Mr. Laco Halterman
Mr. J. Arnold Helm
John Herrell
Mr. Lloyd Hofer
Mr. Philip R. Holmes

Mr. & Mrs. E. D. Hopkins
Page Howdershell
Mrs. Lucy Steptoe Blackwell McClung Jones
Joe Lawler
Mrs. Allison Lee
Jackie Lee
Richard Mayberry
Miss Molly McCarty
Chilton McDonald
Arthur E. Miller
Moscow Minor
Miss Gladys Neill
Alice C. Nichols
Mr. Meade Palmer
Mr. & Mrs. L. Armistead Pearson
Miss Connie Pearson
Miss Pearle Perry
Mrs. Emily Ramey
Martha H. Robeson
Henry Robinson
Ripley Robinson
Mrs. Ann Rumbaugh
Marilyn Rumpf
Mrs. Alice Russell
Mrs. Leslie Sanders
John Shoemaker
Mrs. Kate Smith
Kathy Smith
Mr. & Mrs. Lewis Smith
Preston Smith
Chas. Sprindle III
Pauline Stewart
Mrs. Elizabeth A. Tharpe
Mr. & Mrs. George Richard Thompson, Sr.
Alice Tines
Mrs. Chas. Tompkins
Reginald Vickers
Harold Williams
Jackson Williams
Mrs. Ells Downey White
Miss Gladys Winfield

I wish to express my special appreciation to Kathy and Joe Scherer, Phyllis Scott, and Katherine Taylor for their help in entering data on the computer. Phyllis also helped in rechecking the Warrenton Cemetery and locating others. Joe Scherer spent many hours scanning information from the 1970 edition and also did the page design and layout of subsequent editions.

Nancy Chappelear Baird

Contents

CONTENTS

CONTENTS

CONTENTS

Contents

Contents

Contents

CONTENTS

CONTENTS

CONTENTS

CONTENTS

CONTENTS

CONTENTS

Contents

Contents

Contents

Contents

Ada Episcopal Mission Cemetery, Ada, Virginia
Located on Route 647 in Ada to East of Church. Resurveyed October 25, 1993.

LATHAM, William M 1858–1941 Hester L. 1856–1940

Adams Cemetery, Delaplane - Marshall, Virginia
Located North East intersection of Routes 732 and 724 in grove of locust in field, overgrown, periwinkle, tombstones scattered about. Resurveyed October 29, 1993.

Anna R. Wife of George ADAMS Born Oct. 17, 1801 Died Jan. 15, 1879 aged 77 yrs. 2 mos. & 29 days

George ADAMS Son of Littleton and Elizabeth ADAMS Born March 12, 1786 Died October 5, 1868 aged 82 years 6 months and 17 days

Mary W. ADAMS Daughter of George & Ann R. ADAMS Born August 29, 1848 Died May 4, 1862 aged 18 years 5 mos. & 4 days *(not visible 1993)*

George L. ADAMS Son of George & Ann R. ADAMS Born July 13, 1835 Died April 14, 1864 aged 26 years 9 months *(not visible 1993)*

Mildred D. ADAMS Daughter of George & Ann R. ADAMS Born April 2, 1828 Died April 10, 1862 aged 34 years & 8 days

Ellen D. ADAMS Daughter of George & Ann R. ADAMS Born October 8th 1830 Died September 30th 1859 aged 28 years 11 mos. & 22 dys.

Adaline H. Daughter of George & Ann R. ADAMS Born March 21, 1825 Died Feby. 28, 1859 aged 32 years 11 months 8 days *(not visible 1993)*

Allan Cemetery, Morrisville, Virginia
Located East Route 17 just North of Morrisville Methodist Church. Enclosed by aluminum painted metal fence, honeysuckle overgrowth. Beside the drive to Coventry. Resurveyed April 23, 1994.

Josephine T. ALLAN Born July 15, 1848 Died March 3, 1926

J. W. ALLAN Born May 23, 1834 Died Oct 23, 1893 Aged 59 years 5 months

Landon Tyack ALLAN Born Dec. 8, 1873 Died Jan. 5, 1902

David M. ALLAN *(female)* Dec. 8, 1873 Aug. 11, 1915

Jennie ALLAN Wife of E. S. ALLAN Feb. 21, 1875 Feb. 6, 1933

Edward S. ALLAN 1875–1927

Oswald F. EMBREY Born Mar. 15, 1828 Died Nov. 27, 1890 Aged 69 years 8 months 12 days; Mary Ann Wife of Oswald P. EMBREY Born Mar. 31, 1820 Died Feb. 27, 1862; E. B. EMBREY Born July 17, 1824 Died May 3, 1899

Luther B. EMBREY Born Mar. 29, 1852 Died Dec. 3, 1886

Martha R. ALLAN Died Dec. 1900 Aged 87 years

Susan ALLAN May 10, 1789 Jan. 31, 1868

Capt. Landon ALLAN July 21, 1786 Feb. 2, 1862

Allison Cemetery, Dudie, Virginia
Located on Route 738 (traveling northeast), turn right on Route 741 about 2 miles to driveway on right, cemetery in field behind house on slope on hill in grove of trees. No stones or fence (removed in 1960s per Mr. Allison). Source of information: Basil Allison, Natalie Stevenson, and Madeline Haley, descendants.

Annie ALLISON MONROE Annie Ruth CORDER Died 4 monthe

Maria CORDER Born 1841 Died March 19, 1912

PAYNE infants (3), *one set of twins and one other all daughters of Wade PAYNE and Rosie ALLISON PAYNE)*

John P ALLISON *(father of Basil was buried here but grave later moved to Marshall Cemetery)*

Anderson Cemetery, Markham, Virginia

Located on North side Route 55 at East end of Markham between two houses. Stone fence fallen down, ground hog holes, overgrown. Resurveyed September 6, 1993.

Thomas A. SMITH Born March 6, 1802 Died Dec. 18, 1888
Willie B. Son of Thos. E. & Martha A. ANDERSON born June 13, 1858 died January 1, 1862 aged 3 years 6 months & 18 days
Martha A. MEGEATH Wife of Thos. E. ANDERSON Nov. 20, 1835 July 9, 1911
T. [Thos.] E. ANDERSON Born Sept. 9, 1834 Died Sept. 23, 1864
Thomas E. Son of Thos. E. and Martha ANDERSON Dec. 8, 1862 August 9, 1906 *(tombstone broken 1993)*
Lula H. Wife of George S. CABLE Born Sept. 4, 1869 Died Mar. 4, 1888 aged 27 years & 6 months
Lula ANDERSON Daughter of Geo. S. & Lula CABLE Born Mar. 2, 1888 Died Sept. 19, 1894
W. T. OVERBY Mosby's Command Co. D killed at Front Royal Sept. 23, 1864
Our Father George W. MARSHALL; Our Mother Mary Ellen MARSHALL
Angelina MARSHALL
Kate MARSHALL
Eli ANDERSON who was born March 11, 1803 and departed this life January 15th 1854 aged 50 years 10 months and 4 days
Nancy KILE Wife of Eli ANDERSON
2 rock markers 2 depressions

Note: General Custer had Thos. E. Anderson and W. T. Overby killed while prisoners. Overby was hanged and Custer had Anderson's feet tied to the trace chains and dragged to death at the heels of a horse through the streets of Front Royal. (Southern Cavalry Review Vol. XI, No. 4, January 1994)

Anderson Cemetery, Delaplane, Virginia
Located North of Route 724 in edge of field just East of Route 729, enclosed by stone wall.

Thomas H. ANDERSON 1881–1964
W. G. ANDERSON Feb. 6, 1846 Mar. 10, 1923
Lucy D. TURNER Wife of W. G. ANDERSON Jan. 17, 1852 Nov. 13, 1917
Jane E. ANDERSON Died April 4th 1952 Aged -- yrs. 1 mo

Shelby and Crave ANDERSON buried in unmarked graves.

Armistead Cemetery, between Paris and Upperville, Virginia
Located South side of Route 710 2 miles East of Route 17 on knoll far side of stream, Gap Run, stone fence fallen down. Weeds taken over. Resurveyed October 14, 1993.

Brevet Brigadier General Walker Keith ARMISTEAD Colonel of the U. S. 3d Regiment of Artillery Son of John and Lucy BAYLOR ARMISTEAD of Caroline County Virginia born 25th March 1773 and died 13th October 1845 General Armistead entered the Army a second lieutenant of Engineers in 1804 and in a long career was…duties…correct military deportment and for right moral excellence He left four sons and five daughters to mourn his death.
Joseph G. CARR Born Aug. 19, 1812 died Sept. 13, 1878
Lucinda Stanley CARR consort of Joseph G. CARR Daughter of the late Gen. W. K. ARMISTEAD, U.S.A. Born Nov. 1st 1815 Died Jan. 3, 1850
Lewis ARMISTEAD Son of Joseph G & Lucinda S. CARR born Sept 17, 1845 died Jany 28, 1858
Elizabeth STANLEY relict of Gen W. K. ARMISTEAD Born November 1791 Died Sept. 30, 1861
Elizabeth Daughter of John and Mary FRANCK and relict of Hon. John STANLEY of No. Car. She was a Christian and died in the residence of Her Son in law Gen. W. K. ARMISTEAD on the 30th of August 1845 AE 63
Armstrong Cemetery, Catlett, Virginia
Located West Route 667 200 yards North Route 605, wire fence, overgrown. Resurveyed August 15, 1994 by Mr.

Tim Parup.

Mabel V. BEYDLER Oct. 27, 1884 July 4, 1931
Ella ARMSTRONG July 27, 1898 Aged 30 yrs.
E. E. ARMSTRONG 1908–1909

Armstrong - Leach Cemetery, Warrenton, Virginia

Located between Bethel and Little Georgetown 0.8 mile South East Route 628 in bend of Route 674 about 50 yards in from corner in grove of lovely pines. Excellent mortared stone fence, periwinkle, boxwood. Many rock markers. Entire cemetery filled with graves. Resurveyed June 5, 1991.

John ARMSTRONG Oct. 26, 1821 age 80 years
Joseph ARMSTRONG *(huge evergreen blocked rest)*
Simon D. ARMSTRONG Feb. 19, 1825 July 8, 1904; Sarah A. Aug. 5, 1827 June 25, 1880
8 fieldstone marked graves
Wm. LEACH June 6, 1825 Oct. 24, 1915
Mary A. LEACH Age 84 years
Joseph Son of John & Hannah CARNALL Born June 6, 1855 *(rest in ground)*
John CARNALL Died February 26, 1871 Aged 80 years
ARMSTRONG Our parents Simeon D. Feb. 19, 1825–July 8, 1864 Sarah A. Aug. 6, 1827–June 25, 1880 Children of S. D. & S. A. ARMSTRONG Isabella B. May 25, 1854 Pelle C. Feb. 6, 1859 Infant Son
Nannie NORRIS ARMSTRONG June 10, 1866 March 1, 1927 Our precious sister
Joseph Warren ARMSTRONG June 4, 1852 June 14, 1928
Edward Ashby ARMSTRONG Jan. 15, 1863 June 18, 1927 His Wife Lillie JACKSON ARMSTRONG June 15, 1864 April 4, 1930

Arnold - Oliver - Chapman Cemetery, near Catlett, Virginia

Located West Route 616 1 mile North Route 607, North West house at edge of woods. Resurveyed August 15, 1994 by Mr. Carson.

GIBSON, ARNOLD, & SMITH *families buried in unmarked or fieldstone marked graves.*

Eva M. JOHNSON 1887-1939
Horace W. CHAPMAN 1912-1970

Ashby (Nimrod) Cemetery, Delaplane, Virginia

Located West Route 17, about 0.6 mile North Delaplane at edge of woods in second field. About 14 rock markers. Surveyed September 13, 1993.

Ashby (Nimrod) Cemetery, Marshall, Virginia

Located 0.5 mile West of Route 738 on Route 741 in field below barn, wire fence, well kept. Mr. Bryan Ashby has blueprint of cemetery showing who is buried in each grave. Resurveyed February 1993 by Phyllis Scott.

Millard ASHBY Born Jan. 23, 1928 Died Jan. 16, 1929
Nimrod T. [Thompson] ASHBY [2nd] Aug. 18, 1876 March 1, 1947
Mary ROBINSON ASHBY devoted wife, mother, humanitarian Mar. 12, 1884 Jan. 22, 1969
John M. [Marshall] ASHBY May 17, 1855 March 30, 1927
Wilford W. OLINGER Beloved Son of Nannie & C. E. OLINGER Dec. 8, 1912 Apr. 9, 1917
Infant Daughter of C. E. & N. R. OLINGER Feb. 2, 1910
Unmarked graves of:
James Theodore ASHBY, infant Son of Nimrod ASHBY
Mattie Virginia ASHBY

Nimrod Tyson ASHBY
Mattie HELUNGER ASHBY
Mildred MOREHEAD ASHBY
Charles Burrough ASHBY
Robert SEAY Cno relationCof Richmond, VA
John Edward OLINGER
Louise ASHBY OLINGER
Nimrod Thomas ASHBY
Louise SMITH ASHBY
3 children of John Edward OLINGER & Daniel J. MOFFETT
6 children of Jeanette & Nimrod Turner ASHBY
Nimrod Turner ASHBY
Sarah ENGLISH servant

Richard & Betty MOREHEAD ASHBY *are buried in the pine grove to North of old house with their infant child in unmarked graves.*

Ashby Cemetery

Located on Route 737 just East of Route 699 on left. Data obtained from Joe Lawler, Marshall.

Ashby Cemetery, "Yew Hill", Delaplane, Virginia

Located at intersection of Route 17 & 731. Thomas ASHBY *settled here, but burying ground has vanished into meadow.*

Ashe Cemetery & Indian Burying Ground, Delaplane, Virginia

Located on East side of Route 17, on hill South of Goose Creek by oak tree. Across from "The Meadows". Rock markers, several obvious graves.

Assembly of God Cemetery (originally called Boo Hoo or Free Church), Middleburg, Virginia

Located East Route 629 0.4 mile North of Route 776, church now burned (since 1970), well fenced, 3 fieldstone markers. Excellent condition. Resurveyed November 29, 1993.

Mary J. GREGG Baby Mary Born and Died Dec. 17, 1926
Baby Annie GREGG Born and Died Feb. 28, 1934
Mother July 16, 1894 Oct. 11, 1964 *(evidently wife of Curley GREGG)*
Father Curley H. GREGG Nov. 25, 1869 July 16, 1936

John H. CAMPBELL Jan. 19, 1861 July 9, 1933
Robert T. CAMPBELL Mar. 18, 1888 Jan. 8, 1955
Effie D. CAMPBELL Oct. 12, 1893 Dec. 8, 1956

Donald L. LOVETT Oct. 15, 1939 Jan. 12, 1940
LOVETT Harold Gill Oct. 7, 1914 Jan. 27, 1986; Alice GREGG Nov. 23, 1929

Athey Cemetery, Orlean, Virginia

Located on left of Route 732 about 0.25 miles North of Route 772 beside road, open to livestock. Several rock markers and unmarked graves. Approximately 66 feet x 40 feet. Resurveyed February 16, 1990 by Phyllis Scott.

Gertrude ATHEY LAYCOCK Beloved Wife of James Henry LAYCOCK Born Nov. 18, 1867 Died Mar. 26, 1898
Rev. S. M. ATHEY 1844–1922; His Wife Emma E. 1843–1924
Walter 1884–1902
Genevieve 1877–1888

Herbert 1904–1905
Margaret A. DOUGLAS 1877–1957 *(fhm)*

Bailey Cemetery, Marshall, Virginia
Located on Route 732 about 1 mile West Route 17 - 55 in field back of Ramey barn. Few rocks and one unreadable tombstone with footstone S. B. for Samuel BAILEY, according to Jack Ramey, owner of property.

Baker Cemetery, Marshall, Virginia
Located at intersections of Routes 778 & 737 in field beside house. Wire fence, overgrown, some unmarked graves.

Bessie B. AINSWORTH 1909–1967
Clarunce W. WELCH Died July 7, 1959

Baker Family Cemetery, New Baltimore, Virginia
Located at bend in Route 674 South Route 29 near New Baltimore. Now a strawberry bed according to Mr. Edward Furlong, 50 year resident.

Baldwin Ridge Episcopal Church Cemetery, Warrenton, Virginia
Located South East side Route 827 about 0.25 mile East Route 605. Church gone, in woods just beyond bend in road and large oak tree, overgrown, honeysuckle, two plots with iron fence. Resurveyed January 23, 1993.

Walter Montagu LUARD of Lancashire, England Died Jan. 14, 1887 Age 27
William ASSHETON Born in Lancashire, England October 22, 1826 entered into rest November 9, 1887
Elizabeth ASSHETON late of Lancashire, England Born November 13, 1825 entered into rest November 3, 1894
W. Herbert ASSHETON Lancashire, England August 2, 1851 January 29, 1910
Mary HUNT Died February 24, 1890 Aged 77 years; M. R. footstone

Footstone MR. At least 4 unmarked graves.

These were some distance from others:

Robert MITCHELL April 10, 1833 March 27, 1915
Ella MITCHELL May 28, 1827 died about 1905
R. Tasker MITCHELL, M. D. Feb. 14, 1831 Died about Sept. 1891
Julia Sophia Daughter of Richard Tasker & Charlotte MITCHELL Born May 11, 1828 Died April 17, [1883?]
(stone broken 1993)

Ball - Creel - Griffith Cemetery, near The Plains, Hopewell, Virginia
Located West Route 628 0.7 mile North Route 601 0.5 mile off road, wire fence and trees, poorly cared for. Numerous fieldstone markers. Resurveyed November 22, 1993.

Joseph Peyton BALL Dec. 22, 1874 April 17, 1935
Nancy Jane BALL Aug. 27, 1868 Jan. 12, 1911
Joseph BALL Born Nov. 22, 185__ *(rest of inscription sunk in ground)*
Lucy Jane Wife of Joseph BALL Born April 13, 1833 *(rest sunk in ground)* 1899

Rose HURST Born May 9, 1872 Died Feb. 20, 1877
Martha Wife of Evan CREEL Born Aug. 13, 1832 Died Mar. 11, 1903

Balthorpe Cemetery, "Marley", Marshall, Virginia
Located East of Route 710 North of Marshall just beyond Route 722 between stables and house. Stone and cinder block fence, well kept, 6 fieldstone markers. Resurveyed April 23, 1994.

Daniel H. Son of Jeremiah and Sarah BALTHORPE Born Mar. 3, 1822 Died Feb. 3, 1880 leaving a wife and 8 children
Sarah BALTHORPE Born Sept. 6, 1783 Died Nov. 20, 1869
Jeremaih BALLTHORPE who departed this life Sept. 28th 1849 In the 74th year of his age
Susan S BALTHORPE Born Feb. 1819 Died Oct. 15, 1908
Rebecca E. BALTHORPE Born April 3, 1818 Died Jan. 8, 1901
Jane M. Wife of J. H.. DAY Born July 5, 1826 Died Apr. 12, 1898
John H. DAY Born Aug. 15, 1807 Died April 28, 1891
Charles A. BALTHORPE who departed this life March 15th 1850 aged 13
One base stone missing

Baxter Cemetery, Bristersburg, Virginia
Located .5 mile North East of Bristersburg on Route 233, then 1.8 miles East on Route 609, then 1.15 miles South East on Route 609, then .5 mile South on Route 612, on West side of road. Surveyed by M. D. Gore, Sumerduck, November 10, 1937.

"There is an old graveyard about one hundred yards South of the old Baxter home, but there are no inscriptions. Doubtless, William BAXTER and his two sons are buried here."

Beachy Cemetery, Bealeton, Virginia
Located South Route 28 0.25 mile East Route 745 in field at end of private road through woods, aluminum painted iron fence, briars.

Son of S. & S. BEACHY Sept. 19, 1895 Sept. 21, 1895
Henry SWARTZENTRUBER Nov. 21, 1898 Feb. 8, 1899
N. C. BEACHY Dec. 17, 1898 A. 4-10-1913
A Wacler RAUC 1894 D.A.P. May 189–

Beale Cemetery, Midland, Virginia
Located 0.9 mile South Route 650 West Route 649 at end of private road back of lovely old colonial large frame house around old boxwood. Previous owner pulled up all tombstones and put them behind shed. Rock markers and 4 marble inscriptions found.

Hannah G. BEALE Wife of William E. GASKINS Born Sept. 29, 1833 Died Feb. 4, 1876
Eliza LEE BEALE Born March 31, 1819 Died Sept. 18, 1883
John Beale GORDON Professor Applied Mathematics in the Arkansas University Born Mar. 15, 1855 Died Sept. 11, 1880
William BEALE Born Jan. 19, 1818 Died Aug. 12, 188[6?]

These inscriptions from WPA book. Tombstones now missing:

Mary CATLETT Wife of Charles H. GORDON and Daughter of John G. BEALE and Mary Lee GILLISON Born October 4, 1826 Died July 26, 1892
Charles H. GORDON Born Jan. 17, 1829 Died Jan. 23, 1897 a soldier of the Confederacy

Beale Cemetery, Remington, Virginia
Located on Route 660 1 mile North Route 651 at "Medfield" in field at end of private road. Seven fieldstone markers in clump of trees near pond. Resurveyed April 21, 1994.

J. Edward BEALE April 4th 1857 Oct. 23, 1945 Comander for Life of Black Horse Camp. S.C.B.
Our Father & Mother Ritchie K. BEALE Born 1838 Died 1917 S. F. C. BEALE Born 1830 Died 1914

Bendemeer Farm Cemeteries, Delaplane, Virginia
Located 1 mile North of Delapane on West side of Route 17, families unknown, no markers. Harry McCarty states that there are several cemeteries there. The Nimrod ASHBY family buried here. Resurveyed September 12, 1993.

Bennett Cemetery, Morrisville, Virginia
Located West Route 17 down private drive just North Route 637 back of house on left at edge of woods, fence fallen down, overgrown. Now moved to Cedar Grove, Bealeton Cox plot.

Brother Sister James KEYS Died June 20, 1888 Aged 53 years 5 months & 20 days Almira J. KEYS His Wife Died June 12, 1889 Aged 52 years 6 months & 17 days
Henry T. BENNETT Born Nov. 23, 1828 Died July 9, 1893
Husband Charles T. TRIPLETT Died Sept. 19, 1896 Aged 36 years
Robert H. GREEN Born Mar. 28, 1854 died Sept. 24, 1865 aged 10 years
Our Father A. F. B. [BENNETT]; Our MotherBF. B.; Our Sister Isabella
Our dear Aunt Susan ROGERS Died Nov. 21, 1858
Oscar A. BENNETT Died July 6, 1864 at Richmond Aged 33 years

Bethel Cemetery (Black), Bethel, Virginia
Located 1.5 mile West Route 17 South Route 690 below a Lodge Club of cinder block on steep hill in grove.

Bessie BLAND April 7, 1887 Dec. 11, 1968
Shedrick BLAND July 9, 1865 April 4, 1958
Emily BLAND Died Mar. 30 1916 Aged 81 yrs.
Mary WALDEN Died May 14, 1924 Aged 86 years
William BLAND Died May 4, 1965 Age 64 years Malvina MATTHEWS 1891–1956
Grace D. DOORES 1950–1951
Mrs Eppie J. FREEMAN Died February 26, 1940
Stacey EWELL 1896–1960

Robert L. ROBINSON Jr. May 30, 1960 Feb. 1, 1967
Maria CURTIS ROBINSON May 1, 1875 Jan. 16, 1959
John E. CURTIS Feb. 14, 1872 Oct. 21, 1945
Agnes CURTIS Died Feb. 17, 1941 Aged 90 years
David R. GREEN Oct. 11, 1882 June 29, 1952

John FREEMAN 1877–1953
Sarah R. Beloved Wife of Cronje HELM   –1931

Elizabeth J. RAY Born Sept. 25, 1875 Died Feb. 12, 1923
William WALDEN Died Jan. 2, 1927 Aged 26 years

Julia CURTIS Died April 16, 1930 Aged 19 yrs.
Agnes CURTIS May 28, 1894 June 30, 1934

James Henry KENNEDY, Jr. VIRGINIA CPL HQ CO 367 INFANTRY WORLD WAR I Aug 13 1884 Jan 17 1963

Frank YOUNG Died Jan. 19, 1959 Aged 7 years 4 months 20 days
Amanda YOUNG WINES 1907–1930
Fannie YOUNG 1847–1929; Frank YOUNG 1868–1917

Henry JACKSON 1884–1961

Sallie HARRIS Died 1917 Aged 27 years
Albert WALKER 1883–1952
Doris BUTLER 1907–1958; Jacob BUTLER Died January 12, 1959 Aged
Jacob BUTLER Died January 12, 1959 Aged

Joseph CORAM 1955–1955

Blackwell Cemetery, Orlean, Virginia

Located 1.5 miles South East of Orlean on East side of Route 688 in field with stone wall, boxwood fieldstone markers with no inscriptions. Mr. and Mrs. Wesley Blackwell, present owners knew who were buried there and obtained the following dates from the Family Bible owned by his brother, Edward Blackwell, Lincoln, Virginia.

Joseph A. BLACKWELL died Sept. 13, 1896
William Horton BLACKWELL died Sept. 18, 1901
Willis Horton BLACKWELL died Sept. 23, 1882
Nettie May BLACKWELL JAMES died Feb. 2, 1924
Edward A. JAMES died March 28, 1903
James Joel BLACKWELL died June 19, 1941
Lena Bessie HUME BLACKWELL Born March 2, 1881 died Nov. 6, 1961
Anna BLACKWELL MARSHALL Born July 7, 1914 Died March 15, 1943

Three unmarked infant graves.

Blackwell (Joseph) Cemetery, "The Meadows", Bethel, Warrenton, Virginia

Located East Route 628 at first farm past Bethel Methodist Church, on edge of field at back of stone house, fenced, about 50 fieldstone markers, quite large plot. Well kept with board fence around it. Resurveyed October 28, 1993.

Joseph BLACKWELL Jr. 2ndLt 3rd Va Regt Contl Line 1752–1826 and his wife Ann Eustace (HULL) BLACKWELL 1761–1840 *(Joseph BLACKWELL Jr. also served as a major in the Virginia militia and was a son of the first sheriff of Fauquier County; headstone was placed in Aug. 1989)*
Henry Lee GASKINS who departed this life in a full surrender to a blessed immortality July 24th A. D. 1846 in the 34th year of his age husband, a dutiful son, affectionate fatherY *(Grandson of Joseph BLACKWELL Jr. Son of John Hancock GASKINS and Ann BLACKWELL)*
Lucy Gaskins JORDAN born Sept 6, 1808 died Feb 6, 1887 Daughter of John Hancock GASKINS and Ann BLACKWELL *(Grand-daughter of Joseph BLACKWELL Jr.)*
W. E. GASKINS born May 3, 1821 died Mar 28, 1893 Son of John Hancock GASKINS and Ann BLACKWELL born near Warrenton *(Grandson of Joseph BLACKWELL Jr.)*
Joseph JEFFRIES Born Sept 20, 1816 Died May 28, 1897 *(Grandson of Maj. Joseph BLACKWELL & Son of Enoch JEFFRIES & Agatha BLACKWELL)*
Joseph Hancock BLACKWELL 43rd Bn Va Cav C.S.A. 1832–1905 *(buried 17 Mar 1905. Grandson of Joseph BLACKWELL Jr. New headstone placed in Sept. 1989)*

Some fifty or more unmarked graves may be indicated by rough fieldstones. Brigadier General John B. ROSE, great-grandson of Joseph BLACKWELL Jr., was born at The Meadows in 1885 and lived there fifteen years after World War II; he listed the following as also having been buried there:

John BLACKWELL 1791–1866 *(Son of Joseph BLACKWELL Jr.) and his first wife Rebecca DAVENPORT (died 1831)*
William Steptoe BLACKWELL 1800– *(Son of Joseph BLACKWELL Jr.) and his wife Ann Sparke GORDAN*
James BLACKWELL 1805–1864 *(Son of Joseph BLACKWELL Jr.) and his wife Elizabeth CARTER (1808–1877)*
Benjamin BLACKWELL 1825–c.1890 *(Son of John BLACKWELL and Rebecca DAVENPORT)*

General Rose, who owned The Meadows, had a lot of data prior to his death, but his notes on the cemetery are not available. Joseph BLACKWELL 1752–1826 married Anne Eustace HULL 1766–1840. Hardee's ref. according to Mrs. Jones. Descendents and relatives who lived at "Clifton", "Road Island", "West View", "Loretta", etc., were buried here, at Alton or in Warrenton cemeteries.

Bland - Grant Cemetery, "Bunker Hill", The Plains, Virginia
Located on North of Route 55 in area called Bunker Hill 0.5 mile West Route 704. Very well kept and mowed area opposite frame house. Mrs. Minnie Grant Bolden states that the MUSE family is buried there. A number of graves. Resurveyed October 25, 1993.

Robert Lee LOGAN 1894–1969 *(missing 1993)*
LAMBERT Lofton H., Sr. 1905–1972; Sophie R. 1907–1958
Mattie S. CLARK 1904–1957 *(fhm)*
Albert STROTHER 1903–1961 *(fhm)*
Minnie G. BOLDEN 1889–1985 *(fhm)*
Will GRANT 1885–1942
GRANT Katie Ellen G. March 3, 1886 October 17, 1970; James S. March 5, 1882 March 21, 1938
   (fhm had E. J.)
George Edward GRANT US NAVY WORLD WAR II Jan. 18, 1926 Sep. 12, 1945
Ruth B. BLAND 1924–1983 *(fhm)*
William BLAND, Jr. 1921–1989 *(fhm)*
Michael E. MOORE 1950–1976 *(fhm)*
William BLAND VIRGINIA PFC US ARMY WORLD WAR I April 15, 1894 February 19, 1954
Ruth B. BLAND 1896–1974

Blue Cemetery (Black), Markham, Virginia
Located at West end of Route 728, down private drive, at edge of woods, 300 feet South of Robert Hinkel's house. Mack BLUE buried in fieldstone marked grave. Resurveyed September 20, 1993.

Blue Ridge Farm Cemetery, Upperville, Virginia
Located on Route 623 3 miles South Route 50 in field to right of entrance walled stone cemetery with fieldstone markers, one with E. B. 1899 on it. Another cemetery believed to have been Fletcher cemetery with rock markers near barn by Fountain Hill house. Barn now used as a machine shop. No tombstones or rock markers. Resurveyed March 19, 1989.

Botts Cemetery, Somerville, Virginia
Located 0.5 mile South East Route 637 South Route 610, iron fence, unmarked graves, overgrown.

Thornton S. BOTTS Born Nov. 27, 1822 Died Feb. 1, 1888
Idan BOTTS Born April 4, 1859 Died May 16, 1895 Samuel A. BOTTS Born Dec. 19, 1853 Died Jan. 10, 1912
Mrs. Thornton Benjamin BOTTS June 2, 1858 Died April 19, 1933
Boteler Cemetery, "Belle Valle Farm", Bristersburg, Virginia
Located North Route 806 1 mile West Route 616 back of house, brick topped cinder block fence.

Anna May PETERS Feb. 27, 1893 Oct. 2, 1942
Elmer H. PETERS Aug. 14, 1893 April 23, 1939
Ida Elizabeth PETERS Born April 16, 1857 Died March 10, 1916 Edward E. PETERS Born Feb. 16, 1855 Died
   Jan. 24, 1940
Thomas Catlett GIBSON Born May 16, 1827 Died Feb. 15, 1899
Myrtle Gibson BOTELER Born May 29, 1908 Aug. 16, 1910
Thomas Smoot BOTELER Born Jan. 23, 1897 Died May 4, 1911
Eustace M. BOTELER 1855–1931

Susan A. BOTELER Jan. 18, 1863 Nov. 26, 1936 Stephen Isaac BOTELER May 1, 1852 Dec. 31, 1923
Norman BOTELER Born June 14, 1892 Died Feb. 5, 1920
Alexander A. BOTELER Born Aug. 28, 1894 Died Oct. 1913 PVT 1ST CL MED DEPT Died USA Base Hospital
   Camp Meade, Md.
Zadie Elizabeth Daughter of Stephen I. & Susan B. BOTELER Mar. 8, 1887 Feb. 23, 1912
Minnie E. PETERS Feb. 14, 1865 Oct. 23, 1938
John H. BOTELER Born June 19, 1850 Died Oct. 16, 1935
Frances PETERS Wife of J. H.. BOTELER Born Oct. 16, 1858 Died Oct. 1, 1927
Frances E. Daughter of J. H.. & Frances P. BOTELER Born May 19, 1891 Died Feb. 23, 1908 Aged 16 yrs.
Wm. H. BOTELER Born June 19, 1800 Died Jan. 20, 1883...Husband...Father
Elizabeth A. BOTELER Born March 21, 1818 Died April 14, 1888

Bowen Cemetery, Calverton, Virginia
*Located 3 miles South East of Calverton Route 616 North East 300 Yards by private road 120 yards to cemetery.
2nd cemetery on property 0.25 mile East or North East of old house. Mother of Mrs. Mary EUSTACE buried
here. Research by M. D. Gore April 30, 1936 for WPA.*

Eliza G. BOWEN consort of William A. BOWEN who departed this life February 27th 1836 in the 31st year of her
   age
Buckner A SMITH who departed this life April 12, 1842 aged 17 years

Bowersett Cemetery, Ashville, Virginia
*Located West of Route 731 in field on top hill just beyond Route 723. Enclosed with good stone wall, boxwood and
trees, several fieldstone markers. Homeowner says that the Bowesett family have been taking care of the
cemetery, but did not come up this summer. They put black plastic down all over cemetery, but the weeds came up
through it. A development built up in field in 1993. Wall in good condition. Cemetery overgrown, 50 feet x 60 feet.
Markers all knocked down. Resurveyed October 3, 1993.*

John BOWERSETT Died March 20, 1867 aged 85 years 3 months & 10 days
Elizabeth Wife of John BOWERSETT Died December 29, 1866 aged 78 years 6 months & 9 days She was for 50
   years a member of Lutheran Church.
Sarah J. Daughter of J. & E. BOWERSETT Died May 26, 1864 aged 40 years & 22 days
Julia A. Daughter of John & Elizabeth BOWERSETT who departed this life December 29th 1860 aged 39 years 4
   months & 17 days
Susannah Catherine BOWERSETT who departed this life October 1st 1853 aged 37 years & 10 months
George W. Son of Simon & Jane S. BOWERSETT Departed this life Aug. 1, 1859 aged 4 years
George W. BOWERSETT who departed this life August 19th 1833 aged 6 years 9 months & 21 days
Mary BOWERSETT who departed this life November 14th 1826 aged 8 years 6 months and 8 days
Simon BOWERSETT died 1887 His Wife Jane S. FLEMING died 1905
Gillard Son of _____ & _____ BOWERSETT died Oct. 1, 1853 aged 3 years

Bradford - Robinson Cemetery, Midland, Virginia
*Located North East intersections of Routes 667 & 674 in field in back of first farm house on East side Route 674.
Mortared stone wall, overgrown, some stone markers.*

Thomas G. BRADFORD 1785–1850 His Wife Catharine 1786–1851
Catharine B. ROBINSON 1851–1870
Husband George W. JACKSON Born May 5, 1823 Died June 19, 1869
Ida ROBINSON Daughter of Thos. H. & Laura B. ROBINSON Born April 4, 1820 Died June 28, 1881
W. B. R.; C. B.; I. H. B.; M. L. B.; S. R.

Additional graves found by Ripley Robinson:

Samuel ROBINSON born Jan. 7th 1803–Died May 24, 1858
Caroline Adelaide [BRADFORD] ROBINSON Born Sept. 2, 1817–Died March 1908

Fieldstone marker dated from Robinson family Bible owned by Ripley Robinson:

Catherine Ann ROBINSON July 14, 1840–Dec. 16, 1843
Ida ROBINSON April 20, 1874–Aug. 28, 1881
Wm. Bradford ROBINSON July 14, 1840–Dec. 16, 1843

Brainerd Cemetery, Bristersburg, Virginia
Located 3 miles North East of Bristersburg on Route 233 East 200 yards on private road in field 190 yards from house. Research by M. D. Gore, April 6, 1937.

Tyrus BRAINERD Born in Haddam Ct. Mar. 12, 1806 Died in this place July 19, 1846

Braxton Cemetery (Black)
Located on Route 741. Data obtained from Joe Lawler, Marshall.

Brick Baptist Church, Little Georgetown, Virginia
Located North East corner of Routes 674 and 628. Owner of church, now house, states some Civil War soldiers may possibly be buried between house and creek. Surveyed November 29, 1993.

Broad Run Baptist Church, New Baltimore, Virginia
Located at intersections of Routes 600 & 29-211 to rear of church. At least 150 graves marked by fieldstone markers. Resurveyed July 18, 1990.

Alfred GLASCOCK Born Sept. 26, 1799 Died Nov. 12, 1868; also His Wife Margaret Born June 22, 1802 Died
    Aug. 25, 1878 *(missing 1990)*
S. G.; A. M. G.; M. G.; J. T. M. *(on tombstones)*
Devoted Mother Susan BAILY MINTER Wife of Jas. R. GOUGH Jan. 8, 1820 July 21, 1913
Our Sister Margaret GOUGH Dec. 8, 1839 Nov. 18, 1925
LUNSFORD Martin L. 1857–1924; Lutie A. 1875–1941; Son Hunton LUNSFORD
J. W. ALLISON Born Jan. 10, 1840 Died Aug. 18, 1927
S. R. GARRETT 1877–1922; Beaulah N. His Wife 1882–1922
Baby 1916
Baby 1915
Lilley Blanch CAMPBELL July 8, 1900 Oct. 21, 1966
Samuel B. CRUMMETT September 11, 1865 February 11, 1942
Arthur Wayland CAMPBELL Oct. 18, 1893 Nov. 11, 1984
LUNSFORD Hallie C. Dec. 5, 1903 Dec. 6, 1983; Margaret T. Sept. 5, 1919
Henry W. GOUGH 1885–1931
Levi H. GOUGH Jan. 3, 1847 Oct. 12, 1916; Virginia W. Aug. 5, 1857 June 21, 1926
Flora F. GOUGH 1884–1973
DOUGLAS Oscar M. Feb. 9, 1866 Nov. 4, 1928; Daisie G. Aug 26, 1884 Aug. 18, 1984
LaGlaire BURGESS Jan. 18, 1895 July 14, 1925
Edward Allen GRIMSLEY Born Sept. 18, 1925 Died Apr. 7, 1927
Sanford EMBREY 1885–1965 *(missing 1990)*
Melvil Wilson LUNSFORD US ARMY WORLD WAR II July 17, 1918 Nov. 23, 1972
LUNSFORD Roy Bennett Dec. 14, 1893 July 27, 1971; Mary GRUMMETT Feb. 1, 1894 Mar. 23, 1976
GRAY Julian V. Apr. 22, 1915 Mar. 31, 1976; Lucille B. May 24, 1919 May 24, 1982
Ora F. CARNEAL Born Aug. 17, 1901 Died Nov. 24, 1902

Mother Mary F. CARTER Born Jan. 30, 1821 Died July 7, 1902
Father George CARTER Born Sept. 25, 1820 Died July 1, 1911
Isabella F. CARTER Feb. 16, 1851 Nov. 25, 1935
Corrie E. SOMERS March 16, 1892 April 18, 1939
Samuel M. CARRICO Oct. 25, 1906 Aug. 5, 1927
Mrs. T. S. CARRICO July 3, 1867 Dec. 7, 1927
FURLONG William S. 1855–1935; Cora E. 1875–1966; Edward R. 1905–1982; Mary F. 1908–
THORPE F. Gwynn May 17, 1888 April 8, 1963; Nora A. November 22, 1899
Fannie B. MILTON October 11, 1869 July 31, 1942
Randolph A. MILTON August 13, 1859 February 22, 1940
Father Morton Douglas MILTON March 28, 1906 March 8, 1960
G. A. COOK
H. V. COOK
J. E. COOK Jan. 22, 1860 Dec. 22, 1932; His Wife Mollie CARTER Dec. 29, 1860 Dec. 30, 1937
COOK Benjamin F. Dec. 14, 1868 July 30, 1941; Mary E. Dec. 6, 1869 Jan. 5, 1950
Conrad B. CARTER Mar. 23, 1913 Feb. 14, 1915
SULLIVAN Estelle A. Aug. 9, 1862 Oct. 15, 1955; Laura L. Dec. 26, 1870 Nov. 10, 1961
Geo. T. GRANT 1884–1928; His Wife Mary J. SULLIVAN 1859–1948
Lula E. w o Robert J. SULLIVAN; b. Aug. 9, 1872 d. Feb. 20, 1896
Elmer J. SULLIVAN VIRGINIA PVT L CL 315 INF. L9 DIV March 14, 1957
John T. COOK 1826–1894; Sarah F. His Wife 1837–1929
Evoline V. Wife of G. W. DOUGLAS Born Aug. 31, 1886 Died Jan. 15, 1892
Mary Lillian GRANT March 15, 1896 Aug. 23, 1985
Tombstone face down
3 sandstone tombstones, inscriptions unreadable
Joseph A. FRANCIS born Aug. 28th 1821 died Jan. 3rd 1856 aged 34 years 4 months & 5 days
Mary FRANCIS born March 24th 1842 died March 25th 1856 aged 44 years
Margaret FRANCIS born 1763 died May 6th 1850
Andrey FRANCIS born Feb. 25th 1783 died Dec. 17th 1852
Mary FRANCIS born June 6th 1852 died May 10th 1853
William FRANCIS born Feb. 25th 1854 died May 15th 1854 aged 2 mos & 20 days
Sarah WHARTON Wife of John CARNALL Born Nov. 11, 1785 Died Dec. 20, 1851
Kate HOWISON Wife of Thos H. CARNALL Born Mar. 23, 1834 Died July 9, 1872
T. H. CARNALL Born Jany. 20, 1828 Died Sept. 4, 1865 *(missing 1990)*

Bronaugh Cemetery, Bristersburg, Virginia
Located 2 miles South of Bristersburg on West side of Route 616 0.25 mile from road near old French house, in field, grove of trees, overgrown, 0.25 acre. Many rock markers. Data from Kenneth Eskridge.

John BRONAUGH Born the 15th day of January 1743 Departed this life the 24th of November 1777 Age 34 years

Brooke Cemetery, "Ingleside", Casanova, Virginia
Located West Route 602 about 2 miles North Casanova, in second field behind Victorian house in grove of trees. Rock markers, one flat marker buried in ground on face, with footstone "W. D.", one marker retrieved from vandals and now behind garage, about six more with inscriptions have been stolen.

Francis W. BROOKE Son of Francis & Ann BROOKE Born October 27th 1795 Died July 27th 1828
Francis BROOKE Died October 1800 aged 33 years and of Ann Whiting Daughter of Francis and Ann BROOKE
    Born June 27th 1800 Died March 20th 1802

Brooks - Brown - Wilburn - Jones Cemetery, Sumerduck, Virginia
Located North side Route 651 just East of Route 631 through gate about 150 feet. Chain link fence, well kept, large

holly tree.

BROWN Betty A. Feb. 24, 1870 Sept. 7, 1946 Henry H. Dec. 5, 1862 Apr. 13, 1958
D. L. BROWN Mar. 5, 1868 July 22, 1950
Ashley Wesley Son of Mr. & Mrs. R. J.. LATHAM Oct 13, 1912 Oct. 18, 1912
Mother Queen BROWN Died 1915; Father Thomas BROWN Died 1897
JACOBS William A. Dec. 19, 1863 Nov. 22, 1943 Lizzie A. May 22, 1866 April 20, 1927
Thomas A. BROOKS 1830-1898 His Wife Mary Jane 1835-1905
Lydia R. BROOKS 1872-1886
Inez G. WILBURN 1886-1887; Claude C. WILBURN 1888-1890
Nellie B. WILBURN 1890-1891
Mattie E. JONES Wife of L. J.. BROOKS 1871-1955
L. J. BROOKS 1863-1942
Annie Lou Wife of L. J.. BROOKS 1860-1906
SMITH
WILBURN William F. Feb. 25, 1843 June 12, 1913 His Wife Mary T. May 28, 1858 Oct. 24, 1956

Brown Cemetery, Morrisville, Virginia
Located South Route 637 0.5 mile West Route 806 150 feet in woods opposite house, 60 feet x 60 feet, full of rock markers, wire fence. Moved to Morrisville Methodist.

Father John T. BROWN Born June 24, 1839 Died Nov. 8, 1915; Lucy BROWN Born Aug. 17, 1846 Died June 12, 1890

Brown Cemetery, Morrisville, Virginia
Located 1 mile North West from Morrisville on Route 17, then about 1.2 miles North East on Route 637, "The William Rector Place." Surveyed by M. D. Gore March 16, 1938.

"Eighty yards North of the house is a graveyard."

George R. BROWN Born Dec. 20, 1870 Killed by lightning July 22, 1881
Susan BROWN Born March 5, 1812 Died Dec. 5, 1851

Bundy Family Cemetery, between Sumerduck & Remington, Virginia
Located 100' from Rappahannock South Route 651 between Sumerduck & Remington.

Burying Ground at the Springs, Fauquier Springs, Virginia
Located about 0.25 mile from Fauquier Springs. Research by Louise Lewis, Rectortown, September 7, 1936.

"About 0.25 mile from what was once Fauquier Sulphur Springs, is an old burying ground. There aren't any markers there, so no one knows just who is buried in it. One night, Mr. Jim Hood, who lived at the Springs, was drunk. He started a fight with one of the soldiers and they killed him. He was buried in this cemetery."

Calvary Pentecostal Church Cemetery, Bristersburg, Virginia
Located North East Route 610 at intersection with Route 637, wire fence. Resurveyed May 27, 1990.

Our Father Charles E. BIRD Aug. 22, 1854 Mar. 2, 1923; Mother Ida P. Wife of Charles E. BIRD 1858–1933
Alfred MESSICK Born Aug. 27, 1845 Died Aug. 3, 1922 Elizabeth BILLER MESSICK Born Aug. 8, 1858 Died Jan. 6, 1929 Carrie E. MESSICK Born Feb. 7, 1898 Died Nov. 8, 1926
Samuel Franklin MESSICK Died Oct. 8, 1918 Aged 36 years *(tombstone face down 1990)*
Susan T. Wife of E. R. BRYAN Nov. 26, 1839 Feb. 24, 1902
Benjamin Fairfield BRYAN Aug. 22, 1846 Mar. 24, 1916

Elizabeth TULLOSS COX Oct. 3, 1860 Feb. 10, 1921 Mary TULLOSS REDD Dec. 9, 1857 July 4, 1919
Polk Dallas REDD 1844–1919 Doddridge David REDD 1901–1926

Carper Cemetery, Hume, Virginia
Located on Route 734 on first hill behind Mary Wright's house. CARPERs were early property owners. Rock
markers approximately 38 graves. One very large depression along fence line. Many other depressions and rock
markers on hillside. Mary Wright informed us that she was told early on that this cemetery existed but she is
unsure of family buried here. April 7, 1991

Carr Cemetery, Upperville, Virginia
Located on Route 50 back of 4th building South East of Route 712. Resurveyed September 20, 1993.

Caldwell CARR who was born Feb. 12th 1791 and departed this life August 28th 1855 In the 61st year of his age
Mrs. Cornelia CARR Wife of Caldwell CARR who departed this life on the 17th day of April 1839 in the 30th year
of her age
2 fieldstone marked infant graves

Carroll Cemetery, Turnbull, Virginia
Located 0.3 mile East Route 657 North Route 802, 100 yards back of house near fence in woods. Obliterated by
overgrowth. Resurveyed April 1, 1994.
General HARMON 1864-1941
Rev. L. M.. CARROLL 1884-1961
VELAZQUEZ Rev. Carlos R. February 20, 1894 February 16, 1966; Maria C. [CARROLL] May 5, 1894 January
17, 1964
William TOMES 1891-1956
Arlene C. WILLIS 1890-1963

Marie WEBSTER and others of her family buried to North of next house going north in Turnbull.

Carter Cemetery, Opal, Virginia
Located East Route 806 near end North East Route 17 in woods to left of new house, number sandstone markers,
well kept.

Here lieth the body of Rebecca CARTER consort of John CARTER who departed this life Feby--th 1800 in the 26th
year of her age

Carter Cemetery, Delaplane, Virginia
Located 1.5 miles East of Delaplane on Route 623 on South side of road at bottom of woods behind farm house. No
fence, cattle can graze in area, many rock markers. Resurveyed September 12, 1993.

Moore F. [Fauntleroy] CARTER born December 4th 1771 at Pittsylvania Prince William Co. Va. died September
10th 1820 aged 48 years 8 months and 6 days
John H. CARTER died April 24th 1818 aged 4 months

Carter Cemetery, Delaplane, Virginia
Located Route 712, 1.75 miles North West of Delaplane on Upperville Rd. on line between Rucker and Chappalear
at "Ridgeville" (abandoned), 300 feet behind house in corner of old orchard. Triangular shaped. One distinct
grave approximately 6 obviously marked graves (rock markers). Cemetery dates before Civil War. Surveyed
October 30, 1991.

Carter Slave Cemetery, Delaplane, Virginia
Located Route 712, 1.75 miles North West of Delaplane. John Rucker's "Crest Hill" in corner with Plaskitt, Rucker

and former Johnson property. Size 50 feet by 100 feet. Quartz markers scattered. Stone foundation of slave quarters nearby. Some old fenceposts define cemetery. Surveyed November 1991.

Carter Cemetery, Turnbull, Virginia
Located 0.5 mile East Route 803 about 0.3 mile in woods at end of lane. Terribly overgrown, briars. Tornado has been through recently and knocked down trees. Four fieldstone markers. Tina E. Slamilla and Luther Olinger assisted. Resurveyed April 1, 1994.

Milton C. SANKER 1930–1965
Mrs. Hattie M. CARTER 1903–1964
Thornton CARTER 1935–1968
Jack GRAYSON VIRGINIA PFC 427 RES LABOR BN. QMC WORLD WAR I 1899–1956
Mamie F. TURNER 1882–1968; John Israel TURNER 1909–1968
Whalen CARTER Died Feby. 6, 19--; Mary Frances CARTER 1885–1969
Marshall GRAY 1909–1960
Asberry D. SANKER
Susie Mae CARTER 1891–1976
Pete CARTER 1921–1985
Mary Frances CARTER 1885–1969
Morton CARTER 1911–1981
Rodney CARTER 1989–1991
Taylor CARTER 1914–1980
Thomas BRAGG 1960–1989

Carter Cemetery, "Belmont", Warrenton, Virginia
Located 6 miles West of Warrenton. Data compiled by Helen Jeffries Klitch from pages 192-193 Joseph Arthur Jeffries' "Fauquier County 1840–1919."

Captain William Walden CARTER Died 1902 *(buried "beside his wife in the family burying ground at his late home")*

Carter - Cassell Cemetery, Marshall, Virginia
Located 1 mile South of Marshall on West side of Route 17 on fence line between 2 fields South of Meadow Grove house of Alex. Beverley. Excellent stone wall, overgrown, boxwood. Impossible to enter. Resurveyed October 8, 1993.

William Erasmus CASSELL Born Mar. 15, 1799 Died Aug. 26, 1885
Harriet WHITING CASSELL Wife of W. E. CASSELL Died Aug. 2, 1878 In the 78th year of her age
Anne Maria WILSON Born In Carlisle, England Jany. 1804 Died July 25, 1885
I. B. C. *(on footstone, headstone missing)*
Eliza Brooke CARTER Daughter of Fanny T. & Edward CARTER Died at Meadow Grove Feb. 21, 1907 aged 80 years
Edward CARTER who died June 16th 1843 in the 57th year of his age
Fanny T. SCOTT Wife of Edward CARTER Died at Meadow Grove April 21, 1864 in her 66th year
Virginia Alexander CARTER Daughter of Fanny T. & Edward CARTER Died at Meadow Grove Nov. 12, 1908 in her 84th year
Josiah CARTER Died June 30, 1885 age 67 years

Carver Cemetery, Sowego, Virginia
Located North Route 610 at Stafford County Line. Property of U. S. Marine Corps, very well kept, cinder blocks set in ground to indicate unmarked graves. Surveyed 1993.

Nora B. TUELL April 9, 1893 April 23, 1961

Manora B. Wife of J. W. GRAYSON 1871–1936
Ernest Landon TUELL VIRGINIA A1C US AIR FORCE KOREA Dec 30 1930 March 9, 1966
Maria Virginia MARTIN 1915–1967
Our Parents Herman RUMBEAU Nov. 26, 1932 Nellie E. RUMBEAU May 6, 1940
Mother Nancy GRAYSON; Father William GRAYSON
Isabell HILL Born 1921 Died in 1951 Wife of Ben HILL
Haywood GRAYSON Died at the age of 66

Malviney Wife of Andrew WHITBY Died September 8, 1919 aged 58 years
Rev. Wm. PANNELL 1875–1943
Mary Ella WASHINGTON 1922–1966; Clifton WASHINGTON 1926–1968
John Wesley WASHINGTON January 23, 1947 June 22, 1968

Lueser Wife of Charley GRAYSON Died Apr 20, 1922 Aged 70 years
Rev. Jack BYRD Mt. Zion Church March 3, 1900
Lee Robert WASHINGTON Born in June 10, 1915 Died June 26, 1937
W. H. BUMBRAY was born Jan. 8, 1881 Died June 20, 1900

Caton Cemetery, Somerville, Virginia
Located 0.5 mile South East Route 637 on North side Route 610, iron fence, boxwood, right of house.

Cornelia T. CATON Jan. 10, 1843 Sept. 28, 1933
Richard H. CATON Sept. 8, 1845 March 9, 1924
CATON Janie Elizabeth Aug. 8, 1886 Sept. 8, 1947 Samuel Houston Sept. 16, 1876 Feb. 12, 1945
Harry Houston CATON Oct. 15, 1911 Feb. 11, 1913

Catlett Cemetery (Black), Catlett, Virginia
Located West end of Catlett on Route 28 between highway and railroad, well kept. Resurveyed 1991.

Harrison D. SKINNER Nov. 29, 1908 Oct. 15, 1980
Robert H. JACKSON
WANSER Marshall E. Apr. 8, 1870 Nov. 2, 1942; Martha E. July 21, 1873 May 28, 1960
Wm. McKinley WANSER Jan. 28, 1900 Dec. 22, 1926
WEBSTER, William H. Mar. 3, 1885 Dec. 12, 1960; Mable W. Aug. 9, 1892 Apr. 8, 1969
Cora M. WANSER 1895–1937
Margaret Ann SMITH 1952–1970 *(fhm)*
Christine V. FRYE 1932–1972 *(fhm)*
Henry POOLE 1909–1986 *(fhm)*
Janie T. BURGESS 1877–1937
William PERRY 1889–1961; Louvena B. PERRY 1896–1968
three fieldstone markers
George RAYMOND Died June 15, 1929 Aged 54 years
Chapman LEWIS 1905–1967 erected by his employer Mrs. Laws *(fieldstone marker)*
Belle ANDERSON 1905–1980
Norvell C. ANDERSON, Sr. 1899–1969
Norvell C. ANDERSON, Jr. Born Feb. 19, 1930 Died Nov. 1951
Philip G. GREEN Dec. 17, 1891 Mar. 8, 1941
James H. BUTLER 1851–1956
Estelle WILLIAMS 1923–1966 *(fhm)*
Simon ADDISON WILLIAMS VIRGINIA PVT US ARMY KOREA Feb. 24, 1925 July 9, 1973
William T. TAYLOR 1899–1955
William M. HALEY 1910–1936

BAKER Pearl H. Dec. 27, 1897 Feb. 1, 1990 Mother; Vivian L. July 16, 1926 July 16, 1927 Daughter *(fieldstone marker)*
WILLIAMS Father George W. 1884–1962; Mother Mary A. 1894–
Charles WILLIAMS 1929–1969 VIRGINIA PFC INFANTRY KOREA October 10, 1929 October 25, 1969
WALLER Charles M. 1865–1957; Emma R. 1870–1947
Will MONROE 1882–1969
Charles H. BALL 1960–1986 *(fhm)*
Rosie Lee WILLIAMS 1932–1989 *(fhm)*
2 unmarked graves
Mother Eliza FOUTZ BURGESS Oct. 6, 1883 Feb. 2, 1965
Leon Hampton SHILLINGTON, Jr. 1940–1987
Leon H. SHILLINGTON, Sr. 1915–1984 *(fhm)*
Mother: Mamie SHILLINGTON 1890–1969
Mamie Virginia THORNTON 1944–1987 *(fhm)*
Willie Monroe JACKSON 1882–1969 *(fhm)*
Wilhelmina L. BEVERLY June 1, 1904–February 29, 1988
Willie ROSS 1911–1987 *(fhm)*
Mother Viola ROSS 1906–1962
Jimmie ROSS 1948–1959
Ann Elizabeth LEWIS 1931–1984 *(fhm)*
Mother Virginia JACKSON 1913–1986 *(fhm)*
Baby Ivory K. BLACKWELL 1986–1986 *(fhm)*
Douglas Edwin CORUM 1949–1988
Marlo Deane SKINNER May 2, 1968 Oct. 5, 1987
Baby Girl SKINNER 1990 *(fhm)*
Davon Alexander MORRISEY 1987–1987 *(fhm)*
Viola G. PORTER Wife & Mother Sept. 10, 1911 Dec. 7, 1980
James Thomas PORTER VIRGINIA COX U.S.N. RESERVE WORLD WAR II Jan. 7, 1911 Oct. 6, 1973
Rosalie E. LOMAX February 14, 1900 September 15, 1956
Mrs. Ida V. LOMAX 1877–1962

Cattlett Cemetery, Catlett, Virginia
Located 1 mile North West of Route 28 on North of Route 667 back of house and outbuildings. Weedy, but enclosed by barbed wire fence. Resurveyed August 15, 1994 by Mr. Carson.

Elizabeth McCORMICK CATTLETT
John Madison CATTLETT Died Dec. 19, 1870 aged 76 years
Mary Emily CATTLETT Died Dec. 17, 1905 aged 50 years
Lourella Wife of John Madison CATTLETT Died Sep. 12, 1906 Aged 78 years
Charlotte Vivian Beloved Wife of Samuel CATTLETT Died June 12, 1853 aged 63 years
Samuel CATTLETT Died Sept. 16, 1855 aged 75 years
Archie Son of S. G. & E. McCORMICK Died June 25, 1865 Aged 20 months
Lottie Daughter of S. G. & E. McCORMICK who ended her brief and gentle life in Jesus June 10, 1873 in her 15th year
S. Gibson CATTLETT Born Sept. 3, 1818 Died Oct. 22, 1894
Agnes E. McCORMICK Beloved Wife of Judge E. T. DUNCAN of Mo. Died Jan. 9, 1911 Aged 89 years

Cedar Grove, Bealeton, Virginia
Located on Route 17, South West of Route 28. Surveyed 1991.

Thomas Albert FANT C.S.A. Co. H 4th Va. Cav. Born Sept. 27, 1841 Died January 2, 1935 Alexander
    WILLINGHAM C.S.A. 11th Va. Inf. Born 1823 Died Jan. 22, 1894 James W. GILKERSON Born July 6, 1822

Died April 20, 1901

No markers for:
George W. WILLIS
Morris Dodd WILLIS
Kathleen WILLIS
Annie FANT
Thomas FANT
Arthur FANT
Susan Washington GREEN
Thomas WALDEN C.S.A.
Frank HACKLEY C.S.A.
Horace JOHNSON C.S.A. [Co. H 4th Va. Cav. Born 1823 Died   ] *(Ripley Robinson will apply for Veterans*
   Administration stone when date of death is known)
George HACKLEY
Mrs. George HACKLEY
George Washington GOFF
Mrs. George Washington GOFF
Geo. Washington DIGGS C.S.A.
Mrs. Geo. Washington DIGGS

Cedar Grove Cemetery, Bealeton, Virginia
Southwest corner of intersection of Rts. 17 & 28. Survey completed Oct. 20, 1994. Nicely kept community cemetery with stone wall on two sides. Driveway gates kept padlocked. This cemetery has a number of monuments with photographs enameled on the stones. There are also several monuments with interesting artwork reflecting the interests or occupation of the deceased carved on the stones.

Beginning at front (Rt 17), east corner:
HESS Henry P. Aug. 8, 1919 Sept. 13, 1992; Fannie M. Aug. 2, 1917 Sept. 13, 1992
CATLIN Carl Franklin July 28, 1916 January 6, 1985; Roma WRIGHT April 21 1911
Bernard Allen son of Bernard & Elnora JAMES July 27, 1907 April 11, 1985
JAMES W. Randolph Sr. Feb. 24, 1923 Dec 5, 1993; Mildred I. "Tommie" June 1, 1925
CUNNINGHAM Rufus A. Dec. 1, 1916 June 12, 1976; Helen M. Feb. 21, 1918
Robert STRETIGHTIFF 1922 1993 *(fhm)*
Father BANKE Lawrence F. Apr. 15, 1924– ; Mother Barbara M. May 27, 1929 Jan. 26, 1988
BUTLER Clarence Feb. 4, 1922– ; Mary Dec. 17, 1921–
SMITH Henry Hancock Lee Mar. 25, 1905 Dec. 1, 1986; Watkins Donnell COX Sept, 26, 1907 Apr. 17, 1984
BUTLER Guy F. Aug. 31, 1905 Nov. 6, 1993; Nellie V. March 11, 1899 Feb. 19, 1985
Scott V. PAYNE 1912 1988 *(fhm)*
Lorraine E. PAYNE 1927 1984 *(fhm)*
Mary T. JENNINGS Jan. 21, 1922 Sept. 12, 1982
Edward B. WILLINGHAM husband 1870 1947
Anna V. WILLINGHAM wife 1873 1946
Ruby V. WILLINGHAM daughter 1902 1940
Grayson Bradford ROBINSON May 1, 1904 May 15, 1972
Olga WHITE ROBINSON Nov. 11, 1897 Dec. 16, 1968
under boxwood thicket:
Robert Edward LEE Jan. 15, 1866 April 8, 1926
Meia SHUMATE LEE Nov. 2, 1869 Nov. 30, 1937

Caroline E. daughter of H.W. & C.B. HEFLIN 1886 1908
Caroline B. HEFLIN December 19, 1849 August 9, 1931

Annie R. wife of Austin A. COLBERT May 20, 1846 Feb. 15, 1913

My husband Austin A. COLBERT June 1, 1842 Jan. 14, 1904

Infant Daisy C. [ROBINSON] Aug. 8, 1908 Oct. 8, 1908; Daisy V. wife of L.B. ROBINSON Nov. 9, 1875 Dec. 20, 1908

grave marked by 3 broom handles [Ruby W. BEACH 1902 1941]

DOWDEN Charles H. Sept. 21, 1909 Dec. 16, 1982; Grace H. Apr. 28, 1909 Dec. 24, 1977

Pearl V. HOLDER 1897 1907

HOLDER William T. Mar. 20, 1869 Jan. 26, 1948; Viola H. June 8, 1877 May 18, 1963

Margaret HANBACK 1824 1908 *(fhm)*

Molly HANBACK JACOBS *(fhm)*

C BROWN 1896 1911 [Mary O.] *(fhm)*

Murry P. BROWN 1892 1916 *(fhm)*

----- ------ 1865 1941 [Lucy E. BROWN] *(fhm)*

Infant Oct. 7, 1908; Sanford D. Sept. 21, 1902 July 20, 1903

Clayton M. CRUMP Oct. 23, 1878 Aug. 17, 1904

America V. wife of G.W. CRUMP May 15, 1853 Mar. 28, 1915

G.W. CRUMP, Sr. July 29, 1851 Nov. 13, 1935

Alma C. wife of R.H. WYTHES daughter of G.W. & A.V. CRUMP July 24, 1879 Dec. 6, 1925

KING William T. Nov. 8, 1875 Apr. 5, 1956; Maggie M. Feb. 4, 1878 Nov. 14, 1954

Harriet G. daughter of Wm. Tyler and Birdie E. KING Oct. 6, 1910 Nov. 26, 1916

COOPER E. Christine CLEAR May 22, 1922 November 11, 1976; Albert G. August 26, 1916 November 29, 1982

Julia Rebecca MARSHALL CLEAR May 4, 1895 June 30, 1993 *(fhm)*

CLEAR Christopher H. December 28, 1899 March 16, 1976; J. Rebecca ADAMS May 4, 1895

Wm. H. HARRISON 1870 1944

Sophie Lee BROWN March 9, 1885 Nov. 2, 1961

Charles Douglas BROWN April 14, 1883 June 11, 1950

Alfred C. CORDER Oct. 21, 1858 April 24, 1918; Margaret O. CORDER Mar. 4, 1861 Dec. 13, 1939

Mary C. CALLISON Jan. 3, 1895 Jan. 1, 1935

Julia C. PATTERSON Dec. 7, 1887 April 5, 1942

Louisa Jane wife of D TURK Jan. 25, 1847 Feb. 25, 1920; DeWitt C. TURK Oct. 18, 1842 Oct. 12, 1926

Delilah Pearl PERRY March 18, 1896 Feb. 28, 1988

PERRY Pearl March 18, 1876 Feb. 28, 1988 sister; Charles F. Oct. 11, 1890 Jan. 17, 1986 brother

PERRY William F. July 1, 1850 Jan. 29, 1920; Annie W. Sept. 18, 1855 March 3, 1941

SMITH George Harry Oct. 12, 1880 Feb. 3, 1931; Cora BELL Oct. 14, 1892 June 6 1957

Edward L. KANE 1873 1930; Lillian W. KANE 1879 1947; Walter KANE 1916 1930; Leonard KANE 1923 1944; Oscar KANE 1924 1949

Walter H. PERRY November 11, 1916 October 6, 1984

Juliet HUMPHRIES wife of John W. PERRY July 6, 1881 June 23, 1965

John W. PERRY Oct. 20, 1885 Oct. 31, 1933

Garland J. HOFFMAN June 16, 1933 Jan. 28, 1986

UTTERBACK Richard E. July 8, 1929 Mar. 24, 1986; Louise L. July 14, 1936–

Susie M. HOFFMAN 1909 1993 *(fhm)*

UMBERGER Dallas Kemp "Dick" 1901 1985; Margaret McALLISTER "Peggy" 1909 1983

Mary F. RITCHIE (UMBERGER) 1914 1976

ANNS Samuel K. Feb. 18, 1863 Nov. 16, 1949; Mary C. Feb. 22, 1865 Nov. 2, 1944

Dwight E. UMBERGER Virginia Pvt Btry D 406 CABN (AH) Dec 4 1903 Feb 24 1963

Allen Lee RITCHIE Apr. 14, 1944 Apr. 13, 1950

Pearl UMBERGER 1894 1944 (Erected by Benny MAZZA)

Mother Mary Jane FISHER wife of James H. UMBERGER September 3, 1873 November 24, 1954

Willie E. UMBERGER 1910 1932

Alice Virginia CUNNINGHAM July 31 1869 March 30, 1936

Joseph R. CUNNINGHAM Mar. 17, 1940 Dec. 23, 1940

Charles DOVELL 1872 1951

Joseph A. CUNNINGHAM May 15, 1973 May 17 1973

PERRY William F. July 1, 1850 Jan. 29, 1920; Annie W. Sept. 18, 1855 March 3, 1941

PERRY Pearl March 18, 1896 Feb. 28, 1988 sister; Charles F. Oct. 11, 1890 Jan. 17, 1986 brother

J. Franklin EDWARDS Dec. 14, 1870 Jan. 6, 1936; Martha Z. EDWARDS April 6, 1878 March 30, 1965

John Franklin, Jr. son of J.F. & M.Z. EDWARDS Sept. 4, 1909 Dec. 2, 1923

Joseph Hamilton son of J.F. & Martha Z. EDWARDS July 19, 1914 Dec. 18, 1916

Oswald M. PRICE Mar. 7, 1889 Feb. 12, 1957

Iva CORDER PRICE Feb. 23, 1890 Sept. 28, 1982

Raymond BORGMANN US Navy Apr 9 1904 Apr 1 1987

Laura Willis ROBINSON Oct. 10, 1915 Sept. 6, 1916

Thos. H. ROBINSON Co C 49th Regt Virginia Inf 1861-65 May 22, 1842 June 15, 1916

Laura B. ROBINSON wife of Thos. H. ROBINSON Dec. 12, 1846 Feb. 2, 1913

George Clearence CORDER Oct. 26, 1892 Oct. 30, 1892

Edgar Alexander EMBREY 1836 1921

Josephine CROPP EMBREY 1837 1927

Lizzie daughter of E.A. & T.T.J. EMBREY Sept. 1, 1876 Sept. 26, 1899

HOLMES Monroe J. 1837 1897 4th Va Cav CSA; wife Bettie M. 1856 1913

Mother Elizabeth A. BOWERS April 27, 1826 June 30, 1900; Margaret L. BOWERS Jan. 3, 1851 Nov. 11, 1939

Charles M. CROCKETT, Sr.

CROCKETT Charlie M. May 29, 1901 May 23, 1994; Mary W. [WEAVER] Aug. 31, 1907 Apr. 15, 1992

Cecil Pilcher HOLMES Feb. 4, 1895 Sept. 30, 1961

Annie Louise daughter of Geo. & L.R. SHANNON Jul. 14, 1898 Feb. 17, 1900

Alfred M. JOHNSON September 9, 1880 November 24, 1957

Susie C. JOHNSON August 22, 1893 March 14, 1961

Eliza A. WALDEN Nov. 27, 1813 Jan. 28, 1903

Thomas WALDEN *homemade marker*

Thomas Walden JOHNSON October 24, 1860 November 16, 1935

W. Morgan JOHNSON December 29, 1867 Aug. 30, 1919 husband

Joseph Moncure JOHNSON Sept. 25, 1913 June 16, 1982

Joseph E. JOHNSON Nov. 22, 1870 March 11, 1924

Horace Edward JOHNSON Mar. 20, 1864 Jan. 30, 1913

Francis E. WALDEN wife of Thomas JOHNSON Dec. 25, 1839 June 1, 1916

Thomas JOHNSON Sept. 17, 1830 June 17, 1902

SMITH Walter A. Jr. Oct. 29, 1901 Sept. 2, 1903

Evelyn SMITH HOLMES May 7, 1867 Dec. 4, 1931

A. Lewis SMITH June 29, 1868 Sept. 16, 1896

Mother Ellen OVERTON SMITH Feb. 18, 1844 July 26, 1902

Andrew Jackson SMITH Feb. 14, 1911 aged 64 years 1st Lt of Cal Co K 11th VA Reg CSA 62-65

Mary Elizabeth daughter of W.B. & Eloise H. Deatherage Feby. 20, 1895 July 26, 1895

Alice ROBINSON McDANIEL Feb. 10, 1892 Oct. 21, 1963

Margaret E. ROBINSON Sept. 9, 1848 Jan. 28, 1933

Jessie B. ROBINSON Mar. 8, 1844 Feb. 26, 1915

Maurice 1831 1887

4 unmarked graves

NEALE J. Claybrook Apr. 26, 1904 June 23, 1970; Lucille SMITH Sept. 10, 1909 Dec. 20, 1974

Roberta J. wife of J.W. JONES Feb. 2, 1846 Mar. 20, 1899

J.W. [JONES]

Randolph B. SMITH 1900 1918

Percy G. SMITH April 21, 1872 April 3, 1946

Lula M. SMITH 1875 1954
Sarah F. wife of Capt. H.H. OLINGER Nov. 23, 1824 Mar. 23, 1901
Capt H.H. OLINGER Sept. 16, 1816 April 18, 1878
Mrs. L.E. GUY 1819 1897
Carrie E. wife of G.E. KING Nov. 1, 1880 June 14, 1904
Annie C. PRIEST 1852 1891
Alban C. PRIEST 1860 1939
Julia A. 1866 1938
Berry Thomas PRIEST Aug. 4, 1881 Dec. 1, 1905 (*Masonic emblem*)
Butler CORDER Nov. 19, 1819 Dec. 25, 1899; Eliza CORDER Aug. 10, 1825 Dec. 20, 1900
FISHER Anthony Dec. 20, 1894 Nov. 26, 1984; Bertha V. Feb. 17, 1894 June 29, 1978
John H. WILSON 1848 1892
George W. HEFLIN 1846 1920
Josephine HEFLIN 1850 1927
Mary Louise R. GOFF Sept. 17, 1903 Aug. 7, 1939 mother
Harry C. GOFF, Sr. August 30, 1897 December 24, 1968
Irene BUSCH wife of Herbert F. EARLY July 9, 1897 Feb. 20, 1919
Herbert Franklin EARLY Jan. 7, 1893 June 28, 1956
Esther SMITH EARLY July 25, 1903 June 28, 1956
L.B. DOVELL 1866 1939; Hazel A. DOVELL 1903 1930
GREEN Walter T. January 14, 1884 August 8, 1955; Stella V. June 25, 1892 February 13, 1980
ADAMS George L. Sept. 12, 1877 Dec. 19, 1960; Ethel R. Jan. 11, 1897
ELKINS Earl F. April 12, 1929 June 16, 1988; Bertha M. Sept. 16, 1928
Mother Eva P. D'AGNENICA Dec. 26, 1906 Feb. 28, 1982
Sadie K. WHITT May 20, 1893 June 21, 1929
Robert K. DOVELL 1860 1940
Nora L. DOVELL 1880 1945

Menefee plot:
John W. WRIGHT June 2, 1905 April 12, 1989
Vera E. WRIGHT December 12, 1914 March 8, 1975
Charles B. MENEFEE April 13, 1879 April 30, 1954
Lesbia B. MENEFEE Jan. 13, 1887 Feb. 16, 1930

HACKLEY George A. Oct. 28, 1908 Jan. 23, 1992 World War II US Army 182nd Combat Eng South Pacific
    1943-1945; Lena F. Nov. 14, 1906 Jan. 21, 1992
EARLY Robert Edward Oct. 1, 1935 Mar. 3, 1991; Alice BUCHANAN May 21, 1944
EARLY David F. 1860 1943 father; mother P. Cordelia 1863 1938
George MILLMAN April 7, 1851 Dec. 19, 1910
Lucy Jane MILLMAN Aug. 7, 1862 Oct. 20, 1957
Wilfrid John MILLMAN Aug. 4, 1888 Feb. 10, 1934
William Richard MILLMAN Aug. 7, 1883 July 29, 1940
Gilbert L. MILLMAN Virginia Pvt Base Hosp World War I Sept 13 1895 Aug 9 1968
Robert Ray WILLIS Aug. 25, 1857 March 23, 1925
Robt. WILLIS Sept. 20, 1815 July 29, 1897
Martha J. WILLIS July 31, 1821 Dec. 19, 1892
WILLIS Bluchter Feb. 21, 1849 Jan. 21, 1891
Mary Lee WILLIS October 20, 1867 November 27, 1949
GREEN Andrew 1855 Feb. 11, 1927; Susie W. May 23, 1854 Dec. 26, 1923
Mamie daughter of J.M. & V.E. HALL June 7, 1876 June 29, 1878
Virginia Alice daughter of J.M. & V.E. HALL April 2, 1871 Nov. 11, 1873

DODD Lucy S. Sept. 11, 1854 Sept. 24, 1951; Joseph H. Mar. 12, 1847 June 28 1926
Mrs. Louisa EBBINHOUSEN erected by her children & grandchildren
Father Amon W, TEATES March 12, 1870 Nov. 19, 1939
Mother Maud OLINGER TEATES February 19, 1872 February 15, 1966
Lulu E. TEATES October 4, 1911–
Theodore P. TEATES March 13, 1898 Jan. 31, 1992
Sanford D.EMBREY June 27, 1843 March 15, 1924
Cassandria D. EMBREY June 9, 1851 Sept. 27, 1882 wife & mother
Agnes J. daughter of S.D. & C.D. EMBREY Oct. 25, 1875 Nov. 11, 1891
Sallie E. wife of S.E. EMBREY June 21, 1861 Sept 18, 1893
Mary Lucy daughter of G.N. & N.B. COLBERT Jan. 10, 1876 Dec. 6, 1876
E.L. TEMPLEMAN Dec. 29, 1819 Aug. 20, 1883 aged 63 yrs 7 mos & 21 dys
Mrs. F.A. TEMPLEMAN Nov. 6, 1824 Feb. 1, 1919
W.E. PRICE 1882 1944
Anna T. PRICE July 18, 1882 Aug. 9, 1968
BURKE Walter E. 1878 1960; Rosa L. 1877 1957
Grace Elizabeth 9 months Feb. 16, 1908
Catharine BROOKS Feb. 25, 1801 July 9, 1888
WILLINGHAM James A. Apr. 16, 1850 June 24, 1935; Lucetta F. Feb. 6, 1851 Feb. 24, 1935
Rev. Stockton W. COLE 1860 1929; Fannie PRICE COLE 1874 1964
James Lee son of J.M. & J.D. PRICE Sept. 6, 1887 Feb. 14, 1893
James M. PRICE Aug. 7, 1847 June 23, 1921; Julia D. PRICE Jan. 16, 1854 Nov. 7, 1939
Thomas F. SAUNDERS July 21, 1864 Jan. 21, 1908
Gladys Irene SAUNDERS March 19 1905 June 13, 1936
Earnest E. SUTHARD Feb. 25, 1866 Jan. 25, 1895
William E. EDWARDS December 12, 1850 June 29, 1897
Martha Ann EDWARDS May 18, 1853 April 29, 1949
E.T. EDWARDS 1887 1926

Matilda L. ROBINSON 1857 1903
Willis W. JOHNSON August 1, 1907 August 20, 1937
Flora WILLIS wife of A.M. JOHNSON Oct. 18, 1881 Oct. 18, 1919
Fannie F. wife of Chas. Brown WILLIS 1848 1899
Mabel Iona WILLIS May 24, 1880 Nov. 6, 1969
Fannie J. wife of S.R. MOXLEY Died Oct. 22, 1891 aged 58 years; Solomon R. MOXLEY Died Feb. 18, 1882 aged
    57 years
Horace JOHNSON Co H 4 Va Cav CSA 1823 1895
Mary Elizabeth widow of A.J. SILLING Sept. 22, 1840 Aug. 11, 1919
Clement A. SILLING Oct. 30, 1865 Feb. 26, 1891
BURKE Decatur Markell 1879 1953; William Herbert 1874 1960
PIQUET Howard Samuel 1903 1983; Dorothy V. BURKE 1906 1990
Mother Ann E. wife of Geo. T. SHANNON Dec. 13, 1845 Sept. 23, 1888
Father George T. SHANNON May 4, 1832 Aug. 15, 1897
KENT Graham Barlow July 15, 1911 July 11, 1984; Catherine PRICE Sept. 19, 1916–
Constance Barlow KENT March 10 1884 June 29, 1972
Mary Magdolene wife of John LINDNER died April 26, 1880 aged 63 years 6 months & 10 days
Louise daughter of F & Caroline LINDNER died Feby 10, 1874 aged 4 months and 17 days

Chas. F. HOLDER Sept. 16, 1872 Nov. 6, 1890
MOORE Webster H. Sept. 1, 1916– ; Bernice HALL Jul. 4, 1916 Apr. 24, 1976
Mildred LEHEW Sept. 14, 1896 Aug. 11, 1982
Matthew B. BROWN 1895 1963 *(fhm)*

Charles Philip son of Chas. Wm. & Harvey V. EMBREY (nee BRAWNER) Sept. 23, 1907 June 19, 1909
Margaret C. COLBERT Dec. 3, 1829 May 8, 1890
Husband Wm. Strother COLBERT July 22, 1807 Jan. 16, 1886
Forrest J. TEATES, Jr. Sept 21, 1946
Marguerite O. TEATES Aug. 23, 1910
Forrest J. TEATES SF2 US Navy World War II Aug 16 1909 Dec 16 1991
Mother Nannie M. JAMES Aug. 4, 1829 Sept. 9, 1903
Benjamin H. JAMES Oct. 11, 1829 Jan. 13, 1898
HORD mother Elizabeth B. wife of Dr. Ambrose HORD died April 12, 1889 aged 61 years
Aldridge James HORD April 11, 1848 Feb. 18, 1900
HORD Annie R. Feb. 14, 1887 July 4, 1972; Eugene L. Feb. 16, 1893 Nov. 29, 1978
A.J.F.
Thomas Albert FANT Co H 4 Va Cav CSA Sep. 27, 1841 Jan. 2, 1935
Blanche HUME PAYNE January 29, 1894 February 22, 1937
George Clifton PAYNE September 21, 1891 October 29, 1966
Roberta HACKLEY PAYNE June 10, 1856 June 17, 1935
James Edward PAYNE Sept. 1, 1855 Jan. 30, 1913
Daniel Clifton CULLEN December 17, 1891 December 16, 1924
Daniel Clifton CULLEN, Jr. Aug. 24, 1922 Mar. 22, 1923
Irma M. HACKLEY wife of K.V. DEMASTERS Dec. 21, 1905 Nov. 6, 1928
DEMASTERS Winnie I. March 28, 1899 March 9, 1992; Kembrough V. March 27, 1874 February 13, 1949
Herbert L. KANE Arpil 8, 1937 Dec. 8, 1988
HEFLIN Viola C. 1900 1928; William J. 1875 1969
Lawrence BROWN son of H & Fanny BROWN Nov. 12, 1919 July 9, 1936
BROWN Frances Jane (Fannie) February 13, 1894 May 17, 1981 mother; Henry Clay October 2, 1875 October 25, 1939 father
Thomas E. BROWN Jan. 24, 1924 Nov. 25, 1957
Dorothy S. TROW 1982 1991 *(fhm)*

Robert Lee HAMILTON Aug. 22, 1981 Jan. 12, 1982
Daniel Lee ELKINS Sept. 18, 1985 Nov. 7, 1985
Charles H. MASON 1905 1976
David M. HENSLEY Sept. 1928 Feb. 12, 1930 our baby
HENSLEY Herman W. son of L.R. and Florence HENSLEY Aug. 21, 1908 April 1, 1929
Hazel Florence HENSLEY 1925 1926
HENSLEY Elsie Lee Oct. 8, 1912 Mar. 1934; Leroy Nov. 19, 1883 Feb. 2, 1972; Amanda Bell Dec. 31, 1901 July 2, 1963
WEIMER Amzi April 2, 1875 Aug. 10, 1955; Hettie E. July 14, 1878 April 11, 1960
GRYMES Haywood L. May 28, 1903 Nov. 21, 1972; Vada C. Mar. 27, 1905 June 20, 1982
Pvt Edward Teates PALMER Nov. 21, 1922 killed in action April 19, 1945 Germany
Arthur H. PALMER May 3, 1883 June 8, 1950
Grover E. TEATES Jan. 15, 1889 Oct. 19, 1918
TEATES William W. Oct. 4, 1868 Nov. 15, 1939; May L. May 11, 1875 Dec. 1, 1957
Henry Anna wife of G.W. LOWRY Aug. 23, 1850 Sept. 5, 1928
Andrew T. JONES 1882 1909; Mary Alma JONES 1884 1909
BARRON Robert M. 1902 1955; Blanche J. 1904 1987
George E. DUVALL husband of Bettie DUVALL Jan. 18, 1855 Sept. 29, 189-
Mary A. DUVALL Dec. 30, 1842 Mar. 17, 1913
Tandy DUVALL Sept. 17, 1842 Jan. 12, 1909
William H. DUVALL April 19, 1866 March 24, 1898
Jennie DUVALL wife of William H. DUVALL March 18, 1868 Dec. 8, 1897
Mary Susan wife of Fitzhugh L. DUVALL died March 10, 1893

Henry Hancock LEE Aug. 26, 1837 July 23, 1911 (CSA marker); Olivia D. NUTT wife of Henry H. LEE Nov. 8, 1839 Feb. 9, 1922

Frank son of Henry & Olivia LEE Jan. 1, 1879 Sept. 10, 1899

Alice LEE wife of J.W. SMITH Mar. 8, 1882 Sept. 21, 1914

Rev. William Field BAIN born in Williamsburg, Va. July 20, 1831 died in Charlottesville, Va. January 17, 1902. Entered the Virginia Conference, Methodist Episcopal church, South in October 1851. A true minister of the gospel of Christ for half a century. He gave best years and unstinted labor to add to the sum of human happiness and moral elevation. In the pulpit he declared the whole counsel of God. His sermons were the outgivings of a man bent on aequitting himself of a hugh responsibility. In prayer he was especially gifted. As a pastor he was conscientious and diligent. this dear headed, large hearted, firm and indefatigable minister brought a blessing wherever he labored. Our father

Mrs. Lucie C. wife of Rev. W.F. BAIN of the Virginia Annual Conference died in Richmond, Va. Oct. 2nd 1890 age 56 years

Mattie Florence BAIN daughter of Rev. W.F. and Lucy C. BAIN August 19, 1861 November 11, 1931

Richard SHANNON 1836 1908; Mary Ellen SHANNON 1846 1924

Emma SHANNON Feb. 7, 1869 Feb. 13, 1943

Grayson E. OLINGER Nov. 11, 1823 Sept. 16, 1920 (CSA marker)

Mother Martha A. wife of Grayson E. OLINGER Nov. 1, 1836 Mar. 6, 1894

William Y. SMITH June 19, 1896 Jan. 21, 1945

P.L. PILCHER July 24, 1827 April 29, 1903

James H. LOFLAND May 29, 1854 May 25, 1887; Millard F. LOFLAND Sept. 28, 1856 Oct. 10, 1877

Hugh Leroy CAMERON son of Hugh B. & Martha D. CAMERON Sept. 6, 1880 Oct. 28, 1908

Hugh B. CAMERON Sept. 10, 1836 January 20, 1892(masonic emblem)

Martha D. wife of H.B. CAMERON Feb. 7, 1838 Mar. 9, 1922

Victoria CAMERON JONES Oct. 26, 1863 March 17, 1935

Sara CAMERON JOHNSON March 5, 1877 March 14, 1967

Father & mother Thos. H. DOWELL May 8, 1827 Aug. 12, 1892; Mary J. DOWELL Jan. 10, 1831 Sept. 18, 1891

Arthur E. DOWELL May 25, 1856 March 13, 1918

William Lee DOWELL 1836 1942

Anna R. daughter of J.E. & Ida M. DOWELL Oct. 28, 1898 Nov. 27, 1898

Sallie Bowling KING Jul. 1, 1858 Sept. 7, 1893

Infant son of Leonard & Lena KEMPER December 11, 1922 December 12, 1922

Mary M. KEMPER January 30, 1853 June 25, 1921

Rufus W. KEMPER May 20, 1852 March 12, 1921

Adeline C. KEMPER July 8, 1820 July 9, 1903

CLOPTON Annie M. 1861 1899; Nathaniel V. 1850 1925

Columbia McCONCHIE LESSER 1869 1944

Martha B. McCONCHIE April 3, 1842 Feb. 16, 1920; James H. McCONCHIE Mar. 5, 1841 Dec. 27, 1897

Lucy BROWN 1830 1920

Frederick P. DUVALL Sept. 22, 1874 Jan. 5, 1900

Elmo Floyd McCONCHIE July 19, 1879 March 31, 1924 father

Mary C. McCONCHIE died June 13, 1893 aged 52 years; Robert McCONCHIE died July 20, 1901 aged 65 years

GILKERSON Harry J. 1856 1939; Ann LEE 1864 1944

Mary F. WRIGHT Oct. 15, 1827 Sept. 6, 1895; James W. GILKERSON July 6, 1822 April 20, 1901

Mary H. GILKERSON Feb. 27, 1861 Dec. 25, 1908

Mother Susan N. wife of D.B. CROUSHORN Nov. 27, 1820 Apr. 1, 1876 aged 55 yrs. 4 mo. & 4d

Father David B. CROUSHORN 1823 1911 aged 88 years

Virginia EASTHAM entered into rest Dec. 29, 1894

Virgil T. BAIN son of Rev. W.F. and Lucie C. BAIN September 12, 1866 February 8, 1933

Martha EASTHAM entered into rest Mar. 4, 1895

William TEATS Feb. 14, 1810 June 15, 1897; Robert M. TEATS Feb. 21, 1848 Nov. 30, 1913; Elizabeth W.

TEATS Aug. 22, 1846 April 8, 1935

Tandy E. DUVALL Feby. 11, 1871 Sept. 22, 1894

A loving remembrance of her daughter Sarah C. DUVALL April 10, 1879 Feb. 25, 1900

Infant son of Preston & Dorothy DUVALL

DUVALL C. Preston Oct. 22, 1911 Oct. 24, 1988; H. Dorothy Mar. 1, 1915–

Mary Taylor BOTTS July 21, 1860 June 10, 1922

Brother Kenneth L. BOTTS May 2, 1871 Nov. 8, 1903

Father William F. BOTTS April 21, 1819 May 17, 1887

BOTTS J. Frederick Aug. 31, 1896 Mar. 9, 1948; Bessie BELL Dec. 9, 1861 Nov. 24, 1946; Kate A. Nov. 20, 1863

Lottie TEATES April 26, 1881 January 26, 1964

Olinger plot:

Alice G. SMITH Sept. 23, 1936 Aug. 10, 1955

Roland T. OLINGER Mar. 20, 1902 Dec. 14, 1954

Alice T. OLINGER Feb. 9, 1874 April 1, 1944

Stonewall G. OLINGER Dec. 14, 1863 Jan. 27, 1965

Gene G. OLINGER SSGT US Air Force 1940 1991

Jesse W. TEATES Dec. 17, 1883 Nov. 26, 1915

blank *(fhm)*

Carrie J. WILLIS 1882 1961

Turner A. WILLIS 1862 1948

Jamie Selma infant daughter of T.A. & Kate F. WILLIS Mar. 21, 1887 July 14, 1887 *Lying next to above stone, and on its side*

Wyllian E. TEATES wife of W. Earl MARTIN June 4, 1895 Aug. 4, 1925; W. Earl MARTIN, Jr. July 4, 1919 Feb. 15, 1926

Otelia WOOD THORN May 18, 1863 June 28, 1941; Minnie THORN HARRIS June 14, 1883 March 30, 1928

PAYNE Hugh Hunter May 19, 1901 December 28, 1972; Mary Elizabeth September 1, 1895 January 12, 1981

John W. BURGESS 1855 1937; his wife Mary E. HEFLIN 1860 1944

Katherine B. BECK 1915 1984

PAYNE Gordon R. Mar. 6, 1897 Nov. 20, 1970; Golder M. July 9, 1909–

Norman Lee son of Gordon R. & Golder M. PAYNE June 13, 1930 Oct. 19, 1931

Mary Ellen DOUGLAS CARTER November 13, 1926 March 4, 1994 age 67 *(fhm)*

Bertha E. ADAMS April 10, 1891 March 1, 1985

John F. ADAMS July 13, 1881 April 6, 1958

Ellen D. CATLIN 1890 1934

Anna HARRISON ADAMS September 11, 1853 April 30, 1928

Bernard P. HARRISON 1856 1925

Virginia W. ADAMS 1843 1918

Mildred T. MILLER 1893 1934

Agnes Lee ADAMS 1887 1923

Virginia W. ADAMS Nov. 18, 1879 Oct. 31, 1915

Edwin T. ADAMS Feb. 20, 1833 June 3, 1914; Ann R. daughter of E.T. & Anna S. ADAMS Sept. 12, 1884 May 24, 1915

Basil G. WHITE husband of Jennie WHITE (*stone sunkenB rest of inscription underground*)

Edith P. CHAPMAN June 26, 1922 Jan. 22, 1926; Orville C. CHAPMAN Dec. 12, 1875 Mch. 14, 1929; Olive H. HUNT Dec. 25, 1893 May 27, 1955

Lizzie B. DOVELL March 3, 1865 Dec. 12, 1894

Mrs. Kathern DUVAL October 14, 1800 August 8, 1898 beloved wife of Tandy DUVAL

William A. DRUMMOND August 13, 1882 June 2, 1902 beloved son of Daniel W. DRUMMOND Nov. 13, 1856 Dec. 27, 1949; his wife Laura M. DRUMMOND Aug. 27, 1851 Sept. 19, 1937

Kitty Nora DRUMMOND June 19, 1880 January 26, 1882 beloved daughter of Daniel W. DRUMMOND and Laura M. DRUMMOND

William Robert CHAPMAN, Jr. Born near Lois, Fauquier County, Va. September 6, 1908 died in Clarksville,

Mecklenburg County, Va. November 19, 1913 age 5 years 2 months & 13 days; In loving memory of our darling little son W.R. CHAPMAN, Jr. erected by his father W.R. CHAPMAN, Sr.

Miss Mary Frances ANDERSON Jan. 11, 1827 married Robt. R. CHAPMAN June 23, 1842. He died June 5, 1857. On Sept. 2, 1869 she married Wm. D. BENNETT God called her home Sept. 14, 1899.

James Jackson MILLER died Feb. 15, 1897 aged 67 yrs. 2 mos. & 10 ds.

Mother Sarah MILLER July 9, 1830 March 25, 1912

John Hensel MILLER Sept. 22, 1859 June 4, 1943

Chas. Luther CULLEN May 16, 1877 March 25, 1879

Daniel C. CULLEN May 24, 1847 June 26, 1904; L. Jennie P. CULLEN Jan. 16, 1848 June 14, 1902

James H. CULLEN Mar. 3, 1873 Jan. 29, 1909

Sara Lydia CULLEN Dec. 15, 1881 Apr. 3, 1960

Francillo ROUTT May 20, 1854 June 5, 1921

Mother Mary J. McCONCHIE wife of Geo. W. McCONCHIE died Sept. 12, 1886 in the 56th year of her age

Little Everette son of Lula A. & S.M. McCONCHIE died Jan. 9, 1896 aged 5 yrs & 5 mos.

Jennie M. McCONCHIE April 15, 1860 April 30, 1919

WYNANT Emma V. 1867 1956; Lelia R. 1862 1939

Mother Rebecca P. WYNANT Mar. 30, 1827 April 15, 1901

Allen H. WYNANT April 18, 1860 Aug. 12, 1927; Geo. Edward J. son of H.H. & R. WYNANT Dec. 8, 1870 July 26, 1893

George W. BUSSELL 1839 1922

Susanna O. BUSSELL 1853 1895

W. Allen BUSSELL 1873 1897

Isabell BUSSELL 1902 1896

W.A. KANE Dec. 6, 1860 Feb. 19, 1891; his son John A. April 30, 1886 Mar. 30, 1906

Matilda wife of A. KANE June 22, 1825 Aug. 4, 1906; Ambrose KANE June 8, 1830 July 16, 1904

Aura W. MASON Mar. 20, 1880 Mar. 6, 1972

George H. MASON Virginia Pvt Hospital Corps Spanish America War March 24 1874 Aug 19 1951

Lelia P. daughter of George D. & Josephine KANE May 15, 1887 April 25, 1888

George D. KANE May 10, 1855 April 8, 1916; Josephine KANE Nov. 16, 1858 Jan. 16, 1944

TIMMONS (*no further inscription*)

TIMMONS (*no further inscription*)

Lucy A. TIMMONS Apr. 13, 1836 Dec. 15, 1912

TIMMONS (*no further inscription*)

HANBACK John W. died Mar. 25, 1940 age 72 yrs: Annie LEE died Aug. 12, 1904 age 41 yrs.

Homer H. HANBACK May 11, 1885 Oct. 23, 1967

Marye Arey wife of Adolphus MOORE died May 1889 aged 30 years

EDDINS Abram F. 1869 1948; Pearl B. 1877 1956

Mary A. wife of James A. SPEER Sept. 4, 1835 Sept. 3, 1891

Mother Alice ROUTT June 7, 1858 Dec. 16, 1936

Huldah C. CLARK wife of Geo. W. CLARK Jan. 24, 1837 Jan. 22, 1916; Geo. W. CLARK husband of Huldah C. CLARK Mar. 19, 1835 Feb. 18, 1913

Ladoma DAWSON son of O.F. & Lillian H. CLARK Dec. 9, 1900 Feb. 22, 1902

Susan H. DODD wife of French DODD died Aug. 25, 1902 aged 73 years

HALL Susie Braund December 13, 1873 March 10, 1925; Edward Fletcher October 26, 1871 September 24, 1959

William GROVES died Aug. 24, 1905 aged 82 years

GROVES George Hampton July 10, 1864 Oct. 19, 1937; Myrtie Carolina Oct. 4, 1866 April 27, 1936

Frances W. LEE wife of Robt. B. SMITH Feb. 22, 1874 June 14, 1927

Robert B. SMITH April 27, 1887 Sept. 11, 1960

Mabel T. SMITH May 1, 1884 Sept. 3, 1968

George Lee BRYANT 1917 1918

BRYANT Gertrude L. 1898 1987; Gales M. 1893 1969
Elizabeth HATHAWAY June 19, 1919 Oct. 21, 1966
Julia T. BLACKWELL July 1, 1836 Nov. 16, 1913
C. Gordon BLACKWELL July 30, 1862 March 8, 1929
Wm. M. BLACKWELL Nov. 15, 1860 Sept. 21, 1931; Olivia L. May 3, 1873 July 31, 1953
ZIRKE plot:
Earl S. 1895 1930
Homer L. 1893 1918
Mother Fannie L. 1864 1927
Father Daniel T. 1858 1929
Irvin L. 1905 1931

Samuel T. SHERMAN 1859 1946
SHERMAN Cora B. 1896 1920; Willard 1888 19--
Willie W. DODD daughter of John and Sallie MANUEL October 3, 1900 November 29, 1926
DODD Nellie REEVES August 5, 1903 December 19, 1982; James Ray May 16, 1892 November 25, 1974
Julian D. DODD Aug. 8, 1888 June 20, 1928
Julia Ann daughter of James and Joan DODD May 15, 1965 September 17, 1965

SISK Bernard Ashby Oct. 9, 1905 Aug. 18, 1971; Edna RHODES Oct. 24, 1908 June 30, 1993
RHODES Charles N. 1874 1936; Jannie L. 1869 1929
DOWELL James C. 1874 1943; Lucy T. 1864 1950
Enoch G. DOORES 1887 1938
Maude L. DOORES 1893 1970

COFFMAN plot:
 Joseph A. Nov. 7, 1866 Dec. 3, 1918
 Mary E. July 21, 1867 April 5, 1952
 Charles C. Mar. 13, 1895 Mar. 14, 1931

Charlotte P. BROWN April 10, 1890 June 11, 1973
Gertrude EGERTON BROWN Dec. 4, 1893 Oct. 21, 1918
Lesbia A. BROWN 1861 1910; H. Clay BROWN 1841 1923 [*CSA marker*]
Susie G. infant of J.D. & Lula A. BAILEY Feb. 23, 1911 Aug. 20, 1911
James D. BAILEY May 13, 1885 Dec. 2, 1925
Travis J. HOFFMAN Dec. 11, 1876 Oct. 26, 1961
Ethel W. HOFFMAN Sept. 14, 1885 June 15, 1963
Hettie E. WYNANT June 23, 1860 July 18, 1932
WYNANT Edward L. Jan. 22, 1896 Nov. 21, 1908; W.P. Jan. 7, 1857 Nov. 9, 1907
J.P.F. MILLER Oct. 26, 1865 July 10, 1946
Nellie CAMERON wife of J.P.F. MILLER Aug. 14, 1874 Dec. 20, 1976
MILLER Giles S. 1898 1956
John J. HEFLIN 1906 1973 *(fhm)*
Sallie W. HEFLIN 1874 1955 *(fhm)*
HEFLIN Ida. L. Jan. 7, 1862 Sept. 9, 1902; her husband John T. July 25, 1860 Dec. 15, 1917
Rosa E. WILLINGHAM Nov. 18, 1870 Nov. 8, 1879
Richard WILLINGHAM Jan. 5, 1852 Aug. 26, 1924
Thomas E. WILLINGHAM Jan. 5, 1852 Aug. 26, 1924
Lizzie Olive GROVES 1880 1932
Ada BERRYMAN WILLINGHAM Feb. 22, 1848 April 28, 1942
Claudia W. GROVES Dec. 2, 1888 Aug. 1, 1950
Ivan Leonard GROVES May 21, 1894 Feb. 27, 1975

Alexander WILLINGHAM Co I 11 Va Inf CSA 1823 1894

Elizabeth WILLINGHAM the wife of A. WILLINGHAM died July 1880 in the 49 year [*stone found broken 1994*]

JACOBS Howard A. Aug. 5, 1895 Nov. 15, 1973; Erva GROVES Feb. 26, 1902 July 27, 1987

Alma GROVES Dec. 13. 1911–

Vida GROVES Dec. 6, 1899 Jan. 8, 1978

Elwood GROVES SSgt U.S. Army World War II Mar 12 1923 Oct 30 1993 8th Air Force

GROVES Lewis Ray Apr. 3, 1856 Sept. 11, 1930; Martha Ida GROVES July 16, 1876 July 17, 1957

Radford son of Lewis & Ida GROVES Dec. 13, 1911 Aug. 7, 1912

Fielding Ray son of Lewis & Ida GROVES Jan. 21, 1905 Feb. 26, 1908

Abigail GROVES May 16, 1818 Dec. 20, 1889

Ray son of John & Evie SMITH 1926 1927

Baby daughter of A.D. & M.S. KANE Nov. 9, 1896 Nov. 18, 1896

Alexander D. KANE Jan. 15, 1857 Feb. 14, 1922; Margaret S. KANE Sept. 30, 1875 Mar. 3, 1966

Helen K.H. TOLBERT Feb. 21, 1903 Jun. 25, 1990 daughter of A.D. & M.S. KANE mother of Scott Christian HUMPHREY

Virginia KANE Mar. 21, 1863 Feb. 20, 1942

Stephen ROGERS Mar. 3, 1842 Mar. 23, 1924; Matilda ROGERS Aug. 31, 1858 Dec. 16, 1941

Lula G. May 22, 1891 Dec. 10, 1891; J. Astor Aug. 28, 1895 Sept. 21, 1896; Lelia s. Jan. 2, 1898 May 26, 1898

William M. son of G.W. & A.J. WHITE Sept. 19, 1903 May 19, 1907 baby

WHITE George W. Nov. 1, 1857 July 18, 1942; Alice J. Dec. 10, 1860 March 27, 1930

two unmarked graves

Murry L. WHITE 1878 1934

BUTLER Flora G. 1874 1945; Julius L. 1871 1941

Elizabeth C. JAMES Jan. 11, 1904 Feb. 22, 1962

JAMES Fannie Chilton Sept. 22, 1861 Aug. 10, 1931; John Spilman May 5, 1861 Feb. 16, 1932

L.E. JAMES Feb. 15, 1838 July 10, 1921

T.F. JAMES Oct. 31, 1832 Aug. 20, 1892 [*CSA marker found in 1968, now gone*]

rock marker

Elizabeth BERRYMAN Nov. 19, 1823 June 17, 1910 (*concrete marker - 1968 inscription, no inscription 1994*)

Mother Sarah J. RUFFNER wife of James W. RUFFNER Feb. 7, 1842 Apr. 19, 1903; Father James W. RUFFNER June 17, 1844 March 24, 1926

Charles E. RUFFNER July 15, 1872 Feb. 2, 1952

MILLER J. Walter Jr. Aug. 15, 1932 Sept. 7, 1990; Marjorie H. June 29, 1935 April 21, 1990

MILLER James Walter March 31, 1909 June 6, 1973

Clarence L. HOTTEL husband of Edmonia J. COCKRILL Sept. 30, 1886 April 24, 1946

HOTTEL Pleasant Magruder September 29, 1854 August 26, 1929; Catharine LARKINS October 19, 1858 January 1, 1935

Cora E. wife of W.H. HERNDON Sept. 1, 1882 Mar. 21, 1925

Willie H.B. son of Mr. & Mrs. P.M. HOTTEL born Oct. 26, 1897 at "Oranda", Shenandoah Co., Va. died Nov. 20, 1913 aged 16 yrs. & 25 days

William E. Case died July 16, 1908 aged 68 yr's., husband; Agnes R. CASE died Oct. 12, 1950 aged 74 yr's., wife

Mother Caroline V. KANE wife of Homer B. SHIPP died Feb. 15, 1925 aged 47 years

OLINGER W. Randolph Oct. 12, 1897 May 24, 1984; Ruth W. Oct. 11, 1901 Mar. 19. 1990

J.H. BAYLES Mar. 15, 1846 July 21, 1914; W.H. BAYLES Jan. 21, 1878 July 17, 1923; Josephine BAYLES July 30, 1843 Sept. 16, 1923

Randolph SMITH Virginia Tec5 Field Arty World War II JUly 11 1921 April 15 1945

SMITH Bruce W. 1888 1954; Ester L. 1887 1953

Aubrey M. SMITH Sept. 4, 1912 June 23, 1914

BRYANT Benjamin T. 1893 1931; Laura V. BRYANT 1896 1960

David Allen FIELDING Mar. 3, 1900 May 28, 1976

Audrey JENKINS FIELDING Nov. 6, 1905 Mar. 26, 1991
FIELDING Reginald S. Oct. 30, 1890 Jan. 5, 1967; Susan HENRY May 2, 1890 Sept. 30, 1983
Leslie F. FIELDING April 1, 1860 July 16, 1925; Laura ALLEN FIELDING June 15, 1859 Aug. 9, 1939 (*obelisk
   broken 1994, inscription from 1968 face down*)

GRAY plot:
Eloise G. HERRELL 1902 1979
Louise Elizabeth 1871 1925
James Thomas 1867 1914

Rosser M. KANE May 28, 1901 Feb. 21, 1971
Clyde Franklin KANE Dec. 13, 1888 June 10, 1921 (*American Legion marker*)
KANE Annie B. Jan. 18, 1869 July 14, 1934; Rosser F. July 18, 1864 Oct. 10, 1936
Aunt Mary Virginia KANE February 8, 1874 February 26, 1961
Mother Martha KANE O'ROARK February 23, 1880 January 21, 1955
Martha Jane KANE Oct.30, 1849 Sept. 3, 1943; James T. KANE Feb. 12, 1946 Apr. 27,1915
BURKE A. Clayton May 7, 1887 Dec. 13, 1973; Madeline K. Jan. 17, 1893 Jan. 15, 1972
BURKE Jennings P. Dec. 9, 1906 Aug. 10, 1988; Margaret Sept. 14, 1915 Sept. 10, 1979
Ida Virginia LAWTON Jan. 20, 1883 Oct. 11, 1957
Father Alpheus BRAY; mother Frances BRAY; brother Austin BRAY; sister-in-law Emma BRAY (*dates unknown*)
Pauline daughter of Geo. W. & Carrie E. HEFLIN Feb. 24, 1906 Aug. 18, 1906
HEFLIN Irvin W. July 1, 1899 Feb. 24, 1921; George W. HEFLIN Sept. 27, 1876 Feb. 6, 1953; Carrie E. HEFLIN
   Dec. 28, 1877 Dec. 11, 1970
Husband T. Walter SWART Jan. 14, 1868 Sept. 17, 1907
Ella SWART BENNETT Feb. 27. 1870 June 30, 1919
William H. BENNETT Oct. 7, 1874 June 15, 1944
M. Clay BENNETT Feb. 24, 1834 May 5, 1898; Julia F. BENNETT Nov. 13, 1842 July 7, 1906
Addie H. wife of J.N. KEISER died June 2, 1905 aged 61 yrs, 8 mos 13 days
WHITE Harvey A. January 23, 1891 October 24, 1966; Lena R. February 14, 1894 April 14, 1978
BERRYMAN Kate 1861 1937; Chas. M. 1845 1897
Robert S. FINKS Jan. 7, 1860 married June 4, 1889 died Nov. 1, 1891
several unmarked graves
Maud daughter of A.W. & Laura SPRINGER Dec. 21, 1877 Oc. 5, 1898
Ernest C. HAZEL October 31, 1898 September 12, 1953 (*Masonic emblem*)
Walter W. HAZEL August 2, 1903 July 7, 1954 (*Masonic emblem*)
Elizabeth HAZEL
John F. HAZEL
John M. HAZEL
Frederick B. HAZEL April 29, 1897 March 12, 1964 (*Masonic emblem*)
Frank HACKLEY *metal marker*
William H. husband of Fannie G. HACKLEY & son of Frank & Sallie HACKLEY Sept. 27, 1878 Sept. 23,1901
WILLINGHAM Annie B. 1877 1916; James R. 1877 1928
Mary E. wife of Patrick CLARK Nov. 29, 1901 aged 69 years
Annie D. HERRELL May 7, 1861 Jan. 26, 1908; William C. HERRELL April 25, 1845 Aug. 14, 1910
C.H infant son of H.H. & M.J. CLAGGETT Sept. 25, 1913
Louise GROVES EMBREY Mar. 28, 1908 Aug. 2, 1970
Joseph Ray GROVES Nov. 15, 1879 Jan. 23, 1961
GROVES John J. 1847 1902; Virginia MERCER 1855 1956; Wilbur H. 1898 1940
Nannie TAYLOR BOWER Feb. 11, 1865 Feb. 17, 1956
William O. BOWER Dec. 25, 1848 Nov. 6, 1913
Mary T. BOWER 1852 Jan. 30, 1910
Our father and mother Alexander P. BOWER and Elizabeth ROTHROCK his wife

Ida M. wife of W.O. SHUMATE Mar. 29, 1854 Sept. 10, 1911
Robert Clay son of F.G. & Ida M. MIDDLETON Feb 17, 1879 Jan. 23, 1902
Baby Ada Virginia infant daughter of W.O. & Ida M. SHUMATE Jan. 4, 1890 July 16, 1890
Edith B. wife of O.W. SHUMATE Jan. 14, 1881 June 21, 1906; infant of O.W. & Edith B. SHUMATE June 15, 1904
Father W.J. SHUMATE April 22, 1822 April 20, 1883
Maggie B. wife of C.W. YATES Sept. 7, 1876 Sept. 2, 1902
YATES Charles W. 1864 1953; Blanch B. 1880 1971
Hester H. RANKIN wife of William S. RANKIN July 3, 1833 Feb. 12, 1907
Wilda BURTON 1870 1911
Laura LEPREUX 1892 1935
Brother W.D. BENNETT
Annie BENNETT COX January 17, 1873 March 31, 1952
John I. COX September 5, 1874 August 5, 1945
Brother and sister James KEYS died June 20, 1888 aged 53 years 5 months & 20 days; Almira J. KEYS his wife died June 12, 1883 aged 52 years 6 months & 12 days
Aunt Susan ROGERS Nov. 21, 1855 BENNETT
Husband Charlie S. TRIPLETT Sept. 19, 1896 aged 36 years

Charles Avery TROUGHTON Oct. 22, 1884 Sept. 1, 1942 (*missing 1994*)
Edmond Seymour TROUGHTON Aug. 17, 1886 Jan. 8, 1908
Edmond Skillman TROUGHTON June 24, 1848 March 13, 1918
Jennie Avery TROUGHTON Dec. 1, 1856 June 5, 1943
Permelia RHODES died April 7, 1909 age 43 yrs, 6 mo. 19 days
Raymond A. BURKE Aug. 3, 1891 Feb. 21, 1922
Daughter Susan Roberta BURKE April 6, 1869 Oct. 17, 1888; daughter Mary Ella BURKE April 18, 1876 Oct. 7, 1892
George W. BURKE Nov. 21, 1842 Oct. 17, 1908; Ida R. BURKE June 25, 1852 Jan. 9, 1942
Sarah JACOBS wife of James R. EDWARDS September 15, 1866 May 12, 1939
Sarah McDONALD JACOBS 1834 1922
Frank C. SMITH Dec. 27, 1909 May 30, 1917
George Shelby TANNEHILL 1822 1914
WMW *rock marker*
WILLINGHAM John L. 1891 1968; Annie B. 1904 1986
S. FLETCHER April 25, 1879
W.R. HALL April 26, 1877 May 12, 1883
J.M. HALL born Jan. 16, 1881 (*rest in ground*)
C.E. HALL Jan. 22, 1849 Nov. 5, 1934; Sarah H. HALL June 18, 1879 Nov. 16, 1933
HALL Charles H. Aug. 3, 1875 June 26, 1960 father; Sarah C. June 11,1879 Aug. 3, 1967 mother
Lee D. HALL Sept. 6, 1883 Feb. 11, 1945
Mary S. BOELYN 1865 1956 (*missing 1994*)

Lucinda STRIBLING Mar. 7, 1836 July 2, 1928
William Oscar son of Wm. J. & V.E. BOWER SHUMATE Aug. 17, 1858 Apr. 17, 1928
Hattie T. SHUMATE June 28, 1868 April 19, 1954
Thomas Jackson SHUMATE Jan. 10, 1887 Jan. 25, 1935
Irena CHANDLER Aug. 4, 1896 Sept. 2, 1896 (*stone lying on ground near stone outbuilding 1994, not in plot*)
L.E. wife of J.A. CHANDLER Apr. 10, 1864 Oct. 2, 1896
Susan F. wife of J.A. CHANDLER Apr. 30, 1860 July 11, 1923
Ann F. wife of L.A. RHINE died Dec. 26, 1897 age 74 years
Father William A. WHITE March 9, 1866 April 23, 1935
Mother Lillian Early Oct. 5, 1865 April 1, 1930

Fauquier County, Virginia Tombstone Inscriptions Volume 2

Permelia F. WHITE Sept. 15, 1904 Sept. 18, 1924
Anne L. WHITE Sept. 18, 1899 Aug. 22, 1932
James L. SUTHARD 1863 1945
Laura SUTHARD 1863 1926
C.M. SUTHARD 1898 1945
Grace SUTHARD BROWN 1900–
E.T. SUTHARD 1893 1930
Frank J. LOMAX 1844 1923; Cornelia J. LOMAX 1853 1925
James T. LOMAX 1882 1943
unmarked grave
Helen L. DIGGES 1875 1897
DIGGES George W. July 31, 1835 July 17, 1922 (*CSA marker*);Mary Frances 1825 1897; Mary W. 1866 Oct. 21,
    1902; Bettie M. Dec. 1870 1925
David W. JAMES July 24, 1855–; his wife Annie Elizabeth LEE JAMES daughter of Duncan JAMES May 15, 1862
    Sept. 13, 1928
Thomas H. JAMES son of David W. & Betty JAMES July 5, 1880 July 12, 1903
NEALE Wayland Dunaway Jan. 7, 1875 May 2, 1948; Mary Virginia JAMES May 13, 1886 Feb. 11, 1973
Silas Claybrooke NEALE Oct. 28, 1828 May 20, 1919; Bettie HARRISON NEALE July 4, 1839 April 15, 1907
Mary A. daughter of Silas A. & Bettie H. NEALE July 18, 1884 Biv, 28, 1898
Mary Lucy McCONCHIE June 8, 1912 September 27 1928; Lena Edwards McCONCHIE October 4, 1882
    December 31, 1977
BYERS Rosa L. Aug. 10, 1914 May 6, 1986; Woodrow W. July 15, 1915 Nov. 3, 1985
Blanche A. MORAN 1871 1918
John T. SOUTHARD Jan. 17, 1832 Jan. 8, 1908; Elizabeth S. SOUTHARD Jan. 1, 1840 Nov. 28, 1906
SMITH
Dora Louise ADAMS Sept. 24, 1925 Apr. 6, 1984

Luther Brook COMPTON Sept. 20, 1886 Mar. 7, 1909
Richard E. COMPTON Aug. 11, 1891 Aug. 16, 1955
Ursa B. COMPTON Nov. 1, 1875 Jan. 30, 1962
L. McCONCHIE bornB died Aug. 1907
Bettie RYAN wife of W McCONCHIE Dec. 18, 1874 Feb. 25, 1915
W. Cooper McCONCHIE May 6, 1881 October 11, 1953
James Ryan McCONCHIE July 28, 1904 Feb. 4, 1923
R.L. McCONCHIE Feb. 25, 1915 Mar. 29, 1915
WHITE Cliffie ROUTT Feb. 8, 1878 Oct. 15, 1963

BUTLER plot:
Edwin Julian Apr. 5, 1880 May 10, 1938
Wade Kyle Feb. 3, 1887 March 15, 1914
Winter Payne July 18, 1853 June 25, 1914
Amelia Speer Jan. 16, 1863 Jan. 5, 1948
William Delaware March 11, 1899 July 9, 1956

Jesse James BUTLER Feb. 7, 1891 Oct. 25, 1966 a loving uncle
Ready RECTOR killed by cars Mar. 28, 1903 in his 16 year
Miss Laura Ellen RECTOR died August 21, 1967 aged 72 years (*missing 1994*)
Mrs. Susan RECTOR died December 31, 1932 aged 81 yrs. 10 mos. 7 days (*missing 1994*)
Eliza H. McCONCHIE wife of J.R. McCONCHIE Jan. 29, 1872 Dec. 4, 1900 wife, mother, friend
Mary MARTIN wife of John J. NEWMAN Apr. 26, 1883 Nov. 7, 1918
Laura D. MARTIN Dec. 2, 1880 Jan. 4, 1982
Richard C. MARTIN Mar. 18, 1849 Jan. 19, 1921

Mary C. MARTIN Jan. 4, 1856 Apr. 28, 1945
John Homer GUY Oct. 6, 1898 Aug. 23, 1918
GUY Lorena WITMER October 7, 1878 December 20, 1952; John Henry August 9, 1876 March 16, 1944
Nina WITMER OREBAUGH November 24, 1866 June 10, 1958
homemade wooden stake
Lottie M. 1908 1909 (*wood marker inscription from 1968*)
CURTIS B. Thomas June 25, 1865 June 28, 1944; Ella M. Dec. 30, 1870
Walter REID 1889 1964
DOVELL Robert K. 1898– ; Elsie I. 1905 1975
DODD Charles Aubrey March 7, 1881 October 21, 1964; Kitty Cheston January 21, 1884 July 31, 1982
Hazel HALDEMAN BOWER July 1, 1895 Dec. 5, 1971
William C. BOWER March 13, 1893 March 15, 1949
Neva N. WEAKLEY wife of Hubert S. WEAKLEY Apr. 6, 1880 Jan. 16, 1919
wooden marker, no inscription
Branch BROWN (*rest in ground*)
James Franklin MYERS, Jr. son of James and Betty MYERS Sept. 16, 1963 Sept. 16, 1963
James Lonnie TATE Nov. 10, 1897 Aug. 27, 1987
Laura Virginia MASON 1872 1953
Lora E. STRICKLER wife of W.P. STRICKLER Mar. 1, 1873 July 21, 1921
Herbert F. STRICKLER Feb. 6, 1908 adopted son of Lora E. STRICKLER
Clifford James SUTHARD April 15, 1889 Dec. 4, 1925
Hazael GRIFFITH died June 1912; Rosie GRIFFITH 1853 1937
William WHITMER 1824 1905; daughter Sallie May 1870 1906
John H. WHITMER 1865 1938; Alice G. WHITMER 1870 1906
Gussie WHITMER SMITH 1893 1976
LEE Ludwell A. June 24, 1876 Nov. 18, 1958; Margaret L. June 29, 1970 July 8, 1922
James W. LEE Nov. 18, 1851 Feb. 5, 1907
Lucy LEE wife of Edward T. EMBREY April 15, 1870 July 12, 1938
Abbie MARTIN 1862 1941
R. Granville MARTIN 1856 1924
Malvina MARTIN 1855 1922
Hezekiah E. MARTIN 1854 1921
Lucy MARTIN 1844 1914
Myrtle Ivy [FIELDS] March 13, 1913 April 13, 1914
Elnora Virginia [FIELDS] March 22, 1872 June 11, 1947
Benjamin Douglas [FIELDS] May 4, 1867 Feb. 9, 1940
Robert Henry [FIELDS] June 6, 1869 August 2, 1927
Welford E. OLIVER 1902 1967
C.W. OLIVER 1872 1948; wife Annie Lee GROVES 1874 1939
William Newton BERRYMAN Jan. 30, 1833 Sept. 29, 1911
rock marker

Monument: 1956 Perpetual care for their family plot established by owners and/or survivors of these honored ones:

Carlton McKee BOWER
Edward O. BOWER
William O. BOWER
H. Clay BROWN
Gertrude L. BRYANT
Charles E. BUICKEROOD
George W. BURKE
Walter E. BURKE

W. Herbert BURKE
William E. BUTLER
Winter P. BUTLER
Thomas W. JOHNSON
Alexander D. KANE
J. Taylor KANE
Rosser F. KANE
William A. KANE
Leonard C. KEMPER
Robert E. LEE
Frank J. LOMAX
Richard C. MARTIN
George H. MASON
Robert McCONCHIE
Hugh B. CAMERON
A. Claudius CHAPMAN
W. Guy CHANDLER
Nathaniel v. CLOPTON
Rev. Stockton W. COLE
John I. COX
Daniel G. CULLEN
Alice CUNNINGHAM
Thomas D. DIGGES
Enoch G. DOORES
Ernest P. DOVELL
Arthur DOWELL
Clay DOWELL
Daniel W. DRUMMOND
Herbert F. EARLY
Rev. A.F. EDDINS
Sanford D. EMBREY
Benjamin D. FIELD
John T. GRAY
Thomas GREEN
John GUY
Charles E. HALL
Edward F. HALL
John W. HANBACK
Frederick B. HAZEL
George W. HEFLIN
William T. HOLDER
Monroe HOLMES
James Aldridge HORD
Charles B. MENEFEE
J.P. Fletcher MILLER
Wayland D. NEALE
Charles W. OLINGER
Stonewall G. OLINGER
Arthur H. PALMER
Charles F. PERRY
Pearl PERRY
William F. PERRY

Hon. James M. PRICE
Charles RHODES
Jesse B. ROBINSON
J.W. RUFFNER
Clifton SHANNON
S. Thomas SHERMAN
William O. SHUMATE
Percy G. SMITH
Walter A. SMITH
Willis P. STRICKLER
James L. SUTHARD
John T. SUTHARD
Amon W. TEATES
Lottie TEATES
Robert M. TEATES
Richard WILLINGHAM, Sr.
W. Harvey WISE
William E. WYNANT

MILLER James C. October 11, 1929 May 21, 1985
JAMES Bernard M. 1884 1964; Elnora B. 1884 1973
Lawrence H. BURROWS May 24, 1900 February 12, 1973
Percy A. RILEY November 7, 1896 December 25, 1966
Mary E. RILEY March 10, 1877 April 4, 1963
Emmet C. RILEY December 7, 1867 July 19, 1912
Mary A. WHITMER 1831 1890; Edwin B. WHITMER 1857 1883
Infant boy REID 1970 1970 *(fhm)*
unmarked grave
Amy Beth LEMLEY July 25, 1970 July 26, 1970
rock marker
GROVES James H. March 24, 1902 October 10, 1983; Clara V. July 21, 1898–
MURRAY Ebert E. Dec. 26, 1897 Feb. 17, 1987; Sadie M. May 12, 1897 Nov. 8, 1993
Matthew CULBERTSON May 5, 1972 November 12, 1978
McINTURFF Ernest R. May 23, 1892 May 28, 1961
Archie J. FANT 1877 195- *(fhm)*
Lottie C. FANT Dec. 17, 1877 April 29, 1938
Pearl JONES ELLIS Aug. 5, 1914 Dec. 10, 1937
Mary K. JONES 1876 1968
Samuel H. JONES 1878 1961
William L. JONES 1905 1961
Charles Taylor BOWER 1889 1939
BOWER Eleanor RHODES Dec. 19, 1899 May 29, 1986; Edward Hill Jan. 14, 1896 Apr. 22, 1952
Carlton MacRae BOWER Aug. 12, 1899 Dec. 14, 1959

WHITE William Lee Oct. 27, 1915 Oct. 5, 1989; Emma MASON Feb. 2, 1927– married Sept. 14, 1944
THORN Lula Y. 1878 1966; Wesley C. 1885 1950
TEATES Bryan Womer July 9, 1904– ; Mae Afton BENNETT June 2, 1903–
Roy WHITE
Lizzie B. SOUTTER August 31, 1881 March 7, 1957
Moses R. WHITE Virginia Cpl 353 Infantry World War II May 26 1920 March 27 1945
Mary WISE
WISE Dr. William Harvey Sept. 24, 1872 June 19, 1944; Margaret CULLEN WISE Sept. 26, 1875 Sept. 11, 1936

Clyde E. EARLY Pfc U.S. Army Jan. 14, 1935 Aug. 2, 1993
DUVALL Johnnie Washington April 26, 1910 Dec. 17, 1937 son of Richard W. & Laura A. DUVALL
DUVALL Laura BAILEY Oct. 24, 1876 June 22, 1950; Richard W. Dec. 22, 1868 Jan. 25, 1943
Son Lieut. James Elmer DUVALL Dec. 13, 1915 Sept. 7, 1944 who died in the service of his country in the South
    West Pacific area [*Purple Heart emblem*]
homemade cross
James L. BOSTIC Jan. 11, 1956 Apr. 28, 1981 son; Annie F. BOSTIC Dec. 24, 1916 Nov. 16, 1978 mother
Son Walter R. GAINES 1935–; Father Eppie GAINES 1902 1940
TAPP Nolan Harding May 22, 1921 Dec. 20, 1943
Josie P. TAPP Oct. 15, 1890 Nov. 1, 1962
Charlie TAPP April 2, 1885 March 19, 1944
TAPP Irven Earl Aug. 30, 1941 July 7, 1944; Mary Francis March 26, 1945 April 20, 1946
EARLY Frankie F.; Giles M. Aug. 17, 1925 Apr. 27, 1985
EARLY Wade Rankin May 4, 1900 December 7, 1989; Helen MILLER July 25, 1899 January 22, 1893
WHITE Newton c. 1866 1943; Robert W. 1866 1917
BARBER Lloyd Lendol Sept. 18, 1900 Dec. 24, 1986; Clara WHITE Jan. 10, 1904–
Mildred Letita CAMPBELL Mar. 14, 1876 May 31, 1950
CAMPBELL Ned Burns 1896 1958; Katherine F. 1895 1984
James Harvey WEEKS, Jr. October 9, 1903 July 24, 1981
Hazel MANKEY WEEKS September 14, 1904 April 27, 1987
James Harvey WEEKS Aug. 1, 1861 Jan. 14, 1945
Edith M. WEEKS Jan. 21, 1871 Nov. 1939
Luther R. COMPTON May 6, 1887 Mar. 1, 1953
Elizabeth M. COMPTON Jan. 31, 1891 May 7, 1973
COMPTON Clyde Richard Oct. 13, 1911–; Clara BROWN Sept. 15, 1911 Aug. 17, 1993
Elizabeth COMPTON REID Oct. 16, 1914 Sept. 10, 1937

BUTLER Mary Elizabeth May 28, 1918 March 1, 1939
BUTLER Willam E. Sr. Mar. 10, 1896 Jan. 24, 1993; Agnes L. Sept. 2, 1901 Nov. 3, 1984
Lucy F. BUTLER Jan. 8, 1874 Sept. 28, 1953
Edward G. BUTLER May 21, 1872 Nov. 29, 1952
Lendel H. HOLSCLAW Sept. 26, 1898 August 23, 1942
Emma R. HOLSCLAW Nov. 29, 1898 Jan. 7, 1978
Elizabeth Jane ROHR EARLY Aug. 27, 1892 Aug. 4, 1973
Willis Embry EARLY June 26, 1896 Jan. 22, 1962
Garry Clark EARLY Virginia Adan U.S. Navy March 24 1937 Dec 2 1959
Phoebe Jean DIGGES Aug. 14, 1935 Jan. 21, 1946
DIGGES Roscoe A. Jan. 5, 1908–; Louise F. Sept. 24, 1907 Oct. 19, 1980
Charles Dwight RITCHIE TSgt U.S. Army World War II Aug 8 1916 Feb. 6 1989
RITCHIE Wilbur Early Aug. 30, 1883 Nov. 27, 1963; Ethel LEE March 2, 1888 Jan. 4, 1967
Baby DANAHY Nov. 22, 1946
Doug COOPY 1970 1992 *(fhm)*
Mary Olive FAULCONER Oct. 4, 1901 Dec. 17, 1991
Richard Elmer FAULCONER June 5, 1895 June 1, 1949
DOWNS Clyde Leo Nov. 25, 1880 June 5, 1960; Jennie C. April 8, 1884 June 21, 1972
HOLMES Nolan R. Feb. 9, 1918 July 23, 1982; Elizabeth H. Sept. 10, 1917 Jan. 12, 1992
DOVELL Cleveland O. Dec. 26, 1907 Dec. 17, 1945; Zella R. Jan. 6, 1910 June 15, 1988
Shirley E. EARLY 1943 1994 *(fhm)*
W. Edgar BURKE 1909 1959
Robert T. BURKE Nov. 2, 1944 Dec. 14, 1944
Roy Isaac KIPPS December 23, 1923 December 1, 1949
Mary V. CLOPTON 1879 1957

CLOPTON John T. Nov. 11, 1903 Dec. 23, 1991; Mattie Nov. 3, 1906 Sept. 1, 1994
JONES Mattie V. Oct. 28, 1888 Oct. 24, 1965; Morgan K. June 16, 1884 Dec. 2, 1949
THORN Nora R. March 1, 1901 March 26, 1961; William N. June 14, 1898 June 26, 1960
Aldridge "Buster" DYE 1919 1962
COX John D. Nov. 3, 1886 Jan. 2, 1968; Mamie E. Feb. 5, 1895–
George N. GROVES 1909 1964 *(fhm)*
OGDEN Robert F. 1886 1964; Katie F. 1886 1975
SMITH John M. 1924 1982

Lottie M. 1906 1909 (o*n top of dirt pile outside of fenced cemetery*)

SMITH John Wesley Jan. 11, 1876 Jan. 24, 1968; Evie GROVES Nov. 2, 1897 Aug. 16, 1983
EARLY Conway Houston July 8, 1920 May 5, 1984; Catherine Oberta EDWARDS SMITH March 2, 1919–
BOLEY Golder Beverly March 16, 1905 July 29, 1977; Verean GROVES July 12, 1909 March 30, 1992
KIPPS Lawrence Ray May 21, 1927–; Norma NEESE March 1, 1931–
Michael Howard COCKERILL Feb. 14, 1956 Sept. 8, 1990
McCONCHIE William C. Nov. 9, 1901 Dec. 29, 1973; Ola J. Aug 7, 1903–
John H.McCONCHIE Aug. 2, 1912 Feb. 24, 1950
Alma N. McCONCHIE Apr. 9, 1903 Aug. 12, 1969
KANE Irving H. Aug. 31, 1906–; Rubie M. Sept. 24, 1908 May 2, 1975
John Keith KANE August 7, 1898 January 26, 1951
Rosie Virginia KANE July 19, 1908 April 9, 1975
TANNEHILL Oscar L. 1986 1959; Alice G. 1902 1989
TANNEHILL William C. July 17, 1869 Dec. 19, 1956; Virginia C. Oct. 17, 1874 May 3, 1950
George Clifton TANNEHILL May 16, 1902 Dec. 4, 1975
HANBACK James Stewart Oct. 5, 1918–; Nell EARLY May 12, 1923 Oct. 13, 1989; Margaret Ann June 27, 1959
   Dec. 3, 1982
EDWARDS Albert George Dec. 3, 1916–; Margaret EARLY Sept. 2, 1920–; William Cameron Oct. 8, 1954 Nov.
   10, 1978
SHERMAN Elmer Ray Feb. 18, 1891 Apr. 22, 1957; Odessa E. Dec. 27, 1892 June 18, 1980
NICHOLS Walter Melvin July 24, 1879 Dec. 23, 1951; wife Elizabeth COMPTON Feb. 23, 1886 June 27, 1969
NICHOLS Clinton R. Sept. 11, 1909 Mar. 27, 1963
NICHOLS James Dudley Jan. 22, 1916 Nov. 22, 1966
SCHINDEL Rosie L. June 12, 1892 Dec. 12, 1983; Lee Burton, Sr. Aug. 1, 1902 Oct. 12, 1971
Laura V. SCHINDEL Oct. 25, 1875 July 28, 1925
Patricia Gail daughter of James & Dorothy WHITE Feb. 25, 1947 Dec. 9, 1954
James F. WHITE Oct. 18, 1925 Feb. 23, 1971
James Floyd WHITE Virginia Sgt Co A 15 Infantry World War II Oct 18 1925 Feb 23 1971
ABERNATHY husband Wilbur Joe Dec. 16, 1917 June 25, 1979
BERRY Edgar K May 21, 1891 May 15, 1970; Edward K. Jan. 2, 1915 Dec. 12, 1944; Sadie E. Sept. 25, 1893 July
   16, 1965
GARTNER Wallace P. June 15, 1888 Mar. 13, 1956; Clara E. July 23, 1889 May 14, 1956
John T. DOVELL June 22, 1951 Nov. 25, 1956
Donald L. DOVELL Aug. 27, 1949 June 23, 1961
Sadie I. DOVELL Sept. 10, 1932 Jan. 28, 1984
James Alfred BUTLER Dec. 15, 1905 Feb. 26, 1984
SOUTHARD Charlie W. Aug. 29, 1908 Feb. 17, 1985; Frances F. Aug. 23, 1911 July 19, 1980
McDONALD Carey K. July 16, 1898 May 14, 1957; Elton A. January 2, 1902 February 4, 1972
TRUMBO Jacob F. December 14, 1886 February 4, 1959; Barbara R. February 5, 1888 October 24, 1964
SMOOT Norman A. 1894 1961; Gertrude E. 1894 1963
GRAY Walter M. April 27, 1894 August 15, 1960; Florence W. August 23, 1896 October 21, 1978
GRAY Rixey F. Jan. 29, 1900 Jan. 23, 1975; Ruth E. Mar. 14, 1901

PEREZ Daniel May 17, 1902–; Viola W. January 12, 1914–
WILLINGHAM Roland E. April 30, 1907 October 30, 1967; Minnie June 14, 1918–
EDWARDS James C. November 10, 1918–; Annie P. June 20, 1918–; married Aug. 17, 1940
Edgar R. EDWARDS 1921 1992
EDWARDS Lenes C. July 30, 1887 Jan. 13, 1968; Mabel F. Dec. 14, 1895 Apr. 15, 1971

Frank Deale SWIFT February 13, 1930 September 29, 1987
Robert B. BOWLES, Jr. July 4, 1939 June 11, 1986
EICHER Lloyd H. June 20, 1892 April 4, 1974; Lutie W. June 4, 1893 Feb. 9,. 1983
G. Delmore GRIMES September 7, 1930 October 31, 1991
Peggy MARTIN GRIMES January 2, 1931 October 30, 1966
NEESE Ralph P. 1906 1974; Frances L. 1907–
CLEM G. Roland May 18, 1895 April 23, 1977; Elizabeth C. April 12, 1897 Feb. 19, 1988
Gilbert Roland CLEM Pfc US Army World War I May 18 1895 Apr 23 1977
· H. Evelyn COCKERILL Jan. 18, 1916 Jan. 5, 1979
GREENSTREET Herman 1909 1990; wife Emma Matilda 1907 1977
Augusta R. CULLEN 1887 1964
CULLEN James A. Apr. 30, 1921 Aug. 11, 1983; Helen K. Aug. 27, 1919-
COOK Ellwood R. Jan. 17, 1895 Dec. 28, 1966; Ruth L. Mar. 27, 1894 Apr. 19, 1967
Leonard James CLATTERBUCK Aug. 19, 1912 Oct. 5, 1965
Raymond E. TANNEHILL Sgt US Army World War II July 13, 1911 May 11, 1976
TANNEHILL Raymond July 13, 1911 May 11, 1976; Jean F. Aug. 25, 1922 March 23, 1988
SICHERT Joseph Mar. 13, 1903 June 1, 1986; Willie May 10, 1905 Jan. 28, 1981
BALLARD Kermit H. July 11, 1914 May 25, 1985; Anna T. August 11, 1914-
DODSON George W. May 10, 1891 Apr. 5, 1958; Ethel R. May 18, 1895 Aug. 28, 1987
KANE James D. Mar. 20, 1886 Feb. 19, 1976; Nannie R. Feb. 28, 1892 Dec. 22, 1985
Rosie L. KANE July 20, 1888 March 2, 1975
HALL Carol T. Sept. 25, 1938–; Ruby V. April 18, 1927 Dec. 31, 1989
WHITE Floyd E. April 25, 1901 Feb. 1, 1963; Jessie E. Dec. 21, 1906 April 27, 1989

Clarence R. WILLINGHAM Dec. 19, 1899 Jan. 10, 1938
Flora B. JENKINS March 2, 1889 Nov. 1, 1966
JENKINS Malcolm L. Aug. 24, 1911 July 1, 1964; Grace M. AVERETT Jan. 30, 1914 May 27, 1993
Carolyn K. MARTIN May 22, 1948 Sept. 4, 1976
Father John Z. COFFMAN October 5, 1905 March 18, 1984
HIGHLANDER Charlie E. Apr. 27, 1903 June 5, 1966; Janie P. Dec. 24, 1903 Nov. 30, 1974
Michael Wayne son of Alton & Ruth WHITE Sept. 25, 1970 Sept. 30, 1970
WHITE George A. Dec. 6, 1921–; Olive H. May 8, 1926–
McARTOR Robert W. 1897 1984; Mary Louise 1906 1984 married Apr. 14, 1924
Sidney C. FALLER 1954 1985 *(fhm)*
Sidney Carl FALLER January 5, 1909 December 18, 1976
Betty M. BECKER 1931 1994 *(fhm)*
MILSTEAD James A. Dec. 22, 1904 Oct. 29, 1986; Naomi C. Dec. 22, 1903–
Judy Lee MAUCK Dec. 17, 1950 Oct. 27, 1968
Earl S. MENEFEE Pvt US Army World War II 1915 1976
SHIPP William Jefferson June 18, 1904 Nov. 19, 1971; Irene LITTLE Jan. 3, 1911 Nov. 6, 1990
KIPPS John Robert December 9, 1919–; Wilma HANBACK August 15, 1922–
Jackie Lynn daughter of Robert & Cora COFFMAN Dec. 7, 1962 Nov. 12, 1970
COFFMAN Floyd R. May 21, 1913 June 26, 1993; Anne EVANS November 4, 1917–
Gracen Nevitt HANBACK April 11, 1921 June 19, 1982
HANBACK Herman G. Oct. 28, 1887 May 21, 1973; Charlotte N. Sept. 23, 1893 Dec. 29, 1968
Husband/son John Wesley BOGGS Nov. 27, 1966 July 4, 1993 "Wes" father of Wesley Brian

Sharon E. LACY 1933 1992

Edgar T. LACY, Sr. 1927 1981

Edgar T. LACY US Marine Corps World War II Jun 28 1927 Apr 29 1981

FIELD Milton H. Oct. 21, 1915–; Edith W. May 2, 1920 Aug. 21, 1991

Raymond S. FIELD July 29, 1905 Aug. 29, 1981

monument base, monument gone

RITCHIE Homer N. March 1, 1887 September 8, 1980; Christine E. July 14, 1897 January 12, 1993

Thomas Michael Ritchie Glaettli McDANIEL July 7, 1967 Sept. 26, 1993

Carl Rollo GLAETTLI "Bill" Jan. 10, 1913 Dec. 17, 1983; Miriam RITCHIE GLAETTLI Dec. 4, 1916–;
  granddaughter Melissa Deanna GLAETTLI May 5, 1986

Paul H. STILLWELL Virginia Pfc US Army World War II June 11 1915 May 9 1973

Margaret M. STILLWELL Aug. 31, 1926–

McDANIEL Marvin D. April 6, 1911 April 29, 1985; Minnie L. July 30, 1908 March 13, 1971

Daddy William Kemper GOULDTHORPE April 6, 1901 January 12, 1981

Mother Lesbie Louise GOULDTHORPE May 12, 1908 April 16, 1971

KELLY Carl Barlow Oct. 27, 1922–; Edna ARMENTROUT July 9, 1910 Apr. 3, 1987

McKinley CUNNINGHAM May 17, 1898 April 14, 1971

Nellie CUNNINGHAM Oct. 7, 1914 July 13, 1980

FOX Leroy E. Nov. 15, 1902 Oct. 7, 1989; Ruth HAINES Jan 13, 1908

BELL J. Edwin May 17, 1906 June 5, 1978; Hazel R. October 12, 1914–

GLASGOW Rossell Alvin Oct. 12, 1909 Aug. 16, 1977; Louise DODSON July 24, 1918 Nov. 14, 1987

MAYHUGH Pendleton B. Sept. 21, 1903 July 2, 1972; Nettie M. Sept. 22, 1908 Feb. 28, 1990

Herbert Lloyd MAYHUGH Sept. 16, 1928 July 27, 1965

Ronald B. MAYHUGH Sp4 US Army Vietnam Oct. 19, 1947 Aug. 3, 1989

GRAY Hampton S. 1900 1973; Marion P. 1901 1981

Bernard Allen TAYLOR, Jr. May 3, 1965 May 23, 1987

TAYLOR William H. 1909 1973; Louise G. 1910 1986

Harry M. OLINGER Virginia Tec5 Med Sup Depot World War II June 22 1917 Sept. 11 1972

MOORE Amos Mar. 8, 1902 May 12, 1985; Daisy I. Sept. 9, 1905 Oct. 18, 1984

Charles W. BOSWELL 1927 1971 *(fhm)*

Andrew Wayne BARNETTE July 4, 1964 April 2, 1973

Matthew R. CORBIN 1908 1990 *(fhm)*

Lawrence B. CORBIN May 20, 1890 July 7, 1971

James Bill HOPKINS 1940 1991 *(fhm)*

Reynolds R. FRAZIER Pvt US Army World War II *(no dates)*

CHAPMAN C. Edwin July 20, 1923–; Joan G. October 20, 1923–

CHAPMAN T. Kenneth Mar. 15, 1928 Dec. 11, 1985; Barbara C. Apr. 25, 1936– ; married Jan. 8, 1954

BOGGS Rebecca Nov. 11, 1908 Aug. 22, 1991; Arnold Feb. 23, 1906 Jan. 24, 1986

Son Mikael Warren BOGGS Aug. 3, 1965 July 4, 1993 "Mike"

Carlis MULLINS Feb. 9, 1946 Jan. 9, 1992 grandson

Otella MULLINS Sept. 13, 1896–

GOBER George R. Dec. 20, 1911 Dec. 2, 1993; Snowball Apr. 19, 1972 Oct. 14, 1986; Beulah S. Apr. 19, 1915–

WILLINGHAM Auburn A. Sept. 10, 1910 July 30, 1979; Marion V. Oct. 15, 1916 Jan. 2, 1989 "Sis"

Edith BARB WHITT Apr. 6, 1923 July 7, 1974

William Labon BARB July 6, 1901 January 12, 1981

Rosa NICHOLS BARB May 29, 1907 August 17, 1973

MAY Luther Aldine May 11, 1900 July 26, 1976; Jessie NICHOLS Mar. 10, 1902 Jan. 23, 1989, married June 17,
  1920

MULLINS Tennie Mar. 24, 1913 Feb. 2, 1987; Marie Apr. 5, 1918–

Keith Anthony infant son of Tonie & Delorace MULLINS July 11, 1976 Aug. 27, 1976
Richard D. EDDINS Tec4 US Army World War II 1914 1979
TAPP Earl S. Aug. 15, 1914 Jan. 18, 1987; Anna M. Mar. 25, 1923 Nov. 12, 1988 married Sept. 25, 1937
Alton E. TIMBERLAKE 1917 1979 *(fhm)*
Joseph P. MAYHUGH March 1, 1932 December 6, 1973
Fred L. EPPARD Mar. 18, 1909 Oct. 10, 1984 father
HEFLIN George M. 1901 1974; Laura M. 1902–; George E. 1938–
KIRBY Joseph E. [Sr.] Feb. 2, 1921 Aug. 14, 1978; Betty J. Nov. 30, 1930–
MOORE Herman M. June 8, 1925–; Helen M. Oct. 13, 1926–

Floyd E. COFFMAN July 17, 1927 Dec. 16, 1976
Mother Mary E. BARNETTE Jan. 4, 1938 Sept4, 1975
Debra Lynn GOULDTHORPE June 10, 1965 November 21, 1981 daughter
Richard Austin WILT Dec. 19, 1942 Jan. 11, 1980
CORNWELL "Bill" Iden F. 1915 1989; Ruth E. 1923 1992
Daughter Gale M. ROMINE September 13, 1943 December 31, 1980
Mother Margaret M. PETERS July 25, 1896 April 10, 1985
Louis B. ENNIS, Sr. Cm5 US Navy World War II 1921 1976
Son Glen F. KIDD Nov. 6, 1961 Aug. 8, 1978
Shawn T[yler] CORSARO June 17, 1981 Feb. 25, 1991
HARRIS Samuel R. Apr. 25, 1915 May 9, 1980; Mildred L. Mar. 31, 1921 Dec. 18, 1982
monument base, no monument
Brother John Edward TYREE Nov. 19, 1959 Oct. 8, 1984

Velman Lynn WILLIAMS Mar. 25, 1939 Sept. 30, 1986
William J. HITE Sept. 8, 1935 Oct. 20, 1978
William J. HITE Oct. 17, 1911 Mar. 2, 1987
BALLANCE Audrey Floyd May 23, 1917– "Daddy Pop"; Norma Caroline Dec. 29, 1929 Sept. 3, 1992 "Mommy Pop"
Nora Lynn NEALE Jan. 6, 1964 Nov. 20, 1981 beloved daughter of James C. and Donna L. NEALE
WHITE James J. 1906 1984; Mamie C. 1905 1991
MILLER Carl B. Apr. 20, 1935 July 6, 1990; Lavon K. Oct. 12, 1940 Liz P. CUNNINGHAM COOKE March 25, 1906–
BYRD Jerome B. Jul. 10, 1911–; Irene I. Feb. 14, 1910 Aug. 13, 1982
Mother Flossie N. SMITH July 23, 1908 Dec. 21, 1985
Ida MILLER HICKS April 28, 1901 November 5, 1982
Chester A. HICKS MD February 16, 1900 September 13, 1988
Lucy M. DODD Sept. 12, 1899 Jan 23, 1987
May Erva DODD PIRIE May 26, 1890 May 12, 1985; Raymond Matthews PIRIE March 11, 1894 July 2, 1988
Daughter Vernece R. McCONCHIE Feb. 23, 1957 Sept. 4, 1981
McCONCHIE Elmo F. November 12, 1923 June 20, 1976; Helen L. March 17, 1927

Larry Arnett DEAN, Jr. February 15, 1966 October 14, 1984; Gregory Scott DEAN September 22, 1967 April 6, 1983
EARLY Donald Francis April 30, 1927 February 14, 1992
Richard L. PERRY Sept. 17, 1945 Nov. 18, 1988
Terry Ann KNIPFER 1965 1990 *(fhm)*
Walter B. WHITESIDE February 20, 1925 October 8, 1982
Heyward E. WALDROP September 13, 1923 July 18, 1975

Richard Warfield DUVALL Dec. 22, 1868 Jan. 25, 1943 *(behind stone outbuilding)*

Chappelear (Benjamin Garner) Slave Cemetery, near Delaplane, Virginia
Located 2.5 miles North of Delaplane on Route 712 on the South side of Route 712 on knoll with several trees in 2nd field of "Brookside", called The Graveyard Field, about 50 feet from farm lane South of Gap Run. . There were 5 visible grave depressions. The field has been heavily cultivated during the years. Surveyed September 6, 1993.

Childs Cemetery, Casanova, Virginia
Located just West of Casanova on North side of Route 616. Data collected by Mr. & Mrs. Ernest Childs, who owns property and gave data from family Bible for the fieldstone marked graves.

James H. CHILDS born April 15, 1833 Died July 19, 1878
Nancy CHILDS
fieldstone markers for:
John W. CHILDS born May 22, 1874 died Oct. 5, 1874
James H. CHILDS infant Son of James H. CHILDS died Sept. 27, 1874
Ida May CHILDS born Dec. 22, 1871 died Dec. 8, 1874
Wm. H. CHILDS Born 1859 Died 1906 [*brother of James H. CHILDS*]

Chinn Cemetery, Middleburg, Virginia
Located on Route 50 West of Middleburg at "Bittersweet." Markers have been moved and reset; location of original cemetery site nearby may contain additional graves and markers not discovered.
Charles CHINN Born Sep 1756 Died 3 May 1844 aged 88 years
Sarah CHINN Wife of Charles CHINN Born 11 Jan. 1767 Died 1 Aug. 1858
Charles J. Son of Samuel PULLER and Sarah His Wife aged 6 yrs. 1 mo. & 10 days
John E. Son of John H. & Frances A. CARR Born 22 July 1846 Died 22 Aug. 1853
William D. Son of W. L. T. EVANS and Jane Evans Died 20 Jul. 1851 aged 6 mo. & 10 days
Sarah _____ & Daughter of Margaret R. McMekin Died 8 Jan. 1851 aged 21 years
EVANS *(small stone)*
two illegible due to covering of moss

Church Of Our Savior Cemetery, Little Georgetown, Virginia
Located off Route 55 on Route 601 at Route 628. Resurvey completed April 20, 1989.

North side:
Alwylda ADAMS Aug. 7, 1917 Nov. 10, 1945
John Buchanan Floyd ADAMS Mar. 3, 1866 Oct. 3, 1954
Lewis Lyde Thompson ADAMS July 25, 1879 Nov. 7, 1958
Marie Thompson ADAMS Oct. 17, 1955 Oct. 1, 1957
John Thompson ADAMS Oct. 1, 1904 July 4, 1963
Father M. Bruce WHITMORE 1868–1947
Webster Franklin EDWARDS October 18, 1879 February 14, 1946
Ethel M. EDWARDS HERRELL February 10, 1901 February 11, 1969
VAN HORN William D. October 2, 1876 August 17, 1964; Fannie W. June 29, 1898 October 2, 1962
James D. VAN HORN, Sr. VIRGINIA CORPORAL US ARMY WORLD WAR II KOREA May 21 1926 Oct 15
    1968
RUTLEDGE Ann TURNER of Kinloch beloved Mother of James T. & Carlton, Jr. 1898–1949
Bertha E. BURKE 1898–1952
George N. CAMPBELL 1891–1969 age 68
Pearl F. CAMPBELL 1901–1962 age 61
Charles W. CAMPBELL 1921–1985 age 63
John Edgar ADAMS October 16, 1896
Lucille M. MANUEL 1907–1961
Robert S. BALL Mar. 6, 1914 June 7, 1956

VAN HORN William T. May 29, 1900; Elizabeth B. May 28, 1899 November 13, 1963
Ernest E. S. FLETCHER Sept. 27, 1890 Nov. 16, 1957
John S. LAMBERT September 23, 1877 January 14, 1958
MOORE Elias Milton July 17, 1873 October 10, 1909; Susie Lee November 16, 1883 October 17,1955
Infant Son of Mr. & Mrs. S. J. PAYNE, III Dec. 30, 1958
Infant girl PAYNE 1961–1961
John Thomas JEFFRIES VIRGINIA PVT CO C 127 ENGINEERS WORLD WAR I Jan 1 1896 July 14 1960
John Richard CORBIN 1896–1967
Enich Henry LUNSFORD 1899–1967
Father James O. VERTS January 21, 1901 September 28, 1965
Mother Dorothy Jane ASHBY 1906–1964
Lee F. RECTOR Mar. 7, 1963 age 63
Lawrence BRADFORD 1947–1963
William LEACH 1890–1963
Rebecca C. LEACH 1891–1962
Bessie JONES OWENS January 2, 1880 September 20, 1963
Winter OWENS September 23, 1875 February 6, 1966
Penny E. LEACH 1965–1967
Robert Baldy OWENS 1927–1969
Clyde Lester PEARSON January 16, 1910 October 21, 1968
Mary Ball LUNCEFORD April 18, 1910 November 20, 1966
Robert M. TAYLOR 1890–1968
Carl Turner ANDERSON 1971–1987
Helen Turner ANDERSON 1938–1986
PROCTOR Harvey E. Aug. 17, 1934 Aug. 28, 1985; Shirley E. Oct. 17, 1936
ALLEN Lawson Ira 1929–; George Richards 1881–1941
Robert M. LAWSON VIRGINIA TEC5 US ARMY WORLD WAR II Dec 13 1912 May 11 1972
THORNBERRY Claude D. 1905–1970; Geraldine V. 1907–
KANNARD Shirley L. Sept. 2, 1925 Feb. 25, 1978; Doris M. June 1, 1931 June 4, 1975
GRAY Floyd 1914–1980; Kate E. 1917–
ADAMS Teddy R. Feb. 24, 1911 married June 14, 1933; Minnie Lee Sept. 11, 1907 March 24, 1983
ALTMANN Rozier B. Jr July 19, 1930 January 12, 1984; Lillian F. January 29, 1934
Elijah W. CREEL "Happy" June 13, 1896 Aug. 29, 1984
Dolan Brans MOORE July 9, 1904 Dec. 18, 1975
CURTIS Shirley A. 1917–1977; Frances R. 1919–1977
HEFLIN Edgar B. Feb. 12, 1900 Oct. 29, 1974; Elizabeth V. Jan. 25, 1906
Mrs. Susan B. AYNTON Wife of John Hill CARTER who departed this life on the 25th of February 1826 in the 26th year of her age
James Leo WALTER TSgt. USA WORLD WAR II Sep. 27 1906 Apr. 5, 1988
LUNCEFORD John T., Sr. April 13, 1907 April 21, 1988; Bessie T. May 23, 1909
Robert Beverley HERBERT, Jr. July 23, 1916 July 3, 1977 of Columbia SC and "Avenel" Fauquier
William Henry LEWIS July 27, 1909 July 16, 1987
Eugene Cowper LEWIS April 8, 1911 July 5, 1985
Son Wallace Preston Whitmore Mar. 6, 1902 Nov. 19, 1984
Mother Anne Silling WHITMORE 1868–1947
Jeffrey Scott VAIL June 6, 1968 March 11, 1985
T. Scott GRAHAM 1968–1988 *(fhm)*
HUTCHINS Nelson Jan. 15, 1895 Dec. 20, 1983; Josephine ADAMS Jul. 28, 1915
Laura Lyde Thompson ADAMS July 25, 1879 Nov 7, 1958
Ann Lyde Adams COOPER Apr. 30, 1902 Sept. 23, 1982
LOCKWOOD James Glase Dec. 12, 1904 March 1, 1978; Hannah MALGREM Dec. 7, 1903 Aug. 11, 1987
TURNER William Fisher October 8, 1888 July 2, 1970; Sarah BEVERLEY February 24, 1895 March 24, 1985

Clarence B. RECTOR 1898–1983; Ethel M. MILTON 1910–1985
Mary M. TURNER July 24, 1918 June 27, 1988
Charles Green TURNER Born Kinloch Nov. 26, 1893 Aug. 15, 1980
rock marker
William Virginius MASON Sept. 16, 1855 May 9, 1930
Anna Dorsey MARSTELLER Jan. 14, 1855 March 12 1938
Cyrus C. MARSTELLER 1797–1871; Elise H. MARSTELLER 1814–1899
Cyrus MARSTELLER died July 28th 1845 Aged 4 months & 8 days
unknown
unknown
Frederick W. DUNCAN MSgt USA WORLD WAR II Jul 10, 1926 Aug. 29, 1882
Frances DUNCAN 1925–1984 *(fhm)*

Middle section:
Leela E ROUTZAHN May 30, 1892 January 22, 1971
BLAXTON, Stamper D. 1875-1931; Elizabeth 1888-1976
Barbara Vaughn NELSON Sept 22, 1933 Aug 20, 1982
VAUGHN, Frank Emmett Feb 7, 1905 Nov 29, 1973; Rachel Cockey MITCHELL June 19, 1907
rock marker
BRAWNER, Philip Daw 1853-1936;C. Estelle 1856-1898
Thomas Turner FOSTER "Glenville" August 1, 1900 November 28, 1978
Elizabeth ROBINS FOSTER August 9, 1905 July 1, 1973
HARPER, Fletcher 1874-1963; Harriet W. 1881-1975 {Wadsworth}
Aunt Effie Ann HERRELL July 15, 1902 February 29, 1976

William LEWIS 1750-1830; Ann MONTGOMERY LEWIS 1759-1820 Revolutionary War Patroits Whose Graves are located one mile southwest marked by Elizabeth McIntosh Hammill Chapter DAR 1970. This plaque is erected by lineal descendents 1971.

HERRELL, Gertrude S. Aug 2, 1907 Jun 13, 1982; J Edward Mar 21, 1904 Jul 27, 1985
John Stevens MASON born Washington, D Nov 19, 1914 died Washington, D Jan 12, 1984
James Timberlake LEWIS Aug 13, 1912 Nov 1, 1939
Richard LEWIS March 29, 1878 Feb 18, 1929
Margaret T. LEWIS Apr 28, 1881 Feb 8, 1960
Richard LEWIS, Jr. July 9, 1911 April 8, 1946

North Side C new section near fence:
Joyce Ann LEONARD 1952-1988 *(fhm)*

fenced plot stone and wrought iron BOWMAN *- no marker*

G. Dandridge Kennedy MASON born Washington, D Oct 25, 1912 died Dallas, Texas June 1, 1978

TURNER, Ruby Toms; Loughborough III May 8, 1917 May 26, 1973

J. Bradshaw BEVERLEY WDTL on the 15th of June 1853

SHAFER, Robert Lemuel

Edward Carter TURNER 1886- 1969
James F. TURNER Virginia Captain 10 ARmd Calvary Div WORLD WAR II Jan 19, 1919 Nov 2, 1972
LEWIS, Nicholas Moore July 13, 1905 October 8, 1971

BURGESS, Littleton 1862-1941; Minnie 1866-1905
Andrew W. "Tom" Sampsell 1918-1960
Howard C. BALL Sr. Nov 22, 1967 Sept 2, 1938
Fannie F. BALL Sept 4, 1872 Mar 27, 1947
SARGENT, James S. Aug 12, 1920; Clark K Jan 9, 1922 Oct 15, 1985

Bryan GLASCOCK April 5, 1896 July 3, 1987
Fannie GLASCOCK Feb 7, 1900 March 5, 1984
Lacy D. SINCLAIR January 30, 1872 April 27, 1933; Albert E. SINCLAIR December 15, 1872 December 22, 1957
Morton H. REED 1891-1956
Beryl T. REED 1896-1986
Peter L. CONWAY, Jr. 1916-1979

WISER, Clarence E. 1894-1974; Bettie T. 1895-1969
Walter D. WISER S1 US NAVY WORLD WAR II Nov 12, 1923 Jun 5, 1979
SCHELLENBERG, Theodore R. 1903-1970;Alma G. 1904-1970
Anna Mary DENLINGER Dec 24, 1899 Apr 10, 1984
COFLIN, Thomas E. 1905-1970; Grace BALL
STILLIONS, Omer A. Feb 16, 1886 Jan 19, 1919; William C. Aug 11, 1902 Mar 18, 1982; Albert F. Apr 7, 1909
    May 10, 1934; Dora Feb 24, 1919 Jan 8, 1928; Bertha L. Apr 5, 1908 Jan 21, 1919; Betty J. Aug 11, 1938 Mar
    1942

EDWARDS, Maurice M. 1907-1931; Ralph M. 1910-1936; Beverly W. 1919-1934; Eugene E. 1918-1934 Children
    of R. M. & Mary EDWARDS
Rose Mae Frances NEVILLE November 4, 1914 February 13, 1971
Henry Richard NEVILLE November 14, 1914 February 13, 1971
Rose Mae Frances NEVILLE Born July 2, 1915 Died April 19, 1976

William Gordon LEWIS March 3, 1906 March 8, 1981
Judith BEVERLEY LEWIS November 6, 1908 May 22, 1985

Carol Johnson LEMMER November 29, 1945 March 3, 1874; beloved wife of William C. LEMMER, mother of
    Christine A. LEWIS, mother of Howard J. and Florence C. JOHNSON

Audrey FURR KERR June 10, 1895 October 29, 1976
Charles Graig FURR Died July 9, 1972

SMITH, Annie C. Wife of Howard W. April 13, 1901 April 9, 1977
SMITH, Howard Worth Feb. 2, 1883 Oct. 3, 1976

Juliet W. ALLEN March 8, 1881 April 4, 1973

Anna T. PAGE, beloved wife of Richard C. TURNER March 2, 1883 Jan. 10, 1937
Richard Carter TURNER of "Netherlands" September 19, 1883 December 8, 1962

Byron J. BANKS (Cmdr) US NAVY WORLD WAR II Korea Sep. 31, 1914 Jun 22, 1986

Henry Fairfax LYNN Nov. 8, 1842 Oct. 5, 1914 and wife Mary HOLMES LYNN Feb. 10, 1846 Jan. 6, 1920
Rita ROBERTSON BRASHEARS Feb. 2, 1898 Aug. 9, 1979
Rolph ROBERTSON
PULLEN, L. May Nov. 5, 1925 Lewis H. Feb 4, 1921 Feb 21, 195k
FUNK, George Rm 1898-1972

Ruth PAGE MALMO 1928-1979
DOWNS, William A. Sept. 25, 1887 Oct. 30, 1939
Robert D. DOWNS Sep 3 USA Sep . 29, 1951 May 14, 1983
DOWNS, Hilleary V. Mar. 20, 1884 Apr. 10, 1931; June V. April 1891 Dec. 1, 1963

Civil War Cemetery, Delaplane, Virginia
Located on Route 713 between Delaplane and Rectortown at "Flint Hill" farm; cemetery along side of road around base of dead tree.

Hugh FLYNN
Charles WALL age 31 May 8, 1862 [U. S. Army shield]

Clark Cemetery, The Plains, Virginia
Located East Route 626 opposite Montrose, The Plains. Fieldstone markers only.

Cochran Cemetery, Middleburg, Virginia
Located between Routes 776 & 629 on top of wooded hill back of first farm house on West side of Route 629, home of Roger Lee Elgin, Jr. Difficult to find if Mr. Roger L. Elgin, Sr. had not guided me. Overgrown, stone wall fallen down to South of trail through woods. Mrs. Richard Wallach says there are no changes - conditions overgrown, wall still in fallen down state. Resurveyed November 24, 1993.

Stephen COCHRAN Died Feby 15, 1835 In the 77th year of his age
Mary Ann Daughter of J. S. PRIEST died Feb. 23, 1804 aged 4 years 5 mos. 17 ds
Nathan Son of John and Ellen COCHRAN Born Oct. 18, 1829 Died Oct. 8, 1854
Robert Son of John and Ellen COCHRAN Born Oct. 15, 1814 Died Oct. 18, 1845
Anne E. PRIEST Wife of John PRIEST who departed this life August 22nd 1846 Aged 29 years 2 months and 8 Days
Ellen COCHRAN departed this life Jany. 7th, 1844 Aged 57 years 10 mos. & 6 Days
John COCHRAN Born Dec. 23, 1781 Died Novr. 21, 1856 Aged 74 years 11 months and 28 days
Stephen R. Son of John and Ellen COCHRAN Born April 7, 1824 Died 1827 Aged 3 years
Joseph Son of John and Ellen COCHRAN Born July 8, 1812 Died Jany. 23, 1842
Edna Daughter of John and Ellen COCHRAN Born Jan. 27, 1822 Died 1824 *(not found 1993)*

Cocke Cemetery, Middleburg, Virginia
Located 1 mile South of Route 50 on East side of Route 709, by West side of Lake Ann, on other side of which is a deserted house. Walled on one side. Wall buried by earthen dam. 2 or maybe more unmarked stones. Overgrown, dead tree in corner. Resurveyed January 12, 1992.

Infant Son of Washington & Sally COCKE *(stone not found 1992)*
Washington COCKE who died March 31st 1848

Colbert Cemetery, Turnbull, Virginia
Located on North West side Route 802 at Colbert residence, 100 feet off Springs Rd. on fence line. Surveyed April 1, 1994.

John H. COLBERT Sr. March 4, 1890 July 26, 1974
John H. COLBERT [Jr.] 1921–1979 *(fhm)*

Colvin Cemetery, Catlett, Virginia
Located on South side Route 806 about 1 mile South East Route 28. Cemetery fenced, but in poor condition. Mrs. Lois Heflin Alterton collected the data. Resurveyed April 1, 1991

Our grandfather Richard COLVIN Died July 29, 1825

Our grandmother Leah Maria COLVIN nee WILLIAMS Born Dec. 8, 1819 Died April 28, 1885

Milton E. COLVIN Born April 25, 1859 Died October 10, 1917 In the U. S. Marine service 30 years erected by his children

Thomas Byron COLVIN April 8, 1854 March 16, 1926

Lillie COLVIN (nee) WEAVER May 29, 1859 April 29, 1902 erected by her children

William Wilkens COLVIN Dec. 8, 1877 May 20, 1885

WWC *footstone*

William Henry COLVIN Oct. 30, 1848 Nov. 15, 1925

Virginia Catherine Wife of Henry COLVIN Born Feb. 25, 1849 Died July 24, 1912

Alonza Luther COLVIN Beloved Husband of Mary Oliver COLVIN and Son of B. F. COLVIN died Feb. 12, 1901 Aged 24 years 4 mos. 21 days

May V. OLIVER Beloved Wife of Alonza L. COLVIN Daughter of Alexander W. and Charlotte V. OLIVER Born May 16, 1826 died Feb. 13, 1917

W. COLVIN died Feb. 10, 1808

COLVIN, "Bud" Litell Christy beloved husband of Blanche HORTON Born July 21, 1860 Died Jan. 26, 1914

To our father William COLVIN Born Jan 9, 1812 Died Feb. 20, 1888

footstone "Papa"; overturned stone 1860–1914

There are 28 unmarked graves, some of which contain the following verified by family Bibles for dates:

Thomas Leroy COLVIN born July 17 1785 died Oct. 3, 1938

Lemar COLVIN b. July 20 1885 d. June 14 1935

Martha M. COLVIN b. March 27, 1924 d. March 24, 1929

Helen B. COLVIN LLOYD b. April 29, 1906 d. April 25, 1943

Etta May COLVIN REYES b. February 7, 1920 died December 16, 1963

Floyd R. COLVIN b. May 5, 1898 d. November 18, 1898

William Rufus COLVIN b. Jan. 6, 1850 d. July 15, 1894

Milton E. COLVIN b. Jan. 1, 1885 d. April 17, 1935

Rosa E. COLVIN b. Feb. 15, 1880 d. Dec. 27, 1938

Alpheus Burton COLVIN b. Nov. 21, 1839 d. Nov. 9, 1895

Mary Oliver COLVIN

Charles Mason COLVIN b. Dec. 10, 1876

Gussie COLVIN ROSS

Earl R. ROSS b. April 22, 1894

Jessie Louise COLVIN b. June 5, 1888 d. April 4, 1892

Clinton COLVIN b. Nov. 11, 1937

Litell C. COLVIN b. July 21, 1960

Combs Cemetery, Bristersburg, Virginia

Located Route 609 South East 2 miles, then West, South West .5 mile by private road at the "Kendrick Combs Place." Research by M. D. Gore, Sumerduck, May 17, 1937.

"This graveyard is hard to find. It is in the woods perhaps 0.75 mile South West of the house. There are many graves, but no tombstones with inscriptions. The main graveyard is surrounded by a stone wall, but this was partly torn down some years ago by Ed. Birey (?) and the stones hauled away for building purposes. There was an iron gate, but this is now leaning against a nearby tree. Just outside the stone wall on the East are three graves surrounded by a plank fence. The most westerly grave is that of Seth COMBS, brother of Kendrick. The middle one is that of Kendrick, and the other is that of Mrs. Stark GEORGE, sister of Seth and Kendrick. Some ten yards to the South West are many graves of slaves and colored people. There is no fence around these."

Combs Cemetery, Hopewell, Virginia

Located at end of Route 700, Creels Lane. AWe (Marvin Creel) parked at the end of that road and went into a field (owned by Clarence Payne I think) not more than a hundred yards from a locked gate, opposite the gate to the old Creel homestead.

Mr. Creel informed me that during his youth there were engraved stones with the name Combs, possibly the graves of Robert Combs (1753–13 May 1842) and his wife, Sarah (Linton) Combs. Robert Combs was a soldier in the Revolution. I have a copy of his application for a pension (1832).

However, if engraved stones to the graves of Robert and Sarah Combs ever existed they are now vanished, or possibly covered with earth. There are several graves in the area marked by unusually large field, or flag, stones. The only engraved stone seems to have been "homemade" of an ancient design, with the inscription:

> *Sacred to the Memory of*
> *Sarah H.* CORBIN *daughter of*
> *Elias and Sarah* BRUIN *who departed*
> *this life April 5th 1853 aged 30 yr.*
> *7 mo. 13 days.*

The Fauquier County Marriage Licenses show that license was issued to Sarah H. BRUIN *and George N.* CORBIN *on 24 July 1851. The Bruin family lived at "Mountain End" at the foot of the Bull Run Mts. east of HopewellCthe house is beautifully preserved. A member of this family was a very infamous slave dealer, Joseph* BRUIN, *and another daughter married Thomas Ford and was the mother of Robert (Bob) and Charlie Ford, the outlaws who shot Jesse James.*

There was no connection with the Combs family and the Bruin family. Information supplied by John Gott, May 2, 1994.

Comer Cemetery, Sumerduck, Virginia

Located East Route 632 at end of third private lane on knoll on right, iron fence, brambles.

Dorothy E. Daughter of G. A. & A. V. COMER Nov. 29, 1892 Jan. 2, 1896

Cornwell Cemetery, near Crest Hill, Orlean, Virginia

Located on Route 647 1 mile West Route 688 in field back of old school across lane, enclosed in iron fence. Resurveyed October 30, 1988.

CORNWELL Joseph A. Feb 14, 1864 Jan. 20, 1935 Mary I. Dec. 13, 1874 .Jan. 22, 1928
Our Father Jonas CORNWELL Died Feb. 17, 1890 aged 62 ys 5 mo & 20 ds
Our Mother Lucinda Wife of Jonas CORNWELL Born In 1825 Died Feb 21, 1901
Joshua T. GORE Died Dec. 21, 1918 In his 73rd yr.

Other graves without markers.

Courtney Family Cemetery, near Sumerduck, Virginia

Located South West intersection of Routes 651 & 637 near Sumerduck, stones. Cemetery located on the property of Mr. Maurice Willingham. He stated that the Courtney Cemetery was mentioned in the deed to his property. We found three stones in the fenced cemetery: howver, no infomation on the stones. Mr. Willingham also mentioned another cemetery at the end of his property line near the large tower. He said it might be another cmetery for the EMBREY *'s or possibly another one for the* COURTNEY *family. He seemed to know quite a few cemeteries in the area. He is a good contact person since he and his family have lived in the area for a long time. Information submitted by Karen Nyce and Lisa Desper. Surveyed April 16, 1994*

Courtney Family Cemetery, Somerville, Virginia
Located West of Route 614 and Hartwood Airfield. Vanished

Revolutionary War Soldier William COURTNEY buried in his family cemetery

Cowne Family Cemetery, Midland, Virginia
Located South Route 648 0.8 mile West Route 610 near end of private road to old house on left in field, wire and iron bar fence.

William COWNE Born Nov. 28, 1823 Died Nov. 11, 1860
Our Mother Amanda A. COWNE Born January 26, 1832 Died February 15, 1892

Cox Family Cemetery, Somerville, Virginia
Located South Route 616 2 miles East Route 610 in field. Stone markers individual graves. One marker "The COX Family."

Craig Cemetery, Opal, Virginia
Located 2.1 miles West Route 687 North Route 637 back of house, no markers. CRAIG

Credemore Cemeteries, Warrenton, Virginia
Located at intersection of Routes 674 & 670 back of barn at end of private macadam road. Cemetery to right of barn disappeared. Left cemetery has high mortared stone wall, periwinkle, some rocks possibly fieldstone markers, about 0.25 acre. Large wooden cross set in stone marking one grave with American Legion emblem.

Nelson FELL [*died on return from trip to Guatemala in March or April 1928 CA. V. B.*]

Creel Cemetery, Marshall, Virginia
Located 1 mile off Route 737 on left of 778 in field before house, fenced, overgrown.

Mildred P. Daughter of Geo. C. & Gracie L. CREEL Born Aug. 10, 1914 Died Sept. 18, 1914
Rebecca P. Dau. of Geo. E. & Eliza P. CREEL Born Mar. 29, 1893 Died May 27, 1893 aged 2 years and 3 days
Lizzie P. Wife of Geo. E. CREEL Born Sept. 3, 1868 Died June 26, 1893 aged 24 years 9 months & 23 days
Mildred M. Wife of Wm. L. CREEL Born June 5, 1842 Died April 1, 1904
W. L. CREEL Born April 30, 1842 Died Feb. 3, 1920
Elijah CREEL Died Jan. 1, 1890 Aged 54 years
Margaret D. CREEL March 2, 1844 Jan. 4, 1927
Lucie A. Dau. of Wm. G. & Darcus CREEL Born Jan. 24, 1848 Died Sept. 22, 1895 Aged 47 yrs. 7 mos & 28 dys
Darcus Wife of Wm. G. CREEL Born Aug. 12, 1812 Died Mar. 9, 1885 Aged 72 yrs. 6 mo. & 27 ds
William G. CREEL Born Jan. 19, 1811 Died Sept. 27 1874 Aged 63 ys 8 mo. & 8 dys
Mrs. L. G. LUNCEFORD Dec. 27, 1859 Sept. 20, 1882
Elijah C. ANDERSON Born July 8, 1836 Died March 16, 1890
Avalenel ANDERSON Born Oct. 21, 1838 Died Jan. 15, 1903

About twenty fieldstone markers.

Cross Road Baptist Church Cemetery (Black), Calverton, Virginia
Located intersection of Routes 616 & 607 East of church and to rear, many unmarked. Resurveyed May 27, 1990.

Douglas WASHINGTON Jr. VIRGINIA PFC CO E 168 ENGINEER BN December 6, 1934 April 7 1961
William H. GIBSON 1896–1978 *(fhm)*
Armistead WASHINGTON 1883–1979 *(fhm)*

Annie Oakley TYLER 1907–1983; Spurgeon M. TYLER 1894–1982
rock marker
Walter A. BUMBREY PVT USA WORLD WAR II May 7, 1918 Apr. 7, 1983
Turner H. GIBSON PFC USA WORLD WAR II 1914–1977
Douglas WASHINGTON 1910–1988 *(fhm)*
Lauretha WASHINGTON 1932–1976 *(fhm)*
Nettie Ethel CORUM April 1, 1892 August 2, 1970
Margaret R. SMITH April 20, 1886 November 2, 1984
Florence RICHARDSON Mar. 21, 1912 Jan. 8, 1984
James W. CORUM 1881–1972 *(fhm)*

Crupper Cemetery, Markham, Virginia
Located East side Route 688 3 miles South West Route 17 in back of cattle chute at site of old house, rock wall collapsed, fieldstone markers, cattle grazing. Disappeared by October 25, 1993.

Frances consort of Eli CRUPPER who departed this life October 19th 1857 in the 57th year of her age

Cummins Cemetery, Morrisville, Virginia
Located 16 miles South East of Warrenton, 2.5 miles North East of White Ridge. From White Ridge 0.45 mile on Route 616, then East about a mile on Route 610 to near the Waple place, then 1.5 miles North on a by-road through the woods. Surveyed by M. D. Gore, Sumerduck, October 15, 1937.

"Jeptha Burl CUMMINS is buried in the family burying ground about 75 yards North East of house. There is a square banked-up portion of this graveyard and his grave is in the South East corner of it. There are no tombstones with inscriptions."

Davis Cemetery, Marshall, Virginia
Located on left of Route 647 0.3 mile West of Route 638 to East of house in excellent stone walled area and well kept with boxwood and arbor vitae. Overgrown. Resurveyed October 25, 1993.

Sally Ann Lucy Wife of George W. DAVIS Born June 10, 1827 Died Easter Sunday April 15, 1900
John Morgan DAVIS 1864–1953
DAVIS W. Golder 1857–1945; Edwina HADDOX 1858–1909; W. Clinton 1887–1958; A. Warren 1885–1964;
  Clarence E. 1893–1968

Dennis (Jim) Cemetery
Located on Route 741 dead end on left. Data obtained from Joe Lawler, Marshall. ·

Dixon Cemetery, "Glenarra", Marshall, Virginia
Located 0.2 mile West of Route 635 and Route 647. Vanished from near the house. Located in stone wall to left of house; large unmarked flagstones lying on ground. Disappeared by 1993. Per John Gott, Turner DIXON and his wife Maria TURNER DIXON and probably others: Mary Jane DIXON SCOTT, William DIXON, son of Turner and Maria DIXON, other unmarried DIXON children, and Turner Dixon SCOTT who was the son of A. B. and Mary Jane DIXON SCOTT.

Douglas Family Cemetery
Located South Route 606 near Prince William County line 1 mile East Route 28, east side private road, rocks for markers.

Dowdy Cemetery, Turnbull, Virginia
Located 1 mile South Route 637 West Route 685 at end of road, rock markers, in clump of trees in field. Mrs. Emma Dowdy Jones states her parents, William & Sally FOUTZ DOWDY, Va. Halley DOWDY, Ethel BAILEY, "Boss" BARBOUR, and other Barbours, MYLES & DOWDY graves.

Downing Cemetery, Hume, Virginia
Located in orchard of 2nd farm on North side of Route 635 just West of Route 726. Wire fence, overgrown, trees. Mr. Theodore Kosting, owner, said the graves have been moved to Prospect Hill Cemetery in Front Royal. Contacted October 9, 1993.

Sarah L. HUDNALL Died Mar. 2, 1909 Aged 65 years
Bettie J. BRADY Died Dec. 17, 1919 Aged 85 years
Henry Hawkins Son of John & Fannie DOWNING Born Jan. 29, 1829 Died Dec. 23, 1900

Downing Cemetery, Linden, Virginia
From Hume, Route 635 to intersection of Route 522 in Rappahannock County. Right on 522 to right on Black Rock Ford Rd. (about 1 mile). Continue about 0.75 mile to private drive on right. Follow to Black Rock Ford on Rappahannock River. Farm called "Black Rock" originally "Cool Hill." Cemetery is about 0.25 mile across field. Appears to be called "Bradley Cemetery" on Scheels' map.

John H. DOWNING Born Jan. 14, 1813 Died July 23, 1893 Decision and Resolution of Character and Purpose
  Were Distinguishing Traits As Parent and Husband Tender and Affectionate A True Friend
Arthelia Irene BERRYMAN Beloved Wife of John H. DOWNING Born Oct. 31, 1843 Died June 30, 1901 Thy Will
  Be Done
Hamilton Son of J. H. and A. I. DOWNING Born Sept. 5, 1887 Died April 13, 1896
Linden Kent Son of John H. and A. I. DOWNING Born June 7, 1881 Died March 31, 1882
Lena E. Daughter of J. H. and A. I. DOWNING Oct. 25, 1878 July 31, 1880
Ariett A. Daughter of J. H. and A. I. DOWNING Mar. 7, 1876 June 16, 1880
Fannie S. HUDNALL Wife of John H. DOWNING Born May 3, 1816 Married June 1, 1852 Died July 20, 1865
William G. DOWNING Son of John H. and Fannie S. DOWNING Born April 20, 1858 Died Feb. 15, 1892 He Was
  Without Guile Open Frank True
Ann HUDNALL Born Aug. 10, 1810 Married John H. DOWNING Dec. 19, 1838 Died Oct. 21, 1851
Bettie F. Daughter of John H. and Ann G. DOWNING Born Mar. 4, 1842 Died Oct. 1, 1861
Ariett A. Daughter of J. H. and A. I. DOWNING April 2, 1870 Mar. 5, 1875
Charles R. Son of J. H. and A. I. DOWNING July 27, 1874 Mar. 31, 1875
Bedford M. Son of J. H. and A. I. DOWNING Apr. 3, 1873 Apr. 6, 1875
James Erskins BRADLEY Born Nov. 12, 1885 Died Jan. 20, 1966
Elizabeth F. DOWNING Wife of J. Erskins BRADLEY Born Jan. 10, 1885 Died Jan. 7, 1951
5 stones with no inscriptions (2 broken and missing top)

Downman Cemetery, Morrisville, Virginia
Located 0.75 mile South Route 634, 50 yards West Route 756 beside abandoned road, stone wall, lots of rock markers.

Mrs. Lucy S. DOWNMAN Wife of R. W. DOWNMAN of Lancaster County who died the 11th of Sept. 1817 in the
  32nd year of her age.

Downman Cemetery, Remington, Virginia
Located North Route 657 0.5 mile West Route 29 back of two brick houses in field, cinder block wall, recently cleaned up, with much periwinkle cut back to ground.

DOWNMAN John B. DOWNMAN 1793–1859; Harriot J. His Wife 1793–1869; Ada M. THOM 1824–1850 Wife
  of J. C. THOM and Daughter of J. B. & H. J. DOWNMAN; Ellyson CURRIE 1839–1844; George Yates

HAMILTON 1845–1854; Julian Romney HAMILTON 1855–1859; John Catesby THOM 1846–1855 grandson of
   J. B. & H. J. DOWNMAN; Augusta W. DOWNMAN 1826–1846; Georgiana R. F. DOWNMAN 1828–1844;
   Infant 1819–1819 Daughter of J. B. & H. J. DOWNMAN; Cynthia R. DOWNMAN 1841–1902
Priscilla C. JONES Daughter of Wm. & Frances JONES Died Sept. 26, 1859 Aged 5 years & 1 month
Christopher T. JONES Son of Wm. & Frances JONES Died 7 August 1838 Aged 7 years 3 months & 23 days
William D. JONES Son of Wm. & Frances JONES Died 28th Sept. 1838 Aged 6 years 1 month and 4 days
Ellyson Son of E. A. & Olivia Jane CURRIE Died Aug. 18th 1844 Aged 5 yrs. & 2 months
Ada Matilda the lamented Wife of John Catesby THOM and Daughter of J. B. & H. J. DOWNMAN Born Novr.
   14th 1824 Died April 13th 1850
J. Catesby THOM, Jr. Son of J. C. & A. M. THOM Born July 20, 1840 Died Oct. 20, 18?5
Cynthia Ravenscroft DOWNMAN Feb. 26, 1841 April 20, 1902
John B. DOWNMAN Esq. Born in Lancaster Co., Va. May 9th 1793 Died in Fauquier Co., Va. Nov. 23rd 1859

Dulin Cemetery, Morrisville, Virginia
Located, from Morrisville, North East 2.4 miles on Route 233, then North West 3.5 miles on Route 602, Then South West .25 mile on private road. Research by M. D. Gore, Sumerduck May 14, 1937.

"Two DULIN boys were killed in the Confederate Army and brought back and buried on the home place, but there are no tombstones with inscriptions."

Duncan Cemetery, Dudie, Virginia
Located back of old house on right of Route 738 going North East of Dudie. Data obtained from Joe Lawler, Marshall.

Duncan Cemetery, Marshall, Virginia
Located on Route 55 east of town across from entrance to Marshall Community Cemetery. Located to right of farmhouse near fence. Tombstones removed many years ago according to current resident. Some depressions still evident, but heavily damaged by groundhogs. Surveyed October 13, 1990.

Dye Cemetery, Morrisville, Virginia
Located Route 17 West side, 2 miles South of Morrisville. No markers.

Eastham Cemetery, Warrenton - Bealeton, Virginia
Located North West corner Routes 17 & 660, 13.5 miles South East of Warrenton. Surveyed by M. D. Gore, Sumerduck, February 25, 1938.

"Graveyard about 150 yards East of present house and near the site of the old 'Woodside' home. (George Eastham married Susan Woodside August 28, 1815.) The southern part of the cemetery was for slaves."

Our Father George EASTHAM died Jan 1st 1841

Elizabeth Daughter of George & Susan EASTHAM died Feb 28, 1850

Other family members are buried in Bealeton Cemetery, Cedar Grove.

Ebenezer Church, between Midland and Somerville, Virginia
Located 0.33 mile West Route 610 near junction of Routes 646 & 648, fenced, back of church. Resurveyed July 3, 1990.

David Judson BROWN January 13, 1885 February 4, 1944
Mabel Pauline BROWN September 26, 1918 May 30, 1939
Jesse WHITE 1882–1961
Hattie WEAVER 1876–1958

Irene Mae BROOKS 1921–1965

Tina Irene TAVIS 1964

Babe's children

Emma CHAPMAN 1867–1927; Lewis H. Husband of Emma CHAPMAN Jan. 1, 1854 June 2, 1924

Lidia DAWSON Wife of James DAWSON 1840–1914

Grant ROBERSON 1868–1959; Elizabeth H. ROBERSON 1876–1956

George Leroy GIBSON 1911–1969

Mamie PATTERSON 1900–1953; James A. PATTERSON 1885–1956

Ada JOHNSON 1856–1908

Mary FRIE 1890–1964

Landon N. COLES 1896–1965

Ruth WEBSTER May 22, 1939 Aged 18 years

Father Rev. G. M. TYLER Mar. 1851–Feb. 1917; Mother Fannie J. Wife of Rev. G. M. TYLER May 19, 1855–Jan. 27, 1918

Our Father Gus. D. WILLIAMS Feb. 22, 1932 Aged 82 yrs.

Margarette L. WILLIAMS Wife of G. D. WILLIAMS Born Sept. 11, 1854 Died Sept. 4, 1907

Maudie R. C. WILLIAMS Born Mar. 20, 1889 Died June 16, 1890

Private Meriamans WILLIAMS 48TH CO 158TH DB Born Dec. 30, 1894 Died Oct. 3, 1918 Camp Sherman, Ohio

Jennie L. TURNER April 26, 1881 May 29, 1923; John M. WILLIAMS Sept. 3, 1874 May 25, 1924

Nannie BROWN Beloved Wife of Tyler BROWN Born July 25, 1851 Died Nov. 26, 1907

Everett E. WASHINGTON Born June 15, 1861 Departed this life Jan. 1, 1910 erected by Cornelia THOMPSON & Sebastian EDWARDS

Henry GLASSOE 1845–1934; Hester GLASSOE 1850–19

Henry W. LEWIS VIRGINIA CPL 4096 QM SERVICE WORLD WAR II April 9, 1912–July 11, 1962

James B. LEWIS 1910–1982

George LEWIS 1913–1976 *(fhm)*

Annie E. LEWIS –1976 *(fhm)*

Blanche E. LEWIS 1898–1973 *(fhm)*

GRAYSON Dorothy Mae Feb. 24, 1910–Sept. 19, 1972

Roger H. GRAYSON 1900–1983 *(fhm)*

Audrey W. EDWARDS 1919–1981 *(fhm)*

Edward D. NEVERDON Apr. 18, 1908–Mar. 25, 1965

Father William T. NEVERDON 1867–1957

Mother Cinda E. NEVERDON 1867–1940

Son William C. NEVERDON 1898–1950

Robert Luther WASHINGTON PFC US ARMY WORLD WAR I 1893–1977

Henry PARKER 1900–1975 *(fhm)*

George E. THOMAS 1936–1981 *(fhm)*

Joseph Lewis MILES (1939–1983)

Mitchell CARTER US ARMY 1890–1979

Alice R. CARTER Dec 4, 1862 July 29, 1952

James R. CARTER, Sr. Mar. 11, 1856 July 6, 1932

Nannie C. SCROGGINS June 6, 1906 June 17, 1960

James Richard CARTER MARYLAND PVT. US ARMY WORLD WAR I May 11, 1891 Dec. 5, 1967

Bessie B. JENKINS Apr. 14, 1895 May 30, 1977

Denis Alpheus BUTLER VIRGINIA PVT CO F 6L PIONEER INF WORLD WAR I May 17, 1889 April 2, 1949

Martha BUTLER October 20, 1853 June 5, 1925; Daisy L. BUTLER May 18, 1887; May 17, 1926; Kate D. FITZHUGH October 30, 1881 March 23, 1962; Arpearlia M. SMITH August 11, 1884 September 19, 1971; Coridy D. BUTLER June 23, 1894 August 27, 1986

James R. CARRIER 1891–1967

Miss Olive Roberta CARTER Died July 28, 19__ Aged 88 yrs. 7 mos 9 dys

Sandy Alexander FIELDS 1887–1962; Mary L. FIELDS; Robert L. FIELDS; Thomas M. FIELDS

E. C. WASHINGTON 1886–1928
Timothy JACKSON 1923–1966
Elmo MILES 1889–1957
John I. HARRIS 1899–1967
Annie BENTON Died Oct. 23, 1908 Aged 65 by her daughter
Jacob WASHINGTON Aged 69 years erected by a friend T. C. PILCHER whom he served faithfully for thirty years
Miss Nellie WEAVER 1916–1965
Horace R. JOHNSON 1925–1967
Herbert Louis BYRD VIRGINIA QUARTERMASTER CORPS WORLD WAR I July 3, 1893 Aug 27 1967
Allen Tyler SWEPSON Feb. 17, 1901 Feb. 2, 1957
Ernest Linwood YATES May 24, 1905 Aug. 22, 1977
WEBSTER Mitchell E. Jr. July l3, 1981 July 13, l981; Martha June Oct. 5, 1952 Oct. 5, 1988
Frank WEBSTER 1948–1975 *(fhm)*
Alex E. ROBINSON 1897–1977 *(fhm)*
Willie Lee ROBINSON 1939–1988 *(fhm)*
Alma JOHNSON 1906–1989 *(fhm)*
Samuel W. EDWARDS 1908–1984 *(fhm)*
Minnie B. GIBSON 1903–1980 *(fhm)*
Charles E. LEWIS, Sr. PVT US ARMY WORLD WAR II Jan l5. 1924 Feb. 13, 1977
Virginia GIBSON 1898–1976 *(fhm)*
Jaunietta M. GRIMM Nov. 29. 1956 Jan. 14, 1982
Stanley H. GIBSON Apr. 2, 1936 Oct. 1, 1987
Rev. William RAYMOND *(fhm)*
Elizabeth H. ROBINSON 1876–1956 *(fhm)*
Macie V. PATTERSON 1900–1953 *(fhm)*
Landon N. COLES 1896–1965 *(fhm)*
Bradford PETERRSON 1894–1978 *(fhm)*
Bertha Ann GARRETT 1921–1984 *(fhm)*
Rosevelt Sidney PATTERSON SP4 US ARMY Mar 27, 1956 Feb 24, 1989
Rosie Vernice WEBSTER Feb. 23, 1928 Jan 11, 1984
Baby girl WEBSTER July 6, 1959
Harry WEBSTER, Jr. 1956–1976; Frances A. WEBSTER 1952–1976; Timmy A. WEDSTER 1974–1976
John Lee WASHINGTON 1912–1982 *(fhm)*
Mother Flossie E. WASHINGTON Feb. 15, 1895 Aug. 31, 1947
Douglas WASHINGTON 1884–1979 *(fhm)*
Mary T. WEBSTER 1926–1990 *(fhm)*
Esther I. JOHNSON 1924–1987 *(fhm)*
Edward R. JOHNSON 1941–1985 *(fhm)*
Leroy JOHNSON May 4, 1922 Feb. 12, 1980
Eva N. WILLIAMS 1928–1978 *(fhm)*
Clarence BLACKWELL VIRGINIA PVT US ARMY WORLD WAR I August 10, 1889 May 7, 1971
John Buck JOHNSON l919–1961 *(fhm)*
Eva JOHNSON 1893–1966 *(fhm)*
Charlie JOHNSON *(fhm)*
Walter JACKSON 1912–1971 *(fhm)*
George JACKSON 1906–1972 *(fhm)*
Estelle M. BROWN ADDISON May 21, 1894 Sept. 8, 1982
Benjamin PATTERSON 1889–1968
Alexander WEBSTER 1890–1968; Virginia WEBSTER 1879–1966
Mother Maggie WEBSTER Sept. 5, 1908 Sept. 13, 1963
Lucy R. BUMBRAY April 5, 1954 October 15, 1957
Silas DOWNNELL April 15, 1891 July 3, 1961

Mary E. DOWNNELL July 14, 1893 July 22, 1893

Addie Lynn PARKER May 20, 1906 January 8, 1976

Fay JOHNSON 1898–1972 *(fhm)*

Paul David PARKER SKG US NAVY 1935–1978

Theodore WEBSTER 1917–1988 *(fhm)*

Elmer D. TAYLOR, Jr. 1932–1985 *(fhm)*

Rev. Elma D. TYLER April 29, 1907 Dec. 23, 1968

Mr. Louis M. JOHNSON 1880–1961

William H. ALLEN, Sr. April 29, 1876 July 20, 1954 Father; Virginia V. ALLEN September 11, 1883 January 10, 1967 Mother

OLIVER Virginia D. Feb. 6, 1892 July 17, l976; James F. Sept. 21, 1898 Dec. 11, 1977

William F. OLIVER, Jr. MA7Tl US NAVY WORLD WAR I Dec. 8, 1894 Mar. 31, 1982

Dicey M. WHITE 1896–1966

Mother Emma C. BUTLER 1856–1958; Daughter Amanda E. BUTLER 1894–1965

James Richard CARTER VIRGINIA PVT CO B 808 PIONEER INFANTRY WORLD WAR I February 8, 1892 February 17, 1966

Robert H. POLLARD Nov. 1916 Oct. 1975

Rev. John W. THORNTON May 1908 March 1978

Edna Mae THORNTON May 1911 June 1983

Margaret CLIFTON 1913–1988 *(fhm)*

Edna P. THORNTON l911–1983 *(fhm)*

Rev. John W. THORNTON 1908–1978 *(fhm)*

Robert POLLARD 1916–l975 *(fhm)*

Ella P. CARTER Feb. 23, 1892 Oct. 18, 1953; Florence M. WILLIAMS Mar. 11, 1887 Mar. 3. 1954

C. N. WADE 1952 April 24, 1952

Curtis Henry BROWN Sept. 25, 1918 March 11, 1973

Cornelius B. BROWN 1879–1955; Mamie L. 1893–1979

William ROBINSON 1892–1974 *(fhm)*

Maude CARPENTER 1897–1981 *(fhm)*

Thad W. ROBINSON 1907–1986 *(fhm)*

MARTIN Alfred H. March 4, 1903 January 1, 1987

Florence B. BLACKWELL June 11, 1893 July 19, 1986

Esther E. TYLER May 10, 1896 June 24, 1986

Curtis Henry BROWN Sept. 25, 1918 March 11, 1973

Nellie B. BROWN Jan. 9, 1911 Dec. 15, 1975

Maggie E. WILLIAMS Nov. 8, 1881 July 8, 1970 Mother

Laura E. WASHINGTON *(fhm)*

Charlie WASHINGTON 1900–1980 *(fhm)*

Robert JAMES CPL US ARMY WORLD WAR II 1912–1987

Tate G. BALLENTINE VIRGINIA TEC 5 US ARMY WORLD WAR II Jan. 9, 1909 Dec. 6, 1973

Julia B. TYLER Wife of Wise L. WASHINGTON 1880–1960

Mrs. Emma BLACKWELL 1895–1963

Ada MOORE 1920–1967

Frank WASHINGTON 1933–1951

Robert H. POLLARD Nov. 1916–Oct. 1975

Rev. John W. THORNTON May 1908 March 1978

Edna Mae THORNTON May 1911–June 1983

Margaret CLIFTON 1913–1988 *(fhm)*

Edna P. THORNTON 1911–1983 *(fhm)*

WOODSON Charlotte GREEN Jan. 25, 1952 Feb. 23, 1977

Sharra N. CARTER March 19, 1973 Nov. 3, 1982

James Anthony YATES 1968–1987 *(fhm)*

Jessie R. WILLIAMS 1924–1987 *(fhm)*
Addie W. WILLIAMS May 16, 1926 April 26, 1951
Mary E. JONES 1905–1951
Sarah E. THOMPSON 1877–1956
Louie A. THOMPSON Oct. 6, 1896 Feb. 21, 1984
Mrs. Maria REDD 1874–1948; Mr. James D. REDD 1877–1949 *(missing marker)*
Ernestine W. BLUE 1899–1986 *(fhm)*
Joshua B. BLUE 1900–1978 *(fhm)*
Rosie Dell BLUE JAMES Mother of J. B. BLUE Oct. 27, 1880 Oct. 9, 1950
Annie Mae BLUE 1920–1981 *(fhm)*
Grace E. ROBINSON 1882–1979
James D. REDD 1877–1949 *(fhm)*
Alice M. WILLS 1892–1990 *(fhm)*
R. I. J. 10–27–80
Annah WEST TYLER 1878–1961; Mrs. Esther W. TYLER 1888–1956
Sandy GIBSON August 4, 1965; Jennie TYLER GIBSON 1888–1962
James E. TYLER Aug. 15, 1892 Oct. 31, 1958
Ada YATES BAKER March 17, 1885 July 8, 1965 a native of Stafford Co., Va.
Bollin ROBINSON June 1954 Oct. 1958; Yates 1956–1956

Edmonds Family Cemetery, near Warrenton, Virginia
Located in South East corner of yard of old house on North side Route 674 near Warrenton. Apparently a garden area. William Fitzhugh, Eggleston & Edmonds GRAY were buried here.

Edmonds - Settle - Chappelear Cemetery, "Belle Grove", Paris, Virginia
Located 2 miles South of Route 50 on West side of Route 17 within stone fence on line between 2 fields, boxwood, overgrown, many unmarked or fieldstone marked graves. Resurveyed September 23, 1990.

Elizabeth N [Naomi] L [Lee] [CHAPPELEAR] GRAY 1879–1940 Our Sister
Our Mother Amanda Virginia EDMONDS Wife of John Armistead CHAPPELEAR Born January 13, 1839 Died
    July 13, 1921
Our Father John Armistead CHAPPELEAR Born Dec. 1, 1835 Died June 1, 1916
Our Sister Zulieme Edmonds CHAPPELEAR Born May 20, 1873 Died Nov. 17, 1922 Daughter of John Armistead
    and A. Virginia CHAPPELEAR
Our Brother Clement West EDMONDS [Born 1846] Died Dec. 4, 1875 In the 29th year of his age
Our Mother Elizabeth S. [SETTLE] Wife of Lewis EDMONDS Died March 14, 1874 In the 68th year of her age
My Dear Husband Lewis EDMONDS Died August 27th, 1857 In the 57th year of his age
Isaac SETTLE [Born July 15, 1779] Died Dec 7, 1852 Aged 75 yrs.
Mary [H.] Wife of Isaac SETTLE Born Feb 13, 1775 Died Jany 16, 1847
Helen Winnifred BRADFORD Daughter of Elias EDMONDS and consort of C.BRADFORD 21 Feby 1801 married
    15th Dec 1825 & departed this life 31st of Oct 1826
H. W. B. *(footstone)*
Bessie Lee CHAPPELEAR Born June 6, 1879 Died March 10, 1940 *(missing)*

The following are buried at "Belle Grove", but there are no headstones *(information from Alice Nichols)*:
George Washington EDMONDS Son of John EDMONDS I
Alexander EDMONDS [Uncle Sandy]   –1892 Brother of Lewis
Elizabeth Lou EDMONDS Daughter of Lewis Died June 29, 1896
Dr. Daniel PAYNE Son of Dr. Albert S. PAYNE

Edwards Cemetery, Sumerduck, Virginia
Located West Route 788 West Route 637. 4 rock markers, board fence, overgrown, in second field behind house,

fenced.

Edwards - Brooks Cemetery, Morrisville, Virginia
Located North Route 637 1.5 mile West Route 17 0.3 mile in woods behind old road site. Mrs. Elmer Anns states Henry BROOKS, Freddy BROOKS, Josephine KEMPER, and EDWARDS family buried here.

Elgin Cemetery, Middleburg, Virginia
Located 2 miles North of Route 776 on East side of Route 629 in field back of house, enclosed by a stone wall, trees, periwinkle. Some of the unmarked graves are of the CURLE family, Roger L. Elgin states. Resurveyed November 24, 1993.

Walter R. ELGIN *(rest in ground)*
Gustavia G. Daughter of G. L. and P. C. ELGIN born June 28, 1861 died Mar. 1, 1862
Annie D. ELGIN Daughter of G. L. and P. C. ELGIN born July 2, 1856 died April 14, 1863
Lydia J. Daughter of R. & R. J. WHITACRE Born Feb. 15, 1861 Died Aug. 9, 1861
Minnie R. Daughter of R. & R. J. WHITACRE Born May 21, 1867 Died July 2, 1867
Rebecca J. Wife of Robert WHITACRE Born Mar. 12, 1827 Died July 16, 1867
John C. Son of G. L. & P. C. ELGIN Born Aug. 16, 1853 Died Jan. 31, 1854
Gustavus L. ELGIN Born June 18, 1824 Died May 26, 1863
Pamela E. Dau. of G. L. & P. C. ELGIN Born May 1, 1846 Died Jan. 14, 1869
Pamelia C. Wife of Gustavus L. ELGIN Born Mar. 2, 1825 Died Mar. 16, 1881
Ziban NEAL Oct. 22, 1975

Elk Run Anglican Church Cemetery, Elk Run, Virginia
Located 300 yards South Elk Run on Route 806. Turn East 50 feet. All markers gone. Church and cemetery have almost vanished.

Rev. Mr. James KEITH of Petershead, Scot. Came to Fauquier in 1773. He was the first rector of Hamilton Parish *(at Elk Run Church).* Died in 1761 and is buried under the Altar.

Ellis Grave
Located 0.7 mile South of Orlean on East of Route 688 in box bushes near house. Data obtained from Joe Lawler, Marshall. ELLIS

Embrey (George W.) Cemetery, Sumerduck, Virginia
Located 0.5 miles West Sumerduck North Route 651 to West of house, cinder block wall. Information submitted by Karen Nyce and Lisa Desper. Surveyed April 23, 1994

George W. EMBREY 1884–1960 *(fhm)*
EMBREY Amelia E.; Isham Keith
T. S. E. *(footstone)*

Embrey (Leonard), Morrisville, Virginia
Located North East Route 795 0.7 mile North Route 637 North of house. Board fence, rock markers only. Information submitted by Karen Nyce and Lisa Desper. Resurveyed April 16, 1994

Four markers (only one identified)
Leonard EMBREY Died Mar. 26, 1962 Aged 67 Years

Embrey Cemetery, Sumerduck, Virginia
Located 1 mile North East of Sumerduck on Route 632. The house "The Robert Embrey Place" is 10 yards North West of highway. Research by M. D. Gore, Sumerduck, May 14, 1936. This cemetery is quite old and in very

bad conditions. As noted many of the stones have been broken and turned over and scattered. Information submitted by Karen Nyce and Lisa Desper. Resurveyed April 16, 1994

"There is a graveyard in a corner of the garden, West of the house. One inscription reads as follows:

Rob EMRY Died 1852 Aged 84 yrs.

Robert D. EMBREY, *Son of Rob (or Robert Emry), is also buried here. He was born* Oct. 23, 1825 *and died in* June 2, 1911" *(headstone broken in two pieces in different places)*
R. D. EMBREY
Adied 79 years" *(no other information given)*
Mary G. EMBREY Born Sept. 26, 1848 Died Jan. 31, 1932 *(3 stones pieced together)*
Sarah, wife of R. EMBREY died *(no further information - stone broken)*

9 unmarked grave markers

Embrey - Smith Cemetery, Sumerduck, Virginia
Located on left at end of first private road on East side of Route 632 South of Route 651. Iron fence, overgrown with honeysuckle, and some stones down, fieldstones.

Hezekiah EMBREY Born Dec. 25, 1836 Died Feb. 26, 1914
Susan J. Daughter of Robt. & Jane E. EMBREY David M. Son of Robt. & Jane E. EMBREY Died 1869 In his 40th year
Our Brother Robert H. SMITH Born May 12, 1876 Died May 12, 1939
Emma E. Wife of J. Robt. SMITH Died Feb. 10, 1931 In her 78 year
Florence Daughter of J. R. & E. E. SMITH 1886–1892
Norah B. Daughter of J. R. & E. E. SMITH 1884–1898
J. R. SMITH Born Sept. 20, 1848 Died April 23, 1917
Jane E. Wife of Robt. EMBREY Died 1894 In her 75 yr. Robert EMBREY Died in his 77 year
Robert EMBREY Died Dec. 24, 1916 aged 72 years

Emmanuel Episcopal Church Cemetery, Delaplane, Virginia
Located at the intersection of Routes 17 & 713. Congregation met at Cool Spring Church prior to erection of present church in 1858. Resurveyed September 29, 1993.

Richard Henry McCARTY June 9, 1889 July 28,1968
Delmer Lee THOMPSON DISTRICT OF COLUMBIA C.P.H.M. USNR WORLD WAR II October 24, 1917 Feb. 23, 1953 *(Son-in-law of Richard H. McCARTY)*
Charles Francis WHEAT Norwood Hall Sheffield, England Feb. 6, 1864 Oct. 11, 1936

Mollie V. CURLETTE Wife of B. E. CURLETTE Born May 10, 1847 Died Sept. 17, 1928
B. Elliott CURLETTE Born May 23, 1831 Died Aug. 10, 1918
James W. WOODWARD Oct. 2, 1876 July 18, 1960 His Wife Isabelle M. EDMONDS Feb. 24, 1888 Oct. 16, 1918
Mary Evelina HARVEY Wife of W. H. F. HARVEY Daughter of E. S. & A. B. EDMONDS Born May 17, 1884 Died October 14, 1918
James Benjamin McCARTY III Jan. 1, 1958 Dec. 18, 1973

Infant Dau. of J. B. Jr. & J. L. McCARTY Mar. 10, 1951
Chas. Carrington Son of Ben & Clara McCARTY Oct. 2, 1916 July 15, 1917
J. Benjamin McCARTY May 26, 1887–Aug. 5, 1960
Clara STOVEY McCARTY Feb. 2, 1884 April 23, 1982
Edmund Joseph HORGAN Col. US ARMY WORLD WAR I and WORLD WAR II 1884–1978

John Barcroft McCARTY July 9, 1918 May 5, 1990; Virginia GOFF McCARTY Nov. 4, 1923 Jan. 22, 1991

Roberta CHUNN Beloved Wife of Lloyd O. GOLD Born Sept. 24, 1860 Died Jan. 24, 1956
Lloyd O. GOLD Born June 23, 1853 Died Feb. 19, 1899
Roberta GOLD Beloved Wife of N. Frank NEER Born July 3, 1887 Died Aug. 26, 1964
W. Frank NEER Beloved Husband of Roberta GOLD Born July 1, 1882 Died Aug. 9, 1965
Isabelle A. NEER Beloved Wife of Robert B. SEMPLE born Feb. 16, 1911 died Aug. 4, 1983

Mary BARRETT Wife of Edward HERBERT Nov. 27, 1831 May 31, 1890
Rebecca Beverley Daughter of W. P. & Rebecca HERBERT Died at Woodside Nov. 25, 1891 In the 9th year of her age
William P. HERBERT Aug. 1, 1852 April 3, 1898
John Carlisle Infant Son of Wm. P. & Rebecca HERBERT Died in Columbia S. C. Aug. 18, 1892 Aged 10 months
Rebecca Beverley Wife of Wm. P. HERBERT Died at Woodside Jan. 22, 1892 In the 37th year of her age
Rebecca HERBERT VAUGHAN May 22, 1911 May 15, 1941
Edward HERBERT October 2, 1877 October 28, 1959
Clara LYLE HERBERT August 11, 1879 April 11, 1965
Robert Beverley HERBERT born at "Avenel" The Plains, Va. July 25, 1879 Son of William Pinckney and Rebecca Beverley HERBERT Died in Columbia, S. C. March 4, 1974 Lawyer for more than 75 years
Georgia Rucker HULL Wife of Robert Beverley HERBERT born in Augusta, Georgia April 3, 1894 Daughter of Mary Baldwin LYONS and James Meriweather HULL M. D. Died at Columbia, South Carolina October 12, 1988

James E. CURLETTE Born Sept. 27, 1874 Died Feb. 10, 1902
Richard G. CURLETTE Born July 26, 1889 Died June 6, 1893
Henrietta P. CURLETTE Wife of P. E. CURLETTE Born June 24, 1832 Died Mar. 21, 1889
Mattie CURLETTE Born Jan. 18, 1857 Died June 11, 1893

Mary Elizabeth Beloved Daughter of Channing M. & Lucy D. SMITH Dec. 14, 1873 July 14, 1902
Robert G. Son of Channing M. and Lucy D. SMITH Aug. 10, 1871 May 24, 1889
Channing M. SMITH May 22, 1842 Nov. 8, 1932 His Wife Lucy D. SMITH Dec. 12, 1846 Nov. 25, 1923
Susie A. SMITH Oct. 15, 1878 Sept. 30, 1962
Harry Lee SMITH May 27, 1886 Oct. 28, 1944
Jane S. McGUIRE Wife of Wm. Fitzgerald JONES Daughter of Dr. R. L. McGUIRE Born June 8, 1835 Died May 21, 1887
Minnie Delaplane SMITH May 27, 1894 Nov. 27, 1975
Corinne BAYLY CHEEK 1900–1928
Nannie Lee BAYLY born May 12, 1895 died Sept. 13, 1921
Susan CURLETTE Wife of H. Clay BAYLEY 1895–1906
H. Clay BAYLEY Sr. 1848–1920
Nannie CURLETTE Wife of H. Clay BAYLY 1861–1893
Corinne CURLETTE 1867–1910
Henry Clay BAYLY Jr. 1884–1957
Ann B. C. BAYLY 1888–1962
Rawson KAY BAIRD Oct. 30, 1883–Mar. 9, 1964 Alvin Voris BAIRD Dec. 3, 1882–June 5, 1964

Margaret Lewis Daughter of James F. and Ann L. JONES Born July 11, 1832 Died May 15, 1888

Ann Lewis MARSHALL Wife of James Francis JONES Born August 22, 1821 Died Nov. 11, 188[0]
James F. JONES Died October 9th, 1866 in the [4]7 year of his age
John Daniel McCARTY April 3, 1896 October 1, 1974

Agnes DOUTHAT Wife of Dr. R. L. McGUIRE Born April 14, 1824 Died July 27, 1885

Dr. Robert L. McGUIRE Born April 14, 1822 Died April 10, 1870
Susan Lewis MARSHALL consort of Bowles E. ARMISTEAD Daughter of F. Lewis MARSHALL Born Dec. 11, 1848 Died July 8, 1868
Rebecca COKE Wife of F. L. MARSHALL and their Daughter Margaret, Mary, Susan, Evelyn and Eleanor

Esther MADDOX TRIBLE January 11, 1900 November 13, 1976
Jay NASH Jan. 27, 1947 Jun. 5, 1969
Mavis SCOTT ROBINSON 1911–1981
Ruth JONES McCARTY Mar. 28, 1895 Oct. 21, 1962
Samuel Williamson McCARTY Sept. 6, 1880 April 3, 1974

North side of church:
Arietta JEDAVIE BAYLY Born Jan. 24, 1836 Died Oct. 13, 1905
Emma Rosa BAYLY Born June 1, 1868 Died Aug. 28, 1918
Jessie W. Daughter of E. H. & Nannie BLACKMORE Born Aug. 11, 1887 Died Dec. 31, 1918
Nannie BAYLY Wife of E. H. BLACKMORE Jan 25, 1856 Dec. 7, 1924

John Loring BAYLY 1879–1885 Fannie BAYLY 1884–1891
Sampson P. BAYLY, Jr. 1850–1921 Elise CLAGGETT Beloved Wife of Sampson P. BAYLY 1857–1890
Pierce BAYLY 1886–1891

Rozier C. BAYLY, M. D. 1881–1920

John Brice BAYLY 1889–1959
W. J. Ward BAYLY June 12, 1869 Sept. 2, 1929

Bessie BAYLY Mar. 18, 187__ Mar. 27, 1952
Edith R. FERGUSON Mar. 11, 1887 Dec. 2, 1976

Edith G. BAYLY ____ 15, 1866 Mar. 21, 1969

Richard H. McCARTY, Jr. 1924–1991 *(fhm)*
Eleanor R. FOLLEY 1907–1991 *(fhm)*
Carl Franklin L'ORANGE October 24, 1910 July 9, 1989
Matt VANDERZON

Judith A. LEMASTER July 19, 1944 Dec. 23, 1989
Robert Baylor SEMPLE Aug. 18, 1910 Nov. 4, 1988 Born in St. Louis eminent citizen of Detroit resident of Pohick Farm, Delaplane Husband; Isabelle SEMPLE NEER 1933–1983; Isabelle A. NEER Beloved Wife of Robert B. SEMPLE Born Feb. 16, 1911 died Aug. 4, 1988
Holly REID FOWLER 1985–1988

Ensor Cemetery, Somerville, Virginia
Located 0.4 mile South East Route 637 North Route 610, back of house, iron fence, 2 rock markers, well kept. Resurveyed by L. Arthur Grove February 1994.

Mary A. E. GROVE Nov. 8, 1889 Nov. 22, 1952
Madelene GROVE Jun 2, 1922 Aug. 15, 1923
Martha ENSOR Apr. 15, 1850 Nov. 3, 1901
George W. ENSOR Feb. 25, 1859 Aug. 21 1929
John H. ENSOR Born Mar. 3, 1820 Died Mar. 9, 1904
Mary J. ENSOR Born Feb. 1, 1829 Died June 10, 1881

David L. ENSOR Born May 22, 1871 Died June 22, 1873
Anna F. ENSOR Born Mar. 13, 1861 Died July 24, 1862
John W. ENSOR Born Apr. 14, 1855 Died July 17, 1862
Vernon B. McCONCHIE Nov. 21, 1901 May 23, 1922
Bessie C. ENSOR Feb. 28, 1874 Nov. 21, 1925
H. Lloyd GROVE Born Sept. 25, 1890 Died July 5, 1972
Willie L. GROVE Born July 14, 1926 Died Nov. 2, 1988

Eskridge Cemetery, Bristersburg, Virginia
Located East Route 616 1 mile North Route 806, in field back of house, fenced, boxwood.

John S. THOMPSON Died July 16, 1896 Aged 26 years Beloved Husband
Mary H. SPICER Aug. 13, 1869 Feb. 23, 1916 [*1st married John S. Thompson according to Kenneth Eskridge*]
John W. ESKRIDGE April 1, 1831 Mar. 27, 1889
Henrietta M. ESKRIDGE Oct. 10, 1841 Dec. 16, 1893
Baby THOMPSON *(fieldstone marker)*

Eskridge Cemetery, Bristersburg, Virginia
Located East Route 616 1 mile North Route 806, in field back of house, fenced, boxwood. In addition to the Eskridge family, there are two unmarked cemeteries on this farm, a Negro one and PETERS family, both with fieldstone markers only. Source: Kenneth Eskridge, owner.

Eskridge Cemetery, Morrisville, Virginia
Located 1 mile North East of Morrisville on Route 233, East 360 yards. In poor condition near house on edge of woods by 2 oaks. Research by M. D. Gore, April 22, 1937.

Milton B. Son of John & Elizabeth ESKRIDGE who died Sept. 1819 aged 4 years 8 mo.

Eskridge Cemetery, Morrisville, Virginia
Located diagonally across road from Oliver's house, which is located between Bleak and Mt. Carmel Church. Research by M. D. Gore, March 16, 1938.

"The old Eskridge burying ground is a hundred yards or so back of where the burnt chimneys stood, but there are no tombstones with inscriptions."

Eustace Cemetery, Elk Run, Virginia
Located South of Elk Run. Go South of Elk Run on Route 806 to Route 644, 0.5 mile South West down Route 644 turn right through woods that are being cleared, West about 0.5 mile to cemetery in open field with one large tree. This cemetery has been bulldozed. The marble marker has been moved to the base of the tree, about 250 feet South from chimney of Eustace house to cemetery. One fieldstone grave still visible. Six feet from tree is a large pile of dirt, logs, and stones. Some of the stones are believed to be grave markers. Marble marker says:
Sacred to the memory of Mary, beloved wife of W. H. EUSTACE Departed this life Sept 2nd 1869 in the 66th year
    of her age.

Farrow Cemetery, Markham, Virginia
Located 4 miles North of Route 55 on Route 688 in field on right and to North of house. Four gargoyles have been added to excellent stone wall to cemetery and gate filled in. Covered with honeysuckle. Resurveyed September 13, 1993.

Dorothea G. FARROW Wife of the late Nimrod FARROW departed this life on the 12th day of January 1843 in the
    79th year of her age
Nimrod FARROW who died June 10th 1830 Aged 64 years 10 months and 23 days

Kitty Short BALL who was born the 17th day of September 1798 and departed this life 30th day of May 1830 *(moved from Oakwood Cemetery, Delaplane)*

On a hill to the North were a number of fieldstone marked graves, probably slaves.

Farrow - Hansborough Cemetery, Bristersburg, Virginia
Located 2 miles South Bristersburg East Route 639. Data obtained by L. Arthur Grove.

R. S. GORRELL Departed this life Sept. 13, 1873 In the 72nd year of his age

Thomas Mortimer Son of George A. & Amanda S. FARROW who died Jan. 21st 1845 In the 22nd year of his life

George M. 2nd Son of George A. & Amanda S. FARROW who died April 10th 1848 in the 4th year of his age

Lucy Levenia Daughter of Geo. A. & Amanda S. FARROW who died April 3rd 1848 in the 6th year of her age

Monteray Taylor 2nd Daughter of Geo. A. & Amanda S. FARROW who died April 21st 1848 In the 2nd year of her age.

Margaret Starke Wife of Elder Elijah HANSBOROUGH who was born March 18, 1788 Departed this life July 16, 1835

Enoch Infant Son of Elijah & Margaret HANSBOROUGH who died July 16, 1814

Phinehas HANSBOROUGH who was born 5th July 1820 and departed this life 10th Sept. 1851

Ann Elizabeth 3rd Daughter of Eldon & Elizabeth HANSBOROUGH Wife of Thomas M. FARROW who was born March 7th 1828 & died Feb. 1848

Elder Elijah HANSBOROUGH Minister of the Gospel of Jesus Christ who was born on the 16th of August 1774 and fell asleep in Christ on the 22nd of July 1848

Fauquier County Poor Farm
Located 1 mile North of Route 738 on Route 721. It is large and enclosed with an excellent stone wall. It was burying ground for people who died at the county Alms House. Data obtained from Joe Lawler, Marshall. Thelma Adams Bussey states Elvey PAYNE *in his nineties is buried in Poor House Farm.*

Ferguson Cemetery, Delaplane, Virginia
Located on West side of Route 688 North of George Richard Thompson lake. Tombstones fallen down in middle of cattle field, some partially buried, overgrown, in clump of locust trees. Resurveyed September 3, 1993.

William H. FERGUSON March 23rd 1809 Aug. 8th 1816

Elizabeth Wife of Josias FERGUSON Oct. 21, 1784 Mar. 26, 1856

Harriet FERGUSON Sep. 5th 1803 August 6th 1864

Eliza Wife of James FERGUSON June 5th 1807 Aug 30, 1842

Also stone with "J. F."

Molly A. O. FERGUSON Aug 26th 1816 June 6th 1841

Josias FERGUSON born in Prince William Co. Feb 15 1775 died in Fauquier Dec 14th 1849 "Having no confidence in the flesh"

Ficklin Cemetery, Bealeton, Virginia
Located at family residence near Bealeton. Data obtained from page 194 Joseph Arthur Jeffries' AFauquier County 1840–1919. William L. FICKLIN *died 1904 (C. S. A.) and buried in family cemetery. His remains later moved to Warrenton Cemetery and buried with wife and daughter.*

Finch - Smith Cemetery, Halfway, Virginia
Located on East side of Route 624 south of Route   about 300 feet east of road by gate in field. Unfenced. 3 fieldstone markers, some tombstones at base of tree. Larin Mack helped us find the cemetery. Seems to be located off Creel Cemetery on Scheel's map of Fauquier County. Surveyed November 15, 1993.

John son of Marshall B. and Margaret L. FINCH born June 30, 1865 died Sept. 30, 1894

Roba T. SMITH born May 16, 1820 died April 12. 1907

Jane E. SMITH born 1825 died Sept. 1870
Margaret Lucinda born Oct. 29, 1826 died Sept. 9, 1872

First Baptist Church Cemetery, The Plains, Virginia

Located East side of Route 626 on North side of the town. Organized in 1870. Many fieldstone markers. Well kept located to rear of church building. Rear of cemetery overgrown with honeysuckle and brambles. Forty-two fieldstone markers. Resurveyed October 25, 1990.

Jerry Myer WANZER 1906–1960 *(fhm)*
Grant BOWLES Jan. 20, 1858 age 92 *(missing 1990)*
Betty G. CORN Dec. 8, 1893 July 13, 1977
Georgia B. GANT March 8, 1889 Feb. 26, 1973
Sarah G. Taylor Dec. 12, 1898 Aug. 23, 1970
fieldstone markers
Rev. J. H. FAIRFAX 1892–1966 Pastor First Baptist Church The Plains 1940–1966
James MILLER 1896–1977
Katie M. DADE 1900–1946
Henry WARD 1827–1902; Mary J. WARD 1820–1898
Lena BRADFORD 1905–1982 *(fhm)*
Mary Frances TIBBS Mar. 15, 1902 Aug. 24, 1978
William GARNER Born 1881 Died Aug. 13, 1917
Hattie E. W. GARNER Born 1880 Died Nov. 2, 1965
Philip REELS Died 1917
Marie REELS Died 1938
Rose BROWN

Queen Augusta WARD Born May 28, 1872 Died Oct'r 30, 1891
Gary L. MITCHELL 1858–1913 *(missing 1990)*
Louise SHORTS Nov. 29, 1915 Sept. 11, 1961

GANT Ella Died 1925 Peter 1940 Sarah 1953 and family
Charles GANT April 16, 1903 May 26, 1965
James J. JACKSON 1942–1964 *(missing 1990)*
Amelia CARTER 1910–1961 *(missing 1990)*
Mae Virginia CARTER May 4, 1951 Aug. 1, 1965
InfantCJames LAMBERT Mar. 19, 1958 Aged 6 months
Elizabeth WILLIAMS January 21, 1955 aged 4 years
Norris LAMBERT 1903–1953 *(missing 1990)*
Birtie L. THOMPSON Wife of Thomas Hathaway Born Dec. 1, 1890 Died May 24, 1909
Lettie BOLDEN Wife of Joseph THOMPSON Died Nov. 19, 1916 aged 49 years
William DAW Feb. 19, 1947 Aged 81
Rosie M. THOMAS Daughter of Ross & Blanche THOMAS Born Aug. 16, 1871 Died Mar. 16, 1917
Mose LACEY July 9, 1953 Aged 65 years
Mother Nancy LAMBERT BUTLER December 26, 1934 May 23, 1957

Charles L. CARTER Died July 3, 1959 aged 10 days
Mittie M. BURGESS 1882–1951
Chadwell CARTER 1915–1968 *(missing 1990)*
Charles Henry JOHNSON 1920–1965
William Edward TIBBS PFC 3142 QM Service Co. World War II Sept 19, 1925 June 20, 1953
James Henry CARTER VIRGINIA PVT 350 FIELD RMT SQ QMC WORLD WAR I March 1 1897 October 28 1950
Hattie F. CARTER 1938–1968 *(missing 1990)*

Fletcher (William) & Slaves Cemetery, Upperville, Virginia

Located at intersection of Routes 710 & 623 in south field on a knoll with trees. No fence, graves fallen in with only one marker remaining. About 1991, a four panel creosote board fence put around cemetery which, on 9/6/93, was overgrown with poison ivy, ailanthus trees, and briars. The graves of about seven of William Fletcher's slaves are buried around him in fieldstone marked graves. Resurveyed September 6, 1993.

William FLETCHER Born July 13th 1784 Died Aug. 10th 1850 aged 72 years & 27 days
W. W. PHILLIPS born July 18, 1825 died Aug. 27, 1876

Fletcher Cemetery, "Oak Spring", near Upperville, Virginia

Located 0.6 mile off Route 623 on East side of road and about 2.5 miles South Route 50. Stone enclosed, well kept. Cemetery established by Robert Fletcher (1777–1845). Some unmarked graves. Resurveyed August 19, 1990.

Our Brother Alpheus FLETCHER Son of Wm. & Harriet FLETCHER Born Jan. 7, 1827 Died Sept. 10, 1908
William H. Beloved Son of Wm. & Harriet FLETCHER Sept. 18, 1830 Nov. 15, 1892
Robert beloved Son of Wm. & Harriet FLETCHER May 27, 1833 Feb. 8, 1890
Our Brother F. Marion beloved Son of Wm. & Harriet FLETCHER July 20, 1841 July 1, 1881
Our Baby Edgar E. Son of W. H. & M. V. FLETCHER Feb. 12, 1867 Aug. 3, 1867
Our babe Harriet G. Daughter of L. & M. L. FLETCHER Dec. 23, 1862 Sept. 11, 1863
Catharine A. Wife of Elias H. FLETCHER, decd. Born Jan. 18, 1821 departed this life Sept. 4, 1862
Elias W. FLETCHER who was born July 7th 1815 and departed this life March 12th 1854 aged 40 years 8 months and 5 days
Robert FLETCHER born October 16th 1777 died August 18th 1845
Elizabeth [WHITEFORD] FLETCHER Wife of Robert FLETCHER Born December 1784 Died April 27th 1841
Harriet Ann Daughter of William & Harriet FLETCHER Born August 27th 1839 Died August 18th 1877
Infant Son of William & Harriet FLETCHER was born July 2d & died July the 9th 1848
Harriet Wife of William FLETCHER and Daughter of Isaac & Sally LAKE who was born October 16th 1808 Departed this life July 30th 1857
Father William Son of Robert & Elizabeth FLETCHER Jan. 1, 1804 Sept. 21, 1886
Eliza V. Daughter of Wm. & Harriet FLETCHER Oct. 26, 1828 May 8, 1887
Our Brother B. Frank FLETCHER Son of William & Harriet FLETCHER Born Oct. 16, 1843 Departed this life Feb. 11, 1913
Our Sister Sarah E. FLETCHER Daughter of Wm. & Harriet FLETCHER Born Mar 23, 1833 Died April 15, 1917
Our Sister Mollie C. FLETCHER Daughter of Wm. & Harriet FLETCHER Born Nov. 28, 1845 Died Dec. 11, 1920
Agnes FLETCHER Wife of John G. ROBINSON 1808–1895
John G. ROBINSON was born March 24th 1806 and departed this life Aug. 7th 1857 Aged 51 years 4 months & 13 days
Edmonia Daughter of John G. & A. ROBINSON was born June 27, 1848 and departed this life Jan. 15, 1854 Aged 5 years 6 months and 18 days
Infant Son of Richard L. & Ann E. LAKE died Jan. 1st, 1845
Ella B. Daughter of Richard L. & Ann. E. LAKE born Nov. 29th 1852 died Nov 14th 1856 aged 3 years 11 months & 15 days
Alice Maude Daughter of R. E. & Ann E. LAKE Born March 19, 1857 Died July 17, 1858 age 1 year 3 months & 28 days
Ann E. Wife of R. E. LAKE and Daughter of Robert & Elizabeth FLETCHER Born June 23, 1825 Died July 11, 1863
Richard E. LAKE Born May 10, 1823 Died Nov. 19, 1889
Marietta Theresa Daughter of R. E. & L. E. LAKE Born Sept. 9, 1849 Died Feb. 1, 1872
James Robert Son of R. E. & L. E. LAKE Born Dec. 14, 1845 Died Nov. 3, 1869 aged 23 years 19 months & 20 days
Our Sister Catherine L. FLETCHER Daughter of William & Harriet FLETCHER Born April 21, 1847 Died Aug. 12,

1922

Benjamin [Garner] CHAPPELEAR Born Mar. 3, 1803 Died May 28, 1895

Matilda [FLETCHER] Wife of Benjamin CHAPPELEAR Born August 26, 1800 Died August 17, 1872

James P. [Pendleton] CHAPPELEAR Co. A 6th Virginia Cav. Fell at Dranesville Feb. 22nd 1864 Aged 31 years 2 months & 11 days *(Masonic emblem)*

Henry C. Son of G. W. & N. CHAPPELEAR Died June 7, 1880 aged 9 months & 26 days

Willie W. [Winston] CHAPPELEAR Son of G. [Geo. Warren] & N. [Nannie BARRETT] CHAPPELEAR Died June 22, 1880 aged 10 months & 19 days

H. S. RUCKER Son of W. A. & Annie C. [CHAPPELEAR] RUCKER Born Sept. 25, 1875 Died June 9, 1876

Andrew William MELLON 1855–1937 Secretary of Treasury Ambassador Court of St. James Founder of the National Gallery of Art

Mary CONOVER MELLON May 25, 1904 October 11, 1946

Nora McMULLEN MELLON 1873–1973 Born Hertford, England

Ailoa MELLON BRUCE 1901–1969

Florance Cemetery, Broad Run, Virginia

Located 2.1 miles South of Broad Run on West side of Route 600 at "Cerro Verde". Research by Frances B. Foster July 2, 1937.

In the yard are several unmarked graves, and one tombstone which reads:

Jane H. Wife of Alfred FLORANCE Born Sept. 26, 1807 Died March 25, 1881

Foster Cemetery, Warrenton, Virginia

Located South West intersection of Routes 29 - 17 & 744 in South West corner of woods to right of house. Some unmarked graves. Excellent condition. High board fence around 2 sides. Parking lot other 2 sides. Resurveyed December 3, 1993.

Larry FOSTER 1950–1969; Shirley FOSTER 1944–1963 *(fhm) (children of Wade FOSTER)*

Carrie B. PAGE 1873–1966

Amanda V. FOSTER 1907–1972 *(fhm)*

Wade Hamilton FOSTER PVT US ARMY WORLD WAR I May 8, 1898 May 1, 1978

Fox (John M.) Cemetery, Opal, Virginia

Located in second field West Route 661 just South Route 662. Stone wall, honeysuckle, fieldstone markers.

Freestate Battlefield Cemetery, Dudie, Virginia

Located on Route 689. Civil War soldiers buried here. Cemetery approximately 1.75 acres in size, next to old road bed, across from old Mt. Airy Property. Stone markers now gone, piled up next to old tree stump, some markers have initials. Tree in area about 200 years old. March 17, 1991

Furcron Cemetery, "The Glebe", The Plains, Virginia

Located across from the intersection of Route 50 and the East end of Route 763. Grave enclosed with stone wall.

Annie KINCHELOE FURCRON 1834–1893 Wife of A. S. FURCRON Daughter of Brandt and Mary Rawlings KINCHELOE

Gaddis - Okie Cemetery, Delaplane, Virginia

Located on farm at dead end of Route 731 where it intersects Route 732, in field on left. Excellent stone fence, well kept, boxwood in corners. Resurveyed October 29, 1993.

Fred W. OAKIE Sept. 1, 1872 July 15, 1919
Saint Claire OAKIE Daughter of Pauline and Fred W. OAKIE Dec. 23, 1911 July 17, 1913
Houston L. GADDIS Feb. 19, 1879 Mar. 15, 1957
Pauline D. PLATT 1881–1977 Wife of Fred W. OAKIE and Houston L. GADDIS
Robert J. Riordan 1936–1991 Son of Francine RIORDAN OAKIE and John B. OAKIE

Gaines (Black) Cemetery, New Baltimore, Virginia
Located 26 degrees South East of Route 29 on Route 673. Millie and George Gaines were the last two buried in this graveyard. Surveyed by Justin Frazier, August 27, 1994.

Garrison Cemetery, Halfway, Virginia
Located Halfway on road back of Long Branch Baptist Church. Has fieldstone markers only.

Gaskins Cemetery, Bethel, Virginia
Located at intersection of Routes 17 & 690 back of Humblestone on top of hill in second field behind house near fence line, in grove of trees. The inscriptions that were on the sandstone ones have sheeted away and there are a number of rock markers. GASKINS family probably are buried there.

Gaskins Cemetery, Catlett, Virginia
Located on Route 767. Formerly marked with rock markers. Monuments moved to Catlett Cemetery. Dec. 5, 1990

William GASKINS & wife
6 GASKINS *children*
Douglas CHILD
2 WISE *children*

Gaskins Cemetery, The Plains, Virginia
Located 0.7 mile South on Route 776 on West side of Route 629. Bulldozed away.

George Cemetery, Elk Run, Virginia
Located 1 mile South East Route 616 South Route 806 at end of private road to left rear of old house, old fence, very briary and overgrown, fieldstone markers, aspen & cedars.

Franklin GEORGE Born July 31, 1841 Died December 18, 1892
Mary C. GEORGE Born April 21, 1820 Died December 19, 1886
Weeden S. GEORGE Born January 24, 1819 Died August 5, 1880
Montgomery GEORGE Born September 13, 1843 Died Nov. 20, 1881

George Cemetery, near Bristersburg, Virginia
Located East Route 616 about 1 mile South Route 607 next to Boteler - Peters Cemetery. Tombstones destroyed years ago. Groundhogs and honeysuckle covered. Information supplied by May Afton Teates March 8, 1996.

Benjamin GEORGE Jr. and wife Mary SMITH GEORGE and some of their children and grandchildren.

George Cemetery, Catlett, Virginia
Located off Route 806, across the railroad track at Catlett. Go South to Route 611. On left side of road near Dowell's Run. In pine grove beside a cattle loafing parlour. The cattle destroyed the tombstones. Information supplied by May Afton Teates March 8, 1996.

Benjamin GEORGE, a Revolutionary War soldier, his wife Hannah GEORGE, his grand son Bernard GEORGE, and his wife Sarah STARK GEORGE, some grandchildren named SMITH, and a greatgrandchild named BENNETT.

Germantown Cemetery, Midland, Virginia

Located on Route 643 to West of Licking Run at end of old abandoned road in grove in field where stock have run. Many fieldstone markers, and others all broken off. One large marker buried too deep to lift. Resurveyed April 23, 1994.

Mrs. Ann FOWKE Departed this life Feby 1, 1859 Aged 31 years 5 months 20 days *(weathered badly cannot read dates)*

Mrs. Adelaide L. HALLEY who departed this life July 13, 1866 aged 13 yrs. 2 mos. 11 days "Blessed are they who put their trust in the Saviour"

Emily WEAVER Born April _____ Died December *(rest slated off)*

Mrs. Sarah W. WEAVER Born in Alexandria, Va. March 29, 1795 Died February 9, 1878 *(headstone and footstone with initials)*

Fannie WEAVER Daughter of Joseph W. & Sarah WEAVER Born in Germantown Fauquier Co., Va. June 12, 1821 Died June 10, 1909 *"A faithful servant of her generation"*

The following members of the 1714 group and their relatives and descendants died at Germantown. The people who died prior to 1760 and possible some years later, were probably buried in the Germantown cemetery on the glebe. Later burials, particularly those of the Martin and Weaver families, and perhaps the Darnalls, were probably in their respective family burying grounds.

— From the Germanna Record, April 1962

Melchior BRUMBACK, b. Sept. 2, 1695 at Muesen, d. 1740–45 at Germantown.

Elizabeth His Wife d. before 1745 at Germantown. *(She was probably Mary Elizabeth FISHBACK, b. April 7, 1696 younger sister of Mrs. RECTOR and of John and Harman FISHBACK).*

Agnes BRUMBACK, their daughter, wife of Henry UTTERBACK. She was born about 1720–25 and died at Germantown 1790–1804.

Henry UTTERBACK, Sr., her husband, b. at Trupbach 1698, d. at Germantowm 1762–1770; he was a first cousin of Mrs. KEMPER and Mrs. HOLTZCLAW.

Frances, wife of Henry UTTERBACK, Jr. She died at Germantown 1774–92.

Joseph CUNTZE, b. about 1680 at Niedernorf, d. 1731 at Germantown.

Catherine, his second wife, d. before 1730 at Germantown.

John CUNTZE, eldest son of Joseph CUNTZE by his first wife, b. 1706 at Niederndorf, d. before 1730 at Germantown.

Henry CUNTZE, son of Joseph, d. probably at Germantown after 1746.

Tilman CUNTZE, son of Joseph, d. before 1762, probably at Germantown.

John FISHBACK, b. July 12, 1691 at Trupbach, d. 1735 at Germantown.

Agnes HAEGER, his first wife, b. Oct. 26, 1697 at Siegen, d. 1724–9 at Germantown.

Mary Dorothea FITER, his second wife, d. before 1753 at Germantown.

Henry FISHBACK, son of John FISHBACK by his first wife, d. before 1753 at Germantown, unmarried.

Catherine FISHBACK, first wife of Harman Fishback, d. before 1745 at Germantown. *(She was probably Anna Catherine OTTERBACH, b. Jan. 2, 1705, sister of Mrs KEMPER and Mrs. HOLTZCLAW).*

Mary Clara NOEH, widow of John NOEH, the second wife of Harman FISHBACK, probably died at Germantown before her husband moved to Culpeper Co. around 1760. She was born in Nassau-Siegen in 1694.

Rev. Henry HAEGER b. 1644 at Antzhausen, d. 1737 at Germantown about 93 years.

Anna Catherine FRIESENHAGEN, his wife, born at Freudenberg, d. at Germantown after 1737.

Peter HITT, b. about 1683 at Rehbach, d. 1772 at Germantown.

Mary Elizabeth FREUDENBERG, his wife, b. at Ferndorf, d. after 1773 at Germantown.

Anna Catherine HAEGER, first wife of John HOFFMAN. She was b. May 15, 1702 at Siegen, d. Feb. 9, at Germantown.
John Henry HOFFMAN, son of John and Anna Catherine HOFFMAN, b. Jan. 18, 1724, d. Jan. 27, 1724.

Hans Jacob HOLTZCLAW, b. 1683 at Trupbach, d. 1760 at Germantown, aged over 76 years.
Anna Margaret OTTERBACH, his wife, b. 1686 at Trupbach, d. 1724–29 at Germantown.
Catherine, second wife of Jacob HOLTZCLAW, d. 1754–59 at Germantown.
Catherine HOLTZCLAW, daughter of Jacob HOLTZCLAW and his first wife, and wife of Jeremiah DARNALL; she was b. ca. 1720–25 and d. at Germantown in 1810.
Jeremiah DARNALL, Gent, her husband, b. 1720, d. at Germantown 1795.
Rosamund DARNALL, their daughter, wife of Thomas LATHAM, d. at Germantown prior to 1809.
Catherine DARNALL, their daughter, d. unmarried at Germantown 1824.

John KEMPER, b. July 8, 1692 at Meusen, d. 1758–9 at Germantown.
Alice Catherine OTTERBACH, his wife, b. April 16, 1692 at Trupbach, d. around 1745–50 at Germantown.
Gertrud, second wife of John KEMPER, d. probably at Germantown about 1755–60. She may have been Gertrud NOEH, b. 1718, eldest daughter of John NOEH and his wife, Mary Clara, who m. Harman FISHBACK.

John Joseph MARTIN, b. May 24, 1691 at Meusen, d. 1758–59 at Germantown.
Mary Catherine, his first wife. She was probably Maria Cathrina OTTERBACH, b. Nov. 5, 1699 at Trupbach, sister of Mrs. KEMPER and Mrs. HOLTZCLAW.
Eve, second wife of John Joseph MARTIN, d. 1777–83 at Germantown.
Tilman MARTIN, b. 1730–35, d. at Germantown, son of John Joseph MARTIN.
John MARTIN, b. 1735–40, d. 1823 at Germantown, son of John Joseph MARTIN.
Catherine, first wife of John MARTIN, d. at Germantown after 1785.
Margaret Elliott, second wife of John MARTIN, d. about 1830 at Germantown.

Hans Jacob RECTOR, b. 1679 at Trupbach, d. 1724–29 at Germantown.
Mary Elizabeth FISHBACK, his wife, b. 1687 at Trupbach, married (2) John MARR, d. soon after 1760 at Germantown.
John MARR, her second husband, probably buried at Germantown, d. 1744.
Harman RECTOR, son of Hans Jacob RECTOR, b. ca. 1720–25, d. 1789 at Germantown.
The wife of Harman RECTOR, name unknown, d. prior to 1789 at Germantown.
John RECTOR, probably a nephew of Hans Jacob RECTOR, b. 1708 in Nassau-Siegen, d. 1743.
His wife, name unknown, who married (2) Timothy REDDING, and d. 1760 at Germantown. She may have been a daughter of John SPILMAN.
Timothy REDDING, second husband of the above, d. 1760 at Germantown.
John SPILMAN, b. 1678 at Oberfischbach, d. 1724–29 at Germantown.
Mary Gertrud HOLTZCLAW, his wife, b. at Salchendorf in the "Free Ground", south of Nassau-Siegen, d. about 1762–3 at Germantown; she married George GENT.
Anna WEAVER, widow of Jacob WEAVER and mother of Tilman WEAVER.
Tilman WEAVER, b. ca. 1703 in Nassau-Siegen, d. 1760 at Germantown.
Ann Elizabeth CUNTZE, his wife, b. 1708 at Niederndorf, d. 1777–83 at Germantown.
Capt. Tilman WEAVER of the Revolution, son of Tilamn WEAVER, b. ca. 1746-48, d. 1809 in Germantown.
Elizabeth, wife of Capt. Tilman WEAVER, d. before 1809 at Germantown.
James WEAVER, their son, d. unmarried 1814 at Germantown.
Many other Weavers of this family in the Weaver burying ground.

Gibson (Lucy) Cemetery, Calverton, Virginia
Located 1.2 miles North Route 806 East Route 616 North of house, 6 fieldstone marked graves.

Ella WOOD 1880–1952

Lucy GIBSON 1854–1943; Elizabeth GIBSON 1894–1910

Glascock Cemetery, "Rockburn Farm", Rectortown, Virginia
Located on Route 674 near barn. Data obtained May 23, 1930 by Eleanor Glascock Thompson.

H. G. 1813 _____ H. G. 1821 *(evidently head & footstones of same grave)*

George GLASCOCK who departed this life 4th of March 1826 in the 85th year of his age

Hannah GLASCOCK / formerly Hannah RECTOR Consort of George GLASCOCK She died in September 1816 in the 66th year of her age

Louis Son of Thomas and Emily A. T. GLASCOCK Born October 30, 1861 Died December 24,1865

Aquila Son of George and H. GLASCOCK Born November 4th 1786 Died September 14, 1867 Aged 80 years 11 months and 10 days

Mary wire of Aquila GLASCOCK Born May 3, 1796 Died September 14, 1870 Aged 74 years 3 months and 1 day

Susanna GLASCOCK Consort of Aquila GLASCOCK Daughter of James and Elizabeth LAKE She died December 22nd 1835 Aged 45 years 1 month and 7 days

Elizabeth LAKE Consort of James LAKE Formerly Elizabeth GLASCOCK Who died Jan. 28th 1837 In the 74th year of her age

James LAKE Son of John and Susannah LAKE Husband of Elizabeth LAKE Born January 6, 1762 Died June 7, 1843

Elias Son of James and Elizabeth LAKE Born January 14, 1793 Died October 15th 1865 Aged 72 years 7 months and 1 day

Davy Boy GLASCOCK Son of Aquila and Susannah GLASCOCK Born June 2, 1827 Died June 4, 1842

William GLASCOCK Son of Aquilla and Susannah GLASCOCK Born November 22, 1822 Died August 15, 1843

Eliza Daughter of Thomas and Emily A. T. GLASCOCK Born December 11, 1842 Died August 17, 1847 Aged 4 years 8 months and 3 days

Aquilla Son of Thomas and Emily A. T. GLASCOCK Born November 21, 1851 Died March 13, 1865

John GLASCOCK Born July 19, 1855 Died Aged 28 years 7 months 14 days

May GLASCOCK Wife of John GLASCOCK Aged 30 years 2 months and 15 days [Died about May 2, 1884]

Roddie Son of John and May GLASCOCK Born September 28, 1877 Aged 6 years 5 months and 4 days

Emma Daughter of John and May GLASCOCK Born May 15, 1880 Aged 3 years 9 months and 18 days

Estella Daughter of Jno. and May GLASCOCK Born November 7th 1878 Died July 15, 1880

Thomas Son of John and May GLASCOCK Born April 11, 1882 Aged 1 year 10 months and 21 days

Emily Daughter of Thomas & Emily A. T. GLASCOCK Born December 11, 1842 Died October 25, 1846 Aged 3 months and 25 days

Glascock Cemetery, "Glenmore", Rectortown, Virginia
Located on left of Route 624 in second field North East of Rectortown 1.3 miles, many with fieldstone markers. Stone fence gone. Tombstones leaning against wall for protection from cattle. Resurveyed Octobewr 9, 1993.

Hezekiah GLASSCOCK Died Aug. 1, 1818 Aged 72 years 1 month and 10 days (missing 1993)

Sarah Wife of Hezekiah GLASSCOCK Died Oct. 13, 1815

John GLASSCOCK Died Jan. 29, 1871 In the 84th year of his age

William GLASSCOCK Born May 20th 1785 Died Feb. 17th 1857 In his 72nd year

Lucy DAVIS Died Jan. 29, 1842

10 unmarked graves

Glascock Cemetery, Belvoir, Virginia
Located on old Route 55, (Bunker Hill Road) between Brooke's Corner and east outlet on Route 55, in field, in clump of cedar trees. Cemetery is to left of Corder home, (old Spencer home) some distance from road. Information from John Gott.

Here is buried:

Thomas GLASCOCK died 1793
Agatha RECTOR GLASCOCK died 1828
John Thomes GLASCOCK, son
Benjamin GLASCOCK, son

Glascock - Carver Cemetery, Old Tavern, Virginia
Located on Route 703, Old Tavern, rear of Ed Saunders home. The following is a list of burials in this cemetery from John Gott. According to a phone call the Mrs. Saunders, November 11, 1990, a prior property owner obliterated the cemetery.

Ann COMBS GLASCOCK
Ann GLASCOCK daughter of Spencer and Ann COMBS GLASCOCK
----------- CARVER daughter of Bailey CARVER {stone with lamb moved to Marshall by Pauline Carter Shumate after John Lunceford bulldozed the cemetery for Bill Leachman}

Maria GLASCOCK daughter of John S. & Louisa LAKE GLASCOCK born17 December 1850 died 19 November 1854
Infant son unnamed of John S. & Louisa LAKE GLASCOCK born 27 December 1852 died 7 January 1853
Armistead GLASCOCK son of Spencer and Ann COMBS GLASCOCK {served in Black Horse Cavalry}

Goolrich Cemetery, Somerville, Virginia
Located 3 miles East of Somerville South Route 610 near Stafford Co. line. Data obtained by Arthur Grove.

R. Montgomery Son of P. and J. GOOLRICK Died May 11, 1851 Age 1 year 11 mo. 29 days
Eliza Daughter of P. and J. GOOLRICK Died June 23, 1851 age 3 mo. 11 days

Gordonsdale Cemeteries, The Plains, Virginia
Located 1.8 mile South of The Plains on West of Route 245 on Route 750. Both cemeteries are stone enclosed and well kept. VICKERS is South East of house and PEYTON is South of house and garden.
4 fieldstone markers and one old grave without stone in PEYTON cemetery.

Margaret C. GLASSELL Dau. of Rev. John SCOTT who died in faith Oct. 11th 1843 ... Erected by her children
Robert Eden PEYTON, M. D. the Beloved Physician 3rd Son of Dr. C. & E. D. PEYTON Born Feb. 9, 1804 Died July 15, 1872
Ann Lee PEYTON Wife of Robert Eden PEYTON, M. D. of Gordonsdale and Daughter of Genl. Walter JONES and Ann Lucinda LEE His Wife Born in Washington, D. C. April 5, 1812 and departed this life at Yelverton May 21, 1905, in the 94th year of her age
Ann Lee PEYTON Eldest child of Doctor Robert E. PEYTON of Gordonsdale and Ann Lee PEYTON His Wife Born August 3, 1836 Died October 29, 1919
Virginia Jones PEYTON 1852–1925 Daughter of Dr. Robert E. and Ann Lee PEYTON
Eliza Gordon Scott PEYTON 1841–1926 Daughter of Dr. Robert E. and Ann Lee PEYTON
Robert E. PEYTON Son of Robert Eden & Ann Lee PEYTON August 8, 1843 April 28, 1934
Cornelia G. FOSTER Wife of Robert E. PEYTON Feb. 12, 1846 July 18, 1932
Thomas R. F. PEYTON July 8, 1875 Feb. 19, 1957
Grace HOOD PEYTON 1878–1962
Henry PEYTON 1744–1814 and Susanna FOWKE His Wife
Richard H. PEYTON SMITH nephew & adopted child of Margaret C. PEYTON Born Feb. 8th 1840 Died Oct. 18th 1855
Margaret Christian PEYTON youngest Daughter of Eliza B. SCOTT and Dr. Chandler PEYTON of Fauquier Co., Va. Born Sept. 4, 1809 Died July 22, 1881
Walter Jones PEYTON died July 4th 1853 aged 6 years & Edward Marshall PEYTON died July 6th 1853 aged 4 years sons of Robert E. & Nannie L. PEYTON victims of the epidemic Dysentera which then prevailed

Mrs. Elizabeth SCOTT Daughter of Professor Thomas GORDON of Old Aberdeen Scotland Ob 1802 aged 52 years
Mrs. Eliza C. SMITH oldest Daughter of Chandler & Eliza B. PEYTON who departed this life Ob 14th Feb. 1840 aged 32 years
Capt. Richard H. PEYTON Asst. Or. Master of the U. S. Army who was born in Fauquier Co., Va. and died in Tampa, C. F. on the 11th of Nov. 1839 of the fever of the climate whilst actively engaged in the service of his country aged 28 years
Dr. C. PEYTON OB June 16th 1827 Aged 58
Mrs. Eliza B. PEYTON Relict of Dr. C. PEYTON & eldest Daughter of the Rev. John SCOTT. She departed this life March 9, 1842 In the 70th year of her age
Kate J. PACKARD Born Aug. 22, 1856 Died Oct. 4, 1862
Louis W. GRAFFLIN Oct. 8, 1867 Nov. 18, 1930
Nannette Lee PEYTON GRAFFLIN 1871–1961
Katherine "Kate" FOSTER PEYTON 1880–1960
Corrie FOSTER PEYTON 1883–1962

Tombstones built in stone wall in VICKERS cemetery.

Lucy Voris VICKERS February 1, 1923 November 22, 1923
Helen BAIRD VICKERS August 30, 1884 May 25, 1856 [*Dr. Reginald VICKERS, her husband, born May 16, 1885 died June 23, 1968 and is buried there also*]
Reginald J. VICKERS, Jr. July 7, 1924 October 4, 1978

Gore & Hitt Cemeteries, Crest Hill, Virginia
Located on Route 645 on farm adjacent to Rappahannock River on East side of road. No fence, many fieldstone markers, originally two cemeteries separated by fence.

Lucy A. Wife of John W. GORE Born September 6, 1851 Died January 24, 1892
H AG. 31 1802
H H G AG 96 1846
JJ ON

Grace Episcopal Church, Casanova, Virginia
Located North Route 664 just North Route 602, well-kept, fenced, around church. Resurveyed 1990.

Catharine ALLPORT WEBER December 26, 1870 March 13, 1947
Marie K. FOWKE Aug. 26, 1850 March 6, 1918
Charles Hook THOMPKINS June 8, 1919 January 28, 1968
John Francis RIBBLE, Jr. PVT US ARMY WORLD WAR I Jan. 19, 1900 Feb. 20, 1972; Wife Nell May ALLEN Nov. 14, 1907
John Gordon BEALE February 1910 September 10, 1956
Susan V. GORDON BEALE 1847–1927
Mary GORDON BEALE Wife of Rev. J. Francis RIBBLE Born Nov. 19, 1872 Entered into rest Dec. 25, 1904
John Gordon BEALE 1845–1942 *(C.S.A. marker)*
Ludwell Digges BEALE 1842–1899
Eliza BEALE GORDON 1868–1898; Edward Peagram GORDON 1866–1900
John Gillison BEALE 1870–1925; Sallie Lee TURNER BEALE 1870–1930
Mary AURELTON BEALE 1839–1933
Fannie WHITE Feb. 5, 1857 April 7, 1917
The Rev. David CAMPBELL June 10, 1874 March 12, 1961; Josephine Hart MAYERS Feb. 10, 1877 Sept. 28, 1966
Violet Regina MOORE Wife of J. Alex MAYERS Dec. 12, 1890 Oct. 29, 1926
Millicent DRAYTON THORNE July 23, 1890 Barbados, B.W.I. Dec. 16,. 1911 Richmond, Va.

Ursula DRAYTON THORN April l2, 1901 Barbados, B. W. I. May l5, l985 New York, N. Y.
Buchanon Magill RANDOLPH May 29, 1903 March 24, 1979
Roberta LEE RANDOLPH February 16, 1878 November 18, 1978
Winslow Hoxton RANDOLPH born October 29, 1869 died October 24, 1989
Margaret DUNCAN ROBINSON Wife of Winslow Hoxton RANDOLPH born Feb. 24, 1871 died April 17, l937
Buckner Magill RANDOLPH Physician Son of Bucker Magill and Mary Hoxton RANDOLPH August 21, 1871 July 1, 1931
Rev. Buckner Magill RANDOLPH July 28, 1842 August ll, 1903
Mary Hoxton RANDOLPH Daughter of Eliza L. GRIFFITH and Dr. William HOXTON born in Alexandria, Va. November 23, l846 entered into life eternal January 11, 1930
Clara Pauline RANDOLPH born RATHBONE Sept. 15, 1872 April 25, 1918
Beverley RANDOLPH Son of Robert Lee & Mary Magill RANDOLPH of Eastern View April 1839 Feb. 1917
Bettie BURWELL NICOLSON Daughter of Charles & Mary C. WELLFORD of Fredericksburg, Va. Wife of George Llewellyn NICOLSON, M. D. of Deer Creek, Middlesex County, Va. earthly life Jan. 14, 1827 Aug. 11, 1897
Robert Wormeley Son of G. Llewellyn and Betty NICOLSON died Dec. 25, 1911
Eleanor Tayloe WORMELEY NICOLSON departed this life Dec. 13, 1906
Sallie BERKELEY WILLIAMS beloved Wife of George Thurston WILLIAMS and Daughter of George Llewellyn NICOLSON and Betty BURWELL NICOLSON born at Deer Creek Middlesex County, Va. Sept. 25, 1851 departed this earthly life May 13, 1928

George WILLIAMS of London, England, eldest son of Lt. Colonel Monier WILLIAMS born in India May 14, 1814 died in Virginia April 7, 1898
George Thurston WILLIAMS beloved Husband of Sallie BERKELEY WILLIAMS of Deer Creek, Middlesex and Son of George WILLIAMS and Amelia CHAUNCEY of London, England August 15, 1852 departed this earthly life September 22, 1926 at his home River Hill near Casanova
Mary Welford Daughter of George Llewellyn and Bettie WELFORD NICOLSON Earthly life Sept. 6, 1858 Sept. 19, 1932
Lucy Gray Daughter of George Llewellyn and Bettie WELLFORD NICHOLSON May 26, 1862 July 15, 1938
John Chauncey WILLIAMS 24 January 1884–23 January 1957 Son of Sallie BEAKLEY and George Thurston WILLIAMS of Deer Creek and Rockhill
Elizabeth SPILMAN WILLIAMS Wife of John Chauncey WILLIAMS of Rockhill 25 August 1890 1 June 1964 Daughter of Baldwin Day SPILMAN and Annie CAMDEN SPILMAN of Elway
Amelia Chauncey WILLIAMS Daughter of George and Sallie WILLIAMS of Rockhill 2 February 1879 4 July 1967
Mary MAXWELL GULICK Dec. 15, 1912 June 6, 1958
John Claybrook RICHARDS born Oct. 5, 1962 Died Jan. 31, 1986
William Withers GULICK May l6, 1912 Nov. 30, 1982
George Maxwell GULICK Jan. 26, 1951 May 2, 1982
Rev. Stanley E. ASHTON April 30, 1907 May 3, 1986
Mary GULICK ASHTON April 3, 1909 Sept. 29, 1987
Alan JOHNSTONE, Junior Born at Newberry, South Carolina July 11, 1890 Died at Casanova, Virginia January 4, 1966 Son of Lilla RALL KENNERLY and Alan JOHNSTONE and Husband of Lalla ROOK SIMMONS
Lalla Rook SIMMONS JOHNSTONE Born in Newberry, South Carolina July 29, 1889 Died in Washington, D September 20, 1949 Daughter of Joshua Ward Motte SIMMONS and Lalla Rook and Wife of Alan JOHNSTONE, Junior
Lalla ROOK BACH 1920–1975

THOMPSON Plot:
James Cammina ALPORT Dec. 20, 1911 Died Nov. 28, 1986; Winifred Emily MARTIN Born Bristol, England Nov. 29, 1921 Died Warrenton, Virginia Nov. 10, 1984 Married Jan. 22, 1945 in Salisbury, England
Matilda S. BOSWELL 1836–1896; Charles H. GORDON Jan. 17, 1929 Died Jan. 23, 1897; Mary B. GORDON 1865–1960

Terry Lee LEMMEL Dec. 10, 1951 Aug. 1, 1963
Samuel GOULDTHORPE 1907–1985 *(fhm)*
Jackie F. GOULDTHORPE June 19, 1931 August 6, 1940
Edith I. HILABARD 1884–1962
M. Gertrude MacKNUTT 1884–1960
Viola MacKNUTT 1855–1957
Irene HORSELY CLOPTON 1870–1912
Mary TAYLOR March 27, 1876 Jan. 12, 1961
Eliza TAYLOR RENOUF July 13, 1869 Oct. 16, 1951
Thomas TAYLOR September 22, 1843 October 11, 1907
Annie LAWRASON TAYLOR January 16, 1844 Jan. 5, 1907
THOMPSON Thomas Weston Oct. 6, 1849 Nov. 2, 1931; Sarah Bell ALLPORT Oct. 12, 1875 Sept. 10, 1953
    Married Oct. 24, 1901
Frederick W. TURNBULL 1907–1978
Curtis Lawton TURNBULL 1932–1954
Ellen WRENN COSNAHAN 1837–1912
Louisa M. W. COSNAHAN 1859–1925
Eliza Virginia REDD 1861–1949
Annie CARROLL NOURSE 1858–1935
Charlotte St.George NOURSE 1894–1959
Anne Constance NOURSE 1886–1959; Sallie WALLACE SIMPSON 1844–1907
Charles Joseph NOURSE 1825–1906; Mary Pemberton NOURSE 1891–1916
James Crammond ALLPORT 1833–1918; Mary Jane MORRISON His Wife 1833–1910; Dora Bell ALLPORT
    Daughter 1864–1919
Daisy B. Nov. 7, 1877 Died June 6, 1878
Chas. H. GORDON Born Jan. 7, 1829 Died Jan. 23, 1897
Bernard MOORE Son of B. M. & E. J. CAMPBELL Born Mar. 17, 1869 Died Jan. 8, 1881
Emily J. MOORE Wife of Bernard M. CAMPBELL Mar. 6, 1826 Died Jan. 9, 1912
Bernard Moore CAMPBELL Born Limrick Co., Ga. November 23, 1810 Died May 30, 1890
M. E. JONES 1888–1915
Ada JONES Sept. 28, 1915 Nov. 10, 1915
Mauda GRAY daughter of R. A. & T. L. HART Born Nov. 12, 1868 Died Jan. 28, 1875

Grace Methodist Church Cemetery, Somerville. Virginia
Located West intersections of routes 614 & 616 to North of church, fenced, well kept. Some data taken from
    "Stafford Co., Va. Cemeteries V1" p 75 by Cynthia L. Musselman. Resurveyed June 11, 1994.

Hosier Sumpter COURTNEY Aug. 20, 1921 May 11, 1947
Elizabeth MASON COURTNEY May 28, 1896 Sept. 8, 1951

COOPER Walter J. Aug. 11, 1878 Jan. 23, 1956 Ida H. Feb. 20, 1884 Feb. 2, 1963
Infant Elzia COOPER; Infant Edward COOPER
Mother Dora BEACH COOPER Sept. 14, 1880 Feb. 2, 1928
BEACH James L. May 11, 1876 Sept. 19, 1965 Lula Mae May 10, 1891 May 14, 1939
David COOPER November 30, 1877 January 8, 1958
Fred COOPER Sept. 6, 1852 June 2, 1902
Alice COOPER MASON Julu 14, 1876 Oct. 21, 1924 Mother
Lawrence John COOPER Died Feb. 12, 1968 Aged 60 yrs. 1 mo. 19 days
Bessie COOPER MASON Aug. 13, 1878 Dec. 20, 1903
William W. MASON June 14, 1871 Oct. 31, 1944
Infant MASON
Carlin T. MASON ECC5 US ARMY WORLD WAR II May 22 1914 Nov 28, 1988

Myrtle HEFLIN Mar. 7, 1925 Jan. 8, 1926
2 fieldstone markers
DYE Hughie D. Nov. 29, 1894 Aug. 22, 1960 Father Katie A. Sept. 24, 1909 Oct. 11, 1964 Mother
    Bessie H. DYE Sept. 28, 1898 Aug. 17, 1923
COURTNEY Thaddeus Edward COURTNEY Oct 13, 1884–Dec. 19, 1960 His Wife Corrinne BEACH
    COURTNEY Dec. 28, 1883 Sept. 3, 1972
Ella Lee Wife of Cash H. HEFLIN Sept. 7, 1869 Jan. 16, 1946

BETTIS Thomas J. 1826–1893 His Wife Sarah J. 1838–1917 erected by children
Virgie J. BEACH Mar. 8, 1908 Apr. 3, 1969
Infant Annabell FLETCHER Sept. 6, 1931
MOUNTJOY Infant; MOUNTJOY Infant; MOUNTJOY Infant
Norris O. BEACH Aug. 19, 1898 Dec. 25, 1960
George Irving ARMSTRONG Feb. 20, 1908 Feb. 6, 1969
BEACH Camilla 1881–1919 Henry L. 1890–1937
BEACH Douglas W. Jan. 11, 1884 July 2, 1973; Sallie B. Aug. 29, 1889 Mar. 20, 1982
BEACH Richard H. 1849–1924 Sarah S. 1853–1938
Richard Harry BEACH Born Feb. 20, 1892 Died July 3, 1969 Age 99
Gertrude A. BEACH Aug. 28, 1880 Jan. 18, 1959

STEPHENS William B. July 22, 1874 Jan. 31, 1942 Ella C. Mar. 30, 1876 Oct. 22, 1964
BEACH William B. 1874–1953 Mary L. 1878–1908

WAMSLEY Willie Hawkens S. 1859–1944 Mary Virginia 1852–1931
Benjamin WAMSLEY 1895–1970 *(fhm)*

Earl Wilson COOPER Sept. 21, 1931 June 25, 1965
SKINNER Lawrence Ashton March 1884 November 1957
Frank M. DUFFY Dec. 3, 1889 Nov. 27, 1940
Sallie B. SKINNER Died February 10, 1933
L. A. SKINNER Departed this life July 6, 1915
Mother Addie Belle DUFFEY March 1893 June 1957

WAMSLEY Corabell Feb. 4, 1890 Mar. 9, 1962 Oscar Lee Aug. 6, 1890 Nov. 21, 1967 [*by Hawkens & Mary*
    Virginia WAMSLEY]

Betty Ann Daughter of W. B. and Hazel STEPHENS Feb. 21, 1931 Aug. 10, 1933
2 fieldstone markers
Lizzie BEACH HEFLIN Jan. 2, 1873 July 27, 1942
Thad A. BEACH Sept. 11, 1878 Nov. 19, 1951

Infant of Charles & Ella SMITH; Infant of Lindell & Robena SMITH
Mary E. SMITH Feb. 9, 1844 Jan. 25, 1923

Orion HEFLIN Oct. 6, 1898 Sept. 23, 1920
Earle Ralph HEFLIN Oct. 9, 1913 July 12, 1937
Mollie E. HEFLIN Feb. 26, 1874 Jan. 25, 1923
George William HEFLIN Aug. 28, 1872 July 3, 1948

SMITH Virginia November 9, 1866 August 26, 1933 John W. December 23, 1866 March 18, 1939
MASON George William Dec. 13, 1883 Nov. 5, 1957 Esther STEPHENS Sept. 29, 1897

Fannie A. CRINNAN Born Aug. 1, 1893 Died Sept. 3, 1905
J. Wesley DODD Born Jan. 5, 1887 Died March 25, 1955 Aged 82 yrs, 2 mos 27 days

Nora Lee COOPER Wife of Walter R. ELLIS August 14, 1896 February 2, 1952

Bolivar H. RANDALL Beloved Husband of Mattie B. RANDALL Born Oct. 3, 1895 Died Oct. 23, 1916
DYE Henry W. July 4, 1861 Apr. 7, 1917 Mary E. Feb. 18, 1866 Oct. 2, 1966 Father Mother
Lizzie M. ENNIS Apr. 26, 1886 Dec. 11, 1926
Etta M. ENNIS June 25, 1912 Sept. 11, 1929
Stansbury DYE June 13, 1920 June 2, 1937
Andrew W. DYE VIRGINIA CPL BTRNY F 38 ARTY CAC WORLD WAR I Sept. 16, 1890 May 31, 1953
John DYE June 26, 1885–March 26, 1946 WORLD WAR I Pvt, 6th Engrs, 3rd Div
Son Murkle DYE departed this life Dec. 7, 1911 Aged 21 yrs.
Mother Blanch POSEY Nov. 2, 1889 Sept. 15, 1920
Beauregard DYE Mar. 17, 1861 Mar. 25, 1935 Father
Cecil DYE May 22, 1910 Nov. 25, 1940

Patsey LENOX MASON July 20, 1884 July 6, 1916
Floyd D. MASON Oct. 8, 1881 Feb. 28, 1946
8 fieldstone markers
Rosa Belle PATTON 1879–1957

Hallie Beach CROPP JEWELL June 10, 1873 Oct. 8, 1938
George W. CROPP Aug. 29, 1859 June 27, 1910
John N. CROPP 1907–1908
Alberta JEWELL 1912–1916
CROPP Carter 1820–1903 Mary Francis 1831–1923
Bertie L. BROWN 1882–1959; Louis G. BROWN 1914–1966
Ethel BROWN HOLMES Died March 9, 1969 Aged 51 yrs. 6 mos. 23 ds

Thomas E. O'MALLEY Aug. 14, 1917 July 8, 1861 Son

Donna Mae BEACH Oct. 5, 1961 Oct. 8, 1961
Edward Albert BEACH VIRGINIA PFC 2 BBL RAF BEST CO. WORLD WAR II OCT. 28, 1924 MAY 27, 1966
Leslie HEFLIN June 1, 1904–Dec 31, 1961 His Wife Ethel CROPP Dec. 6, 1907–Feb. 14, 1986
Willard M. COOPER VIRGINIA S1 USNR WORLD WAR II Sept 22, 1924 June 13, 1963
Dorrick Danielle Daughter of Mary Ellen & Wm. DUTY Born & Died April 12, 1964
DUTY William H. 1913–1977 Mary Ellen 1926

Paul T. MITCHEM July 26, 1852 March 2, 1968
George Erwin BREEDEN VIRGINIA PFC CO I 116 INF 29 DIV WORLD WAR I Sept 11, 1893 March 31 1956
Charles Lee CLARK Nov. 25, 1942 May 4, 1955
Richard Merrick TEATES June 11, 1945 Nov. 8, 1954
HEFLIN Maurice Sept. 26, 1900 Aug. 2, 1954 Margaret B. Jan. 14, 1911

Father William Peyton LENOX July 24, 1870 December 25, 1956
William Edward LENOX Died October 30, 1969 Aged 59 yrs. 1 day
Mrs. Lorrie Virginia LENOX Died July 7, 1955 Aged 69 years
Harry Lee GREEN VIRGINIA A3C US AIR FORCE Dec. 6, 1941 Oct 5, 1963
COOPER Ambous S. Nov. 4, 1897 Apr. 14, 1972 Virginia B. July 18, 1893 Jan 15, 1959 Husband Wife
Lucille C. MOSS Aug. 5, 1917 Aug. 25, 1962 Gertrude C. CORBIN Mar. 29, 1910
Elizabeth SHELTON DYE Oct. 21, 1935 June 10, 1962

Arthur Marion DYE Feb. 7, 1929 May 31, 1953
Martha Ada DYE Nov. 25, 1896
Henry Willard DYE Dec. 8, 1924 Dec. 27, 1965

Charles W. BEACH Mar. 18, 1883 Feb. 14, 1946
George W. CROPP June 4, 1900 Jan. 14, 1965
Jeptha Allen COOPER July 3, 1889 March 8, 1950

Larry Eugene Infant Son of John & Pearl DODD Feb. 16, 1850 Mar. 18, 1950
James Lewis Infant Son of Stafford & Ellen M. DODD Dec. 22, 1850 Dec. 24, 1950
John Lewis DODD Jan. 22, 1883 Feb. 20, 1960 Lillian Sept. 8, 1932
Lonnie Ashton WILSON Died May 24, 1908 Aged 61 yrs. 5 mos. 1 day

Mrs. Lillie Mae HEFLIN Died March 13, 1969 Aged 60 yrs. 7 mos. 9 days
Welford HEFLIN PVT CO D 18 INFANTRY WORLD WAR I Feb. 6, 1897 April 13, 1967

Roderick S. SMITH May 7, 1923 March 19, 1948
Delores Jane ETHERIDGE Nov. 4, 1941 April 16, 1943
James Harrison STEPHENS Jan 2, 1891 Feb. 9, 1960
Ruth Marie Daughter of Lennie & Mary HEFLIN July 31, 1942 November 11, 1942
DODD Allen R. Apr. 16, 1900 Feb. 11, 1967 Macie O. June 30, 1904 Dec. 14, 1972

HEFLIN Benjamin F. April 7, 1890 Sept. 2, 1965 Alberta J. May 21, 1895
Barbara J. HEFLIN June 7, 1939 Jan. 16, 1955
Edward HEFLIN May 10, 1923 July 1, 1945

LENOX Walter Scott May 9, 1872 March 23, 1952 Susan DODD November 10, 1877 January 15, 1947 Father
   Mother
Louise L. LENOX May 22, 1912 June 17, 1944 Daughter
Mrs. Edwin M. LENOX Mar. 8, 1925 July 12, 1892
Michael M. LENOX Mar. 23, 1897 Aug. 23, 1937
ANDERSON, Minnie F. June 12, 1935 April 21, 1992: Vincent L. June 13, 1927

Walter Sylvester BEACH VIRGINIA PFC BTRY B 43 COAST ARTY BN WORLD WAR II June 29, 1919 August
   19, 1965
Father Mother BEACH Walter C. Aug. 7, 1874 May 21, 1954 Roberta Mar. 27, 1879 Nov. 7, 1939
J. Herman BEACH Sept. 30, 1905 July 16, 1940
Shirley STEPHENS 1936–1939
STEPHENS, Dophia Sept. 3, 1893 Oct. 17, 1938: Lindsey C. June 21, 1912 July 6, 1976
Stacey Leroy STEPHENS Jan. 24, 1935 Nov. 17, 1951
Leonard F. HEFLIN May 26, 1912 August 21, 1940

Ernest R. MASON Born Nov. 6, 1902 Died April 19, 1968 Aged 65 years
Franklin D. MASON Died March 26, 1969 Aged 33 years 3 mos. 18 dys.

REID Cornelius F. April 23, 1895 Aug. 24, 1966 Olive HEFLIN June 4, 1904 May 23, 1982 Husband Wife
Harry S. HEFLIN Aug. 11, 1906 Nov. 5, 1963
Sadie DODD HEFLIN Jan. 15, 1885 June 8, 1966
Elliott T. HEFLIN April 10, 1880 Sept. 11, 1953
William M. SMITH Oct. 15, 1870 Dec. 15, 1947
Ida DODD ECKERT 1882–1964 Mother

COOPER Androw N. May 21, 1898 Jan. 7, 1969 Mamie M. Aug. 12, 1903 Jan. 7, 1969
Kathleen SMITH WHITE June 26, 1953 Jan. 10, 1992 Sweet Lady
CARRINGTON Luther 1871–1947 Anna 1876–1949
Son Herbert CARRINGTON 1908–1936

Annie E. COOPER March 11, 1936 May 10, 1937

C. L. JEWELL Born July 11, 1897
M. V. JEWELL Born 7 02 92 Died Sept. 8, 1935
Willie J. JEWELL; Agnes JEWELL Born June 7, 1891 Died Feb. 10, 1954

Thomas L. BETTIS Nov. 25, 1918 April 12, 1937
BETTIS David 1875–1952 Bertie 1885–1957 Father Mother

ENNIS Dallie M. May 10, 1897 John M. Dec. 24, 1882 Oct. 20, 1958

Raleigh S. COOPER Feb. 16, 1939 Nov. 5, 1961; Glen Francis COOPER Aug. 28, 1935 April 17, 1939
William Robert COOPER, Sr. April 3, 1891 Oct 6, 1968 Frances Copage COOPER March 30, 1905 June 11, 1959
Hoover R. COOPER June 22, 1930 Nov. 4, 1968
Edgar Charles COOPER Born Mar 7, 1925 Died December 29, 1969 Aged 44 yrs. 9 mos. 22 dys

James C. HEFLIN February 2, 1931 June 9, 1931 Infant Son of H. L. HEFLIN
Anna M. HEFLIN May 9, 1933 July 9, 1934 Infant Daughter of H. L. HEFLIN

Percy Linwood CLARK Sept. 18, 1925 Apr. 29, 1930
Percy Payne CLARK Mar. 16, 1893 Oct. 4, 1968
Mamie GROVE March 26, 1888 May 20, 1970
HEFLIN J. Luther July 23, 1873 Died Sept. 8, 1930 His Wife Sarah E. Born July 26, 1876 Died June 9, 1959
BEARD Clara H. Mar. 4, 1879 June 16, 1931 James G. Dec. 30 1867 June 6, 1947 Mother Father
Sarah E. BEACH dau. of D. F. & E. F. SILLAMAN 1914–1936
Sister Mazie B. JONES Aug. 11, 1908 Feb. 21, 1939
Brother Willie R. BEACH July 5, 1911 April 12, 1940

Kendrick HEFLIN June 15, 1860 December 15, 1931
Irene ENNIS BEACH September 19, 1892 August 8, 1953
James H. HEFLIN Dec. 13, 1900 Apr. 6, 1959 Jimmie
Johnson P. HEFLIN July 8, 1862 May 6, 1943 Father
Julia B. HEFLIN Feb. 14, 1872 Nov. 23, 1936
HEFLIN John R. April 28, 1869 May 17, 1932 Susan A. December 18, 1867 March 15, 1933 Father Mother
Elwood Kerne HEFLIN Mar. 11, 1920 Mar. 18, 1945
HEFLIN Ruby E. Oct. 31, 1902 Apr. 21, 1963 Larkin T. Oct. 11, 1892 July 4, 1964 Mother Father

BEACH Albert H. June 24, 1882 March 17, 1961 Bertha E. May 11, 1887 February 1, 1960
[Powhatan Lee ARMSTRONG Born Sept. 17, 1891 Died November 13, 1969 Aged 78 yrs. 1 mo. 27 dys]
ARMSTRONG, Powhatan Lee Sept 17, 1891 Nov 13, 1969: Lillie C. Oct. 18, 1893 Oct. 1, 1979
Susan Virginia MANUEL 1860–1930
Mother Susan R. MANUEL Mar. 24, 1830 Aug. 20, 1902
Father Silas A. MANUEL Mar. 30, 1828 Dec. 21, 1901
Silas A. MANUEL, Jr. 1864–1938

Daughter Esther E. HEFLIN Aug. 5, 1895 Aug. 16, 1910
Charles Marshall HEFLIN 1862–1937 His Wife Cornelia Frances MANUEL 1868–1936

Ella L. GROVE Aug. 3, 1855 Aug. 24, 1931
Noah GROVE May 17, 1854 Mar. 28, 1908

PEARSON Samuel H. July 6, 1890 Jan. 16, 1918 Edith A. Aug. 28, 1895 Jan. 21, 1968
PEARSON Horner L. August 4, 1903 March 13, 1965 Dorothy F. December 3, 1906 October 31, 1966
PEARSON Samuel 1867–1937 Sarah A. 1871–1945

Catherine J. EMBREY Nov. 28, 1860 Dec. 14, 1943
Will H. EMBREY June 25, 1865 Dec. 3, 1936

SCHOOLER Samuel B. March 28, 1858 September 3, 1924
SCHOOLER Armanda SIMPSON Wife of Samuel SCHOOLER August 14, 1845 August 16, 1938
Mother Sallie M. WOOD

William H. TEATES Apr. 8, 1916 June 9, 1917
Estelle S. TEATES BROOKS Feb. 20, 1879 Jan. 11, 1943
Henry W. TEATES Nov. 24, 1858 Aug. 17, 1919
Clifton E. TEATES Aug. 23, 1913 Jan. 31, 1921

Dulcenia D. DEAN May 10, 1872 Feb. 20, 1935
Son James G. DYE July 22, 1931 Dec. 7, 1951
Florence Margaret COOPER Jan. 19, 1931 Mar. 21, 1934 Daughter
Peter JEWELL 1860–1937
ANDERSON Archie S. 1881–1965 Ethel D. 1890–1970
TEATES, Noah Grove Jan. 9, 1909 July 9, 1989: Edna MERRICK Jan. 13, 1913
ANDERSON, Pearl Gray Oct. 24, 1899 Jun. 29, 1972
ARMSTRONG, Gearge W. May 22, 1864 Aug. 28, 1939: Lulie C. May 1, 1874 Dec. 7, 1953
ARMSTRONG, Lillie C. Oct 18, 1893 Oct. 1, 1978

BEACH, Agnes C. Jun. 18, 1892 Jan. 17, 1981
BEACH, Douglas W. Jan. 11, 1884 Jul. 2, 1973: Sallie B. Aug. 29, 1889
BEACH, Isaac F. 1890-1960; Mary J. 1883-1959
BEACH, Martha COOPER Jun. 10, 1885 Jun. 20, 1968
BEACH, Silas E. 1893-1942; BEACH, Myrtle 1891-1967
BEACH, WESLEY S. 1844-1922; BEACH, Betty C. 1846-1930
BOTTS, Frank T. Sept. 30, 1897 Feb. 3, 1975; Lora H. Aug. 19, 1912
BROWN, Laura SMITH Mar. 20, 1860 Nov. 27, 1936
BUTLER, Rena MASON 1890-1967

COOPER, Alvin R. 1881-1970
COOPER, C. Ramey Sept. 19, 1898 Jan. 20, 1973
COOPER, Charlie 1865-1929; Susie C. 1873-1941
COOPER, Jane H. 1894-1974
COOPER, Nellie Aug. 30, 1901 Aug. 7, 1972
COURTNEY, J. Sumpter 1895-1974
COURTNEY, John T. Oct. 14, 1857 Sept. 6, 1913; Sallie J. June 25, 1858 Sug. 16, 1937

DODD, J. Wesley Mar. 22, 1855 Jan. 5, 1948
DUFFEY, Frank M. Dec. 3, 1889 Nov. 27, 1940
DYE, Alfred W. Sept. 16, 1890 May 31, 1953 WORLD WAR I, Cpl, Batry F, 38th Art CAC
DYE, Dessie Sept. 28, 1898 Aug 17, 1923

DYE, J. Broaddus 1892-1917; Alice
DYE, Eliza CROPP Jan. 24, 1858 June 2, 1930
DYE, J. Strother May 9, 1899 Jan. 22, 1960; Bessie M. Apr. 4, 1904 June 18, 1974
DYE, Louis Andrew Aug. 10, 1892 Jan. 23, 1971 WORLD WAR I, Pvt, US ARMY
DYE, Lucy B. May 1, 1867 Feb. 1, 1954

ENNIS, Alice S. May 27, 1895 Apr. 24 1957

GAY, Mary Lee Nov. 7, 1895 Oct. 17, 1949; James GAY
GRINNAN, Fannie A. Aug. 1, 1863 Sept. 3, 1905

HEFLIN, Asa L. Died 1934; Lilly R. Died 1932
HEFLIN, Lillie WILSON May 24, 1908 Mar. 13, 1969

LENOX, John Edward 1890-1975
LENOX, Wallace May 17, 1899 Oct. 18, 1980

MASON, A. Mae May 11, 1892 July 15, 1973
MASON, George Lewis 1858-1924; Emma JACKSON 1861-1904
MILLER, Lillian DODD Sept. 4, 1892 Jan. 2, 1940

OLIVER, Curtis Lee Nov. 17, 1880 July 12, 1937; Emma Jean W. Nov. 16, 1888

SMITH, Thomas H. Jan. 18, 1896 Mar. 21, 1979; Eunice I. Mar. 27, 1902
SMITH, Mary Brown Oct. 23, 1829 Apr. 21, 1921
SPRINKLE, Abbie LENOX Feb. 19, 1898 May 29, 1971
SWIM, Hurburt Apr, 3, 1898Apr. 14, 1972
SWIM, Maxine. W. Apr. 13, 1902

TATE, Wm. H. [Dr.] Jan. 12, 1841 Jan. 23, 1923; Mrs. L. M. Oct. 23, 1850 Apr. 15, 1918

Grant Cemetery, "Bunker Hill", The Plains, Virginia
Located South Route 55 about 2 miles West of The Plains in yard of frame house. Many unmarked graves, well kept.
Resurveyed Fall 1993.

William BLANTON VIRGINIA PFC US ARMY WORLD WAR I April 15 1894 February 19 1954
Albert STROTHER 1905–1964

Mrs. Minnie GRANT BOLDEN states that the unmarked graves contain among others, her in-laws: Mr. & Mrs.
Edward GRANT; Sophia Lambert, Janie STROTHER, Buck BLAND, Albert STROTHER and his daughter Mittie;
Jim GRANT and his 3 sons, Edward GRANT & 2 daughters, Will GRANT & baby. Mrs. Bolden also states that the
MUSE family is buried across the road in unmarked graves in overgrown thicket.

Grant - Chloe Cemetery (Black), Marshall, Virginia
Located on Route 710 on both sides of Grant - Chloe driveway. Right side along stone wall. February 2, 1991

right side
Theodore R. TINES 1902-1979 *(fhm)*
Elsie Elizabeth HERRING 1925-1984 *(fhm)*
Charles Edward TINES CPL USA WORLD WAR II Oct. 14, 1926 Sept. 14, 1986
2 rock markers

1 unmarked grave

left side
Morvitza BRIDGETT 1915-1980 *(fhm)*
STEWART Clara 1913-1978
Ethel M. TRACY 1914-1985 *(fhm)*
unmarked grave
Darrell Lane CAISON 1982-1982 *(fhm)*
mother Sally Ann CAISON June 11, 1926 May 17, 1971
2 funeral home markers inscriptions gone
Antonette D. MASON 1973-1973 *(fhm)*
Our sister Florence TALLEY Died June 28, 1899 Aged 29 years
rock marker
Robert MOXLEY 1910-1977 *(fhm)*
Gertrude E. CAISON 1894-1965 *(fhm)*
Mattie M. BRIDGETT 1938-1978 *(fhm)*
Nimrod CAISON 1889-1970 *(fhm)*
other unmarked graves in briar

Gray Cemetery, Somerville, Virginia
Located 2 miles South of Somerville at the intersection of Routes 752 and 617, 300 yards East in field. Surveyed by L. Arthur Grove February 1994.

3 unmarked field stone markers

Gregg Cemetery, Halfway, Virginia
Located West Route 626, just South Route 628 to left of yard and house, fenced, overgrown.

Myrtle M. Daughter of R. L. & G. T. GREGG Born Nov. 5, 1906 Died Feb. 25, 1919
Harlan M. Husband of Elmore V. GREGG Born April 8, 1848 Died Aged 61 years
Minnie D. Daughter of H. M. & E. F. GREGG Born May 18, 1888 Aged 29 years
Donnie M. Daughter of H. M. & E. F. GREGG Born May 26, 1896 Aged 12 years

Gregg Cemetery, The Plains, Virginia
Located West Route 626 North of Montrose near The Plains. Vanished.

Gregg Cemetery, near Halfway, Virginia
Note: Mr. Roger Lee Elgin, Sr. tells me that the overgrown and inaccessible cemetery to the left of the stone house at the intersections of Routes 773 & 702 South of Halfway on the North West was owned by the GREGG family as far back as he remembers.

Griffith Cemetery, Halfway, Virginia
Located East Route 626, 0.5 mile South Route 628 at end of private road, directly back of shingle house and to the left of old house ruins about 50 yards. Stone wall fallen down, boxwood, very overgrown. Barbed wire fence enclosure. Resurveyed November 22, 1993.

Elijah W. GRIFFITH Born June 21, 1859 Died April 28 1915
Abner Lee GRIFFITH Died September 1925 Aged 71 years
GRIFFITH James M. Born May 16, 1866 Died Aug. 3, 1910
Father GRIFFITH Abner G. Born April 28, 1823 Died Jan. 24, 1888
GRIFFITH Mother Judith Frances Wife of Abner G. Born Feb. 22, 1822 Died Mar. 3, 1916
Mary H. GRIFFITH, age 42 years

(FLYNN)

M. H. G. & W. F. G. *(footstones to tombstone on face buried in ground)*

DOWNS Harvey H. Died Feb. 21, 1905 Aged 31 years; Hugh Hunton Died Feb. 11, 1895 Aged 22 yrs.; Mary
   Hunter GRIFFITH Wife of J. H. DOWNS Born Feby. 2, 1849 Died June 24, 1912

W. E. GRIFFITH Born Oct. 9, 1839 Died Mar. 22, 1912

Fieldstone North East intersection of Routes 626 & 628 slave cemetery with rock markers.

Grove Presbyterian Church Cemetery, Goldvein, Virginia
Located South East intersection of Route 813 & 615 just off Route 17 behind church. Well-kept.

Father McClellen REESE Born Sept. 24, 1882 Died April 21, 1943

Mother Fannie Ann REESE Born Dec. 24, 1829 Died April 25, 1921

HOLMES Mary Roberta July 2, 1862 July 23, 1933; Ferdinand N. May 7, 1857 May 24, 1941 Mother Father

Joseph H. EDWARDS Aug. 15, 1834 Dec. 16, 1909

Mother Ann EDWARDS beloved Wife of Joseph EDWARDS Born Feb. 10, 1840 Died Aug. 24, 1910

JONES Susan EDWARDS July 3, 1866 May 28, 1934; James Thomas Dec. 28, 1865 July 5, 1939

Anna Floribel beloved Wife of Jas. R. MONROE Born May 16, 1878 Died Oct. 16, 1908

Nora Blanche Wife of D. J. HUMPHREY Dec. 7, 1880 Feb. 3, 1920

Hugh H. EDWARDS July 23, 1875 Aug. 10, 1942; Emma LODS Wife of H. H. EDWARDS July 15, 1883 Feb. 6,
   1920

Hugh H. Son of H. H. & Emma L. EDWARDS July 26, 1911 Sept. 1, 1923

COOKE G. Keith Feb. 26, 1883 Nov. 1, 1950; Ida M. July 29, 1885 Mar. 10, 1951

Golder RANDALL 1898–1963

Violet V. RANDALL Born May 10, 1908 Died Nov. 27, 1984

Ben RANDALL 1903–1964

James W. RANDALL Aug. 6, 1901 Nov. 13, 1967

ACTION Lloyd P. Sept. 1, 1909; Louse A. April 28, 1909 April 16, 1980

CURTIS J. Hezziekiah May 25, 1856 July 12, 1939; Lucy D. Nov. 5, 1854 Oct. 5, 1944

Lena Edna BALLARD May 13, 1908 July 8, 1951

Raymond Lee BALLARD Dec. 23, 1898 Oct. 26, 1951

Patrick M. ENNIS VIRGINIA PVT 320 INF 80 DIV WORLD WAR 1 July 4, 1888 November 14, 1948

Lelia B. NOBLE ENNIS April 12, 1890 December 14, 1966

William ENNIS April 15, 1886 June 1, 1947

Clarence Lee "Bill" WHITE January 27, 1909 January 30, 1986; Lelia Doris September 24, 1915 May 25, 1985

G. W. HEFLIN Born 1822 Died 1920

Joshua Earl COLLINS Aug. 20, 1985 Nov. 16, 1987

Ronald Carter SMITH July 5, 1954 Feb. 25, 1983

Violet Pearl RANDALL July 4, 1927 June 19, 1980

George Samuel FREEMAN May 20, 1883 Jan. 8, 1953

Ruby E. FREEMAN July 20, 1919 June 20, 1921

Rosa BOLING April 14, 1859 March 12, 1927

Catherine ENNIS Feb. 13, 1918 June 21, 1932

Lola J. CORBIN June 29, 1885 Dec. 9, 1945

HEFLIN George W. June 22, 1856 Sept. 6, 1920; Mary M. June 10, 1857 Feb. 17, 1927

Norma Belle ENNIS Aug. 26, 1912 June 21, 1932

Elizabeth BROWN FREEMAN Sept. 16, 1887 Dec. 25, 1963

Father Archie Thomas FREEMAN Dec. 3, 1907 Jan. 16, 1974

Rachel Annie Wife of J. D. TULLOSS May 12, 1835 Oct. 10, 1910

Mary Jane Wife of J. D. TULLOSS Died Dec. 4, 1862

ROYALL Rev. J. J.; Anna K

John G. COOKE Born May 2, 1824 Died Aug. 18, 1904; Helen M. COOKE Born Dec. 22, 1842 Died Feb. 6, 1900

her children ariseY
Rev. J. R. COOKE Jan. 15, 1870 May 16, 1949
Sadie P. FREEMAN March 7, 1906 Apr. 20, 1927
Julia R. Wife of Samuel FREEMAN Died May 17, 1913 Aged 75 years
Silas M. HOLMES US NAVY
Miss FIELD Ruby E. FREEMAN July 20, 1919 June 20, 1921; Queen L. FREEMAN Dec. 1, 1917 Dec. 22, 1925
LIGHTNER William Stuart Born Sept. 1832 Died Dec. 1908; Mary Martha Born May 1849 Died Dec. 1899
Elizabeth HUNTER AREY Born Nov. 17, 1900 Died Jan. 3, 1901
Gustav MIDDELTHON July 25, 1867 May 20, 1920; Nannie KEITH MIDDLETHON Dec. 9, 1867 Dec. 19, 1963
Charles H. HOUGHTON Co B 6 Va Cav

Groves Cemetery, Remington, Virginia
Located on Route 658 2.5 miles North West of Remington on North side of road, iron fence, overgrown.

William A. GROVES Born Jan. 20, 1849 Died July 13, 1906 His Wife Cynthia J. PARLSON Born May 13, 1853
   Died Sept. 29, 1926
Barbara A. GROVES Died 1945

Some fieldstone markers.

Groves Cemetery, Sowego, Virginia
Located South Route 611 East Route 694 in grove back of an electronics installation, no markers.

Halby Cemetery, Warrenton, Virginia
Located by pump house by tree. Mr. Budd, farmer, stated that niece of Mrs. Halby was buried here. Tombstone was upside down and embedded in ground. Resurveyed December 3, 1993.

Haley Cemetery (Black), Markham, Virginia
Located at West end of Route 728. Turn right into Robert Hinkel's property. Go about 150 feet to a walking trail on right. Continue on trail to pond. Go North West about 50 yards to huge poplar tree. About 25 feet by 25 feet in woods. Resurveyed September 13, 1993.

B. F. FORD born July 20, 1883 died Nov. 30, 1898
Nelson HALEY died Aug. 24, 1884 aged 19 years
Frank HALEY born Oct. 27, 1868 died Oct. 18, 1886
12 fieldstone markers or sunken graves

Hall Cemetery, Orlean, Virginia
Located on Route 741 off Route 739 2.5 miles on abandoned farm South of house in field, fieldstone markers. Data obtained from Joe Lawler, Marshall.

Hall Cemetery (Black), The Plains, Virginia
Located back of 3rd house North of First Baptist Church on right side of Route 626. Top of hill, back of house in cedar grove. Surveyed November 22, 1993.
Louie Gotford HALL PVT US Army WORLD WAR II Aug. 5, 1928 Oct. 11, 1987
Robert Lee HALL TEC5 Engineers WORLD WAR II Mar. 23, 1926 June 19, 1954
Mary HALL MITCHELL Apr. 29, 1917 Mar. 11, 1948
Henry HALL Feb. 28, 1911 April 15, 1937

Unmarked graves:
Katherine HALL HILMAN
Davis HILMAN, Jr.

David HILMAN, Sr.
Edward MITCHELL
Roberta MITCHELL
"Baby" GRANT

Halley Family Cemetery, Opal, Virginia
Located 2.1 miles West Route 687 North Route 637 back of house, no markers.

Halley Cemetery, Rectortown, Virginia
Located across from post office in yard of old Kincheloe house on Route 710. Tombstones propped up against tree surrounded by day lillies. Resurveyed October 9, 1993.

Dr. Samuel H. HALLEY Born December 10, 1822 Died March 5, 1885

Halley Cemetery, "Hunting Ridge", Warrenton, Virginia
Located 3 miles South Route 802 on Route 744. Mrs. Francis Greene, owner, gave data: This place called "The Poplars" was given to Mrs. Halley for a dowry by her father, Mr. Hutton.

Elizabeth Wife of Henry S. HALLEY Born May 25, 1792 Died July 17, 1869

Hamilton Cemetery, Remington, Virginia
Located about 2 miles West of Remington on South side Route 651 on farm of Mr. & Mrs. E. D. Hopkins, who took the data from the tombstones for me. Cinderblock wall in field North West of barn. Clean condition. Resurveyed October 16, 1993.

Ferguson HAMILTON Born in the County of Fauquier Nov. 30, 1843 Died Nov. 21, 1892
Anne Berry Daughter of Hugh & Janet HAMILTON Died May 26, 1851 17 years
Hugh HAMILTON Born Aug. 21, 1859 Died Mar. 2, 1926
Virginia P. Wife of Hugh HAMILTON Born Dec. 15, 1857 Died Nov. 27, 1891
John S. HAMILTON Born Feb. 27, 1832 Died May 29, 1910
Virginia J. HAMILTON Born Feb. 28, 1888 Died July 22, 1936
Mary W. HAMILTON Born Dec. 11, 1862 Died Oct. 22, 1936

Hamm Family Cemetery (Black), Bethel, Virginia
Located in the vicinity of Route 690 and Route 628, Cannon Ball Gate Rd. George HAMM says his father, who died c. 1969 is buried in this cemetery. Data obtained from John Gott August 15, 1990.

Hamm - Foster Cemetery, Turnbull, Virginia
Located in North East intersections of Routes 688 & 802 in front yard of old house, overgrown. Resurveyed April 2, 1994.

Mrs. Lucy P. HAMM 1898–1962; Jack HAMM 1888–1956
Lorraine S. HAMM 1919–1946; Mrs. Lynn HAMM 1899–1963
William I. FOSTER Jan. 17, 1877–1966 [*daughter Maggie Foster gave month and day*]
Betsy Rose DORES Dec. 1907 Sept. 1964
Karen Betsy SETTLE 1965–1967

Hansborough Cemetery, Midland, Virginia
Located North Route 806 0.4 mile East Route 610 in North East corner of field, cemetery covers 50 feet x 50 feet has been cultivated, only one marker lying flat. Information supplied by Ripley Robinson 1991.

Mary E. Daughter of Elijah T. & Sallie E. HANSBOROUGH Born Nov. 22, 1881 Died July 18, 1882 *(stone stolen since book was last published)*

No stones for the following. Information is from family Bible. Note spelling of last name.

Elijah Thomas HANSBROUGH Born Sept. 14, 1842 Died May 31 1912 69 yrs 8 mos
Sally Elizabeth HANSBROUGH *(wife)* Born June 2, 1850 Died *(could not find death of date)*
Lottie May HANSBROUGH (granddaughter) Born Sept. 7, 1919 Died November 19, 1919

Hardin Cemetery, Elk Run (Blackwelltown), Virginia

Located on Route 610, 1 mile North West of Elk Run. House is 40 or 50 feet South West of the road. Surveyed by M. D. Gore, Sumerduck, August 12, 1937.

"Near garden and ten steps from the road; it is lying flat and partly covered with dirt":

Here lies the body of Lydia HARDIN who departed this life in the 38th year of her age 1766 March ye 22 d.

Harrison - Hume - Rector - Bowersett Cemetery, "Monterey", Marshall, Virginia

Located South West of Route 66 overpass of Route 723 about 2 miles North of Marshall at end of Route 184 on old Hume Farm in field to North of house. Brambles, rock markers no fence, one obelisk. Resurveyed February 1992 by Marianna & Jack Alcock.

William HARRISON 1795–1833; Burr HARRISON Died 1842
George P. HARRISON 1797–1834; George Wm. HARRISON 1832–1842
Leonore HARRISON 1804–1881
Arrianna RECTOR 1823- 1893
Daniel Burr HARRISON 1825–1903; Lucy Pickett HARRISON 1827–1835
Benjamin HARRISON 1829–1900
Thomas Allen RECTOR 1803–1884
Nannie RECTOR HUME 1840–1918
Battle RECTOR 1843–1918; Mary RECTOR 1842–1842
Eliza RECTOR 1846–1883; Randolph RECTOR 1848–1854
Robinson RECTOR 1856–1874; Thomas Allen RECTOR, Jr. 1860–1860
Pratt RECTOR 1859–1934
William M. HUME 1823–1872; William M. HUME 1867–1933
Wm. Hume BOWERSETT 1902–1902
Thomas Rector HUME 1869–1934; Anna HUME BOWERSETT 1866–1947

Marianna & Jack Alcock, present owners, have counted 52 graves. Among those with no markers:

William HARRISON *(who was killed by his slaves)*
Thomas Grayson HARRISON *(who committed suicide)*

Slave cemetery adjacent

Hathaway Cemetery, "Denton", Halfway, Virginia

Located on Route 702 at "Denton" in paddock directly behind house. Cemetery disappeared. Several small rock markers and one large rock monument scattered in vicinity. January 12, 1992

Hathaway - Adams Cemetery, Middleburg, Virginia

Located 0.2 mile South of Route 776 on Route 629 West side in field in front of modern house by old boxwood bush with periwinkle covering much of ground. Both Mrs. Ralph D. Chadwick and Roger L. Elgin, Sr. state that it was a large cemetery, and Mrs. Elgin says there were a number of tall tombstones which were stolen except for one buried in ground. Resurveyed November 22, 1993.

Sarah Frances consort of James A. HATHAWAY Departed this life May 12th 1841 Aged 28 years 8 mos. & 11 Days *(missing 1993)*

Heale - Weaver Cemetery, Greenwich, Virginia
Located Route 694 Burwell Rd. South of Greenwich at old log house on property which has been known at various times as the Weaver Plantation and Squires Home. (Weaver bought it from Heale). Cemetery located along fence line behind house under 2 walnut trees. Area covered with daffodils, daylillies, and periwinkle. Surveyed March 18, 1992.

There is only one rock marker, but Martha BECKER FOX, Wife of George FOX is buried here. There is a stone leaning against the front yard gate which appears to be a tombstone. It reads: S. FOX 1836 (the last 2 digits are difficult to discern). According to Minnie Squires McMichaels, who grew up in this house, a George FOX lived here and married Martha BECKER. Martha's former suitor, a young man named Caleb, fought and died in the Civil War at age 31.

Caleb's ghost came back to find Martha, now married, and has remained, lingering, ever since. This information came from a medium consulted by a McMichaels family member. Caleb's ghost has been seen a recently as 1991.

Heart's Delight Church Cemetery, Sowego, Virginia
Located South Route 612 0.2 mile of church on Quantico Marine Base. This cemetery has many homemade tombstones with inscriptions of poured concrete and numerous rock markers of all types of stone. Well-kept. About 150 feet square. Goes back into woods. Resurveyed 1992.

Mr. James BUNBRAY Nov. 18, 1928 July 8, 1950
Maria WILLIAMS 1886–1968
Mrs. Liza A. D____ died January 6, 1954 aged 84 yrs 10 mos 1 day
Calvin USTERS June 15, 1887 June 21, 1952
Selener REDD born Mar. 15, 1869 died Oct. 29, 1949
Milton REDD born Aug. 15, 1870 died Jan. 1, 1917?
Miss Mary HEDGMAN May 22, 1919 died 1939?
Mrs. Mettie WILLIAMS born 1868 died March 9, 1934
Geo. WILLIAMS born Mar. 1821 died July 19, 1879
Mary BURGESS WILLIAMS May 27, 1879 Nov. 22, 1933
Miss Emily HEDGMAN June 9, 1924 died
Algirty Lucious WILLIAMS
Miss M. C. REDD USTERS born Aug. 8, 1902 die July 10, 1924
Robert Lacy GREEN born Oct. 10, 1902 died Dec. 27, 1946
Rettie Mae BUMBRAY born Sept. 18, 1931 died June 12, 1939 Daughter of Earl & Frances
Miss Mary BROWN born Dec. 17, 1893 died Apr. 15, 1958
Mr. Robert BUMBRAY died March 12, 1950 age 70
Herier BUMBRAY 1880–1965
Mother: Mary P. WEBSTER Feb. 16, 1917 Jul 9, 1984
Husband & Father James H. WEBSTER June 28, 1909 March 21, 1978
Charlotte M. WEBSTER Dec. 15, 1915 June 9, 1979
Rev. William A. GIBSON departed Jan. 20, 1944 He was a kind father and a staunch minister. Erected by Hart Delight, Sowego, Cross Roads, Calverton. Mt. Zion, Warrenton, Ebenzer, Midland, First Mt. Zion, Stafford, St. Johns, Hurleytown, Silver Hill, Morrisville
Jessie E. THORNTON 1903–1990 *(fhm)*
Grant Hampton TAYLOR 1933–1968 *(fhm and fieldstone rock)*
Edward M. MORTON March 25, 1876 May 15, 1934; Fannie JACKSON His Wife

MORTON Seth R. Nov. 13, 1882 April 14, 1954; Mary E. July 12, 1891 July 28, 1963
Lucy Ella BROOK 1900–1985 *(fhm)*
Mr. J. L. WILLIAMS bor Apr 8, 1840 died Apr 18, 1894
E. O. REDD born 1872 died Mar. 5, 1890
Matha A. E. EDWARDS REDD born December 1st 1841 died Nov. 12, 1896
John Thomas GIBSON born Mar 4th 1865 died Aug 1st 1954
Edw. M. FOUTS born Mar 29, 1870 died June 25, 1941
Everett A. FOUTZ Jan. 15 1868 May 30, 1961
Mr. Thomas FOUT born June 7, 1876 died Feb. 16, 1955
Virginia Morton FOUTZ Aug. 30, 1886 July 15, 1971
Bessie V. BROWN Oct. 28, 1917 Sept.26. 1981
Helen E. BROWN Oct. 23, 1925 Dec. 20, 1987
Bertie May BUMBRAY 1937–1977 *(fhm)*
David W. TAYLOR Nov. 1, 1903 Feb. 6, 1985
Eva Mae GORDON Jan. 18, 1902 June 3, 1989
Avera A. GORDON 1978–1978 *(fhm)*
Mr. J. Aaron BROWN born Feb. 5, 1875 died Dec. 23, 1954
Eddie S. SHELTON born on Sept. 2, 1948 di Feb. 25, 1951
Carrie Ella HENRY 1894–1967 *(fhm)*
Clarence L. EDWARDS 1899–1965; Smoot D. EDWARDS 1886–1960
George M WASHINGTON born Nov. 10, 1907 died Nov. 7, 1957
Father Grandson EDWARDS died Jan. 23, 1943
Mother Lucy EDWARDS died Jan 18, 1939
Clark W. GRIGSBY died April 7, 1969 aged 35 years
Thomas N. GORDON April 26, 1876 July 22, 1953
Ethel GORDON KING born Mar 9, 1900 died Nov. 5, 1925
Massie TAYLOR Died Mar. 20, 1932
William T. GORDON May 3, 1908 April 12, 1971; Iva V. GORDON Nov. 29, 1908 Apr. 3, 1988
Lester ODELL 1894–1987 *(fhm)*
Henry *(fhm)*
Susie MORTON GORDON Feb. 16, 1884 July 1, 1981
Robert Stanley MORTON 1905–1985
Robert J. GRIGSBY June 9, 1907 Sept. 17, 1980 *(fhm)*
Malcolm I. STREET Dec. 6, 1977 9 months *(fhm)*
Tona May GORDON Died October 6, 1959 Aged 15 years
Louise GORDON May 11, 1914 July 1, 1962
Creola Alma GORDON 1924–1968
Florence May BUMBRAY 1911–1970
Clarence Homer LEE 1914–1985 *(fhm)*
Frederick HEDGEMAN 1903–1980 *(fhm)*
David H. WASHINGTON 1868–1945; Minnie His Wife 1873–19
Alice WASHINGTON 1881–1969; William Carter WASHINGTON 1897–1964
Nelson C. WASHINGTON 1909–1965
Mother Ella BLACKWELL Died Feb. 19, 1929
Mother Roberta BUMBRAY Died April 11, 1929; Thomas BUMBRAY 1870–1961
Florence BUMBRAY 1883–1962; James BUMBRAY 1917–1967
Ardella EINES 1890–1968
John T. RUSSELL Born February 4, 1881 Died Aug. 29, 1961
Charles Richard EDWARDS SP5 US ARMY VIETNAM 1951–1985
Mother: Henrietta BUMBRAY May 11, 1900 July 1, 1982
Husband: Monroe BUMBRAY Apr. 17, 1906 Dec. 26, 1977
Mother: Bessie M. BUMBRAY May 22, 1937 Aug. 12, 1977

Blanche JACKSON 1890–1961
Ella REDD Wife and Maria
Mrs. S. W. WEBSTER Born on May 6, 1876 Di Dec. 21, 1927
Rosie G. WEBSTER 1885–1961
Banny TAYLOR 1886–1961; Grant Hampton TAYLOR 1898–1968
Albert D. REDD 1913–1970
Herbert PRICE Born March 19, 1912 Died May 19, 1930
Mrs. Jane WANSER GIBSON MOORE Bor Aug 8, 1913 Die July 22, 1955
John WANSER Born Mar. 30, 1873 Died Mar. 30, 1953
Josephine W. SIMMS 1872–1944 Devoted Mother
Edward M. LEE Bor Oct. 22, 1908 Die Jun 30, 1958
Bessie COLLINS Born Nov. 5, 1893 Died April 12, 1934
Addie OLIVER Born Sept. 23, 189_ *(rest in the ground)*
H. C. LEE Born Dec. 2, 1899 Died May 2, 19__ *(in ground)*
Martha LEE Born Aug. 10, 1871 Died Feb. 13, 1942
Zack LEE Born Oct. 30, 1861 Died June 26, 1945
Florence A. BUMBRAY 1931–1970 *(fhm)*
Howard BUMBRAY 1918–1986 *(fhm)*
Stanley BUMBRAY 1927–1958 *(fhm)*
Maurice BUMBRAY CPL US ARMY WORLD WAR II 1924–1987
Russell O. PAYNE 1929–1988 *(fhm)*
Charles Walter PAYNE S7 M3 US NAVY WORLD WAR II 1920–1982
Dolly Virginia BUMBRAY 1904–1978 *(fhm)*
Sydney EDWARDS 1895–1951
Rev. T. T. HEDGMAN Bor Sept. 7, 1871 Die Jan. 23, 1943
Margaret F. HEDGMAN 1881–1961
FMY *(on a wooden cross)*
Mary M. BUMBRAY 1886–1982 *(fhm)*
Nelson M. BUMBRAY 1901–1971 *(fhm)*
Beatrice EUSTACE PITTS July 8, 1924 July 15, 1978
Robert Wilson BUMBRAY 1939–1974 *(fhm)*

Heflin Cemetery, Somerville, Virginia

Located 0.4 mile North Route 616 West Route 610 on hill in field, wire fence, oak trees. Resurveyed by L. Arthur Grove February 1994.

HEFLIN George W. HEFLIN Katherine SMALLWOOD HEFLIN Harry HEFLIN John R. HEFLIN
    Frank HEFLIN James W. HEFLIN Mary CORBIN HEFLIN Golder HEFLIN Beulah COOK
    Dora A. REDD Dora's Baby Charles SCHOOLER Kate GROVE John SMALLWOOD
G. L. H. Died April 26, 1911; F. D. H. Died --12
Beulah HEFLIN Born May 1th 1875
EFFLER Ruth HEFLIN May 1, 1895–Nov. 30, 1966 Edward M. Oct. 18, 1881–Aug. 14, 1966
Rev. J. W. HEFLIN Born Oct. 8th 1851 Died Sept. 29, 1930 Ordained 1889 7 day Feb.
Mary Fannie Wife of J. W. HEFLIN Born Dec. 10, 1812 Died 19
------ REDD Died April 1909
Kate GROVE Born July 20, 1884 Departed this life Feb. 19, 1886
J. E. H. Died Nov. 6th 1918; H. W. H. Died Jan. 1, 1889
G. W. H. Died Jan. 21, 1884; C. E. H. Died Oct. 1, 1887
-------- Died Jan [31?] 1862
Harry H. JOHNSON May 11, 1884 Nov. 1, 1950

Heflin (Blanch) Cemetery, Cromwell, Virginia
Located West Route 612 just below Route 639. As near as we could make out, buried in white board fenced plot South West of house. Resurveyed by L. Arthur Grove February 1994.

Blanch HEFLIN Died January 4th, 1954 Aged 66 yrs. 1 mos 3 days

Heflin - Moffett Cemetery, Marshall, Virginia
Located on left of Route 691 2.1 miles North of Route 689. 1 acre, many deep depressions. Some unfenced graves and two iron fenced sections in open field near road.

Thomas COCKRILL Born Mar. 22, 1822 Died Jan. 1, 1885 *(stone not found)*
Mrs. Letitia COCKRILL Daughter of Henry E. & Nancy Alice BAILEY Born March 12, 1826 Died December 20, 1895 *(stone not found)*
Jessie MOFFETT Mar 24, 1798 June 10, 1880; wives Elizabeth HITT; Martha RYAN Oct. 29, 1817 Feb. 18, 1889
Jessie MOFFETT Mar. 2, 1759 Aug. 31. 1832; Wife Elizabeth SMITH *(stone not found)*
Captain Lawson Alex. HEFLIN Son of Wm. & Lucy HEFLIN Born June 25, 1804 Died Jan. 15, 1877 *(stone not found)*
Murray J. Son of J. M. & A. A. HEFLIN Born July 3, 1888 Died July 15, 1888 *(stone not found)*

Footstones:
L. F. H.; J. L. H.

Rozier L. Son of J. M. & A. A. HEFLIN Born Jan. 3, 1898 Died Jan. 10, 1889
Florrie T. Daughter of J. M. & A. A. HEFLIN Born July 3, 1882 Died April 4, 1902
Robert F. HEFLIN Born Dec. 10, 1844 Died Jan. 1, 1922 Member of Mosby's Command 43rd Battalion Virginia Cavalry He was a devoted husband and a faithful member of Enon Baptist Church
Tabitha HEFLIN Daughter of Jas. & Frances HILL Wife of B. J. HANBACK & Robert HEFLIN Born April 1, 1848 Died Dec. 17, 1919 *(stone down)*

Jos. WELCH Oct. 18, 1833 Dec. 6, 1907; His Wife Sallie Mar. 10, 1855 Oct. 12, 1915

Heflin Family Cemetery, near Midland, Virginia
Located South West intersections of Routes 610 & 616 near Midland, stone markers.

Helm - Jones Cemetery, "Old Tannehill Place", Somerville, Virginia
Located South Route 637 between Routes 610 & 634 0.5 mile off road, rock wall fallen down, somewhat overgrown, rock markers. Data obtained from Robert Cooper and Kenneth Eskridge.

Thomas HELM Born July 19, 1790 Departed this life Sept. 24th 1848
Joanna HELM Wife of Thomas HELM Born August 22, 1792 Died July 15, 1860

Annette G. JONES Daughter off W. A. & Elizabeth JONES Born April 24, 1850 Departed this life March 11, 1859
Annie T. JONES Daughter of P. F. & A. JONES Born Jan. 13, 1856 Departed this life August 29, 1857

Henson Family Cemetery, Little Georgetown, Virginia
Located South intersection Routes 628 & 674 in corner of yard to front of house. The source is Nell Lewis. Beautifully kept. Resurveyed November 29, 1993.

HENSON Thos. J. 1840–1908; Mary N. 1843–1921; Luther B. 1882–1929
N. B. HENSON Died 1907; Mary HENSON Died 1909
Lewis N. HENSON Born Feb. 8, 1869 Died June 7, 1925
Mary HENSON and Virginia HENSON *(2 maiden HENSON aunts in unmarked graves)*

Emma HENSON CALLAN *(sister to Lewis)*

Herndon Cemetery, Delaplane, Virginia

Located back of house on Wm. W. Triplett farm just North of Pleasant Vale Baptist Church on Route 628. Stone fence fallen down, but owner is going to put up wire fence. Overgrown, trees collapsed on cemetery. Resurveyed September 13, 1993.

Margaret A. Wife of Lyne S. BROTHERTON Born Aug. 12, 1838 Died Mar. 16, 1882
A. W. HERNDON Born June 2, 1865 Died June 28, 1910
Julia K. CHANCELLOR Sept. 26, 1845 Aug. 24, 1940
Sue M. HERNDON Oct. 25, 1853 Jan. 22, 1948
Emma E. HERNDON Born July 17, 1855 Died Sept. 7, 1865
Wm. K. HERNDON Born Dec. 27, 1866 Died Feb. 28, 1867
J. T. HERNDON Born Nov. 6, 1875 Died Aug. 26, 1876 *(missing in 1993)*
C. D. HERNDON Oct. 15, 1880 Died Feb. 21, 1882 *(missing in 1993)*
Laura H. MARSHALL 1848–1934
Robert A. MARSHALL Trp. H 2 Rgt. Mo. Cav. C.S.A.
Frances C. MARSHALL 1872–19 *(actually buried in Upperville Cemetery)*
Anna MARSHALL 1879–1970
Charles M. GIBSON Born March 7, 1792 Died Dec. 6, 1872
Judith GIBSON Wife of Charles M. GIBSON Born Dec. 19, 1802 Died July 21, 1891
M. F. HERNDON Wife of Thaddeus HERNDON Born Sept. 18, 1822 Died July 16, 1888
Thaddeus HERNDON Born May 9th, 1807 Died June 2nd 1878

Hicks - Edmonds Cemetery, Paris, Virginia

Located in a clump of trees in field South West of intersection of Routes 17 & 50. In 1969 the stone wall around cemetery has disintegrated, cattle have apparently gotten into the cemetery and the gravestones are in bits and pieces and over grown with honeysuckle. In the WPA Historical Inventory of 1937–1938 Mrs. Carter Foster got the inscriptions on this cemetery on Liberty Farm. From the pieces that are still decipherable they agree with her findings. Wire fence erected around remains of stone wall. Overgrown, numerous stones piled around old tree and a few lying down. Resurveyed October 1, 1993.

Thomas SHERMAN who was born March 19, 1780 and departed this life May 10, 1854
Celia consort of Thomas SHERMAN [Died July 17, 1851 age 68] *(broken stone)*
Stephen HICKS Departed this life January 5, 1857 aged 25 years
[Sacred to the memory of] Israel HICKS Died 1810 aged 31 years [who departed this life Dec. 25, 1810 34 years]
   Isiah HICKS who departed this life July 12, 1830 in the [61] year of age
[Sacred to the memory of] Thomas Sherman HICKS Son of Kimble and Amanda HICKS who departed this life
   August 21, 1838 aged 2 years [21 days] - [Ann] Celia Daughter of Kimble and Amanda HICKS [died] who
   departed this life August 8, 1842 aged 23 months
[Sacred to the memory of] Matilda consort of Kimble HICKS who departed this life September 27, 1824 in the 74th
   year of her age
Kimble HICKS who departed this life February 2, 1837 In the 91st year of his age
[Sacred to the memory of] Maria A. BLACKWELL consort of J. E. S. [Jno Edward Shephard] BLACKWELL Born
   June 17, 1799 Died in Knoxville, Tennessee April 23, 1845 aged 45 years 10 months and 6 days These her mortal
   remains were removed from Knoxville, Tenn. to her native county and state, by her husband.
Stephen HICKS Died 1833 aged 45 years

The following were not found in the October 1, 1993 survey. Information was obtained from other sources:

In memory of Ann Virginia EDMONDS a native of Fauquier County, Va. she was a member of the Knoxville
   Female Academy and died in Tenn. on the 8th of Nov. 1831 being 16 years on the day of her death.

Ann and Thomas HICKS *(a small brick vault enclosing two children)*

John EDMONDS *(buried on West side. Father of Maj. EDMONDS. He married twice—Miss Frances Jane*
    WILDER and Mrs. "Helen Shephard" HACK an English actress of note)
4 rock markers
Unmarked grave to the left of Stephen Hicks (1/5/1857)
Unmarked grave to Maria Blackwell's right. It may be her father, Major Jno EDMONDS, as her husband was not
    brought to Virginia.
Emma HICKS Wife of Stephen HICKS who departed this life March 26, 1856 in the 64 year of her age
Stephen HICKS Died October 1833 46 years old
Unmarked grave to the right of Israel HICKS (probably his wife)
2 unmarked graves to the left of Celia Sherman
Aunt Celia EDMONDS *(Daughter of Maj. Jno EDMONDS. She weighed nearly 300 pounds and was put there as*
    late as 1880). The lot must have been full, for she was put on the outside.
Aunt Harriet EDMONDS MURRAY *and her husband William MURRAY and Daughter Miss Eliza MURRAY (a*
    Belle) are put there.

Hicks Cemetery, Poplar Springs, Casanova, Virginia
Located West Route 602 about 100' off Route 616. Only fieldstone markers. Data obtained from Joe Lawler,
    Marshall.

Hinson (George) Cemetery
Located on mountain off Route 741 on left. Data obtained from Joe Lawler, Marshall

Hitt (Peter) Cemetery
Located on Route 645 across from old house, near the Rappahannock River. On hillside next to road in area
    covered with briars. One old large persimmon tree standing in cemetery. The lower side was once fenced with
    stone but all evidence of fence is gone. Briars are too thick to determine approximately how many graves may be
    contained here. Local people were not aware of the family name of those buried in this cemetery. The ruins of a
    log cabin are nearby that belonged to HOPPER family, before the HITT. HOPPERs are probably buried in this
    cemetery also. Within sight of the "the Chimneys." Resurveyed December 29, 1992.

P. H. [Peter HITT] AG. 31 1802 [Revolutionary War Soldier]
[Hannah] H. HITT AG. 25 1846
2 large rock markers
1 small rock marker
1 quartz rock marker

Holmes Cemetery, Marshall, Virginia
Located at Route 55, 0.5 mile West of Marshall. House and barn sit on top of hill at bend in the highway. Per John
    Gott, on knoll to the right of the house in the field John Holmes and his wife Catherine STROTHER HOLMES
    are buried here. It was on this knoll that Stonewall Jackson sat on his horse and watched his men come into the
    present Route 55 from the old road to Ada and Orlean in August 1862 on their way to 2nd Manassas in Jackson's
    famous march around Pope's army. There may be other Strothers buried here. No tombstones. There may be an
    UTTERBACK cemetery to the left of the barn.

Holtzclaw Cemetery, Meetze, Virginia
Located East Route 643 3 miles South Warrenton North East of calf shed and milking parlour, grove of trees,
    several fieldstone markers.

J. M. HOLTZCLAW Son of Bennett & Ann HOLTZCLAW Died Dec. 3, 1821 Aged 54 years

Holtzclaw Cemetery, Warrenton, Virginia
Located in field South East intersections of Routes 211 & 681. Good stone wall, owner said Mr. Holtzclaw's grave had been moved elsewhere, some fieldstone markers.

Hooe Family Cemetery, Catlett, Virginia
Located West Route 605 1.5 miles North 603 0.3 mile in woods back of field & house. Iron fence, periwinkle, fallen and decaying trees. Resurveyed August 15, 1994 by Mr. Aaron Chichester.

Richd. Johnson Son of R. T. & E. A. NALLE who died May 30, 1840 aged 1 year 2 months 20 days
Ellen Ann NALLE Wife of R. T. NALLE Daughter of R & E. HOOE who died Feb. 24, 1847 in her 52d year
Elizabeth Daughter of Rice & Elizabeth HOOE Departed this life October 23d 1836 aged 2 years 2 days
Elizabeth consort of Rice HOOE, Esquire who departed this life on the 19th of February 1851 in the 55th year of her age
Rice HOOE Died on the 28th day of March 1874 at his residence near Fredericksburg, Va. in the 90th year of his age

Huddleton Cemetery, Opal, Virginia
Located 2 miles from Opal (no other directions). Research by Louise Lewis, Rectortown, August 1, 1936.

"She (Sophie HUDDLETON) is buried with the rest of the family in the old family graveyard, which is about 100 yards from the front yard.

Hume - Eaton Cemetery, Sumerduck, Virginia
Located near end of Route 632 South Route 651 on East side back of barn and old house by a sycamore tree, no fence, cattle grazing, few fieldstone markers.

Geo. A. HUME July 31, 1820 Nov. 7, 1896; Susan HUME June 20, 1826 Jan. 11, 1899; Susan HUME Jan. 20, 1851 Mar. 8, 1915; Joseph H. HUME July 31, 1855 Aug. 17, 1918

Hurleyville Cemeteries, Midland, Virginia
Located 0.2 mile South St. John the Baptist Church on West side Route 674 on North side private road, many fieldstone markers and:

Maria Beloved Wife of R. J. HUNGERFORD Died May 10, 1907 aged 35 years

Located 0.5 mile down same private road.
Nannine Wife of Kevin RECTOR and baby.

Located 0.2 mile South of St. John the Baptist Church on East side Route 674, 100 yards from edge of road at the edge of the woods.

Clifton S. SMITH 1916-1969
Rev. W. W. SCHAEFFER 1903-1964
Elizabeth S. CRAIG 1893-1953; John I CRAIG 1887-1955

Located 0.3 mile North of St. John the Baptist Church on East side Route 674, bordering private road. Wire fence has fallen down, well kept.

J. A. CREW Born Oct. 1 or 7, 1800 Died Dec. 3, 1881
Mary P. CREW Born May 10, 1829 Died Jan. 8, 1900
Bell SMITH Wife of Sam SMITH March 2, 1858 August 2, 1949

Samuel E. SMITH Feb. 17, 1852 Sept. 17, 1923
Mae G. BELL 1901-1963

Hunton Cemetery, New Baltimore, Virginia

Located on Route 674 0.5 mile North Route 694 to rear of house on East side of road. Wall fallen down, has been overgrown, but owners are cleaning it up. 50' by 100' One side has American fence and barbed-wire fence, rest gone. 20 fieldstone markers. Resurveyed March 12, 1994.

Elizabeth M. Wife of James M. MOREHEAD Died June 9, 1879 In her 49th year
Little Lizzie *(rest in ground)*
James Marye Son of J. M. and E. M. MOREHEAD born April 18, died June 21st 1851
James HUNTON Born September 30, 1820 Died February 18, 1875
Matilda C. Wife of James HUNTON Born July 10, 1828 Died March 24, 1877
Little Mollie
Robert M. Son of J. I. & M. C. HUNTON Born Sept. 15, 1861 Died in Socorro, N. Mex. Dec. 1, 1885
J. Heath Son of James I. & M. C. HUNTON Born July 24, 1857 Died October 17, 1886
Hugh C. HUNTON Born June 30, 1858 Died Sept. 26, 1889
Matilda C. HUNTON Born Sept. 16, 1883 Died Dec. 21, 1888
George W. HUNTON who entered into rest May 6, 1903
Mrs. M. V. HUNTON Beloved Wife of George W. HUNTON Born June 6, 1832 Died Feb. 24, 1879
Elizabeth HUNTON Wife of Maj. Eppa HUNTON who died March 6, 1866 in the 72nd year of her age
Eppa HUNTON was born the 31st January 1789 and departed this life on the 8th of April 1830
Silas Brown HUNTON Born April 23, 1819 Died August 4, 1900
Margaret Ann Wife of Silas B. HUNTON Born December 24, 1821 Died April 3, 1890 Aged Sixty-nine years 3 months and 10 days
Mary Brent HUNTON aged 10 years & 7 months
Elizabeth M. HUNTON Born Jan. 3, 1889 Died March 20, 1889
Laura HUNTON 1851-1938
Ann Eliza HUNTON Wife of John B. HUNTON departed this life September 12, 1860 in the 41st year of her age *(tombstone falling over)*
Mary BROOK

Hunton Cemetery, New Baltimore, Virginia

Located on Route 29 just East of Route 600 on North side in second field behind brick house and barns on crest of hill in burned cedar grove, overgrown.
Thomas HUNTON 1845–1924
Louise HUNTON COX June 22, 1851 Apr. 29, 1930
Thomas E. HUNTON Born May 28, 1813 Died 1882?
Mrs. Jane C. HUNTON Beloved Wife of Thos. E. HUNTON Died May 6, 1906 aged 81 yrs. & 6 months
Ernest C. HUNTON Son of Thos. E. & Jane HUNTON Born April 5, 1847 wantonly assassinated October 22, 1867
Matilda BROWN widow of Thomas HUNTON and John BROWN who departed this life April 19, 1854 In the 55th year of her age
John BROWN who departed this life June 5th 1849 In the 78th year of his age
WELLS family
20 fieldstone markers.

Hunton (Charles) Cemetery, New Baltimore, Virginia

Located off Routes 29 0.5 mile West Route 600 South Route 975 on left of private drive in middle of field, stone wall coming down, overgrown, scrub trees.

Charles HUNTON Born January 4, 1787 Died June 16, 1853
Hannah B. HUNTON Born March 29, 1789 Died March 24, 1957

Lizzie LEACHE Daughter of J. Willet & Jane R. LEACHE Born Aug. 12, 1835 Died Jan. 15, 1873
Jane Roberts HUNTON Wife of Dr. J. W. LEACHE Aged 47 years
Eugenia HUNTON Born 19th April 1835 Died 25th April 1854
Mary HUNTON Born May 16, 1826 Died March 23, 1853

Hunton (Joseph) Family Cemetery, "Fairview Farm", New Baltimore, Virginia
Located on Route 600 0.25 mile North Routes 29-211, at end of private drive to right of old brick house in front of stone barn, perwinkle over whole cemetery, honeysuckle. Partially collapsed stone wall, 100 ft. x 100 ft. Resurveyed March 12, 1994.

Joseph G. HUNTON Born at Fairview, Va. July 25, 1826 Died Jan. 23, 1906
Mildred J. Wife of Dr. Edgar MOSS Born Sept. 17, 1820 Died Oct. 16, 1891 *(collapsed and broken)*
Dr. Edgar MOSS Died Feby 19, 1872
Thomas HUNTON who departed this life Oct. 27, 1826 in the 55th year of his age
James HUNTON Born the 4th of September 1810 and Died on the 26th of July 1839

There are at least 23 stone markers in this large cemetery.

Ivy Hill Cemetery, Upperville, Virginia
Located on North side Route 50 at east end of town. Well kept community cemetery. Resurvey completed August 11, 1993.

Center section:
William D. FRASIER Feb. 10, 1878 Feb. 6, 1937
Gibson F. FRASIER July 20, 1875 Apr. 30, 1948 sons of George & Emily FRASIER
Etta B. GULICK Wife of Gibson FRASIER Oct. 8, 1879 May 7,1968
George FRASIER Sept. 27, 1844 May 20, 1922 *(C S A marker)*
Emily FLETCHER Wife of Geo. FRASIER Feb. 12, 1847 Nov. 1, 1908
Thomas FRASIER Sept. 14, 1794 Sept. 2, 1849
Catharine Wife of Thomas FRASIER April 4, 1804 July 1, 1896
Tacy Daughter of Thomas and Catharine FRASIER Oct. 30, 1832 Mar. 27, 1911
W. Hunter DAUGHTREY Jan. 28, 1903 Jan. 5, 1965
Kate AIKEN FRASIER Apr. 10, 1863 Dec. 30, 1960

LLEWELLYN Paul Parks 1886–1966; Irene Eleanor 1906–1991

Beloved Mother Vidie Wife of Conrad B. KINCHELOE Died July 23, 1894 aged 58 ys. 8 mos. & 7 dys
Ella S. HUMPHREY 1871–1941
Blanche M. KINCHELOE 1860–1940
Minnie L. KINCHELOE 1866–1963
KINCHELOE John Wm. 1868–1939; Annie May 1873–1956
Mother
Father *(C.S.A. marker)* [Conrad B. KINCHELOE] 1835–1904

George W. [Warren] CHAPPELEAR Sept. 8, 1842 Nov. 5, 1922 *(C.S.A. marker)*
Nannie O. [Overton BARRETT] CHAPPELEAR June 14, 1851 Aug. 16, 1925
George W. CHAPPELEAR, Jr. Aug. 23, 1889 Oct. 4, 1944
Nannie BINFORD CHAPPELEAR Mar. 16, 1880 Dec. 31, 1961
Lyle L. CHAPPELEAR March 10, 1881 Sept. 21, 1927
CHAPPELEAR Gladys C. [CHAPPELEAR] 1884–1972; B. [Benjamin] Curtis 1877–1954 *(U.D marker)*

Alice J. Daughter of Wm. & Sarah KENDALL Died Sept. 6, 1892 aged 33 years and 12 days

Dr. Willie KENDALL Born Feb. 8, 1862 Died Feb. 20, 1907

E. V. McCORMICK Eldest Daughter of Wm. & Sarah C. KENDALL Died Feb. 25, 1893 In her 41st year

Wm. KENDALL Born Nov. 29, 1823 Died Sept. 23, 1915

Sarah C. Wife of Wm. KENDALL born Jan. 28, 1826 died May 2, 1911 Aged 85 years 3 mos. and 4 days

Edwin Lee KENDALL July 21, 1862 March 1, 1943

Mary J. FLETCHER Daughter of R. L. & M. A. FLETCHER Born June 10, 1902 Died Jan.28, 1903

Vidie K. Daughter of R. L. & M. A. FLETCHER Born Mar. 12, 1896 Died Jan. 21, 1916

FLETCHER Robert L. 1853–1923; Mary Ann 1863–1960

Alice J. FLETCHER Born Dec. 28, 1820 Died July 27, 1896 our Mother; our Father John C. FLETCHER Born
    Mar. 13, 1818 Died Feb. 16, 1856

Irva Lee FLETCHER Feb. 20, 1889 July 13, 1978

Thomas J. FLETCHER 1892–1976

John C. FLETCHER Oct. 28, 1890 Oct. 28, 1957

Charles Warren Son of Winter & Jennie SCOTT ROGERS Born Dec. 13, 1880 Died April 11, 1900

Jennie SCOTT beloved Wife of Winter ROGERS Born May 18, 1849 Died Oct. 21, 1900

Rachael H. [HOLMES] PEARSON 1905–

C. Austin PEARSON 1906–1976

Edward M. HOLMES 1867–1942

Mary S. HOLMES 1877–1939

Oakley E. HOLMES 1898–1952

Edythe A. HOLMES 1899–1975

HYNSON - AUTY Plot:

Orra MASON HYNSON Jan. 31, 1894 Oct. 15, 1968

Read HYNSON PFC PENNSYLVANIA ORDINANCE DEPARTMENT WORLD WAR I July 5 1888 July 25
    1953

Ada A. AUTY Mar. 26, 1891 Jan. 27, 1981

Fred Sawyer AUTY Mar. 2, 1895 July 14, 1950

James M. KINCHELOE Sept. 4, 1861 July 4, 1944

Annie W. G. KINCHELOE Sept. 13, 1868 May 7, 1932

Esther N. KINCHELOE 1896–1898

J. Gibson KINCHELOE Jan. 26, 1900 June 30, 1935

Anne M. RUMP 1947–1948

John Rogers GIBSON Feb. 12, 1874 July 13, 1904

John Nelson GIBSON Sept. 1, 1835 May 10, 1889 *(C.S.A. marker)*

Eliza ROGERS GIBSON Oct. 21, 1842 April 17, 1931

Helen GIBSON Wife of William A. REID March 17, 1884 March 10, 1954

William Alfred REID June 16, 1871 January 13, 1954

Brooke B. GOCHNAUER August 16, 1875 June 18, 1935

Virginia GIBSON Wife of Brooke B. GOCHNAUER Apr. 2, 1876 Jan. 19, 1953

Lillie Virginia beloved Wife of R. J. DWYER Born July 6, 1869 Died Feb. 28, 1911

Richard Joseph beloved Husband of Lillie Virginia DWYER Born Jan. 1, 1866 Died Jan. 3, 1954

Philip W. DWYER 1891–1963

Thomas Milton DWYER VIRGINIA PVT US ARMY WORLD WAR II Aug. 3 1902 Aug. 6 1963

Dorothy DWYER 1928–1966 *(missing 1993)*

Preston M. BROWNING Born Oct. 7, 1854 Died Sept. 13, 1894

Tacie FLETCHER Wife of P. M. BROWNING Born July 3, 1852 Died April 2, 1915

Emily V. WELFLEY Oct. 9, 1903 Dec. 12, 1974

WELFLEY John D. [Dixie] 1871 1954; Bertha V. [KINCHELOE] 1878–1954

Emily A. [CHAPPELEAR] KINCHELOE 1840–1904
Elisha D. KINCHELOE 1837–1919 *(C.S.A. marker)*
Helen Welfley HATCHER 1910–1944
Bertha ELGIN born Sept. 23, 1864 died Sept. 4, 1884
William H. ROBINSON Co. A 8 Va. Cav. C.S.A.
William L. ROBINSON 1867–1939
Milton Garner ROBINSON 1862–1947
Alice E. ROBINSON 1846–1907
A. Elizabeth ROBINSON 1835–1926
Mary Robinson BUCKNER 1872–1973
Dennis McCARTY Jan. 19, 1855 Sept. 1, 1930
Catharine beloved Wife of Dennis McCARTY Born Dec. 26, 1853 Died April 19, 1909
Elizabeth JACKSON McCARTY 1844–1922
McCARTY Elizabeth L. [LOCKE] 1902; Dennis D. 1884–1959

James Lewis STROTHER Born Dec. 15, 1850 Died Aug. 16, 1916
Mary Elizabeth STROTHER Born Mar. 1, 1849 Died Sept. 3, 1917
William Smith STROTHER May 21, 1882 Sept. 19, 1972; Louis Delaplane STROTHER June 26, 1889 Feb. 8,
    1984
Jackson GIBSON Born Apr. 10, 1847 Died May 15, 1914
GIBSON Rush J. 1892–1960; Rosa P. 1892–1990
Georgia G. GIBSON 1894–1986
John W. STROTHER Jun. 13, 1835 Nov. 9, 1915
Jas. W. STROTHER Feb. 1833 Feb. 24, 1918
Florence S. Wife of Geo. W. GREEN 1868 June 8, 1942
George W. GREEN 1867–1948
Infant Son of J. C. & Bennett H. GREEN Born Sept. 11, 1917
Anna Belle CAMPBELL 1889–1980
Herman Douglas GIBSON Died Oct. 29, 1920 *(C.S.A. marker)*; Helen J. Wife of H. Douglas GIBSON Born Feb.
    11, 1840 Died Feb. 11, 1916
Ada WARREN Wife of J. C. JONES Born Oct. 31, 1866 Died Dec. 25, 1890
Daniel Howe JONES Born Apr. 27, 1918 Died July 11, 1927
John Clay JONES 1ST LT. 175TH INF 29 DIV Born Apr. 18, 1920 Died Sept. 11, 1944 Buried in Brittany France
Warren Gibson JONES, Sr. Born Dec. 25, 1890 Died Mar. 1956
Sally HOWE Wife of W. G. JONES, Sr. Born Mar. 27, 1890 Died Jan. 21, 1968

Pearl PEAK Wife of F. GOCHNAUER May 31, 1880 Jan. 9, 1971
George Robert FLETCHER died 1992 *(no marker 1993)*
Mirriam GIBSON born Aug. 25, 1868 died Aug. 25, 1868
Norma E. GIBSON born Nov. 25, 1871 died Nov. 26, 1881
Bessie V. GIBSON born Feb. 3, 1877 died Dec. 22, 1882
Warren Gibson JONES, Jr. Dec. 23, 1913 Oct. 28, 1982
Douglas Gibson JONES CPL US ARMY WORLD WAR II Jan 11 1925 Jan 26 1989
Jane JONES BULL Sep. 7, 1916 Apr. 3, 1981

Frederick GOCHNAUER, M. D. Born April 11, 1879 Died Oct. 9, 1945
Kate FRASIER beloved Wife of P. S. GOCHNAUER Born Jany. 3, 1842 Died April 1, 1895
Pembroke S. GOCHNAUER Born Aug. 10, 1841 Died Oct. 16, 1919 8th Va. Regt. C.S.A. wounded 2nd Manassas
    1862

William Glascock FLETCHER May 26, 1877 Sept. 4, 1970 His Wife Louise MOBLEY FLETCHER Dec. 30, 1894
    June 6, 1982

Bedford FLETCHER May 17, 1884 Sept. 25, 1955
William FLETCHER Son of Joshua & Eliza FLETCHER Aug. 24, 1845 Mar. 19, 1915
Annie G. Wife of Wm. FLETCHER July 17, 1848 Apr. 1, 1947

PEACH Richard S. June 2, 1897 Oct. 15, 1972
Paul Seldon PEACH Oct. 14, 1904 Jan. 9, 1988
Clinton Miller PEACH Aug. 16, 1866 Sept. 10, 1926
Daisy R. Wife of C. M. PEACH June 24, 1886 Nov. 2, 1943
Robert Murphy PEACH May 19, 1860 Mar. 28, 1913; His Wife Zella DICE Oct. 7, 1870 Feb. 15, 1951 Robert
    Murphy PEACH 1904–1983
Joseph Norton WALTON Aug. 14, 1890 Oct. 19, 1947
William Selden PEACH April 3, 1833 July 5, 1890
Tacie Anne FLETCHER Wife of W. Selden PEACH June 15, 1837 Oct. 8, 1907
Dorothy Daughter of Clinton and Daisy PEACH April 6, 1896 April 7, 1896
Irene J. Wife of R. S. PEACH 1900–1981
PEACH WALDON Feb. 15, 1893 Sept. 29, 1982
Geraldine E. PEACH Feb. 27, 1904 Dec. 24, 1973
Lulu GLASCOCK McCOY July 24, 1929 Dec. 31, 1968
HEDRICK Douglas W. May 17, 1910; Annie Laurie September 6, 1911 July 5, 1982
John K. HERRELL Died Jan. 27, 1894 Aged 70 ys 1 mo & 27 ds
Martha J. Wife of J. K. HERRELL Died Aug. 2, 1900 Aged 78 years
C. F. SMALLWOOD Born May 11, 1848 Died Jan. 21, 1905
Laura F. Wife of C. F. SMALLWOOD Born Jan. 15, 1845 Died Feb. 19, 1909
Laura G. 1877–1895
1836–1925 Bettie MARABLE Wife of I. B. LAKE; 1837–1922 Isaac B. LAKE Son of Ludwell LAKE Pastor of
    Upperville Baptist Church 50 years
Lula Wife of James L. LAKE and Daughter of Col. J. W. CALDWELL 1866–1906
1861–1952 James L. LAKE Son of Isaac B. LAKE professor of physics Wake Forest College
Virginia Caldwell LAKE 1869–1954
Sallie E. Wife of W. H. LAKE Jan. 31, 1822 Aug. 15, 1903
Wm. H. LAKE Born Nov. 7, 1826 Died Jan. 8, 1897

William FLETCHER Son of Joshua and Eliza FLETCHER Born August 24, 1845 Died March 19, 1915
Joshua FLETCHER Born Sept. 1, 1850 Died April 8, 1913
Lizzie C. Daughter of Joshua & E. A. FLETCHER Died Aug. 23, 1861 aged 19 years
Virginia Daughter of Joshua & E. A. FLETCHER Born Sept. 18, 1848 Died Aug. 3, 1879
Julia Daughter of Joshua & E. A. FLETCHER Born Sept. 18, 1848 Died Sept. 22 1881
Gibson Son of Joshua & E. A. FLETCHER Died Aug. 15, 1866 aged 7 years
Mary E. Daughter of Joshua & E. A. FLETCHER Born June 24, 1842 Died May 9, 1847
Ella Daughter of Joshua & E. A. FLETCHER Born Jan. 21, 1852 Died Jan. 1, 1876
John Son of Joshua & E. A. FLETCHER was killed in the Army May 23, 1862 in the 27th year of his age
Clinton Son of Joshua & E. A. FLETCHER was killed in the Army April 25, 1863 in the 18th year of his age
Joshua FLETCHER Sr. Died Mar. 21, 1862 aged 52 years
Eliza A. Wife of Joshua FLETCHER Sr. Born May 2, 1819 Died June 24, 1893

Thomas Son of Aquilla and Susanna L. GLASCOCK Apr. 22, 1814 July 23, 1885; His Wife Emily Ann T. Daughter
    of John and Tacy P. FLETCHER May 30, 1821 Jan. 11, 1897
Ida FLETCHER Daughter of Joshu and Eliza A. FLETCHER Wife of Bedford GLASCOCK Dec. 30, 1853 June 23,
    1878 Joshua F. their Son Jan. 31, 1878 Aug. 11, 1878
Bedford GLASCOCK Son of Thomas and Emily Ann GLASCOCK Jan. 2, 1850 Jan. 28, 1929; His Wife Lulu
    COCHRAN Daughter of Burr H. and Sarah Josephine RICHARDS Dec. 30, 1859 May 1, 1934

Robert FLETCHER Born Jan. 1, 1839 Died Apr. 20, 1911
Tacie GLASCOCK Wife of Robt. FLETCHER Born Nov. 10, 1844 Died July 23, 1878

George GLASCOCK Mar. 14, 1856 Sept 8, 1935
Andrea GLASCOCK Oct. 28, 1852 Oct 28, 1939
George F. GLASCOCK Jan. 26, 1817 Dec. 29, 1856
Maria L. GLASCOCK Aug. 21, 1820 May 8, 1904
Aquilla GLASCOCK May 16, 1845 May 6, 1865
William GLASCOCK Feb. 9, 1854 March 10, 1873
S. Alice GLASCOCK March 16, 1851 Feb. 8, 1923 *(Note: Her father's Bible gives her birth as March 16, 1850 according to Eleanor Glascock Thompson*
T. S. Aprl. 22, 1814 July 23, 1885 *(missing 1993)*
George Mecham SLATER Born Dec. 25, 1840 "Rose Hill" Frederick Co., Md. Died Jan. 2, 1923 Paris, Va. *(C.S.A. marker)*
Ellen Louisa P. Wife of Geo. M. SLATER Born April 10, 1843 Died June 23, 1899
Katie Daughter of Geo. M. and Ellen SLATER Died Nov. 8, 1883 Aged 14 years 4 months and 12 days
Bedford Fletcher SLATER Dec. 31, 1911 Nov. 27, 1930 St. Christopher's School Class of 31
Henry SLATER Feb. 16, 1916 Feb. 16, 1916
Catherine E. SLATER Nov. 7, 1918 Nov. 20, 1918
George Hoffman SLATER July 19, 1871 May 20, 1923
Tacie FLETCHER SLATER July 15, 1878 Oct. 10, 1952
Dibrell D. CRENSHAW Sept. 8, 1903 Dec. 18, 1903

Elias H. McDONALD Feb. 4, 1844 Jan. 4, 1931
Almedia McDONALD Dec. 30, 1846 Feb. 29, 1928
Earl A. McDONALD Sept. 13, 1885 Jan. 10, 1927
Eppa P. McDONALD Dec. 18, 1881 Jan. 19, 1916
Ida McDONALD SAMPSELL March 17, 1878 Aug. 3, 1939

Harved M. ADAMS Aug. 4, 1914 Mar. 9, 1971; Louise S. Sept. 9, 1914–
Anna Mae ADAMS 1917–1978
Edith L. [LLOYD] ADAMS 1889–1961
Oscar T. ADAMS 1882–1945
Berkley Stuart GLASCOCK March 1, 1980 Nov. 13, 1983
Della V. dau. of E. T. & A. V. ROSE Sept. 14, 1927 July 12, 1928
George Washington beloved Son of Thos. & Lula ROSE Born Feb. 23, 1917 Died Dec. 15, 1928
Ralph Rinker ROSE Born Aug. 2, 1921 Died Aug. 8, 1923 *(missing 1993)*
ROSE John T. 1872–1931; Mary L. His Wife 1874–1949
JONES, Evelyn R. 1918–; James D. 1926–1992
ROSE Minnie W. Dec. 1, 1907; Welton M., Jr. Sept. 3, 1907 Jan. 4, 1980
ROSE Nannie E. 1880–1967; Welton M. 1879–1966
ROSE Mabel C. 1894–1975; Charles W. 1894–1962
ROSE Rozella C. 1855–1936; Charles A. 1851–1932
ROSE Agnes B. June 29, 1908 March 31, 1983; Edward T. Mar. 2, 1901 Sept. 29, 1976

Ann Virginia Wife of W. W. ROGERS Born Aug. 25, 1819 Died May 28, 1883
Wm. M. ROGERS Born April 8, 1819 died July 30, 1889
Ella ROGERS Died Feb. 5, 1910
Laura B. ROGERS Died Dec. 11, 1920
Hannah LAKENA Died 1877
Mary L. ROGERS Died Nov. 13, 1925
Wm. ROGERS Died 1863

Joseph GIBSON Born Oct. 29, 1799 Died Aug. 12, 1879; Mariah GIBSON Born Aug. 5, 1808 Died Oct. 5, 1882
Geo. W. GIBSON Born May 27, 1826 Died Sept. 29, 1895; M. L. GIBSON Born Mar. 24, 1829 Died July 19, 1898
Gilbert B. GIBSON Born April 19, 1842 Died Mar. 14, 1907; Margaret V. GIBSON April 10, 1837 Dec. 19, 1911
Nellie R. GIBSON 1848–1938
Fannie E. GIBSON 1841–1926
Mary J. GIBSON 1828–1920

Wallace PHILLIPS Sept. 14, 1830 Sept. 14, 1891
Our Mother Anceline PHILLIPS Jan. 8, 1838 Jan. 10, 1906; A. Wallace PHILLIPS Sept. 14, 1830 Sept. 19, 1891
Lucinda Wife of Evan PHILLIPS Jun. 14, 1800 Mar. 11, 1889
Francis Levi NICHOLS July 12, 1853 Nov. 17, 1918
Susan IDEN Wife of F. L. Nichols Oct. 24, 1871 Aug. 28, 1917
Abner IDEN Died Feb. 15, 1910 Aged 71 years; Sarah K. IDEN Jan. 13, 1839 June 22, 1912
Lulah B. IDEN Dec. 27, 1876 May 31, 1962
Annie G. IDEN Jan. 2, 1882 Aug. 27, 1960
Gladys I. SILCOTT Sept. 6, 1901 Dec. 16, 1968

Mildred KEENE Sept. 6, 1896 Feb. 22, 1967
Francis Land GALT M. D. December 13, 1833 November 18, 1915
Lucy RANDOLPH GALT beloved Wife of Francis Land GALT August 13, 1851 April 18, 1922
Eva GALT NEVILLE Oct. 18, 1884 Mar. 17, 1931 Wife of Henry R. NEVILLE
Susan RANDOLPH ELGIN October 30, 1850 June 22, 1923

Thomas Lee SETTLE 1836–1920; Louisa H. SETTLE 1833–1884 *(C.S.A. marker)*
Addie M. SETTLE Born April 1, 1861 Died Aug. 7, 1868
Joe Gales SETTLE; Addie M. SETTLE; Louisa P. SETTLE; Kathleen SETTLE

William H. ANDERSON Born Jan. 2, 1872 Died Feb. 16, 1906

Nannie E. WILSON Daughter of Thalomiah and Louisa WILSON Feb. 5, 1849 June 3, 1928
Baby Boy ROSE August 7, 1975
HEFLIN William F. 1904–1972; Bessie C. 1910
Lillie H. FEWELL Jan. 22, 1896 Oct. 13, 1973 "Grannie"
THOMPSON Walter S. Jan. 21, 1919 Oct. 1, 1983 married May 17, 1939; Evelyn S. Aug. 8, 1918 Apr. 5, 1989
Dmitri Emmanuel SHAHEEN August 4-5, 1987
Dale Gordon JOHNSON 1949–1979
LUKENS Paul F. 1897–1979; Helen C. 1899–1986
WRIGHT Thomas E. Dec. 8, 1913 Sept. 12, 1982; Elizabeth J. March 14, 1922 July 8, 1985
Ephraim L. SHIPE TEC4 US ARMY WORLD WAR II Dec 2 1910 Jun 16 1982
Bronnie M. SHIPE beloved Wife and Mother Apr. 4, 1909 Aug. 22, 1983
George W. REID, Sr. CPL US ARMY WORLD WAR II KOREA Sep 9 1926 Jul 30 1984
Roger E. FEWELL May 14, 1925 Aug. 7, 1984
PAYNE L. Rebecca 1920–1985 "Becky"; Mason L. Aug. 31, 1909
Zora Belle PEARSON 1922–1985 *(fhm)*
Elijah Theodore PEARSON PFC US ARMY WORLD WAR II Sep 16 1922 Jul 18 1976 *(a playmate of mine)*
KNIGHT Thomas J. April 12, 1919; March 9, 1986; Maude V. Nov. 15, 1923 Sept. 11, 1979
Joseph M. LEGG Nov. 12, 1938 Feb. 24, 1962
LEGG James E. 1907–1960; Josephine A. 1911

SMALLWOOD Samuel B. 1882–1957; Minnie G. 1897 1975
SMALLWOOD Charles B. Mar. 31, 1915 Aug. 18, 1978; Mary C. June 22, 1921 May 29, 1983

GRIMES Rick A. Mar. 24, 1963 Feb. 15, 1990 Linda S. Sept. 14, 1955
"Biddy" Eleanor A. Adams LANHAM April 30, 1920 July 14, 1992
Patricia L. [Lanham] EDMONDS July 15, 1947 Feb. 12, 1989
Edward F. LANHAM Dec. 22, 1922 Apr. 4, 1974
Russell Sydney COOKE 1915–1981
Minnie K. SHAFFER May 5, 1920 June 2, 1982
Mary H. HAYWARD Dec. 5, 1914 Dec. 17, 1985
Richard H. HAYWARD LT COL US AIR FORCE WORLD WAR II Jun 17 1903 May 10 1981
NALLS Wayne Sr. 1943 Gracie S. 1944
SHAFFER Mary Virginia 1925; George H. "Bus" 1909–1989
Mary Lou EAST 1923–1962 *(fhm)*
William B. SHAFFER September 15, 1907 November 17, 1981
Clinton C. JACKSON Dec. 28, 1918 Nov. 16, 1985
William Henry JACKSON Mar. 25, 1907 Aug. 24, 1968; 1938 Alice Virginia BETTIS 1985
WRIGHT William N. Dec. 9, 1911 Apr. 19, 1969; Elsie V. Aug. 1, 1912
Mollie Katherine PEARSON SIMONIN Nov. 30, 1909 Jan. 23, 1982
George W. CANARD 1899–1973
BROWN Henry Edwin 1894–1952; Hilda Mae 1907

JACKSON Walter J. Nov. 9, 1897 May 28, 1953; Florence E. Jul 14, 1891 Apr. 30, 1965
DARNELL Curtis H. Apr. 23, 1929 Jan. 3, 1984; Elsie V. Jan. 31, 1932 married April 26, 1949

Roger L. T. BUDD VIRGINIA EMFN US NAVY Aug 29 1935 Jan 1 1958
BUDD Thomas E. April 21, 1990; Ethel F. February 9, 1903 July 3, 1985
Allen Vincent BUDD VIRGINIA PVT 31 AA REPL TNG BN CAC WORLD WAR II Oct 25 1922 Aug 11 1964

William J. WRIGHT Feb. 13, 1919 July 1, 1989
WRIGHT Betty L. 1938–1952; James W. 1930–1956
WRIGHT Joseph M. 1889–1965; Zula L.

William Henry JACKSON 1907–1968 *(missing 1993) (fhm)*

A. Weadon SAMPSELL Feb. 5, 1873 March 13, 1954; Annie Sept. 4, 1885 Feb. 17, 1979
Paul C. FRAME June 14, 1911 Aug. 2, 1987 *(Masonic emblem)*
T. D. FRAME Dec. 18, 1877 Sept. 25, 1962
Otis Homer ELLIS "The Deacon" Nov. 25, 1912 Feb. 17, 1982 our Father 1ST LT. US ARMY WORLD WAR II
Richard Lee CORDER PVT WORLD WAR I 1895–1982; Marie PEARSON CORDER 1918–1987
George Warren BEARD PVT US ARMY WORLD WAR I Dec 26 1896 Mar 31 1987
HUTCHISON J. Julian May 20, 1911; Josie G. Oct. 11, 1913
TRIPLETT Charles S. Dec. 8, 1890 Jan. 30, 1983; married Sept. 17, 1919; Kathleen H. Mar. 27, 1900
TRIPLETT James W. Apr. 21, 1907 June 13, 1986; married July 6, 1929; Virginia L. Sept. 13, 1908

Theodore U. FRAME 1961–1962 *(missing 1993) (fhm)*
Archie A. McGUINN US NAVY WORLD WAR II Feb 17 1927 June 16 1987

LACKEY William G. 1883–1974 ; Bertha E. 1883–1958
EDWARDS Thurman P. 1888–1954; Mary F. 1885–1962
Jeffrey G. Son of F. C. & B. [Betty] H. [HINSON] SLACK 1959
EDWARDS John 1911–1976; Beulah S. 1900–1979
EDWARDS Marguerite A. [ADAMS] 1912–1979; Jesse H. 1915–1971
Hazel B. ADAMS 1904–1972
Carroll S. ADAMS 1884–1953

BUDD Emma L. 1910–; Herbert V. 1904–1984
Fannie Pauline Daughter of J. T. & Fannie V. BROWN Born Feb. 5, 1874 Died May 27, 1917
Charles L. BROWN 1864–1941
Erma L. BROWN Nov. 23, 1884 Nov. 2, 1967
George Lambert BROWN 1904–1959
Charlie G. BROWN 1907–1981

Harrison C. LUNCEFORD Aug. 26, 1803 Jun. 20, 1893
Julia A. LUNCEFORD Born Feb. 17, 1819 Died May 3, 1900
Robert M. SEATON Died Mar. 28, 1897 Aged 76 years
Amanda F. Wife of R. M. SEATON Born Nov. 30, 1822 Died Dec. 22, 1893
Augusta B. Wife of G. A. TIMBERLAKE and Daughter of R. M. & Amanda F. SEATON Born Dec. 19, 1844 Died
    Aug. 11, 1894
Dr. Norman Powell LAKE Son of R. R. & Katie LAKE Born June 18, 1876 Died Jan. 7, 1911
R. R. LAKE 1847–1924; Katie E. His Wife 1853–1934

Betty Ray DELAPLANE 1907–1977
Channing L. DELAPLANE Born Feb. 25, 1897 Died Nov. 22, 1983; Elizabeth Ray Wife of C. L. DELAPLANE
    Born February 28, 1907 Died July 31, 1977
Channing C. DELAPLANE Born Mar. 19, 1850 Died April 11, 1920
Mary W. DELAPLANE Born Jan. 26, 1863 Died July 12, 1930
Infant of C. C. & M. W. DELAPLANE July 15, 1898 Aug. 1, 1900
Charles H. FRAZL Born Nov. 1, 1844 Prague, Bohemia Died Dec. 7, 1929 Front Royal, Virginia USA

Dr. Wm. M. LUPTON Dec. 30, 1824 Aug. 1, 1881; Josephine K. LUPTON July 23, 1837 Feb. 20, 1882

Samuel Moore SHUTE D. D. 1823–1901
Samuel Moore SHUTE, Jr. 1860–1908
Daniel Kerfoot SHUTE, M. D. 1858–1935
Augusta Pettigrew SHUTE 1869–1943
Delia Bayne SHUTE 1861–1947
Edith SHUTE 1863–1952
Nella Bayne SHUTE 1870–1960
Jane KERFOOT SHUTE 1831–1895

Sarah M. Wife of William LACKEY Died Dec. 23, 1934
Bobby L. LACKEY Feb. 27, 1926 Nov. 23, 1951
Maude M. LACKEY June 9, 1905 May 29, 1986
Harry E. C. LACKEY Feb. 21, 1924 Dec. 3, 1925
Robert C. LACKEY May 20, 1899 Dec. 17, 1976
Harry Edwards Son of E. D. & M. LACKEY Born Feb. 2, 1902 Died Mar. 9, 1912 *(missing 1993)*

Lewis STROTHER 1839–1910; His Wife Sarah A. STROTHER 1838–1915

Lucinda M. FLEMING Died June 1, 1910 age 70 years
Littleton FRASIER Nov. 2, 1847 May 1, 1918
Laura Daughter of Townsend & Sarah E. FRASIER Died Dec. 18, 1906 aged [?] years and 8 days
Townsend D. FRASIER Sept. 14, 1822 Nov. 27, 1907
Sarah Elizabeth Wife of Townsend FRASIER June 29, 1822 Sept. 22, 1885
Catherine FRASIER 1861–1941
Townsend FRASIER 1867–1937

SUTPHIN Edward F. 1908–1978; Eleanor K. [KERFOOT] 1918–1982
Lena RAMEY KERFOOT 1879–1947
Daniel Brown KERFOOT 1873–1955
Maria C. KERFOOT Born Apl. 28, 1845 Died May 19, 1862
Margaret D. KERFOOT 1848–1925
Ella KERFOOT 1848–1916
Daniel S. KERFOOT Born Jan. 16, 1802 Died Aug. 26, 1884
Maria CARR Wife of D. S. KERFOOT Born May 10, 1807 Died Dec. 4, 1865
Wm. F. KERFOOT Born Dec. 22, 1843 Died June 14, 1890
Emily Carr KERFOOT Born Jan. 10, 1840 Died Jan. 2, 1900
William Benedict SMITH Born February 22, 1855 Died March 16, 1916
Rosa Jane Wife of William Benedict SMITH Born March 12, 1852 Died May 17, 1932
Eleanora E. SMITH beloved Daughter of W. B. SMITH & Rosa J. SMITH Born Sept. 26, 1878 Died Apl. 17, 1920
Lucy E. GIBSON Died Nov. 28, 1911 aged 73 years
Mary A. GIBSON Born May 30, 1826 Died Feb. 1, 1899
Margaret A. Wife of Mahlon GIBSON Died Jan. 9, 1915 aged 76 years
Mahlon GIBSON Died Sept. 1, 1892 aged 52 years
Judith A. GIBSON Born Oct. 18, 1832 Died Feb. 16, 1916
one sunken headstone

beloved Aunt Smildia J. SEATON Wife of S. W. TRIPLETT Born Feb. 26, 1853 Died May 5, 1920
S. W. TRIPLETT Died Nov. 11, 1913 aged 64 years
Sarah A. Wife of Urial TRIPLETT Born Sept. 4, 1814 Died June 24, 1892
Urial TRIPLETT Born Jan. 16, 1803 Died Jan. 9, 1874

BRADFIELD Plot:
Lucy Wife of Mandley BROWN Born Feb. 24, 1825 Died Jan. 25, 1894
Lucie M. BRADFIELD June 2, 1868 Oct. 1, 1954
Susie F. MEALING Dec. 31, 1862 Aug. 14, 1934
Grafton B. BRADFIELD July 26, 1890 March 25, 1928
Corrine B. BURTON July 12, 1905 Sept. 16, 1964
J. E. BRADFIELD Aug. 26, 1860 Dec. 28, 1951
Ray B. KENNER June 24, 1888 May 28, 1939

Nancy L. BRADFIELD July 31, 1917 November 14, 1984
Urcell M. BRADFIELD October 27, 1889 December 4, 1976
John A. BURTON II Feb. 3, 1906 Jan. 9, 1980
Richard C. ROZELL 1886–1944
Florence GIBSON ROZELL 1875–1959
Arthur E. GIBSON Son of J. A. & F. L. GIBSON Born Dec. 12, 1869 Died July 27, 1870
Florence L. Wife of Jos. A. GIBSON Born Oct. 2, 1847 Died Oct. 8, 1894 aged 47 years & 6 ds.
Jos. A. GIBSON Born Dec. 13, 1833 Died July 13, 1907
Father William Blakeley GIBSON January 15, 1871 December 19, 1964
Mother May LEITH GIBSON May 10, 1874 December 2, 1956
Lieut. Joseph A. GIBSON Co. A 6 Va. Cav. C.S.A.N.
Arthur B. Son of Jos. A. & F. L. GIBSON Born Dec. 12, 1869 Died July 27, 1870

DOSTER Albert F. April 11, 1914 July 20, 1990; Dorothy S. Jan. 10, 1922
Henry FRASIER Jan. 26, 1860 March 27, 1929
Lizzie J. HAMBLIN Wife of Henry FRASIER Feb. 11, 1866 Feb. 11, 1905
Townsend Son of Henry & L. J. FRASIER Died Aug. 26, 1891
Richard C. Son of H. & L. J. FRASIER Born Dec. 1, 1888 Died July 19, 1889

Mary Esther FRASIER Dec. 8, 1902 Feb. 6, 1905
Ruth LIGHTFOOT FRASIER Wife of William Pickney BERRY Oct. 20, 1884 Nov. 12, 1963
R. L. S. BERRY 1884–1963
Evelyn BERRY REID Daughter of William & Ruth FRASIER BERRY August 28, 1910 November 7, 1924
Elizabeth Smith FRASIER Daughter of John & Susan FRASIER Febry. 27, 1886 October 24, 1983
Susan Isler FRASIER Daughter of John & Susan FRASIER April 30, 1891 November 5, 1977
STICKLES G. Leonard Oct. 16, 1909; Pauline S. Dec. 13, 1909 Jan. 2, 1974
Maude L. FRASIER Wife of Nathl. H. RUSSELL Sept. 8, 1889 March 11, 1929
Susan SMITH FRASIER June 4, 1862 Dec. 19, 1935
John FRASIER April 30, 1857 March 12, 1927

FILLER Mason S. 1903–1968; Helen S. 1908
SIMPSON John F. 1883–1965; Rosie P. 1884–1975
Armason V. SIMPSON Jan. 23, 1904 Mar. 23, 1915
Rev. Herman C. SIMPSON Sept. 11, 1906 July 11, 1970

MOORE Pauline SETTLE Dec. 6, 1869 Feb. 21, 1955
MOORE Edgar Ackley M. D. May 12, 1878 Oct. 24, 1924
Thomas Settle MOORE Feb. 15, 1912 Oct. 31, 1990
Edgar Milburn Son of Nicholas and Olive M. MOORE Jan. 31, 1914 March 15, 1915
Olive MILBORN June 3, 1883 Sept. 10, 1956
Nicholas MOORE March 19, 1882 April 1, 1963
Isabelle SHUTZ WOODS November 21, 1906 June 5, 1969

Died on Tuesday the 17th day of Aug. 1858 Lucinda Daughter of John M. & Mary M. SCOTT aged 3 years 4
    months & 13 days
Died on Saturday the 31st day of July 1858 John Marshall Son of John M. & Mary M. SCOTT aged 8 months & 10
    days

Irene DUVALL SCOTT 1871–1953
Henry Martyn SCOTT 1868–1934
James Williams SCOTT Born Feb. 18, 1859 Died Oct. 10, 1882 *(missing 1993)*
Walter Williams SCOTT Born Feb. 18, 1859 Died Oct. 16, 1932
Mary Mildred Wife of John SCOTT Born Jan. 13, 1832 Died July 17, 1905
John M. SCOTT Born Jan. 22, 1833 Died Feb. 11, 1924
Henry Martyn SCOTT Dec. 22, 1909 Feb. 10, 1985
Mary Scott McKILLITS Oct. 22, 1903 June 24, 1990

Chas. Floyd Son of C. W. & Bertha F. WILTSHIRE Born Feb. 16, 1904 Died June 10, 1919
Thomas W. FLEMING Born April 17, 1838 Died November 9, 1909 *(C.S.A. marker)*
Thomas W. Son of W. C. & A. C. FLEMING Aug. 16, 1918 Oct. 28, 1918
Catherine L. FLEMING Born Feb. 18, 1851 Died Mar. 21, 1937
FLEMING Leola B. Oct. 12, 1888 Dec. 2, 1964; Fred H. Aug. 19, 1886 July 7, 1940
Leola SEATON FLEMING March 27, 1896 Sept. 8, 1925
Ann Rebecca Wife of Geo. FLEMING Born Aug. 6, 1813 Died Feb. 23, 1903
Kendall C. Son of C. T. & L. L. FLEMING Sept. 30, 1891 aged 5 months 2 days
Bessie May dau. of C. T. & L. L. FLEMING Born Feb. 21, 1906 Died Oct. 18, 1906
Gladys G. FLEMING Daughter of C. T. & L. L. FLEMING Born Feb. 6, 1900 Died Jan. 2, 1928
FLEMING Charles T. April 11, 1866 Oct. 24, 1950; Lizzie L. Oct. 16, 1872 March 12, 1950
F. M. KENDALL Born Jan. 6, 1836 Died May 11, 1903; R. E. KENDALL Born Jan. 17, 1845

Imogene JOHNSTON Wife of John Rush CROCKETT April 19, 1898 Sept. 30, 1964

John Rush CROCKETT March 6, 1898 April 25, 1957
Nancy CROCKETT HARRISON May 19, 1927 July 20, 1967
James Abner JOHNSTON March 27, 1861 December 5, 1933
Fannie HAINES JOHNSTON February 18, 1858 December 28, 1934
JOHNSTON Lester VIRGINIA BN SGT MAJ HDQ TROOP 29 DIV WORLD WAR I Dec. 1, 1894 Sept. 30, 1957

FLETCHER Plot:
Lula P. FOSTER beloved Wife of Joshua FLETCHER Oct. 24, 1857 July 23, 1892
Joshua FLETCHER Sept. 5, 1850 April 8, 1913
Marion P. CARTER beloved Wife of Joshua A. FLETCHER Jan. 21, 1875 Nov. 21, 1948
Lula Foster beloved dau. of Lula P. F. & Joshua FLETCHER July 20, 1891 Sept. 24, 1907
Mary FLETCHER GLASCOCK Oct. 9, 1888 Dec. 6, 1974
Robert FLETCHER July 14, 1902 Feb. 20, 1979; Betty GIBSON beloved Wife of R. C. FLETCHER Oct. 29, 1910

Benj. E. THOMPSON March 21, 1869 Aug. 14, 1940
Lula A. LEE Wife of B. E. THOMPSON Nov. 14, 1869 March 26, 1936
Baylis THOMPSON May 30, 1841 Feb. 8, 1893; Amanda V. His Wife July 31, 1845 May 21, 1920
Carrie M. THOMPSON 1882–1906
Uncle Ben THOMPSON 1847–1936

SMALLWOOD Clarence William 1899–1964
COSTELLO: Francis A. "Paw Paw" Feb. 16, 1923 Aug. 21, 1990; "Rissy" Charlotte S. May 3, 1925

East Side:
Eliza A. TRIPLETT Wife of C. L. SEATON Born Sept. 7, 1852 Died June 22, 1916
Tacie M. FLETCHER LESTER June 26, 1894 Dec. 3, 1973
FLETCHER Dixie P. 1908; Elizabeth B. [BROWNING] 1917
Davis W. THOMPSON July 10, 1899 October 14, 1985
Myrtle A. THOMPSON March 29, 1905 March 29, 1971
Tyrone B. Thompson SGT US ARMY WORLD WAR I Aug 7, 1896 Dec 30 1975
E. Idell REID May 16, 1875 Aug. 26, 1967
Dora Alice REID [died] Sept. 1, 1949
Florence G. REID Aug. 21, 1906
Arthur Cook REID Feb. 21, 1874 Feb. 2, 1947
Minnie M. REID Nov. 29, 1954
William P. REID July 21, 1903
Amanda E. REID Feb. 6, 1892

Capt. James E. TOWNSEND Co. G 17 Va. Inf. C.S.A.
Husband Allen S. TOWNSEND June 4, 1866 Sept. 28, 1908
Julia D. YOWELL September 4, 1958
Cecil L. YOWELL 1890–1978
Margaret A. YOWELL June 9, 1930 July 26, 1989

S. Virginia BISHOP Daughter of William F. & Anne V. BISHOP Mar. 19, 1898 Oct. 30, 1967
William F. BISHOP July 29, 1876 Aug. 16, 1959
Annie V. BISHOP Wife of W. F. BISHOP Mar. 5, 1868 Jan. 4, 1944
Ada L. BISHOP May 1901 Aug. 1902

Elijah G. CREEL Born Aug. 11, 1835 Died April 15, 1895
Elizabeth P. CREEL Born Dec. 22, 1832 Died June 24, 1903

Mandley IDEN Died July 3, 1884 aged 87 years; His Wife Elizabeth PIERCE Died 1882 and daugh. Florida 1837–1875

Robert G. IDEN Sept. 3, 1910 Jan. 19, 1911

Twin daughters of R. C. & Lucy J. IDEN Oct. 24, 1912

Richard J. IDEN Mar. 18, 1914 July 11, 1914

Catherine E. IDEN June 30, 1922 Nov. 17, 1922

Carroll Samuel IDEN Feb. 21, 1918 Nov. 17, 1972

IDEN Lucy Dora JOHNSTON Sept. 18, 1883 April 12, 1956; Robert Carroll Jan. 27, 1879 Apr. 19, 1976

Genevieve R. [JOHNSTON] CHAPPELEAR 1870–1949

Henry Welby Son of H. L. & Ann R. JOHNSTON Born Sept. 11, 1858 Died Jan. 20, 1894

Our Father H. L. JOHNSTON Mar 10, 1827 Apl. 12, 1905

Our Mother Ann R. JOHNSTON Sept. 16, 1829 July 28, 1905

Henry H. Son of M. P. & A. E. JOHNSTON Born Mar. 4, 1885 Died July 24, 1885

Mandley Allen JOHNSTON Aug. 24, 1888 Jan. 20, 1937

Elizabeth JOHNSTON May 3, 1886 Nov. 5, 1973

Mandley Pierce JOHNSTON Mar. 24, 1856 Mar. 19, 1926

Annie Elizabeth JOHNSTON Mar. 16, 1853 Aug. 3, 1922

Wilmer Pierce JOHNSTON Oct. 10, 1881 Sept. 18, 1946

Anna KEARNEY JOHNSTON June 14, 1879

Henry Hamilton JOHNSTON March 24, 1885 July 24, 1885

Joseph Carr CALVERT Born June 15, 1826 Died Aug. 18, 1892 *(C.S.A. marker)*

Anna M. Wife of Dr. S. K. JACKSON and Daughter of George & Elizabeth CALVERT Born Dec. 2, 1822 Died Feb. 7, 1900

Amanda Carr CALVERT Daughter of George & Elizabeth CALVERT Born Nov. 18, 1823 Died Jan. 22, 1904

Bessie Stanley dau. of Daniel & Mary CALVERT Oct. 12, 1851 Apl. 3, 1904

Mary Landon Armistead ROSSER Wife of C. C. CALVERT Daughter of J. Travis & Mary ARMISTEAD ROSSER May 14, 1844 Dec. 23, 1917 *(broken in 1993)*

Caldwell Carr CALVERT Son of George & Elizabeth CALVERT Jan. 28, 1831 Sept. 14, 1909

Mary Rosser CALVERT June 13, 1881 Nov. 16, 1955

Landon Ralls CALVERT May 26, 1884 Nov. 25, 1960

Charlotte Mary EDWARDS May 14, 1867 July 5, 1953

Mary E. RYLEY 1897 September 7, 1954

Mary M. HUNTER Died Aug. 26, 1874 aged 84 years 7 months & 18 days

Melbourne HUNTER Born July 6, 1848 Died Dec. 27, 1920

Sallie AYRE Wife of Melbourne HUNTER Born Aug. 31, 1859 Died Oct. 16, 1939

Elsie AYRE Born Sept. _ 1895 Died July 19, 1896

Marie AYRE Dau. of E. A. & Annie AYRE aged 7 months & 9 days

William T. AYRE Born Aug. 22, 1842 wounded at Gettysburg Died at Chester PA July 25, 1863 aged 29 years 11 mo. & 3 dys *(C.S.A. no marker)*

Nathaniel B. BIDGOOD b. 1865 June 5, 1938

AYRE Edward V. b 1857 May 7, 1930; Annie B. b 1859 May 3, 1946

Mary Ann Wife of Geo. S. AYRE Born Dec. 10, 1817 Died Apr. 18. 1904 aged 81 yrs 11 mns & 4 dys

Joseph F. FLEMING Born Oct. 13, 1834 Died Aug. 2, 1913

Lucinda Wife of Joseph F. FLEMING Born April 16, 1840 Died June 5, 1904

Robert COSTELLO Born Jan. 26, 1820 Died Sept. 22, 1892

Mary A. Wife of Robert COSTELLO Born Aug. 16, 1822 Died Feb. 26, 1892

W. L. COSTELLO Born Aug. 2, 1864 Died Dec. 19, 1949

Sarah Margaret Wife of W. L. COSTELLO Born Nov. 18, 1872 Died Dec. 22, 1931

COSTELLO George C. Feb. 22, 1862 Oct. 13, 1935; Susan V. April 23, 1863 Nov. 14, 1937

COSTELLO Walter S. 1887–1956; Elizabeth T. 1894–1973
Bertha May COSTELLO Nov. 7, 1894 July 14, 1979

Samuel R. TRIPLETT Died Jan. 7, 1893 aged 67 yrs. 6 mos. 10 days
Frances A. Wife of William TRIPLETT Born Jan. 17, 1798 Died Sept. 5, 1872
Martha F. LUCIUS Sept. 10, 1862 Aug. 8, 1846
Harvey D. LUCIUS Mar. 23, 1894 Nov. 4, 1945
Hunter W. LUCIUS Nov. 18, 1866 Apr. 22, 1951
Betty V. LUCIUS Wife of William F. ENTWISTLE July 11, 1917 Oct. 27, 1959
William F. ENTWISTLE, Sr. Husband of Betty V. LUCIUS May 16, 1911 Jan. 12, 1975
Mary Elizabeth LUCIUS Born Aug. 21, 1893 died Aug. 27, 1918
LUCIUS Sarah Frances Dec. 10, 1898 July 20, 1982; Lewis Beverley Aug. 31, 1891 May 23, 1951
LUCIUS Lela S. 1902–1985; Robert M. 1896–1977

Lula V. DUNBAR Jan. 9, 1876 Sept. 20, 1960
H. Beverley DUNBAR Oct. 2, 1879 Nov. 16, 1940
Mollie A. DUNBAR Nov. 13, 1864 March 9, 1940
Ann Elizabeth Wife of H. H. DUNBAR Nov. 24, 1849 May 28, 1925
Harvey DUNBAR died Sept. 3, 1891 aged 72 yrs 16 d

William MOSS Born Jan. 29, 1812 Died Oct. 5, 1900
Catherine E. Wife of William MOSS
Edith MOSS Daughter of F. M. & S. E. TINSMAN born June 30, 1894 died Jan. 26, 1898

Eben Taylor LAWS Born Aug. 12, 1816 Died June 1, 1921
Elmira C. LAWS Born Mar. 12, 1840 Died June 15, 1881
Sarah T. TINSMAN Dec. 10, 1853 April 20, 1946
Francis M. TINSMAN July 30, 1839 Feb. 13, 1914
Mary Joseph ABRIBAT Feb. 19, 1889 Feb. 10, 1954
Clarice TINSMAN ABRIBAT Aug. 8, 1896 July 30, 1953
Otis TINSMAN May 1, 1885 Sept. 10, 1942
Wells TINSMAN March 18, 1883 July 9, 1913
Eva Daughter of F. M. & S. E. TINSMAN Born Jan. 16, 1892 Died Sept. 1, 1893
Carl Son of F. M. & S. E. TINSMAN Born Nov. 30, 1890 Died Aug. 30, 1893
Lettie Daughter of F. M. & S. E. TINSMAN Born Oct. 28, 1886 Died Mar. 1, 1891
Hepsie H. Daughter of C. R. & S. E. WALKER Nov. 1, 1899 Aug. 20, 1881
Viola PIET TINSMAN June 16, 1882 Aug. 27, 1968

James W. LEE Born May 29, 1836 Died Aug. 7, 1904
Charlotte E. Wife of James W. LEE Born Jan. 1, 1839 Died Mar. 6, 1895
Ludwell Letcher LEE July 3, 1859 Feb. 27, 1923; Sarah Anne LEE Mar. 22, 1863 Mar. 22, 1942
Beulah Mae LEE beloved Daughter of Ludwell Letcher LEE and Sarah Ann LEE Apr. 18, 1890 Mar. 21, 1962
Annie G. LEE 1901–1902
Infant LEE 1903

Eliza Jane Wife of W. E. WILLIS Dec. 2, 1870 Apr. 4, 1930
W. G. BYRD Born Feb. 18, 1800 Died Feb. 11, 1875
Lucy BYRD Born May 16, 1860 Died Mar. 3, 1923
Flotilla Daughter of W. G. & Barbara BYRD Born June 18, 1866 Died Nov. 22, 1893
L. Stanley WILLIS Nov. 2, 1900 July, 9, 1948
W. Edward WILLIS May 26, 1872 Feb. 2, 1950
Isabella CRAUN Daughter of H. O. and Hattie CRAUN born Jan. 5, 1896 died Jan. 6, 1896

Franklin D. Son of P. H. CRAUN born & died Nov. 7, 1933
Robert Edward CRAUN Born Sept. 14, 1923 died Aug. 13, 1925
CRAUN Samuel Daniel SGT CO G 59 PIONEER INF WORLD WAR I March 3 1892 Dec. 6 1953; Susie Ellen
    May 4, 1902 Jan. 5, 1933
Samuel O. CRAUN born May 6, 1858 died Dec. 30, 1904 aged 46 yrs 7 mos & 24 da; Hattie CRAUN born May 9,
    1863 died April 6, 1905 aged 41 yrs 10 mos & 27 ds

W. Hampton PIERCE Nov. 5, 1902 Jan. 14, 1975
Daniel C. PIERCE Dec. 1907 Apr. 23, 1983
Graham PIERCE Jan. 29, 1873 Dec. 13, 1951
Kate G. PIERCE Aug. 6, 1875 Feb. 18, 1958
Abner C. PIERCE Born Sept. 11, 1838 Died Nov. 7, 1906
Sarah C. Wife of A. C. PIERCE Born Aug. 14, 1842 Died Dec. 21, 1900
Nellie Daughter of A. C. & Sarah C. PIERCE Born Mar. 13, 1828 Died Oct. 23, 1880
R. G. PIERCE Born Feb. 4, 1899 Died Oct. 31, 1959

Richard D. CRENSHAW 1911–1973
Dibrell D. CRENSHAW 1868–1934
Fanny Q. CRENSHAW 1879–1942
George Rutledge CRENSHAW Sept. 8, 1903 Dec. 18, 1903
Ellen R. TRIPLETT Mar. 3, 1859 Oct. 25, 1939
James W. TRIPLETT Died July 11, 1907 aged 71 years C.S.A.; Margaret J. TRIPLETT Died Nov. 17, 1907 aged
    83 years
Annie F. TRIPLETT Jan. 2, 1862 Jan. 4, 1923 aged 61 years
Fred H. DUNCAN Sept. 9, 1901 June 21, 1854
Clarence William TRIPLETT Sept. 2, 1893 Dec. 11, 1948
Laura B. TRIPLETT Sept. 12, 1873 Nov. 10, 1951; J. Edward TRIPLETT Jan. 29, 1886 May 12, 1939
Mabel Irene TRIPLETT Sept. 22, 1890 June 2, 1988

Father Marvin H. BROWN 1910–1967
BROWN Bessie T. 1875–1949; Jacob L. 1873–1951
Mabel A. BROWN Mar. 18, 1918 Mar. 23, 1918
Sarah BROWN Mar. 24, 1841 July 14, 1925
Jno. S. BROWN Mar. 18, 1831 July 31, 1904

Ida D. LEGG 1873–1958
James E. LEGG Born Sept. 25, 1835 Died July 19, 1915
Cornelia A. Wife of James E. LEGG Born Mar. 2, 1835 Died Jan. 6, 1907

Holcombe Douglas GIBSON Born 1896 "Brookland" Upperville Died 1952
May HOLCOMBE LAWSON Wife of Herman Douglas GIBSON Died June 27, 1934
Herman Douglas GIBSON Sept. 18, 1869 Nov. 7, 1926
Richard Bitton LAWSON Born Oct. 22, 1840 Died in Fredericksburg, Va. April 23, 1924 Confederate veteran
    1861–1865 [C.S.A.]
Mattie ROBERTSON LAWSON Born in Amelia Co. Jan. 19, 1844 Died in Fredericksburg, Va. Feb. 16, 1919
1 stone in parts, no data visble
John Dice LAWSON Born "Willow Brook" Upperville, Va. May 1, 1899 Died Vero Beach, Florida Nov. 18, 1964
Richard Brook LAWSON Born "Willow Brook", Upperville, Va. April 25, 1896 Died Sarasota Florida March 2,
    1954
Mary Elizabeth LAWSON Born "Willow Brook", Upperville, Va. Mar. 1, 1901 Died Upperville, Va. Feb. 8, 1962
Anthony Brooke LAWSON Born Wytheville, Va. Jan. 9, 1868 Died "Willow Brook" Upperville, Va. Feb. 21, 1947
Alice DICE Wife of A. Brooke LAWSON Born Staunton, Va. Nov. 15, 1863 Died "Willow Brook" Dec, 18, 1943

Roszelle Robertson Daughter of Brooke and Alice LAWSON May 1, 1899 July 22, 1901

Marion Joseph DOAK Son of James & Eliza DOAK COMPTON Canada died Oct 2, 1905
Martha April 8, 1894
Ann Eliza CARTER Jan. 25, 1872 June 26, 1946
Shelby Hill CARTER May 26, 1872 Oct. 30, 1951
William Fred CARTER September 28, 1904 October 24, 1987
Juliet Yates CARTER March 26, 1900 Dec. 11, 1982
Richard Mason CARTER Oct. 16, 1902 April 22, 1979
Herbert Lee Son of Shelby & Annie CARTER Born Feb. 11, 1903 Died May 30, 1904
B. Addison TRIPLETT Born Feb. 28, 1837 Died Dec. 24, 1929 aged 92 yrs. 9 mos. 24 days; His Wife Amanda M.
   Born Feb. 28, 1845 Died May 29, 1909 aged 64 yrs 3 mos. 1 day *(C.S.A. marker)*
Bertha S. dau. of B. A. & Amanda TRIPLETT Died Nov. 11, 1888 aged 13 years 8 months & 7 days

M. Katherine LEAR March 19, 1919 July 19, 1973
Mary Virginia Dau. of R. C. & M. E. McCARTY May 20, 1878 Nov. 18, 1905
Martha E. Wife of R. C. McCARTY Dec. 24, 1839 Feb. 15, 1897 Mother
Father Robert C. McCARTY
M. Katherine McCARTY June 4, 1892 Sept. 24, 1966
R. Mason McCARTY Feb. 19, 1876 July 7, 1966
Marion H. McCARTY June 9, 1874 March 29, 1959
Ernest R. McCARTY March 5, 1868 May 3, 1939

RIDGEWAY Robert Powell, Sr. Dec. 3, 1906 Jan. 4, 1991; Anna Mae June 11, 1904 April 5, 1987
RIDGEWAY Thomas Apl. 28, 1902 Feb. 16, 1903
Hattie V. RIDGEWAY 1870–1958
Andrew J. RIDGEWAY 1865–1943
Frances E. RIDGEWAY Mar. 14, 1952
RIDGEWAY Lila Payne Apr. 25, 1896 Sept. 30, 1981; Jacob Glen Oct. 27, 1896 Sept. 28, 1988 PVT US ARMY
   WORLD WAR I

Sophie K. WOOLF Nov. 16, 1845 Aug. 10, 1924
Francis M. WOOLF June 22, 1844 July 7, 1901
Virginia HEADLEY WOOLF Mar. 23, 1885 Jan. 7, 1969
William Stanley WOOLF Dec. 24, 1885 Aug. 9, 1966

EMBREY Mollie L. 1866–1942; Meredith E. 1865–1942
Clifton M. EMBREY May 5, 1901 Mar. 27, 1925
Theresa M. dau. of Meredith & Mollie L. EMBREY Born Apr. 26, 1900 Died Aug. 10, 1900
HANNA William B. 1914 Dorothy C. 1913

Joseph McARTOR Aug. 14, 1849 Jan. 17, 1914
McARTOR Olivia Jane Apr. 4, 1840 Feb. 7, 1912; Joseph WILLOUGHBY Aug. 14, 1849 Jan. 17, 1914; Maria
   Thomas July 13, 1854 Aug. 28, 1926

HURST Fannie L. 1878–1898; Cordelia A. 1858–1893; George W. 1848–1904
Father Snowden E. McGUINN 1878–1960
Mother Susie B. McGUINN 1891–1938
Thomas C. McGUINN 1923–1940
Snowden E. McGUINN, Jr. 1911–1950

Mary Augusta SCOTT Aug. 19, 1899 April 27, 1973

Ann D. Daughter of C. T. & Annie SCOTT Died Oct. 8, 1891 aged 11 months
Margaret Daughter of C. T. & Annie SCOTT Died July 10, 1896 aged 1 year
Nellie Virginia Daughter of C. T. & Annie SCOTT Born Aug. 11, 1887 Died Mar. 22, 1901
SCOTT Anna M. 1884–1950; Charles T. 1857–1936
Gabrella SCOTT 1860–1934
Rebecca Jane Wife of Moses SCOTT Born September 29, 1825 Died Apr. 26, 1902
Moses SCOTT Died May 8, 1897 aged 89 years

Mother S. Louise PAGE SETTLE Died Oct. 27th 1926
Mother Ida E. HALEY 1847–1908; Walter Clyde 1873–1875; R. D. HALEY 1844–1901 Father *(C.S.A. marker)*;
    Maude H. [HALEY] ANDERSON 1869–1939; Edward F. ANDERSON 1876–1944; Blanche HALEY 1871–
    1938
Father R. D. HALEY 1844–1901 C.S.A.
Our sons Walter Clyde 1873–1875; John Arthur 1872–1889

Lee Roy SISK Born Aug. 21, 1871 Died March 1, 1922
Annie L. CARVER 1879–1966

Nelson MAXWELL RICHARDS July 9, 1881 November 14, 1957; Jesse Washington RICHARDS August 26, 1878
    July 14, 1960 *(U.D marker)*
Washington L. RICHARDS Born June 29, 1835 Died Sept. 15, 1904 aged 69 years; Martha C. RICHARDS Born
    Sept. 21, 1841 Died Jan. 10, 1926 aged 84 years
Hume B. BROUN Died Sept. 1, 1916 aged 32 years
Lena M. beloved Wife of Hume B. BROUN July 4, 1883 Oct. 11, 1979
Hume T. BROUN 1910–1935
Mary Lena dau. of H. B. & L. M. BROUN Nov. 16, 1906 June 10, 1910
TAVENNER M. Thorton 1833–1916; Lucy T. His Wife 1838–1925

Infant Daughter died 1913
Infant Daughter of J. S. & F. C. KINES Mar. 13, 1906 Apl. 24, 1906
KINES Fannie C. 1880–1964
KINES Joseph S. 1879–1963
James S. SLACK Born May 9, 1896 died Nov. 22, 1896

TAVENNER Plot:
Lela Virginia Daughter of Lizzie M. & Ralph D. TAVENNER 1900–1906
Grace TAVENNER WILEY Wife of Winter W. WILEY Jan. 12, 1897 Oct. 3, 1970
Ruby KINES SCOTT July 22, 1915
Earl A. SCOTT, Jr. Sept. 17, 1942 May 4, 1992 our Son
Earl A. SCOTT PVT US WORLD WAR II Jul. 20 1911 Oct 26 1984
Elizabeth B. SIMPSON Wife of William E. SIMPSON aunt of William E. TAVENNER Jan. 19, 1928 Sept. 15,
    1992
Winter W. WILEY DISTRICT OF COLUMBIA PVT CO B 112 ENGINEERS WORLD WAR I Oct 3 1890 March
    5 1956
TAVENNER John M. 1901–1941
Eugene M. TAVENNER Oct. 30, 1868 Feb. 22, 1957
Jennie W. Wife of E. M. TAVENNER 1866–1935

Mary I. LLEWELLYN March 6, 1917
Mary C. LLEWELLYN July 20, 1888 January 30, 1960
Edith Moss Daughter of *(rest in ground)*

J. Norman HURST 1894–1958 *(missing 1993)*
James W. HURST 1861–1950
Mary F. HURST 1861–1938
Henry Clay HURST May 5, 1887 Nov. 2, 1896
Mary A. HURST Mar. 6, 1904 aged 67 years
Frances FORREST Died July 5, 1905 aged 84 years
Jno. W. HURST Died Nov. 2, 1901 aged 71 years
Annie H. BURGESS May 11, 1889 Dec. 22, 1958
Rosa Lee Wife Henry HURST Died Mar. 19, 1905 aged 38 yrs 1 month 11 ds

Dr. C. F. RINKER Nov. 13, 1859 Nov. 11, 1930; Dora Wife of Dr. C. F. RINKER Mar. 14, 1860 Jan. 7, 1907;
   Lizzie 1893–1895

Roberta J. GLASCOCK March 29, 1847 Oct. 9, 1930
Luther B. GLASCOCK April 20, 1853 Oct. 12, 1925
Doris L. GLASCOCK Dec. 9, 1857 March 11, 1927
Fanny I. GLASCOCK Aug. 12, 1828 Sept. 22, 1900
Thomas J. GLASCOCK April 5, 1823 March 4, 1906
Emma W. GLASCOCK Nov. 20, 1865 July 3, 1946
Elizabeth Wife of Jos. J. GRIMES Died Sept 15, 1909 aged 82 years
Joseph J. GRIMES Co. K 11 Rgt. Va. Cav. C.S.A. July 9, 1839 Aug, 3, 1922
FERGUSON Abner 1839–1911; Mary E. His Wife 1840–1906

Mary Rosalie FERGUSON 1881–1915
Wade Hampton FERGUSON 1867–1925
Lila M. FERGUSON 1862–1937
Josephine FERGUSON 1871–1949
Betty FERGUSON 1872–1956
Lucille FERGUSON 1874–1954
W. P. FERGUSON 1879–1941
A. H. FERGUSON 1875–1949
Anna M. FERGUSON 1879–1959
MAUCK David Martin Mar. 6, 1871 Aug. 2, 1955; Ellie ATHEY Nov. 24, 1869 Nov. 9, 1955
Henry M. Son of H. M. & M. C. LLOYD Jan. 30, 1920
Henry M. LLOYD 1878–1949; His Wife Mabel C. 1883–1967 aged 84
OLIVER Irene E. Nov. 17, 1908 Aug. 5, 1975; Roy W. Oct. 3, 1903 Feb. 19, 1983
Lester E. Son of H. M. & M. C. LLOYD Died Dec. 31, 1918 aged 14 years & 4 mos.
Norman Rinker Son of H. M. & M. C. LLOYD Born Oct. 15, 1912 Died Nov. 17, 1914
Raymond S. Son of H. M. & M. C LLOYD Born & Died Oct. 15, 1915
Esther P. Daughter of H. M. & M. C. LLOYD Born Aug. 24, 1901 Died July 22, 1912
Cathy Daughter of H. M. & M. C. LLOYD Born Aug. 24, 1894 Died July 22, 1912 *(stone face down 1988 & 1993)*

WILSON Daniel B. [Boone] June 23, 1859 Feb. 4, 1949
John WILSON Born June 26, 1859 Died Oct. 19, 1929
Joseph R. WILSON Born Feb. 8, 1853 Died Oct. 21, 1924
Susan C. WILSON Died Dec. 6, 1907 aged 77 years; Fannie PEER Died Jan. 29, 1910 aged 75 years
WILSON Norah Lee Dec. 4, 1864 Feb. 13, 1936
Herbert R. JOHNSON 1898–1913

Mother Lille R. THOMAS July 8, 1867 July 29, 1957
Father John C. THOMAS January 30, 1851 June 25, 1923
Mary Jane REED Born July 29, 1851 Died Nov. 3, 1941; Lewis Jackson REED Born Sept. 8, 1862 Died Jan. 8,

1945; Lille REED THOMAS Born July 8, 1867 Died July 29, 1957; John Milton REED Born Nov. 4, 1818 Died July 28, 1876; Sarah Ann STROTHER REED Born Aug. 8, 1831 Died Dec. 28, 1906; Richard A. Born May 12, 1855 Died Oct. 18, 1867 Bettie A. Born Sep. 2, 1859 Died Sep. 21, 1881 Children of J. M. & S. A. REED; Anna E. Born April 18, 1865 Died Feb. 25, 1912; Edwin S. Born Dec. 18, 1869 Died Oct. 1, 1914

LEACH Rose H. 1875–1954; J. Thomas 1869–1944
WHITE Walter S. 1874–1931; Janie L. 1883–1956

William T. GREY Born Nov. 22, 1853 June 13, 1938; Annie E. GREY Born Jan. 21, 1857 Dec. 13, 1942
Marie LOTZ KRANZLER Dec. 28, 1883 April 6, 1951
Mother Kathryn Lindsey FRASIER HOLMAN April 30, 1888 October 6, 1974
Father Bruce A. DUESENBERRY 1881–1955
BOLEN Sadie M. June 21, 1889 June 29, 1971 Mother; William T. E. Dec. 12, 1887 Aug. 20, 1856 Father

Howard TRUSSELL Born Aug. 3, 1833 Died Oct. 24, 1903 Father *(C.S.A. marker)*
Lucy E. TRUSSELL Born May 12, 1848 Died Dec. 5, 1912 Mother
Panama TRUSSELL 1884–1958
TRUSSELL Delia DOVE May 23, 1882 June 15, 1958; Francis M. Nov. 1, 1882 July 26, 1971
M. S. G. & A. T. G. footstones

Alfred Kent GREEN Mar. 7, 1856 May 16, 1944
Elizabeth RICE Wife of Alfred K. GREEN April 1, 1864 July 27, 1949
W. W. GREEN

JEFFRIES - GRIMES Plot:
GRIMES George R. 1898–1971; Chrystal E. 1905
Baby Annie Elizabeth daug. of M. W. & J. E. GRIMES Nov. 5 & 6 , 1896
George J. GRIMES Feb. 18, 1866 Oct. 7, 1931 age 65 years 8 mos. 11 ds.
Bertha Virginia Daughter of G. J. & A. V. GRIMES Sept. 26, 1888 April 1, 1912 aged 24 yrs. 5 mos. 25 ds.; James E. GRIMES 1874–1942; Eliz. LEACH GRIMES 1871–1960; McNeece E. GRIMES 1939–1939; McNeece W. GRIMES 1899–1970; Josie G. HUTCHISON 1913–; J. E. GRIMES
NEFF John M. 1876–1952; Daisie M. 1879–1963
Shelby J. NEFF 1936–1938

Maggie I. Wife of W. W. LEACH Feb. 19, 1869 Mar. 21, 1911; Children of W. W. & M. I. LEACH Wade H. Aug. 28, 1891 Aug. 9, 1893; Mary M. Aug. 1, 1892 Aug. 18, 1893; James E. Oct. 23, 1900; Roberta V. D. Jan. 15, 1908
Annie C. Wife of T. B. LEACH Born Oct. 23, 1871 Died Mar. 4, 1891
LEACH Rosie H. 1875–1954 J. Thomas

R. C. LUCIUS Co. B Mosby's Virginia Cav. C.S.A.
Martha E. DUNBAR Died Feb. 12, 1907 aged 78 years; T. S. DUNBAR Died July 20, 1908 aged 83 years; John DUNBAR Died June 16, 1868 aged 75 years; Lydia DUNBAR Died Oct. 2, 1886 aged 96 years; John A. DUNBAR Died June 13, 1879 aged 46 years

Elizabeth A. HANES Born April 8, 1812 Died Feb. 17, 1909; Ella V. HANES Born June 3, 1845 Died April 3, 1915; H. S. HANES Born Nov. 8, 1852 Died Aug. 23, 1917

William C. GIBSON Nov. 18, 1845 Dec. 18, 1925
Mary J. GIBSON Mar. 10, 1848 Nov. 18, 1934

FLEMING T. William Feb. 3, 1908 July 13, 1983; C. ODEAN Nov. 13, 1912

Boulder monument, no inscription
LARRICK Richard R. 1875–1957; Mary DUNBAR 1877–1949

Margaret Pickering TEELE Died Sept. 23, 1962 aged 85 *(missing 1988 & 1993) (fhm)*
Father Reuben B. EMBREY 1852–
Mother Josephine EMBREY 1853–1927
A. F. ROBEY Born Sept. 6, 1810 Died Mar. 27, 1894
Sarah E. Wife of William S. ROBEY Born April 6, 1851 Died April 11, 1893
Mary Jane Wife of William S. ROBEY Born Nov. 10, 1854 Died April 30, 1897

J. W. GRIMES Born Dec. 24, 1831 Died April 5, 1892; Mary JOHNSTON Wife of J. W. GRIMES Born Jan. 13, 1836 Died Oct. 1, 1914 Daughter of J. W. & M. J. JOHNSTON who was a Daughter of Geo. J. JOHNSTON who was a Revolutionary soldier buried with honor of war Charles Town Presbyterian Church yard Evie Roberta Daughter of J. W. & M. J. GRIMES Dec. 12, 1872 April 26, 1894 Inez Newton Daughter of J. W. & M. J. GRIMES Oct. 27, 1882 Sept. 10, 1896

Horace Milton Son of W. E & M. P. MILLER Died Jan. 27, 1892 aged 29 days
William E. MILLER Sept. 3, 1865 Oct. 5, 1952
Mattie P. Wife of W. E. MILLER Born July 8, 1868 Died April 19, 1896
Hugh P. MILLER 1893–1975

SLATER Hylton RUCKER Oct. 1, 1912 Apr. 30, 1983; Thomas Glascock Aug. 14, 1908 Apr. 19, 1984

Laura Battaile KERRICK Wife of C. C. KERRICK Born June 18, 1839 Died Nov. 27, 1907

Chas. C. KERRICK Born Apr. 7, 1852 Died Oct. 8, 1900

John W. GREEN Born Feb. 18, 1844 Died Dec. 6, 1919 *(C.S.A. marker)*
Eliza H. Wife of J. W. GREEN Born Oct. 16, 1854 Died Dec. 16, 1935
William A. Son of J. W. & Addie GREEN Died Oct. 16, 1904 aged 18 years
William J. Son of Monte & Mary G. LLOYD Oct. 8, 1930 Nov. 2, 1935

William L. EMBREY May 16, 1917 May 5, 1990
EMBREY Joseph A. 1879–1925; Alice C. 1882–1969
LLOYD Mary G. Dec. 14, 1899 Mar. 1, 1977; Monte F. Oct. 9, 1900 Dec. 8, 1979 *(Masonic emblem)*
EMBREY Carroll June 30, 1905 October 21, 1975

Our Father & Mother Romulus R. RIDGEWAY 1822–1899; His Wife Elizabeth STILLIONS 1824–1907
James William RIDGEWAY Died April 28, 1863 aged 35 *(missing 1988 & 1993)*

Henry J. aged 35 years; Wm. W. aged 23 years; sons of J. A. & H. J. HUFF

Katie Wife of J. E. JACKSON Died May 5, 1907 aged 29 years

CARTER Sallie L. 1869–1956; Turner A. 1859–1938

Herbert MANN Son of M. M. & J. L. M. BALL born Sept. 24, 1906 died Jan. 5, 1910
Addie P. NALLS 1866–1915
John T. NALLS 1854–1936
Pearl D. NALLS 1889–1950
Mother Gladys V. YOWELL 1918–1957; Edgar Warren NALLS US ARMY KOREA Oct 12 1920 Feb 6 1984

Ethel CLARKE NALLS Mar. 4, 1894 July 21, 1979 Mother
John Preston NALLS Aug. 31, 1893 Nov. 16, 1966 Father

WILLIAMS Ruth E. 1895–1988; Thomas E. 1889–1961
James Henry WILLIAMS Died June 3, 1960 aged 94 years *(stone face down 1988 & 1993)*
Melville Wife of J. Henry WILLIAMS Died Jan. 8, 1912 aged 44 years 11 months 6 dys

Wm. E. BALL CO. C. USMTD RIFLES MEX. WAR
Harriet B. BALL Wife of Wm. E. BALL Born Feb. 13, 1831 Died Sept. 19, 1910
Father Humphrey Marshall BALL Oct. 10, 1867 Dec. 27, 1912
Mother Lillian LUNCEFORD BALL July 15, 1871 May 22, 1944
Son Phillip Preston BALL Dec. 16, 1909 Mar. 11, 1962

John Thomas SLACK July 17, 1841 July 9, 1907; His Wife Ann Cornelia Jane Aug. 12, 1842 Jan. 20, 1917
SLACK Belle G. 1889–1932; Walter H. 1874–1940
Ann Belinda SLACK Oct. 23, 1872 Nov. 23, 1965
Frederick Thomas SLACK CPL US ARMY WORLD WAR II Jan 1 1922 Apr 5 1985
SLACK Corinne H.[HINSON] July 7, 1916; Richard H. June 30, 1917 July 7, 1977

Geo. Raymond THOMAS Son of Clinton & Betty THOMAS July 8, 1905 December 12, 1955
CLOTHIER Mary E. 1860–1937
Nimrod SHAFER Mar. 28, 1851 Mar. 28, 1937; Martha HAUS His Wife Sept. 7, 1854 Jan. 16, 1933
Fred THOMAS Died Sept. 23, 1912 aged 21 mos 9 ds
Chas. Wilton BUCKNER Son of Chas. & Elizabeth BUCKNER 1913–1943
THOMAS Betty SHAFFER May 10, 1869 March 10, 1956; Albert Clinton October 26, 1862 February 17, 1947
Elizabeth T. KIDWELL 1892–1972

McRAE Maj. John Hampden C.S.A. 1824–1904; His Wife Sheldena Amanda BEACH 1840–1922; Children Euphan
    Washington PH. B. M. A. M. Ed. 1862–1935; Martha Beach 1868–1950; Sheldena Amanda CLARK 1874–1911;
    Richard Moncure, M. D. 1877–1957
Dr. Pierre Numa CHARBONNET Oct. 19, 1894 Feb. 1954; His Wife Blanche Joan CHARBONNET May 20, 1893
    July 9, 1972; Matilda Charbonnet LIEBEL October 5, 1925 July 26, 1983
HARPER Frances 1798–1878; Joel Zane 1794–1864 John W. 1831–1898
Frances Wife of Joel Z. HARPER Born May 1, 1798 Died Dec. 3, 1878
Joel Zane HARPER Born May 7, 1794 Died Oct. 18, 1864; John W. HARPER Born 1831 Died Jan. 16, 1898 aged
    63 years
Sarah Marye HARPER Died Oct. 24, 1911
Frances [HARPER] age 70 years May 1, 1799 Dec. 5, 1878

Henry Arthur HALL Born Crednal, Va. April 15, 1825 Died Clermont, Va. April 16, 1913; and His Wife Susan
    Fitzhugh GRAYSON Born Newstead, Va. May ,13, 1835 Died Clermont, Va. Jany. 19, 1914
Robert Carter HALL Born Oct. 22, 1862 Died Dec. 30, 1931
James D. HALL Born near Upperville, Va. Mar. 19, 1867 Died Grasslands near Linden, Va. Jany. 15, 1914
Edward D. HALL Born Grasslands near Linden, Va. Dec. 6, 1869 Died Philadelphia, Pa. April 23, 1906
Louisa HALL RINKER Born Aug. 15, 1871 Died Nov. 8, 1961

Ella Lee GRIMES Born & Died 1922
GRIMES Ada B. June 6, 1900 September 10, 1961 Mother; Thomas E. August 14, 1890 June 10, 1964 Father
NALLS Sam April 4, 1918 Ethel G. Jan. 20, 1922

William Carroll Son of A. C. & E. A. ELLIS Born Dec. 2, 1911 Died Feb. 23, 1915
ELLIS Edith PAYNE 1892–1931; Ruby ELLIS PIERCE 1916; Jesse Lee 1917–1984

Benjamin Arthur GULLICK S. SGT US ARMY WORLD WAR II Aug 8 1906 July 20 1988
John Samuel OWENS VIRGINIA PFC US ARMY WORLD WAR II Nov 22 1924 Aug 11 1973
Leslie H. OWENS PFC US ARMY Aug 6 1887 Nov 11 1974
Ella G. OWENS 1909–1990
Edwin H. OWENS 1895–1968
PEARSON Randolph F. 1906–1970; Hester H. 1907

James H. COSTELLO Dec. 26, 1846 Jan. 30, 1928; Sarah C. His Wife Sept. 28, 1872

HINSON Maurice M. 1920–1937; Wilbur S. 1881–1958; Kate G. 1883–1937
Linda Sue dau. of E. C. & B. M. KINSLER 1961
HINSON Neville G. Mar. 16, 1912 May 24, 1977; Ethel M. Feb. 28, 1914 Oct. 7, 1987

THOMAS Plot:
Leslie GRAY WRIGHT Died April 25, 1964 age 82 years Mother
John Robert WRIGHT Died May 28, 1966 aged 87 years
Curtis H. WRIGHT 1939–1956
Aubrey Stanton THOMAS Feb. 15, 1889 Feb. 14, 1983

M. Cornelia LARRICK 1907–1963
Frances LARRICK ARRIGONI Sept. 30, 1905 Mar. 26, 1956
Lydia E. REID November 5, 1872 April 12, 1963
Harold J. ARRIGONI Oct. 27, 1903 Oct. 28, 1986

Bertram Carroll TAVENNER October 3, 1904 October 1, 1955
CORRIE John W. 1894–1962; Evelyn T. 1900–1948
Walter Elbert SAUNDERS January 30, 1895 April 18, 1951; Margaret Thelma Oct. 7, 1901 Apr. 21, 1977
Margaret LOMA TAVENNER November 23, 1873 July 17, 1949
Dodge TAVENNER August 18, 1874 February 28, 1939
Herbert E. CORRIE 1900–1953
Charles W. SCHAFFER Feb. 12, 1909 Oct. 2, 1964
Dorothy SCHAFFER GOODWIN Feb. 10, 1913 Jan. 30, 1979
Thomas A. SHAFFER July 15, 1910 November 30, 1981

Lewis Addison ARMISTEAD Son of Elizabeth MARSHALL and Capt. Bowles Edward ARMISTEAD Born
    January 2, 1876 Died November 18, 1943 *(stone found broken 1988 & 1993)*
Capt. Bowles Edward ARMISTEAD Son of Geo. Walker Keith ARMISTEAD and Elizabeth STANLEY April 26,
    1838 Oct. 16, 1916 *(stone found broken 1988 & 1993)*
Elizabeth LEWIS ARMISTEAD Wife of Capt. B. E. ARMISTEAD Daughter of Henry Morris MARSHALL and
    Elizabeth Whiting BROOKE May 25, 1846 Dec. 10, 1919

Confederate monument:(soldiers killed in battle at Upperville.Erected 1894 by Upperville Confederate veterans)
E. HANMON, N A. McDANIEL, N S. TARRAINES, N S. P. FINK, N T. HIGGINS, N A. F. KING, N A. M.
    SHEFFIELD, Ga.; S. S. RICE, Va.; I. C. EDWARDS, Va.; F. J. DUNSTON, Va.; BALL,   Va.; C.
    MITTIER, Va.; A. J. HOOD, S W. D. HOLLAND, [S]; 2 unknown

William Walter GULICK 1876–1958
Mildred STROTHER GULICK 1884–1954
Attaway WITHERS GULICK Daughter of Margaret Ann BAGGOTT and Walter WITHERS Born in
    Fredericksburg, Va. Dec. 9, 1843 Died July 28, 1920
Julia TOLSON GULICK 1871–1929
Katherine WITHERS GULICK 1882–1977

L. A. ASHBY 1850–1923
Capt. J. T. ASHBY, C.S.A. 1841–1928 *(C.S.A. marker)*
ASHBY H. J. 1884–1928
Frances G. MARSHALL 1872–1968
Sallie J. ASHBURY 1880–1972

TAVENNER Lycurgus Oct. 29, 1871 July 14, 1952; Belle THOMPSON April 3, 1872 Mar. 22, 1966
TAVENNER Thomas H. Oct. 22, 1908 Feb. 20, 1971; Hilda V. March 31, 1921
JONES Charles Hill Jan. 22, 1897 Mar. 22, 1981

POWERS Wife September 17, 1905 Ann joined God's angels 3/21/[19]92
Henry J. PILLION 1926–1963
H. Bradley DAVIDSON, Jr. Sept. 10, 1892 Aug. 8, 1972 BETHESDA MARYLAND WORLD WAR I - WORLD
   WAR II LT. COLONEL *(VFW marker)*
LEE Grover C. 1893–1926; A. Ethel 1895–1967

Fenton A. THOMAS Oct. 25, 1927 Sept. 24, 1988
THOMAS Alice K. 1898–1919; Joseph L. 1894–1967
David Ferguson THOMAS May 24, 1937 April 10, 1984
stone cross, no inscription
Curtis H. THOMAS 1939–1956
Aubrey Fenton THOMAS Feb. 15, 1889 Feb. 14, 1983
WRIGHT: Mother Lissie GRAY Father John Robert

Bertha LARRICK MILLER Aug. 7, 1909 Aug. 13, 1988
Baby MILLER 1967 *(marker missing 1988)*
Leslie P. BURDEN July 1, 1949 July 5, 1988 Granddaughter of Anne T. DAVIS Daughter of Rhoda D. [DAVIS]
   BURDEN Mother of Leo K. NAPIOR
RUSSELL Harvey H. Jan. 10, 1887 Jan. 8, 1980; Caroline V. Feb. 27, 1894 Sept. 7, 1954
Lurline TINSLEY Feb. 22, 1897 May 2, 1940
Anna T. DAVIS May 18, 1892 Jan. 23, 1980
T. Brody TINSLEY May 18, 1892 Aug. 29, 1976
Thomas B. TINSLEY, Jr. June 15, 1916 May 31, 1971 *(Masonic emblem)*

Sarah V. Wife of James P. YOWELL 1868–1943
Amy YOWELL MILTON 1930–1963
YOWELL Infant 1920; Infant 1921; Infant 1940
Hazel Lee YOWELL 1928–1929
Kenneth Ray YOWELL 1935–1971
James Edward YOWELL US ARMY WORLD WAR II Oct 2 1888 Nov 8 1983

James M.[Morris] HATCHER 1872–1946; Lucy R.[RUST] HATCHER 1873–1947
Lily ADAMS Born prior to 1860 died 1930
Maysie HATCHER WARREN 1902–1979
James M. HATCHER, Jr. Mar. 19, 1906 Mar. 13, 1985
TIPPETT Colonel C. J. Feb. 14, 1913; Mary Elizabeth June 18, 1906 Oct. 30, 1988

ASHWORTH Frederick L. 1925– ; Katherine K. 1923–1975
Charles Ray MORRIS, Sr. Nov. 8, 1914 May 8, 1981
McELROY Rev. Charles Wm. Sept. 3, 1874 Aug. 11, 1949; Jenny Emma Aug. 26, 1874 Feb. 17, 1968
MOATEN F. Morris VIRGINIA PVT QUARTERMASTER CORPS WORLD WAR II Sept 30 1909 Feb 27 1955
Elizabeth C. MORRIS Sept. 4, 1911 Aug. 25, 1955

Stump by Confederate Monument:

Arthur L. CHEEKE April 22, 1905 Oct. 16, 1966

Rev. Edward B. BURWELL Born Feb. 25, 1857 Died Feb. 24, 1945 Son of J. Armistead BURWELL and Lucy Penn GUY; Rosa B. SNEED Born April 16, 1860 Died Jan. 2, 1946 Wife of Rev. Edward B. BURWELL Daughter of William B. SNEED and Louisa Ann HOWARD

John Armistead BURWELL Son of Rev. Edward B. and Rosa SNEED BURWELL April 16, 1891 December 20, 1953

Mary POWELL BURWELL Wife of John Armistead BURWELL Daughter of Robert B. and Anne BURWELL POWELL March 18, 1906 September 10, 1988

Howard Spotswood BURWELL Son of Rev. Edward B. BURWELL and Rosa SNEED BURWELL June 27, 1900 Aug. 14, 1959

BURWELL Mary Elmslie SCOTT Aug. 5, 1912 May 15, 1991; Edward Bouldin BURWELL, Jr. Dec. 17, 1894 March 20, 1964

Isham KEITH beloved Husband of Lucy Guy BURWELL Son of Julian Chilton KEITH and Mary Alberta LAPSLEY June 22, 1897 August 23, 1979

Lucy Guy BURWELL KEITH Wife of Isham KEITH Daughter of Rev. Edward B. BURWELL and Rosa B. SNEED January 2, 1890 Aug. 22, 1989

Mary Armistead BURWELL Mar. 18, 1968 Sept. 19, 1969 little Daughter of Ethel OGDEN and John Armistead BURWELL, Jr.

William Sneed Conrad BURWELL Son of Rev. Edward B. BURWELL and Rosa S. BURWELL November 29, 1904 November 13, 1971

Mabel Eleanor HIBBERT Wife of Howard Spotswood BURWELL March 27, 1904 July 5, 1982

GREYER Mamie [Virginia CHAPPELEAR] May 22, 1876 Jan. 5, 1946 Charles P.[Peyton] Mar. 22, 1876 Oct. 5, 1940

Mary CLEGG Sept 8, 1934

Joseph W. Mar. 31, 1911 Aug, 18, 1889

William TAYLOE TEC 4 US ARMY WORLD WAR II Jan 10 1917 Jul 8 1990

H. Gwynne TAYLOE of Mt. Airy May 3, 1874 January 4, 1961

Grace LEMMON TAYLOE Wife of H. Gwynne TAYLOE November 7, 1881 November 4, 1967

OWENS Nellie B. 1891–1959; Harry T. 1891–1979

Thomas F. OWENS 1912–1963 Age 51

Daniel H. EDMONDS 1888–1964 Age 76

William F. OWENS S2 US NAVY WORLD WAR II Dec 20 1916 May 6 1985

PEARSON William H. 1886–1975; Corrie O.[OWENS] 1893–1984

Raymond S. OWENS, Jr. Oct. 18, 1962 March 11, 1982

Helen POWERS de BUTTS Wife of Richard Earle de BUTTS, M. D. Born Shrewsbury, NJ September 19, 1922 July 5, 1979

Constance W. GLAYSHER 1905–1987

George W. GLAYSHER 1900–1977

Virginia Eugenia GRANT Died Oct. 11, 1965 aged 98 yrs 6 mos. *(missing 1988)*

Daniel Delaney de BUTTS Son of Dulaney Forrest & Emma ASHBY de BUTTS March 14, 1906 September 30, 1968

William Hunter de BUTTS Son of Forrest and Emma ASHBY de BUTTS October 23, 1899 November 23, 1987

HOWREY Edward F. Sept. 5, 1903 May 27, 1991

Robert Vanderpoel CLARK, Jr. October 2, 1940 October 4, 1964

Robert Eugene COX July 3, 1914 Oct. 22, 1965

Dorothy Louise WATERS April 18, 1965
Suzanne DeLASALLE CLARK Wife of Robert V. CLARK Aug. 20, 1901 Sept. 2, 1982 Born Lille France

Mother Afton Delois BRADY June 14, 1916 April 4, 1960
Father Thurman V. BRADY July 13, 1910 November 10, 1987
Betty H. SCARLETT Oct. 10, 1919 Aug. 22, 1962
Alice B. COLEMAN Jan. 26, 1906 Nov. 21, 1974
Fannie EMBREY DENNIS Sept. 10, 1903 May 1, 1988
Eugene B. DENNIS Feb. 5, 1911 Nov. 10, 1968
ROSE Mary S. 1910; Fred C. 1905 –1972
Ruben E. BUDD 1913–1968
THOMAS Alice K. 1898–1974; Joseph L. 1894–1967
Hubert B. PHIPPS November 12, 1905 August 15, 1969
Arthur Henry ADAMS III Dec. 12, 1924 Nov. 8, 1966; Arthur Henry ADAMS Oct. 16, 1891 June 18, 1931
GRIMES Willie A. 1912–1968
Harvey R. TRUSSELL 1936–1962
O'BANNON Harry Lee January 19, 1888 July 14, 1960; Annie WINE February 24, 1890 January 22, 1970
George T. O'BANNON VIRGINIA PFC CO E 290 INFANTRY WORLD WAR II Sept 4 1917 June 18 1971
Mother Kittie G. JOHNSON August 29, 1909 June 15, 1988
Rozier E. LUNCEFORD, Jr. VIRGINIA PVT 22 TRP CARR SC AAF WORLD WAR II Sept 25 1928 Aug 20
    1968
Rozier E. LUNCEFORD Apr. 20, 1904 Feb. 12, 1976
Anita Louise LUNCEFORD Dec. 5, 1966 Aug. 20, 1968
Father Thomas W. ROSE Dec. 29, 1918 June 13, 1968
Daisy HUFF MITCHELL Nov. 8, 1888 Jan. 22, 1962
Walter Armstead JOHNSON 1885–1960
Larry D. ROSE Jan. 2–3, 1959

William Jackson MANN, Jr. Born Fauquier County, Virginia July 12, 1888 Died & Baltimore County, Md. March
    30, 1958
Emma Jessimond GAMBLE Wife of Charles Harrison MANN Daughter of Elisha F. Jackson GAMBLE and Annie
    HARRISON His Wife Born Natchitochee Parish Louisiana November 16, 1879 Died Jacksonville, Florida March
    30, 1954
Charles Harrison MANN Son of William Jackson MANN and Sally Bruce SMITH His Wife Born Fauquier County,
    Virginia September 15, 1882 Died Jacksonville, Florida November 21, 1967
MANN Amy RINKER December 12, 1891 August 28, 1973; Thomas Armistead January 7, 1894 June 14, 1977
Elizabeth BOUGHER SILITCH 1908–1976
G. Clarke WATSON 1907–1966
George Riggs GAITHER 1883–1953
James Francis TINSMAN June 2, 1915 Feb. 5, 1990
Ethel LEMMON GAITHER 1885–1960
George Edward Tabb Son of Wm. J. & Sally B. MANN Born Oct. 4th 1880 Died Aug. 24, 1917
Martha Tabb dau. of Wm. J. & Sally B. MANN Born Apr. 7, 1878 Died Mar. 8, 1893
William Jackson MANN Born Feb. 23rd 1843 Gloucester C.H., Va. Son of Rev. Charles MANN and Mary
    Congreve JACKSON Died Feb. 9, 1930 Granite, Md. a private in the Second Cavalry of Richmond Howitzers
    C.S.A. 1862–1865
Sally Bruce MANN Wife of William Jackson MANN Born Glen Roy, Gloucester County, Virginia Sept. 23, 1851
    Daughter of William Patterson SMITH and Marion Morsen Andrea SEDDON His Wife Died Oct. 27, 1937
Lizzie Jackson Daughter of Charles & Mary MANN Born Dec. 8, 1832 Died July 11, 1900
MANN Charles Harrison, Jr. Son of Jessimond GAMBLE and Charles Harrison MANN Introduced legislation
    creating George Mason University January 15, 1908 died Arlington, Va. November 28, 1977; Frances HART
    Daughter of Lavela SLICER and George Luzerne HART Born Roanoke, Va. July 8, 1909 died Alexandria Va.

Oct. 3, 1990

HART Lavela SLICER 1878–1961 *(D.A.R. marker)* Born Fincastle, Va. Daughter of Carrie Hale CARPER, Fincastle, Va. 1856–1947 and John Neff SLICER Lonaconing, Md. 1854–1926 Interred Fincastle, Va.; George Luzerne 1874–1968 Born Corning, N.Y. Son of Pluma THAYER, Linesville, Pa. 1839–1916 and Dr. Henry Clay HART, Wayne, Ohio 1837–1919 interred Roanoke, Va.

Infant Son of George & Lavela HART May 17, 1903 interred Fincastle, Va.

GATES Thomas L.; Betty MANN Daughter of Frances HART MANN and Charles; Harrison MANN, Jr. Born Sept. 14, 1936 Died Feb. 16, 1986

Mary Maria Daughter of Charles & Mary MANN Born Dec. 8, 1832 Died July 11, 1900

Lorie Ann BUDD Died 1-13-65 [1965] Aged 4 yrs. 3 mos. 12 days

Alice Ellen RECTOR February 3, 1964

Daughter Ethel YOWELL KINES 1893–1931

James P. YOWELL Husband of Sarah V. YOWELL 1858–1950

Ada C. dau. of J. P. & S. YOWELL Nov. 18, 1902 Dec. 5, 1903

Ernest L. Son of J. P. & S. YOWELL July 4, 1889 Sept. 3, 1904

Lester N. Son of J. P. & S. YOWELL Feb. 26, 1910 June 22, 1916

Ludwell LEE Died Aug. 27, 1905 aged 63 years

Taylor Scott HARDIN March 26, 1904 September 18, 1976; Katherine BLISS HARDIN June 30, 1901 June 12, 1977

Geoffrey Hart HARTWOOD died November 16, 1987 aged 37 years 0 months 29 days *(fhm)*

HOWREY Edward F. Sept. 6, 1903 Jane Gould Aug. 31, 1903 May 27, 1991

Thomas Monroe GOULD May 1, 1966 June 19, 1990

Roger J. WILLIAMS Dec. 31, 1932 Dec. 8, 1987; Charlotte M. Dec. 3, 1935

Charles V. B. CUSHMAN LT COL US AIR FORCE WORLD WAR II KOREA May 4 1902 Jan 13 1987

William Hunter de BUTTS Son of Dulaney Forrest and Emma ASHBY de BUTTS October 23, 1899 November 23, 1987

ARCHBOLD-SAUNDERSON of County Cavan, Ireland Plot:

Anne MILLS ARCHBOLD Born November 24, 1873 Titusville, Pennsylvania Wife of Armar Dayrolles SAUNDERSON 1906–1922 Died March 26, 1968 Nassau, Bahamas Mother of Lydia, Armar, John, Moira

Armar Edward ARCHBOLD 1909–1957

Bertrande BENOIST ARCHBOLD beloved Wife of John Dana ARCHBOLD Daughter of Geraldine Grace & Louis Auguste BENOIST Born October 2, 1931 San Francisco, California Died April 8, 1966

Infant Son of John & Bertrande ARCHBOLD November 23, 1962

William Cabell GRAYSON of Blue Ridge Farm May 28, 1921 April 15, 1980

Moira ARCHBOLD born July 9, 1911 Santa Barbara, CA died March 30, 1988 Washington, DC former Wife of F. Nicol SMITH

West Side:

Robert D. GOLDEN June 14, 1918

Helen R. GOLDEN Oct. 3, 1895 Dec. 7, 1974

Walter D. GOLDEN Mar. 12, 1895 Dec. 22, 1988

Alice L. GOLDEN Jan. 17, 1863 Jan. 19, 1952

William J. GOLDEN Aug. 16, 1865 Jan. 3, 1946

Richard Lee JONES 1949–1967

GOLDEN Virginia R. 1894–1961; George W. 1887–1971

Ruby L. GOLDEN 1923–1937

Infant Fred GOLDEN 1917

Paul F. LACKEY June 19, 1911 May 24 1913 Moses R. LACKEY Feb. 21, 1915 July 29, 1922 Moses F. P.
   LACKEY May 11, 1886 Jan. 3d 1921
Thomas W. LACKEY US ARMY WORLD WAR II 1912–1979
Paul F. LACKEY June 19, 1911 May 24, 1913
Moses R. LACKEY Feb. 21, 1915 July 29, 1922

Harold Hubert SMALLWOOD Jan. 17, 1918 July 19, 1918
Carrie HARRIS SMALLWOOD 1850–1934
Thomas William SMALLWOOD 1856–1941
Joseph Earl SMALLWOOD 1879–1945
Nina LANHAM SMALLWOOD 1878–1969; Little Nina Daughter of R. L. & R. M. SMALLWOOD 1956–1961
Elizabeth S. WHEELER 1910–1983

KERNS Plot:
F. L. KERNS March 30, 1859 Oct. 4, 1923,Josephine KERNS Dec. 5, 1862 Dec. 10, 1940
Charles W. EDWARDS 1881–1953,Evelyn B. Wife of C. W. EDWARDS 1891–1933
William E. KERNS Feb. 16, 1888 Apr. 8, 1943

M. Moselle GRIMES March 30, 1886 April 26, 1956
Agnes K. SMALLWOOD Mar. 18, 1898 Mar. 22, 1965
George F. SMALLWOOD Oct. 21, 1892 Nov. 19, 1943
George SMALLWOOD, Jr. June 7, 1937 June 15, 1948
Hugh C. GRIMES July 2, 1884 July 25, 1957

George F. CHAPELLE Jan. 5, 1879 Mar. 28, 1948
Ethel M. CHAPPELLE Dec. 23, 1878 Aug. 2, 1966
Mary Agnes WELSH Feb. 2, 1866 Jan. 12, 1952
ANDERSON Y. Consuelo June 10, 1903 Oct. 10, 1985
ANDERSON James Gilmore July 20, 1884 Apr. 25, 1964
ANDERSON James Gary Jan. 7, 1936 Oct. 25, 1954
Virginia A. Wife of Samuel S. PECK July 28, 1858 Oct. 30, 1919
Mary A. LYNCH nee GEIMAN Jan. 8, 1837 Oct. 8, 1928

RAWLINGS Plot:
Infant Arthur A. RAWLINGS Oct. 21, 1873 Aug. 25, 1923
Laura P. RAWLINGS Aug. 26, 1871 May 28, 1953
John C. RAWLINGS Dec. 10, 1904 April 19, 1942
Cordelia RAWLINGS June 16, 1906 March 23, 1969

Thurston B. WILLIS US ARMY WORLD WAR I Oct 23 1897 Sep 26 1978
Amy MOORE WILLIS July 16 1899 January 15 1982

WOOLF James F. Nov. 7, 1897 April 28, 1948; Lula M. Aug. 29, 1900 Jan. 26, 1978
D. E. GREEN Born Aug. 11, 1879 Died Jan. 9, 1922; Daniel H. GREEN Born Nov. 10, 1835 Died Jan. 31, 1917;
   Mary E. GREEN Born Sept. 14, 1837 Died Feb. 8, 1899
Frances Katherine FANTASKI Dec. 5, 1921 Dec. 2, 1977
Cleon Luck WOOLF March 10, 1898 Feb. 26, 1978; LISTON Edward Richard 1903–1965; Blanche M. 1910–1976

Conrad Pendleton KINCHELOE April 8, 1914 July 22, 1967
HUFF Charles William 1924–1942 Son

116

Son Emmett L. McGUINN 1887–19
Daughter Agnes McG. BRADY 1904
J. W. McGUINN June 25, 1851 March 17, 1917 ·
Son Norman D. McGUINN 1902–1962
Jerry Strother B. McGUINN 1901–1936
Strother F. McGUINN 1942–1945
Mother Adella C. McGUINN 1867–1952
Father John W. McGUINN 1851–1917

S. Rebecca GREEN Born Jan. 27, 1858 Died Dec. 20, 1935
William JARDINE beloved Husband of Alice JARDINE Born Mar. 24, 1853 Dumbartonshire, Scotland Died Dec.
  8, 1916 Upperville, Va.

H. W. THOMPSON Born Sept. 6, 1867 Died July 16, 1918
Emma R. THOMPSON March 21, 1870 Aug. 4, 1925
Baylis John THOMPSON Dec. 27, 1892 Jan. 22, 1968; Jennie Mae Jan. 17, 1904 Nov. 7, 1984
Florence M. LANHAM October 4, 1890 June 23, 1976

Welby J. HALL 1895–1943
Phoebia E. LOCKE 1878–1960
Welby Thompson HALL VIRGINIA TEC5 BTRY B 247 AAA SL BN WORLD WAR II Sept 7 1920 April 9 1969

SMALLWOOD Benjamin F. 1872–1920
Ella V. THOMPSON Jan. 21, 1884 Jan. 30, 1963
Mary E. THOMPSON Sept. 3, 1864 Jan. 11, 1949
John P. THOMPSON Nov. 24, 1852 June 16, 1924
Leda E. THOMPSON Wife of Carl E. HUGHES Feb. 14, 1901 Feb. 19, 1933
THOMPSON Hubert W. Mar. 14, 1886 Jan. 30, 1971; Julia F. May 26, 1883 Jan. 28, 1966

SWART James W. 1883–1947; Maude J. 1886–1967

John F. LANHAM 1891–1930; Nellie E. LANHAM 1899–1988
Herman R. LANHAM February 13, 1891 December 3, 1945; Nellie E. LANHAM MARTZ 1899–1988
LANHAM Anna H. Mar. 7, 1867 Sept. 20, 1920; John W. Apr. 28, 1857 Dec. 13, 1939

Madge LAUGHLIN Mother of John LAUGHLIN 1885–1974 *(missing 1993)*
LEWIS John T. 1906–1972; Grace B. 1912–1968
LEWIS William Henry Feb. 22, 1865 Jan. 29, 1940; Wife Alys TURNER May 2, 1873 Feb. 10, 1951 *(U.D marker)*
LAUGHLIN John 1907–1958; Louise L. 1910 VIRGINIA TEC5 ENGINEER WORLD WAR II
LEWIS William Franklin Feb. 13, 1901 Oct. 13, 1979; beloved Wife Rubye E. COATES Oct. 3, 1900 Nov. 5, 1925
Infant dau. of Ruby C. & W. F. LEWIS Born & Died Oct. 13, 1925

MAUCK Catherine 1914–1964; Morton S. 1893–1966
Grace SHAFFER 1886–1976 Mother
George KEMP 1876–1957
Lewis RECTOR June 27, 1883 July 18, 1963
Mamie T. RECTOR Dec. 23, 1883 Nov. 30, 1950
Helen Theresa Daughter of Louis and Mamie RECTOR Born Mar. 22, 1917 Died Aug. 29, 1917
SISK Smith H. 1887–1966; Emma E. 1892–1962
Charles F. SISK Oct. 19, 1924 Dec. 14, 1924
Phyllis RAY 1934–1940
HINSON Bessie J. 1884–1958; Claude C. 1883–1936

HINSON James E. 1830–1903; Mary A. 1856–1941
HINSON Ambrose B. Mar. 6, 1895 Oct. 31, 1970; Addie G. [GREEN] Oct. 31, 1896 Mar. 19, 1980
Thomas PAYNE Dec. 25, 1881 May 10, 1949 Father
Pearl C. PAYNE Jan. 29, 1885 Sept. 1, 1957 Mother
Carlton J. PAYNE Feb. 11, 1902 Nov. 24, 1973; Mae P. PAYNE Oct. 7, 1904

Joseph R. CORDER VIRGINIA PVT US ARMY WORLD WAR I Sept 14 1893 June 18 1970
Charles William HUFF 1924–1942; Elva S. 1906–1981; W. Andrew 1897–1963
PFC George B. SMALLWOOD 1907–1947
Margaret Lanham CORDER June 26, 1911 Nov. 19, 1992
Moffett YOUNG Sept 9, 1904
Senah V. YOUNG Jan. 24, 1909 Sept 30, 1981
Mildred L. CUNNINGHAM Aug. 25, 1913 Mar. 18, 1946
JENKINS M. Louise Dec. 10, 1932; Claude R. Oct. 16, 1907 Jan. 15, 1987
Ada I. ASHBY 1899–1978 *(missing 1993)*
Calvin W. MORRIS VIRGINIA PFC 190 MIL POLICE CO WORLD WAR II BSM PH Aug 30 1912 March 19, 1959
Frida W. MORRIS 1908–1953
Arthur W. MORRIS 1917–1942
"Tipper" John H. MORRIS 1881–1967
Moaten F. MORRIS VIRGINIA PVT QUARTERMASTER CORPS WORLD WAR II Sept 30 1909 Feb 17 1935
Elizabeth C. MORRIS Sept. 4, 1911 Aug. 25, 1955
Charles Ray MORRIS, Sr. Nov. 8, 1914 May 8, 1981
Ida P. MORRIS 1887–1971
Homer H. MORRIS TEC5 US ARMY WORLD WAR II 1918 1981
E. Ackley STICKLES Feb. 7, 1909 Dec. 28, 1973
STICKLES Mary J. 1863–1934; Simon J. 1859–1938
THOMAS Edith 1905–; Shirley 1909–1977
ELLIS Alpheus O. 1860–1940; Lucy A. 1872–1962
Gregory S. PULLEN Mar. 15, 1971 Mar. 17, 1971
KENDALL George E. 1904–1954; His Wife Lillie G. 1900–1975
McELROY Rev. Charles Wm. Sept. 3, 1874 Aug. 11, 1949 *(Upperville Baptist :Church minister)*; Jenny Emma Aug. 26, 1874 Feb. 17, 1958

North side of drive:
Charles M. REID 1916–1989
Stephen D. THOMAS Feb. 27, 1957 Aug. 19, 1990
OLIVER "Jimmy" Roy W. Jr. Sept. 25, 1928 Oct. 3, 1990; Elizabeth A. L. "Annie" Apr. 10, 1928
Ernest D. MONEYMAKER 1939–1991 *(fhm)*
REID Beuford R. 1932–1990; Mary Ellen 1940
Garner D. HUFF US NAVY KOREA Jul 19 1933 Mar 11 1991
DENNIS Gloria Jean Sept. 21, 1965 Mar. 13, 1991
Henry L. KIRBY TEC 5 WORLD WAR II Apr. 12, 1914 Sept. 22, 1991; Betty D. Wife & Mother Aug. 30, 1930
Harry Alfred RUST August 15, 1902 April 24, 1989
GRIMES Kenneth L. Aug. 13, 1924; Mattie A. Sept. 24, 1920 Nov. 12, 1992
Thomas W. SUDDUTH 1942–1993 *(fhm)*
Elizabeth T. WHITE Wife & Mother Dec. 18, 1917 Feb. 7, 1991
Leslie E. SHOEMAKER US NAVY Sept 3 1919 Mar 7 1990
Jordan Elizabeth ROSE February 1, 1990 our precious with sunshine
Donald William ROSE "Little Donny" Oct. 19, 1987 Dec. 29, 1987
Hazel B. McCOY 1920–1992 *(fhm)*

Southwest Corner:
HINSON Thomas C. 1871–1949; Louisa G. 1879–1969
NEFF Carl M. 1904–1967 *(Masonic emblem)*; Louise H. 1915–1984
James W. HINSON Jan. 7, 1906 Feb. 24, 1954
HINSON Channing T. 1902–1976; Alice Rose 1910–1987
KING Saunders S. 1912–1984; Irene H. 1914–1962
HINSON Charles E. 1880–1967; Alice C. 1882–1954
GALE Thelma H. 1910–1970; James J. 1912–1983
Joseph M. HYNSON 1908–1984
HYNSON John E. 1901–1984; Jessie L. 1910–1988
George E. KIRKPATRICK May 26, 1947 March 31, 1985; Hans LIMBECK Jr. October 18, 1962 May 18, 1991
KIRKPATRICK James A. Dec. 11, 1873 Mar. 9, 1950; Grace M. Oct. 10, 1889 Dec. 27, 1981

PHILLIPS Pamela Kaye 1953–1968; Artemous 1917–1958
Joseph ROSE Nov. 27, 1876 June 13, 1946
Addie C. ROSE Oct. 9, 1880 Dec. 24, 1964
Minnie L. Wife of Thomas DENNIS *(rest in ground)*
John T. ROSE Sept. 10, 1904 Nov. 26, 1979
Opal E. ROSE Dec. 20, 1910 July 5, 1979
Ted R. ROSE Oct. 4, 1908 Oct. 2, 1978
Eliza R. ROSE Mar. 7, 1911 May 28, 1992
Jane Edna ADKINS 1912–1962
STRICKLAND Mary J. 1863–1934; Simon I. 1859–1938 Father

Wm. A.[Ambrose] RUCKER 1840–1928 *(C.S.A. marker)*
Annie C.[CHAPPELEAR] RUCKER Wife of Wm. A. RUCKER 1838–1922
Bayard A.[Ambrose] RUCKER July 28, 1877 Aug. 5, 1951
Minnie VARNER RUCKER Sept. 16, 1879 Dec. 9, 1960

Minnie THOMAS DELAPLANE March 26, 1865 Nov. 22, 1929
George Albert DELAPLANE Dec. 26, 1863 Dec. 15, 1937
George A. DELAPLANE Jr. June 6, 1892 Feb. 2, 1931
Minnie HALL DELAPLANE Aug. 31, 1893 July 15, 1970
John W. DELAPLANE CAPT US ARMY WORLD WAR I 1897 1977
Elizabeth NEWTON DELAPLANE Feb 7 1900 June 10 1981

SEATON Floyd Eugen Oct. 25, 1872 Nov. 14, 1943; Effie SAMPSELL Nov. 26, 1872 Nov. 11, 1938
Hazel S. ALLEN Wife of Dr. J. R. ALLEN Feb. 4, 1904 Jan. 13, 1957
Effie SEATON McCABE Wife of Thomas McCABE Sept. 1, 1901 Mar. 8, 1932
WINES Harry M. 1897–1965; Beatrice E. 1906–1985
Harry M. Son of H. M. & B. E. WINES Mar. 31, 1938 Jan. 9, 1939
Otto SCHMIDBAUER Oct. 28, 1909 Nov. 27, 1959
FARGIS Larnie B. 1902–1957; Pauline M. 1904–

Mother Mattie B. CHILDRESS May 15, 1889 Aug. 29, 1973
Daughter Rhonda Hope WILLIAMS July 16, 1951 Sept. 6, 1969
WILLIAMS Anna K. Feb. 12, 1923; Ralph Hutchinson PFC US ARMY WORLD WAR II Mar. 1 1911 Jul. 31 1981
LEE John Donald October 6, 1920 August 14, 1974; Jessie WILTSHIRE December 16, 1909 September 12, 1990
EMBREY Aquila I. June 15, 1856 March 1, 1936; Mary P. Sept. 12, 1862 May 20, 1935

Stevie F. ASHBY 1891–1949
Sgt. E. N. Dudley EMBREY VIRGINIA 116 INFANTRY Jan 15 1918 June 25 1945

Father Harvey C. EMBREY Feb. 15, 1882 June 21, 1959
Willie Lee EMBREY Sept. 27, 1886 August 31, 1944
Harvey M. EMBREY Oct. 22, 1909 Apr. 12, 1976
Mother Mariah K. EMBREY June 7, 1880 Sept. 7, 1974

ROYSTON Plot:
ROYSTON Malinda TRUSSELL 1874–1962
ROYSTON M. Burnadette 1918–1928
ROYSTON Joseph Robert 1869–1948
Pauline R. Oct. 1907 Nov. 1982
Son Albert Lee KIRKPATRICK July 9, 1944 June 8, 1970

Bennett H. GREEN beloved Wife of W. Clyde GREEN 1885–1935
William Henry SEELBACH 1874–1946

Catherine L. RANDLE Aug. 27, 1916 July 19, 1981
Richard Adam LOUGHBOROUGH Feb. 18, 1891 March 3, 1946
Ella Muri LOUGHBOROUGH Oct. 24, 1896 Sept. 10, 1966
HAWES Charles R. Oct. 1, 1905 April 28, 1955; Marie E. Apr. 11, 1919

SINGHAS Frank A. 1890–1957; Leora C. 1892–1966
William H. CLEMONS Apr. 13, 1913 Sept. 3, 1955

LANHAM James F. 1882–1957; Bertha I. 1900–1970
LANHAM Florence October 4, 1890 June 23, 1976

Mandley PIERCE Born May 4, 1804 Died June 28, 1869 aged 65 years 1 mo. & 24 days
Harriet PIERCE consort of Mandley PIERCE Born April 1, 1804 Died June 11, 1866 aged 62 years 1 mo. 11 days
John A. PIERCE Died August 6, 1864 aged 34 years 10 mos. & 20 days
James W. PIERCE Died March 10, 1863 aged 26 years 8 mos. & 19 days
1847 Zachary Taylor PIERCE 1915; 1845 Ann DOWDELL PIERCE 1929; Their Children: 1872 Carroll PIERCE
    1937; 1874 Harriet PIERCE GRASTY 1966; 1875 Mary Dowdell PIERCE 1966; 1876 Cordella PIERCE ROSS
    1963; 1881 Ann PIERCE GREGG 1969

Orra H. GIBBONS July 13, 1862 Feb. 7, 1938
EBHARDT William C. Sept. 25, 1885 Jan. 10, 1957; Grace E. Dec. 25, 1891 Dec. 22, 1961
Father Thomas Manley DARNELL June 29, 1896 February 29, 1968 ROBINSON C. Willie 1913–1935
DARNALL John T. 1856–1931; Janie K. 1863–1935
Ernest M. GRIFFITH Nov. 26, 1864 June 5, 1923

Paul P. Son of Paul P. & Audrey M. PIERCE April 24, 1925 April 5, 1929
PIERCE Graham Jr. Aug. 23, 1905 Aug. 23, 1977; Katherine D. Aug. 14, 1903
Paul P. PIERCE Sept. 19, 1900 July 1, 1980
Audrey M. A. PIERCE June 18, 1904 Dec. 8, 1992

WATTS Effie T. September 20, 1866 April 14, 1967; William H. March 14, 1861 May 20, 1940

Virginia SPITLER August 16, 1848 March 9, 1934
Bushrod J. ----LEY November 5, 1926 *(missing 1988 & 1993)*
Anne Carter LEE Wife of Hanson E. ELY, Jr. July 21, 1897 November 8, 1978
Hanson Edward ELY III October 26, 1923 December 8, 1963-
Jackson LLOYD July 12, 1874 May 26, 1944-

Charles D. LLOYD 1884–1961
LLOYD Father Herman A. 1903–; Mother Margaret D. 1894–1976
Melvina P. LLOYD 1933–1934

George BROWN 1874–1936
Elizabeth F. Wife of Geo. BROWN 1878–1935
BROWN George A. Dec. 3, 1905 Sept. 12, 1961; Catherine W. June 20, 1912
Hugh L. WHITE 1908–1965
J. Brooke ANDERSON 1871–1943
Elizabeth E. ANDERSON 1879–1958
R. Wesley ANDERSON 1899–1978

HOYT John C. 1874–1946; Jennie K. 1878–1960
Elizabeth H. HOYT 1898–1983

John C. GALL Feb. 1, 1901 Dec. 13, 1957
Elsie ROSENBERGER GALL June 3, 1901 March 30, 1964
Amos WINES 1900–1960 *(fhm)*
Mary B. WINES 1908–1986 *(fhm)*
ATWOOD Howard Jackson 1898–1982
Etta E. ATWOOD July 27, 1903 Oct. 10, 1988
Mary B. ATWOOD Dec. 2, 1921
WEEKS Anderson R. Apr. 10, 1916 May 21, 1983; Elizabeth A. Sept. 22, 1923
ATWOOD V. Blanche TRUSSELL 1869–1943
Thomas Blackwell SMITH Born Mar. 28, 1880 Died Sept. 15, 1939
Anne Catherine SMITH Born June 26, 1890 Died July 29, 1961

Bessie SCOTT BALL January 19, 1864 November 15, 1954
Mason Fitzhugh BALL June 28, 1897 August 17, 1958
Grace LEE BALL December 1, 1884 February 10, 1965
Hugh H. HOLMES 1873–1946
Raymond HOLMES 1899–1959
Raymond K. HOLMES TEC5 US ARMY May 24 1924 Nov 1 1976
Meta A. HOLMES 1903–1944
Infant Son of C. W. & C. G. HALL Born June 5, 1931
HALL Clarence Wellington May 9, 1896 March 7, 1982; Goldie LAWRENCE Dec. 19, 1898 Jan. 20, 1991
Mary E. WINE Jan. 21, 1838 Feb. 18, 1932
LAWRENCE Emily Ann May 1, 1868 Sept. 23, 1956; James Henry June 30, 1870 Jan. 7, 1964
Thomas H. LAWRENCE VIRGINIA PVT CO. I 56 ENGINEERS WORLD WAR I June 29 1895 May 10 1960
Andrew F. LAWRENCE PFC US ARMY WORLD WAR II 1910 1976

Julia Cameron GATEWOOD September 19, 1903 March 19, 1968
Marie Louise Daughter of Harry HEWLINGS and Julia Tyler TYSON January 26, 1875 May 16, 1954
Grace Tyson GATEWOOD Daughter of Harry HEWLINGS and Julia Tyler TYSON June 20, 1878 October 18, 1962
Eugene Cameron GATEWOOD Son of William Byas and Mary Welby de BUTTS GATEWOOD August 27, 1877 November 30, 1926
Dulaney Forrest de BUTTS, Jr. July 2, 1898 Nov. 3, 1938; His Wife Mary Stuart MARSHALL de BUTTS March 24, 1900 March 30, 1972
Henry Marshall de BUTTS Aug. 21, 1928 Jan. 18, 1984 dearly loved Husband of Lois BROWNING de BUTTS
James Marshall PLASKITT Nov. 12, 1897 Apr. 17, 1978; his beloved Wife Mary Welby de BUTTS of Kirkby, Upperville, Virginia Feb. 22, 1897 Sept. 30, 1975

PLASKITT Mary Morris MARSHALL of "Mont Blanc" Fauquier County Wife of Joshua PLASKITT Jan. 29, 1872
    Jan. 10, 1950
Dennis McCARTY III Born Willow Hill Sept. 25, 1927 June 17, 1986
Henry Starr WATTLES, III February 1, 1915 December 17, 1950
John Heath de BUTTS Son of Dulaney Forrest and Emma ASHBY de BUTTS January 29, 1902 January 24, 1958
Rozelle HUDD de BUTTS Wife of John Heath de BUTTS February 12, 1906 August 22, 1918
Margaret BLAIR de BUTTS Wife of Harry Ashby de BUTTS July 17, 1900 September 20, 1951
Emma ASHBY de BUTTS Wife of Dulaney Forrest de BUTTS March 28, 1872 May 9, 1947
Dulaney Forrest de BUTTS Son of Richard Earl and Sarah HALL de BUTTS April 15, 1860 September 10, 1926
Harry Ashby de BUTTS Son of Dulaney Forrest and Emma ASHBY de BUTTS October 13, 1895 August 25, 1983

Betty Kelly BARON ADAMS March 1930 Oct. 12, 1970 Wife *(fhm)*
Emma D. ADAMS January 1, 1852 May 28, 1939; John W. DELAPLANE May 5, 1861 August 12, 1934
Anne E. SMITH Nov. 20, 1849 June 14, 1917
Gibson F. SMITH Sept. 10, 1880 Feb. 5, 1924
Maria L. SMITH Oct. 27, 1882 Mar. 11, 1967

Chas. W. WILTSHIRE April 10, 1873 Dec. 30, 1935
Bertha FLEMING WILTSHIRE Aug. 27, 1877 Mar. 20, 1971
Charles Stuart LANHAM March 5, 1909 September 5, 1964
WILSON Warren W. 1914–1965; Mary W. 1900–1980
PEARSON Curtis M. 1891–1964; Ruth L. 1892–1971
FAVRE Edward T. Mar. 31, 1916 Jan. 8, 1978; married Apr. 29, 1955; Alice R. Jan. 25, 1919
Bengie M. RECTOR CPL US ARMY Oct 11 1914 Feb 26 1945
RECTOR Major B. June 16, 1887 Aug. 11, 1971; Lena G. June 27, 1888 Feb. 6, 1923
Joseph H. RECTOR May 16, 1917 Aug. 1,, 1951
Thomas G. RECTOR Sept. 19, 1910 Aug. 22, 1927

EDMONDS Edmon S. 1849–1942; Ada B. 1864–1958

Ann V. EMBREY Died June 6, 1917 aged 87 years
EMBREY Minnie L. 1873–1956; Edward L. 1871–1961
Howard Moatz BALLENGER Nov. 11, 1916 Jan. 31, 1985
Robert W. CAYLOR VIRGINIA SGT US MARINE CORPS WORLD WAR II PH Aug 26 1926 July 14 1971

KINES Plot:
Avice LEE 1903–1982
KINES Shirley Lyndon 1909–1965
Ada FLEMING 1884–1961
William G. FLEMING 1889–1955
Hazel G. FLEMING 1891–1981
Grandson Dennis Yates TAYLOR 1945–1982
KINES J. Shirley 1885–1969
Will T. 1883–1964
Dora FLEMING 1879–1965
Fitzhugh C. KINES Apr. 25, 1889 Aug. 27, 1933
Edith K. STRICKLER Dec. 24, 1876 July 28, 1946

Father Earl M. EMBREY 1901–1967

PYNE Marshall M. 1848–1928; Amanda E. 1850–1939
FURR Buckner M. 1882–1960; Mabel E. 1883–1964

Edward WOOLSTON Born at Rayleigh, Essex Co. England June 3, 1874 Died in Virginia Mar. 3, 1937
Emmie DEGROVE WOOLSTON Born July 9, 1875 St John's County, Florida Died Aug. 11, 1947 Fauquier
  County, Va.
William Reginald WOOLSTON Born at Rayleigh, Essex, England Dec. 9, 1871 Died Oct. 1, 1945

MILLS Charles Thomas 1871–1940
MILLS Martha Jane 1873–1957
Ida Belle MILLS 1895–1968
Charles C. KENNEY 1893–1972
Colin MacLEOD beloved Husband of Katharine WRIGHT July 13, 1881 January 10, 1948 Father of Jane and Colin,
  Jr.
Katharine WRIGHT MacLEOD March 31, 1888 October 29, 1976
Colin MacLEOD, Jr. Februuary 28, 1915 December 12, 1977 Husband of Ann Father of Colin Bruce
SPINKS Thomas A. 1882–1954; Mary W. 1887–1963
William S. SPINKS Jan. 29, 1913 April 18, 1984
Elizabeth WOOLSTON TRIPLETT beloved Wife of Harry B. TRIPLETT Aug. 19, 1902 Mar. 19, 1957
Francis Woolston TRIPLETT beloved Son of Harry B. and Elizabeth W. TRIPLETT Nov. 1, 1927 June 21, 1949
Willie M. GLASCOCK Feb. 21, 1913 June 15, 1981
Lucy B. GLASCOCK 1927–1992 *(fhm)*
Mary B. WINES 1908–1986 *(fhm)*
Joseph R. HARRINGTON 1915–1981 *(fhm)*
Harry Benjamin TRIPLETT Aug. 18, 1896 Apr. 28, 1975

Matilda JONES de BUTTS Born Jan. 1, 1881 Died June 3, 1939
Richard Henry de BUTTS Born Oct. 2, 1875 Died Dec. 18, 1954

LEACH Thorton B. 1871–1951; Ida B. 1877–1964
Edwin Earl LEACH 1901–1968
REID Willie J. 1894–1962; Ada G. 1895–1970; Willie T. 1915–1970
Baby Brian Lee PAYNE Aug. 18, 1966 Aug. 18, 1966
Fred Carl RETTBERG CPL US ARMY KOREA April 16 1928 August 30 1969; Lucille Leonard August 23, 1930
EMBREY Father Eugene F. August 1, 1898 December 8, 1980; Mother Lillie M. April 7, 1900 July 27, 1961
Wade Bradshaw LEACH 1905–1970
Nannie LEACH KIRBY Mar. 15, 1903 Feb. 9, 1975
Ethel LEACH SMITH 1898–1973
Mother Hattie E. CARPER May 7, 1887 January 4, 1949
J. William EMBREY 1893–1923; Emma HOGAN EMBREY 1891–1983
Mother Mary V. REID 1907–1960
FATHER Cary T. REID 1899–1985
REID Norman F. July 17, 1910 March 18, 1986; Anna M. Sept. 2, 1920 March 19, 1992
Infant Son of N. F. & A. M. REID 1959
REID Lewis Smith 1866–1924; Rosei EDWARDS 1870–1941
EMBREY Sherman G. Jan. 27, 1915; Grace M. Dec. 7, 1919; Augustine Feb. 17, 1929 Sept. 15, 1930; Sherman H.
  May 18, 1889 Jan. 8, 1976; Sarah J. Jun. 16, 1892 Jun. 25, 1969; Leonard died Sept. 30, 1913
Rosalie REID RAMSEY 1918–1954
REID, Willie J. 1894–1952; Ada G. 1895–1970; Willie T. 1915–1978

Bertha G. LANHAM 1918–1952 Mother

P. Richard ROSE 1903–1975
Annie Lee THOMPSON 1894–1985 *(fhm)*
THOMPSON Frank T. 1865–1938

THOMPSON Cora E. 1889–1938
THOMPSON Sarah M. 1902–1929
Annie L. THOMPSON Sept. 8, 1894 Feb. 9, 1985
THOMPSON Ollie Settle Nov. 28, 1892 Nov. 12, 1961; His Wife Annie V. ROSE June 26, 1899 May 9, 1979
PEARSON Charles A. 1893–1973; Ursula L. 1898–1983

BETTIS Lillie B. 1882–1928; Lee Roy 1882–1959
John Hamiltonn BETTIS
May Francis BETTIS
Alfred T. LLOYD 1906–1957
Andrew Jackson BETTIS US MARINE CORPS WORLD WAR II Feb 6 1918 May 27 1985
EMBREY Augustine Feb. 17, 1929 Sept. 15, 1930; Leonard Died Sept. 30, 1913
Infant beloved Son of Leonard EMBREY Died June 16, 1952
Rosie L. BETTIS 1873–1941
Lewis S. EMBREY 1866–1924
John EMBREY 1898–1923
Mother Mary V. REID 1907–1960
RECTOR, Major B. June 16, 1887 Aug. 11, 1971; Lena G. June 27, 1868 Feb. 6, 1923
Joseph H. RECTOR May 16, 1917 Aug. 1, 1951
Thomas G. RECTOR Sept. 19, 1910 Aug. 22, 1927

THOMAS Plot:
William Howard THOMAS 1915–1978
Lena POSTEN THOMAS 1917
Alice Isabelle POSTEN 1918–1966
Mary E. STEELE 1877–1958
Lelia J. THOMPSONN 1898–1957
Lucille Marie GREY 1928–1989 *(fhm)*
Mason E. THOMPSON 1897–1950
Charles Stewart LANHAM March 5, 1909 September 5, 1964
WILSON Warren W. 1914–1965; Mary W. 1900–1980
J. Frank GRAY Son of John C. & Nancy GRAY April 3, 1857 July 23, 1931; Elizabeth Daughter of H. M. &
    Winnie DIGGS Wife of J. Frank GRAY July 19, 1859 Jan. 31, 1946
GARTRELL G. Donald Sept. 3, 1890 Feb. 28, 1966; Dixie GRAY Apr. 4, 1892 Sept. 4, 1979
Winnie Gray GARTRELL beloved Wife of Leonard L. LIGHTCAP July 21, 1913 Nov. 8, 1950
GARTRELL Winnie GRAY May 6, 1890 Oct. 3, 1979; Arthur Apr. 28, 1887 Sept. 11, 1966

Melbourne R. McCARTY Oct. 27, 1885 July 12, 1958
R. Page McCARTY July 15, 1890 Jan. 22, 1956
R. Eugene McCARTY Jan. 30, 1888 Feb. 29, 1948
Ida ROBINSON McCARTY Aug. 4, 1857 Nov. 12, 1929
Robert W. McCARTY Nov. 27, 1849 Nov. 17, 1921
Eugene D. FLETCHER 1892–1918

Husband Josh A. ROSE 1908–1958
Father Ryland R. RIDGEWAY 1878–1954
Daughter Katherine RIDGEWAY 1912–1939
Wife Mozelle R. ROSE 1914–1942
Mother Mary C. RIDGEWAY 1889–1922
Susan L. THOMAS 1920–1923
THOMAS William T. Aug. 8, 1887 Nov. 9, 1945; V. Grace Nov. 10, 1893 Jan. 18, 1951
Claude N. THOMAS 1919–1923

Roy Brandt DALE May 24, 1975 July 22, 1975

Isabelle GRANT KELLEY 1871–1929
John B. KELLEY 1877–1971
Lillian S. KELLEY 1899–1979 *(Americal Legion Auxilliary)*
Edward A. KELLEY 1902–1979
Elizabeth KELLEY SOWERS 1900–1928

William J. PEARSON 1865–1947; His Wife Elizabeth 1863–1928
Mildred Ann Daughter of Mason E. & Lelia THOMPSON Feb. 23, 1931 Oct. 24, 1931
PEARSON Beverly T. 1893–1986; Nancy HUFF 1892–1981

William L. GRIMM VIRGINIA GM3 USNR WORLD WAR II Aug 29 1920 Aug 2 1969
Edward Marshall EMBREY PVT US ARMY WORLD WAR II Jun 7 1924 Jul 28 1988
EMBREY James F. Jan. 9, 1923; EllaLee D. Dec. 2, 1911 Nov. 17, 1988 Married March 5, 1945
Son Samuel H. FIGGINS April 28, 1927 March 22, 1986
Mother Ada E. MOYER March 9, 1906 Jan. 3, 1984

Rivers Randolph WRIGHT July 12, 1885 Feb. 4, 1969
Daisy J. WRIGHT Feb. 27, 1895 Apr. 26, 1928
WRIGHT Elizabeth C. Dec. 19, 1923 Jan. 16, 1989; Pershing G. Oct. 25, 1919

Wallace B. BROWN 1909–1949
George G. BROWN CPL US ARMY WORLD WAR II 1919 1976
Thelma BROWN GRIGSBY Jan. 10, 1906 Feb. 8, 1927
Mother Susan F. BROWN Born Jan. 17, 1879 Died Oct. 5, 1939
Father T. Benton BROWN Born July 7, 1871 Died Sept. 14, 1941
Renzo D. SISK Oct. 11, 1895 May 19, 1963
Myrtle E. SISK May 13, 1898 Oct. 18, 1980
J. Thornton EMBREY 1890–1968
BROWN Herbert H. 1917–1977
William L. GRIMM VIRGINIA GM3 USNR WORLD WAR II Aug 29 1920 Aug 2 1969
SCHRIVER, Dr. Alfred Bradron Nov. 11, 1914 Sept. 5, 1991; Elizabeth KINCHLOE SCHRIVER Sept. 19, 1920
    Aug. 25, 1992

John T. HENDERSON Sept. 24, 1947 Mar. 10, 1978
McGUINN Samuel H. Dec. 17, 1891 Nov. 9, 1977; Nellie Lee Sept. 15, 1890 April 17, 1978
McGUINN Samuel Burns 1914–1976
William B. KINCHELOE Mar. 3, 1898 Dec. 12, 1954; His Wife Elizabeth H. & KINCHELOE Apr. 25, 1901 Feb.
    2, 1977
FORD Clyde E. 1917–; Ruby A. 1916–1974
Adaline R. THOMAS 1918–1980 *(fhm)*
THOMPSON William M. July 18, 1914 Dec. 6, 1984; Susie A. July 5, 1924 Feb. 3, 1976
HURST Carl R. Dec. 22, 1898 May 16, 1976; Cora B. Jan. 20, 1904 Mar. 21, 1990
ALLISON J. Adrian 1910–1982; Mary Y. 1913–1979
Audrey T. ROLES Dec. 7, 1928 Aug. 3, 1978
BURNS Charles Joseph Sept. 1, 1920 Sept. 19, 1981; Dorothy Lee Feb. 14, 1915
"Tommy" Thomas L. FEWELL Feb. 11, 1953 June 5, 1987 Husband, Father, Son, Brother
UMBEL Kay F. May 1943 April 1985 beloved Daughter of Merill & Elsie Umbel

Adrian Louis SWART his beloved Wife Martha Elen and his ancestors…22 unknown men and women –10 unknown children…burials dating 1700–1900s family cemetery on "Swart Farm", banks of Broad Run…remains moved and reinterred Ivy Hill Cemetery, Upperville, Virginia December 3rd, 1987

SWART Adrian Louis Aug. 4, 1822–1908; Martha Elen Oct. 16, 1822 Sept. 30, 1892

DAVIDS Charles O. Oct. 20, 1912 Mar. 9, 1993; Dorothy B. Apr. 21, 1913 Oct. 31, 1979

Milton Oakley THOMPSON TEC 5 US ARMY WORLD WAR II Jan 10 1917 Nov 10 1989

Diane M. ROLES June 16, 1961 Aug. 22, 1981

William Malcolm THOMPSON PFC US ARMY WORLD WAR II 1914–1984

William Franklin ELLIS Jan. 2, 1942 Oct. 12, 1973

KELLOGG Charles Edward 1890–1978; Harriet Catherine 1891–1984

Ellen E. VINCENT Oct. 19, 1917 Jan. 7, 1985

Paul Leo VINCENT CONNECTICUT SFC US ARMY KOREA Jan 6 1922 Aug 19 1973

Amos CROSS Aug. 10, 1900 May 5, 1988

THOMPSON John Rinker Dec. 2, 1920 Dec. 5, 1991; Mabel C. Nov. 6, 1916 Nov. 30, 1987

Edna CARTER HERRING Mar. 28, 1911 May 26, 1973

BRADY Milton H. 1901–1974; Minnie H. 1902 -

SINGHAS Thomas L. 1914–1977; Ruth L. 1918

Maggie S. LEWIS Dec. 6, 1888 Nov. 16, 1968

J. Elmer NALLS April 18, 1909 Sept. 15, 1989

NALLS Ellie G. July 14, 1903 June 27, 1971

HURST Edgar Randolph PVT US ARMY KOREA Apr 28 1928 Jan 14 1986

Melvin A. DAWSON Sept. 9, 1970 Sept. 9, 1970

JEFFRIES Elsie M. T. Sept. 13, 1918 Feb. 10, 1985; John B. [Barrett] Oct. 27, 1908 April 28, 1992

Adah HANSCOM KEENE 1910–1985 Wife of Arthur G. KEENE

Mary S. BROWN 1851–1926; James B. BROWN 1850–1938

Susan I. KEENE 1872–1943

Mary E. BROWN 1840–1922

Yvonne KILLINGSWORTH WILLIS Apr. 6, 1936 Dec. 19, 1980 Wife of Arthur R. WILLIS

FLEMING Ernest Ross Aug. 22, 1897 Mar. 28, 1974; Grace JOHNSTON Nov. 6, 1903 Feb. 25, 1990

UMBEL, Kenneth E. 1940; Carol A. 1943–1988 wed March 2, 1959

Elsie N. SNIDER 1917– Mother

Dewitt T. SMEDLEY 1890–1971

MOORE George W. May 25, 1908 Apr. 2, 1982; Virginia S. Feb. 12, 1909

"Buzzy" Harrison B. MOORE Oct. 23, 1933 June 19, 1968

ROSE John R. Aug. 24, 1933 Apr. 4, 1985; married Sept. 6, 1959; Karis L. July 29, 1940

LEONARD Forrest Leslie Oct. 9, 1919 Father; Louise THOMPSON May 23, 1924 Mother

Son David Wayne LEONARD September 23, 1953 January 31, 1969

Katherine B. McGUINN Feb. 17, 1913 Mar. 24, 1983

WINES Robert D. Sept. 12, 1903 Oct. 23, 1979; Virginia S. Feb. 16, 1914

PAYNE Luther S. 1901–1984; Lillie S. 1906–1979

DARNELL James A. 1925–; Rosie Lee 1931–1985 married July 1, 1950

Channing A. THOMPSON S2 US NAVY WORLD WAR II Sep 27 1923 May 1 1987

SWART William Martin Jan. 31, 1913 Aug. 6, 1986; Nancy Ruth Oct. 26, 1918

THOMAS Walter S. Dec. 13, 1911 Apr. 4, 1987; Irene K. Sept. 16, 1919

John T. WRIGHT 1909–1987; Frances B. 1921

George Pomeroy KINGSLEY September 23, 1897 October 3, 1991

Albert J. PAYNE, Jr. Oct. 18, 1946 "Juddy" Jan. 3, 1989

PAYNE Albert Judson, Sr. July 7, 1927; Marie BRADY May 15, 1926 Aug. 5, 1982

CARTY Earl T. Mar. 29, 1907 Aug. 6, 1989; Clara B. July 3, 1893 Sept. 5, 1973

Nellie FLEMING WARD 1919

Morris S. WARD TEXAS SF1 USNR WORLD WAR I & II May 18 1903 Dec 21 1970

PEARSON Silas H. 1907–1988; Katherine U. 1906–1976

Pauline A. FOGLE Sept. 24, 1909 Sept. 12, 1967

LUNSFORD Wilson Fairfax Dec. 25, 1913; Edith BRADY Mar. 27, 1922 Jan. 28, 1985

Thomas F. McGUINN S2 US NAVY WORLD WAR II Nov 6 1906 Jan 14 1976

NALLS Carl R. 1888–1955; Rachel F. 1890–1957

YOWELL Daniel R. May 7, 1956 Apr. 29, 1989; James L. Sept. 26, 1954 Brothers

YOWELL Hilton W. Feb. 27, 1896 Sept. 4, 1977; Mary E. Dec. 16, 1907 Apr. 9, 1990

Robert William EMBREY July 3, 1925 August 10, 1974

ROSE R. Frank Jan. 2, 1904 Apr. 29, 1977; Mary B. May 31, 1912

KEELS Jack D. Dec. 1, 1932 Feb. 17, 1978

EMBREY Elmer E. Nov. 10, 1915 Feb. 28, 1980; married July 28, 1945; Eula L. Mar. 11, 1927

Charles S. WRIGHT May 3, 1933 August 15, 1985

Irving E. WRIGHT PFC US ARMY WORLD WAR II Oct 9 1923 Aug 23 1985

William A. WRIGHT September 29, 1930 July 21, 1977

ROSE Suphorn; Marty

Hugh V. JOHNSON, Jr. Dec. 20, 1917 Mar. 17, 1988

Effie Lee HUFF May 20 -- aged 58 *(fhm)*

de BUTTS John Dulaney April 10, 1915 December 17, 1986; Gertrude WALKE July 22, 1914 August 10, 1990

NALLS Hugh Mason TEC5 US ARMY WORLD WAR II Oct 6 1921 Jun 9 1983

WILLIAMS Andrew J. Feb. 11, 1910 March 16, 1985; Pearlie M. May 3, 1910

WELCH William H. 1913–1972; Mary E. 1911

SISK Ollie 1916–1970; Lizzie 1919–19

Nathan Roger SISK VIRGINIA PFC BTRY B 103 FIELD ARTY WORLD WAR II Aug 13 1912 March 29 1970

William D. HUFF 1959–1972 *(fhm)*

NALLS John N. 1912–1986; Edna W. 1914

BROWN Willie F. 1908–1978; Ethel M. 1904

Tellis WELCH 1905–1978; Bertha WELCH 1909–1969

Aldrich H. SUTPHIN, Jr. STC US ARMY KOREA Feb. 1 1934 Aug. 22 1988

SUTPHIN Aldrich H. 1892–1970; Wave G. 1902–1972

BUDD George Sidney 1906–1976; Lucille DOWNS 1913–1977

KESTNER Sarah E. Aug. 5, 1922; Douglas R. Oct. 10, 1920 Feb. 24, 1980

William F. EDWARDS PFC US ARMY WORLD WAR II May 21 1921 Sep 11 1976

REID Cary A. Oct. 24, 1921 Oct. 29, 1982; Elizabeth E. Jul. 16, 1929 Sept. 6, 1985

Ella Virginia EMBREY Feb. 15, 1897 July 16, 1987

Vernon W. JONES 1904–1982 *(fhm)*

Doris Judy JONES 1942–1983 *(fhm)*

George T. HENDERSON 1915–1983 *(fhm)*

Nannie Frances HUFF 1909–1980 *(fhm)*

Carroll Davis HUFF 1916–1984 *(fhm)*

Duncan T. WINES 1992–1992 *(fhm)*

Douglas R. KESTNER PFC US ARMY WORLD WAR II 1920 1980

John T. WRIGHT Jan. 12, 1913 July 24, 1976

Pauline Butler BELL May 27, 1915 Mar. 15, 1992

ESOVSKI Martin E. 1911–1986; Jane C. 1915

CAMPBELL John W., Sr. Nov. 5, 1892 Apr. 4, 1980; Wife Virginia Peach Oct. 27, 1896 Dec. 18, 1972; daughters
    Virginia MILLARD Apr. 13, 1926; Jean NICKLAS May 9, 1927; Son John W., Jr. July 31, 1928; Son-in-law
    Wayne R. MILLARD March 29, 1924

Eugene David THORPE, Sr. PFC US ARMY WORLD WAR II Feb 12 1918 July 7 1988
Eugene David THORP, Jr. July 5, 1944 May 15, 1972
THORP Eugene D. 1918–; Lucy E. 1914–1969
HUFF Grover Lee 1917; Elizabeth Anne 1915–1980
Roy Lee JEFFRIES March 13, 1950 June 27, 1973
Amos W. THOMPSON CPL US ARMY KOREA 1930 1976
WOODWARD Harold C. Oct. 15, 1916; Dorothy B. May 5, 1920
WOODWARD Clemma S. March 15, 1891 December 5, 1979
PILKERTON Della GOLDEN Dec. 14, 1889 Sept. 17, 1975
Daddy Rinker A. JOHNSON May 5, 1919 December 23, 1972
Enoch C. CANARD TEC5 WORLD WAR II APR 18 1918 Jun 13 1990
Jim THOMAS 1888–1978 *(fhm)*
Mabel F. HENDERSON 1950–1987
Mary E. WRIGHT 1915–1978 *(fhm)*
WILLIAMS Wilmer W. July 17, 1912 Apr. 28 1988; Audrey C. Mar. 9, 1913
Robert Frederick MELTON PVT US ARMY Oct 10 1926 Sept 10 1989

Robert D. JOHNSTON Oct. 5, 1851 Feb. 15, 1925; His Wife Maria M. KERFOOT May 30, 1872 Aug. 1, 1935
HOUGHTON Gideon B. Nov. 6, 1876 Jan. 31, 1955; Beulah A. Nov. 11, 1881 Jan. 13, 1929

PEARSON Bruce P. September 17, 1882 March 17, 1953; Julia M. February 12, 1888 March 21, 1967
PEARSON Arthur Warren Apr. 28, 1938 Feb. 28, 1954
Nellie PEARSON Died June 14, 1986 aged 76 years *(fhm)(missing 1993)*
Mollie Katherine PEARSON SIMMONS Nov. 30, 1909 Jan. 25, 1982

Michael M. WISNIESWKI and family
Bessie E. EMBREY Oct. 7, 1909 June 19, 1980
William John EMBREY MECH CO D 2 INF VA NG WORLD WAR I December 5, 1890 October 19, 1956
LEE Brooke E. 1899–1950; Zella 1898–1970
Morris H. GRAY 1915–1992
Mollie R. HUFF 1880–1953
Robert L. HUFF 1875–1943

Emma P. BRADY May 4, 1883 Oct. 17, 1934
Ernest D. BRADY Jan. 24, 1892 Aug. 18, 1966
Beulah W. BRADY Feb. 28, 1893 Jan. 22, 1957

John HANNA Aug. 8, 1900 Jan. 1, 1969

Harrison B. MOORE "Buzzy" Oct. 23, 1873 June 19, 1968
Francis D. REID 1925–1965
Edward D. SMEDLEY 1911–1966; Adeline A. SMEDLEY 1917
Harry DEMAWBY, Jr. Jan. 12, 1917 Jan. 20, 1976
THOMAS Wade Hampton 1899–1919; Elsie TOMBLIN 1906–1967
Pauline A. FOGLE Sept. 24, 1909 Sept. 12, 1967; Son Thomas Edward RIDGEWAY 1928 Died Feb. 28, 1969 age 40
RIDGEWAY Thomas L. 1897–1964; Katie H. 1900–1972

DOHNER John B. 1907–1964
PEARSON George Owen 1904–; Lucy ELLIS 1913–1966
Charles A. WYNES Sept. 27, 1903 May 10, 1963

Mother Emma P. CHADWELL Sept. 7, 1886 June 1, 1971
Sister Madeline C. HOLZAPFEL May 12, 1918 Sept. 29, 1962

Lucy Josephine THORP 1914–1969; Eugene D. 1918–1988

Edward S. THOMPSON VIRGINIA SSGT US ARMY WORLD WAR II May 22 1911 Sept 16 1966
Edward M. THOMPSON VIRGINIA FIREMAN 1CL US NAVY Dec 4 1886 May 31 1943
THOMPSON: Clifford Curtis July 22, 1885 July 2, 1956; Ellis Pearle March 17, 1888 July 4, 1957

Peggy M. DAVIS 1943–1946
DAVIS Charles I. 1888–1964; Thelma F. 1909 -
Sydnor Gladstone HODGIN May 31, 1900 June 16, 1958
DEMAWBY Harry 1878–1961; Beatrice 1889–1978
JONES Hugh E. 1910–1971; Elizabeth L. 1915–1961
Theodore Ellis WRIGHT June 21, 1939 April 17, 1964
TABRUM William W. 1893–1968; Daisy BUDD 1896–1961
William Smithson BROADHEAD Born Barrow-in-Furness England November 24, 1888 June 17, 1960

TRIPLETT Elwood W. 1896–1963; Helen G. 1913
COOK Walter 1921–1965
THOMPSON, Walter S. Jan. 21, 1919 Oct. 1, 1983; married May 17, 1939; Evelyn S. Aug. 8, 1918 Apr. 5, 1989
Dmitri Emmanuel SHAHEEN Augt. 5, 1987
Dale Gordon JOHNSON 1949–1974
LUKENS, Paul F. 1897–1979; Helen C. 1899–1986
WRIGHT, Thomas E. Dec. 8, 1913 Sept. 12, 1982; Elizabeth J. March 14, 1922 July 8, 1985
Ephraim L. SHIPE TEC 4 US ARMY WORLD WAR II Dec 2 1910 June 16 1982
Bronnie M. SHIPE Wife & Mother Apr. 4, 1909 Aug. 22, 1983
Betty L. DWYER Oct. 9, 1947 June 23, 1948
William H. PHELPS June 2, 1946 July 17, 1964
Willie Monroe PHELPS 1911–1964 Died Nov. 19, 1964 Aged 53 years
Elizabeth SLACK PHELPS Feb. 9, 1916 Sept. 25, 1976
George W. PEARSON 1899–1973
Agnes V. OTT "Marnie"1912–1990
William E. NEFF Feb. 10, 1916 Apr. 8, 1990
NEFF Nevia A. Feb. 11, 1908 Sept. 19, 1991; Ruby B. June 25, 1910 Mar. 11, 1988
Mary V. POSTON "Ma" Oct. 3, 1888 Apr. 24, 1976

Ruby M. NEFF 1910–1988 *(fhm)*
John EDWARDS PFC US ARMY WORLD WAR II Dec. 7, 1911 Feb. 5, 1976
Jeffrey G. Son of E. G. & B. H. SLACK 1959
KEYTON Herbert L. Oct. 3, 1931; Mildred M. June 11, 1930
Debbie D. POPKINS 1955–1972 Daughter of Carla Rena POPKINS Died May 14, 1972
Scott E. WINES June 1, 1907–April 24, 1971

J. Thomas FRASIER October 20, 1895 June 1, 1947; Marjorie DICKEY FRASIER October 6, 1893 February 10, 1947
E. Alben SMALLWOOD Nov. 22, 1919 Mar. 5, 1941
Arthur C. SMALLWOOD May 22, 1886 Feb. 24, 1971
FEWELL John Sullivan Feb. 28, 1892 April 30, 1938; Susie ROBINSON March 30, 1894 Jan. 2, 1978
WINES R. Scott 1877–1953; Dixie S. 1878–1952
Kimberly A. KIRKPATRICK March 8, 1968 July 13, 1980
Amos S. KIRKPATRICK 1923–1984 *(fhm)*

Clarence Edward TINSMAN May 10, 1921 June 16, 1981; Our family Mary; Clarence; Clarence III; Nancy; Gloria; Hilda
FEWELL Charles W. 1908–1988; Maty E. 1911

Ashton TAVENNER June 6, 1870 March 8, 1966
Charles A. TAVENNER 1909–1962
NEFF Leonard L. 1906–1980; Minnie V. 1911
PEARSON William H. Nov. 20, 1913; Julia Apr. 11, 1913 Sept. 23, 1975
James S. SOAPER March 30, 1946 Feb. 9, 1984 beloved Son & Brother
Mary Agnes RIDGEWAY 1897–1969; Luther E. RIDGEWAY 1899–1976
Warren Lee OLIFF 1915–1983 *(fhm)*
FURR George G. July 9, 1929 Dec. 31, 1983; married March 1, 1955; Mary E. March 13, 1939
RECTOR Maurice B. Sept. 19, 1898 Nov. 20, 1982; Thelma L. Dec. 9, 1905 Aug. 1, 1985
Father Jake I. DUNIVAN May 25, 1929 March 31, 1983
Frederick H. THOMAS VIRGINIA TEC5 HQ BTRY 232 FA BN WORLD WAR II Dec 4 1912 May 14 1955

WRIGHT William N. Jr. Sept. 18, 1934 Oct. 13, 1983; Joan E. Feb. 17, 1938 April 15, 1988
Reginald E. WRIGHT Aug. 6, 1922 Sept. 14, 1940
Roberta Lee WRIGHT 1918–1967 *(missing 1993)*
William J. WRIGHT VIRGINIA PFC AIR SERVICE WORLD WAR I October 9 1899 December 23 1946; Ida Elizabeth Sept. 2, 1900
Father Bedford James WRIGHT June 2, 1915 Feb. 4, 1974
FLEMING: J. Melvin Jan. 28, 1902; Alma B. Dec. 20, 1912 Sept. 21, 1990
Meta E. Daughter of J. Melvin & Alma B. FLEMING June 25, 1935 Sept. 5, 1936
NEFF Bernard H. 1910–1988; Marion E. 1912–1973
Delbert A. NEFF 1937–1938
Charles E. GLASCOCK AR US NAVY Nov 16 1939 Aug 18 1974
Father Eppa H. GLASCOCK Feb. 20, 1908 Aug. 26, 1985
Joseph P. ABELLE 1878–1936
Cora E. ABELLE 1880–1936
Charles W. STAPILER 1910–1983 *(fhm)*
Stanley R. LUNCEFORD SP5 US ARMY Jul 12 1931 Jul 25 1974
LUNCEFORD Preston R. Sept. 30, 1904 Apr. 11, 1972; Nina T. Aug. 10, 1913
Janet N. KIRBY 1948–1993 *(fhm)*
Mary Ellen LUNCEFORD Apr. 4, 1949
BUTLER Joseph K. 1900–1974; Sara T. 1908–1984

Jackson Cemetery, Delaplane, Virginia

Located 1 mile South of Pleasant Vale Baptist Church on Route 724 on right in field. About 75 feet from Route 724 by farm lane; many large rocks. Cemetery a mess. Some fieldstone markers. Resurveyed September 13, 1993.

Geo. JACKSON Born Aug. 7, 1813 Died April 4, 1875 Aged 61 yrs. 7 mos. & 27 Dys. *(missing 1993)*
Margaret Wife of Geo. JACKSON Born May 19, 1812 Died July 15, 1866
M. A. J.
F. A.
C. A.
Mary Ann consort of Geo. JACKSON who departed this life January 20th 1847 Aged 43 years & (3?) months & 13 days *(missing 1993)*
Susan CHINN Daughter of Hugh & Margaret CHINN was born 1st day of Oct. 1804 and died the 24th of Oct. 1852 Aged 48 years and 6 days

Jacksonville Cemetery (Black), Delaplane, Virginia

Located 1.2 miles West of Route 17 on Route 623 on left of and beside road. Some fieldstone markers, overgrown with honeysuckle. Resurveyed in October 29, 1993.

Willie ASHBY William Earl ASHBY Died June 19, 1967 Aged 71 years *(not visible in 1993)*

James Cemetery, "Elk Run", near Midland, Virginia

Located, from Elk Run, 0.24 mile South East on Route 610, then 400 yards North East by private road, "The Thomas Helm Place." Surveyed by M. D. Gore, Sumerduck, July 30, 1937.

"There is an old graveyard in the woods about a quarter of a mile East of Tom Helm's house. Part of it was surrounded by an earth embankment which can still be seen. A broad, flat tombstone has inscriptions on both sides."

To the memory of John JAMES who was born March the 16th, 1709 and departed this life Jan the 2, 1778–Age 68 years

May 16th day 1800 departed this life Dinah JAMES who was Wife to John JAMES Decd., Born 1716–aged 80 [83?] years and 7 mo.

James Cemetery, Midland, Virginia

Located East side Route 649 about 1 mile North Route 28. About 400 yards East of Route 649 in open field. Fieldstone markers are now gone. Information obtained from Ripley Robinson.

Duncan JAMES
Allen HEFLIN

James Cemetery, Midland, Virginia

From Route 643 take 602 West to Licking Run, up Run (North) about 0.5 mile turn East 0.25 mile. Cemetery on top of hill. All fieldstone markers, no inscriptions. Information supplied by Ripley Robinson 1991.

Jarman (or German) Cemetery

Located between Routes 721 & 741. Billy Jake JARMAN Cemetery nearby. Data obtained from Joe Lawler, Marshall.

Johnson Cemetery (Black), Markham, Virginia

Located on left side of Route 28 1 mile up a terrible old road, across from pond, near West end of Route 728 on right. About 25 feet by 25 feet. Barbed wire fence in bad condition. Resurveyed September 13, 1993.

Henry JOHNSON Family *(African Cross above name, not usually seen this far North)*
Herbert JOHNSON -19-- *(fhm in bad shape)*
8 or 10 depressions about 5 for children

Johnson (Charlie) Cemetery, Turnbull, Virginia

Located South Route 803, 0.5 mile East Route 637, no markers.

Jeffries Cemetery (Black), Markham, Virginia

Located at West end of Route 728 in a field to the South of Robert Hinkel's ranch style home. Resurveyed September 20, 1993.

Jeffries - Moore Cemetery

Located on Route 737 north of Route 738, on right 300 yards Paul Ashby place, no fence. Large area of graves in yard, about 25 fieldstone markers. Suzanna Ashby (wife of Paul) said some graves were moved to Orlean

Cemetery. Large sunken hole in center of graveyard.

field stone marker - J. W. E. *maybe footstone*
Betrtha B. wife of H. L. KEMP Died Jan 21, 1904 Aged 28 yrs. 4 months 24 days
M. A. JEFFRIES Born Dec. 18, 1828 Died May 25, 18 (*stone broken*)

Kelley (Kelly) Cemetery, Opal, Virginia
Located on land once used as county landfill Route 674 in Opal according to 1979 deed. Cemetery was reserved out by family. Included in legal descriptions as far back as 1902. No cemetery found February 12, 1989. On February 3, 1990 Linda BURDA found exact location of cemetery. No markers. Now under a skateboard ramp.

According to the Marriage Bond book, Dinah THOMPSON married Alexander KELLEY Dec. 13, 1802 Daughter of James. Tax District A 1787. Dinah CONWAY married John KELLY Aug. 29, 1797 Daughter of Peter. Tax District A 1787.

Kelly - James Cemetery, Bealeton, Virginia
Located 1 mile North West Route 28 North Route 745 in middle of field, overgrown. Both Rush Boyer and Obrey Messick state that was originally 2 acres in size. Major James WRIGHT was buried here in the first Masonic funeral. During the Civil War, the Union troops pulled up the tombstones to use for stepping stones in their camp. The people were outraged and their officers made them put them back. Later they vanished, and the cemetery is now about 30 feet x 40 feet.

Elizabeth nee WRIGHT widow of John JAMES Died Feby 28, 1828 aged 65 years 9 mos. and 28 days
Margaret 2nd Daughter of John P. & Margaret KELLY Died Octr. 28, 1848 Aged 24 yrs. 4 mos. and 25 days
Margaret Wife of John P. KELLY Died May 19, 1827 Aged 30 yrs. 8 mos. and 17 days

Kemper Cemetery, Warrenton, Virginia
Located on Route 802 just East of "North Wales" to East of mansion, fenced, well kept. Fieldstone markers, some with initials: H. M.

Charles KEMPER Born June 27th 1756 Married Nov. 30th 1786 Died Dec. 1st 1841
Susanna MAUZY Wife of Charles KEMPER Born Sept. 24th 1765 Died July 14th 1843
Mary Ellen McCORMICK Wife of Charles KEMPER, Jr. Born February 10th 1802 Died July 20th 1854

Kemper - Claxton - Edwards Cemetery, Sumerduck, Virginia
Located 0.5 mile South Route 651 at intersection of private lane on South & Route 631 to North. Link wire fence, well kept.

CLAXTON Martha A. Sept. 11, 1855 Oct. 10, 1940 Richard E. Oct. 2, 1851 July 2, 1929
Mary Ann KEMPER the beloved Wife of Richard KEMPER Born April 16, 1826 Departed this life May 7, 1892 aged 66 years & 22 days
Richard KEMPER Born May 5, 1827 Died July 10, 1903
Norman C. EDWARDS July 4, 1910 Oct. 20, 1915 Honor EDWARDS Nov. 6, 1902 Jan. 28, 1903
William H. EDWARDS Apr. 23, 1879 Oct. 1, 1924
Hugh K. CLAXTON Jan. 6, 1883 Apr. 11, 1960

Kendall Cemetery
Located on Route 738 near Route 721 on North side of road. Another unmarked cemetery just North of this farm. Data obtained from Joe Lawler, Marshall.

Kenner Grave, Somerville, Virginia
Located 0.5 mile North Somerville, West Route 610 in woods about 300 yards down trail. The inscription below is

exactly as it appears on the tombstone. Resurveyed by L. Arthur Grove February 1994.

This drery vault stranger contains the body of Capt. Howson KENNER who descendid to the dust in a good old age for he saw from his loins the third generat" He departed hence 24 of May 1778 age 66 This stone from a sence of his goodnes is humbly dedicated to his memory by his youngest son Rodham KENNER

Kercheval - Ferguson Cemetery, Delaplane, Virginia
Located in yard of farm just to South of Pleasant Vale Baptist Church on Route 724. Overgrown with tombstones scattered near fence, Jean (Goode) Shoemaker, the owner, stated that some Kincheloes buried there. Cemetery almost vanished when resurveyed September 13, 1993.

James H. KERCHEVAL Died Dec. 2, 18[8?] 1 aged 6[1?] yrs. 7 mo. and 11 days
Sarah A. KERCHEVAL Died Dec. 16, 1861 Aged 22 yrs. 4 mo. & 2 days
John D. FERGUSON Departed this life June 4, 1860. In his 55th year
Edna A. FERGUSON Died May 3, 1881 Aged 72 years

Some rock markers

Kerns Cemetery, Halfway, Virginia
Located on Route 706. Nine graves marked with rock markers.. Possibly 3 unmarked graves.November 11, 1990

The following are buried here:
John W. KERNS 1917-1918
Hazel E. KERNS 1924-1929
Harry R. KERNS 1886-1948
Virginia L (LEE) KERNS 1887-1968
Annie Taylor KERNS 1868-1929
J. R. Teel KERNS 1888-1956
I. [Ira] KERNS 1913-1979
Infant daughter of W. D. & M. S. DARR 1957
James Herny LEE 1889-1956 *(fhm)*

Kerns Cemetery, Midland, Virginia
Located South East intersection 650 & 649 in middle of field in grove of trees, no fence, about 0.25 acre of fieldstone marked graves. Reuben Miller stated that it was Kerns family cemetery and about 1950, Reuben WINES was buried there. Resurveyed April 23, 1994

Lillian SMITH Died July 19, 1904 Age 11 years
at least 11 tombstone most have no inscriptions

Buried there before 1905, no stones. Fieldstone markers for (information reported by Ripley Robinson 1991):
Greely JAMES *(buried in the 1930's)*
Billy KERNS
Virginia "Jinny" KERNS *(wife of Billy KERNS, was married first to Duncan JAMES)*
Mrs. Scott KANE

Kincheloe Cemetery, Rectortown, Virginia
Located 0.5 mile East of Route 713 on South side Route 716 at "Greendale" behind and to the left of house on hill in open field. 3 illegible markers, verified by copy made by Dr. A. S. Furcron August 5, 1933. Overgrown. Resurveyed October 9, 1993.

Sergeant Wickliffe KINCHELOE Co. B 8th Reg. Va. Volunteers Pickett's Brigade, Longstreet's Division Born in

Fauquier Co. Virginia Wounded at Williamsburg May 5, 1862 Died a prisoner at the Chesapeake Hospital Sept. 22, 1862 He lies buried in the U. S. National Cemetery near Fort Monroe, Va.

Lieutenant D. James KINCHELOE Co. C 49th Reg. Va. Volunteers Peagram's Brigade Ramsuer's Div. Early's Corps Born in Fauquier Co. on March 13, 1836 Killed Aug. 29, 1864 near Smithfield, Jefferson Co. West Va. He lies buried in the old burying ground of village of Smithfield.

Brandt KINCHELOE Born Aug. 18, 1801 Died May 29th 1874

R. W. P. KINCHELOE Son of Brandt and Mary KINCHELOE born Sept. 30, 1848 died Feb. 8th 1923

Louisa KINCHELOE Daughter of Brandt and Mary RAWLINGS KINCHELOE born Aug. 13, 1832 died May 9th 1894

Mary RAWLINGS KINCHELOE Born July 9th 1801 Died Aug. 29, 1884

Rebecca KINCHELOE Born at "Texas" near The Plains, Fauquier Co. Va. Feb. 1840 died at the invalids Hotel, Buffalo, N. Y. at 5 o'clock in the morning of Oct. 16, 1899 She was the third Daughter of Brandt and Mary RAWLINGS KINCHELOE

Travis DAVIS who died June 2d 1851 Aged 66 years

Julius KINCHELOE He lies buried in the cemetery at Booth Bay, Maine near the home of his wife Born in Virginia Jan. 28, 1831 Drowned in Oregon May 20, 1867 together with his boat's crew while engaged in the U. S. Coast survey off Tillamook Bar. Only one rescued from the sea. It was due to his reluctance to leave uncertainty of his result and for this he risked the danger of the sea in which....

Elizabeth KINCHELOE who was born Dec. 27th 1765 and departed this life March 29th 1844 Aged 78 years 3 months & 2 days

Enoch KINCHELOE who departed this life Aug. -d 1830 aged 3[0?] years

John W. H. PATTIE who was born March 4, 1828 and departed this life the 13th 1838 aged 10 years 7 months and 9 days

William PATTIE was born June 2d 1789 and departed this life Sept. 12, 1839 Aged 50 years 3 months & 10 days

H. K. *(footstone)*

Klipstein - Bartenstein Cemetery, New Baltimore, Virginia

Located 0.4 mile South West Routes 29 North West Route 674 in overgrown wooded area at crest of hill to left of old house about 200 yards, near site of old house. Shale markers were used for most of the graves that were left, but a neighbor to East helped himself to a number of them for a cement walk according to Mr. Edward Furlong, who gave the only inscription that was left. Many of the graves have been moved to the Warrenton cemetery, I expect, as I picked up the family there. Surveyed in 1969 by Nancy Baird and Tom Browning.

J. B. KLIPSTEIN Oct. 31, 1861

Lacey Cemetery, Marshall, Virginia

Located South West intersection of Routes 55 & 691 near Marshall Community Cemetery in field which has no other markers. Overgrow. Resurveyed October 9, 1993.

Hugh B. LACEY VIRGINIA PVT CO F 63 PIONEER INF WORLD WAR I June 5 1894 October 16, 1957 *(grave moved 1994CCommercial Tool & Die now located on cemetery site.)*

Lake Cemetery, Atoka, Virginia

Located 0.4 mile West Route 714, 1.5 miles South Route 50 in second field. Board fence, wrought iron fence on side, overgrown,grass, with many unmarked graves. 4 field stone markers. Resurveyed November 15, 1993.

1804–1852 48 years 1 month 10 days *(top missing)*

Dewitt C. [Clinton] LAKE Born Dec. 10, 1829 Died Dec. 15, 1862

Eleanor BREWER LAKE second Wife of Isaac LAKE Born July 26, 1804 Died Nov. 5, 1858

Inside wrought iron fence:

Isaac LAKE Died March 26, 1851 Aged 68 years 2 months & 28 days

Sallie LAKE Died May 18, 1821 Aged 35 years 11 months & 28 days

Susan LAKE Born March 28, 1814 Died 4 April 1882 Aged 68 years and 7 days

Lake Family Cemetery, Warrenton, Virginia
Located at Bellevue near Warrenton. Moved to Warrenton.

Lawler Cemetery, Marshall, Virginia
Located at end of Route 737 on left 0. 5 mi. up dirt road in field to left of old Lawler home, fenced.

Ronald H. ASHBY 1949–1949
Lettie F. LAWLER 1861–1938
George C. LAWLER 1860–1922
Sarah R. LAWLER 1870–1924
Lawrence D. LAWLER 1901-1917
Ethel R. JEFFRIES 1895–1930
Mary E. LAWLER 1867–1960
Joseph H. LAWLER 1863 1934
Mary A. LAWLER 1863–1883
James W. LAWLER 1826–1909
Sarah A. LAWLER 1831–1916
Jane E. LAWLER 1859–1951
Paul L. LAWLER 1897–1898
Eveline LAWLER Died Mar. 1880

Joe Lawler stated that the Walker family are no relation, but asked to be here:

In memory of children of Robert & Mary WALKER
Maude F. WALKER Born Sept. 28, 1884 Died Nov. 15, 1889
Lizzie WALKER 6 days
Clara W. WALKER Born July 16, 1897 Died Jan. 19, 1902
Ora J. WALKER Born Mar. 5, 1904 Died June 17, 1920

Lawrence - Utterback Cemetery, Marshall, Virginia
Located 1 mile North East of Marshall on Routes 17 - 55 on Norht side of lane in woods back of field, with excellent stone fence and large wood. Down old lane between Russell property and Mary Cunningham farm. Trees and gate fallen down, branches and vines all over the place. Resurveyed April 2, 1994.

Richard M. Son of James R. & Virginia A. WOODWARD Born Jan. 27, 1863 Died Feb. 11, 1865 *(very hard to read B still has footstone)*
Presley M. JEFFRIES Born November 17, 1805 Died December 28, 1887 *(can read very well- still standing by itself leaning a little forward - footstone still intact)*
Nancy W. JEFFRIES Died June 17, 1877 In the 73 year of her age *(still standing by itself B footstone still intact)*
Susan GLASCOCK Wife of Bryant O. UTTERBACK Born Sept. 21, 1814 Died Nov. 29, 1892 *(still can read well B leaning and held up by tree behind)*
Willie B. UTTERBACK only child of Bryant & Sue UTTERBACK Born Sept. 8, 1862 Died Feb. 1, 1870 *(can still read most - held by pipe and wire wrapped around it)*
Bryant O. UTTERBACK Born March 19, 1812 Died June 17, 1898 *(broke in half B can still read everything clearly B held up by pipe)*
Mary E. Wife of P. N. LAWRENCE Born Feb. 1, 1853 Died Sept. 29, 1886 *(can still read, but stone is lying on back B otherwise good)*
Drucilla Wife of Wilfred UTTERBACK Died Sept. 23, 1876 aged 65 years 1 month & 19 days *(very easy to read B broken horizontally through middle B held up by two iron posts and wire)*
Wilfred N. UTTERBACK Born Aug. 4, 1816 Died Nov. 1 1890 *(very easy to read has big letters B still standing*

straight on its own B tree has fallen in front of it)
Nancy MASON Beloved Wife of W. N. UTTERBACK Born Sept. 23, 1841 Died Mar. 2, 1891 *(half of it is easy to read, but last and bottom half is hard to read. Surrounded by trees and brush)*

Laws Family Cemetery, Catlett, Virginia

Located .3 miles on Route 603 at Intersections Routes 667 and 603, 0.25 mile North St. Stephen's Church by barn, stones down, in bad condition. Resurveyed August 15, 1994 by Mr. Ben McGee.

Mary JACKSON LAWS June 20, 1813 Died Sept. 24, 1872
Ann LAWS Born July 15th 1813 Died Jan. 13th 1864
Elizabeth Wife of Newton LAWS Born February 24, 1824 Died Nov. 15, 1902
P. A. DULIN Dept. this life Sept. 28, 1863 aged 15 yrs. 2 months & 2 days
Mollie Daughter of B. J. & A. V. LAWS Died Sept. 25, 1865 Aged 8 years
Virginia Daughter of Newton & Ann LAWS Born June 20, 1845 Died Aug. 30 1895

Leach Cemetery, Virginia

Located at end of Route 697 West Route 628 at top of hill in woods past house. Resurveyed December 29, 1993.

Unmarked graves
Mrs. Becky LEACH
Wade LEACH
Thornton LEACH
Josh LEACH

Lee (Henry Hancock) Cemetery, "Greenview", near Warrenton, Virginia

Located bear Botha on Route 651 to right of "Greenview." The cemetery has disappeared, bulldozed by one time owner. Ripley Robinson says Henry Hancock LEE IV and family were buried here. Ripley is a descendant.

Lee - Strother Cemetery, "Shady Valley", Warrenton, Virginia

Located 1 mile South West Route 17 on North West side Route 699 in fenced yard North of house, well kept. Mrs. Alison Lee, wife of James S. Lee, owner, states that there are some graves marked with 10 fieldstone markers for which she gave the data in brackets, based on family genealogical records. There is also a slave cemetery behind the barn with about 85 fieldstone markers, well kept. Resurveyed February 7, 1994.

Our beloved Sister Caroline V. STROTHER Died January 16, 1894
Angeline V. STROTHER Died Oct. 1, 1909
Upton D. COLLINS born Jan. 9, 1831 died Oct. 3, 1862 [a soldier who ate too much honey & died]
LEE, Ruth Lunceford LEE Oct. 3, 1899–May 13, 1966; her Husband James Strother LEE Sept. 26, 1865–Nov. 16, 1938
Richard Henry LEE Jan. 2, 1873–April 9, 1952
Alexander STROTHER born Sept. 30, 1807 died April 12, 1891
Maria STROTHER Born May 5, 1830 Died April 15, 1907
James T. LEE Born March 26, 1834 Died Dec. 19, 1897 Infant Son Aged 27 days Infant Daughter Aged 14 days
Mother Susannah STROTHER Born Sept. 2, 1779 Died Feb. 11, 1855
JSTBRU 1918 ---- *(Handmade marker. 9-5 after date. Illegible letters on first three lines)*
LUNSFORD Minnie MARTIN July 28, 1874 Jan. 23, 1927 John S. Oct. 18, 1865 May 29, 1926
Octavia [STROTHER] Wife of John C. DOWELL Died May 18, 1879 In her 59th year *(fieldstone marker)*
[Mollie Virginia LEE Aug. 9, 1868–Nov. 29, 1928] *(fieldstone marker)*
LEE, Lewis Francis Jan. 4, 1919 July 3, 1990 Elizabeth Poland
DUNDON, Fannie [Alice] LEE Feb. 15, 1863 Nov. 12, 1946; Joseph W. 1865 May 25, 1938
James Leonard FOSTER VIRGINIA PFC US MARINE CORPS WORLD WAR II Apr. 3, 1918 Mar. 11, 1973
Garnett F. FOSTER 1921–1992 *(fhm)*

LUNSFORD, Minnie MARTIN July 28, 187- Jun. 23, 1927; John S. Oct. 18, 1865 May 29, 1926
Mrs. M. E. HINTERSON Born May 23, 1835 Died March 31, 1860

Lewis Cemetery, Little Georgetown, near The Plains, Virginia
Located South East on Route 55, left on Route 674, right on Route 676 about 1 mi. Cemetery on right enclosed with iron fence, partly down, cattle have been in.

William LEWIS Born 1750 Died 1830 Son of Thomas and Sarah HAWLEY of Douguecreek, Fairfax Co.
Nannie L. Wife of William LEWIS Born Dec. 2, 1842 Deceased 1870
Harry LEWIS Feb. 28, 1801 Dec. 8, 1853 Aged 52 years and 14 days
Ann MONTGOMERY Born Sept. 3, 1759 Wife of William LEWIS Daughter of Capt. Wm. MONTGOMERY of Rosemont and Catherine MARRS
Lucy Ann LEWIS Born Sept. 8, 1813 Died Dec. 17, 1904

Lewis Family Cemetery, Little Georgetown, Virginia
Located off of Route 674 West on Route 696 0.5 mile. Rock & iron fence, 0.25 acre, boxwood and oak trees. Judge Smith keeping it up. About 10 fieldstone markers. Data obtained by Frank Lewis & H. Thomas Browning.

Mother Anne M. LYNN Born Aug. 1, 1820 Died July 21, 1908
Nannie L. Wife of William H. LEWIS Born December 2, 1842 Died June 10, 1870
N. L. L. *(footstone)*
Lucy Anne LEWIS Sept. 8, 1812 Dec. 17, 1904
Thomas Son of W. H. & Susan
Henry L. LEWIS Born October 25, 1801 Died December 9th 1853 Age 52 years 2 months and 14 days
Nannie STROTHER LEWIS Wife of G. W. JOHNSTON Born June 3, 1860 Died Aug. 13, 1882
Mary Conway Daughter of G. W. & N. S. JOHNSTON Born Mar. 11, 1882 Died Aug. 13, 1882
Ann MONTGOMERY Born Sept. 3, 1759 Wife of William LEWIS Daughter of Capt. Wm. MONTGOMERY of "Rosemont" Prince William Co., Va. and His Wife Catherine MORRIS
William LEWIS Born 1750–Died 1830 Son of Thomas LEWIS and His Wife Sarah HAWLEY HARRISON of Dogues Creek Fairfax Co., Va.
Josephine LEWIS Daughter of Henry M. & Lucy A. LEWIS Born November 13th 1850 Died July 4, 1854 Age 3 yrs. 7 months and 21 days
Mary LEWIS Daughter of Henry and Frances H. LEWIS Born January 1, 1840 and died the same year
Frances LEWIS Wife of Henry M. LEWIS Died Mar. 15, 1840 Age 32 years 9 months and 7 days
about 10 stone markers in cemetery

Linden Community Cemetery, Linden, Virginia
Route 638, Fiery Run Road, 0.25 mile on left past bridge over railroad tracks. Survey completed March 29, 1989

Left Section
Fannie HAINES died Aug. 1870 aged 50 yrs.
Lucy Wife of W. B. WALTER died Mar. 1862 aged 40 yrs.
Henry ODER this monument is erected by his children Born January 28, 1815 died February 15, 1875
William Hanson RAMEY VIRGINIA PVT US ARMY WORLD WAR I Nov 4 1895 Oct 4 1973
MILLS John T. 1906–1968; Lillian M. 1917
Mother Annie Marion WALTER 1844–1919; Father James Edward WALTER 1838–1916
Jennifer Lynn BUTLER June 28, 1959 June 29, 1959
James Edward WALTER, Jr. 1878–1954
Ruby M. C. WALTER 1882–1960
Sarah G. WALTER died Feb. 1900 aged about 65 years
Carroll L. SMITH Sept. 17, 1891 July 20, 1978
HUDNALL Russell Turner 1907–1970; Gladys TILDEN 1894–

W. B. WALTER born Apr. 22, 1821 died Mar. 13, 1899

Sophie DALMAS WREDEN April 5, 1896 Sept. 28, 1966

Wife Maude WALTER HALL July 18, 1871 May 26, 1946; Husband Frederic Thomas HALL July 9, 1890 Oct. 13, 1959

DALMAS Walter Haines Nov. 19, 1904 Aug. 29, 1979; Ann DIEMER June 14, 1904

Louise WALTER BUTLER 1905–1961

Anne DALMAS 1900–1934

Rebecca STERRETT 1888 –1892

Henry Little Son of Henry A. & Maud DALMAS *(rest in ground)*

PRITCHARD James W. 1853–1921; Louise C. 1858–1930

Joseph Haslup PRITCHARD born Jan. 22, 1899 died Oct. 14, 1918 aged 19 yrs.8 mos. 22 ds.

Henry COOPER Mar. 5, 1828 June 27, 1905

COOPER Martha Wife of Henry COOPER born Dec. 10, 1835 died Apr. 3, 1896

E. Everett WALTER born July 27, 1859 died Aug. 15, 1924

William O. WALTER 1854–1919

Annie B. WALTER 1853–1909

Margaret H. WALTER 1826–1903

John T. WALTER 1823–1901

WRIGHT Frances WALTER 1905–; Kenneth Adams 1906–1976

WALTER Annie GREEN 1871–1962; Carroll Winter 1863–1929

Elisabeth Winter daut. of Carroll W. and Annie E. WALTER Born Jan. 12––Died July 2, 1896

WALTER Carroll Kennedy 1897–1976; Lillian LEHEW 1896–1930

Lucy M. WALTER 1847–1942

James L. WALTER Nov. 3, 1893 June 17, 1959

Carrie V. WALTER Wife of S. P. WALTER Sept. 16, 1870 Oct. 18, 1957

Stuart P. WALTER 1866–1937

Shirley Miller WALTER 1899–1929; Wife Lucy Hilda HUDNALL Mar. 1, 1901

Mary E. BROWN Born Aug. 6, 1881 Died Oct. 19, 1881

Gussie HOTCHKISS 1876–1903

HOTCHKISS Charles Strother Oct 22, 1872–July 13, 1916; His Wife Augusta Estelle 1876–1903; Lillie HOTCHKISS 1865–1951; Jean HOTCHKISS ROSSER 1869–1953; Martha Jane KIDWELL Sister of M. E. H. July 21, 1844 July 28, 1896; Eli James Jan. 8, 1830 July 10, 1896; His Wife Mary Elizabeth Apr. 25, 1839–June 3, 1893; Samuel Davis Aug. 25, 1858–Dec. 25, 1870; Sarah Elizabeth Nov. 8, 1859–June 8, 1900

Jas. P. A. J. 1885–1906

JOHNSTON 1898

John S. J.

Margaret J.

P. J.

George C. BERRYMAN July 5, 1883 Oct. 17, 1935

M. Alma BERRYMAN Born Mar. 8, 1881 Died Jan. 11, 1919; D. Thomas BERRYMAN Born Sept. 23, 1838 Died Oct. 16, 1917

Marcellous O. BERRYMAN Born May 9, 1845 Died *(rest in ground)*

Louisa PHILLIPS Born Mar. 16, 1820 Died Sept 21, 1901

Benjamin F. BERRYMAN June 22, 1879 April 21, 1950

BERRYMAN Landon L. 1881–1953; Leslie F. 1882–19--

BROWN John W. Born Mar. 12, 1846 Died July 4, 1895; S. Ada BROWN Born July 22, 1856 Died May 13, 1894

HOFFMAN Father Wesley A. July 18, 1844 Dec. 2, 1896; Mother Bettie M. Oct. 8, 1848 Dec. 19, 1914; Esser M. Nov. 1, 1869 May 13, 1927; Mary K. May 14, 1872 Apr. 23, 1934; Ruth Anna July 16, 1882 Jan. 27, 1891; Sallie Nov. 13, 1880 Aug. 18, 1900

BERRYMAN A. W. BERRYMAN and Family

H. H. B.

A. B.

S. M. B.

A. W. B.

RILEY E. Millison Born July 16, 1848 Died Sept. 25, 1924; Robert Van RILEY Born Aug. 10, 1897 Died Mar. 21, 1919

Cora Lee REDMOND February 12, 1892 March 31, 1965

Nora S. BALDWIN Feb. 28, 1882 May 14, 1957; William H. BALDWIN July 25, 1879 Jan. 5, 1958

Edna P. BALDWIN Nov. 5, 1911 Mar. 31, 1926

S. Henley SMITH 1845–1934; Virginia LLOYD His Wife 1856–1948; Grandson S. Marvin GRADY 1907–1925

Nora J. SMITH Born May 30, 1880 Died Sept. 9, 1906

John W. SMITH Born Dec. 10, 1842 Died Feb. 25, 1915

Mother Martha Jane beloved Wife of John W. SMITH Born July 19, 1844 Died Aug. 27, 1924

Allie J. SMITH Born Sept. 8, 1871 Died Feb. 5, 1934

John W. SMITH, Jr. Born July 14, 1880 Apr. 19, 1934

William T. BARBER Born Sep. 19, 1831 Died Sep. 29, 1899

Louise A. Wife of W. T. BARBER Born Apr. 9, 1837 Died Oct. 22, 1909

Mariah Wife of Jefferson SMITH Born Feb 4, 1808 *(rest in ground)*

L. BERRYMAN Born July 27, 1810 Died Sept. 14, 1891; A. B. BERRYMAN 1850–1927; N. J. BERRYMAN 1849–1927; Mary Jane His Wife Born July 10, 1815 íDied Mar. 11, 1901

Sallie Gabrella BERRYMAN Born Aug. 19, 1885 Died Jan. 13, 1919

BERRYMAN A. Douglas 1888–1966; Nannie M. 1895–1977

Douglas Roy BERRYMAN Oct. 25, 1914 July 29, 1930 aged 24 years

Mary L. Wife of J. W. SHIPE second husband

Robert WINE Mar. 10, 1848 Dec. 9, 1937

Olive Lela Daughter of J. W. & M. L. SHIPE died May 10, 1903 in her 21 year

S. H. S. *(footstone with confederate marker)*

William A. SMITH VIRGINIA CPL 43N REPL TNG CENTER WORLD WAR I Dec 7 1887 May 3 1957

A. Betty HUDNALL SMITH Feb. 21, 1894 May 7, 1977

E. Kingston SALISBURY, Preston, Lancashire England Born Nov. 15, 1845 Died Dec. 13, 1916

Lucy Josephine SALISBURY Wife of E. Kingston SALISBURY of England Born July 14, 1855 Died March 10, 1915

Dulaney B. KENNEY 1906–1965 *(fhm)*

KENNEY Ella Mae 1886–1926; Richard W. 1878–1963

Mable GATEWOOD

Gracie Massie Daughter of W. B. & M. W. GATEWOOD Born July 15, 1884 Died July 28, 1900

W. B. [GATEWOOD] enter-- *(rest broken)*

Mary WELBY Wife of W. B. GATEWOOD Born Dec. 18, 1852 Died July 22, 1900

Ida de BUTTS Daughter of W. B. & M. W. GATEWOOD Born July 20, 1888 Died Mar. 1890

Frances SYDNOR Wife of D. D. de BUTTS Born June 29, 1854 Died Nov. 2, 1932

Daniel Dulaney de BUTTS Born Apr. 3, 1848 Died Feb. 10, 1913

Carrie Snowden Daughter of D. D. & Fannie T. D. de BUTTS Born Aug. 16, 1885 Died July 27, 1887

Dulaney Forrest de BUTTS Born Oct. 8, 1887 Died July 17, 1890

Sydnor de BUTTS Aug. 20, 1891 June 19, 1948

Sara Earl de BUTTS Wife of C. H. TRUMBO Sept. 29, 1879 Oct. 3, 1949

Richard L. TRUMBO Aug. 18, 1920 Apr. 7, 1950; Richard L. TRUMBO Born Sept. 11, 1877 Died Apr. 27, 1919

Margaret de BUTTS Wife of Richard Louis TRUMBO July 24, 1877 June 28, 1939; Richard K Son of R L. & M. D. TRUMBO Born 1903 Died 1907

Gertrude de BUTTS MARSHALL 1906–1927

Nellie TRUMBO MARSHALL 1870–1937

Millicent Welby Daughter of E. H. & J. F. de BUTTS Feb. 5, 1906 Oct. 25, 1919

E. Herbert de BUTTS Husband of Julia FRENCE de BUTTS July 22, 1865 Apr. 2, 1920

Julia FRENCE de BUTTS Apr. 18, 1867 July 16, 1958

John Addison de BUTTS Aug. 15, 1891 Aug. 31, 1950
Rebecca de BUTTS LEACH Dec. 25, 1900 Jan. 3, 1975
Carlyle Whiting de BUTTS Mar. 22, 1898 Mar. 6, 1961
Richard Earl de BUTTS June 1, 1890 Jan. 27, 1955
John Peyton de BUTTS Aug. 9, 1894 Sept. 26, 1954–
Charles L. WOODWARD 1920–1943
Edgar L. WOODWARD VIRGINIA PFC 48 ARTILLERY CAC WORLD WAR I May 6 1882 May 13 1959
Mollie A. WOODWARD 1885–1949
Robert L. WOODWARD Born Aug. 1, 1882 Died Aug. 30, 1921 aged 39 years
RUTHERFORD Mark, Lucy, Joe, Julie, & AnnieRaymond A. TRUMBO 1882–1947
George H. TRUMBO March 16, 1874 Feb. 27, 1943
G. H. TRUMBO Born Aug. 1, 1840 Died Aug. 26, 1899 *(Masonic emblem)*
Margaret Daughter of George & Sara TRUMBO Born July 18, 1916
BEATY
MILLS Father William H. March 12, 1876 August 6, 1948; Mother Mary F. August 2, 1878 August 31, 1961
Ruby M. R. W. D
Martha J. Wife of R. J. KIRBY born Apr. 24, 1893 died Nov. 22, 1917
Sarah Metcalfe MAUPIN Daughter of Jere. G. HATCHER born at Thaxton, Bedford County, Va.. March 3, 1845
    died at Linden, Warren County, Va. Sept. 6, 1912 Wife of Wm. Carey MAUPIN
Robert Carter HALL 1880–1941
HALL William Hunter 1852–1927; Ida de BUTTS HALL 1853–1933
Eliza F. CARTER born Jan. 16, 1822 died Feb. 17, 1902
Robert CARTER born Oct. 15, 1817 died Feb. 13, 1898
Gertrude H. HALL 1878–1950
Guy de BUTTS HALL 1882–1967
Infant Son of I. H. & Victor DEMURGUIONDO 1929

Little Zion Baptist Church, Greenville, Virginia
Located North of Route 28 on Route 603. Resurveyed 1990.

TURNER Edward C. 1887–1932; Lucy C. 1889–1961
2 fieldstone markers
John Lucien GRIGSBY 1900–1988 *(fhm)*
NICKENS William F. Nov. 13, 1878 Jan. 20, 1968; Victoria M. July 29, 1887 Dec. 19, 1982
Dollie B. NICKENS April 13, 1892 Nov. 5, 1980
Macon G. NICKENS Dec. 23, 1891 May 17, 1965
Juanita T. DANIELS Oct. 2, 1919 Nov. 23, 1985; Marion E. NICKENS May 16, 1921 July 5, 1949
NICKENS Kate Mar. 16, 1954 Mar. 24, 1948; James M., Sr. May 28, 1852 Sept. 15, 1934
NELSON Rowena May 10, 1893 Mar. 15, 1954; Shirley B. Nov. 3, 1892 Mar. 25, 1971
Macon G. NICKENS, Jr. PVT US ARMY Mar. 8, 1926 Oct. 28, 1968
John Cook NICKENS Born May 11, 1874 Died Dec. 5, 1961
Nannie B. NICKENS November 2, 1896 September 11, 1965
Frederick D. NICKENS Feb. 16, 1895 August 5, 1958
Geneva WALKER NICKENS Born January 24, 1881 Died March 9, 1966
Helen 1950–1956
One fieldstone marker
GASKINS Sarah E. July 13, 1888 January 29, 1986; Thomas S. July 7, 1879 April 28, 1949
Mollie G. NICKENS Dec. 23, 1891 May 13, 1965
James A. NICKENS Born May 28, 1852 Died Sept. 15, 1934
Laura Virginia SMITH 1881–1964
Horace GREEN Oct. 20, 1914 Sept. 5, 1958
Henrietta LUCAS 1916–1964

Emmanuel PAYNE 1911–1960
John H. SMITH 1886–1955
Henrietta Olive GROOMS 1956–1967
Harriet GROOMS October 7, 1956 January 1, 1967
Michael C. ASH 1955–1967
Robert MATTHEWS 1877–1964
Mary Catherine SMITH January 23, 1877 April 7, 1962
Eliza Beloved Wife of Charles DAVIS Born 1864 Died Oct. 28, 1906
GREEN Deacon R. Leroy Mar. 1, 1894 Feb. 19, 1955; Mary C. PAYNE Dec. 26, 1896
TOLER W. Henry June 24, 1844 Aug. 4, 1922; Allvia A. Jan. 31, 1858 June 21, 1943
Mary E. KEYS May 20, 1881 March 10, 1945
William M. KEYS Dec. 7, 1878 Aug. 17, 1970
Edwin TURNER Aug. 8, 1924 Aug. 11, 1924
Rev. TURNER Died Oct. 21, 1927
15 rock markers West of fence and seems to be full of unmarked graves, probably at least 30

Unfenced new area:
Wife & Mother Georgia E. TURNER Sept. 2, 1909 Jan. 12, 1982
Maladean B. TURNER 1909–1982 *(fhm)*
Pearl HARRIS Aug. 8, 1937 Aug. 16, 1982 Daughter & Sister
Johnny Lee QUINN Jun 1, 1947 Nov. 25, 1984 Son, Brother & Father
Frank W. QUINN, Jr. SL US NAVY WORLD WAR II 1911–1990
John W. BALL 1900–1985 *(fhm)*
Earl T. SMITH Jan. 6, 1904 Feb. 27, 1988
Verbena S. JOHNSON Oct. 16, 1901 Jan. 32, 1989
Mary E. HOLBROOK 1918–1990 *(fhm)*
John Kennedy GROOMS 1961–1990 *(fhm)*
Bernice Riley MILES 1910–1982 *(fhm)*
Rebecca HARLEY July 4, 1908 April 1, 1975
William David KNAPPER PVT US ARMY WORLD WAR II Jun. 13, 1907 Mar. 1, 1976
William W. MATTHEWS 1911–1976 *(fhm)*
Michael C. ASHE 1955–1967 *(fhm)*
Lillian SKINNER Jan. 9, 1977 *(fhm)*
William "Nick" GRIGSBY Feb. 17, 1923 May 15, 1978
William R. TASKER 1899–1980 *(fhm)*
Sarah Frances HOOPER 1941–1988 *(fhm)*
Mother: Irene G. WALLACE May 23, 1920 Sept. 1, 1986
Ernest BARBER 1A US NAVY 1937–1986
James Franklin LOFTY SGT. US ARMY WORLD WAR II May 4, 1907 Aug. 16, 1989
Helen V. LOFTY July 14, 1920 Dec. 9, 1980
Genara T. GRANT Feb. 1, 1908 Nov. 8, 1977
Aaron Alfonzo GRANT 1885–1980 *(fhm)*
Lora GRANT Dec. 17, 1884 Dec. 4, 1975
Baby girl TURNER 1964 *(fhm)*
Daddy Charles E. TURNER June 13, 1916 March 29, 1980
Ella P. TURNER April 20, 1916 July 20, 1965
Charles B. WALLACE, Sr. 1916–1982 *(fhm)*
Roxie Ann WALLACE 1899–1972 *(fhm)*
Linesay Marie GRIGSBY 1936–1965 *(fhm)*
Mother Rovena QUINN Aug. 14, 1934 Aug. 8, 1965
Walter QUINN 1935–1965
Charles E. PAYNE 1872–1966 *(fhm)*

Mary E. ROBERTSON 1885–1970 *(fhm)*
ULYESSES G. Wallace 1897–1970 *(fhm)*
Mary QUINN Dec. 22, 1910 July 13, 1972 [*by Henry Poole*]
Robertson AMES 1908–1973 *(fhm)*
Dora Ann BUCHANAN 1922–1974 *(fhm)*
Theodore SMITH 1914–1970 *(fhm)*
Henrietta Ann CRAFT 1935–1978 *(fhm)*

Lomax Cemetery, Bristersburg, Virginia
Located 0.75 mile West Route 616 South Route 806. Wire fence, end of private lane, North West garage & house, well kept. 2 fieldstone markers.

Spurgeon M. LOMAX 1859–1935
Eugene G. LOMAX Aug. 16, 1867 Nov. 7, 1943

Longbranch Baptist Church, Halfway, Virginia
Rock markers in pile with biulding stone from church addition. Although there are references to the cemetery here in old records, the church or other sources have not been contacted for names of those interred.

Love Cemetery, Middleburg, Virginia
Located East on Route 649 3 miles North of Route 702 in Woods to South of house, mortared stone wall, well kept. Resurveyed March 31, 1993

Mary Wife of Augustine LOVE Born Jany 22, 1756 Died May 31, 1851
Augustine LOVE Born July 1, 1753 Died Feb. 11, 1820
Sarah S. LOVE Daughter of Augustine and Mary LOVE Died June 16, 1873 Age 87 years 12 days
Martha Daughter of Augustine and Mary LOVE Born May 18, 1784 Died Sept. 17, 1853
Jane HALE Daughter of Augustine and Mary LOVE Born Aug. 26, 1788 Died Jany. 12, 1828

MacRae - Tomlin Cemetery, Warrenton, Virginia
0.25 acre in size. Resurveyed November 29, 1993.

Sarah ALLANIA
Stephen TOMLIN 14th February 23 January

Malvin Cemetery, Turnbull, Virginia
Located North of Turnbull, rock markers.

Manor Lane Farm Graveyard, Warrenton, Virginia
From Warrenton, go west on Route 211 3.8 miles, go left at Route 681, go approximately 0.9 mile. Take a right turn into Smith drive, mailbox says SMITH Box 597. Go up lane past stream and Smith barn bear right, go up hill, bear left at top of hill, go 50 yards. Graveyard is adjacent to small tenant house. This information taken on April 16, 1994 by Stephan W. Smith and David K. Atkinson.

Thomas NELSON Died Dec. 21, 1856 Aged 79 Years 7 Days "He that hath clean hands shall be stronger and stronger"
Martha E. CARTER Born Nov. 3, 1816 Died July 7, 1873 "Weep not, she is not dead, but sleepeth, asleep in Jesus; Blessed sleep, from which none ever wake to weep."
In memory of Elizabeth - Wife of Thomas NELSON - Died Jany. 5th, 1837 Aged 55 Years 21 Days – "Her children rise up and call her blessed"
In memory of our father - Capt. W. W. CARTER Born April 27, 1815 Died Feb. 19, 1903 "He is at rest"

Mark Cemetery, Catlett, Virginia

Located North Route 806 0.5 mile South Route 767 opposite brick rambler in grove, unfenced, in field. Resurveyed August 15, 1994 by Mr. Carson.

Mary H. MARK Born Dec. 26, 1837 Died Mar. 7, 1896

Isabella Wife of Nimrod MARK Born Oct. 17, 1817 Died Sept. 14, 1896 Nimrod MARK Born Feb. 21, 1912 Died Mar. 22, 1871

Sarah F. DUVALL Born April 12, 1812 Died Jan 1, 1888

Marshall Cemetery, "Locust Hill", Markham, Virginia

Located South of Route 728 1.5. miles West Route 688 in grove of trees back of house, barbed wire fence. We could not find it September 28, 1993. Catherine Dodd, former resident said some of the Marshall family was at the cemetery several years ago and they couldn't find it either.

Thos. H. MARSHALL Born April 26th 1800 Died July 8, 1880

Anne Eliza Wife of Thos. G. MARSHALL and Daughter of George & Mary H. HARRIS who was born the 17th of Aug. 1801 and died the 28th of June 1853 Aged 48 years 10 months 11 days

Mary Ali-- eldest Daughter of T. G. & A. E. MARSHALL Born April 18th 1825 and died the 20th Oct. 1830 aged 5 years 6 months & 8 days

Anne Eliza 2d Daughter of T. G. & A. E. MARSHALL Born Nov. 15th 1826 Died Nov. 18th 1830

Robert Whitehead MOSS Nov. 29, 1885 Mar. 29, 1886

Elvira Adams Daughter of T. G. & A. E. MARSHALL Born Feby. 20th 1838 & died July 10th 1838 Aged 4 mos. & 20 days

Note: There is a slave cemetery at the MOSS home just East of Locust Hill with fieldstone markers.

Marshall Cemetery, "Mont Blanc", Delaplane, Virginia

Located at junction of Routes 729 & 724 back of barns, manager's office on Cobbler Mt. Farm on edge of field with good stone fence. Overgrown. Resurveyed October 7, 1992.

John MARSHALL Son of John MARSHALL & Mary Willis AMBLER Born 15th Jan. 1798 and died 25th Nov. 1833 aged 35 years 10 months and 10 days

This stone indicates where are interred the mortal remains of Hanson Contee fourth son of John & Elizabeth M. MARSHALL Born May 29th 1828 Died July 29th 1831 Aged 3 years & 2 months & 18 days

Catharine Thomas oldest Daughter of John & Elizabeth M. MARSHALL born Nov. 9th 1832 died Jan. 27th 1833 aged 2 months

There is evidence of several other graves, but no markers for them.

Marshall Cemetery, "Oak Hill", Delaplane, Virginia

Located 3.9 miles North Marshall, Va. Located on Route 55 East service road to Route 66 back of the Oak Hill mansion built by John Marshall. Cemetery between house and barns in good stone wall enclosure, much overgrown with tree debris covering graves. Resurveyed March 1992.

Thomas MARSHALL who died in Baltimore on the 29th of June 1835 in the 51st [54th?] year of his age while on his way to see his venerable father, then ill in Philadelphia. He left seven motherless children to mourn his untimely death. While in him were united all the ---- which rendered him eminent in the discharge of every private duty. By this stroke of death has fallen ripe scholar the very devoted patriot, the libral philanthropist the humble servant of God. July 21 1781 *(probably date of his birth)*

Margaret W. MARSHALL consort of Thomas MARSHALL of Oak Hill she died February 2d AD 1829 in the 37th year of her age

Mrs. Agnes LEWIS consort of Fielding LEWIS of Weyonoke who departed this life on the 11th day of August in the year MDCCCXXII *(rest broken 1992)*

Alvin V. Baird, Jr. remembers there being another grave there.

Marshall Cemetery, halfway between Hume and Orlean, Virginia
Located at intersection of Routes 647 & 688. Resurveyed January 29, 1992.

Wallie [MARSHALL] age 2 years Feb. 5, 1920 March 1, 1923

Martin Cemetery, Midland, Virginia
Located West side Route 674 0. 5 mile South of County Dump on South side farm lane, stone wall down, overgrown with honeysuckle and briars, about 25 feet x 60 feet apparently full, stone markers. Resurveyed November 28, 1983.

Inscriptions found by Ripley Robinson and Scott Carter in cleaning up Confederate Black Horse Troopers graves.

George W. MARTIN on four sides of obelisk the inscription:
[Front] In Memoriam George W. MARTIN Born Feb. 2, 1844 Died Feb. 24, 1898 the most famous of the Black Horsemen [Southwest side] The lamb of the household the lion in battle He looked friend and foe in the face [North side] The Martin boys the pride of old Fauquier
Susan A. MARTIN was born March 10, 1803 Died Aug. 9, 1879 aged 76 yrs. 5 mos.
R. E. M. *(fieldstone marker with no dates [Robert E. MARTIN, Co. H 4th Va. Cav.]*
E. M. Age 68 Died Nov. 26, 1832 *(fieldstone set near NW wall)*
M. F. M. *(fieldstone marker set near NW wall about half way down)*

Outside of stone wall in wrought iron enclosure:
William BOWEN Co. H 4th Va. Cav. C. S. A.

Mauzy Cemetery, Bristersburg, Virginia
Located North West intersections of Routes 616 & 806 on farm of Homer George. Has stone markers only, Kenneth Eskridge stated.

McCormick Cemetery, "Auburn", Catlett, Virginia
Located 100 yards West intersection of Routes 670 & 602 at top of hill. Resurveyed August 15, 1994 by Mr. Tim Parup

Mary F. Daughter of Stephen & Elizabeth McCORMICK Born Sept. 5, 1820 Died Sept. 20, 1856
Elizabeth M. Wife of Stephen McCORMICK Born July 28, 1790 Died June 19, 1865
Stephen McCORMICK Died Augt. 29, 1878 Aged 92 years

McKennie Cemetery, Marshall, Virginia
Located in field to left of house on Winterset Farm off Route 772 about 1.5 miles North of Route 732. Enclosed with good stone wall.

Mrs. Mary McKENNIE Wife of Doctor Matthew McKENNIE Died May 6th 1862 Aged 86 years & 4 months
Matthew McKENNIE, M. D. Sept. 17, 1757 May 31, 1812
L. Eliza Wife of John PAYNE and Wife of Mason HURST *(no dates)*
John Cumberland PAYNE Born January 27th 1811 Died January 8th 1867
I. W. B 1731 D 1821

Many fieldstone markers in grove outside wall, possibly for slaves.

Miller Cemetery, Bristersburg, Virginia
Located 0.7 mile West Route 616 South Route 806 about 1 mile West of Bristersburg on way to Elk Run. In field back of frame house, fenced, well kept. Data from Arthur E. Miller.

Gladys E. MILLER Aug. 22, 1873 March 15, 1967
Reamy B. MILLER May 9, 1911 July 5, 1922
Gladys MILLER Born May 9, 1914 Died May 12, 1914; Ralph A. MILLER 1917 *(died 3 months after birth)*;
   Charles MILLER 1930–1932
John N. MILLER Feb. 22, 1872 June 3, 1958
Sallie B. MILLER Born April 7, 1838 Died January 4, 1907
G. Allen MILLER Born July 1, 1830 Died Sept. 13, 1914
Gladys Eva MILLER 1873–1967

Moffett Cemetery, Marshall, Virginia
Located to left of Route 738 1.6 miles North of Route 689 to rear of house, enclosed by iron fence, overgrown. Resurveyed February 1991 by Phyllis Scott.

Daniel Jackson MOFFETT Born March 15, 1846 Died Nov. 2, 1928
Bettie T. ASHBY Wife of D. J. MOFFETT Born June 19, 1851 Died May 8, 1921
W. S. ARCHER Son of M. B. & Mary MARSHALL ARCHER Born March 23, 1840 Died March 20, 1906
William L. MOFFETT 1872–1955 *(stone not found 1991)*
Nimrod Ashby MOFFETT VIRGINIA PFC CO F 104 AMMO TN 29 DIV WORLD WAR I June 5, 1891 Dec. 5, 1962
Samuel R. MOFFETT 1887–1966
Daniel Thomas Son of D. J. & Betty Ashby MOFFETT Born Feb. 10, 1878 Died Dec. 25, 1898

Moffett - Swain Cemetery, Marshall, Virginia
Located 0. 8 mile North of Route 739 on Route 691 in field on left.

SWAIN James E. Feb. 27, 1872 August 3, 1958 Mary Jane May 1, 1871 August 7, 1947
Clara Belle SWAIN Feb. 27,1907 May 11, 1961
MENEFEE Henry Turner Sept. 2, 1877 Oct. 20, 1880 His Wife Susan MOFFETT Jan. 3, 1880 April 17, 1913
Robert F. MOFFETT Dec. 11, 1842 Feb. 25, 1907
Susie B. MOFFETT Jan. 3, 1880 April 17, 1913
Fannie MOFFETT BALL May 6, 1877 Oct. 1, 1902
Susie Roberts BALL Mar. 13, 1902 June 4, 1902
Ethel M. JENKINS 1910–1966

Moore Cemetery
Located to right on Route 799. Data obtained from Joe Lawler, Marshall.

Moore Cemetery, Orlean, Virginia
Located in field on Route 732 across from Orlean Cemetery, well kept.

Ella M. HALL July 25, 1893 June 6, 1965
Lena Wife of Adolphus MOORE Sept. 17, 1862 April 18, 1926
Adolphus MOORE Nov. 23, 1868 Jan. 17, 1939

Footstones: Baby, Mattie, Minnie, John T. and 6 fieldstone markers.

Moore Cemetery, Orlean, Virginia
Located at intersection South West of Routes 737 & 739 in back of house in small grove of trees. Markers have been

moved according to Norris Wilson, Culpeper, Va. Thelma Adams Bussey, family genealogist, states that her great great grandparents were buried in fieldstone marked graves. They were:

Emily [PARKER] MOORE
James MOORE

Morehead Cemetery, New Baltimore, Virginia

Located on farm just North Route 694 on Route 674 in field to North of house, only tombstone stored in shed and plan to move to above HUNTON cemetery.

Unable to locate. There is a new housing development called "Valley Green." There were no old farm houses around. No sign of a "Valley View" farm. Stopped and asked localsCno knowledge of location of cemetery or of tombstones. Resurveyed by Paul and Mark Cameron, August 15, 1994.

Presley Washington MOREHEAD Born Mar. 20, 1818 Died Feb. 25, 1891
Mildred MOREHEAD His Wife Born Mar. 8, 1817 Died Jan. 28, 1886

Morrisville Methodist Church Cemetery, Morrisville, Virginia

Located between Routes 17 & 835 North of Morrisville to rear and side of church. Excellent condition. Resurveyed 1990.

Vernon Clyde VARNAU Born May 12, 1925 Died January 21, 1989 aged 63
Norman R. EDWARDS 1873–1957
Allford Clopton EMBREY 1871–1934; Edmonia LIMERICK EMBREY 1878–1951
Whitson G. SHUMATE Feb. 5, 1842 Aug. 28, 1928; His Wife Virginia EMBREY Jan. 18, 1844 Jan. 25, 1935
DAVIS George Milton 1880–1950; Elsie THOMAS 1889–1977

Stanley William SMITH 1881 Died October 4, 1965 aged 78 years; Sister Mary B. 1885–1973
SMITH Father Thomas W. 1850–1926; Mother Emma J. 1850–1936

WALTER William Ward July 18, 1873 July 28, 1943; Annie Catherine Jan. 3, 1879–July 20, 1965 Father Mother
George M. WALTER Son of W. W. & A. C. WALTER April 13, 1899 Jan. 25, 1919
WALTER Raymond W. Sept. 2, 1897 Jan. 14, 1975; Verlie E. Dec. 20, 1904 Oct. 12, 1977
Mary V. KANE Nov. 20, 1852 May 30, 1936
James T. WALTER 1897–1978
Mary V. WALTER 1900–1989

ETHERIDGE Charles R. May 30, 1905; Grace B. Aug. 29, 1905 Feb. 12, 1989

HALTERMAN W. B. Nov. 27, 1902 Jan. 3, 1984; Margie V. Apr. 22, 1915
Moved from BROWN family cemetery:
John T. BROWN Born June 24, 1839 died Nov. 5, 1915; Lucy C. BROWN born Aug. 17, 1846 died June 12, 1890
Austin Loco HALTERMAN TEC 5 US ARMY WORLD WAR II Jan. 13, 1916 Dec. 24, 1982 *(a helper on the first edition of this book)*
Simon L. HALTERMAN 1878–1938
HALTERMAN Leander H. Sept. 19, 1916 Dec. 13, 1982; Margaret G. Nov. 24, 1917

HOLDER Thomas Winfield June 9, 1899 Mar. 5, 1981; Victoria EDWARDS Aug. 15, 1900 Mar. 5, 1989
William B. HERNDON 1867–1950
Victor JAMES Died Jan. 25, 1935; Emma JAMES Died Feb. 13, 1935
George Melvin BROWN September 14, 1880 Feberuary 29, 1961

Lester T. CUPP US ARMY July 31, 1904 June 11, 1985
Leroy J. Son of Marcus & Ollie CUPP Oct. 20, 1910 Feb. 4, 1932
Russell E. Son of Marcus & Ollie CUPP Sept. 8, 1908 June 22, 1935
Mother Ollie E. CUPP Nov. 2, 1882 Dec. 9, 1974
Mabel E. CUPP June 13, 1902 Sept. 6, 1986
Harold C. Beloved Son of Ashby & Audrey WILLIAMS April 26, 1921 June 2, 1924

Ashby Deming Son of Ashby & Audrey WILLIAMS Aug. 29, 1919 Mar. 29, 1920
Grace Belle Daughter of Ashby & Audrey WILLIAMS Dec. 15, 1917 Jan.. 15, 1919
Audrey BROWNE WILLIAMS November 22, 1892 April 10, 1931
Turner Ashby WILLIAMS Sept. 30, 1896 June 13, 1965

Leathe L. KERNS April 7, 1862 Nov. 15, 1915
William D. KERNS Dec. 15, 1855 Feb. 8, 1915
Mattie EMBREY NUICK 1864–1948
Lucy STRIBLING EMBREY 1827–1895; Edna Harriet STRIBLING 1838–1922
Martha STRIBLING JOHNS 1844–1921
THARPE Father Smith Henry 1847–1925; Penelope DRAKE 1860–1934; Lucian Everett 1889–1940 Brother
FINNALL Webb S. Apr. 3, 1865 Nov. 26, 1938; Susan E. Sept. 14, 1869
Lewis Thomas FINNALL Mar. 3, 1904 June 11, 1979
Wilmer D. DINGLE DISTRICT OF COLUMBIA S2 US NAVY WORLD WAR II Oct. 3, 1926 Mar. 18, 1974
McMAHON Bernard L. June 26, 1909 Oct. 23, 1986; Louise W. July 28, 1904 Dec. 20, 1975
Samuel H. EDWARDS July 31, 1866 Sept. 20, 1951

Susie D. EDWARDS Feb. 18, 1877 Aug. 7,. 1956
Edward S. EDWARDS Jan. 3, 1912 July 7, 1945
Samuel H. EDWARDS June 24, 1910 July 4, 1911

Beverly Russell BROWNE August 16, 1903 June 28, 1929
Emma Florence Wife of Philip J. BROWNE July 4, 1869 Feb. 27, 1927
Philip Deming BROWNE April 24, 1890–March 15, 1917
Hugh Cameron BROWNE March 28, 1895 Aug. 16, 1924
Philip Jackson BROWNE March 9, 1864 May 5, 1935
Hurst Herbert CLAYPOOL 1883–1942
Christopher C. CLAYPOOL 1856–1945
Martha ANDERSON CLAYPOOL 1861–1949
Edsell Hayward COPPAGE Nov. 3, 1931; Kathryn Louise COPPAGE March 9, 1926 Dec. 14, 1989

Della C. POE 1884–1964
PRICE Jesse R. Sept. 13, 1881 May 27, 1948; Anna G. June 13, 1887 Jan. 27, 1965 Father Mother
Wesley Harold GIERSDORF Feb. 13, 1896 Sept. 28, 1961
Lottie EBERT Wife of William L. GIERSDORF Nov. 22, 1871 Oct. 11, 1961
CLARK Elvira G. Dec. 12, 1897 July 9, 1964; John Lindsay Sept. 13, 1902 May 24, 1965
LACY William Kenneth June 26, 1929 Nov. 25, 1989
SHOLL Lyman David Jan. 24, 1914; Jane EDWARDS Mar. 21, 1916
PRICE Claude Lee, Sr. Sept. 3, 1907 Oct. 12, 1977
Geneva L.GLASCOCK 1965–1965
Roscoe H. PRICE August 19, 1920 September 6, 1968
Steven A. JEFFRIES 1986–1986 *(fhm)*
Haskell Robert, Jr. Son of Haskell & Hilda CARMICHAEL Feb 9, 1940 Jan., 1942
DINKLE William Allen Jan. 6, 1874 Dec. 25, 1941; Pearl PHILLIPS May 13, 1877 Oct. 31, 1969
Reathy M. DINKLE July 25, 1906 Jan. 16, 1988

Haskell Robert CARMICHAEL M SGT US MARINE CORPS WORLD WAR II 1908 1976
Hilda BREEDEN CARMICHAEL Sept. 26, 1917 Sept. 29, 1978
Joseph Ford THOMPSON April 4, 1893 December 7, 1959
Frances M. RILEY April 18, 1847 March 6, 1926; His Wife Amelia F. RILEY December 27, 1856 October 12,1918

Snowden FINNALL Sept. 13, 1862 Jan. 1, 1927
Mary E. ESKRIDGE Wife of Morgan L. FINNALL Born Dec. 25, 1830 Died Aug. 28, 1912
FINNALL Clarence W. Oct. 5, 1859 Feb. 9, 1942
Morgan I. FINNALL Born April 13, 1830 Died March 17, 1901

Ann F. beloved Wife of Lemuel PETTY Born Feb, 15, 1829 Died Nov. 15, 1913
Lemuel PETTY Born July 25, 1827 Died Mar. 28, 1902

ANDERSON Catherine T. June 12, 1908; Andie F. June 26, 1898 May 2, 1947
Everett Lee ANDERSON Aug. 1888 Dec. 8, 1936
Benjamin Hiter ANDERSON Feb. 18, 1858 Sept. 8, 1927
Olive Ettie ANDERSON Jan. 6, 1866 July 30, 1946
Jane Hunter ANDERSON Infant Daughter of B. H. & O. E. ANDERSON Born July 16, 1895 Died May 10, 1897 Aged 1 yr. 9 mos.

Andrew ANNS Born June 13, 1834 Died April 20, 1904
Mary Jane ANNS Aug. 28, 1839 June 1, 1927
BOLEN Newman Earl Aug. 21, 1926 Dec. 10, 1980; Bertha (Bette) Mar. 27, 1929
John F. RILEY Co C 8 Va Inf C. S. A.

Thomas T. JONES Co A 9 Va Cav C. S. A.
T. T. JONES 1846–1924; Byrdie JONES 1851–1884
Hugh Clifton Son of T. T. & Byrdie JONES Born June 30, 1874 Died May 15, 1897
Alonzo T. JONES Born April 3, 1876 Died July 18, 1876 aged 3 months 15 days
Manuel Edward GARRETT March 20, 1896 February 24, 1971
Edward R. PETERS VIRGINIA PFC CO L 163 INFANTRY WORLD WAR I Sept. 22, 1895 May 3, 1967; Esther H. Sept. 27, 1898
HELM Cornelius H. July 25, 1859 Dec. 1, 1938; Fannie Belle June 18, 1856 June 28, 1946
Laura E. HELM Jan. 28, 1896 June 1, 1956

Bessie CROPP SMITH July 2, 1884 Oct. 6, 1957
SMITH Ray E. February 2, 1908 April 28, 1982; Gladys E. January 27, 1908 December 27, 1968
SMITH James W. Dec, 2, 1918; Audrey S. July 5, 1927 May 8, 1979

HANSBOROUGH Ida B. June 28, 1887 Dec. 4, 1955; H. Ashton Oct. 27, 1878 Aug. 10, 1956
Ashton H. HANSBOROUGH, Jr. April 12, 1901 Oct. 26, 1979
Elijah Thomas HANSBOROUGH VIRGINIA TEC 5 BTRY A 573 AA BN CAC WORLD WAR II Feb. 1, 1922 Oct. 24, 1972; Marianne W.

Herman Lee CAMPBELL Sept. 6, 1906 Mar. 22, 1976
KEMPER W. Leonard Oct. 10, 1888 Feb. 7, 1970; Cora S. Oct. 28, 1888 May 19, 1974
Susan A. SHUMATE Mar. 9, 1850 Jan. 17, 1941
Ollie J. SMITH Sept. 20, 1949; Everett J. SMITH Nov. 7, 1943
SMITH Everett Saxton May 8, 1911 Sept. 6, 1979

Edward GARRETT 1925–1935
Bessie V. GARRETT HURST November 1, 1907 May 21, 1968
Dorothy Jane GARRETT February 19, 1932 July 2, 1950

JOHNS William Henry October 14, 1882 December 12, 1961; Olive BROWNE February 15, 1888 February 7, 1968
Lawrence B. ANNS Sept. 5, 1860–June 8, 1924; His Wife Emma J. ANNS Feb. 18, 1867 March 7, 1944

Barbara Jane BOLEN Dau. of Earl & Bette Feb. 4, 1953 June 30, 1979
BOLEN Newman B. Sept. 15, 1896 Died Oct. 17, 1970; Pearl A. June 26, 1898 Aug. 21, 1964
John A. BOLEN 1950–1968 Son of Earl and Bette June 21, 1950 September 14, 1968

John H. YATES 1866–1939; His Wife Zella McCONCHIE 1886–1964
Colbert Powell Son of John & Mary YATES Aug. 8, 1942 Aug. 26, 1942
W. B. McCONCHIE
Robert A. McCONCHIE Born 1837 Died Aug. 20, 1908; Mary I. His Wife Born Mar. 20, 1848 Died Mar. 15, 1909

D. A. EDWARDS Mar. 10, 1867–July 15, 1942
B. A. EDWARDS Jan. 6, 1857–Feb. 18, 1929
Lucy Ann EDWARDS Jan. 24, 1826 Nov. 14, 1901; William G. EDWARDS Sept. 24, 1828 Mar. 6, 1912

W. J. MANUEL Born June 14, 1823 Died March 21, 1906
Sarah J. MANUEL Sept. 14, 1827 Dec. 1, 1913
Rosa V. MANUEL Jan. 5, 1864 Mar. 20, 1915
G. H. MANUEL Born March 29, 1861 Died June 3, 1898

Raymond EMBREY 1907–1907
Warner L. KEMPER 1914–1914
Rufus J. EMBREY Apr. 13. 1952 Feb. 1, 1934
Catherine E. EMBREY March 14, 1855 June 28, 1935
Ida J. EMBREY Sept. 4, 1879 Sept. 17, 1961
Arthur W. EMBREY May 21, 1881 Aug. 27, 1910
Estelle E. RICKER Apr. 3, 1877 Nov. 24, 1953
A. Leslie EMBREY July 21, 1907 Oct. 7, 1936

EDWARDS Charles Carlin June 12, 1908 Sept. 23, 1985; Louise JAMES June 29, 1909
Eugene Elwood KEMPER VIRGINIA S2 USNR WORLD WAR II Sept. 20, 1915 April 17, 1949
David R. KEMPER VIRGINIA PFC CO L 31 INF 7 INF DIV KOREA PH May 4, 1926 June 4, 1951
John Vincent Son of John & Caroline GARRETT May 29, 1963 February 12, 1968
ANNS Baby Boy Born Dec. 31, 1971
ANNS Elmer H. Nov. 19, 1905 Dec. 4, 1967; Myrtle A. Sept. 22, 1902 March 11, 1986
Samuel H. GARRETT Aug. 21, 1930 Aug. 2, 1986
June Ivan GROVE May 20, 1943 July 18, 1943
William Clarence EMBREY VIRGINIA SGT QMC WORLD WAR I June 1, 1888 February 25, 1951
Wallace W. EMBREY Aug. 9, 1845 Jan. 8, 1912

HELM James Thomas August 15, 1869 Jan. 31, 1947; Florence J. Dec. 4, 1868 July 25, 1965
Virginia A. HELM Born Aug. 9, 1828 Died Feb. 12, 1904
James H. HELM Born June 28, 1830 Nov. 13, 1900

Lucian M. MANUEL Co A 12 Va Cav C.S.A. 1845–1907
MANUEL Lucian M. 1845–1907; Mary S., 1847–1905; Garland L. 1867–1899; William L. 1872–1912; Maud J. 1872–1906; Frank E. 1884–1925; Herman C. 1895–1923; Flossie M. 1900–1944; Gertrude J. 1878–1948; Anna

Mae 1865–1968

W. C. RALLS Born March 1, 1852 Died Aug. 6, 1931
Merle R. MOFFETT 1887–1959 *(fhm)*
John E. MOFFETT July 18, 1899 Oct. 11, 1944
BROOKS Zoraida T. 1878–1919; Joseph W. 1874–1948

Lucretia B. Wife of Dr. C. D. RICKER July 26, 1866 Mar. 5, 1912
Chas D. RICKER MAJOR MED CORPS USA Husband of Estelle H. RICKER Mar. 16, 1876 Aug. 4, 1919
COX James William March 7, 1889 Sept. 23, 1937; Florence RALLS May 25, 1890 July 21, 1944
GONZALES Marie COX Mar. 31, 1921; John Vincent Aug. 14, 1920 Mar. 12, 1984
JACOBS Hugh T. Dec. 13, 1897 Oct. 7, 1955; Olive M. Oct. 25, 1900
Anna M. BROOKS 1877–1959
Nannie T. LEE Born Feb. 28, 1841 Died July 7, 1968
Harry STRIBLING PFC US ARMY Jan. 13, 1921 Dec. 25, 1976 served in WORLD WAR II 29TH DIV
STRIBLING Hugo Nov. 26, 1912; Edith E. April 5, 1920
Elizabeth COX HENNIGH Oct. 7, 1898 March 5, 1970
LOMAX Mother Nellie M. Nov. 2, 1889 June 30, 1976
Nannie T. COX 1891–1918
Martha E. BROOKS
Alonzo H. BROOKS
EMBREY Sumpter M. June 6, 1890 Jan. 2, 1973; Emma P. Feb. 20, 1919 Nov. 24, 1919; Lucy K. May 3, 1890
   April 8, 1976
William WILCIE Oct. 7, 1895; Minnie E. Sept. 17, 1897 Apr. 22, 1989
LAWS Father Rex Aug. 13, 1920; Maybelle S. May 12, 1922 Dec. 13, 1983
EMBREY Leo Ray Sept. 8, 1909 Aug. 7, 1986; Lucy Arlene Nov. 20, 1911 Oct. 31, 1983
Ruby Mae Nov. 30, 1924 July 18, 1925 Daughter of J. J. & Blanche STRIBLING
Bernice [STRIBLING] Aug. 18, 1923 Oct. 31, 1923
STRIBLING Joseph Jasper Sept. 5, 1877 Feb. 12, 1936; Blanche RECTOR Feb. 7, 1889 Dec. 11, 1968
Leroy STRIBLING July 18, 1915 Jan. 8, 1937
Elnora OLIVER RECTOR Dec. 28, 1847 Died Nov. 25, 1947; Daniel B. RECTOR 1879–1969 *(fhm)*
Janice Ann Daughter of Wm. F. & Dorothy C. JOHNS Nov. 23, 1942 Nov. 27, 1942
John W. GUY Born Mar. 1840 Died July 1914
Susan Ann Beloved Wife of J. W. GUY Died Dec. 11, 1906 aged 65 yrs. 14 days
Mary LEWIS FINNALL Dec. 17, 1871 Aug. 30, 1958
Hattie Isabel FINNALL April 9, 1867 Nov. 17, 1948
Frances Elizabeth Daughter of Howe & Mary FINNALL July 3, 1911 Nov. 1, 1915
Infant Son of Howe & Marie FINNALL Aug. 30, 1907
Beulah Elizabeth FINNALL Born Feb. 3, 1902 Died Dec. 28, 1902
Norman R. EDWARDS 1873–1957

Morgan Cemetery, Delaplane, Virginia
Located on Route 724 on farm next to above on top of hill back of barn and very old house. Stone and wire fences
   both long down and cattle in field. Many stone markers and several broken bottoms of marble markers. Slightly
   cleaned up. Resurveyed September 13, 1993.
footstone: J. A. W. S. and another S. M.

Susan MORGAN Born December 20th 1770 Died February 11th 1840
Joseph MORGAN *(no dates)*
John A. W. SMITH Born June 2, 1781 Died Sept. 1, 1892

Mosby - Waugh - Whitfield Cemetery, Somerville, Virginia
Located 1 mile South Somerville, North Route 617. Source: L. Arthur Grove. 9 unmarked graves. Resurveyed

Fannie MOSBY Apr. 12, 1857 Aug. 14, 1921
Mary WAUGH 1844–1929
Henry WHITFIELD Aug. 10, 1850 June 26, 1927

Mount Airy Cemetery, Dudie, Virginia
Located on Route 689, Dudie Road, behind house (brick) former site of "Pullen" house. Old oak tree on site, day lillies beside section of old stone fence. Approximately one quarter acre. Cemetery vanished March 17, 1991 The following inscriptions were furnished by Mr. George Parr, Warrenton, Virginia, an old inhabitant County Court Records.

William H. WINGFIELD Born June 1, 1844 Died February 9, 1919
His wife, Susan Keith FITZGERALD Born May 11, 1837 Died August 25, 1901
Lucy V. STEVENS Born May 8, 1877 Died September 21, 1881
Our mother Lucy V. Wife of S. S. JONES Born in Culpeper County May 18, 1823 Died in Portsmouth, Virginia
 October 9, 1883 "Asleep dear Mother, thy toils are over, Take thy rest so oft needed before."

Mount Carmel (Black), near Morrisville, Virginia

Rev. T. W. NEWMAN Born July 25, 1832 Died Dec. 6, 1903 *(former pastor of Mt. Carmel, The Grove, & other Baptist churches. Son Cephas buried in same cemetery at 50 years old.)*

Mount Ephraim Cemetery, Goldvein, Virginia
Located at end of Route 803 off Route 615 South of Route 651. Cemetery shown on Land Tax Maps, but could only find flagpole in front yard with azalea garden around it and bronze plaque, although I suspect there must be a ROYALL & COOKE cemetery also.

William J. GLASCOCK 1888–1954 One & big brother to children of Augustine R. and Josephine GLASCOCK
 Augustine Charles Louis Clara Francis Raymond William Russell Frederick Norman

Mount Holly Baptist Church Cemetery, Sumerduck, Virginia
Located West of Sumerduck on Route 651. Some quartz and fieldstone markers. Resurveyed 1991.

Capt. John C. Son of the Rev. J. G. WITHERSPOON of Iredell Co., N. C. Died Nov. 8, 1863 aged 26 years
Velme C. Daughter of John & Lizzie SMITH Died July 26, 1896 aged 9 mos. 7 dys.
My Father Haris FREEMAN, Sr. Died Nov. 16, 1877 aged 81 years

Mount Horeb Church Cemetery, Bristersburg, Virginia
Located South West intersection of Routes 616 & 639 to rear of church. 3 rock markers in old area covered with periwinkle. Two plots fenced. Resurveyed May 27, 1990.

Sarah T. PENNINGTON who departed this life July 1, 1896 Aged 81 years
Pauline PENNINGTON Departed this life March 16, 1895 in the 75th year of her age
Richard Walter TULLOSS June 19, 1884 Oct. 20, 1899 *(stone found broken 1990)*
Susan T. COX 1866–1941; Clarence R. COX 1906–1938
Heyber COX Born Mar. 2, 1867 Died Mar. 3, 1923

Joseph H. GEORGE 1856–1920 Corma M. His Wife 1860–1895 Mary G. VOORHEESE 1883–1913 Hattie G.
 MEGBY 1889–1918 Baby WATTS 1895 Maude M. GEORGE 1888–1889

JAMES William C. Nov. 3, 1860 Mar. 1, 1940 Mary V. June 5, 1868
Fred B. McWELCH Nov. 23, 1942 Dec. 3, 1946 *(stone missing 1990 - unmarked footstone, no headstone)*

The following information is from Barbara Cooper, Kensington, MD taken from family Bible (Mrs. Cooper states cemetery is in terrible condition):
FICKLIN Sallie
COOPER Baby 1946
COOPER Benjamin Born Dec. 16, 1805 Died June 21, 1894
COOPER Sarah C. Born April 2, 1830 Died Aug. 4, 1895

Mount Sterling Slave Cemetery, Warrenton, Virginia
Located South side Route 605 just 10 feet off the road by tree at top of second hill East 29 according to Mary Ann (Gray) Day who grew up there. Rock markers only.

Murray Cemetery, Marshall, Virginia
Located on Route 705 about one mile North of Route 55 on left in field. Eleanore G. Thompson gave me this inscription copies in 1930s but I understand the graves have been since moved to Mashall cemetery.

Reuben MURRAY Died June 13, 184(5?) in the 84th year of his age

Myles - Bailey Cemetery, Orlean, Virginia
Located 2.6 miles South of Orlean 0.2 mile off Route 688 on Route 743, edge of woods on right. Unmarked or fieldstone marked graves of John Henry MYLES & Fanny MYLES

Robert F. MYLES 1884–1960; Turner MYLES 1899–1930
William H. BAILEY VIRGINIA SGT TROOP D 10TH CAV PVT November 22 1872 Mar 1 1917

Nalley - Strother Cemetery, near Paris, Virginia
Located off Route 688 on Route 711 0.4 mile on North West side of road atop hill. Overgrown. Nalley graves individually enclosed in stone walls with wooden roofs. Roofs now fallen in. Strother portion of cemetery enclosed with iron fence. Another Strother cemetery with stone markers only further back on mountain. Resurveyed October 24, 1993.

2 fieldstone markers
John NALLEY Born July 4th 1789 Died March 25th 1855 Aged 65 years 8 months and 21 days
Sarah Wife of Aaron NALLEY Born in 1751 Died Septr. 8th 1834 In the 83rd year of her age
Sarah Wife of Jessie NALLEY Daughter of Jacob & Mary Cornwell Born July 4th 1791 Died August 13th 1850 Aged 59 years 1 mo. & 9 days
Jesse NALLEY was born September 22, 1778 departed this life April 12th 1857
Mary Catherine STROTHER Wife of James F. GREEN Born Nov. 4, 1835 Died Mar. 20, 1872
Alfred M. STROTHER April 1, 1813 Oct. 25, 1912; Sue Vergie Wife of A. M. STROTHER Mar. 12, 1817 Aug. 19, 1880
S. T. S.; J. M. S.; W. J. S.; Infant
Our Father James F. GREEN Born Sept. 3, 1828 Died May 21, 1892
Channing D. STROTHER Dec. 11, 1880 Dec. 11, 1939
Susan E. [EDMONDS] FERGUSON Born Sept. 1, 1821 Died Jan. 12, 1891
William M. FERGUSON Born Oct. 4, 1826 Died Jan. 12, 18[7?]2
George William STROTHER April 24, 1837 March 10, 1900
Sarah Margaret STROTHER March 5, 1840 Dec. 17, 1909
Infant Daughter Dec. 22, 1867
E. May STROTHER March 6, 1869 Sept. 2, 1937
Wilber Jackson STROTHER March 31, 1879 Nov. 28, 1880

John A. Son of John STROTHER Born Dec. 16, 1809 Died Feb. 11, 1891
John STROTHER Born Nov. 6, 1798 Died Dec. 20, 1881
Robert F. STROTHER Born Feb. 15, 1841 Died Mar. 28, 1901 Aged 60 yrs. 1 mo. & 13 dys.
Frances A. Wife of R. F. STROTHER Dec. 23, 1836 Nov. 20, 1912
James R. STROTHER Born Nov. 17, 1838 Died Jan. 10, 1862
Julia A. Wife of John STROTHER Born Dec. 10, 1800 Died Feb. 11, 1891
Mother Sue Wife of Armistead

Newhouse Cemetery, Opal, Virginia
Located West of Route 29 just South of intersection of Routes 17 & 29 in field below house in clump of trees, cleaned up, fence removed Several fieldstone markers. Resurveyed December 3, 1993.

S. H. NEWHOUSE Born Mar. 13, 1814 Died Feb. 20, 1898
Bellfield NEWHOUSE Wife of S. H. NEWHOUSE Born Feb. 11, 1823 Died Feb. 10, 1895

Newhouse Cemetery, Warrenton, Virginia
Well-kept by present owner. Evidence of fence once surrounding it. Resurveyed December 3, 1993.

Nourse Cemetery, "Timberlane". Casanova, Virginia
Located North Route 616 1 mile South Casanova on fence line with "Weston" near house.

Joan W. NOURSE VIRGINIA 2ND LT 554 AAF BASE UNIT WORLD WAR II March 26 1923 Dec 22, 1946
Walter B. NOURSE VIRGINIA 2D LT 320 FIELD ARTY 82 DIV WORLD WAR I April 23 1893 March 3 1945

Oak Grove Baptist Church Cemetery, "Embreys Shop", Somerville, Virginia
Located 0.3 mile South Route 610 East Route 637 to left of church.
Sallie Eva GIBSON 1886–1969; Solomon A. GIBSON 1888–1965
John GIBSON 1935–1965
William TIBBS 1878–1960
J. R. EMBREY 1880–1956
Miss Cecelia Ann GIBSON Died February 6, 1953 Aged 14 yrs. 7 months
Mrs. Oather G. GIBSON Died March 22, ----
Sallie BROWN 1890–1967; Robert L. BROWN 1898–1967
James H. BROWN 1872–1959
Addie EMBREY 1880–1923
Nolan OLIVER 1894–1964; Irva OLIVER 1905–1952; Ella OLIVER 1865–1952
James MORRIS 1946–1960; Richard MORRIS 1949–1960
Eddie L. BOLTON 1865–1965

Oakwood Farm Cemetery, Delaplane, Virginia
Located on North side Route 724 1 mile West of Route 17. Ball tombstone in yard against meat house, others in plot back of house and garden, former iron fence down and evidence of a number of graves. Resurveyed September 12, 1993.

Masieth [?] second Daughter of John H__ND born of September 1832 departed this life on the 15th day of August Anno Domini 1833 aged 11 months and 13 days
Martha Wife of Granville PAGE born January 12, 1821 died Mar. 14 1855
Kitty Short BALL who was born the 17th day of September 1798 and departed this life 30th day of May 1830 *(moved to Farrow Cemetery, Markham)*

O'Bannon Cemetery, "Old Tavern", Warrenton, Virginia
Located 1 mile North Route 17 North East Route 698 at first right angle in road behind garage at second old house

at end of mountain lane, overgrown, only one grave.

Here lyeth the body of [John?] O'BANNON who departed this life Feb. 1791

O'Bannon Cemetery, "Old Tavern", Warrenton, Virginia
Located just East of Route 17 South Route 245 between house and barn, some fieldstone markers.

John O'BANNON Born Oct. 12th 1780 Died Sept. 30th 1821 aged 40 yrs. 11 months & 18 days.

O'Bannon - Glascock Cemetery
Located on Route 698, (O'Bannon's Road) from Meadowville to the Orange County Hunt Kennels on "Chetwood", the Skinker family home. Back of the garage at the old house some distance behind present dwelling.
John O'BANNON member of 1st Vestry of Leeds Parish 1769
Henry GLASCOCK 1790-1880 son of Thomas & Agnes RECTOR GLASCOCK
Jane COMBS GLASCOCK his wife

Ogilvie - Klipstein Cemetery, "Rosevale", New Baltimore, Virginia
Located on Route 694 1 mile West from Route 674. Research by Frances B. Foster September 27, 1937.

"One grave in the lilac bordered garden believed to be a Klipstein child. About 500 yards away is the old slave burying ground, around which was a stone wall, but that has fallen away. The part of the farm on which was the Ogilvie graveyard has been sold long ago and the graves all obliterated by cultivation of the land."

"We went 36 degrees South of Route 674 on Route 694. There were bushes and fences that made it hard for us to find the grave. We could not find the Klipstein childs' grave. The graves we found were just impressions in the ground. There were four impressions. Two had fieldstone markers." Resurveyed August 27, 1994 by Justin Frazier.

Oliver Cemetery, Somerville, Virginia
Located 3 miles South West of Route 616 North Route 617 0.25 mile off road by lane in field on Sillaman farm, poor fence, honeysuckle. Data obtained by Bob Cooper & Kenneth Eskridge.

W. W. OLIVER Born August 4, 1848 Died May 11, 1896
Catherine [E or J or G] OLIVER Born April 29, 1848 Died July 14, 1923

Orlean Methodist Church Cemetery, Orlean, Virginia
Located on Route 689 in Orlean, Va., iron fenced, well kept. Resurveyed March 20, 1991.

Amos G. EWERS Aug. 9, 1909 Aug. 19, 1972
HOLLAND George Louis HOLLAND 1832–1927; His Wife Jacqueline M. PAYNE 1843–1926 Minnie
  HOLLAND BUSHONG 1881–1926 Elizabeth S. HOLLAND 1878–1966
Mother Henrietta PAYNE EWERS 1878–1953
PAYNE Hugh Golder 1847–1928; Charlott V. 1850–1926

ATHEY James Cone 1872–1930; Elizabeth FLEMING 1872–1964
Clara Summerville Beloved Daughter of Benton S. & M. E. FLEMING Born Dec. 20, 1873 Died Jan. 18, 1899
Martha Eugenia FLEMING 1846–1927
Benton Scott FLEMING February 10, 1843 Died July 19, 1886

BANNESTER Mary Barton PAYNE April 20, 1881 Dec. 12, 1942 Mother
Dr. Amos PAYNE Born Sept. 11, 1808 Died Jan. 31, 1887
Elizabeth BARTON Wife of Dr. Amos PAYNE Born March 11, 1817 Died May 12, 1895

Ernestine V. Daughter of Dr. & Elizabeth B. PAYNE Born October 25, 1860 Died November 7, 1883

Edward C. 1868–1873 Amie B. 1870–1873 Catharine 1877–1877 Amos E. 1884–1884 Leslie W. 1887–1887 Beloved children of Upton & Mary C. PAYNE

John Eston PAYNE Beloved Husband of Belle S. PAYNE 1874–1902 Son of Upton & Mary C. PAYNE

Upton PAYNE Born March 13, 1845 Died Jan. 17, 1921 Mary C PAYNE Born March 7, 1845 Died Feb. 20, 1933

Hugh Golder SMITH Son of John P. & Mary G. SMITH Born at Orlean, Va. July 7, 1834 Died at Corder, Mo. March 22, 1900

Lizzie S. Wife of Dr. M. F. HANSBROUGH Born Sept. 6, 1857 Died July 29, 1889 Daughter of Dr. & Elizabeth B. PAYNE

Edward A. PAYNE Born Feby 16, 1838 Killed in the battle of Chancellorsville Nov. 27, 1863 Wm. Undril PAYNE Born Aug. 10, 1850 Died Oct. 1, 1877 Sons of Dr. Amos & E. B. PAYNE

Frances EWERS WHELCHEL Oct. 4, 1916 Oct. 2, 1979

Charlotte EWERS McARDLE Jan. 25, 1899 Jan. 11, 1984

Owens Cemetery, The Plains, Virginia

Located North East intersection of Routes 601 & 628 in second field North East of old house. In grove of trees in cow pasture, unfenced. Accompanied in 1969 by descendants Mrs. Jean Smith Barnes and Mr. Preston Smith. About 0.25 acre filled with graves. 16 or more fieldstone markers. Resurveyed October 18, 1993.

Elizabeth Wife of Cuthbert OWENS Born Nov. 28, 1794 Died May 5th 1860 Aged 65 years 5 months and 6 days *(missing 1993)*

Cuthbert OWENS who departed this life February 22d 1841 in the 55th year of his age

Wm. M. OWENS Born Feb. 22, 1841 Killed at Loudon Heights, Va. Jan. 10, 1864 Cuthbert OWENS Jr. Son of Joshua OWENS Born July 12, 1843 Fell at Battle of Yellow Tavern Aug. 11, 1864 Simon K. OWENS Born March 22, 1839 Fell at Battle of Williamsburg 1862 Cuthbert OWENS Born March 8, 1830 Died Jan. 18, 1899 Wounded in the Battle of the Wilderness

John Samuel OWENS October 8, 1825 August 25, 1910

Caroline A. CALDWELL Wife of John CALDWELL and Daughter of Cuthbert & Elizabeth OWENS Born July 14, 1823 Died January 21, 1857 *(missing 1993)*

Padgett Cemetery, Meetze, Virginia

Located South West intersection of Routes 643 & 574 on a knoll about 400 yards North West of house. Stone wall, 40 feet x 50 feet with several cedars & a Japanese maple. To the West of stone wall crudely marked graves, within wall appears to be full with fieldstone markers. Data obtained by Mr. Meade Palmer, owner.

R. A. PADGETT only Son of Demsey and Sarah PADGETT Born 31 April 1819 Died 7 July 1861

Addine WYMER Daughter of Demsey and Sarah PADGETT Born Jan. 23, 1821 and departed this life May 20, 1853

Payne Cemetery, Marshall, Virginia

Located to left of Route 737 at end of Route 799 to right of house , no fence, boxwood, well kept. 18 feet x 42 feet. Resurveyed November 13, 1990.

Jas. M. PAYNE Mar. 1815 Oct. 10, 1879 His Wife Margaret E. Aug. 18, 1821 Apl. 18, 1897; Cora A. PAYNE Feb. 2, 1851 Apr. 17, 1905; Nellie C. PAYNE 1886–1931

Abraham H. STRINGFELLOW Apl. 5, 1856 Sep. 21, 1911; His Wife Ella Lee Apl. 7, 1863 Mar 15, 1895

Catherine W. STROTHER June, 28, 1846 May 25, 1871

Alexander PAYNE Died Oct. 16, 195[6?] aged 91 yearsBmos 24 ds *(fhm)*

James Son of R. L. & W.? STRINGFELLOW

Mary Fannie PAYNE Born March 22, 1846 Died Sept. 27, 1888

Our parents Latham N. PAYNE March 16, 1857 Jan. 19, 1912; His Wife Mary F. March 22, 1856 Sept. 29, 1888

G. W. S. footstone

Payne Cemetery, Marshall, Virginia

Located on Route 776 1 mile off Route 738 to right in field near house, iron fence, well kept.

Corrie PAYNE CISLER 1885–1930
Annie M. Wife of L. A. PAYNE Born Feb. 3, 1894 Died Feb. 20, 1922
B. Scott PAYNE Born April 1, 1800 Died July 16, 1913
Mildred E. Wife of B. Scott PAYNE Born July 1, 1849 Died July 11, 1921

Payne Cemetery, Marshall, Virginia

Located on Route 738 one half mile north of intersection with Route 741 turn left (traveling north) at driveway at school.. Property of John and Donna Bloom at Fresta Valley Christian School. Picket fence 40 x 40, well maintained, descendants restored some of the stones recently. The following information suppolied by Vinton Everington.

Mary Margaret PAYNE Aug. 5, 1882 May 9, 1941
Ada THORPE wife of Vinton F. PAYNE May 26, 1872 Aug. 7, 1894
Vinton F. PAYNE Nov. 23, 1870 Feb. 25, 1930
Mittie E. wife of U. D. PAYNE Apr. 16, 1888 Aug. 20, 1916
Vriginus PAYNE, Born and Died Aug. 20, 1916
Warren A. PAYNE Oct. 12, 1858 Aug. 10, 1897
Alexander PAYNE Died May 13, 1892 Aged 70 years
Eleanore PAYNE Died Jan. 2, 1891 Aged 60 yrs, 6 mos. 11 das.

Payne (Luvega) Cemetery, Marshall, Virginia

Located to right of Route 721 several miles North of Route 738, in field beyond woods to right of house with stone wall and hemlock tree. Some fieldstone markers.

Georgia A. HERRELL Wife of T. R. PAYNE Born April 30, 1856 Died February 22, 1896
Roy PAYNE Born Nov. 10, 1894 Died Oct. 27, 1895
Thomas Son of R. S. & M. V. PAYNE Born Feb. 5, 1884 Died Aug. 9, 1884
Ethel WILSON July 17, 1920 Dec. 24, 1921 Baby

Payne Cemetery, Midland, Virginia

Located East Route 610 0.5 mile Route 806 North East of house end of private road in field on knoll near 2 cedars and a sycamore.

William S. PAYNE Born Dec. 23, 1811 Died June 27, 1887

Payne Cemetery, Orlean, Virginia

Located on East side of Route 737 between Routes 732 & 799 in stone enclosed wall to South of frame house. Rock markers and unmarked graves. 78 feet x 45 feet. Resurveyed November 13, 1990.

Willie M. UTTERBAGH Born June 16th 1876 Died Aug. 2, 1887
Patsy FISHER Born April 9, 1817 Died Feb. 1, 1887
Francis FISHER Departed this life Dec. 8, 1867 aged 53 years 6 mos. & 13 days
Thomas HIRST Born May 25, 1812 Died Sept. 13, 1881
Lucie M. HURST Born May 31, 1822 Died July 7, 1902
Mother Mrs Margaret PAYNE Born March 4, 1808 Died April 15, 1893
Francis PAYNE Died April 13, 1859 in the 79th year of his age He was a member of the Baptist Church
  Father…,Husband…
Aunt Patsy PAYNE who departed this life 24 May 1836 aged 47 years 3 months and 9 days

Ida PARKER CHAPMAN Feb. 15, 1898 Aug. 2, 1977

Payne Cemetery, Orlean, Virginia
Located 1 mile South of Route 732 on West side of Route 732 in field, enclosed by fallen over stone fence, about 0.25 acre with numerous fieldstone markers. Resurveyed 1993.

Thornton PAYNE Dec. 2, 1798 Nov. 10, 1875; His Wife Lucinda P. 1803– Mar. 11, 1868

Payne Cemetery, Orlean, Virginia
Located on Routes 635 and 730, Stillhouse Hollow Road.In clump of trees. Approximately 10+ graves - some with rock markers - some unmarked. Prior tenent on property said that 15 years ago there were about 8 tombstones all except on has disappeared. Remnants of stone wall surrounding wall around cemetery. Surveyed February 3, 1991.

Mary Jane PAYNE consort of John PAYNE [Jr.] and daughter of MOREHEAD WDTL May 2, 1833 aged 21 years 2 mo. and 27 days

Additional information regarding PAYNE family, John PAYNE, Jr. married Mary Jane MOREHEAD 9 Aug. 1831, per Early Fauquier County, Virginia Marriage Bonds. Also, Jane had sister Elenora married Benjamin RIXEY and sister Lucy Ann married Wm. K. BARBEE 1842

Payne Cemetery, "Bellevue", Warrenton, Virginia
Located at Bellevue on North side Route 628 1.5 mile West of Route 17. PAYNE and LAKE families moved to Warrenton. Data obtained from Joe Lawler, Marshall.

"I went over to 'Bellevue.' I collected some old-timers in the place and learned that there had been a Payne Cemetery there, but that it had been bulldozed some years ago to make way for a tenant house. The story was that the bodies had been removed. I suspect not, but who knows." James O. Hall of McLean, VA, November 16, 1971.

In Fauquier County, Virginia 1759–1959 pages 225–226 [Bellevue] was purchased in 1819 by Captain William [Winter] Payne, as he is not in the Warrenton Cemetery, we think Mr. Hall is correct in this assumption.

Payne Cemetery, "Clifton", Warrenton, Virginia
Located on Route 628 at home of Mrs. Jadwin, Cannonball Gate Road at "Clifton." stone wall enclosure with plague in wall. February 3, 1991

"Family burying ground of Captain William PAYNE of Clifton whose residence occupied the site of present dwelling 400 yards to the north east. The building was completed on June 2, 1799 and destroyed by fire on January 1, 1899.
*   Here lie buried*
Captain William PAYNE 1755-1837
Marion Andrew MORSON, his 2nd wife 1765-1840
Her sister Margaret MORSON, wife of Dr. William KINCAID, died 1822
Mary Conway Mason FITZHUGH, first wife of Arthur Alexander Morson PAYNE 1805-1842
Arthur, their son 1838-1842
Margaret Marion, infant daughter of Arthur A. M. PAYNE by his second wife Mary HUME 1846-1846
Lucy Battaile FITZHUGH sister of Mrs. Arthur A. M. PAYNE and daughter of Judge Nicolas FITZHUGH and his wife Sarah Washington ASHTON died 1852"

This memorial was erected in 1932 by a group of Captain William PAYNE'S descendents.

SAR emblem embedded in stone wall:

William PAYNE, *Captain, Virginia Militia, Revolutionary War*

DAR marker loose on ground for Captain William PAYNE *1775-1783, placed by the Washington-Lewis Chapter*

3 depressions outside of stone wall

Payne Cemetery, "Granville", Warrenton, Virginia
Located on Route 691 0.3 mile South of Route 628 South of house & garden, overgrown, some fieldstone markers.

Ella Daughter of Richards and Alice PAYNE Born the 11th Day of June 1812 Died the 29th day of January 1816
Alice Dixon Daughter of Richards and Alice PAYNE Born the 5th day of September 1815 and died the 28th day of July 1846
Daniel PAYNE Born June 17th 1781 Died Sept. 19th 1860
Elizabeth Winter Wife of Daniel PAYNE born Dec. 3, 1783 Died March 19th 1835
William Eustace Son of John D. and Lucy T. PAYNE Born September 2nd 1856 Died April 15th 1857
Robert Bolling Son of J. T. & Elizabeth MEREDITH died 1860
Elizabeth Winter Daughter of Daniel and Elizabeth PAYNE and Wife of John T. MEREDITH Born May 30, 1846 Died April 11, 1890
Alice PAYNE MEREDITH Daughter of John Taylor and Elizabeth PAYNE MEREDITH Born Apr. 30, 1853 Died July 13, 1906
Robert T. H. PAYNE Born 1811 Died 1814
John Scott PAYNE *(unmarked grave)*

Payne Family Cemetery, "Woodside", Bristersburg, Virginia
Located East Route 615 near intersection with Routes 609 & 639, edge of garden, boxwood.

G. Frank KELLY 1841–1889 Dora E. KELLY 1851–1887 Duff PAYNE 1838–1890 R. L. PAYNE 1848–1903 Annie PAYNE 1839–1878 Georgia PAYNE 1846–1876 Roy H. PAYNE 1841–1869 Rev. R. H. PAYNE 1810–1868 Catherine PAYNE 1815–1869

Payne - Kelly Cemetery, "Chestnut Lawn", Remington, Virginia
Located 3 miles South East of Remington on Route 651 back of field back of barn and house of Barret Weaver. Surrounded by stone wall and barbed wire fence, covered with periwinkle, well kept, some graves with no markers or stone markers.

James Marshall Son of Granville J. & Harriet E. KELLY Died August 19 1848 Aged 4 yrs 9 mos and 25 days
Margaret Daughter of Granville J. & Harriet E. KELLY Died March 17 1840 aged 3 years 3 months and 4 days
Mary Isham Daughter of G. J. & H. E. KELLY Died Nov. 26, 1857 aged 11 years 3 months & 9 days
Granville KELLY Born Jan. 12, 1821 Died Oct. 13, 1898
Harriet E. Wife of Granville J. KELLY Born August 15, 1822 Died April 30, 1900
Mary ISHAM Wife of J. W. JAMES and Daughter of James & Mary I. PAYNE Died Aug. 10, 1855 aged 28 years 5 months and 7 days
Mary J. PAYNE Wife of James PAYNE Born June 13, 1789 Died March 14 1868
James PAYNE Born June 20, 1791 Died April 2, 1869
Thomas Keith PAYNE Mar. 5, 1875 July 28, 1938
Mary Catherine Wife of D. J. PAYNE Dec. 13, 1829 Nov. 11, 1905
Daniel J. Son of Jas. & Mary I. PAYNE Jan. 31, 1825 Feb. 9, 1900
Harriet Judith Daughter of Daniel J. & Mary C. PAYNE Born Feb. 17, [1859?] Died Apl. 21, 1869

Peake Cemetery, "Hopewell Gap," The Plains, Virginia
Located 100' East Route 700 0.8 mile North Route 601 on fence line, slightly overgrown with periwinkle, about 50 feet x 100 feet, 8 fieldstone markers. Resurveyed November 14, 1993.

Mary Eliza PEAKE Jan. 23, 1850 March 22, 1923

Armenia PEAKE Beloved Wife of H. HOWDERSHELL Born Nov. 8, 1840 Died Aug. 6, 1910 [*H. HOWDERSHELL Died Nov. 1919 according to Page Howdershell*] *(missing 1993)*

Eva PEAKE CHAPMAN April 2, 1863 March 5, 1897

William H. YEATMAN Co. C 47 Va. Reg. C. S. A. 1841–1913 His Wife Virginia PEAKE 1847–1924

Cornelia E. Daughter of Joseph & Mary PEAKE Born Jan. 23, 1848 Died Sept. 27, 1877

Cosmella Daughter of Joseph & Mary PEAKE Born Jan. 31, 1857 Died Aug. 21, 1877

Rosa O'BANNON Died Nov. 9, 1891 Aged 86 years *(missing 1993)*

Joseph Milton PEAKE 1854–1929 His Wife Jane F. [Frances] 1850–1950 [P. H.]

Joseph S. SINCLAIR Beloved Husband of Susan L. SINCLAIR Born Sept. 22, 1825 Died July 4, 1905

Susan L. SINCLAIR Beloved Wife of Joseph S. SINCLAIR Born Aug. 22, 1825 Died Oct. 19, 1891

[Thomas A. BELT buried in unmarked grave [P. H.]

Peters Cemetery, Bristersburg, Virginia
Located East Route 616 about 1 mile South Route 607 across private drive from houses. Boteler Peters cemetery fenced and well kept. Bowen cemetery so overgrown that only one marker was visible although area about 50 feet x 50 feet.

Boteler M. PETERS 1886–1933

Infant of Alma LOMAX & Boteler PETERS July 1925

TUCKER *(large markerCno individual inscriptions)*

Margaret Louise REDD Oct. 12, 1838 Nov. 27, 1918

Henly Kenneth PETERS 1912-1913

Elizabeth PETERS June 30, 1914 July 14, 1914

Raymond PETERS June 30, 1914 July 16, 1914

Hugh PETERS 1915–1919

Louise Caroline PETERS 1846–1914 Jesse Mauzy PETERS 1829-1910

Mary PETERS 1883-1904

Bettie PETERS MILLER April 6, 1878 Feb. 15, 1944

Peters Cemetery, Bristersburg, Virginia
Located 0.25 mile West Route 616 North Route 806 back of old house in oak grove on road, fenced, cedars. 1 fieldstone marker.

Whitfield PETERS Born Aug. 21, 1841 Died Apr. 10, 1927 Nannie S. Wife of Whitfield PETERS Born March 1, 1848 Died Feb. 26, 1921

Pettitt - Huffman Cemetery, between Somerville & Elk Run, Virginia
Located 1 mile South of Elk Run, East on Route 637, .6 mile to Reed Farm on South side of Route 637, 200 yards from road under 3 large oak trees. Surveyed by L. Arthur Grove February 1994.

In fenced area:
Mother Susan A. HUFFMAN, Wife of Kendrick HEFLIN Jan. 28, 1860 Aug. 12, 1922
4 graves with field stone markers

Outside fenced area:
Departed this life Des. 30, 1830 John H. PETTITT aged 61

In second fenced area by two large oak trees:
12 field stone markers

Pilcher Cemetery, Midland, Virginia

Located at end of private road opposite intersection of Routes 646 & 610 in cedar grove back of barns, no fence, ponies grazing, all stones knocked down, few fieldstone markers. Cemetery now gone. Stones moved to Midland Cemetery in 1977 by Irene Pilcher Perrow.

Alexander [Spotswood] PILCHER Born Oct. 1, 1803 Died Dec. 2, 1881 Aged 78 years
Fannie P. PILCHER 1805–1897
John T. PILCHER May 12, 1838 Died Dec. 27, 1861
Maria F. PILCHER Born Sept. 12, 1836 Died 1853 aged 17 years

Pilgrim Rest Cemetery At Beulah Baptist Church, Broad Run, Virginia

Located East Route 600 West at end of Route 621 to East of church. Resurveyed July 18, 1990.

William M. FIELDS 1925–1990 *(fhm)*
Helen Ann FIELDS 1923–1973 *(fhm)*
George Levy PAYNE June 23, 1920 July 16, 1980
Alberna H. NELSON 1905–1982; Thurman H. NELSON 1908–1985
Marie F. CAMPBELL Sept. 4, 1904 Dec. 21, 1983
BUTLER, Joseph P. 1878 1946; Eleanor L. 1884–1960
Louise Myrtle CORUM 1924– 1967
Marie MASSIE 1897–1967
BUTLER Landon P. April 25, 1895 July 11, 1966
Constance M. ROSS 1863–1965
PERCELL Samuel, Jr. 1968–1987 *(fhm)*

Kenneth E. BUTLER 1917–1978 *(fhm)*
Norman A. BUTLER 1916–1978 *(fhm)*
Herman S. BUTLER 1905–1975 *(fhm)*

Esther L. ROWE 1921–1988 *(fhm)*
Charles M. BROWN 1912–1983 *(fhm)*
Elsie L. BROWN 1901–1981 *(fhm)*
fieldstone markers
Aubrey M. CARTER 1920–1978 *(fhm)*
fieldstone markers
Marth C. _____ Aged 100 yrs. *(fhm)*

12 fieldstone markers
Sister Carrie E. NELSON 1900–1931 *(fhm)*
Mother Martha A. NELSON 1876–1941
Charles H. NELSON Born Oct. 28, 1855 Died March 12, 1938
16 fieldstone markers
Annie BROWN Born 1879 Died Feb. 14, 1925 Pilgrim Pride Chamber 6081 Broad Run, Va.

Mother Sadie Ann FIELDS Nov. 23, 1895 May 20, 1961
Father John W. FIELDS Apr. 13, 1897 Mar. 27, 1978
Lillie M. WARFIELD April 11, 1893 Feb. 11, 1930
Mrs. George Mason MERCER 1900–1968 *(fhm)*
William H. MERCER PFC US ARMY WORLD WAR I 1898–1977
Keller E. CHRISTIAN 1927–1978 *(fhm)*
Raymond CHRISTIAN 1891–1971 *(fhm)*
Hugh R. PENDELTON Jan. 9, 1895 Mar. 20, 1967

John Willis LONG 1898–1974 *(fhm)*
Lucille L. CAMPBELL 1899–1974 *(fhm)*
Addie A. PENDELTEN Feb. 7, 1905 Oct. 12, 1966
Mary A. FIELDS 1887–1982 *(fhm)*
Vincent Silas GRIGSBY PFC US ARMY WORLD WAR II 1917–1976
Silas GRIGSBY *(fhm)*
Mary E. MERCER 1871- 1971 *(fhm)*
Mamie MERCER CARTER 1896–1976 *(fhm)*
Geneva DADE MERCER June 31, 1887 Jan. 17, 1972 *(fhm)*
Louise M. LAMBERT 1937–1980 *(fhm)*
Kenneth MERCER, Sr. 1930–1984 *(fhm)*
Mary E. JENNINGS 1906–1981 *(fhm)*
Father Hannibal BUTLER 1865–1937; Mother Mary S. BUTLER 1870–1949
Harry CHRISTIAN Died May 5, 1947
George Mason MERCER 1900–1968; Mrs. Frances MERCER 1894–1963
Lillian C. COOK 1919–1966
Cassell F. GRANT 1922–1965
Margaret GRIGSBY 1876 Died 1943; Charles GRIGSBY Died 1943; Silas GRIGSBY

Thomas R. PENDELETON; Mrs. Cora PENDLETON March 1889 August 17, 1963
James PENDLETON Born 1858 Died Nov. 13, 1940 Age 84
Mary PENDLETON Born Dec. 3, 1861 Died July 18, 1932 Mother

Mrs. Arnold LONG Died January 22, 1953 Aged 70 years
Charles E. CHRISTIAN 1881–1955
George W. BROWN 1865–1949; Agnes BROWN 1883–1956

Charles T. MERCER 1869–1932; Jos. P. MERCER 1904–1947
James Edward MERCER Born Jan. 14, 1873 Died Jan. 4, 1939
Mrs. Rosa MERCER 1880–1963

Pinkard Family Cemetery
Located South Route 674 0.5 mile West Route 643 at Meetze Rd. in 2nd field to East of house on slope in grove of trees, small iron fence around part, stone markers only.

Piper Cemetery, Warrenton, Virginia
Located on Route 744 just past Training Center on Shipmiddy St. Monument erected by the family as markers had eroded away.

Poplar Fork Baptist Church Cemetery, near Warrenton, Virginia
Located on Route 670 a few miles South East of Warrenton. Resurveyed November 25, 1990.

Joseph HUDNALL 1872–1961
Charles E. CLARK 1909–1968
Erva W. FLETCHER 1889–1949 *(fhm)*
TAPSCOTT Robert Feb. 18, 1863 Sept. 8, 1946; Mamie A. Dec. 17, 1869 Nov. 15, 1959
Elizabeth DAWSON ADDISON Jan. 19, 1864–July 2, 1935; Rebecca A. PENN Feb. 18, 1896–June 17, 1917;
    Mildred A. STOKES Jan. 17, 1905–Jan. 10, 1931
John H. TAPSCOTT Jan. 18, 1908 Aug. 17, 1967
Aletheal BALL 1900–1964
Louis PENN 1886–1964

RUSSELL George C. Mar. 12, 1866 Dec. 16, 1949; Nannie R
Rachael Ann RECTOR April 29, 1940 May 16, 1942
James Franklin RECTOR February 21, 1946 November 1, 1968 beloved Husband
Spillman CEPHAS 1926–1963
Irene CEPHAS 1922–1950 *(fhm) [missing 1990]*
Ruth V. CEPHAS July 31, 1949 Oct. 18, 1951; Hiawatha CEPHAS 1928–1958 *(fhm)*
Chas. PENN and Family
Russell CHICESTER Born Jan. 15, 1875 Died July 29, 1913
Jeffrey CEPHAS 1916–1966
Sadie V. BROWN Born June 4, 1885 Died Feb. 10, 1912
Mary F. BROWN Born Sept. 11, 1886 Died Oct. 24, 1905
Henretter R. CLARK Born Sept. 11, 1861 Died Feb. 8, 1921
Theodore CLARK May 4, 1860 Sept. 20, 1940 Husband
Theodore CLARK, Jr. July 6, 1883 March 29, 1924
CHICESTER Randolph Dec. 30, 1934; Carrie Mar. 15, 1934
William George JACKSON 1866–1940
Bernard SMITH Sept. 28, 1872 June 8, 1957; Howard SMITH 1906–1956
SMITH Brother Edward B. 1921–1944 Mother Sarah E. 1895–1945
Bony SMITH 1834–1920; His Wife Elizabeth SMITH 1836–1896
Dempsey S. SMITH 1908–1930
Thomas SMITH 1874–1950
Andrew J. CORUM, Jr. Born Aug. 9, 1898 Died April 1, 1920
Mary S. SCOTT
Lethia WALKER Wife of William F. EVANS Died March 12, 1910
William A. EVANS 1902–1910 Age 8 years
Janie C. GREEN Born Feb. 26, 1862 Died Aug. 15, 1911
Alfred Mason GREEN 1892–1948
Mrs. Mamie C. ADDISON 1871–1958

Mary Lena SMITH CAMPBELL Oct. 1, 1881 Feb. 7, 1948
Wilbur D. CAMPBELL July 12, 1920 Oct. 7, 1943
Hamilton CAMPBELL March 30, 1886 February 4, 1966
Edward SMITH July 4, 1876 Aug. 2, 1952
Sarah E. SMITH Mar. 16, 1855 April 13, 1939
Henry Hamilton CAMPBELL VIRGINIA PVT 33 AVN SQ AAF WORLD WAR II December 14, 1904 July 7, 1968
Baby Walter A. CLARK, Jr. April 30, 1927 July 10, 1927
Lucy CLARK Died Dec. 29, 1925
Emily TAPSCOTT Wife of Jack TAPSCOTT Born 1831 Died 1904
Jack TAPSCOTT Died June 23, 1922 Age 78 years
Mamie WOOD Born Feb. 14, 1888 Died July 20, 1919
James Allen WALKER 1855–1939

Dorothy E. DOWELL 1940–1955; Hayward H. DOWELL 1912–1956
Bertha C. DOWELL 1895–1960; Harold W. DOWELL 1880–1969
Annie M. MORAN Born Apr. 19, 1847 Died Dec. 10, 1918
Eppie DOWELL [HUNTON]
Mattie HUNTON Born Dec. 16, 1872 Died Jan. 4, 1912
Little Jack [HUNTON]

M. B. WALKER Dec. 21, 1896
Norman WALKER;

Quintina WALKER Died June 21, 1898 Age 81
Samuel WALKER Born July 4, 1817 Died Oct. 1st 1892

Louise MARSHALL BRADLEY 1894–1938 Mary MARSHALL THOMAS 1870–1953
Mamie F. MARSHALL Born Nov. 11, 1897 Died May 22, 1918
Ed. E. MARSHALL [Died April 9, 1889] *(missing 1990)*
B. D. RUSSELL Feb. 12, 1873 Sept. 28, 1937; Wife Jennie Feb. 24, 1896 Aug. 18, 1975
Mary F. RUSSELL Sept. 2, 1835 Nov. 10, 1915
M. A. RUSSELL Born Aug. 1, 1836 Died Feb. 20, 1929
Annie V. TAPSCOTT Died March 17, 1918 Age 76 yrs.
Philip HOUGHS died February 1888 Age 12 years; T. L. HOUGH *(rest damaged)*
Sallie Ann NICKENS Born Dec. 15, 1828 Died Feb. 3, 1919
Ruth HUGHES Died Oct. 7th, 1874 Age 19 months
Betsy BROWN *(rest illegible)*
Mr. C. COROM Born 1916
Henrietta HOLMES [HOLINS?] Born May 17, 1848 Died June 14, 1898
CHICHESTER Ralph 1915–1977; Evelyn Mae 1916–1980
Elias S. BROOKS Sr. Aug. 2, 1908 Mar. 23, 1977
mother Pauline T. BROOKS July 10, 1913 March 2, 1987
Mrs. Emma WALKER June 1, 1972 aged 78 years *((fhm))*
rock marker
Annie V. TAYLOR 1911-1975 *(fhm)*
2 rock markers
Thomas BLACKWELL VA STM 1 USNR WORLD WAR II July 18, 1909 March 6, 1973
rock marker
W. T. PAYNE Born Dec. 8, 1858 Died Dec. 17, 1892
William Ernest JACKSON USA WORLD WAR II 1911-1977
3 rock markers
Preston I. GREEN 1894-1956
Mabel HARLEY Born April 1877 Died Feb 22, 1979
Nancy M. CHICESTER Died Nov. 14, 1877 age 33 years
T. L. HUGHES [?] *(rest gone)*
Mary E. TAPSCOTT 1866-1923
Halbert BROOKS Se. 1917-1982 *(fhm)*
PERRY Dudley M. Dec 4, 1904 Dec. 5, 1974; Susie F. Oct 22, 1918
Jennie E. RUSSELL Born Nov. 11, 1862 Died Sept. 12, 1900
De Vaughn Abner RUSSELL June 26, 1938 May 20, 1970
HEFLIN Martha 1897-1971; Theodore 1891-1971
James Golden ROWE 1897-1989 *(fhm)*
Virginia D. ROWE 1897-1971 *(fhm)*
Mrs. Mamie A. ADDISON 1871-1958 *(fhm)*
Dorothy E. DOWELL 1941-1955 *(fhm)*
Hayward A. DOWELL 1912-1956 *(fhm)*
Bertha G. DOWELL 1890-1960 *(fhm)*Harold W. DOWELL 1880-1960 *(fhm)*
John W. DOWELL USA WORLD WAR II Dec 3, 1903 Apr 24, 1981
Granville R. DOWELL 1916-1983 *(fhm)*Raymond R. DOWELL 1920-1900 *(fhm)*
Mosker SMITH Jr. Aug. 30, 1917 Aug. 29, 1989
old tombstone face down
Frank B. WALKER 1876-1967 *(fhm)*
Agnes M. SMITH Oct. 2, 1877 Dec. 28, 1975
Mabel L. SMITH July 11, 1909 Feb. 8, 1988
Howard SMITH 1906-1956

Eveline SMITH CURTIS Oct. 1, 1884 April 4, 1963
Rosa W. TAPSCOTT 1875-1981
Celeste M. SMITH Nov. 14, 1930 Dec. 7, 1938
Shirley E. SMITH May 5, 1916 Aug. 22, 1933
Sister Lillian BROWN 1925-1981
Father Mosker [SMITH] Sr. 1886-1970
SMITH Brother Edward B. 1928-1944; mother Sarah E. 1895-1945
sister Sarah E. WARD April 5, 1920 Aug. 2, 1975
mother Gladys Mary CAMPBELL Aug. 17, 1914 Nov. 6, 1983
Susie A. NICKENS Born Jan. 14, 1876 Died Aug. 18, 1891 (?)
Eddie PENN 1897-1966 *(fhm)*
Mabel ADDISON
Jeffrey CHICESTER 1966-1968 *(fhm)*
Aunt Martha V. BROWN Dec. 6, 1862 Aug. 7, 1938
Richard CLARK Sept. 28, 1885 Nov. 25, 1968
mother Ida T. CLARK Nov. 11, 1897 April 25, 1985
Mary HELN 1871-1951 *(fhm)*
Franhn HELM 1861-1967 *(fhm)*
Childs J. ADDISON Jan. 31, 1889 Feb. 9, 1972
Sadie L. ADDISON Nov. 14, 1894 Mar. 29, 1986
Joan A. KENNY March 5, 1935 March 24, 1981
Melvin G. CEPHAS 1912-1982 *(fhm)*

Porter Cemetery, Turnbull, Virginia
Located North of Turnbull, rock markers.

Porter (John) Cemetery, Turnbull, Virginia
Located South Route 802 0.4 mile East Route 637, overgrown, rock markers. Resurveyed April 2, 1994.

Porter (Weathers) Cemetery, Turnbull, Virginia
Located 0.25 mile East Route 637 North Route 802, overgrown, no markers. Resurveyed April 2, 1994

Primm Cemetery, Somerville, Virginia
Located 1.5 miles South West Somerville South Route 617. 12 - 15 unmarked graves. Data obtained by L. Arthur Grove.

Charles P. PRIMM Born June 19, 1803 Died April 27, 1871

Providence Baptist Cemetery (Black), Orlean, Virginia
Located on Route 689 South East of church in grove of trees, unfenced. Resurveyed January 21, 1990 & March 31, 1991.

Henry BURRELL Born September 20, 1876 Died March 20, 1940
Mamie HYNES 1895–1972
L. Ernest ROBINSON 1889–1968
Lemmon E. ROBINSON, Jr. 1926–1926
Mrs. Lula DADE CHAMP 1878–1961
Madie M. SMITH 1897–1960
Leon T. EAMES
Bessie OWENS 1895–1969
Mavinia WASHINGTON 1886–1964
James WASHINGTON 1884–1968

164

Harvey R. WASHINGTON 1902–1953
Henry H. BALTIMORE Died July 6, 1949 Aged 75 years
Ernest F. BAILEY 1907–1969
Bertie CHAMP 1883–1968
Willie ROY 1909–1964
Gabrile ROY 1876–1958
James F. BROOKS VIRGINIA PFC 644 AAA AUTO WPNS UW17 CAC WORLD WAR II May 24, 1926 July 22, 1949
James F. BROOKS PVT US ARMY WORLD WAR II 1890–1976 His Wife Edmonia L. BROOKS 1904–1974
Ernest F. BAILEY Dec. 28, 1907 April 9, 1969
TATES Alice L. A. Dec. 13, 1900 Nov. 8, 1974 Huriah May 17, 1898 Sept. 11, 1981
WHITFIELD Tates US ARMY WORLD WAR I May 6, 1893 Jan. 7, 1983
Charles E. TATES Died Jan. 26, 1988
OLIVER, Conrad H. Feb. 24, 1893 June 3, 1984 Bessie L. July 10, 1898 March 12, 1969
ROBINSON Moore US ARMY WORLD WAR II Aug. 28, 1913 July 24, 1984

Putnam - Hitt Cemetery, Orlean, Virginia
Located back of house on Route 736 at intersection with Route 688. Enclosed with wire fence, well kept, shrubbery, 17 or more fieldstone markers for ancestors of Marshall Putnam, who owned it. Resurveyed October 22, 1993.

Clarence E. PUTNAM 1910–1984 *(fhm)*
Edna R. PUTNAM 1915–1991 *(fhm)*

Mrs. Marshall Putnam says 3 babies buried near Hitt's tombstone. Two Hitt babies and brother of Marshall died of diphtheria.

PUTNAM - HITT monument

Roberta HITT Born Mar. 9, 1861 Died Dec. 18, 1955
Jack HITT Born July 26, 1862 Died May 24, 1904
John Barton PUTNAM
Mrs. Marshall Putnam's 6 family Bibles provided the following information:

From the 1907 American Bible Society Bible:
Lucy PUTNAM July 27, 1868
"Bob" PUTNAM Robert Lee Jan. 12, 1871 died March 7, 1932
Mary Sarah PUTNAM Jan. 29, 1884 Feb. 2, 1971
"Molly" PUTNAM Mary Elizabeth March 8, 1861

From the 1858 Bible of Joseph Harding & Son:
Elizabeth V. PUTNAM March 27, 1874 April 20, 1930

Randolph Cemetery, "Eastern View", near Casanova, Virginia
Located East of Route 643 just South of Route 602 in field to left of manor house. Stone wall and cemetery in excellent condition, periwinkle, grape vines, etc. Resurveyed March 31, 1991

Our Father and Mother Robert Lee RANDOLPH Born 1791 Died Dec. 26, 1857 Mary Buckner THURSTON RANDOLPH Born July 16, 1809 Died Jan. 20, 1890
Col Robert RANDOLPH of "Eastern View" Son of Peter RANDOLPH of Chatsworth 1760–1825 Elizabeth CARTER His Wife Daughter of Charles CARTER of Shirley 1764–1832
Lavinia H. Daughter of Charles & Mary A. E. RANDOLPH Born Jany 20th, 1814 Died July 10th, 1850
Eliza Garret third child of Robert D and Landonia R. MINOR Born Aug. 20th, 1837 Died Aug. 18yh, 1858

Our beloved Brother Norwood B. second Son of Charles and Mary RANDOLPH of Fauquier Co. Va. Born Feb. 27, 1819 Died July 9, 1874

M. A. F. [Mary Anne Fauntleroy] RANDOLPH Consort of Charles C. RANDOLPH Born in Fredericksburg Va. May 9, 1804 Died at "the Grove" August 25th, 1858

Margaret Kemble Daughter of Buckner M. & Mary RANDOLPH Born May 31, 1883 Died June 18, 1884

Llewellyn GRIFFITH Son of Buckner M. & Mary RANDOLPH Born Nov. 2, 1887 Died July 10, 1887 *(stone not found B base in place 3/31/91)*

Robert Lee RANDOLPH Born 1791 died Dec. 26, 1857

Mary BUCKNER THURSTON RANDOLPH Born July 16, 1809 died Jan. 29, 1890

Found buried in underbrush by Randolph Scott Carter:

Elizabeth Carter RANDOLPH Feb. 15, 1835 Aug. 25, 1837 Child of Robert Lee and Mary McGILL RANDOLPH

Elizabeth CARTER MOFFATT Nomini Hall, Born 1760 Died 1847

Anne Marie MOFFATT Born 1762 Died 1846CDaughter of Dr. Charles Mortimer and Sarah Griffin FAUNTLEROY of Fredericksburg

Roberta RANDOLPH MINOR July 20, 1858 Died March 30, 1869CChild of Robert Dabney and Landonia RANDOLPH MINOR

Our beloved Brother Col. Robert the eldest Son of Charles and Mary RANDOLPH of Fauquier County, Va. Born Nov. 18, 1835 Killed in the Cavalry charge at Meadow Bridge, Aug. 12, 1864 while leading his Regiment the 4th Va. Cav. into action

Rector Cemetery, Morrisville, Virginia

Located North East intersection of Routes 637, 602, & 806 deep in woods about 1.5 miles near old house. We were led to it by Mr. Laco Halterman, a woodsman & hunter.

Marshall RECTOR Died May 2nd 1811 In his 65th year

Sally RECTOR Died October 28th 1826 in her 20th year

Susan OLIVER Died February 2, 1837 in her 8th year

Mary OLIVER Died August 8, 1837 in her 3rd year

Elizabeth OLIVER Died December 8, 1881 in her 78th year

Rector Cemetery, Midland, Virginia

Located 0.7 mile South St. John the Baptist Church on West side Route 674 on North side private road, many fieldstone markers and unmarked graves of Nannie RECTOR, wife of Levin RECTOR & baby. See Hurleyville Cemeteries.

Rectortown Cemetery, Rectortown, Virginia

Located in Rectortown on Route 713, cleared but unfenced. Graves located at top of hill. Approximately 50 unmarked graves between tombstones & road & by back fence. Restored in 1991 by Piedmont Valley Ruritans. Resurveyed January 12, 1992.

Thomas O. SAMPSELL Died July 27, 1883

E. S.

K. S.

Hoffman W. Son of G. T. & Nanny KINSEY Aged 5 mos. & 12 dys *(stone missing 1992)*

Nannie Beloved Wife of G. T. KINSEY Born Dec. 22, 1844 Died Sept. 28, 1892

George Thomas KINSEY Born August 26, 1842 Died April 2, 1907

Sgt. J. W. FLOWEREE Co. E 3rd U. S. Cav.

several rock markers

Mabel A. GEORGE Beloved Wife of R. A. GEORGE Died Mar. 29, 1915 Aged 27 years
Mary Dau. of S. M. SEATON Died Jan. 31, 1909 Aged 26 years
J. [John] L. SEATON Beloved Husband of C. A. SEATON Died Feb. 13, 1913 Aged 70 years *(sunken in ground 1992)*
Carrie A. Wife of J. L. SEATON Born July 4, 1855 Died May 27, 1927 *(stone missing 1992)*
J. Lester Son of J. L. & C. A. SEATON Died Feb. 10, 1887 1 year 10 Ds
Margaret FISHBACK Born Dec. 5, 1819 Died Nov. 17, 1882 *(stone missing 1992)*
James P. [Powell] SEATON born June 2nd 1816 Died December 18th 1852 aged 36 years 6 months & 16 days
Elmira F. [FISHBACK] Wife of J. [James] P. SEATON Born Feb. 18, 1810 Died Oct. 8, 1883

Harriet A. Daughter of James H. & Rebecca A. RECTOR who died Jan. 21st 1850 aged 9 years and 9 days
Infant Son of James H. RECTOR & Rebecca Born Feb. 11, 1852
Mary N. Daughter of James H. & Rebecca A. RECTOR who died Nov. 24th 1843 aged 1 year 5 months & 22 days

Redd Cemetery, Bristersburg, Virginia
Located 0.25 mile East Route 616 South Route 607 on private road in field in back of house and woods about 0.5 mile. Size 0.25 acre, fenced, grove of trees. Reuben Heflin owner, states "There are several graves just outside fenced area and about 200 yards East is another cemetery filled with graves with no inscriptions, possibly slaves."

Peter W. REDD May 20, 1820 July 5, 1905
William A REDD Born Apr. 6, 1854 Died Feb. 22, 1919
Jos. A. REDD Feb. 18, 1830 Dec. 24, 1884 Mary E. REDD Nov. 8, 1827 Jan. 17, 1906 Wm. B. REDD Jan. 30, 1818 July 29, 1899

Remington Community Cemetery, Remington, Virginia
Located on Route 651 just North West of Remington. Well kept. Resurveyed 1994.

Wm. W. CAMPBELL April 19, 1861 April 23, 1926
Alice ALLAIRE CAMPBELL Dec. 5, 1864 Nov. 18, 1945
Alexander A. CAMPBELL 1967
Stanley M. MELTON May 3, 1929 July 4, 1976
WOODSON; Lonnie R. Aug. 21 1916; Roberdeau Weaver Mar. 7, 1919 May 7, 1994
WILLINGHAM Mary BATTMANN Nov. 22, 1926 Feb. 14, 1985
WILLINGHAM Richard R. June 15, 1891 Sept. 23, 1973; Willie S.

McCONCHIE, Cecil G. April 22, 1906; Virginia T. Oct. 21, 1911
James M. HEFLIN March 15, 1903 Dec. 5, 1976; Lena E. HEFLIN July 15, 1906 Jan. 17, 1982

OLINGER Lois L. June 21, 1905; Birdie E. Oct. 8, 1897 Dec. 17, 1975
OLINGER Walter A. 1898–1976; Ethel R. 1899–1988

ROSENBERGER Garry M. 1959–1976; Frank L. 1926
FRAZIER Harry W. 1889–1978; Mary C. 1897–1977
JONES, John Henry 1923–1991; Helen Byrn 1930–
Walter L. GRIMES TEC 4 US ARMY WORLD WAR II Sep 30 1923 Dec 5 1991

James A. WEAVER Born Nov. 17, 1879 Died June 22, 1949
Elsie A. WEAVER Born May 18, 1890 Died June 23, 1932
SMITH Lee Thomas July 25, 1892 July 24, 1968; Effie WHITE July 29, 1898

Ralph Taylor McCONCHIE Jan. 14, 1897 Aug. 27, 1963
Rudolph Stanley McCONCHIE Sept. 6, 1899 May 5, 1967
Erva McCONCHIE STRICKLER May 3, 1901 Feb. 4, 1960
Ethel Frances McCONCHIE Sept. 13, 1894 Aug. 7, 1981

HOPKINS David N. March 11, 1847 Dec. 18, 1929; Ellen C. Sept. 20, 1845 Sept. 29, 1930
HOPKINS Elmer David 1922–; Dorothy Davis 1927–
McCONCHIE J. Walter Apr. 6, 1869 Sept. 12, 1937; Ida TAYLOR Sept. 20, 1872 Aug. 20, 1960
Douglas LeRoy HOFFMAN 1944–1945
Wade H. FINKS 1884–1968
CLAXTON Jack T. May 29, 1902 Dec. 5, 1970; Helen S.
John J. FINKS 1857–1944; S. Virginia FINKS 1853–1945
Bertha L. FINKS 1887–1970
HERRING John R., Sr. Oct. 5, 1914 Aug. 14, 1987; Eula D. Oct. 15, 1916
Herbert Chancellor HERRING, Sr. Aug. 26, 1909 Jan. 19, 1984
Jones Frederick HERRING TEC 5 US ARMY WORLD WAR II May 3, 1904 Sept. 15, 1980
Geo. Raymond HERRING Feb. 1, 1900 Feb. 25, 1985

HERRING Woodie E. June 25, 1897 Oct. 6, 1973; Mayme D. Dec. 8, 1897 Jan. 7, 1989
HERRING George A. 1868–1945; Irene J. 1876–1954
Macie L. SUTPHIN June 23, 1920 Feb. 17, 1980
SMITH Mordecahi F. Dec. 11, 1878 Sept. 3, 1967; Annie T. Aug. 31, 1892 Oct. 14, 1979
Ruth E. JAMES 1897–1984 *(fhm)*
Rubin Jesse GARNER 1886–1970 *(fhm)*
Florence TACKETT Dec. 25, 1879 April 5, 1969
PULLIAM Virginia I. June 6, 1914; Joseph B. Sept. 29, 1913 June 6, 1968
Edward W. PULLIAM 1915–1969
SMITH Dick H. Jan. 25, 1896 Jan. 1, 1983; Lillie A. Aug. 21, 1895
Hugh Mercer HAMILTON 1905–1981
Rose HERRING HAMILTON 1915–1977

GORCHEN Charles W. June 8, 1926 married Nov. 16, 1947 Rose M. Apr. 11, 1926 July 12, 1987
James Edward HOFFMAN Nov. 21, 1913 Sept. 4, 1985 *(American Legion marker)*
PULLIAM Mother Carrie Sept. 3, 1879 Jan. 29, 1955; Son Lloyd Mar. 8, 1917 Jan. 31, 1962
FINKS George A. 1869–1944; S. Virginia FINKS 1853–1945; Wade H. 1884–1968; Bertha L. FINKS
SPICER Robert M. Feb. 22, 1884 August 25, 1942; Eula B. March 5, 1889 Sept. 13, 1951
PARKS Garrett M. June 23, 1900 June 4, 1964; Elizabeth M. August 21, 1902 May 24, 1941

Charles Nelson MYERS Feb. 12, 1906 Mar. 27, 1982
MYERS Charles Hamilton Oct. 1, 1878 Jan. 11, 1941; His Wife Susannah BURKE Aug. 29, 1881 July 9, 1977

Douglas Leroy HOFFMAN 1944–1945
William Wyant HOFFMAN July 8, 1912 Dec. 26, 1981
Maxie Smith COOPER January 19, 1885 March 14, 1942
SMITH William M. Oct. 30, 1862 Nov. 30, 1941; Laura ATKINS Oct. 25, 1867 Apr. 3, 1956 *(missing in 1990)*
James S. SMITH Sept. 18, 1886 March 18, 1979
John A. HUMPHREY May 11, 1871 Sept. 20, 1937; Charlotte R. HUMPHREY 1892–1978
Wm. Jete HUMPHREY Nov. 6, 1868 Oct. 20, 1949
Hattie HUMPHREY JORDON 1866–1927
Mandley Keith PAYNE Jan. 23, 1866 May 12, 1935
PAYNE William H. 1915–1942; Sadie C. 1913–; Agnes T. 1857–1956

Information supplied by Ripley Robinson:
Buren M. SOWLES Co. I 5th Vt. Inf. Born Dec. 13, 1840 Died March 11, 1913 *(Veterans Administration stone applied for)*
Sarah Virginia PAYNE Born Nov. 12, 1902 Died Dec. 25, 1981 *(no stone)*

W. Garnet DAVIS 1923–1972
DAVIS Grover L. 1897–1971; Virginia S. 1898–1977

David Hamilton RICH Aug. 7, 1916 June 16, 1983 WORLD WAR II PACIFIC THEATER *(American Legion marker)*
RICH Fleming Keane 1885–1962; Mae Hamilton 1886–1962

SHAW James W. June 24, 1914 June 6, 1981; Thelma T. Dec. 10, 1911

TAYLOR Richard L. Feb. 28, 1876 Aug. 11, 1959; Mary E. Feb. 9, 1890 Dec. 13, 1975
DAVIS Clarence J. Feb. 7, 1894 May 19, 1988; Irene Dumpsey Sept. 11, 1896 July 17, 1957

Eugene R. LONG 1907–1967; Mary E. LONG 1908–1975
Tyson Roosevelt LONG Virginia Pvt. 3 Engineer Co. Bn 24, INF Div Korea PH May 26, 1930 July 16, 1950

ROBINSON Samuel T. Aug. 1910 Jan. 25, 1967 WORLD WAR II Virginia T. Sgt. 526 Bomber Sq. AF
ROBINSON Samuel May 6, 1885 June 3, 1948; Louise C. Feb. 4, 1886 May 6, 1971 Mother

Alice R. CLARK August 4, 1909 June 14, 1964
Cecil A. CLARK August 22, 1907 November 15, 1978

CORNWELL Robert M. May 15, 1865 April 14, 1957; Alice R. Dec. 9, 1871 April 23, 1964 Father and Mother
LAHMON James Allen June 5, 1892 June 21, 1927; Ruth CORNWELL May 1, 1897 March 21, 1983

Edith T. WALLACE 1891–1964
Martha E. WILLINGHAM 1870–1939
Charles H. WILLINGHAM 1868–1935
Carl H. WILLINGHAM 1898–1961 *(Masonic emblem)*

MARTIN William Earl 1892–1946
MARTIN William G. 1869–1900
MARTIN Lillie McDONALD 1863–1943

HEARD James F. Sept. 24, 1929 Aug. 26, 1988; Stasia
Joseph Brian HEARD June 7, 1963 Nov. 8, 1979

OLINGER George P. July 12, 1912 Sept. 26, 1977; Ivia May 26, 1903 Oct. 28, 1983
Son George OLINGER Aug. 28, 1943
Sarah V. PAYNE 1902–1981 *(fhm)*

Charles M. ROBINSON March 5, 1921 May 9, 1967
Thomas M. ROBINSON 1957–1990 *(American Legion marker)*
CHILTON John Berry Jan. 11, 1905; Virginia HILL Oct. 8, 1903 March 12, 1987

Twins James H. WELCH July 6, 1909 July 15, 1909; Andrew J. WELCH July 6, 1909 July 18, 1909
WELCH: William Broadver Nov. 19, 1874 Apr. 9, 1960; Mary McDONALD May 29, 1875 June 25, 1959

KILBY Swarou K. Dec. 25, 1877 Sept. 4, 1960; Sara W. Mar. 8, 1897 Feb. 7, 1983
Mahalia C. HILTON wo Charles E. KINCER Aug. 16, 1874 Nov. 5, 1944
KINCER Charles Edward Sept. 14, 1872 Oct. 27, 1963

John Morgan CURRIER 1864–1942
Ella LOWMAN CURRIER 1878–1956
Ira Lowman CURRIER 1916–1966
John Franklin CURRIER 1900–1939
Fannie LOWMAN ROTRUCK 1877–1944
Edgar Malcolm CURRIER 1906–1976

Arthur B. HERSBURGER Jan. 13, 1912 Sept. 25, 1991
Bena Caskie STINETTE Mar. 24, 1887 May 26, 1966
Harry L. STINETTE Mar. 28, 1880 Jan. 20, 1957
James MAXWELL 1927–1937

McDONALD Wesley Lyons Apr. 2, 1910 Aug. 24, 1985
Willie Lee McDONALD Mar. 9, 1875 Nov. 14, 1949 Father; Susan HARTLEY wo W. L. McDONALD Jan. 25,
    1874 Mar. 31, 1926 Mother

WALKER Warren M. Jan. 28, 1870 Mar. 12, 1935; Susie CHILDRESS Nov. 11, 1869 Nov. 1, 1955
Wm. MANKEY May 7, 1858 May 1, 1938; Ada M. MANKEY Oct. 10, 1867 July 19, 1943
MICKLEY Milton Leroy 1881–1967; Ella BOWER 1890–1988 *(DAR marker)*
Mary MICKLEY AIKEN 1917–1994 *(fhm)*
Mary Elizabeth MICKLEY 1848–1928
Hudson MICKLEY 1846–1919

Edith WILLIS beloved wife of Milton E. FOSTER Mar. 10, 1891 Jan. 14, 1919; Milton E. FOSTER beloved
    husband of Edith WILLIS Apr. 8, 1888 Mar. 14, 1925
Robert Lewis WILLIS 1860–1940
Minnie MELVIN WILLIS 1861–1948
Isabel TAYLOR BALDWIN 1901
Carl Odell BALDWIN 1897–1970
Rebecca GRAYBEAL wife of J. N. BALDWIN Feb. 21, 1863 Feb. 13, 1935
James NELSON May 30, 1860 June 5, 1938
WHITMER Matthew Erwin Jan. 12, 1863 Feb. 11, 1944; Jane LORIMER Dec. 25, 1870 Aug. 18, 1953
Alice L. WHITMER May 16, 1901 Apr. 5, 1995

McCONCHIE Mary CHILDS Sept. 28, 1881 Feb. 7, 1949; Marvin P. Mar. 20, 1878 June 14, 1950
Handy E. PARK Virginia MSgt. Tech Ser Unit WORLD WAR II June 28 1916 Nov 20 1953
SMITH Frank Lee May 31, 1903 Nov. 24. 1953; Edith SOAPER May 28, 1904 July 19, 1991
SOUTHARD Raymond T. June 26, 1913; Lillian H. July 31, 1912

HOPKINS Joseph A. Mar. 2, 1930; Gladys S. July 26, 1933
HOPKINS David Elmer Mar. 10, 1891 Aug. 12, 1990; Mary OLINGER Jan. 16, 1895 Feb. 16, 1922
Robert Lee HOPKINS Nov. 23, 1927 Dec. 12, 1983

Albert Eugene KILBY Aug. 13, 1927 Dec. 28, 1968
Joseph Irwin KILBY Virginia Pfc US ARMY KOREA PH March 19 1931 Oct 22 1969

WILLINGHAM Elizabeth Jan. 1, 1917 April 20, 1994

John Kenneth WELCH Jan. 14, 1906 July 7, 1993
Rudolph A. JENKINS Oct. 6, 1922 May 25, 1990
DWYER Robert M. Aug. 26, 1921 Apr. 9, 1989
GROVES Robert D. born 4–3–31 died 2–28–89
CLOUDER Allen Taylor Apr. 9, 1913 Mar. 22, 1993
GIBSON Kenneth E. 1930–1989; Helen L. 1947–
Jonas Cord SCRUGGS Feb. 6, 1875 Aug. 9, 1991
CLATTERBUCK John W. June 18, 1910 Jan. 19, 1991; Dahlia July 31, 1920

Thomas Munson RANNY Feb. 26, 1928 Feb. 7, 1986
WINGO William Holdman Jr. April 30, 1916 Oct. 8, 1990
Wanda Lynn FERGUS July 22, 1959 Apr. 11, 1990
Carroll S. JENKINS 1954–1994 *(fhm)*

JENKINS Carroll Stevin Aug. 26, 1930 Mar. 28, 1982
James William JENKINS SP US NAVY WORLD WAR II Nov 5 1922 Mar 4 1984 *(American Legion marker)*
JENKINS Egbert H. May 3, 1903 Mar. 5 1983; Lillie E. July 28, 1905 Dec. 23, 1987

EMBREY Clarence W. Apr. 18, 1918 June 27, 1991; Ruth N.
SOUTHLAND Jr. Frank Apr. 21, 1915 Apr. 28, 1995; Vera L. Mar. 20, 1917 Oct. 8, 1982
WILLIAMS Ernest A. born April 6, 1904 deceased July 27, 1963; Velma ELEY born Feb. 20, 1909 deceased Sept. 14, 1994
BAILEY Thomas R. 1935–1993; Lorraine W. 1930
Rusell H. BAILEY Sept. 6, 1910 Mar. 4, 1973 Father

June MILLS BOBYN June 28, 1932 Aug. 9, 1964
STONE Alexander B. 1891–1966; Virginia C. 1894–1971
Roscoe S. STROTHER Feb. 11, 1890 July 1, 1968
REID Dewitt N. July 29, 1902 Oct. 8, 1977; Bertha E. Apr. 30, 1908 Feb. 21, 1978
Harry M. PEARSON 1894-1987
Willie M. HICKS Jan. 13, 1933 Jan. 26, 1990
Lisa Rena HICKS Dec. 19, 1965 Nov. 21, 1985

RICH Robert Allen TSgt US ARMY WORLD WAR II Sep. 17, 1917 Nov. 7, 1993; Billie ASHBY May 23, 1919

Begining at the SE corner:

MUSSELMAN John Monroe 1919; Lois Leona 1921 1990
FERGUSON Forrest F. 1899 1975; Mabel W. 1899 1977
SHIPE Walter R. Sr. April 19, 1898 Feb. 23, 1983; Ruth B. July 1, 1900 Sept. 19, 1990
GROVES Earlene V. 1893 1988; Bitzyer H. 1896 1957
Herman C. GROVES March 11, 1885 May 17, 1961
DWYER son Morris J. Nov. 6, 1893 Nov. 19, 1967; mother Mary E. June 6, 1868 Sept. 14, 1956; father Isiah F. Mar. 12, 1856 Mar. 11, 1905

Frank Elizah EDWARDS March 20, 1888 October 2, 1962
Lena HUMPHREY EDWARDS January 28, 1895 January 18, 1975
Dorothy Mae EDWARDS April 25, 1921 Feb. 15, 1939
Evelyn EDWARDS HOFFMAN April 27, 1928 October 19, 1976
Frank EDWARDS Virginia PVT US Marine Corps Dec 30 1930 April 28 1968

William Lee PAYNE PFC US Army WWII 1906 1987

Mary Courtney wife of Alfred J. PAYNE Oct. 11, 1987 June 23, 1954
Alfred James PAYNE March 22, 1869 Dec. 17, 1948
John Richard PAYNE Jan. 20, 1912 Aug. 31, 1983
James Alfred PAYNE Aug. 28, 1904 June 11, 1940

GRUN James Preston July 7, 1907 May 7, 1978; Cora OLINGER STEPHENS Mar. 4, 1889 Dec. 19, 1981
Katherine STEPHENS BURKE Apr. 17, 1915 Oct. 26, 1990
James P. STEPHENS PFC Air Corps WWII June 10 1920 July 1 1942
James W. STEPHENS Oct. 22, 1889 Aug. 26, 1936
Norma E. STEPHENS July 25, 1913 Jan. 24, 1992

Thelma F. GROVES wife of Merlin BROUSE Apr. 23, 1900 Sept 1, 1957
Grace F. GROVES wife of Norman A. KELLY Sept. 26, 1896 Feb. 9, 1955
Millard GROVES Sept. 25, 1903 Dec. 1, 1920; Raymond GROVES Dec. 2, 1891 July 19, 1923 served in the World
    War Co G 60th Inf A.L.F.; Branwelle O. GROVES Nov. 2, 1855 Dec. 17, 1927; Ada HARRIS GROVES Sept. 6,
    1858 Feb. 12, 1933
Merlin Gray BROUSE May 24, 1887 June 1, 1958
Raymond J. GROVES Virginia PVT Co Inf 5 Div Oct 2 1898 July 1923 *(American Legion marker)*

JASPER Richard A. 1880 1967; Clara E. 1881 1956
Sallie E. JAMESON Nov. 7, 1863 Oct 5, 1948
HARRIS James A. 1872 1957; Irene C. 1877 1959

Florence BROWN wife of J.B. BROWN Nov. 7, 1856 Feb. 23, 1936

Mary BOWEN WHITMAN beloved wife of Paul WHITMAN Dec. 20, 1907 Jan. 12, 1983
Paul WHITMAN Nov. 8, 1903 Mar. 10, 1957
Harry Bowen BRITTLE July 19, 1916 March 5, 1993
BRITTLE Leslie Meade the 4th son of Peyton Oliver BRITTLE & Sallie Nelson STRICKLAND his wife born at
    ____, Va. March 10, 1875 died March 18, 1966; Georgia BOWEN BRITTLE beloved wife of Leslie Merlin?
    BRITTLE the daughter of Harry C. BOWEN and Georgia ROTHROCK his wife born Rappahanock Station
    March 7, 1874 died February 24, 1908
Susan E. STRINGFELLOW Nov. 23, 1830; Elizabeth M. daughter of Jas. & Rachel BOWEN 1789 Jan. 1887;
    George MOORE Mar. 11, 1799 Sept. 12, 1835 buried in Florida; Catherine R. wife of George MOORE Feb. 1,
    1809 Sept. 4, 1883; Elizabeth wife of James BOWEN June 8, 1829 Aug. 8, 1859; J. MOORE July 28, 1859 Mary
    15, 1865; Sally A. Sept. 3, 1832 April 5, 1835; George Feb. 5, 1834 Jan. 5, 1862

MINDER Albert A. Oct. 11, 1898 Dec. 25, 1964; Virginia E. Dec. 16, 1909 Oct. 10, 1976
GROVES Homer M. 1983 1966; Alice F. 1895 1965

Turner Ashby MARTIN April 25, 1897 March 19, 1973
Earl FERGUSON MARTIN March 1, 1897 February 12, 1978
Alma FERGUSON CHAMBERS October 22, 1911 May 15, 1992
Lucile FERGUSON LEWIS 1908 1957

Elizabeth HERDGIN VAUGHAN Ooct. 12, 1882 June 9, 1964
William T. FOSTER Feb. 18, 1886 Feb. 8, 1953
Julia VAUGHAN FOSTER Apr. 16, 1886 Jan. 24, 1967

Harry M. NISSIBRODT July 15, 1920 October 16, 1939

Jack Leonard SPICER PVT WWII Nov 20 1907 May 30 1976

W.A. McDONALD 1857 1938

Eva HOLLINS WILKES August 17, 1910 April 17, 1988
George B. WILKES June 5, 1866 Sept. 25, 1947
Eva EMBREY WILKES Oct. 29, 1870 Nov. 5, 1952

Clyde T. FERGUSON 1901 1932
Samuel Turner FERGUSON April 6, 1868 Nov. 25, 1946
Jane THOMPSON FERGUSON April 4, 1880 Mar. 15, 1959
Belle C. CULP Died May 18, 1909 aged 8 years

Charles W. HITT 1861 1915
Thomas B. HITT 1876 1973
J. Russell HITT 1910–
Louise G. HITT 1909–
Graham F. HITT 1938–

Anna Mae OLINGER Nov. 25, 1873 Mar. 15, 1948
Joseph T. OLINGER 1878 1944; Antoinette D. OLINGER
James Putnam OLINGER July 24, 1850 Dec. 18, 1919
Adelia Rebecca ASHBY wife of J.P. OLINGER Jan 22, 1859 Jan. 17, 1908

SPICER George W. Mar. 11, 1876 June 24, 1961; Mildred TAYLOR Aug. 16, 1871 July 20, 1935
J.B. LOHSE July 5, 1839 Mar. 26, 1906
Anna C.M. LOHSE Jan. 10, 1828 April 18, 1902
George W. DUEY July 6, 1831 Sept. 11, 1903

Benjamin Francis PERROW 1863 1958
Betty WISE PERROW 1869 1961
Robert C. son of F.A. & J.D. BYERLY Mar. 31, 1881 Apr. 13, 1882

ESPES Cynthia Marie Lynn May 4, 1981 May 9, 1981
ELAM Cyrle R. Sept. 25, 1907 Aug. 18, 1940; Maggie V. Nov. 22, 1905 Oct. 14, 1990
Mary Alice BLOCKER Sept. 25, 1933 June 8, 1992

OLINGER Robert Edward Mar. 4, 1912 May 15, 1980; Girly Roy Dec. 25, 1906 June 26, 1987

Infant Milton H. FEAGANS III Oct 11, 1857

H. Ashby BROWN 1885 1969
Elva S. BROWN 1892 1988
William Nelson SHACKLEFORD 1880 1972
Margaret COVINGTON SHACKLEFORD 1895 1988

Hunton TIFFANY 1882 1959; Stuart S. TIFFANY 1884 1971

WHETZEL Rodney Gilmon July 30, 1890 Aug. 12, 1969; Nadine FICKLIN Dec. 10, 1917 -

PORTIS Virginia Ellen Aug. 18, 1912– ; Ira Wilson Aug. 8, 1900 Aug. 14, 1986

James William OLINGER Apr. 27, 1884 July 23, 1970
Lola

Elizabeth BIRKISS Jan 23, 1868 Dec. 6, 1935
Ida

Mother Annie Elizabeth wife of William H. HOUGHTON Jan. 28, 1889 May 15, 1924
Wm. J. HOUGHTON
John W.

Charles Byrd WILLIS
Mary Alice WILLIS March 10, 1869 Oct. 28, 1977]
Infant Harriet

Hal CLARKSON
Nora HEDINGER November 22, 1878 May 11, 1868
T.H. HEDINGER Aug. 11, 1876 Dec. 3, 1916
Peter HEDINGER May 5, 1837 Oct. 14, 1920
Bettie A. HEDINGER Jun. 29, 1842 Jan. 10, 1909

Rev. Richard STEPHENS Mar. 6, 1818 Feb. 5, 1912
Elizabeth H. wife of Rev. R. STEPHENS Jan. 7, 1830 May 16, 1900
Russell C. DAVIS June 5, 1906 July 14, 1906

Clarence W. BAILEY, Jr. Feb. 8, 1953 Feb. 9, 1953
Russell Cottingham ELAM Sept. 4, 1914 June 13, 1983
Eva P. ELAM 1878 1949
Thomas W. ELAM 1876 1939
Eleanor M. REESE 1909 1936
Hugh Daniel ELAM 1910 1975 *(fhm)*
Minnie C. ELAM 1902 1970

Woodland L. CARROLL SGT US Marine Corps WWII Korea Aug 31 1927 Mar 5 1989 *(American Legion marker)*
Mary V. CARROLL Feb. 26, 1926 May 20, 1990 devoted wife to Woodland L. CARROLL and loving mother of
    Wm. Rex and Newton C. CARROLL
LANGE Louis J. 1867 1954; Ella M. 1901 1981
Betrice E. LANGE Oct. 12, 1924 June 23, 1925

FOSTER Ruth FOSTER JENKINS April 2, 1905 Feb. 15, 1923
Herbert Leon FOSTER Virginia PVT 305 Engrs 80 Div November 2 1918
ARMSTRONG Glenn O. Sept. 28, 1891 Nov. 27, 1963; Lena F. Nov. 30, 1890 May 7, 1982
FOSTER James B. July 15, 1856 May 9, 1939; Annie L. STEPHENS June 28, 1861 Feb. 3, 1962

Jackson B. CLATTERBUCK Oct. 15, 1865 Dec. 23, 1931
Mollie Lupton infant of J.M. & S JAMES Jan. 3, 1911 July 25, 1911
Dorothy E. BRUFFY July 13, 1924 Spt. 28, 1928

James A. McCONCHIE 1866 1927
Lilla SCOTT McCONCHIE June 19, 1876 June 11, 1914
Garnet R. McCONCHIE July 31, 1908 Nov. 24, 1960
Ashby Ray REID, Sr. Sept. 16, 1910 Sept. 6, 1962
Mary J. McCONCHIE Oct. 1, 1843 March 4, 1918
Lemuel A. McCONCHIE Dec. 25, 1834 Oct. 7, 1908

Thomas Clay McCONCHIE May 25, 1874 Oct. 19, 1944
Mary B. McCONCHIE May 26, 1881 Feb. 16, 1948
Earl S. McCONCHIE Oct. 22, 1900 Jan. 20, 1926

Father Charles E. BOLEYN April 8, 1875 June 12, 1959
Mother Jennie S. BOLEYN May 3, 1885 Oct. 11, 1959
Opal PENNINGTON BISPHAM Oct. 16, 1892 Lynchburg, S passed away Feb. 9, 1976 Washington, D
Nathaniel C. BISPHAM Feb. 21, 1852 Apr. 12, 1930
Mary S. BISPHAM Oct. 26, 1867 June 25, 1909
Marian N. BISPHAM July 3, 1904 Aug. 18, 1972

Marion Jackson PHILLIPS Sept. 7, 1900 May 29, 1934

Marvin R. BOWEN March 28, 1880 March 28, 1964
Fannie C. BOWEN Aug. 25, 1884 May 19, 1978
James Kinnon beloved son of Marion & Helen CASKIE Sept. 10, 1916 Aug. 31, 1920
William Rixey CASKIE Sept. 17, 1899 Aug. 30, 1900
Olivia Rixey BOWEN Dec. 24, 1905 Apr, 15, 1911
James Alexander CASKIE
Bettie FOSTER CASKIE wife of James A. CASKIE died Aug. 17, 1909
Alice DIMMOCK CASKIE wife of James CASKIE died Feb. 21, 1891
Nannie E. CASKIE died Aug. 29, 1912
James M. CASKIE, M.D. June 3, 1860 Nov. 24, 1930; Olivia RIXEY CASKIE August 23, 1856 Dec. 7, 1943
CASKIE Marion M. 1890 1966; Helen S. 1891 1978
Alice D. CASKIE 1865 1945
Clarence CASKIE Feb. 2, 1872 Apr. 24, 1957 and wife Anna Louise HOUGHTON June 20, 1874 June 12, 1914

CLOPTON Wright J. 1896 1919; John S. 1898 1919
CLOPTON James Keith Feb. 26, 1868 Dec. 23, 1938; Annie JAMES June 19, 1873 May 12, 1942
CLOPTON Marshall Keith 1907 1979; Blanche WILT 1910 1956
John S. CLOPTON; his wife Susie K. CLOPTON

FOSTER, Catherine S. January 20, 1883 January 25, 1965; J. Leonard June 3, 1878 November 17, 1925
Roina wife of John UTTERBACK Sept. 1850 Nov. 1941
Quincy W. husband of Susannah FOSTER Oct. 3, 1874 Oct. 19, 1918

Shirley Jameson ROUSE wife of William Alden ASHBY June 30, 1889 Aug. 11, 1937; William Walden ASHBY
    jan. 9, 1886 Oct. 12, 1918

Roy HOFFMAN 1880 1938; his wife Cora H. HATTON 1883 1967
Anne Mary HOFFMAN Jan. 13, 1873 April 3, 1943
Lucy L. WISE wife of James M. HOFFMAN Dec. 14, 1842 Jan. 20, 1929 mother
James M. HOFFMAN June 5, 1846 Nov. 12, 1913
Minneola HOFFMAN Oct. 27, 1878 Nov. 12, 1962
Our dear brother John Bunyan son of J.M. & Lucy L. HOFFMAN Sept. 18, 1874 Nov. 4, 1914

Elsie JONES BUTLER Sept. 3, 1897 June 18, 1926
JONES James Wesley 1868 1919; Alveria NEALE 1870 1958
Alvina JONES Feb. 14, 1913 Feb. 26, 1913

CORNWELL John Ellis Aug. 10, 1907 Mar. 15, 1969; Bessie JONES Mar. 11, 1907 Dec. 19, 1993
CORNWELL John Milton born in Strayhaven, Scotland

Roberta T. SPINDLE May 6, 1862 March 3, 1949
John E. SPINDLE Apr. 11, 1848 Aug. 5, 1903
sister Mary L. BOSWELL wife of J.E. SPINDLE Dec. 31, 1854 Sept. 15, 1896

David S. HILTON Virginia PVT 2 Inf April 17 1942 *(American Legion marker)*

William C. YATES Dec. 8, 1823 Sept. 9, 1902; Fannie J. YATES June 10, 1832 Jan. 28, 1895; Bettie V. YATES
    Sept. 18, 1861 May 4, 1887

Jesse P. BOWEN 1881 1963
J. McGILL BOWEN 1883 1948
Maie S. BOWEN 1877 1898
George P. BOWEN 1851 1921
Harry C. BOWEN 1846 1928
Champe E. BOWEN 1875 1927
William T. BOWEN 1871 1940
Charlotte GOODLOG BOWEN 1881 1957
Harry Moore BOWEN 1881 1951

Henry PAYNE March 30, 1840 July 12, 1912
Louis French sone of H. & M. PAYNE Feb. 9, 1882 Dec. 14, 1901

Hugh FOSTER 1880 1902
Z.M.P. FOSTER 1853 1931
Ella McD. FOSTER 1859 1947

NASH Perlina CARROLL 1867 1904; William Trent 1863 1938

Susannah WEAVER Mar. 19, 1837 Sept. 17, 1906
Joseph S. WEAVER Feb. 27, 1827 Jan. 14, 1912
Mary Elizabeth BURKE May 21, 1856 Mar. 24, 1934

Mary P. SEYMOUR wife of Joseph S. SEYMOUR June 6, 1875 Jan. 12, 1968
Joseph S. SEYMOUR 1860 1940

HICKERSON David P. 1848 1931; Rosena JONES 1855 1917
Martha EWERS July 27, 1845 Oct. 7, 1917; George H. EWERS Mar. 26, 1841 Nov. 13, 1911
Ernest EWERS 1866 1946

Bettie BARIT FREEMAN May 16, 1851 May 27, 1928
WEAVER Mason Emmett July 14, 1873 Aug. 3, 1945; Ethel FREEMAN Oct. 31, 1873 March 6, 1941

Revis Ethel WEAVER Jan. 9, 1905 Aug. 3, 1912
father Andrew E. GROVES Sept. 30, 1878 Sept, 30, 1918

QUACKENBUSH Dr. Leslie Rasbach Nov. 4, 1844 July 9, 1913; Lillie MARINER his wife Sept. 7, 1941; Mary
    Marriner Jan. 14, 1896 Feb. 22, 1921

SPICER Shirley Ernest January 5, 1880 Nov. 11, 1955; Eddie THOMAS August 6, 1887 July 4, 1962
Lloyd W. SPICER Dec. 7, 1920 April 4, 1942
Shirley SPICER April 28, 1913 July 11, 1923

Marie E. SMITH daughter of V & V.E. SMITH July 14, 1925 Feb. 7,1926
SMITH Broadus Calvin Sept. 27, 1898 Oct. 12, 193____

Infant William H. HITT Dec. 17, 1927 Dec. 23, 1927
Alma H. MOLCHANOFF Nov. 17, 1910 Feb. 9, 1954
Rhoda C. HITT MARTIN Apr. 18, 1887 Mar. 11, 1974
William F. HITT Feb. 18, 1878 May 15, 1953

Mother Rosa Lee MILLS July 5, 1883 Jan. 20, 1938
Father Edward Bailey MILLS Dec. 24, 1879 Nov. 22, 1961
Aubrey L. MILLS Oct. 5, 1907 July 28, 1966
Clarence W. MILLS 1903 1927
George C. MILLS 1913 1932
J. Richard MILLS 1925 1952

ELAM Lorine daughter of Walter T. & Lovelle C. Nov. 28, 1930 Feb. 9, 1931
ELAM Walter T. Sept. 29, 1905 Mar. 30, 1978; Lovelle C. Oct. 30, 1911 Mar. 1976

Nellie GILLIAM McCONCHIE 1869 1933
Katherine E. McCONCHIE Sept. 7, 1896 Jan. 8, 1939
Richard E. McCONCHIE Oct. 9, 1898 May 23, 1945
Charles C. McCONCHIE April 11, 1905 Aug. 2, 1961

Thomas Reed OTT July 21, 1901 June 26, 1966
Agnes CLOPTON OTT June 4, 1904 Nov. 28, 1966

TAYLOR Alexander P. July 28, 1878 Feb. 2, 1942 *father*; *mother* Rosa Frances Nov. 22, 1881 May 12, 1953
WHITE Clay Marshall Mar 22, 1900 Oct. 10, 1979; Anna MYRTLE Nov. 17, 1919; Baby WHITE July 11, 1934
    July 11, 1934

Della M. BOLIN Sept. 4, 1985 July 22, 1933
Floyd A. BOLIN VIRGINIA SGT ENGINEERS WORLD WAR II April 18, 1926 May 18, 1947
Anna L. CARR Aug. 9, 1909 Nov. 28, 1987

Oscar D. EMBREY Mar. 11, 1888 Nov. 23, 1949
father Joseph D. EMBREY b. Feb. 19, 1854 d. Jan. 16, 1911; *mother* Fannie W. EMBREY b. May 15, 1857 d. Sept
    26, 1931

WAGER Hallie E. TIMBERLAKE 1880-1954; J. E. B. WAGER, Sr. 1865-1926

RHODA 1893-1894
M. Catherine WEATHERHEAD 1873-1943
C. L. WEATHERHEAD 1855-1935
Elizabeth br 1665 w/o C. L. WEATHERHEAD Jan. 6, 1866 March 29, 1894
Irving L. WEATHERHEAD Aug. 5, 1899 Aug. 26, 1957
Frank F. WEATHERHEAD 1901-1971
Lilla (WEATHERHEAD) Jan. 16, 1912 July 21, 1928
SHEPHERD Richard James May 18, 1887 Oct. 29, 1969; Janie HUMPHREY Feb. 6, 1885 Mar. 28, 1954
SHEPHERD Richard James Jr. Apr. 10, 1914 Jan. 21, 1975; Alice MYERS Jan. 26, 1920 Mar. 5, 1980
Jas F. SHEPHERD May 19, 1857 Aug. 16, 1928; Alice S. SHEPHERD Nov. 5, 1856 Feb. 5, 1923
HUME William R. Aug. 13, 1851; Mary SHEPHERD Sept. 21, 1884 Aug. 18, 1962

Bwrin M. SOWLES Co. D. Inf. Dec. 13, 1840 Mar. 11, 1913 3 VT. INF. (*Amerigan Legion*)
Alton Alexander WHITE June 14, 1903 Oct. 8, 1977
Floyd SOULE Oct. 30, 1883 Nov. 13, 1952
Lula Allison SOULE Jan. 24, 1888 Mar. 6, 1943
Wm. O. JENNINGS Nov. 2, 1860 Oct. 21, 1891
Mary L. JOHNSON Dec. 15, 1833 Dec. 12, 1902
Jos. L. JENNINGS Apr. 6, 1924 Seot. 22, 1862
Luther Martin ALLISON May 18, 1849 Oct. 20, 1930
Carroll Jennings ALLISON Apr. 2, 1853 Feb. 9, 1898
Carroll JENNINGS Oct. 27, 1884; Robert Layetteu Nov. 17, 1883 *infan*t of M. & C. J. ALLISON

Sodice E. TAYLOR w.o. W. W. TAYLOR b. Jan. 30, 1871 d. Nov. 19, 1929
William W. TAYLOR b. Jan. 21, 1865 d. Dec. 26, 1922
Nella A. Gay daughter of W. W. & S. E. TAYLOR b. Apr. 30, 1894 d. Mar. 12, 1909
Clifton A. TAYLOR b. Mar. 14, 1906 d. Dec. 4, 1922

Lida S. NEWBY b. May 6, 1898 d. Apr. 5, 1911
Annie L. NEWBY Apr. 11, 1858 Jan.16, 1928
John S. NEWBY b. Nov. 17, 1857 d. Apr. 24, 1919
NEWBY Rena James Mar. 10, 1898 May 18, 1964

STANLEY Wade P. Aug. 22, 1911 Aug. 28, 1957; Ruth WEEKS Dec. 18, 1918
HERRELL John M. 1894-1968; Esther V. 1898-1967

Marie COCKRILL BALDWIN Apr. 23, 1917 Jan. 16, 1983
Norman D. COCKRILL 1909-1951
Lewis Jones BALDWIN Dec. 10, 1920 Oct. 12, 1977

Mary F. JASPER 1884-1972 (*fhm*)
Mattie OLINGER CHILDRESS May 15, 1915 Apr. 18, 1961

HOLSTEIN James E. 1920-1969; Frances 1925-

Larkin A. WOOLFREY Aug. 2, 1923 Aug. 18, 1950
Douglas A. WOOLFREY Oct. 8, 1872 May 18, 1958
Mary C. WOOLFREY Sept. 11, 1882 May 21, 1958
Wilfred W. WOOLFREY Nov. 14, 1901 Nov. 25, 1957

Mary CHILDRESS DEWANE Jan. 8, 1905 Jan. 16, 1985
William Henry CHILDRESS May 27, 1880 May 8, 1948

HUME Robert Fisher Oct. 27, 1855 Apr. 29, 1940; Annie E. HUME Jan. 30, 1854 July 22, 1932
John E. BYWATERS Mar. 31, 1842 De. 5, 1924

WEEKS S. Harvey Oct. 27, 1883 Feb. 12, 1923; Florence Sept. 29, 1884 Dec. 31, 1975

Mary A. GRAYSON b. Apr. 10, 1835 d. Sept. 25, 1918
Robert O. GRAYSON March 26, 1830 Mar. 20, 1907 (*broken in half*)

Alford ROGERS b. June 27, 1817 d. Aug. 15, 1918
Flora E. SIMMONS Jan.10, 1862 Nov. 24, 1947

W. Blanche ROGERS Aug. 30, 1891 Apr. 10, 1910

Homer R. THORN 1889-1972
Eunice T. THORN 1896-1955
Alma T. STOCKING 1909-1990

Remington Methodist Church Cemetery, Remington, Virginia
Located end of Church St., Remington. Stones laid flat in ground back of church. Resurveyed 1993.

William E. MARINER Born Nov. 25, 1861 Died Nov. 9, 1885
Infant of W. R. & Fannie S. PERROW Born Sept. 18, 1909 Died Oct. 31, 1909

Richards Cemetery, Warrenton, Virginia
Located 8.5 miles South West of Warrenton and 1.5 miles West of Opal on Route 687 South West 2 miles on Route 651, 150 yards North West of road. Place originally owned by Lee, Marshall, Jefferson, & Chowning families. Research by M. D. Gore, May 4, 1938 for WPA.

Mary W. RICHARDS was born the 18th day of July 1825 departed this life on the 9th day of September 1854 my only child

Rock Hill Cemetery, Casanova, Virginia
Located North side Route 747 1 mile North of Casanova in barnyard, fenced.

Eleanor Daughter of Edward and Louisa MURRY Born April 20, 1851 Died Sept. 15, 1862 Thomas Donaldson Son of Edward and Louisa MURRY Born February 24, 1853 Apl. 1, 1869

Rockland Mission Cemetery, Hume, Virginia
Located 0.6 mile North Route 635 on West side Route 727. Church no longer there, wire fence, laurel and other small trees.

John J. DAWSON 1870–1957
Mrs. Frank SHOWERS Died October 28, 195–Aged 54 years
Jeff Davis PICKRELL Born Dec. 16, 1862 Died Mar 31, 1923; M. P.

Ella S. Wife of C. F. McGUINN July 11, 1882 Sept. 10, 1907; A. B. McG.

Rose Hill Cemetery, Upperville Virginia
Located 0.4 mile West of Goose Creek on Route 50 in orchard. In unfenced area in orchard. Some rock markers. Resurveyed September 20, 1993.

Amy E. consort of Amos DENHAM born July 6, 1786 died Feb. 28, 1851 In the 65 year of her age
Amos DENHAM born Sept. 18th 1768 Died Aug. 31st 1838 In the 64th year of his age
Infant Daughter of Malcolm & Margaret HORTON born Dec. 28th 1853 died March 13th 1854 age 10 months & 5 days *(destroyed by bush hog, now leaning against tree 1993)*
Eliott CASSADEY born April 1st 1816 died August 9th 1847 *(now leaning against tree, shattered 1993)*
Oliver DENHAM born 1765 died March 1847 aged 82 years

Rowles Cemetery, Markham, Virginia
Located at West end of Moss Hollow Road, formerly RAWLS, RALLS, or ROWLES Hollow Rd. Route 728. Vanished.

Revolutionary War soldier Wm. ROWLES buried on his farm 1787 lease from Fairfax proprietory

Rust Cemetery, Upperville, Virginia
Located on farm at end of Route 619 1.5 miles South Route 50 back of barn. Stone wall fallen down and cemetery overrun by cattle, stones destroyed, but evidence or many graves. Found one large base and cemetery almost vanished. Road into it had been changed. No visible and readable tombstones. Resurveyed September 28, 1993.

W. T. C.
Died April 16, 1859 Algernon Carlin [RUST] Aged 2 months
John S. RUST Departed this life 27th day of Jan. in the 19th year if his age
Henry Howell beloved Son of James & Emily B. WILLIAMS Born June 29, 1865 Died Mar. 21, 1880
S. Wright WILLIAMS of Baltimore, Md. Died 30th March 1870 Aged 32 years
Benjamin RUST who departed this life on 21st day of June 1831 in the 85th year of his age
Hannah R. L. RUST who departed this life June 6th 1821 aged years
J. N. R.
Died April 2d 1851 James Alfred CARLIN [?] Aged 7 years

Rutter - Hutchison - Henry Cemetery, Halfway, Virginia
Located about 1 mile West of Route 626 on South side of Route 708, down private road to right of barn lot, fence down in woods, periwinkle covered, fieldstone markers

John T. RUTTER Born Sept. 18, 1846 Died Aug. 5, 1873
Daisy HENRY Age 10 years
James M. HUTCHISON Born Nov. 27, 1851 Died Feb. 14, 1852

Ryan Cemetery
Located 200 feet West of junction of Routes 649 and 650 in woods. Fieldstone marker for Mrs. Ryan.

Saffell Cemetery, Linden, Virginia
Located on North side Route 55 beyond Belle Meade. Department of Highways reports: "On property of Charles R. SAFFELL and Virginia SAFFELL PEARSON 34 graves were disinterred and reinterred in Prospect Hill Cemetery, Front Royal, Virginia. Four of the graves had stone markers and a large marble shaft which were reset at the new graves in the above cemetery." Their names as follows:

Silas SAFFELL, died 7-18-1887; Virginia C. SAFFELL, died 1-3-1882
Jennie E. SAFFELL, died 4-34-1876; Silas E. SAFFELL, died 7-17-1870

Saffell Cemetery (Black), Linden, Virginia
Located on North side Route 55 beyond Belle Meade. Department of Highways reports: "The 30 unknown remains were placed in individual boxes and placed side by side, 6 to a grave."

Sanders Cemetery, New Baltimore, Virginia
Located 0.5 mile North East Route 29 North Route 683 in locust grove on left of drive in field. Dates given by wife, Mrs. Kathleen Sanders.

Leslie Richard SANDERS Born Sept. 24, 1888–Died Mar. 30, 1952

Scott Cemetery, Ada, Virginia
Located South East Route 647 0.75 mile South Route 732 on first fence line past creek, top of hill on left, about 100 feet from road, overgrown with periwinkle, wire fenced with gate - fence mostly down - one rock marker (mother of children?), inscriptions down. Phyllis Scott provided information for unmarked grave. January 19, 1991
Mary A. Wife of J. R. KERNS Died Feb. 25, 1897 Aged 42 years 4 mos. & 25 days
Lillie HOOPER lived to love and died a Christian Wife of W. H. HOOPER July 9, 1896 Aged 31 yrs. & 11 mos.

Henry D. SCOTT Died Oct. 22, 1895 Aged 18 years 1 mo. & 13 dys *(died of typhoid fever)*
Lillie L Dau. of E. & W. SCOTT Died May 7, 1900 age 7 mos. an angel
James C. [Cletis] SCOTT died Sept. 26, 1895 aged 22 yrs. 25 days *(died of typhoid fever)*
Mary EDWARDS SCOTT *(rock marker)*

Scott Cemetery, Warrenton, Virginia
Located on Route 678 0.9 mile South of Route 691 in second field back of house and stable enclosed by excellent cinder block wall painted white.

In memory of honorable John SCOTT Son of Reverend John and Elizabeth SCOTT Born Jan. 1779 Died Feb. 17, 1850
Betsy BLACKWELL Daughter of Martin PICKETT and Wife of Judge John SCOTT Died Sept. 16, 1862
Robert Eden SCOTT Born Apr. 23, 1808 killed by Yankee Deserter May 3, 1862
Margaret Gordon Daughter of Judge John SCOTT and Wife of Robert Eden LEE Died May 17, 1866
Robert Eden Son of the Honorable Charles and Margaret Christiana LEE Born Sep. 1811 Died June 24, 1840
Charles Francis SCOTT Son of the Honorable John and Elizabeth SCOTT Born Aug. 1, 1829 Died Feb. 15, 1846

Shacklett Cemetery, "Rose Hill", Delaplane, Virginia
Located on right of Route 17 about 4.5 miles North of Delaplane, across from old house, "Rose Hill." Cemetery large, with stone wall, but is now open field, stones terribly broken and scattered. Data taken March 7, 1937 by Eleanor Glascock Thompson.

John SHACKLETT Died Aug. 2nd 1817
Elcey BALTHROP Wife of .John BALTHROP born July 29th 1783 and was married Nov. 29th 1800 Departed this life Jany 1st 1802
Hezekiah SHACKLETT departed -------- Decr. 6 ----
El----- SHACKLETT departed this life ----- Janna -- 7th 1828 *(possibly Eliot)*

Shumate Cemetery, Catlett, Virginia
Located 1.25 miles South West of Catlett, in the South angle formed where the railroad crosses Cedar Run, at the "Dan Shumate Place." Research by M. D. Gore, Sumerduck, February 15, 1937. Resurveyed August 15, 1994 by Mr. Feagans.

"About 75 yards North East of the house is the family graveyard, with tombstones to Bailey, Daniel Shumate, and others."

[Bailey SHUMATE, Daniel SHUMATE]

Shumate Cemetery, Marshall, Virginia
Located on left of Route 647 about 1 mile West of Routes 17 - 55, well kept and fenced, some fieldstone markers. Resurveyed October 25, 1993

Taylor S. SHUMATE July 18, 1857 Oct. 16, 1919; Catherine Shumate Aug. 9, 1959 April 1920
Kitty GAINES Born July 7, 1824 Died Mar. 9, 1901
R. S. F. Apr. 17, 1929
H. E. LEE 1870–1956 *((fhm))*
James E. LEE Died June 7, 1956 Aged 85 years 4 mos 5 ds
SMITH Shirley E. Nov. 1889 Jan 1957
Mother Nannie FADLE July 8, 1867 Oct. 5, 1951
E. L. G. Died Dec. 27, 1898
Baby
A. D. [DODSON]; B. D. [DODSON]

Randolph DODSON Born Jan. 25, 1856 Died Oct. 23, 1898
Mother Nannie MASON DODSON Born July 18, 1863 Died Jan. 24, 1927
Georgia E. DODSON 1894–1968
GRANT, W. Irven July 31, 1908 Jan. 31, 1970; Alfreda R. Oct. 18, 1910
Willie E. DODSON 1920-1971 *(fhm)*
Howard DODSON 1908-1974 *(fhm)*
Bailey S. FORD LEE 1886-1958
William Lewis HOLMES 1928-1988 *(fhm)*
Franklin Elmer MILLER US ARMY Kores Aug. 31, 1933 Jan. 13, 1988
Harry M. FORD 1913-1972; Beatrice FORD 1907-
Mary P. MILLER 1906-1991 *(fhm)*
Harry Mason FORD Virginia S. Sgt 507 P. N. Bn TEC WORL WAR II Apr. 3, 1913 Dec. 20, 1972
Lillian ADAMS Spril 26, 1907 July 13, 1968
Carl B. FORD June 22, 1902
DODSON, Dannie V. Nov. 15, 1914; Roger M. Sept. 20, 1912 April 30, 1975

Across Route 647 in field with iron fence and trees:
John SHUMATE Died Jan. 17, 1873 aged 80 years 5 months and 10 days

Shumate Cemetery, Warrenton, Virginia
Located West Route 17 about 0.25 mile South Route 616 in field, some stones outside iron fence. Resurveyed in 1992.

John W. SHUMATE Died March 30, 1930 His Wife Mary W. SHUMATE Died Jan. 10, 1907

Silver Hill Church Cemetery, Morrisville, Virginia
Located at the intersection of Routes 613 & 633 East of Route 17. Many fieldstone markers. Resurveyed 1990.

Robert W. COLE Oct. 10, 1893 July 8, 1951
Bella J. COLE Jan. 1, 1892 May 27, 1942
Thomas H. COLES Born Dec. 25, 1826 Died Feb. 17, 1914
Father Augustus J. COLE Born June 12, 1878 Died Oct. 28, 1927
Mary A. TAYLOR Wife of Thos. H. COLES Mar. 31, 1879 July 12, 1938
Philip H. LEE 1890–May 19, 1958
Idella WALTERS Born 1934 Died Oct. 25, 1979
Irene BROCKLEY Born 1931 Died Apr. 21, 1979

William COLES Born 1924–Aug. 8, 1978
Fred W. COLES US ARMY Oct. 24, 1926 March 20, 1972
Cornelius COLES Died April 17, 1959 aged 70 years
Marvin CARTER MARYLAND EC 4 1963 ENGINEERS AVN DEPOT WORLD WAR II Mar. 11, 1922 May 18, 1968
Mary K. COLES April 24, 1900 Sept. 4, 1981
E. C.; L. H.
Margauerette COLES 1917–1988

William CARSON PVT US ARMY 1926–1976
Kate MILES 1878–1977 *(fhm)*
Harry F. GIBSON 1897–1970 *(fhm)*

Lucille RAYMOND 1917–1980 *(fhm)*
Joseph D. RAYMOND 1935–1982 *(fhm)*

Margaret RAYMOND 1944–1975 *(fhm)*
Edith W. RAYMOND 1893–1972 *(fhm)*

Mary A. TAYLOR Wife of Thomas H. COLES Mar. 31, 1879 July 12, 1938
Albert J. GARNETT, Sr. Jan. 8, 1905 March 22, 1968
Mother ALLA V. WHITE 1893–1956
A. R. E. L.; A. F. C.; H. C.; L. L.; G. H.; E. C.; F. H.; L.H.; M. J. H.
James H. COLES July 21, 1861 Oct. 31, 1938
Clara C. COLES Born 1871 died Feb. 11, 1932
Larry SCOTT 1881–1960
Mr. Floyd HULL August 22, 1953 Aged 74 yrs. 3 mos. 18 days

Ella V. CARTER died May 19, 1944; N. B. C.; C.D J. H.
William CARTER 1915–1961; Marie CARTER 1908–1961
Callie CARTER 1906–1962; Marvin CARTER 1922–1928

Mary HILL died Feb. 7, 1964
Rena H. MANUEL Mar. 29, 1898 Aug. 17, 1970
John Moon GIBSON 1907–1976 PPC US ARMY
Thomas A. SMITH 1926–1990
Mother Florence GAMBLE 1917–1986
Virginia POLLARD 1926 -1988
Delliah V. JACKSON 1905–1986
William W. JACKSON 1885–1975
William G. GIBSON 1911–1987
Powhatan BUCKNER March 22, 1893 February 2, 1986
James D. GIBSON 1910–1980
Carey RUSSELL COLE Mother Mar. 11, 1932 Nov. 26, 1985
Lewis Wilson COLE PFC US ARMY WORLD WAR II 1927–1984
Mortimer MARTIN VIRGINIA WORLD WAR I April 1892 June 2, 1972
James Oscar MARTIN PVT US ARMY WORLD WAR II 1911–1987

Sinclair Cemetery, "Hopewell Gap", The Plains, Virginia
Located on the West side of Route 601 about 1 mile West of Hopewell Gap, on a knoll. Robert Sinclair stated that
his father, George Sinclair, said there were about fifty tombstones with inscriptions at the cemetery, which were
bulldozed away by a later owner. In 1988 the only tombstone Robert Sinclair could find was a fieldstone with:
Robert SINCLAIR B died 18–7.

Robert Sinclair had photo of another:
Martin SINCLAIR died May 24th in yr of Our Lord 1801

Sinclair Cemetery, Midland, Virginia
Located on North side Route 650 0.25 mile South West Route 649. Source: Ripley Robinson. Ripley's grandfather
bought area - 100 acres - in 1905 from Turner Willis. Resurveyed April 23, 1994

Fieldstone markers for:
Stack SINCLAIR and his wife

Sinclair (Charity) Cemetery, Midland, Virginia
Located South East corner of Ball's Mill Rd. and Route 249 in grove of trees. Miss Charity SINCLAIR is buried in
fieldstone marked grave. Source: Ripley Robinson.

Slave Cemeteries
(1) South intersection of Routes 616 & 607 on fence line. Data obtained from Joe Lawler, Marshall.

(2) To left of Route 764 at end of road in field. Other Negroes buried there including Maggie COLE. Data obtained from Joe Lawler, Marshall.

(3) At the Moss home just East of Locust Hill with fieldstone markers.

Smallwood Cemetery
Located 1st private lane South Route 705 West Route 626 100 feet. Vanished.

Smith Cemetery, Halfway, Virginia
Located on Route 702 next to John Cooper place, near stone wall boundary between Nordan & Cooper. Resurveyed 1990.

George H SMITH 8th Va Infantry Co. C 1826-1919 *(UDC marker)*
fieldstone markers for Wife Eliza FOSTER SMITH & grandchild

Smith Cemetery, Orlean, Virginia
Located between Thumb Run and Route 736 on Route 688. Judge John Barton Payne erected the excellent stone wall and monument with all family data on it. Very well kept. Below the cemetery in the woods are buried a number of Union soldiers, apparently killed in an action in which the Baptist church at cemetery site was burned according to Mrs. Mary S. Putnam, owner. All inscriptions on one monument. Resurveyed August 1988.

John Puller SMITH 1782–1838
Elizabeth Barnes BROWN His Wife 1786–1812
John Brown SMITH 1809–1842
Susannah M. FARROW 1810–1891
Alexander SMITH 1812–1880
Mary Gilberth BARTON second Wife 1793–1841
Elizabeth Barton PAYNE 1817–1895
William Undril SMITH 1824–1863
Jackaline Puller BARBEE 1826–1901
Maria Catherine MASSIE 1830–1857
Hugh Goalder SMITH 1834–1900
Mary Virginia SMITH 1818–1820
Sarah Ann SMITH 1820–1821
Robert Puller SMITH 1822–1823
Lucy Lettitia SMITH 1828–1829
James Thomas SMITH 1833–1833

On separate monument:

John SMITH who departed this life Aug __ 1811 66 years 6 mos. 16 days

Smoot Cemetery, Bristersburg, Virginia
Located 1 mile East of Bristersburg on Route 609. House 500 yards South of road. Cemetery in clump of trees 100 yards West of tenant house. Surveyed by M. D. Gore March 17, 1937.

Dr. Horace SMOOT Born Dec. 14, 1830 Died Jan. 14, 1903

Virginia Wife of Dr. H. SMOOT 1841–1930

184

James COOPER Born Feb. 22, 1822 Died July 14, 1904

Marian READ [*sister of Mrs. Smoot and wife of Joe READ*]

Benjamin SMITH who departed this life August 29, 1855 aged 13 years and 7 months

Betty SMITH who departed this life in the 13th year of her age

Squires Cemetery, Plains, Virginia
Located in field East of creek, North West intersection of Routes 601 and 628. Robert Sinclair tried to find it in 1993 but it had vanished.

St. James Church Cemetery, Bealeton, Virginia
Located West Route 29 0.25 mile South Route 663 on West side of Route 661 back of church, fenced.

M. E. WASHINGTON 1900–1957

Jackson THOMAS Died November 15th 1959 Aged 43 yrs 1 month 2 days
Mary [Ellen] THOMAS Died January 1st 1962 Aged 81 yrs.

SAYLES Lonnie Mar. 3, 1895 Pauline HART Apr. 26, 1900 May 18, 1924
Mattie CORUM 1850–1905

Moses FISHER Died 1933; Mildred FISHER 1870–1938
Lucy V. MORGAN Jan. 13, 1890 Nov. 21, 1950

Mother Mary J. TACKETT Feb. 16, 1866 Jan. 22, 1913
Richard TACKETT Born Dec. 24, 1888 Died Oct. 7, 1918

Eva T. HALL Born Aug. 22, 1926 Died Aug. 23, 1927
Lucrecia MUDD Died May 2, 1910

DAWSON Bessie SAYLES Nov. 25, 1885 June 11, 1919
Charles SAYLES 1866–1954

John P. MUDD VIRGINIA PVT CO B 341 SVC BN QMC WORLD WAR I Dec. 1, 1890 Feb. 12, 1960
Grace T. MUDD Feb. 3, 1908 June 12, 1961

Lelia WASHINGTON 1896–1953

James D. BERRY Born March 5, 1910 Died Jan. 12, 1931
Esther BERRY Died July 4, 1937 Aged 51 yrs. 5 mos. 8 dys

Milton Joseph HART VIRGINIA CPL 584 AMN SQ AAF WORLD WAR II July 16 1912 November 9 1968
HART Carrie C. Dec. 25, 1876 May 24, 1959 Charles C. April 19, 1877 July 31, 1952 Mother Father

Irving N. JACKSON Jr. PFC US ARMY January 6 1931 May 16 1954
Fannie F GRANT July 10, 1900–Mar. 11, 1960

Robert M. TAYLOR 1875–1966
Charles O. GRANT 1907–1968; Samuel GRANT June 11, 1937 June 18, 1937

Mother Emma CORAM ROY January 2, 1895 July 13, 1962

Mary F. COLEMAN Sept. 20, 1843 March 20, 1910 Mark COLEMAN May 10, 1831 May 24, 1901
Mattie *(rest in ground)*
THOMAS Martha 1884–1942 Hamie 1884–1941
G. E. THOMAS Born March 2 1833 Died June 3 1939

Bertha JENKINS Died December 1960 Aged 61 yrs 8 months 7 days
Edward JENKINS 1892–1965; Carol W. JENKINS 1893–1967

Heywood FORD 1876–1961
Benjamin MOSELY Born Jan. 11, 1892 Died Oct. 7, 1918 Bintie MOSELY Died May 27, 1901
J. B.
Richard S. GRANT Born Dec. 19, 1891 Died Feb. 10, 1908
William JENKINS Born Dec. 14, 1853 Died Dec. 31, 1921 Anna JENKINS Nov. 7, 1854 October 22, 1961
Raymond R. GRANT July 20, 1912 October 22, 1961
Mary Ella GRANT Oct. 12, 1865 June 11, 1931

St. Stephen's Episcopal Church Cemetery, Catlett, Virginia
Located at the intersection of Routes 667 & 603. Cemetery between church and parish house.

Evelyn ALLSTON BOORMAN Born Dec. 17, 1850 Died May 24, 1881
Robert Henry BOORMAN Born Aug. 1, 1837 Died April 6, 1918

IVEY Henry Jan. 2, 1858 Dec. 22, 1911 Minnie K. Mar. 14, 1879 Jan. 31, 1958
Graham BRYANT, Jr. Dec. 5, 1913 July 13, 1914
Maggie A. AUSTIN Beloved Wife of John L. CARRICO Born Oct. 7, 1855 Died Nov. 6, 1897
Elizabeth DOVALL BOORMAN Aug. 30, 1865 June 1957

Used as a Federal hospital, Union soldiers burned East side of church in garden area.

Strother Cemetery, Marshall, Virginia
Located on Route 647 at "Holly Hill" Farm, formerly owned by Hedgman STROTHER and also the LEE family. Information from John Gott. Cemetery has not been surveyed.

Strother Cemetery, Paris, Virginia
Located on East slope of Blue Ridge about 200 yards South East of signal pole and 100 yards North West of Appalachian Trail just North of spring on trail. Go to the wall around the cemetery. Surveyed by Ranger Irvin Kenyon of Richard Thompson Wildlife Park August 1991.

fieldstone markers for:
Mary Catherine [RAY] STROTHER
James STROTHER
Elizabeth [PURCELL] STROTHER

There appear to be a few infant graves and at least 7 other graves.

Strother - Green Cemetery, Markham, Virginia
Located North of Route F284 about 1 mile West of Route 688 at Markham, VA. Stone wall, full of weeds, about 50 feet from road. Resurveyed September 28, 1993.

Mary G. Infant Daughter of James R. & Annie R. GREEN Born Aug. 3, 1880 Died Aug. 17, 1881

Rebecca Childs Daughter of James R. & Annie R. GREEN Born July 31, 1885 Died Aug. 6, 1885
Alice Montgomery Daughter of James R. & Annie R. GREEN Born July 1, 1890 Died July 2, 1890
Annie Rebecca Wife of James R. GREEN Born Nov. 20, 1847 Died July 5, 1894
James R. GREEN Born Dec. 7, 1844 Died Jan. 14, 1929
M. H. S.; N. D. A.
Catharine E. STROTHER Born June 30, 1866 Died Nov. 18, 1921
Charles Edward STROTHER Born March 13, 1857 Died June 19, 1926
Ann R. Wife of A. G. GREEN Born Oct. 29, 1821 Died June 6, 1857 aged 35 yrs 7 mo 8 days
A. G. GREEN Born June 19, 1812 Died Aug. 5, 1886 Aged 73 yrs nine mos and seven days
William H. STROTHER Born Jan. 15, 1849 Died Aug. 9, 1894 Aged forty-five years four months and twenty-four
    days
Nannie D. ANDERSON Wife of William H. STROTHER Born May 6, 1865 Died May 6, 1895 Aged thirty years
Alice HANK STROTHER of Baltimore Wife of Rev Franklin M. STROTHER of Baltimore Conference of the M.E.
    Ch. Born February 23, 1856 Died September 29, 1948
Rev. Frank M. STROTHER Born March 7, 1852 Died Oct. 20, 1886
John R. STROTHER Born Oct. 24, 1853 Died Mar. 24, 1884 *(Masonic emblem)*
Catharine Mildred CHILDS Wife of James STROTHER Born Feb. 22, 1817 Died Feb. 14, 1904
James STROTHER Born Nov. 18, 1807 Died Feb. 17, 1861
Mary C. IDEN Wife of Wm. TEMPLEMAN April 1831 March 1922
Elizabeth C. Wife of W. P. IDEN Born 1808 Died 1899
Thomas IDEN Born Dec. 13, 1831 Died Jan. 17, 1908
Mary E. STROTHER Wife of Thomas E. IDEN Born Sept. 10, 1839 Died Jan. 5, 1928
Jessee C. BOLEN Died Dec. 14, 1893 His Wife Frances W. BOLEN Died Oct. 6, 1915
Elizabeth WHITE Died Mar. 8, 1904
Della S. TEMPLEMAN 1801–1876
Mary T. CABLE Feb. 21, 1822 Oct. 27, 1872 *(broken in 2 pieces 1993)*
Alfred CABLE Nov. 26, 1810 April 6, 1877

Stone House Primitive Baptist Church Cemetery, Markham, Virginia
*Located on Route 688 South of Route 55 intersection. 2 graves marked with fieldstone markers. Cemetery area
    large, no markers. Rock markers piled up near parking area. Resurveyed October 24, 1989.*

Turner A. ASH VIRGINIA PVT 3 CAV September 7 1873 May 19 1946
Evan Henry KIDWELL Died July 5, 1888 Aged 50 yrs.; Susan D. His Wife Died June 16, 1892 Aged 52 years
Our Mother L. M. PAGE August 6, 1804 May 17, 1884
Col. C. T. PAGE Born Dec. 25, 1798 Died Feb. 21, 1868
F. Page FURR E. C. PAGE sisters members of First Baptist Church

Henry M. BRADY June 23, 1863 March 13, 1934 His Wife Lucy R. BRADY Feb. 29, 1860 August 3, 1938
Mary S. McINTYRE 1870–1940 *(fhm)*

South Run Church Cemetery
Located 0.25 mile North Route 721 on Route 738. Data obtained from Joe Lawler, Marshall. Bulldozed.

Suddeth - Kelly Cemetery, Somerville, Virginia
Located 3 miles South Somerville on Route 617. Found and resurveyed by L. Arthur Grove February 1994.

James W. KELLY Died June 3, 1853 Age 67 years
Asenath SUDDETH Wife of John SUDDETH Died March 11, 1841 Age 57
6–8 unmarked graves

Sumerduck Baptist Church Cemetery, Sumerduck, Virginia
Located on North side of Route 651 in Sumerduck back of church, well kept. Resurveyed 1991.

GREENWOOD Benjamin H. Mar. 17, 1889 June 20, 1953 Olive B. July 8, 1919 Dec. 23, 1947
JACOBS Judson J. Feb. 26, 1906 July 2, 1987Ida M. May 29, 1912 Mar. 24, 1961
Pearl WILSON MANUEL June 23, 1912 Feb. 2, 1969
WILSON George E. Sept. 9,.1882 Apr. 10, 1958 Annie E. Mar. 10, 1890 Nov. 15, 1968 Married Dec. 26, 1906

EMBREY Melvin J. Aug. 1, 1875 July 27, 1955 Rosia B. Apr. 10, 1881
Ernest Ray EMBREY VIRGINIA CPL. 1943 ENGR. UTIL DET WORLD WAR II Sept 21 1925 Nov 4 1961

SMITH Norman C. Aug. 31, 1890 Feb. 13, 1961 Pearl C. Nov. 8, 1896 Mar. 3, 1962
DAY Lesley L. Aug. 29, 1884 May 15, 1962 Blanche C. Oct. 15, 1890
HARDING Myrtle D. Mar. 14, 1912 Feb. 12, 1963
Powell H. JONES VIRGINIA S SGT CO B 3233 ENGR SVC BN WORLD WAR II Oct 15 1911 Oct 2 1966
Arnold C. HOLMES VIRGINIA PFC 234 ESCORT CO ASC WORLD WAR I Dec 17 1886 Oct 24 1965
James D. WARR Apr. 30, 1931 Nov. 11, 1951
Nellie EMBREY 1867–1943
JACOBS Susie J. 1870–1959 Jacob H. 1868–1939
Charles William JACOBS 1898–1959
Lennis Cooper JACOBS VIRGINIA PVT US ARMY WORLD WAR I May 29 1892 Oct 4 1963
Mrs. Alice Gloria JACOBS Died Friday November 14, 1969 Aged 77 yrs.

Henry C. JONES Sept. 10, 1867 Feb. 26, 1941
Theodosia HOLMES JONES July 14, 1873 April 3, 1949
Joseph Hackley JONES April 7, 1870 Feb. 16, 1945
Ottaway Chester JONES VIRGINIA PFC CO A 797 MP BN WORLD WAR II April 2 1906 Feb 5 1957
Linda Jeanette DURNAN Mar. 19, 1902 Aug. 12, 1961 Interred Arlington National Cemetery
Remus Coleman JONES Nov. 17, 1905 Jan. 22, 1956 *(Masonic emblem)*
James C. JONES Sept. 10, 1867 March 13, 1913 Musetta I. JONES June 11, 1877 Feb. 18, 1946

Tackett - Burroughs - Davis Cemetery, Remington, Virginia
Located 0.7 mile South East intersection of Routes 651 & 655 0.5 mile from road in field, chain link fence painted green.

Mary Elizabeth Wife of Charles M. DAVIS Born Dec. 10, 1853 Died June 30, 1900 Charles Mills DAVIS Born
   Dec. 2, 1844 Died July 19, 1900
Mary E. DAVIS Born April 27, 1818 Died July 16, 1887
W. G. M. DAVIS Born May 9, 1912 Died March 11, 1898 erected by daughter
Louisa BURROUGHS PAYNE Born April 20, 1819 Died Oct. 29, 1905
Samuel B. BARBER Oct. 10, 1835 Nov. 8, 1881
Rev. J. F. BRANNIN Died Sept. 1912 aged 86 years
Eliza L. BRANNIN faithful Wife of Rev. J. E. BRANNIN Died March 1904 aged 86 years
SPRINDLE Lena G. beloved Wife of M. W. Born June 22, 1860 Died Sept. 22, 1894 Mary B. Born Dec. 3,1891
   Died May 15, 1894 Milton J. Born Mar. 5, 1894 Died June 17, 1894
Milton W. SPRINDLE Nov. 30, 1854 July 21, 1916
Granville Coleman SPRINDLE Infant child of Milton & Leta SPRINDLE Died July 5, 1910 1 year old
Mary Lena and two children of H. C. & Nannie B. HICKERSON
Everett B. HICKERSON 1891–1964
HICKERSON Lewis W. June 1, 1899 Dec. 27, 1901 J. Aubrey Nov. 11, 1903 Sept. 3, 1911 sons of J. B. & F. B.
   HICKERSON
Florence B. HICKERSON 1858–1920

John B. HICKERSON Jan. 31, 1856 Nov. 27, 1940
Martha L. HICKERSON Born 1863 Died 1956 Florence Virginia Daughter of C. K. & M. F. HICKERSON Born April 10, 1854 Died Nov. 26, 1905
Chas. Kendall HICKERSON Born June 11, 1820 Died Jan. 14, 1892
Martha Frances Wife of Chas. Kendall HICKERSON Born Nov. 4, 1825 Died July 1, 1897

Mary E. BURROUGHS Born Dec. 10, 1832 Died May 19, 1898 John B. BURROUGHS Born Sept. 11, 1820 Died May 8, 1898
CRIGLER Ethel B. Wife of A. M. CRIGLER Dec. 24, 1874 July 3, 1901 East: Mary West: Kathleen North: Robert S.
Rev. John O. TACKETT Born June 24, 1848 Died May 20 1907
Nannie B. Wife of H. C. HICKERSON Jan. 31, 1865 Oct. 23, 1908
Charles A. TACKETT Dec. 4, 1845 Oct. 9, 1920

Tannehill Cemeteries, Somerville, Virginia
Located West Route 752 0.5 mile South West Route 617 between end of private lane and very old house, overgrown with briars.
Brick walled cemetery has fieldstone markers and:

Susan A. E. Daughter of Joseph & Lucy THOMPSON and Wife of Docr. James E. FORD who departed this life 10th Sept. 1845 in the 17th year of her age

Wire fenced cemetery:

Aurelia A. BOTTS Wife of Thornton BOTTS Sept. 1, 1865 May 22, 1957
William A. TANNEHILL Nov. 22, 1859 May 19, 1945
Anson J. TANNEHILL Aug. 23, 1827 Sept. 29, 1889 Jane C. TANNEHILL Sept. 28, 1833 May 13, 1934

Tarman (Denmark) Cemetery
Located off Route 738. Data obtained from Joe Lawler, Marshall.

Tarry Cemetery, Warrenton, Virginia
Located at intersections of Routes 17 - 29 & 744 North West corner back of house, no markers. Wade Foster states that Braxton PORTER, Nannie TARRY FRAZIER and Al FRAZIER are among people buried there.

Taylor Cemetery, Remington, Virginia
Located near intersection of Routes 655 & 656 East of RR in field by fence, good stone wall with stile, poison oak. Fauquier National Bank says money for upkeep gone, so they have let it become overgrown. Resurveyed April 26, 1994.

Eppa H. TAYLOR Born July 5, 1874 Died June 14, 1905
Daniel E. TAYLOR Mar. 26, 1882 Oct. 5, 1944
George W. TAYLOR July 19, 1829 April 3, 1902 Mary F. TAYLOR Dec. 21, 1840 April 3, 1894
Georgianna TAYLOR McCONCHIE

Taylor Cemetery, at the "Highlands", Remington, Virginia
Located on Route 651, 1 mile North of Route 621, North East 400 yards by private road. Research by M. D. Gore, Sumerduck, February 21, 1938.

One tombstone in graveyard in North West corner of yard:

Anna Maria Daughter of E. Shelton & Harriet TAYLOR of Amenca, Dutchess County, New York, Died at this place

June 15, 1851 Whilst engaged as a teacher in the family of Colonel Fant Age 22 years

Taylor Cemetery, Old Tavern, Virginia
Located West side of Route 17 near its north intersection with Merry Oak Road along abandoned roadbed. No markers. Information from John Gott.

William F. TAYLOR & wife Susan

Templeman Cemetery, Orlean, Virginia
Located South East Routes 647 & 688 on Williams farm on hill in back field. All inscriptions on one monument, surrounded by excellent stone wall. Some fieldstone markers. Resurveyed January 29, 1992.

Leroy TEMPLEMAN Aug. 27, 1811–Nov. 21, 1891
Sarah Patton TEMPLEMAN Sept. 15, 1812–Feb. 10, 1906
Edward P. TEMPLEMAN Oct. 26, 1803–July 13, 1896
Fielding TEMPLEMAN Jan. 4, 1780–March 8, 1847
Hannah Hume TEMPLEMAN Sept. 30, 1776–Aug. 29, 1823
Nancy TEMPLEMAN Feb. 22, 1780–April 9, 1845
Sally E. Daughter of Wm. H. & Hattie L. TRIPLETT Born Feb 5, 1876 died February 23, 1884
William H. TRIPLETT Jan. 25, 1833–Jan. 24, 1896

footstones:
H. H. T. N. T.
W. H. T.E. P. T.
S. P. T. L. T.
F. T.

Virgil Dantic says a Confederate soldier had a tombstone marked C. S. A. (marker gone 1992) wounded at Manassas. Made it along road as far as Templeman house, where he died and was buried in family cemetery. He was unable to tell family his name.

Templeman - Nelson Cemetery, Orlean, Virginia
Located on Route 691 1 mile East of Route 739 in field back of barn, unfenced, fieldstone markers. Mr. Irving C. Ashby stated that Templemans had been moved to Warrenton. Resurveyed January 29, 1992.

Sgt. Thomas A. NELSON Co F 12 Va. Inf. C.S.A.

Thomas - Grant Cemetery, Warrenton, Virginia
Located 1.5 miles South Fauquier Springs South East Route 687 about 0.75 mile on dirt lane on left. 14 rock markers. Data collected by Ed Cooper.
Sarah THOMAS Died December 3rd 1884 Aged 84 years Also Her Son Richard Henry GRANT Died July 12th 1880 Aged 55 years

Thomas Cemetery, Paris, Virginia
Located on mountain above "Ovoka.".Possibly on the site of an earlier GREEN cemetery. Surveyed 23 September 1990

Clinton Reed THOMAS born Loudoun County, Virginia March 27, 1901, "Avoka" farm, Fauquier County, Virginia, February 10, 1989
Megan Reed THOMAS beloved daughter of Mary Margaret SWING and Clinton Reed THOMAS born Washington DC June 2, 1940, died San Luis, Obispo County, California July 16, 1977

Thorn Cemetery, Morrisville, Virginia
Located West Route 17 at first farm South Route 668 at end of private road to South West of house, boxwood bush in yard and field.

Thumb Run Baptist (Old School Baptist) Church Cemetery, between Orlean and Marshall, Virginia
Located at intersection of Routes 733 and 732. Cemetery is back of church enclosed by a fence and well kept. 6 rock markers and one unmarked. Resurveyed October 13, 1990.

Peyton Vowell Son of Z. V. & M. P. ROYSTON born October 20, 1910 Died September 3, 1911 *(stone not found 1990)*
Mildred M. Daughter of J. W. & M. E. ROYSTON Jan 14–Dec 25, 1901
Jos A. ROYSTON Jan 14, 1807 September 20, 1880
Harriet ROYSTON Sept 15, 1810 Aug 8, 1896

James K. O'BANNON May 12 or 13 1906 Son of Jos & M. L. O'BANNON

Willis PEARSON *(no dates)*
Pearley M. dau of A. A. & H. J. PEARSON July 3, 1877 Feb 1, 1887
Albert A. PEARSON May 15, 1850 January 11, 1921
PEARSON Morris A. Nov. 15, 1900–01; Baby Boy Nov. 14, 1904
Harriet R. PEARSON 1851–1937

Timbers - Millers, Belvoir, Virginia
Located on Route 709 behind small store near railroad crossing. According to Mollie Jackson, members of her mother's family are buried here, near old house site. Not surveyed - only rock markers.

Tomlin - Macrae Family Cemetery, "Old Tavern", Warrenton, Virginia
Located West Route 698 between Route 17 and Route 695 at top of mountain. High mortared stone wall about 200 feet from site of old house. 1 acre.

John Robert Wallace MacRAE July 19, 1827–April 1, 1887 one honest man very much given to hospitality His Wife Hannah BLANCHMORE TOMLIN Dec. 12, 1819–Dec. 1, 1894
Sarah Allen MacRAE Age 5 years
Ann Edwin MacRAE 1854–1873
Stephen TOMLIN who was born the 4th February 1781 and died on the 21st January 1850 erected by his daughter Sarah TOMLIN Wife of Stephen TOMLIN who died in the 73rd year on the 13th November 1849 erected by her daughter

Trinity, Catlett Cemetery, Catlett, Virginia
Located on the North side of Route 28 in Catlett. Resurveyed January 14, 1995.

NOLAND L. Ford August 25, 1917 May 17, 1978; Madge B. Nov. 15, 1913 August 25, 1980
Woodrow P. BOLIN "Woody" April 22, 1929 April 21, 1981
BOLIN George B. "Bate" Mar 16, 1913 Jan. 3, 1977; Irene C. April 6, 1905
SANFORD William E. May 26, 1921; Bessie B. Aug. 27, 1934 Mar. 24, 1987
Jerald Wm. GRANT April 4, 1942 January 12, 1977
S. E. DETTIN
Mother Lilla CRABTREE PENCE BOLEY Sept. 29, 1898 Dec. 24, 1986
Mary WAYNE BROWN August 17, 1953 November 5, 1976
Joshua R. AVENT 1979 *(fhm)*
German Harrison PENCE October 31, 1887 June 30, 1964
Roy Allen Son of Susan & Loyd BOWER March 9, 1960 September 20, 1964

RUFFNER Jesse P. September 16, 1918 November 25, 1965

Bernard B. FEWELL January 16, 1922 PFC US ARMY WORLD WAR II

Mother Allene N. HAMMILL January 16, 1908 July 12, 1985

Jane F. RUBAS September 22, 1927 January 1, 1987

Paul M. PHILLIPS, Jr. 1898– *(fhm)*

HEFLIN Ruben A. Nov. 8, 1896 Oct. 20, 1988; Evalene Aug. 30, 1914 Mar. 4, 1933

Virginia M. BINNIX August 12, 1918 March 1, 1979

John SATTERFIELD Aug. 6, 1939 Jan. 11, 1984

MARSH Paul R. Aug. 14, 1893 Jan. 9, 1973; Helen RILEY 1895 May 2, 1970

F.A.A.M. John OLIVER, Sr. February 12, 1912 May 31, 1975; O.E.S. *(order of Eastern Star)* Mary Anabel August 31, 1975

Gertrude E. WEEKS Feb. 16, 1915 Nov. 17, 1978

Roland D. WEEKS CPL US ARMY WORLD WAR II May 23, 1914 Sep. 28, 1975

Charles William WILDMAN June 26, 1944 April 23, 1979

Thomas A. WILDMAN May 6, 1915; Cymantha L. WILDMAN Dec. 4, 1911 July 20, 1988

J. Mark MILLER December 10, 1964 September 28, 1989 *(Masons)*

HOLMES M. Russell Aug. 19, 1914 Dec. 5, 1987; A. Frances Nov. 25, 1913

CORNETT Clyde J. October 26, 1906 March 6, 1983; Bertheda N. Nov. 10, 1910

DAY Roya June 5, 1908; Elizabeth W. Feb. 25, 1910 Jan. 14, 1976

Husband Cecil I. FEWELL June 19, 1924 April 12, 1981

Floyd Thomas BOYER WEST VIRGINIA PFC CO A L74 INF REGT WORLD WAR II Sept. 22, 1916 Aug. 2, 1971

EUSTACE Ceryl Price July 31, 1947 March 23, 1981

EUSTACE J. Wagner Jan. 10, 1902 June 17, 1985; Susanna M. Aug. 18, 1910 Dec. 12, 1986

Billy Reece TOWNSEND 1946–1985 *(fhm)*

CHARLES Ulysses G. June 24, 1941 June 28, 1979; Violet S. Feb. 17, 1942

(Butch) Lannie R. CHARLES Sept. 18, 1954 Mar. 13, 1989

Clifton M. HEFLIN Born and died Oct. 28, 1982

Frances ESCHERICH FRANK 1907–1989

STRAWSER Lowell S. April 20, 1918 December 29, 1978; Catherine M. June 1, 1920 November 29, 1989

JENKINS Charles L. April 17, 1896 October 12, 1967; Fleda I. September 10, 1896 May 22, 1980

Wilbur Earl FEWELL January 28, 1911 January 6, 1959

GLAETTLI Alioth R. Jan. 19, 1907 Dec. 14, 1974; Delia W. May 8, 1915

BERRYMAN Richard B. Apr. 18, 1898 Apr. 16, 1989; Grace D. Apr. 30, 1900 Sept. 4, 1988

Daisy Marie FEWELL June 30, 1885 Sept. 24, 1972

David E. FEWELL 1926–1988 *(fhm)*

BEAN (Bud) Bennett Jan. 18, 1896 July 18, 1985

Virgil M. BALDWIN Culpeper County March 24, 1923 July 28, 1969

COLVIN Rufus B. September 15, 1907 January 24, 1974; Constance W. January 17, 1914 December 19, 1963

Judy Ann WINES 1964–1964

Infant Baby WINES 1960–1960

Wanda A. WINES 1966–1966

EMBREY Eugene W. February 9, 1935 October 29, 1965; Virginia W. February 22, 1935

WHETZEL David A. June 12, 1893 February 2, 1963; Lottie C. September 4, 1889 July 9, 1969 Father Mother

Frances ENNIS KILBY May 24, 1915 Oct. 3, 1988 Grandma

Henry Rixey ENNIS April 1, 1911 July 29, 1971 Husband

Emily Grace Daughter of Stan and Faith RUMPH Born & Died July 20, 1978

George Edward NEYHOUS October 10, 1953 October 15, 1978

DUVALL Robert L. Jan. 31, 1934 June 20, 1980; Mabel

WINES Clarence B. November 14, 1903 Aug. 3, 1973; Eva BRAGG Apr. 6, 1911 Aug. 6, 1987

ALLEN Margie L. Feb. 5, 1934; Melvin L. Jun. 30, 1934 Oct. 6, 1987

RAMUY Donald Apr. 6, 1917 Jan. 10, 1981; Eva S. Aug. 1, 1921
FRYE William May 8, 1890 Feb. 23, 1978; Callie J. Feb. 4, 1894 Nov. 26, 1971
EDWARDS Cornelius B. Nov. 15, 1903 June 30, 1970; Theodora R. Oct. 15, 1911
WINES Horace E. Dec. 9, 1930; Annie A. Apr. 3, 1932 Dec. 21, 1984
John William FEWELL May 30, 1909 Nov. 23, 1974
Mary Lee FEWELL November 19, 1915 August 7, 1980
PARSONS Charles C. July 28, 1900 Feb. 15, 1970; Pearl V. Mar. 29, 1906 June 29, 1977
Eugene Warren EMBREY VIRGINIA SP 3 809 ENGR AVN BN Feb. 9, 1935 Oct. 29, 1965
M/Sgt Paul T. EMBREY 31 INFANTRY DIVISION Born October 21, 1924 MISSING IN ACTION KOREA
    November 28, 1950
EMBREY Warren W. October 20, 1894 May 9, 1971; Mable July 26, 1896 October 26, 1988
EMBREY James H. Jan. 29, 1917 Oct. 17, 1988; Della K. Aug. 8, 1924
GRIFFITH Donald C. August 8, 1916 March 1, 1963; Lucille E. October 6, 1916
Ernest E. TIPTON CPL US ARMY WORLD WAR II May 12, 1911 Sep. 2, 1975
Cary Stacy TIPTON May 28, 1962 September 2, 1965
TAPP Mollie D. August 7, 1901 December 7, 1976; C. Elmer July 29, 1906 January 31, 1961
BALILIE Lemuel Apr. 21, 1902 Oct. 19, 1976; Lula S. Jan. 17, 1906
SHERMAN James B. June 22, 1877 Mar. 10, 1959; Annie W., Feb. 22, 1887
MOSELEY Harrison R. Aug. 15, 1908; Gladys L. June 2, 1905
SMITH Robert H. Sept. 14, 1914 Feb. 12, 1983; Lucile LAWS Feb. 23, 1915
BOLEY William 1914–1978
BOLEY Edna 1908
BOLEY Eva 1881–1952
BOLEY William 1885–1951
ARMSTRONG Hughie W. Dec. 1, 1905; Alice M. Nov. 18, 1907 Apr. 6, 1989
LAWS Ira Eugene August 17, 1878 Feb. 14, 1943; Carrie May Sept. 12, 1881 Oct. 18, 1966
Emma A. LAWS Oct. 22, 1907 May 22, 1922
Baby MOSELEY
Avis I. SHERMAN January 9, 1923
Russell H. SHERMAN 1887–1962
MILLER Walter A. July 5, 1902 Sept. 21, 1977; Gladys G. Sept. 24, 1911 Jan. 17, 1983
CHARLES "Dad" William McKinley Oct. 27, 1896 Nov. 18, 1976 Married Sept. 18, 1920; Mom Frances Ann Mar.
    7, 1907 Oct. 6, 1985
Brenda Sue DOTSON Feb. 9, 1949 Feb. 13, 1972
Kerman Passie MULLINS PFC US ARMY WORLD WAR II 1926–1988
WOODWARD John M. Apr. 4, 1911; Mary B. Sept. 21, 1912 June 15, 1983
RIDGLEY Ira G. Aug. 10, 1907 June 17, 1989; Violet P. Aug. 8, 1908

Northwest Section
Leroy Edward LANE Aug. 9, 1956 Jan. 9, 1971
Walter A. ABEL Sept. 23, 1928 Dec. 31, 1975; Neta F. ABELL Jan. 27, 1939
SHIFLETT Stewart Wise April 12, 1915; Beulah BREEDEN July 24, 1912 May 16, 1969
John W. COLVIN June 21, 1875 January 16, 1966 Father
Jaclyn Rae SEIFERT Jan. 25, 1976 May 24, 1976
Daniel Lee CLARK Nov. 5, 1976 Sept. 11, 1976
R. R. STEELE Aug. 31, 1842 Apr. 3, 1919
W. H. STEELE 1837 Dec. 22, 1909
James Rodney ABEL Born Oct. 25, 1860 Died Jan. 9, 1917
HERNDON James D. August 4, 1916 January 26, 1966; Edna K. May 19, 1919
GRIFFITH William L. July 5, 1881 July 25, 1961; Pearl F. May 6, 1884 Sept. 10, 1920
Phillip E. GRIFFITH August 14, 1879 December 13, 1935
Jarrell W. RATLIFF 1958–1989 *(fhm)*

LOMAX Frances C. Feb. 16, 1922 July 19, 1968; Clyde, Jr. June 22, 1929 July 3, 1975

Julia MASSOLETTI Beloved Wife of Clyde LOMAX Born June 28, 1894 Died Jan. 30, 1923

Father Clyde LOMAX Born January 26, 1886 Died Aug. 7, 1957

Janie E. BURGESS Wife of Rev. O. F. BURGESS Sept. 1, 1855 Sept. 9, 1919

Oscar Franklin BURGESS Sept. 15, 1847 May 17, 1935

Norman W. BURGESS October 30, 1885 November 12, 1950

Margaret WILBUR BURGESS Dec. 18, 1854 Jan. 22, 1934 Wife of Rev. O. F. BURGESS

REDD Joseph S. 1859–1937

Sadie B. REDD February 6, 1884 July 5, 1957

REDD Linden July 29, 1915 Oct. 24, 1938

Stephen HARNSBERGER, M. D. 1852–1926

Katherine HOPKINS Wife of Stephen HARNSBERGER 1856–1918

William B. WEAVER Aug. 17, 1877 Sept. 30, 1954

Robert S. WEAVER April 1, 1908 Feb. 28, 1958

Dulcie C. SMITH September 30, 1859 June 23, 1942

Joseph David Son of Joseph and Harietta PETERS April 6, 1931 Sept. 16, 1933

Lille E. MASSOLETTI 1867–1958

Lewis E. MASSOLETTI 1857–1927

Lillie S. MASSOLETTI Jan. 30, 1902 Jan. 5, 1973

Lucy Margaret MASSOLETTI Mar. 16, 1910 Oct. 15, 1983

Luke H. REDD 1857–1937

FICKLEN Florence B. April 12, 1886 January 15, 1959; William A. July 18, 1882 December 15, 1954

TULLOSS Rixey F. Sept. 17, 1904; Ora L. Mar. 8, 1907 May 28, 1985

Blanche COWNE LAWS 1893–1989

Henry B. LAWS Nov. 28, 1892 May 1, 1929 Daddy

MERCER Charles Harvey Jan. 18, 1891 Oct. 16, 1950

CLARK Inez M. Jan. 20, 1920 Dec. 24, 1984

POWERS John Ballard March 3, 1863 Sept. 25, 1934; Eleanora RICHARDS Oct. 19, 1865 March 8, 1950

Elizabeth HARNSBERGER Wife of W. B. WEAVER 1879–1918 *(beside him)*

Newton R. Husband of Delphia S. LAWS Sept. 15, 1874 Apr. 23, 1918

Delphia S. Wife of Newton R. LAWS Apr. 9, 1889 Dec. 2, 1970

SMITH Raymond July 21, 1901 Oct. 28, 1917

SMITH Victor Dec. 5, 1904 Dec. 3, 1930

Cecil S. SMITH Jan. 25, 1866 April 13, 1941; Mina F. SMITH June 3, 1872 June 12, 1958

SMITH Harry C. Oct. 22, 1923 Oct. 11, 1984; Dorothy M. Apr. 4, 1924

SMITH Harold R. June 20, 1896 April 16, 1980; Lucy A. Jan. 22, 1900

Lenie M. BEANE April 17, 1890 December 14, 1936

Cecil B. BEANE April 8, 1895 April 9, 1955

BEANE Samuel W. Born Jan. 31, 1857 Died Mar. 1, 1913; Mattie Jane Born Sept. 11, 1867 Died Nov. 26, 1945
   Father Mother *(footstone)*

Grace BEANE MINNIECE Died July 8, 1944 Abingdon, England

Amy M. BEANE June 9, 1885 Nov. 15, 1941

Mary E. CROSIER April 1835 March 1925

Archibald DENNISON Husband of Ethel IVEY DENNISON September 12, 1884 November 26, 1963 Father

Ethel IVEY DENNISON Wife of Archibald DENNISON June 5, 1890 April 11, 1960 Mother

Richard Corin IVEY Feb. 18, 1859 Dec. 5, 1912; His Wife Elizabeth A. ARTHUR Dec. 16, 1869 Nov. 6, 1929

Charles STOVER McLAUREN Sept. 8, 1866 May 22, 1917

Horace N. McLEAREN Son of Horace McLAUREN and Cynthia Maria Sept. 17, 1881 Oct. 2, 1971

Grace E. McLEAREN Wife of Hampton McINTEER Sept. 3, 1881 July 31, 1970

Dora LAWS McLAUREN Sept. 14, 1868 Feb. 24, 1937

LAWRENCE Bessie McLAUREN August 26, 1884 March 24, 1962; George May 24, 1886 May 30, 1962 Mother
   Father

HOWELL Lloyd J. July 8, 1924 May 20, 1979; Mary F. March 23, 1923
James P. ALLEN Sept. 7, 1903 Nov. 14, 1969
Mother Emma F. ALLEN August 6, 1874 March 20, 1948
Father Luther E. ALLEN February 7, 1869 November 14, 1945
Ruby Isabelle ALLEN Aug. 31, 1912 Oct. 24, 1912
Edward Rankin ALLEN, Jr. July 18, 1931 July 19, 1931
Mary Elizabeth ALLEN born & died Feb. 18, 1935
WILSON Herbert A. Nov. 3, 1880 Jan. 23, 1966; Eva ELTON Nov. 12, 1882 May 14, 1965
Infant Son of Herbert A. & Eva E. WILSON Dec. 26, 1917
Leidy L. WILSON December 9, 1890 September 26, 1965
Robert J. WILSON Aug. 13, 1854 Sept. 27, 1930; Rosa B. His Wife May 1, 1858 Jan. 2, 1940 Father Mother
Naomi M. WILSON Jan. 7, 1896 August 22, 1987
Douglas Lee GRAY April 14, 1926 May 19, 1988
Evelyn Marie WILSON Oct. 21, 1915 July 30, 1917
Lucile W. GRAY May 9, 1894 Aug. 27, 1968
Charles Bell GRAY April 7, 1886 Jan. 18, 1977
WILSON Harry J. Oct. 25, 1909; Elizabeth A. Apr. 8, 1910 July 9, 1989
John Eggleston Son of Lucile & Chas. B. GRAY Sept. 10, 1923 Nov. 7, 1923
Franklin S. ENSOR June 16, 1857 Nov. 15, 1933; Susan Wife of F. S. ENSOR Sept. 9, 1853 Apr. 17, 1933
RUSSELL William M. May 26, 1930 December 5, 1968 Daddy
TRENIS Lemuel W. February 1, 1877 January 24, 1966; Hattie M. May 6, 1880 November 8, 1965 Dad Mother
TRENIS Edwin M. May 27, 1907; Mary C. August 31, 1910 December 8, 1984
Hoyt M. ORNDOFF May 26, 1893 Jan. 16, 1950
Minnie M. ORNDOFF May 24, 1879 Jan. 16, 1964

TRENIS Plot:
Paul LEFAINT TRENIS August 10, 1885 December 11, 1962
Evelyn LaPOINT July 19, 1918 Aug. 30, 1934
GUY Ella C. Feb. 5, 1882 Nov. 7, 1912; Lewis R. Aug. 24, 1878 Mar. 28, 1952
Bessie M. GUY May 12, 1898 January 9, 1983
Elbert L. GUY June 9, 1915 February 2, 1973
HERRELL Richard H. Feb. 25, 1910 Jul. 8, 1987; Loyce G. May 31, 1905 Feb. 5, 1990
SMITH Ralph E. Apr. 14, 1926 Sept. 25, 1985; Sybil D. Apr. 6, 1929
Mildred M. GUY Died May 26, 1910 aged 53 yrs.
Edward ALLEN (Bud) July 5, 1907 April 19, 1979
Thomas Edward ALLEN 1922–1985
Jesse E. ALLEN PVT US ARMY WORLD WAR II June 19, 1922 Aug. 17, 1989
Mary Evelyn Wife of Edward A. ALLEN 1912–1949 Mother
Thomas E. ALLEN, Sr. 1897–1965
Mary Jane DOWELL TRENIS Oct. 1, 1891 July 4, 1988
Rueben E. ALLEN Mar. 11, 1847 Mar. 28, 1929
Emma E. Wife of Rueben E. ALLEN Aug. 22, 1861 Nov. 4, 1939
Twins Emma C. ALLEN June 12, 1913 May 2, 1929; Myra M. ALLEN June 12, 1913 May 2, 1929
Gladys ALLEN Born & Died Mar. 4, 1907
Myra M. and Emma C. ALLEN Born June 12, 1912 Died May 2, 1929
Charles ALLEN Born Dec. 12, 1877 Died in the cyclone May 2, 1929
Dessie May ALLEN March 12, 1878 October 7, 1961 Mother
Rev. Geo. W. CRABTREE 1873–1940
George J. Son of Samuel & Mary HOLLADAY Husband of Sallie HOLLADAY 1868–1902
Sallie HOLLADAY IVEY Mar. 16, 1878 Aug. 7, 1931
John Son of John & Elizabeth IVEY Husband of Sallie HOLLADAY May 4, 1917
Ruby Bernice BURKE May 5, 1895 December 19, 1940

William T. Husband of Ruby H. BURKE Aug. 1, 1893 Jan. 15, 1919

Ralph Harvey BURKE 1924–1989

Gilbert S. ENNIS PVT US ARMY Apr. 13, 1897 Sept. 29, 1974

Joseph S. ENNIS 1855–1919; Mary F. His Wife 1857– 1937

ENNIS Eva HEFLIN March 4, 1882 February 6, 1963; Luther Robert April 26, 1884 October 28, 1926 Father Mother

Robert ENNIS Feb. 8, 1910 Oct. 28, 1910; Howard Corbin May 2, 1929 Jan. 21, 1933

ENNIS Martha E. April 1, 1901 June 3, 1973; William C. August 17, 1905

Mother Fannie E. ISENBERG Nov. 22, 1892 Feb. 10, 1947

Gladys C. ISENBERG July 27, 1924 May 14, 1944

Howard W. ISENBERG September 17, 1916 September 6, 1925

Father Joseph M. ISENBERG Feb. 20, 1869 Apr. 5, 1950

Mother Sallie FOUT Wife of Joseph ISENBERG Feb. 18, 1868 Dec. 19, 1912

Alfred H. WEAVER Died Feb. 16, 1913

Amanda C. Wife of John L. CARRICO Apr. 22, 1850 Oct. 8, 1943

John CARRICO 1856–1934

John Oliver Son of John L. & Margaret CARRICO Jan. 20, 1897 Dec. 23, 1911

Charles Wesley CARRICO September 17, 1883 February 12, 1962 Father

Mamie GUY CARRICO April 30, 1886 December 7, 1961 Mother

WORKMAN Vivian L. Jul. 8, 1908 Jan. 9, 1983; Emory D. Dec. 12, 1902 Jan. 10, 1983

LAWS Virginia Louise July 29, 1917 Jan. 10, 1990; Joseph Arthur May 4, 1913

LAWS Kenneth C. Apr. 18, 1909; Ida J. Oct. 8, 1909

LAWS Vernon E. Sept. 1, 1902; Zola C. Sept. 23, 1905

PACE William T. Mar. 7, 1914 Aug. 1, 1988; Marie K. Mar. 14, 1917

Joseph A. LAWS Oct. 16, 1846 July 21, 1910; India C. LAWS Apr. 23, 1844 Feb. 3, 1908

Emma L. COLVIN May 30, 1895 Feb. 15, 1966

Hoyt ORNDOFF, Jr. 1921–1990 *(fhm)*

Joseph A. Husband of Mabel C. LAWS Mar. 21, 1884 Jan. 14, 1932

Mabel Cora Wife of Joseph A. LAWS Feb. 12, 1882 Mar. 2, 1952

Ebin Taylor LAWS May 17, 1838 Aug. 7, 1921

Emma D. Wife of E. T. LAWS Dec. 7, 1845 Apr. 27, 1922

Ella E. MARK Nov. 22, 1850 Mar. 29. 1916

Alice LAWS Wife of Lewis W. BOODY Oct. 18, 1876 Aug. 6, 1921

Laura Virginia Wife of A. J. CHESNUT Apr. 13, 1855 Dec. 15, 1911

Southwest Section

Chester CORBIN 1909–1980 *(fhm)*

ALLEN Harry D. Nov. 10, 1913 Apr. 2, 1974

Mother Mary R. ENNIS Oct. 6, 1897 Sept. 18, 1969

Father Archie J. ENNIS Oct. 18, 1895 Mar. 30, 1905

Zelma Henrie DANIEL June 16, 1915 Oct. 16, 1915

Ephram G. DANIEL February 23, 1868 September 18, 1954 May 30, 1949

Lula FOSTER DANIEL August 30, 1877 May 30, 1959

Jesse A. J. RUFFNER Jan. 13, 1846 Jan. 23, 1916; His Wife Emma D. BALL July 14, 1854 Sept 14, 1926

RUFFNER Joshua C. Oct. 16, 1884 Sept. 13, 1940; Sallie B. April 3, 1891 Jan. 28, 1963 Mother Father *(footstones)*

Alvin Laws RUFFNER 1915–1990

George McCoy COLVIN November 15, 1877 December 12, 1955

Dora RUFFNER COLVIN February 21, 1877 July 27, 1967

Naomi COLVIN Nov. 12, 1915 Aug. 18, 1916

Roland Knight COLVIN Nov. 23, 1917 Sept. 28, 1918

Emma McCoy COLVIN July 24, 1904

Baby Frances Aileen Dau. of Wallace & Lottie ENNIS Feb. 26, 1916 June 26, 1918

Mary Lottie Nee MACY Wife of Wallace ENNIS Apr. 20, 1891 Feb. 7, 1919
James Wallace ENNIS Oct. 28, 1882 June 8, 1948
Mother Mary Jane ENNIS July 15, 1891 April 20, 1961
CORBIN Rexford L. January 16, 1891 March 14, 1967; Katie C. March 11, 1888 November 26, 1968
CORBIN George Wm. Mar. 1, 1857 Mar. 22, 1933; Ida MAYHUGH Jan. 11, 1866 August 18, 1969
Floyd J. CORBIN Born Feb. 22, 1914 Died Feb. 2, 1919
Gladys E. NEITZEW Jan. 13, 1914 Sept. 20, 1978 She was the summer of our home
ALLEN Harry D. Nov. 10, 1913 Apr. 2, 1974
Mother Mary R. ENNIS Oct. 6 1897 Sept. 18, 19169
Father Archie J. ENNIS Oct. 18, 1895 May 30, 1905
WADE Laura M. April 28, 1894; Fred Dec. 7, 1884 Jan. 7, 1952
Stephen F. WADE VIRGINIA TEC 5 411 INF 103 INF DIV WORLD WAR II Aug 22 1923 Nov 16 1944
Olive H. DABNEY Sept. 3, 1911 Oct. 29, 1978
Ola V. WHITMER April 11, 1918 May 17 1983 .
Jean C. ACHESON 1883–1967
Annie Lorrain CORBIN "Miss Nan" Oct. 9, 1879 Jan. 24, 1970
W. H. TAYLOR 1875–1938

WILLIAMS Plot:
Poca ENNIS 1897 1919
WILLIAMS Elizabeth Aug. 27, 1925 Feb. 17, 1926
Infant 1919
Mother Mary Elizabeth WILLIAMS Dec. 19, 1866 Sept. 27, 1943
Father Robert Lee WILLIAMS Mar 23, 1865 Aug. 14, 1922
Baby Junior D. FOSTER Mar. 14, 1913 May 1, 1913
W. L. CORRELL Apr. 1842 June 10, 1929
CORRELL Emma HALL Died Feb. 9, 1909 Aged 49 yrs.
CORRELL Mary F. Died Feb. 9, 1905 Aged 71 years
John S. BENNETT August 29, 1857 March 26, 1933
Josie R. BENNETT May 3, 1860 Feb. 23, 1935
Dorothy EDMONDS Wife of Burwell BENNETT Dec. 19, 1902 May 1974
Nary C. BENNETT May 27, 1887 June 19, 1922
David John BENNETT Sept. 7, 1898 Oct. 28, 1931
Lena Lee BENNETT Ap[ril 10, 1892 August 7, 1908
Trigg B. BENNETT March 12, 1900 July 29, 1949
Mary Elizabeth Dau. of John & Ethel W. KING Aug. 29., 1914 Mar. 15, 12923
Dorothy Lee Daughter of John & Ethel W. KING Apr. 7, 1922 Dec. 1, 1923
Edward STEELE born June 20, 1876 Died Aug. 5, 1924
WILLIAMS Forrest Glenn August 24, 1904 December10, 1975; Julia TRENIS March 11, 1886 August 3, 1965
Thos. H. R. FOUKE Born Mar. 15, 1797 Died Mar. 17, 1871
Frederick W. FOWKE born Sept. 18, 1848 Died Sept. 17, 1921
Martha O. LUCKETT Died Dec. 19, 1914
CRITTENDEN Fisher Henry, Sr. 1879–1953; Annie J. 1875–1942

Samuel T. KEYS 1817–1920; Virginia A. KEYS 1857–1926
VOGT James W. Jan. 12, 1882 Feb. 21, 1959; Mildred M. June 9, 1887 Apr. 29, 1956
ALMOND Lizzie C. 1902–1952; Wallace W. 1901–1987 "The Lord is my Shepherd I shall not want"
Russell ALMOND July 7, 1927 Sept. 1, 1927
Mary Jane ALMOND Infant Daughter of Wallace W. & Lizzie C. ALMOND
Opal Alberta ALMOND daughter of Wallace W. & Lizzie C. ALMOND 1933–1938
Junior A. ALMOND Infant son of Wallace W. & Lizzie C. ALMOND
Benjamin F. COLVIN 1852–1931; Alice M. COLVIN 1862–1943

F. Leslie COLVIN November 13, 1889 September 30, 1955
Harold Bruce COLVIN May 29, 1898 August 1, 1963
Mary WEAVER COLVIN September 25, 1917 December 29, 1991
Mother Cynthia R. RABER June 14, 1882 February 17, 1959
CORBIN Clementine B. Aug. 12, 1897 Jan. 5, 1962; Eppie P. Sept. 18, 1888 Sept. 16, 1968
Juanita R. GRAY January 19, 1924 September 8, 1992
JEFFERIES Frank L Nov. 3, 1889 Feb. 3, 1973; Susie G. Jan. 30, 1900
Shirley B. JEFFERIES 1915–1994
George R. NESSELRODT 1874–19 ; Cordelia J. His Wife 1879–1932 (C.J.N.)

ARMSTRONG Plot:
Irving R. ARMSTRONG Virginia PVT TRP G 1 Cavalry World War 1 June 28, 1897 Jan. 7, 1970
Charles N. 1853–1904
Josephine S. ARMSTRONG 1853–1943
Gertrude DAY ARMSTRONG 1862–1939
J. Bert ARMSTRONG 1883–1941

NESSELRODT Dorothy FRAZIER Dec. 24, 1932 Nov. 16, 1958
Eleanor NEWMAN DOUGLAS July 16, 1894 October 2, 1984
James Keith DOUGLAS March 11, 1899 August 8, 1954
Ritchier GASKINS Oct. 12, 1857 April 20, 1939
Golder B. HEFLIN 1884–1937
Leola HEFLIN 1889–1965
Virginia DOUGLAS BULKELEY May 12, 1901 August 4, 1979
James S. DOUGLAS June 25, 1836 Feb. 5, 1923
Susan V. DOUGLAS April 3, 1959 May 13, 1912
James Hancock GASKINS 1825–1876; His Wife Fannie KEITH GASKINS 1825–1898
NESSELRODT Branson H. Nov. 10, 1902 Feb. 2, 1976; Nettie M. Sept. 13, 1910 Aug. 18, 1976
Hugh C. SHERMAN 1849–1906
Hannah F. SHERMAN 1854–1931
Belinda LINTHICUM 1820–1904

MARSH Plot:
Rev. William Henry November 1, 1862 October 16, 1958
Mary Ruby MARSH February 10, 1884 March 24, 1970
Majorie MARSH COOPER April 10, 1902 August 26, 1989
HEFLIN Cal T. October 11, 1888 June 13, 1957 (Daddy); Fannie C. April 14, 1892 June 12, 1955 (Mother)
Lucille COLVIN SIMMONS June 20, 1884 December 17, 1961
Leah COLVIN BURNAP December 6, 1888 May 24, 1976
Lois B. ALDERTON Feb. 21, 1912 Sept. 3, 1987 "Our Beloved Aunt"
Paul Wayne PADGETT 1963–1992 *(fhm)*
Matthew Brian SMITH "Matt" Loved 19 February 1967 28 September 1989 "Ever Ready, Ever Willing"
"Dee Dee" Deidre Christine SMITH-STEPHENS October 11, 1961 December 28, 1991
HEFLIN James T. May 16, 1853 July 4, 1919 Father; Lillie B. May 29, 1866 April 15, 1933 Mother
Layton Golden RUFFNER June 16, 1910 June 17, 1937
Wilton S. RUMPH December 1, 1908 May 31, 1970 Daddy
Cassius H. HEFLIN March 16, 1878 June 1, 1955
Carroll Benton HEFLIN July 3, 1891 Sept. 6, 1952
Nellie Estelle HEFLIN Mar. 6, 1894 May 31, 1975 Grandmother
William Thomas GASKINS 1862–1923; His Wife Corinne NEWMAN GASKINS 1857–1955

SHERMAN Plot:

Ethel B. 1916–1924
Susie J. 1894–1946
Donald H. 1893–1942

DAY Chauncey F. Ja. 24, 1886 Dec. 31, 1926; Bessie T. Dec. 20, 1887 Sept. 15, 1969
James W. WOODWARD, Jr. Born May 1, 1885 Died Nov. 3, 1928 "Keep him Jesus in Thy keeping until I reach the
    Heavenly shore, then oh Master let me see him love and hold him as before"
Pauline IVEY WOODWARD Feb. 28, 1898 Sep. 28, 1983
Wife of James W. WOODWARD, Jr. Never met a stanger (J.W.M.)
WOODWARD Nannie M His Wife 1860 1924 Mother; James W. 1860–1934 Father
KEYES John Walter Feb. 1, 1869 Sept. 30, 1936; Mary Virginia Dec. 20, 1882 June 27, 1965
Ray Stephen KEYES July 23, 1908 March 2, 1960
RILEY Plot:
George H. 1878–1952
Grace A. 1887–1965

FREEMAN Plot:
Frank Irvin FREEMAN July 14, 1906 Oct. 4, 1974
Ella RILEY FREEMAN Jan. 2, 1916 Oct. 1989 "Mother nothing is treasured more than love, and no mother is loved
    more than you. Love Always"
Eugene DAVIS ALLEN 1940–1991 (FHM)

DAY Plot:
Beulah A. June 14, 1889 Oct. 25, 1976; William H. Aug. 2, 1872 Mar. 20, 1964; William W. Oct. 14, 1913 Nov. 16,
    1939; Annie O. May 28, 1917 Feb. 16, 1941
Mother Annis O. ORICK May 28, 1917 February 16, 1941
Henry Lewis DAY US Army World War II Dec. 17, 1919 Aug. 17, 1991
Robert L. DAY SGT US Army Korea Jun 1, 1925 Feb. 25, 1994

HUFFMAN Plot:
Clay J. HUFFMAN 1905–1933
Birtie T, HUFFMAN Jan. 31, 1877 Jan. 30, 1951
Frank H. HUFFMAN Sept 17, 1877 Sept. 26, 1961

SMITH Son Robert Jr. Jan. 15, 1960 Dec. 6, 1976; Son Lonnie D. Jan. 17, 1961 Dec. 6, 1976
Flora H. COPPAGE July 16, 1901 April 25, 1980
Joseph Richard COPPAGE November 3, 1896 May 11, 1955 "BUCK"
COPPAGE Hazel Lee Daughter of J. R. & Flora March 12, 1925 March 27, 1926 Asleep in Jesus
McLEAREN Plot:
Alfred Owen McLEAREN October 16, 1889 January 3, 1956
Owen Elliott McLEAREN December 11, 1923 December 11, 1923
George Ray McLEAREN June 17, 1860 October 16, 1929
William Ray McLEAREN June 14, 1911 February 18, 1987
Lorena V. McLEAREN December 13, 1918 January 3, 1990

James W. HEFLIN Born June 11, 1854 Died Dec. 19, 1924
Angeline KANE HEFLIN August 15, 1857 March 20, 1936
HEFLIN Guy G. June 23, 1889 July 22, 1972; Rosa S. Sept. 29, 1895 June 14, 1960
Lewis M. HEFLIN Nov. 9, 1891 June 11, 1981 Age 40 Years
RYAN Lena H. Dec. 22, 1903 Aug. 2, 1984; James M. Dec. 28, 1904 Oct. 3, 1982
Infant son of James & Lena RYAN Nov. 6, 1937 Nov. 6, 1937 (Inf)
Richard M. HAYES, jr. US Navy World War II Oct. 10, 1917 Sept. 27, 1977

James E. SPENCER Aug. 27, 1902; Mary A. SPENCER Sept. 3, 1906 Oct. 20, 1985
Mother Emma DILSAVER Jan. 1, 1910 June 3, 1981
Brother Roy E. VOGT Aug. 8, 1931 Oct. 4, 1979
Mother Dorothy V. MARSHALL Feb. 25, 1919 Feb. 4, 1977
Turner Lee MARSHALL PFC US Army World War II Decv. 2, 1919 Apr. 17, 1979
Basil J. THOMPSON US Army World War II Nov. 27, 1909 Apr. 29, 1978
Anne C. BYRD October 11, 1915 September 4, 1974 (AGB)
Ralston FOSTER August 18, 1901; April 4, 1956; Frances FOSTER THOMPSON April 11, 1912 December 18, 1976
    (R.F. F.F.T)
Mother Helen REEVES KING may 2, 1913 August 4, 1955 "Dukie"
SHIPE Ira G. June 12, 1885 September 16, 1955 Father; Ida E. October 24, 1890 December 31, 1966 Mother
CAMERON James E. March 6, 1906 April 1, 1981; Laura E. Jan 22, 1910
Oca E. HEFLIN 1910–1994
Thurston D. HEFLIN May 12, 1904 July 11, 1953 son

Triplett, near Middleburg, Virginia
Located South Route 50 West Route 709 about 1 mile in garden by long white house, fieldstone markers.

Trough Hill Baptist Church Cemetery, Crest Hill, Virginia
Located on Route 647 just West Route 645. Many fieldstone markers. Well kept. Resurveyed 1990.

William Hugh GREEN 1895–1954
Joseph H. LANE 1890–1950
Minnie Wife of William T. PAYTON Aug. 22, 1889 Dec. 16, 1918
Gordon
William Hugh NELSON VIRGINIA 422 RESER LABOR BN QMC WORLD WAR I July 14, 1896 June 17, 1965
William E. Son of Alexander & Dolley A. RUSSELL Aug. 6, 1886 March 6, 1922
RUSSELL Dolley A. 1869–1938; Alexander 1856–1941

James Henry FRANKLIN 1857–1951
Sarah Roberta FRANKLIN 1870–1939
H. FRANKLIN

Mrs. Mary M. ANDERSON 1895–1962
Charles ANDERSON VIRGINIA PFC 341 QM LAUNDRY DETACHMENT WORLD WAR II Jan 9 1928 Jan 31
    1957
James Franklin ANDERSON Died July 8, 1940 Aged 52 Years
James H. ANDERSON AFC US ARMY WORLD WAR II 1921–1975
Sarah E. ANDERSON 1919–1975
ANDERSON Charles H.; Charlotte widow; James; Alberta; Sarah; C. H., Jr.

Albert B. CAMPBELL Sept. 10, 1917 Dec. 26, 1981
WILLIAMS Mamie Jane GREEN Jan. 15, 1924
GREEN George Isaac Feb. 13, 1929 March 13, 1929
Horton BROOKS PVT US ARMY WW I Jan. 15, 1898 Nov. 7, 1978
2 rock markers

NELSON Lulu L. Nov. 4, 1887 Mar. 30, 1972; William Hugh June 16, 1870 June 13, 1951
Easter NELSON 1825–1928 *(l03 yrs)* Erected Aug. 17, 1985 Mother
    Note: *Easter Nelson's remains are actually located in front yard of adjacent houseCcurrent owner obliterated
    burial plot. Tombstone erected in church cemetery.*
Goldia L. NELSON Aug. 12, 1906 Feb. 22, 1980

fieldstone markers
Douglas NELSON PVT VIRGINIA ART KOREA *(dates in ground)*
Shirley Stewart NELSON VIRGINIA PVC 25 CML DECON Co May 10, 1924 Sept. 6, 1970

RECTOR Mary 1894–1974; Edward 1890–1933
RECTOR Randolph 1918–1942
Carenton E. RECTOR 1915–1989
Lewis A. RECTOR 1922–1974

12 rock markers by Hall grave
Gertrude D. FRANKLIN 1902–1961
Edmonia ADAMS May 8, 1893 Nov. 9, 1937
Mother Lena Virginia BLACK 1891–1960
TYNES
Walter PRICE Died July 16, 1966 Aged 56 years
Audrcy DAVENPORT April 19, 1964 Aged 23 years
Ernest Thomas BALL Died Sept. 20, 194-
    li-n FRANKLIN
Edmond BERRY Born Oct. 1, 1835 Died *(rest in ground)*
Mary Susan WASHINGTON Born Nov. 1852 Died Mar. 12, 1901
Ann Elizabeth RECTOR Born in 1834 Died Oct. 20, 1902
Rex Anner FRANKLIN Born Feb. 15, 1851 Died Oct. 27, 1897
Sarah Daughter of Jake & Mary FRANKLIN Born July 10, 1899 Died Oct. 23, 1918
10 fieldstone markers
George L. WILLIAMS 190_–197_
Barbara ANDERSON December 1, 1949 June 29, 1973
Nettie WILLIAMS April 16, 1900 June 5, 1969; Wistor WILLIAMS April 2, 1889 Feb. 1, 1977
Robert H. LACEY 1843–1960 *(fhm)*
Tina D. RODRIGUEZ Jan. 19, 1948 Jan 23, 1983
Arthur M. CARTER 1912–1982
CORBIN Maggie C. ROBINSON 1894–1961; Mary E. CORBIN 1918
TYNES J. Sylvester 1906–1981; Pauline A. 1918
Robert N. ANDERSON 1907–1972

Father Nathaniel H. BLACK 1891–1969
Mother Lena Virginia BLACK 1891–1960
Evelyn Nathaniel BLACK PFC US ARMY WORLD WAR II 1919–1976

Robert G. Son of Robert C. & Susie HALL Born March 25, 1909 Died Mar. 15, 1925
Bushrod RECTOR Jan. 28, 1876 Sept. 30, 1958

J. R. CORBIN, Jr.
John Clifton CORBIN April 14, 1914 Sept. 2, 1982
Alfred Eric CORBIN TECH 4 US ARMY WORLD WAR II Feb. 2, 1920 Sept. 5, 1979
Father Henry T. CORBIN Aug. 21, 1907 Feb. 25, 1972
Debra E. CORBIN Aug. 30, 1912 Aug. 4, 1975
Henry Ernest CORBIN April 15, 1878 Oct. 25, 1962
Mary Jonsie CORBIN Born May 24, 1886 Died Nov. 2, 1959 Wife of Henry F. CORBIN
CORBIN Henry F. Born April 16, 1878 Died Oct. 25, 1962

ANDERSON Charles L. 1880–1946; Carol E. 1884–1950
Bettie NEWMAN Died Nov. 30, 1916 Aged 65 years

Jerry NEWMAN Born Aug. 1838 Died Feb. 27, 1891 Aged 57 years
John WILLIAMS Son of Nuttie WILLIAMS Born Oct. 21, 1846 Died Jan. 24, 1897
Nuttie WILLIAMS Born Sept. 20, 1817 Died Oct. 18, 1888
Mrs. Alice BALL 1882–1961
Moses LANE Sept. 18, 1864 Oct. 2, 1919
Cara Lee LANE May 21, 1883 Apr. 14, 1941

Contents of Russell Cemetery in near-by yard
George GREEN, Sr. 1929–1987 *(fhm)*
Martha GREEN 1828–1985
William E. Son of Alexander and Dolley RUSSELL Aug. 6, 1886 March 6, 1922

Tulloss Cemetery, "White Ridge", Somerville, Virginia
Located 50 yards West intersection of Routes 610 & 616 in field, fenced. Resurveyed by L. Arthur Grove February 1994.

Effie DUNINGTON TULLOSS Mar. 26, 1868 July 20, 1907 William David TULLOSS Mar. 15, 1852 Jan. 28, 1921
Ida Thelma TULLOSS Sept. 24, 1900 Apr. 25, 1901
Hannah Catherine TULLOSS Aug. 24, 1886 Dec. 9, 1886
Emma Hunton TULLOSS Sept. 21, 1881 June 13, 1882
Hannah Catherine TULLOSS Aug. 17, 1850 Jan. 13, 1922
William H. TULLOSS Son of Rodham & Elizabeth TULLOSS who was born August the 4th 1826 and died Octr. the 2d 1855
Janetta E. TULLOSS Daughter of Richard D. and Emma G. TULLOSS who departed this life March 19th 1858 aged 8 years 8 months & 17 days
Rodham TULLOSS who was born May the 10th 1780 and died May the 15th 1842
Elizabeth TULLOSS who was born July the 8th 1790 and died April the 5th 1885
William David TULLOSS Mar. 15, 1852 Jan. 28, 1821

Tulloss, Somerville, Virginia
Located West Route 610 0.75 mile South Route 616 on private road South West of proposed house in woods. Few fieldstone markers only. Surveyed by L. Arthur Grove February 1994.

Turner Cemetery, Delaplane, Virginia
Located West of Route 724 0.25 mile North of Route 732 South East of old stone and clapboard house. Cemetery area fenced, but stones outside wall.

Agnes TURNER Born November 23, 1819 Died June 23, 1885
James T. TURNER Born February 6, 1819 Died May 25, 1882

Turner Cemetery, "Kinloch", The Plains, Virginia
Located East of The Plains Route 601. Cemetery below house, stone wall, excellent condition. Ivy covered. On the gate "Turner of Kinloch." Resurveyed October 18, 1993.

Major Thomas TURNER who departed this life on the 3rd of Jany 1839 In the 67th year of his age
Our beloved Mother Mrs. Eliza C. TURNER Wife of Maj. Thomas TURNER of Kinloch departed this life July 3d 1866 in the 84th year of her age
Eliza Carter RANDOLPH Wife of Nathaniel LOUGHBOROUGH, Jr. and Daughter of Major Thomas TURNER of Kinloch who departed this life February the 26th 1844 In the 24th year of her age
Bradshaw Son of Robert and Jane E. BEVERLEY who departed this life Dec. 31st 1847 Aged 2 years
Roberta Daughter of Robert & Jane E. BEVERLEY who departed this life 1853 *(tree grown over rest)*

God is Love April 29, 1888 (*on a tombstone*)
Caroline Virginia Daughter of the late Major Thomas TURNER of Kinloch who departed this life the 22nd of October 1850 in the 32nd year of her age
Lucie GREEN Wife of N. [Nathan] Loughborough TURNER Nov. 17, 1860 Died Sept. 28, 1930
Nathan Loughborough TURNER Son of Edward CARTER & Sarah BEVERLEY TURNER Oct. 2, 1920 aged 61 years
[*No name*] April 29, 1838
Wilhelmina EDMONDS colored a faithful servant and devoted friend of the Kinloch family died in 1889 In the 69th year of her age
Charles RANDOLPH a soldier of the War of 1812 He died at Kinloch December 20, 1863 In the 74th year of his age
Charles C. TURNER Son of Edward C. and Sarah J. TURNER who departed this life September 26th 1869 In the 22nd year of his age
Robert Fauntleroy TURNER Son of Edward C. TURNER of Kinloch and Sarah Jane BEVERLEY His WifeDied June 9, 1889 In the 39th year of his age
Pocahontas Wife of Robert T. TURNER Born September 12, 1854 Died June 7, 1896
Elizabeth COCKE who died the 13th of Decr. 1829 In the 60th year of her age
Robert Fauntleroy Son of Edward C. Jr. and Nannie H. TURNER Born May 8, 1890 Died October 16, 1890
Nannie HAMILTON TURNER Wife of Edward Carter TURNER youngest Daughter of Richard Henry CARTER of Glen Welby Aug. 2, 1859 June 3, 1936
Edward C. TURNER Son of Edward C. TURNER of Kinloch & Sarah J. BEVERLEY Died April 23, 1896 in his 42nd year
Mary McGILL RANDOLPH Beloved Wife of Edward C. TURNER Born at Eastern View November 12, 1833 Died at Montrose November 12, 1910
Edward C. TURNER In the 75th year of his age died Mar. 3, 1891
Mrs. Sarah Jane TURNER who died at Kinloch February 20, 1865 In the 45th year of her age
Thomas B. TURNER Died at Kinloch April 29, 1863 In the 20th year of his age

Turner Cemetery, The Plains, Virginia
Located directly back of Montrose on mountain at end of private road South Route 703 North Route 601. Fieldstone markers only, excellent stone wall, well kept.

Upperville Baptist Church Cemetery, Upperville, Virginia
Located on Route 50 in back of church. Tombstones have been beautifully placed flat in ground, so that they are easily readable. Resurveyed August 13, 1990.

Luella Daughter of Rev. Geo. W. and Anna M. HARRIS was born Oct. 21st, 1856 died Aug. 9th 1858
Samuel STEWART Died Aug. 30, 1863 Aged 50 yrs. 2 mos. & 20 Ds.
Eliza STEWART Died Feb. 16, 1876 Aged 67 years 9 mos. & 12 Ds
J. Gales SETTLE Born June 10th 1856 Died Feb. 3rd 1867
Mary A. SETTLE Born May 27th 1817 Died Dec. 13th 1867
Dr. Zachariah J. CHUNN Died Aug. 30th 1849 aged 29 years & 10 months
Mary S. CHUNN Born Feb. 17th 1822 Died Sept. 14th 1858
Our Daughter Jane Strother SINGLETON Born June 22d 1816 Died May 18th 1853
Mollie S. Wife of W. T. WHITTINGTON Died February 16, 1887 Aged 20 years 6 mos. & 3 days
Charles H. SWANN Died Oct. 22, 1872 aged 33 yrs. 1 mo. & 12 Ds.

There is evidence of several more unmarked graves.

Upperville Methodist Church Cemetery, Upperville, Virginia
Located in Upperville on West side of Route 712. Resurveyed August 13, 1990.

Tacie BLEAKLEY Wife of Charles BLEAKLEY Born July 3, 1807 Died Mar. 16, 1887 aged 79 ys, 8 mos., 13 Days

Charles BLEAKLEY Born Jan. 13, 1810 Died Mar. 17, 1876 Aged 66 years 2 mos.

Wm. R. BLEAKLEY Born Oct. 20, 1847 Died Aug. 30, 1863 Aged 15 yr. 10 mos. 10 days

Winefred Wife of Richard HALL Born July 20, 1773 Died Dec. 16, 1860 aged 87 yrs. 4 mos. & 6 Dys

Thomas FRASIER Born September 14, 1794 Died September 2, 1849 aged 54 years 11 months and 19 days

Henry W. Son of P. S. X & C. GOCHENOUR Born Jan. 4, 1874 Died Feb. 2, 1874

Our Mother Elizabeth Wife of Liet. B. F. CONRAD Died Jan. 25, 1881 aged 40 years

Our Father Liet. B. CONRAD Died Nov. 12, 1882 aged 40 years *(C.S.A. marker)*

Frances S. Wife of William C. YERBY Born Nov. 20, 1799 Died July 29, 1868 In the 69th year of her age

Daisy D. Dau. of B. F. & E. S. CONRAD died Oct. 31, 1880

Oscar Son of A. O. and Bettie YERBY of Essex Co., Va. Died June 29, 1851

Adela L. Daughter of A. O. & C. B. YERBY of Richmond Co. Born Dec. 11, 1856 Died Sept. 10, 1857

Wm. H. HOPPER Born March 23, 1823 Died Dec. 13, 1882

Alpheus Calvin Son of Amos & Mahale V. PIERCE died May 25th 1850 aged 14 years 1 month and 1 Day

Joseph Son of Joel & Frances WARD who departed this life October 1, 1848 aged 8 months

Annie G. CROUCH Died Sept. 10, 1888 aged 3 months

Gertrude Daughter of Cuthbert & Virginia A. PETTIT died Sept. 3rd 1853 aged 4 months & 14 days

Roberta Daughter of Franklin & Harriet BALL who was born April 16, 1851 and departed this life Sept. 13th 1852 aged 4 years 4 months & 27 days

Freland Son of Richard & Susan DAVIS who was born Sept. 6th 1853 Departed this life Oct. 25th 1854 Aged 1 year 4 months & 19 days

John Hoffman WAUGH only Son of ---- Hoffman WAUGH *(rest in ground)*

Ann L. Wife of John J. BOWIE who departed this life Dec. 17th 1861 *(rest in ground)*

Aurelia P. BROWN Daughter of Dr. A. P. & M. C. BROWN Born Jan. 6, 1865 Died Jan 7 1884

Clarence E. Son of B. F. & E. C. POSTON Born Mar. 12, 1878 Died Apr. 7, 1885 Our Ellwood

Robert McARTOR Born April 12, 1813 Died March 15, 1888

Sarah McARTOR Wife of Robert C. McARTOR Born August 29, 1815 Died July 5, 1890 Aged 74 yrs 10 mos. & 6 days

Charles Kemp Son of James L. & Rebecca S. DONALD who departed this life on the 6th day of August 1850 aged 20 months & 4 days

Olivia J. C. Wife of William CHAMBLIN Born March 17, 1821 Died April 28, 1881

Lucy Henry GIBSON Died Aug. 15th 1846 aged 1 year 1 month and 23 Days

Armstad C. Son of Harrison & Julia A. LUNCEFORD who was born Dec. 3rd 1849 departed this life May 10th 1850

John Harrison LUNCEFORD was born August 14, 1845 and departed this life April 29th 1847 Aged 1 year 8 months and 14 days

Thomas Son of Edward & Emily COCHRAN Died July 16, 1846 aged 10 years

Samuel Son of Edward & Emily COCHRAN Died July 10, 18[4?]7 Aged 15 years 6 months

Sarah J. Wife of Ebbin T. LAWS who departed this life Sept. 11th 1849 aged 3[0?] years 6 months & 27 days

Our first born Norval Son of Norval & Alice LAWS Died Nov. 10, 1881 aged 8 years

Willie Son of Norval & A. LAWS Died Dec. 12, 1881 Aged 2 years & 8 months

Rose W. LAWS Died Dec. 31, 1888

Evaline Wife of Henry HAINES Died Feb 6, 1850 Aged 75 years

Henry HAINES Died March 9th 1873 aged 73 years

Dr. Thomas W. SMITH Born October 19, 1818 Died July 19, 1866

Eleanora Wife of Dr. Thos. W. SMITH Died Oct. 13, 1855 Aged 23 years

John C. ARMISTEAD Born July 30th 1797 deceased 10th April 184– *(metal support attached here to tombstone)*

Capt. John B. ARMISTEAD Va. Mil. War 1812

Bettie Hale Daughter of Horace H. & Elizabeth H. McKENSTER Died Jan. 31st 1852 aged 1 year 7 months & 2 days

Eliza A. BRUCE Died Oct. 20, 1845 in the 56 year of her age

Mahlon GIBSON who departed this life June 1th 1852 In the [5?] 1st year of his age

Martha L. GIBSON who died Dec. 4th 1855 aged 28 years

Eleanora GIBSON who died Dec. 5th 1855 In the 61st year of her age

Robert Son of George & Elizabeth L. CALVERT Died May 1830 aged 9 months

Ralls CALVERT Born September 22nd 1808 Died July 26th 1849

George CALVERT Born October 20th 1795 September 23rd 1871

Elizabeth LOVELL widow of George CALVERT Daughter of Joseph CARR Born February 26th 1802 Died March 14th 1871

Elizabeth Lovell Daughter of Caldwell & Mary L. CALVERT Born Mar. 31st Died June 5th 1880

One stone face over in ground and too heavy to lift (stone not found 1990)

U. S. Marine Base

Cemeteries (other than CARVER) within the area of the U. S. Marine Base in Fauquier County were relocated to Cedar Run in Prince William County with the exception of one located near G8 on bank above Route 612, which family was to keep up and I could not find.

Utterback Cemetery

Located on Route 721 0.5 mile South of Route 635. Data obtained from Joe Lawler, Marshall.

Utterback Cemetery

Located on Route 735 by old road bed on a knoll.

John N. UTTERBACK Born Jan. 3, 1824 Died Aug. 20, 1902; Maria M. UTTERBACK Born Apr. 1, 1840 Died July 6, 1922

infant grave with rock marker

rock marker

Waite Cemetery, Bristersburg, Virginia

Located 2 miles South Bristersburg East side of road 0.5 mile in woods near stream, no fence, honeysuckle. Some fieldstone markers. Data obtained by Kenneth Eskridge.

Jane WAITE who departed this life the 4th day of November 1794

William WAITE a native of the island of Great Britain Born the 1st of January 1700 came to Virginia 1751 and departed this life the 10th day of November 1782 being nearly 83 years of age

Matthew WAITE Born the 24th of February 1735 and departed this life the 1st day of October 1763 Aged 38 years 7 months

Walker Cemetery, Delaplane, Virginia

Located South of house and barns South West of intersection of Routes 17 & 724.

David T. WALKER Born Oct. 2, 1821 Died Oct. 21, 1870

Blanche L. B. WALKER Died Mar. 26, 1884 aged 12 years 9 months & 6 days

Bessie A. WALKER *(rest sunk in ground firmly)*

Walker Cemetery, Markham, Virginia

Located 1.75 miles North Route 55 on East side Route 688 on hill between two houses, stone wall, covered with wild roses and honeysuckle.

Elijah WALKER Born Mar. 5, 1858 Died Jan. 10, 1929

Mary HALEY Wife of Elijah WALKER Born Feb. 28, 1874 Died May 3, 1939

Walton Family Cemetery, Catlett, Virginia
Located South Route 640 one mile East Route 806. In field, cement buttress wall, wooden cross. Resurveyed August 15, 1994 by Mr. Greg Mercado.

Susan R. WALTON 1814–1904; Melville WALTON 1805–1884
M. N. WALTON 1855–1868
J. B. WALTON C. S. A. Nannie A. WORRELL 1845–1887

Washington Cemetery, Opal, Virginia
Located 0.5 mile West Opal on Route 637 South side back of barn in corner of field, pine & oak. 8 rock markers.

Wesley Beloved Husband of M. F. WASHINGTON March 7, 1842 Sept. 15, 1924

Washington Family Cemetery, Opal, Virginia
Located 2.1 miles West Route 687 North Route 637, back of house, no markers.

Waterman Place Cemetery, Morrisville, Virginia
Located 0.25 mile South Route 806 East Route 634 back of very old house at end of private lane, good stone wall, huge American box bushes, no markers.

Weaver Cemetery, Midland Airport, Midland, Virginia
Located West Route 610 South of Midland in grove to East of hangars, one sandstone marker with inscription sheets away, possibly some fieldstone markers:

Charlott A. WEAVER Departed this life January A. D. 1825 age 3

Weaver Slave Cemetery
Located near Greenwich, partly in Fauquier in Prince William County. Owned in 1984 by Minnie S. McMichael who supplied data recorded in Fauquier County Deed Book. It is on wooded hill side and contains about 100 slave graves. Her grandfather was G. C. Squires, who bought land which he deeded to Mrs. McMichael.

Webster Family Cemetery, Turnbull, Virginia
Located 0.3 mile East Route 657 North 803 100 yards back of house near fence in woods (adjacent to Carroll). Marie WEBSTER and others of her family buried to North of next house going North.

West Cemetery (Black), Catlett, Virginia
Located on Route 767, Catlett behind John Douglas' house. 5 unmarked graves

William WEST Born Dec. 18, 1840 Died July 28, 1911
Mrs. Patricia WEST BORN APRIL 15, 1840 DIED APRIL 28, 1928 *[information from daughter M. Noland]*
Charles D. WEST Born Jan. 20, 1870 Died July 24, 1916

West - Williams Cemetery, Morrisville, Virginia
Located South East Route 634 1 mile West Route 637 to left of house in field, good fence.

Minnie W. WILLIAMS 1851–1930
Estella Daughter of H. M. & E. M. WEST Aug. 24, 1888 Mar. 20, 1898
Horace W. WEST Aug. 10, 1848 July 17, 1915 M. Ellen WILLIAMS Nov. 16, 1848 Apr. 20, 1939

Westminister Presbyterian Church Cemetery, Delaplane, Virginia
Located in Delaplane on Route 712. First church on site dedicated in 1889. Well kept. Church now used by the Delaplane Assembly of God. Resurveyed September 6, 1993.

Anne Green KEMPER 1879–1955
Sarah Catherine Settle, Wife of Hugh GREEN, July 20, 1851–July 27, 1930
H. G. GREEN, M. D.. born April 7, 1842, died Oct. 28, 1916 *(Masonic emblem)*
Robert Berry GREEN, born May 20, 1874 died Dec. 2, 1896
Jane Rebecca GREEN, 1876–1960
David Thomas GREEN, 1882–1970
Frances Walker GREEN, 1914–1976
Edward Hugh GREEN, 1889–1979

John H. LUNCEFORD Co, B. Mosby's Regt. Va. Cav., C.S.A. April 26, 1846-Jan 10, 1934
Mary LUNCEFORD July 24, 1846–Jan. 24, 1930
Alexander ULLMAN [Minnie]

Children of John and Jane ANDERSON, Hugh born Dec. 11, 1895 died June 16, 1896, John born Dec. 11, 1895,
    died June 13, 1896
John ANDERSON died May 28, 1904 aged 84 years
Bessie ANDERSON, May 31, 1879–Aug. 9, 1905
Mildred A. ANDERSON born Aug. 13, 1837 died Dec. 12, 1919
Andrew J. CHUNN Aug. 9, 1817–Apr. 22, 1894
Isabella A. CHUNN, Wife of Andrew J. CHUNN, Feb. 3, 1825–Mar. 28, 1915; Taylor, Son of A. J. & I. A.
    CHUNN died Aug. 2, 1900–Mar. *(rest sunk in ground)*

M. G. ASHBY born June 2, 1834 died April 1, 1918
Mary W. Delaplane ASHBY 1848–1917
Henry S. ASHBY Dec. 20, 1845–July 10, 1909 *(Masonic emblem)*

Samuel Ashby CHANCELLOR Son of G. W. & Rose Briggs CHANCELLOR born June 15, 1871 died Mar. 5, 1912
Josephine BRIGGS, Wife of G. W. Chancellor born Mar. 14, 1839, died Mar. 6, 1892
G. W. CHANCELLOR born Aug. 12, 1837 died Feb. 15, 1915
Charles Lewis Jackson ASHBY Mar. 17, 1834–Sept. 17, 1916
Eliza Vienna Poston ASHBY Sept. 18, 1816 May 2, 1905
Charles Poston ASHBY June 4, 1875–Nov. 20, 1876
Turner Jackson ASHBY Dec. 28, 1869–Mar. 1, 1934
Thomas ASHBY, 1886–1886
Elmer Walker ASHBY June 18, 1871–Feb. 1895
Scott ASHBY Sept. 1878–Oct. 14, 1901

Sarah Ellen MARTIN 1890-1968
Mother Elizabeth FUCHS GOELINER November 16, 1848–October 1, 1936
Maj Wm. H. CARY Feb. 7, 1874–June 26, 1932 His Wife Elizabeth I. *(Salvation Army)*
GOELINER Oct. 11, 1878–Feb. 29, 1956 *(Salvation Army marker)*
ROBINSON, Edward C. 1877–1955 His Wife Lucy M. CARY 1872–1960

Indecipherable marker

Elmer L. LUNCEFORD VIRGINIA CPL. 3889 OMHV TRUCK CO WORLD WAR II Aug. 1, 1916–Sept. 20,
    1966
Jennie T. LUNCEFORD 1879–1964
Robert C. LUNCEFORD 1878–1942
Ruby J. infant dau. of J. B. & G. V. JEFFRIES Jan. 18, 1939
Gladys V. Wife of J. [John] B. JEFFRIES June 21, 1908–Jan. 22, 1939

John B. JEFFRIES Oct. 27, 1908–[*1992 buried in Ivy Hill Cemetery, Virginia with his third wife. Source Nancy C. Baird*]

Westview Cemeteries (Black), Upperville, Virginia
The oldest one is located on South side of Route 50 back of lumber yard at South end of town in a wire fenced area completely overgrown with honeysuckle, with graves sunken and no tombstones visible. There appear to be a great many graves. On the West side of Route 712 at South end of Upperville back of old school converted to a dwelling is a well kept cemetery containing some unmarked and marked graves.

Walter B. MARSHALL 1880–1913 Husband Father
C. Henry GRAYSON 1900–1965
Clifford R. MOTEN Died May 4, 1964 aged 75 years

Abraham ADAMS Died January 8, 1963 Aged 75 years
Virginia S. WILLIAMS 1902–1967
James W. CABELL Sept. 15, 1946 May 19, 1956
Thomas E. SMITH Apr. 1, 1919 May 25, 1950
Henry D. YOUNG Sept. 14, 1889 Apr. 18, 1957
Baby Girl MARLOW Died Sept. 6, 1968 Apparently stillborn
Annie Rose ROSS Died Sep. 23, 195- Aged 76 years
Clyde ROSS Died Jan. 24, 1953 Aged 47 years
Winter Roger ROSS 1916–1967
Cora A. JACKSON June 18, 1881 February 4, 1952
Buford E. SANFORD 1887–1950; Flora SANFORD 1885–1964
Oscar SANFORD Feb. 29, 1856 June 21, 1938

James PROCTOR Died 1934
Harry Cud GRAYSON 1906–1967
Jessie L. EMBERS Died April 29, 1965 Aged 66 years

Gabriel TURNER Died May 21, 1963 Aged 87 years
Milion ---- Died July --, 1963 aged 26

Janet Lue TERRY Died SeptemberC1962 aged 1 year
Della R. GRAYSON 1888–1967
Dennis L. BRIDGETT 1946–1957
Harry GRAYSON 1873–1966
Jacqueline L. YATES 4 months 1963
William WARNER Died July 29, 1969 Aged 78 years
Robert ROBINSON VIRGINIA PFC CO A 330 SVC BN QMC WORLD WAR I Jan 1 1889 Nov 3 1962
Andrew ROBINSON Died February 3rd 1956 Aged 75 years

Joseph Henry BROOKS VIRGINIA WORLD WAR II STM2 USNR WORLD WAR II July 21 1921 July 7 1951
Peggy Lee ALLEN Died June 13 1967 Aged 5 months
Ann W. PAYNE Died June 25, 1943
Edward ALLEN 1915–1969
Beverly THOMAS Died June 30, 1956 Aged 54 years
John W. HOWARD 1847–1922 Ann HOWARD Died May 23, 1921
Ann Josephine HOWARD Born Feb. 2, 1921 Died May 19, 1921

Edward ROBERTS Died August 19, 1969 Aged 50 years
Albert TRACY Died March 19, 1951 Aged 76 years

Lynn TURNER June 20, 1901 November 22, 1961

HOWARD Plot:
Zella DeROSA 1893–1956; Richard [HOWARD] 1899–1903
Betty HOWARD 1871–1954; James [HOWARD] 1906–1925
Herman CHARITY Died July 13, 1966 Aged 53 years
Mary Elizabeth CHARITY Died January 1, 1963 Aged 108 years
Mary F. BARBOUR 1893–1968
William F. BAILEY 1877–1957

Sidney BROOKS 1900–1943

Susie BROOKS 1880–1923; Joseph W. BROOKS 1878–1956

Gabriel L. CHARITY Died March 16, 1966 Aged 84 years Mary PINKETT CHARITY Died March 18, 1869 Aged
    84 years 1860 Virginia C. PINKETT 1941

Father Edward ROBINSON 1871–1942 Son Harry E. ROBINSON 1897–1942
Minnie V. ROBINSON 1871–1951
J.   l.   1965 Aged 47
Louisa WILLIAMS SMITH Died Oct 28, 1968 Aged about 85 years
Channing Richard TURNER Died July 22, 1967 aged 30 years
Charles William PROCTOR Died Oct. 10, 1958 Aged 63 years
Irene Elizabeth COLBERT Died September 1, 1969 Aged 55 years

Wheatley Cemetery, "Belcoir", Remington, Virginia
*Located near Sumerduck 5 miles South East of Remington on Route 781 100 yards East of Brown's Run. Fence
    gone, overgrown. Research by M. D. Gore, Feb. 8, 1937.*

James H. JAMESON Son of Enoch & Fannie E. JAMESON who departed this life September 20 A. D. 1861 aged
    47 years 3 months and 4 days
Sarah Ann Wife of G. T. Wheatley & Daughter of ---- TAYLOR born ____1804, died 23 ___1835[?]
George T. WHEATLEY Born January 28, 1803 Died May 19, 1877
Our dear Mother Catherine P. Wife of George T. WHEATLEY Daughter of Mandley & Catherine TAYLOR Born
    Nov. 12, 1807 Died March 31st 1842
I. or J. WHEATLEY on red rock marker

Whiting Cemetery (Black), Marshall, Virginia
*Located at East end of Route 184 at "Monterey" cattle guard. Funeral home markers that were here, according to
    Jack Alcock, have vanished. In woods to left of cattle guard, remains of stone wall of triangular shaped cemetery
    adjacent to old road. About 5 or 6 graves. Resurveyed September 20, 1993.*

Whittle Chapel Cemetery, "Hopewell Gap", The Plains, Virginia
*Located in Hopewell Gap at site of old Episcopal Church (Hopewell Chapel, now a private home) on Route 601
    East of Route 628 near Route 700 to South West of house, well kept by owner. 13 fieldstone markers. Resurveyed
    October 18, 1993.*

Information in parentheses given by Bob Sinclair:
Elizabeth Jane SINCLAIR Mar. 4, 1880 Aug. 20, 1964 *(Mrs. Sinclair was a DOWNS, daughter of Rush DOWNS)*
Margaret M. SINCLAIR Born Dec. 10, 1834 Died Oct. 9, 1908 *(unmarried daughter of George B. SINCLAIR)*
Virginia E. SINCLAIR Born Aug. 21, 1839 Died Aug. 7, 1907 *(unmarried daughter of George B. SINCLAIR)*
Ann Elizabeth SINCLAIR 1848–1928 *(nee HOWDERSHELL wife of Charles H.)*

Charles H. SINCLAIR 1846–1923

Archibald C. SINCLAIR Dec. 11, 1876 May 15, 1933 *(son of Charles and Ann Elizabeth, husband of E. Jane)*

Lelia Earl SINCLAIR 1901–1902 *(infant daughter of Archie and E. Jane)*

Harvey SINCLAIR Son of Charles and A. E. Died at age 7 December 1891 of diptheria *(unmarked stone)*

Lucy SINCLAIR Daughter of Charles and A. E. Died at age 4 January 1892 of diptheria

HOWDERSHELL & COCHRAN *families are also buried here.*

Wince Cemetery, Orlean, Virginia

Located 0.6 mile North of Orlean on Route 688. Well kept with chain wire fence. Mrs. Virgie GRIMSLEY WINCE made monument on large rock from Family Bible records for fieldstone markers. 75 feet x 75 feet. Five cinderblock markers. Resurveyed October 22, 1993.

Jacob WINCE 1817–1902

Eliza Y. WINCE 1822–1910

Jane E. WINCE 1848–1917

Joe WINCE 1853–1912

Jim WINCE 1854–1923

Henry WINCE 1856–1911

Frank A. WINCE 1899–1937

Lena M.. WINCE 1877–1955

Dan R. WINCE 1869–1958

Mollie W. BRADFORD 1858–19--

Turner R. WINCE 1904–1907

Lena G. BUTLER 1921–1942

Grace BUTLER 10 yrs.

Martha BUTLER 1914–1918

Vance BUTLER, Jr. 5 days

James R. WINCE, Jr. Sept. 14, 1930 Jan. 20, 1955

J. Edgar WINCE 1898–1952

WINCE Franklin A. Dec. 23, 1859 Feb. 20, 1938 Lena SPICER Mar. 8, 1876 June 22, 1955

WINCE Eppa Hunton 1901–1964 Virgie GRIMSLEY 1901–1969

Walter F. WINCE Virginia STAFF SGT. 565 AAF BOMB SQ. WORLD WAR II April 20, 1920 November 26 1943

Julia Maureen WINCE Oct. 1, 1931 Nov. 7, 1936

GRIMSLEY Philip H. July 4, 1910 July 13, 1961 Emma R. Dec. 2, 1919

Daniel R. WINCE April 14, 1869 Dec. 1, 1958

Woodrow W. WINCE VIRGINIA PVT 1 CL. MED. DEPT. January 1, 1921 March 28, 1944

Lucy Ada WINCE July 2, 1885 Jan. 10, 1968

Leah Margaret WINCE August 24, l929 August 26, 1967

Clarence Eugene GRIMSLEY Died June 8, 1966 Aged 29 years *(missing 1993)*

Della WINCE GRIMSLEY Nov. 27, 1906 Mar. 5, 1991

Horace M. WINCE 1908–1990

Clarence Ashby WINCE F1 US Navy WORLD WAR II Mar. 2, 1918 Feb. 25, 1993

William L. WINCE 1912–1993

Dwight Milton ALMAN Aug. 10, 1953 Mar. 29, 1973

BARCON Luther M. July 11, 1906 Nov. 3, 1979; Gracie Dec. 29, 1912 Dec. 23, 1986

Wade Michael BRAGG Oct. 16, 1955 Sept. 16, 1989

Charles W. SCHMIDT Virginia M Sgt. US Marine Corps WORLD WAR II and KOREA Aug. 6, 1920 Nov. 12, 1966

Gertrude F. SCHMIDT Mar. 4, 1922 Dec. 29, 1968

Vance W. BUTLER 1905–1977

Withers - Nelson - Ficklin Cemetery, Warrenton, Virginia

Located 2 miles North of Opal on East side of Route 29 to right end of farm road, fenced, being restored by owners, boxwood, trees and periwinkle on what was called Licking Run Farm, when people were buried here.

Virginia E. FICKLIN Born June 11, 1829 Died Sept. 19, 1915 Daughter of George & Elizabeth PORTER NELSON

Gustavius FICKLIN Died at his house near Warrenton Nov. 18th 1891 in the 78th year of his age

Sarah Daughter of George & E. NELSON Died April 25, 1882 aged 50 years

Elizabeth H. NELSON Died Sept. 12, 1873 aged 80 years

George NELSON Died March 23rd 1860 aged 76 years

Elizabeth WITHERS was born Sept. 22d 1732 Mard Dec. 15 1756 & dyd Oct 17th 1787

W. WITHERS, Sr. was born April vi 1796 Died --- 1801

Atherine WITHERS was born in 1771 Departed this life the -- July 1821

L. WITHERS Died May 4, 1821

James W. FICKLIN April 23, 1852 March 5, 1932; His Wife Lucy F. JASPER Nov. 28, 1867 Jan. 15, 1909

Sarah H. NELSON who departed this life in the 8th day of Sept. 184[5?] in the year of our Lord

1 slate tombstone face down and too heavy to lift

Woods Family Cemetery, Midland, Virginia

Located 1 mile West Route 610 South East Route 806 in woods back of house, fieldstone markers only. Confederate & Union soldiers in fieldstone marked graves at old place across the road.

Woodward Cemetery, Rectortown, Virginia

Located 1.3 miles North of Rectortown on Route 713 on west side of road surrounded by iron fence, much overgrown. Resurveyed September 5, 1993.

Our aunt Eliza A. WOODWARD Wife of Luke WOODWARD Died Oct. 21, 1897 aged about 88 years

Ann E. WOODWARD consort of Luke WOODWARD who was born Dec. 4th 1799 and departed this life October 3, 1854

Annie E. WOODWARD Born Dec. 4, 1799 Died Oct. 3, 1854 Mother

Luke WOODWARD

Luke Son of L. E. & E. E. WOODWARD Born Jan. 11, 1882 Died Aug. 4, 1882

Emma Eugenia Wife of L. E. WOODWARD Born Feb. 11, 1851 Died Sept. 14, 1884

Luke WOODWARD March 6, 1845 Dec. 10, 1934 Capt. Chapman's Co. "Co. F" Mosby's Command, C. S. A.

Lambert E. WOODWARD 1880–1956

Our Mother Nancy Mary GLASCOCK Wife of Enoch GLASCOCK Born Sept. 7, 1793 Died Aug. 15, 1875 ⟵

Mrs. Patsy REID Wife of Alfred REID Born Dec. 23, 1796 Died Feb. 12, 1880

Alfred REID Born Feb. 25, 1794 Died Sept. 1, 1873 Aged 72 years 6 months & 26 days

Annie E. Wife of D. BOYD & Daughter of Luke WOODWARD Born March 1842 Died August 21, 1881

Annie Mamie Daughter of S. D. & A. L. BOYD Born Feb. 12, 1879 Died Sept. 13, 1879

C. W. RIVERCOMB Born July 12, 1853 Died Mar. 31, 1893 Aged 39 years 8 months & 19 days

B. M. B.

A. R. U.

Our little Harriet born July 4, 1852 died July 31, 1847

Ann H. Daughter of T. & R. HERNDON

William RECTOR . born July 15th 1769 and died Jan. 24 d 1834 aged 65 years 6 months and 19 days

Augustine KENNER Son of George A. & Harriet Born July 2, 1861 Died December 22, 1921

Harriet RECTOR Wife of George A. KENNER Born Jan. 12, 1834 Died Sept. 9, 1922

George A. KENNER Son of Rodham F. & Elizabeth JOHNSON KENNER Born July 22, 1818 Died June 8, 1888

Our Alfred Son of Alfred & Catharine A. M. RECTOR was born July 11, 1838 and departed this life Feb. 12, 1846

Zoar Baptist Church Cemetery, Bristersburg, Virginia
Located at intersections of Routes 616 & 806 behind church. Resurveyed May 27, 1990.

Harriet C. SCHOOLER Born Jan. 27, 1837 Died Dec. 13, 1905
Sarah E. CLEMENT Died May 3, 1891 in the 69 year of her age

FRENCH George Lee FRENCH Dec. 31, 1831 June 21, 1903; Martha P. McCOY His Wife Daughter of James R.
   PAYNE June 4, 1832 Dec. 31, 1905 Father Mother

Note: In middle of huge box in French fenced area is a large tombstone face down in dirt. One unmarked grave in
   this area.
P. L. F. footstone

Unknown Family Cemetery
Located on Route 645 one half mile away from Rappahannock on East side of road. Stone fence with two straight
   rows, maybe 3 rows, at least 17 graves, possibly more. Remains of one wooden marker. Cemetery on E. Scheel's
   map. December 29, 1992.

1818 ? - or ca 18
JF JF 1889
JK-F or Jeff

Unknown Family Cemetery (Cliff Mill)
Located near fork of Carter's Run and on hillside above site of Cliff Mill (Blackwell's Mill) directly across run
   from Cliff Mill's house, picnic table on site and two old trees. According to Eugene Scheel's map ca. 1985,
   Carter's Run Battle occurred here. John Gott indicated that this may be a DIGGS family cemetery. If so, then
   Edward DIGGS, Revolutionary War soldier is buried here. Cemetery is approximately 25 feet by 60 feet. 4
   graves marked with fieldstone markers (one adult & one child's grave distinctly marked, side by side) numerous
   depressions. March 20, 1991

Unknown Cemetery, The Plains, Virginia
Located at the edge of the woods uphill North West of Owens Cemetery.

"Dad" carved on rock. Other symbols LE 5.

Unmarked Cemeteries

(1) Route 737 0.5 mile North Route 738 on left in Richard MOORE garden. Data obtained from Joe Lawler,
   Marshall.

(2) Route 721 in woods. Data obtained from Joe Lawler, Marshall.

(3) At Henry Glascock's. 1 unmarked grave. Data obtained from Joe Lawler, Marshall.

Near Catlett, Virginia
Located North Route 767 1 mile East Route 806 on top of hill by road. No inscriptions.

Bealeton, Virginia
Located 1 mile North West 28 North Route 745 200 yards North East of Kelly - James Cemetery, probably slaves.

Hume, Virginia
Located at DeButts place, "Mt. Welby", East side of Route 726 2.5 miles North Route 635. Has fieldstone markers for members of a family trekking to the gold rush who lost some of their family there.

Goldvein, Virginia
Located about 1.5 miles South of Route 651 to East of Route 615 , in second field beyond large woods about 50 feet x 100 feet, overgrown with trees and many fieldstone markers. Mrs. James Clark took me to this cemetery, which is near the Mount Ephraim Cemetery.

Midland, Virginia
Very large Negro slave and white cemeteries in overgrown area to North of old house site South West intersections of Routes 649 & 663.

Near Midland, Virginia
Located 0.75 mile South East of Elk Run on Route 610, 0.25 mile East off of Route 610 by private road. There is a cemetery about 0.25 mile East of house.

Morrisville, Virginia
There is a very large cemetery 150 yards North Route 637 about 1.5 mile East Route 17, by site of ancient road., about 0.125 acre outlined by tall cedars, wire fence around part, deep in woods, to which Ronnie Anns led me, but no markers with inscriptions and he did not know family buried there.

Remington, Virginia
Located on Route 654. Surveyed by M. D. Gore, December 15, 1937. "There is a colored graveyard on the 'Wellington' farm about 0.75 mile South East of house."

Unlocatable Cemeteries

At "Fairfield", the old Marshall place, located on South side of Route 636 East of Route 726.

Miscellaneous Fauquier County Burials
The following information comes from the "Journals of Amanda Virginia Edmonds" edited by Nancy Chappelear Baird :

Upperville, Virginia

Lucy CHILDS
James RUST
Mr. HUTCHINSON *(killed by Yankees April 1862)*
Kim and Sam HICKS Died May 1865

Paris, Virginia

Sally GREEN Died Feb. 1864 [Ovoka?]
John FLETCHER 6th Va. Regt. May 1862

Delaplane, Virginia

James Pendleton CHAPPELEAR May 1865

Burial Locations Unknown

Betty BLACKWELL Died March 1860
Addie O'REAR Died November 17, 1861
Betty ROGERS Died of Tuberculosis Aug. 14, 1862
Albert TRIPLETT Died March 27, 1862 *(accidentally shot himself in camp. Body brought back to Fauquier for burial)*

Confederate Soldiers Buried in Fauquier County Cemeteries

Name	Military Unit	Cemetery	Date of Birth	Date of Death
ADAMS, Henry Clay	Co. B 43rd Bn. Va. Cav.	Adams Family Cemetery, Paris	1834	4/29/1865
ALLISON, Richard	Co. K 17th Va. Inf	Warrenton		
AMES, James F.	Co. F 43rd Bn. Va. Cav.	Delaplane	1831	10/9/1864
ANDERSON, Thomas E.	Co. D 43rd Bn. Va. Cav.	Anderson	9/9/1834	9/23/1864
ANDERSON, William C.	Co. G 43rd Bn. Va. Cav.	Markham	1846	1923
ARMISTEAD, Bowels E.	CPT Co. A 6th Va. Cav.	Ivy Hill	4/26/1838	10/16/1916
ASH, Joseph Adelbert	Co. A 43rd Bn. Va. Cav.	possibly Ash Family	1842	
ASHBY, John T.	CPT Co. B 8th Va. Vol.	Ivy Hill	1841	1928
ASHBY, Henry Stribling	Co. B 8th Va. Inf./43rd Bn. Va. Cav.	Westminster Presbyterian	12/20/1845	7/10/1909
ASHTON, Henry	SGT MAJ Brooke's Battery	Warrenton		
ATHEY, Samuel M.	SGT Beauregard Rifles	Athey	1844	1922
ATKINS, John	43rd Bn. Va. Cav.	Paris Community (unmarked)		10/1864
AYRE, William T.	not stated	Ivy Hill	8/22/1842	7/25/1863
BAKER, William	not stated	Marshall Community	9/17/1842	4/10/1922
BALL, Albin P.	Co. L 43rd Bn. Va. Cav.	Church of Our Savior	1846	2/28/1910
BALL, J. Johnston	Virginia	Ivy Hill		
BALTHORPE, G. R.	Co. C 43rd Bn. Va. Cav.	unknown	1840	
BARBER, Saml. A.	Co. B 43rd Bn. Va. Cav.	unknown	1828	
BARBER, Wm. H.	Co. B 43rd Bn. Va. Cav.	unknown	1832	
BARTENSTEIN, Andrew R.	not stated	Warrenton	10/2/1847	12/10/1916
BAYLEY, James P.	Co. H 43rd Bn. Va. Cav.	unknown	1832	
BAYNE, Richard B.	Co. G 43rd Bn. Va. Cav.	unknown	1839	
BEALE, John G.	Black Horse Cav.	Grace Episcopal	1845	1942
BEAMER, William B.	Co. D 27th Va. Inf	Warrenton	1837	1886
BENDALL, Robert T.	CPL Co. H 13th Va. Cav.	Warrenton	1833	1913
BENNETT, Henry T.	CPL Warrenton Rifles	Warrenton	11/23/1828	7/9/1893
BENNETT, Oscar A.	Kemper Brigade	Warrenton		7/6/1864
BENNETT, Samuel C.	not stated	Warrenton	1827	1896
BERRYMAN, Marcellus	Co. D 43rd Bn. Va. Cav.	Markham	1845	
BISHOP, Hezekiah	Wise's Dragoons	Warrenton	3/9/1843	1/18/1928
BLACK, Ludwell D.	Black Horse Cav.	Grace Episcopal	1842	1899
BLACKWELL, D.	not stated	Warrenton	6/17/1822	6/26/1887
BLACKWELL, Joseph Hancock	Co. D 43rd Bn. Va. Cav.	Blackwell, The Meadow, Bethel	1905	
BLACKWELL Moore C.	Co. D 38th Va. Inf.	Warrenton	1833	1917
BOOTH, G.G.	not stated	Warrenton	1821	1906
BOWEN, Henry Clay "Harry"	Co. H 43rd Bn. Va. Cav.	Remington	4/3/1846	3/5/1928
BOWEN, James W.	CPL Kemper Brigade	Marshall Community	2/16/1840	11/19/1928
BOWEN, William	Co. H 4th Va. Cav.	Martin		
BOWIE, John W.	Co. A 43rd Bn. Va. Cav.	unknown	1846	
BRAGG, Charles P.	Co. K 17th Va. Inf.	Warrenton		
BRAWNER, Henry Newton	Co. A 43rd Bn. Va. Cav.	Church of Our Savior	9/30/1847	2/9/1932
BREDELL, Edward Jr.*	LT 43rd Bn. Va. Cav.	Cool Spring Meth. (unmrkd)	1839	11/16/1864
BRIDGE, James E.	Co. E 43rd Bn. Va. Cav.	unknown		
BRODIE, A.M.	LT Warrenton Rifles	Warrenton	1/14/1829	4/18/1915
BROOKE, James V.	Co. A 12th Battalion	Warrenton	10/10/1824	10/9/1898
BROWN, David F.	Co. B 43rd Bn. Va. Cav.	Marshall	8/?/1842	1/22/1910
BROWN, H. Clay	Black Horse Cav?	Cedar Grove	1841	1923
BROWN, Jessie	Kemper Brigade	Grove Baptist		8/17/1907
BROWN, Jno. S.	Wise's Dragoons	Ivy Hill	3/18/1831	7/31/1904
BROWN, Judson	not stated	Warrenton		
BROWN, W. Johnson	LT Brooke's Battery	Warrenton	1834	1902
BURGESS, Moses	Co. A 43rd Bn. Va. Cav.	unknown	1845	
BURTON, Harrison "Highty"	Co. F 43rd Bn. Va. Cav.	unknown	1840	
CALVERT, Joseph C.	43rd Bn. Va. Cav.	Ivy Hill	7/15/1826	8/18/1892
CALWELL, L.W.	not stated	Warrenton		
CAMPBELL, Alexander S.	SGT Brooke's Battery	Warrenton	3/10/1818	9/10/1890
CAMPBELL, John H.	Co. A 43rd Bn. Va. Cav.	unknown		

Confederate Soldiers Buried in Fauquier County Cemeteries

Name	Military Unit	Cemetery	Date of Birth	Date of Death
CAMPBELL, John W.	Co. D 43rd Bn. Va. Cav.	Warrenton	1845	1883
CARNARD, Walter	not stated	Warrenton		
CARROLL, Gray Lt	unit not stated	Leeds		
CARTER, Cassius	Black Horse Cav.	Warrenton	10/16/1835	12/25/1914
CARTER, Edward C.	CPT Beauregard Rifles	Warrenton	8/19/1832	10/3/1928
CARTER, George H.	Black Horse Cav.	Warrenton	1839	1914
CARTER, Henry Furlong	Co. H 1 Va. Cav./43rd Bn. Va. Cav.	probably in Albba Rd.	1836	
CARTER, Isaiah	Co. E 43rd Bn. Va. Cav.	perhaps in Little Georgetown	1846	
CARTER, Richard H.	MAJ 8th Va. Inf Vol.	Warrenton	4/21/1817	4/7/1880
CARTER, Thomas W.	Co. A 6th Va. Cav?	Warrenton	3/9/1849	1/7/1925
CARTER, Thomas Walden	Co. D 43rd Bn. Va. Cav.	Warrenton	5/3/1847	4/7/1926
CARUTH, James T.	Co. H 43rd Bn. Va. Cav.	probably Warrenton	1846	
CHANCELLOR, George W.	Co. A 7th Va. Cav.	Westminster Presbyterian	8/12/1837	2/15/1915
CHAPPELEAR, George W.	CPL Co. A 6th Va. Cav.	Ivy Hill	9/9/1842	11/5/1922
CHAPPELEAR, James P.	Co. A 6th Va. Cav.	Fletcher		2/22/1864
CHAPPELEAR, John A.	Co. A 6th Va. Cav.	Edmonds	12/1/1835	6/1/1916
CHICHESTER, Thomas T.	Black Horse Cav.	Warrenton	1838	1908
CHICHESTER, Wm. Dodridge	43rd Bn. Va. Cav.	probably Auburn	1837	
CHILDS, James H.	SGT Black Horse Cav.	Childs	4/15/1833	7/19/1878
CHILTON, James V.	SGT Brooke's Battery	Warrenton	5/2/1841	9/9/1905
CHILTON, Samuel	not stated	Warrenton		
CHILTON, William	not stated	Warrenton		
CLATTERBUCK, John M.	not stated	Warrenton	8/13/1845	12/13/1925
COCHRAN, John				
COCHRAN, John H.	Co. A 43rd Bn. Va. Cav.	Marshall	9/22/1845	3/23/1906
COCHRAN, Thomas B.	43rd Bn. Va. Cav.	Marshall Community	3/20/1843	12/10/1870
COCKE, Wm. F.	Co. A 43rd Bn. Va. Cav.		1845	
COCKRELL, John H.	Co. A 43rd Bn. Va. Cav.	Cool Spring	3/26/1837	9/20/1912
COCKRELL, Wm.	Co. F 43rd Bn. Va. Cav.		1834	after 1895
COLBERT, Austin A.	Black Horse Cav.	Cedar Grove	6/1/1842	1/14/1904
COLLINS, Upton D.	not stated	Lee - Strother	11/7/1831	10/3/1862
COLOGNE, Edgar M.	Black Horse Cav.	Warrenton	1842	1907
COLVIN, John R.	not stated	Warrenton	1845	1922
CORDER, Butler	Co. E 43rd Bn. Va. Cav.	Bealeton	11/19/1819	12/25/1889
COX, J.E.	Co. E 43rd Bn. Va. Cav.			
CREEL, Elijah G.	Co B 8th Va. Vol	Ivy Hill	12/22/1832	6/24/1903
CREEL, Eppa	Co. A 43rd Bn. Va. Cav.			
CREEL, Francis	Co. A 43rd Bn. Va. Cav.		1846	
CURTIS, A.M.	not stated	Warrenton	1837	1901
DAVIS, Chas. E. Mills	Co. A 43rd Bn. Va. Cav.	Tackett - Burroughs	12/3/1844	7/19/1900
DAVISSON, Hugh N.	Warrenton Rifles	Warrenton	11/25/1841	2/10/1868
DAY, Alexander	Warrenton Rifles	Warrenton	8/3/1843	7/6/1862
de BUTTS, Richard Earle	43rd Bn. Va. Cav.	Church Hill, Linden	1823	7/6/1892
DIGGES, George W.	LT Black Horse Cav.	Cedar Grove		
DIGGS, Ludwell	Co. F 43rd Bn. Va. Cav.	Warrenton	7/2/1846	3/24/1913
DOUGLAS, Hugh T.	CPT Engineers CSA	Warrenton	4/12/1819	3/14/1898
DOUGLAS, John J.	MAJ U.S. Army	Warrenton	4/11/1834	6/10/1898
DOWELL, Peter G.	Co. A 43rd Bn. Va. Cav.	probably Paris		after 1909
DOWNING, John H.	Co. A 43rd Bn. Va. Cav.	Downing near Black Rock	8/24/1846	7/30/1911
DOWNING, Wm Henry	Co. E 43rd Bn. Va. Cav.	Marshall	7/19/1847	7/28/1879
DOWNMAN, Robert H.	Black Horse Cav.	Warrenton	9/9/1833	10/8/1891
DUNSTON, F.J.	Va.	Ivy Hill		
EDMONDS, John E.	43rd Bn. Va. Cav.	Warrenton	7/29/1910	
EDMONDS, Clement West	Co. B 43rd Bn. Va. Cav.		1845/6	12/4/1875
EDMONDS, Edward G.	Co. A 6th Va. Cav.	Warrenton	10/4/1821	12/23/1895
EDMONDS, J. Robert	Black Horse Cav.	Warrenton	6/13/1835	9/27/1899
EDWARDS, Arthur	not stated	Warrenton		

Confederate Soldiers Buried in Fauquier County Cemeteries

Name	Military Unit	Cemetery	Date of Birth	Date of Death
EDWARDS, I. C.	Virginia	Ivy Hill		
EDWARDS, John T.	Kemper Brigade	Marshall Community	1842	1940
EDWARDS, Joseph H.	CPL Kemper Brigade	Grove Presbyterian	8/15/1834	12/16/1909
ELGIN, James B.	not stated	Warrenton	1839	1910
EMBREY, Frederick	Tr D 4 Va. Cav.	Mt. Carmel Baptist		
EMBREY, Robert E.	Kemper Brigade	Mt. Holly	3/23/1836	12/1/1918
EMBREY, Silus B.	Tr D 4 Va. Cav.	Mt. Carmel Baptist		
FANT, Edward L. Jr.	Beauregard Rifles	Warrenton		6/27/1862
FANT, M.	not stated	Warrenton		
FANT, Thomas A.	11th Va. Inf.	Cedar Grove		
FEWELL, Benjamin F.	Beauregard Rifles	Marshall Community	1837	1898
FICKLIN, William L.	Co. H 4th Va. Cav.	Warrenton	1841	1904
FIELDS, Charles W.	Beauregard Rifles	Warrenton	11/17/1840	1/15/1916
FINKS, S.P.	North Carolina	Ivy Hill		
FISHER, Robert W.	not stated	Warrenton	1835	1907
FLEMING, Thomas W.	not stated	Ivy Hill	4/17/1838	11/9/1909
FLETCHER, Albert	Warrenton Rifles	Warrenton	2/27/1841	10/11/1917
FLETCHER, Benton	Co. C 43rd Va. Cav.	Warrenton	12/4/1832	12/2/1920
FLETCHER, Clinton	Co. A 7th Va. Cav.	Ivy Hill		4/25/1863
FLETCHER, James H.	Brooke's Battery	Warrenton		8/15/1909
FLETCHER, John	6th Va. Regt.	unknown		5/1862
FLETCHER, JohnW.	Co. A 7th Va. Cav.	Ivy Hill		5/23/1862
FLETCHER, Robert	Warrenton Rifles	Warrenton		
FLETCHER, Robert	Co. A 7th Va. Cav.	Ivy Hill	1/1/1839	4/20/1911
FLORANCE, George C.	not stated	Warrenton	4/19/1833	10/23/1884
FLORENCE, Robert G.	Co. H 4th Va. Cav.	Warrenton		
FLOWEREE, J.W.	SGT Co. E 3rd U.S. Cav.	Rectortown		
FLYNN, James B.	not stated	Warrenton	1839	1910
FLYNN, John F.	Co. E 43rd Bn. Va. Cav.		1841	
FOLLEN, Patrick	not stated	Warrenton		3/9/1887
FOSTER, James W.	CPT Co. A 43rd Bn. Va. Cav.	Foster	11/7/1808	4/10/1866
FOSTER, T. Hunton	Co. H 6th Va. Cav.(died as POW)	Foster	8/1864	
FOWLER, W.S.	COL, unit not stated	Warrenton	1810	1895
FRANCIS, Robert	not stated	Warrenton		
FRASIER, George	not stated	Ivy Hill	9/27/1844	5/20/1922
FRAXER, Robert	not stated	Warrenton		1908
FUGGITT, W. P. Gustavus	Co. A 43rd Bn. Va. Cav.		1832	after 1898
FURLONG, Edward P.	not stated	Warrenton	9/16/1854	5/12/1894
FURR, Charles W.	Co. K 8th Va. Cav.	Warrenton		
G. [GASKINS?] T.,	Black Horse Cav?	Warrenton		
GALLOWAY, C.F.	not stated	Warrenton	1842	
GARRISON, Wm. H.	Co. C 43rd Bn. Va. Cav.	Marshall	3/22/1844	8/4/1914
GASKINS, John A.	Black Horse Cav.	Warrenton	9/19/1854	3/14/1895
GEORGE, B.	Co. F 43rd Bn. Va. Cav.		1847	
GEORGE, Montgomery	Black Horse Cav.	George	9/13/1843	11/21/1892
GIBSON, Gilbert B.	Co A 6th Va. Cav.	Ivy Hill	4/19/1842	3/14/1907
GIBSON, Herman D.	not stated	Ivy Hill		10/29/1920
GIBSON, John N.	not stated	Ivy Hill	9/1/1835	5/10/1889
GIBSON, Joseph A.	Co. A 6th Va. Cav.	Ivy Hill	12/13/1833	7/13/1907
GIBSON, Madison Monroe	Co. E 43rd Bn. Va. Cav.		4/11/1829	6/29/1892
GIBSON, Wm. C.	Co. B 43rd Bn. Va. Cav.	Ivy Hill	11/18/1845	12/18/1925
GLASCOCK, Aquilla	Co. A 43rd Bn. Va. Cav.	Ivy Hill	5/16/1845	5/6/1865
GLASCOCK, J. Samuel	Co. A 7th Va. Cav.	Warrenton	1841	1932
GLASCOCK, John S.	Co. A 7th Va. Cav.	Warrenton	1/21/1823	6/11/1880
GLASCOCK, Minor	Beauregard Rifles	Marshall Community		11/22/1863
GOCHNAUER, Pembroke S.	8th Va. Regt	Ivy Hill	8/10/1841	10/16/1919
GOLDSMITH, John M.	CPT, unit not stated	Warrenton	1840	1903

Confederate Soldiers Buried in Fauquier County Cemeteries

Name	Military Unit	Cemetery	Date of Birth	Date of Death
GORDON, Charles	Black Horse Cav.	Grace Episcopal	1/7/1829	1/23/1897
GRAHAM, James M.	not stated	Warrenton	12/23/1844	6/13/1916
GRANT, John N.	not stated	Warrenton		4/10/1898
GRAY, Chas. Henry	Co. D 43rd Bn. Va. Cav.	Marshall	1843	10/4/1916
GRAY, Elias E.	not stated	Warrenton	1835	1899
GRAY, James A.	Co. B 43rd Bn. Va. Cav.			after 1895
GRAY, Thomas	not stated	Warrenton	8/7/1819	11/14/1907
GRAY, William F.	Brooke's Battery	Warrenton	6/15/1843	6/8/1898
GRAYSON, George W.	not stated	Warrenton	12/8/1835	6/22/1919
GREEN, Bernard	Black Horse Cav.	Warrenton	9/9/1842	9/19/1902
GREEN, Daniel H.	Co B 8th Va. Vol	Ivy Hill	11/10/1835	1/31/1917
GREEN, John W.	not stated	Ivy Hill	2/18/1844	10/6/1919
GREEN, Moses	not stated	Warrenton	7/1/1827	7/15/1919
GREEN, T. Richard	Black Horse Cav.	Warrenton	3/2/1838	11/9/1899
GRIMES, Joseph J.	Co. K 11th Rgt Va. Cav.	Ivy Hill	7/9/1839	8/3/1922
GROGAN, Robert Osborne	Co. D 43rd Bn. Va. Cav.	Remington	3/26/1830	3/20/1907
HACKLEY, Frank	Brooke's Battery?	Cedar Grove		
HACKLEY, Geo. Lewis	Co. G 43rd Bn. Va. Cav.		1848	
HALEY, R.D.	not stated	Ivy Hill	1844	1901
HAMILTON, Ferguson	SGT Black Horse Cav.	Ferguson	11/30/1843	11/21/1892
HAMILTON, George S.	not stated	Warrenton	2/21/1830	3/3/1912
HAMILTON, Hugh	Black Horse Cav.	Warrenton	1841	1928
HANMON, E.	North Carolina	Ivy Hill		
HANSBOROUGH, John	Black Horse Cav.	Warrenton		
HARRIS, James K.P.	5th TX Regt	Warrenton		9/18/1862
HARRISON, Daniel	Co. A 7th Va. Cav.	Warrenton		
HART, Robert A.	43rd Bn. Va. Cav.	Warrenton	12/8/1840	6/27/1909
HEFLIN, Albert	Co. I 11th Regt	Warrenton	1/11/1839	4/17/1908
HEFLIN, Robert F.	43rd Bn. Va. Cav.	Heflin - Moffett		1/1/1922
HELM, Edward	not stated	Warrenton	8/8/1844	5/1/1866
HELM, Erasmus	Black Horse Cav.	Warrenton	2/14/1839	9/13/1862
HELM, Franci M.	Co. H 43rd Bn. Va. Cav.	Warrenton	4/7/1848	3/4/1872
HELM, Harry	not stated	Warrenton		
HELM, William P.	Black Horse Cav.	Warrenton	5/26/1836	1/8/1922
HERRELL, Rodlph R	Co. A 43rd Bn. Va. Cav.	Cool Spring	1/21/1836	1/4/1922
HICKS, Robert I.	MAJ, unit not stated	Warrenton	12/31/1831	10/16/1920
HIGGINS, T.	North Carolina	Ivy Hill		
HOFFMAN, James M.	43rd Bn. Va. Cav.	Remington	6/5/1846	11/12/1913
HOLLAND, George L.	Black Horse Cav.	Orlean Methodist	1832	1927
HOLLAND, W.D.	unknown	Ivy Hill		
HOLTZCLAW, Charles	Black Horse Cav.	Warrenton	2/23/1846	5/23/1922
HOOD, A.J.	South Carolina	Ivy Hill		
HORNER, George B.	not stated	Warrenton	7/1/1833	2/7/1892
HORNER, Gustains B.	Co. D 43rd Bn. Va. Cav.	Warrenton		
HORNER, Richard H.	Co. A 7th Va. Cav.	Warrenton	8/20/1839	12/8/1899
HORNER, William E.	not stated	Warrenton	7/6/1823	10/30/1896
HOSKINS, Bradford Smith	43rd Bn. Va. Cav.	Greenwich Presbyterian	1842	6/2/1863
HOUGHENS, Thomas	not stated	Warrenton	3/10/1841	3/24/1913
HOUGHTON Charles H.	Co. B 6th Va. Cav.	Grove Presbyterian		
HUNTON, Emmett C.	Co. D 43rd Bn. Va. Cav.	Hunton		
HUNTON, Henry S.	Black Horse Cav.	Alton	7/2/1846	2/15/1881
HUNTON, Joseph G.	Black Horse Cav.	J. Hunton	7/25/1826	1/23/1906
HUNTON, William S.	Black Horse Cav.	Alton	3/1/1840	10/7/1896
HURXTHAL, William	not stated	Warrenton		
IDEN, Abner	Cpt Stribling's Battery	Ivy Hill		2/15/1910
IDEN, John	8th Va. Inf.		1838	3/13/1865
JAMES, Marshall	Black Horse Cav.	Warrenton	4/16/1839	10/31/1871

Confederate Soldiers Buried in Fauquier County Cemeteries

Name	Military Unit	Cemetery	Date of Birth	Date of Death
JAMES, T.F.	Black Horse Cav.	Cedar Grove	10/31/1832	8/20/1892
JEFFRIES, Enoch J.	Brooke's Battery	Warrenton	1818	1900
JEFFRIES, Frederick	Warrenton Rifles	Warrenton		
JEFFRIES, Joseph	Warrenton Rifles	Warrenton	1840	1919
JENKINS, Frank	not stated	Warrenton		
JENNINGS, W.	not stated	Warrenton		
JOHNSON, Horace	Black Horse Cav.	Cedar Grove		
JOHNSON, Perry M.	not stated	Warrenton	11/15/1845	4/10/1908
JOHNSON, Robert	not stated	Warrenton		
JOHNSON, Smith	Co. G 43rd Bn. Va. Cav.		1824	after 1902
JOHNSON, Thos.		Bealeton	9/17/1830	6/17/1902
JOHNSON, William	Black Horse Cav.	Warrenton	4/29/1824	11/25/1891
JOLLEY, Bushrod E.	not stated	Warrenton	1825	1888
JONES, Andrew J.	MAJ Co. I 11th Va. Vol.	Mt. Holly	1831	1908
JONES, Hilary P.	COL, unit not stated	Leeds	1833	1913
JONES, Strother S.	Bugler, Black Horse Cav.	Warrenton	4/5/1831	10/12/1916
JONES, Thomas T.	Co. A 9th Va. Cav.	Morrisville Methodist		
KEITH, Isham	Black Horse Cav.	Warrenton	9/5/1833	9/19/1902
KEITH, James	Co. H 4th Va. Cav.	probably Warrenton	9/7/1839	
KEITH, Jerome	Co. D 43rd Bn. Va. Cav.	probably Warrenton	1832	
KEMPER, George N.	Warrenton Rifles	Warrenton	12/14/1830	12/12/1913
KEMPER, Hugh T.	Warrenton Rifles	Warrenton	12/15/1832	8/28/1873
KERFOOT, William F.	Piedmont Rifles	Ivy Hill	12/12/1843	6/14/1890
KINCHELOE, Conrad B.	Co. B 8th Va. Vol	Ivy Hill		
KINCHELOE, Elisha D.	Piedmont Rifles	Ivy Hill	1837	1919
KING, A.F.	North Carolina	Ivy Hill		
KINSEY, Geo. Thos.	Co. C 43rd Bn. Va. Cav.	Rectortown	8/26/1846	4/2/1907
KIRBY, James A.	Co. H 6th Va. Cav.	probably Rectortown	1834	after 1902
KIRBY, James D.	CPT Warrenton Rifles	Warrenton	10/13/1838	11/10/1910
KIRKPATRICK, Enoch J.	not stated	Warrenton	4/10/1846	
KIRKPATRICK, Marcellus	Co. H 6th Va. Cav.	Marshall	3/20/1842	1929
KLIPSTEIN, Philip A.	PVT Co. D 8th Regt Va. Inf.	Marshall Community	12/18/1820	7/3/1905
KLOMAN, Edward F.	not stated	Warrenton	1838	1917
LAKE, Isaac N.	Co. D 4th Va. Cav.	Warrenton	8/9/1837	11/23/1905
LAKE, John L.	CPT Beauregard Rifles	Warrenton	10/19/1840	10/14/1913
LAKE, Ludwell	not stated	Warrenton		
LAKE, Luther Branwell	Co. B 8th Va. Cav.		1844	
LAKE, Wm. Henry	43rd Va. Cav.	Ivy Hill	11/7/1825	1/8/1897
LATHAM, John S.	not stated	Warrenton	1844	1918
LAWRENCE, James Montgomery	43rd Va. Cav.	Lawrence-Utterback	4/12/1845	7/21/1863
LAWS, John Shadrach	Co. C 43rd Va. Cav.	probably Paris	1845	
LEAR, Robert	Co. H 4th Va. Cav.	Warrenton		
LEE, Julian P.	CPT 43rd Bn. Va. Cav.	Warrenton	2/27/1840	5/2/1901
LEGG, James E.	Co. A 12th Va. Cav.	Ivy Hill	1835	7/15/1915
LEWIS, R.	Co. B 43rd Bn. Va. Cav.	Ivy Hill		
LEWIS, William H.	Black Horse Cav.	Church of Our Savior	8/18/1838	8/19/1903
LOMAX, Lindsay L.	MAJ GEN unit not stated	Warrenton	11/4/1835	5/28/1913
LUCIUS, Robert C.	Co. B 43rd Va. Cav.	Ivy Hill	1847	
LUNCEFORD, Benjamin R.	not stated	Warrenton	12/8/1837	8/4/1900
LUNCEFORD, Elijah Chilton	Co. E 43rd Va. Cav.	Marshall Community	1827 or 1830	1920
LUNCEFORD, James W.	Co. B 43rd Va. Cav.		1847	
LUNCEFORD, John H.	Co. B 43rd Va. Cav.	Westminster Presbyterian	4/26/1846	1/10/1904
LUNCEFORD, Thos. R.	Co. D 4th Va. Cav.	probably Warrenton	1825	
LYNN, Thaddeus	not stated	Warrenton	4/17/1846	7/26/1929
MADDOX, Robert E.	not stated	Warrenton	11/7/1843	4/26/1928
MADDUX, F. Webster	Co. A 7th Va. Cav.	Marshall Community	10/18/1838	7/18/1905
MADDUX, Henry "Cab"	43rd Bn. Va. Cav.	Marshall Community	7/17/1848	6/24/1901

Confederate Soldiers Buried in Fauquier County Cemeteries

Name	Military Unit	Cemetery	Date of Birth	Date of Death
MADDUX, James Henry	Co. E 43rd Va. Cav.	Warrenton	3/14/1818	4/2/1898
MADDUX, Thomas W.	Co. A 7th Va. Cav.	Marshall Community	1841	1864
MANN, William J.	PVT 2nd Cav. Richmond Howitzers	Ivy Hill	2/23/1843	2/5/1880
MANUEL, Lucian M.	Co. A 12th Va. Cav.	Morrisville Methodist	1845	1907
MANYETTE, Edward A.	not stated	Warrenton	1847	1927
MARKELL, George H.	Black Horse Cav.	Warrenton	11/25/1831	2/11/1895
MARKELL, Milton W.	Co. B 3rd Va. Inf.	Warrenton		
MARR, John Q.	CPT Warrenton Rifles	Warrenton	8/27/1825	6/1/1861
MARSHALL, James Edward	Co. D 43rd Va. Cav.		1831	
MARSHALL, James M.	Black Horse Cav.	Warrenton	9/14/1842	9/6/1862
MARSHALL, R.I. Taylor	Warrenton Rifles	Warrenton		1861
MARSHALL, Robert A.	Trp H, L Regt, MO. Cav.	Herndon		
MARSHALL, Robert M.	not stated	Leeds	7/12/1845	10/12/1863
MARSHALL, William	CPT unit not stated	Leeds	1838	1928
MARSTELLER, LaClaire A.	Black Horse Cav.	Warrenton	1839	1917
MARTIN, George W.	Black Horse Cav.	Martin	2/2/1844	2/24/1898
MARTIN, James R.	Black Horse Cav.	Warrenton		
MARTIN, R.E.	SGT Black Horse Cav.	Martin		
MASON, John Stevens	Co.D 43rd Va. Cav./CoA 17th Va. Inf.	Church of Our Savior	1840	1918
McCABE, John H.I.	not stated	Warrenton	11/4/1845	10/14/1935
McCONCHIE, Benjamin F.	SGT Co. K 17th Va. Cav.	Warrenton	1827	1884
McCONCHIE, John	Kemper Brigade	Mt. Holly	5/16/1841	11/6/1919
McCORMICK, Joe B.	Brooke's Battery	Warrenton	10/27/1844	3/22/1913
McDANIEL, A.	North Carolina	Ivy Hill		
McDONALD, Elias H.	Black Horse Cav.	Ivy Hill	2/4/1844	1/4/1931
McILHANEY, John	not stated	Warrenton		
McINTOSH, B.F.	not stated	Warrenton		
McINTOSH, Charles R.	Warrenton Rifles	Warrenton	1838	1922
McLEAREN, Thomas C.	AWOL Warrenton Rifles	Warrenton	2/10/1819	11/12/1886
McRAE, John Hampden	MAJ unit not stated	Ivy Hill	1824	1904
MILLER, G. Allen	Beauregard Rifles	Miller	7/1/1830	9/13/1914
MITCHELL, Philip	not stated	Warrenton		
MITCHELL, Robert	SGT Black Horse Cav.	Baldwin Ridge	4/10/1833	3/27/1915
MITTIER, C.	Virginia	Ivy Hill		
MOFFETT, Daniel Jackson	Co. A 43rd Bn. Va. Cav.	Remington	5/4/1844	10/18/1927
MOORE, George J.	Kemper Brigade	Remington	2/15/1841	11/6/1919
MOORE, Richard S.	Stribling's Battery	Orlean	1844	1897
MOSBY, John S.	Colonel 43rd Bn. Va. Cav.	Warrenton	12/6/1833	5/30/1916
MOUNTJOY, John W.	Wise's Dragoons	Warrenton	6/5/1838	12/11/1922
MOUNTJOY, R.P.	CPT Co. D 43rd Bn. Va. Cav.	Warrenton	3/15/1842	11/27/1864
NALLS, Enoch	Co. E 43rd Bn. Va. Cav.		1846	after 1893
NALLS, James K.	Co. E 43rd Bn. Va. Cav.		1845	
NELSON, George H.	not stated	Warrenton	1839	1904
NELSON, Joseph H.	43rd Bn. Va. Cav.	Warrenton	1839	1904
NELSON, Thomas A.	SGT Co. F 12th Va. Inf.	Templeman - Nelson		
NORTH, James H.	CPT CSN	Warrenton	9/17/1813	8/1893
OLINGER, Grayson E.	Brooke's Battery	Cedar Grove	11/11/1823	9/16/1920
OLIVER, Peyton L.	not stated	Warrenton	2/25/1835	6/15/1889?
OVERBY, W.T.	Co. D 43rd Bn. Va. Cav.	Anderson		9/23/1864
OWENS, Jr. Cuthbert	Co. A 7th Va. Cav.	Owens	7/12/1843	8/11/1864
OWENS, Simon K.	Piedmont Rifles	Owens	3/8/1830	1/18/1899
OWENS, William M.	not stated	Owens	2/22/1841	1/10/1864
PACK, Benjamin J.	Co. C, Hampton Legion, SC	Warrenton (common grave)	9/18/1862	
PALMER, F. Gendroy	MAJ Holcombe Legion SC	Warrenton		
PARKINSON, John W.	Warrenton Rifles	Warrenton	1817	1904
PATTIE, D.M.	not stated	Warrenton	6/6/1823	1/19/1894
PATTIE, Horace	not stated	Warrenton	11/22/1823	1/7/1885

Confederate Soldiers Buried in Fauquier County Cemeteries

Name	Military Unit	Cemetery	Date of Birth	Date of Death
PATTIE, Otha H.W.	not stated	Warrenton	10/17/1844	9/9/1877
PAYNE, Alexander D.	43rd Bn. Va. Cav.	Warrenton	9/30/1837	3/8/1893
PAYNE, Arthur	Stribling's Battery	Orlean		
PAYNE, Bernard	Stribling's Battery	Orlean		
PAYNE, Berryman	4th Va. Cav.	Orlean		
PAYNE, Charles E.F.	not stated	Warrenton	3/8/1840	7/9/1880
PAYNE, Daniel J.	Kemper Brigade	Payne (Chestnut Lawn)	1/31/1825	2/9/1900
PAYNE, Edward A.	Co. A 7th Va. Cav.	Orlean Methodist	2/16/1838	11/27/1863
PAYNE, Fielding	LT 8th Va.	Orlean		
PAYNE, Hugh G.	Co. A 7th Va. Cav.	Orlean		
PAYNE, Inman	not stated	Warrenton	8/28/1822	10/10/1905
PAYNE, J. Rice	not stated	Orlean		10/21/1914
PAYNE, James W.	Co. A 7th Va. Cav.	Orlean		
PAYNE, Jesse	Stribling's Battery	Orlean		
PAYNE, John D.	Black Horse Cav.	Warrenton	4/22/1823	12/18/1881
PAYNE, John S.	MAJ 5th Cav. U.S. Army	Warrenton	1844	1895
PAYNE, John T.	Co. A. 7th Va. Cav.	Orlean		
PAYNE, Lafayette	Co. A 7th Va. Cav.	Orlean		
PAYNE, Lycurgus	49th Va.	Orlean		
PAYNE, Marshall	9th Va. Cav.	Warrenton	1824	1887
PAYNE, Mason B.	Co. A 7th Va. Cav.	Orlean		
PAYNE, Minor	4th Va. Cav.	Orlean		
PAYNE, Richard C.	Co. A 7th Va. Cav.	Orlean		
PAYNE, Jr. Richards	Warrenton Rifles	Warrenton	9/30/1837	3/8/1893
PAYNE, Robert J.	Co. A 7th Va. Cav.	Orlean		
PAYNE, Robert W.	Co. A 7th Va. Cav.	Orlean		
PAYNE, Thomas	Stribling's Battery	Orlean		
PAYNE, Thomas H.	Co. A 7th Va. Cav.	Orlean		
PAYNE, Upton	Co. A 7th Va. Cav.	Orlean		
PAYNE,	SGT Co. A 7th Va. Cav.	Orlean	4/19/1841	9/11/1935
PAYNE, William E.	Stribling's Battery	Orlean		
PAYNE, William F.	not stated	Warrenton	1/27/1830	3/29/1904
PAYNE, William H.	Stribling's Battery	Orlean		
PAYNE, William Winter	Co. E 43rd Bn. Va. Cav.	Warrenton	12/20/1835	2/4/1889
PAYNE, William W.	not stated	Warrenton	1/8/1807	9/2/1871
PAYNE, Wilson V.	Co. A th Va. Cav.	Orlean		
PEARSON, H. Clay	Co. C 43rd Bn. Va. Cav.	Cool Spring Methodist	8/5/1844	1/3/1933
PEARSON, John W.	Co. C 43rd Bn. Va. Cav.	Marshall	1/25/1843	9/2/1923
PEARSON, Taylor L.	Co. C 43rd Bn. Va. Cav.	Orlean	11/7/1845	5/1/1878
PEARSON, W.G.	Co. C 43rd Bn. Va. Cav.			after 1909
PIERCE, James W.	Lt Co. B 8th Va. Vol	Ivy Hill	3/10/1863	
PILCHER, Theodore C.	Black Horse Cav.	Midland	3/20/1844	12/7/1917
POLLOCK, Thomas G.	ADJ GEN Kemper Brigade	Warrenton		7/3/1863
PRIEST, James G.	Black Horse Cav.	Warrenton	9/20/1833	8/30/1874
RAMEY, John Mason	Co. E 43rd Bn. Va. Cav.	Foster	10/27/1844	3/24/1907
RANDOLPH, Buckner M.	Co. C 49th Va. Inf.	Grace Episcopal	7/23/1842	8/11/1903
RANDOLPH, Robert	COL Black Horse Cav.	Randolph	11/18/1835	8/12/1864
RANDOLPH, William F.	CPT Jackson's Bodyguards	Warrenton	12/7/1831	7/31/1914
REDD, Polk Dallas	Co. E 43rd Bn. Va. Cav.	Ivy Hill	1844	1919
REED, John	Co. A 6th Va. Cav.	Warrenton	4/1/1826	9/19/--
RICE, S.S.	Virginia	Ivy Hill		
RILEY, John F.	Co. C 8th Va. Inf.	Morrisville Methodist		
RISDON, William J.	Warrenton Rifles	Warrenton		3/27/1898
ROBERTSON, Walter H. Rev.	Co. C 43rd Bn. Va. Cav.	Warrenton	1841	7/2/1903
ROBINSON, Thomas H.	Co. C 49th Regt 26th Inf.	Cedar Grove	5/22/1842	6/15/1916
ROBINSON, William B.	not stated	Warrenton	7/6/1842	4/1/1919
ROBINSON, William H.	Co. A 8th Va. Cav.	Ivy Hill		

Confederate Soldiers Buried in Fauquier County Cemeteries

Name	Military Unit	Cemetery	Date of Birth	Date of Death
ROGERS, William Wagoner	Co A 7th Va. Cav.	Ivy Hill		1863
ROSE, Alexander F.	not stated	Warrenton	5/27/1846	4/29/1935
ROSS, John	not stated	Warrenton	6/24/1816	6/22/1902
ROYSTON, James W.	Co. F 43rd Bn. Va. Cav.	Thumb Run Baptist	1835	
ROYSTON, John W.	Co. G 43rd Bn. Va. Cav.		1831	
ROYSTON, Z.V.	Co. B 8th Va. Vol./43rd Bn. Va. Cav.	Marshall Community	4/21/33	12/14/28
RUCKER, William A.	not stated	Ivy Hill	1840	1928
RUSH, R.H.	not stated	Warrenton		
RUSSELL, John W.	Co H 6th Va. Cav./Co. C 43rd Va. Cav	Marshall	6/4/1821	2/1/1864
RUSSELL, Thos. Alfred	Co H 1st Md./Co. F 43rd Bn. Va. Cav	Orlean	1/28/1841	12/29/1919
SAUNDERS, John A.	Co. D 43rd Bn. Va. Cav.	Warrenton	1845	
SAUNDERS, Richard	Co. D 8th Va. Cav.	Warrenton		
SAUNDERS, Thomas E.	Co. D 43rd Bn. Va. Cav.	Warrenton	1822	1906
SCHWAB, Antonio	Black Horse Cav.	Warrenton	1834	1906
SCOTT, John	43rd Bn. Va. Cav.	Warrenton	4/23/1820	5/7/1907
SCOTT, Robert S.	not stated	Warrenton	4/26/1822	2/6/1914
SCOTT, Robert T.	CPT Beauregard Rifles	Warrenton	3/10/1834	8/5/1897
SCOTT, Turner N.	2LT Wise's Dragoons	Warrenton		
SEALOCK, John Thos.	Co. A 43rd Va. Cav./Co. D Fauq Art.	Linden	1836	2/1908
SETTLE, Thomas L.	Surgeon Co. A 7th Va. Cav.	Ivy Hill	1836	1920
SHACKELFORD, B. Howard	Warrenton Rifles	Warrenton	11/10/1819	5/18/1870
SHACKLETT, Edward	Co. C 43rd Bn. Va. Cav.	Cool Spring Methodist	12/12/1845	1/10/1917
SHEFFIELD, A.M.	Georgia	Ivy Hill		
SHEPPARD, Hamilton	not stated	Warrenton		
SIMS, Matthew A.	not stated	Warrenton	12/20/1841	1/12/1917
SISK, James H.	Co. F 43rd Bn. Va. Cav.		1847	after 1898
SKINKER, William K.	Black Horse Cav.	Warrenton	9/22/1839	5/27/1918
SLACK, John Thos.	Co. C 43rd Bn. Va. Cav.	Ivy Hill	7/17/1841	9/9/1907
SLATER, George M.	43rd Bn. Va. Cav.	Ivy Hill	12/25/1840	1/2/1923
SMITH, Albert G.	MAJ 38th Va. Regt	Alton	1/4/1834	5/4/1892
SMITH, Channing M.	Black Horse Cav.	Emmanuel Episcopal	5/22/1842	11/8/1932
SMITH, Charles A.	not stated	Warrenton		
SMITH, David	LT Co. H 49th Va. Vol.	Alton	6/8/1842	5/30/1864
SMITH, Edwin	Warrenton Rifles	Warrenton		
SMITH, George H	8th Va. Infantry Co. C	Smith	1826	1919
SMITH, Henry	Black Horse Cav.	Alton	7/2/1846	2/15/1881
SMITH, Isaac E.	Black Horse Cav.	Alton	7/29/1827	5/13/1872
SMITH, John	Black Horse Cav.?	Warrenton		
SMITH, Norman E.	CPT 43rd Bn. Va. Cav.	Alton	5/24/1845	8/24/1863
SMITH, Thomas B.	Co. A 7th Va. Cav.	Ivy Hill	3/28/18--	9/15/1939
SMITH, Thomas T.	CPT Warrenton Rifles	Warrenton	3/8/1841	6/21/1918
SMITH, William A.	Co. H 49th Va. Vol.	Alton	6/5/1840	5/30/1862
SMITH, William R.	LT Black Horse Cav.	Alton	1/12/1836	1/9/1864
SOWERS, J. Richard	43rd Bn. Va. Cav.	Warrenton	12/13/1837	7/31/1914
SPILLMANN, John R.	Ord. Dept.	Warrenton		
SPILMAN, William M.	Black Horse Cav.	Warrenton	12/3/1893	
STAUNTON, Dr.	not stated	Warrenton		
STEPP, William G.	not stated	Warrenton	11/29/1823	4/23/1911
STRIBLING, Robert M.	COL Stribling's Battery	Leeds	1833	1914
STROTHER, Alfred M.	Co. A 43rd Bn. Va. Cav.	Nally - Strother	4/1/1813	10/25/1912
STROTHER, James M.	Co. A 43rd Bn. Va. Cav.		1837	after 1898
STROTHER, John W.	Co. A 6th Va. Cav.	Ivy Hill	6/1835	11/9/1915
STROTHER, Lewis	12th Va. Cav.	Ivy Hill	1839	1910
TALLIAFERRO, John K.	43rd Bn. Va. Cav.	Remington	5/4/1844	10/18/1927
TARRAINES, S.	North Carolina	Ivy Hill		
TAYLOR, George N.	Black Horse Cav.	Taylor	7/19/1823	4/3/1902
TEMPLEMAN, Madison Monroe	Co. H 43rd Bn. Va. Cav.	Warrenton		5/3/1863

Confederate Soldiers Buried in Fauquier County Cemeteries

Name	Military Unit	Cemetery	Date of Birth	Date of Death
THORTON, Thomas	not stated	Warrenton	5/14/1843	7/11/1910
TONGUE, Johnzie	Black Horse Cav.	Warrenton	2/16/1843	1/27/1925
TONGUE, Thos. Wm.	Co. D 43rd Bn. Va. Cav.	Warrenton	9/16/1846	1/22/1918
TOWNSEND, James E.	CPT Co. G. 17th Va. Inf.	Ivy Hill		
TRIPLETT, Albert		unknown		3/27/1862
TRIPLETT, B. Addison	43rd Bn. Va. Cav.	Ivy Hill	2/28/1837	12/21/1929
TRIPLETT, James W.	not stated	Ivy Hill	7/11/1907	
TRIPLETT, William H.	Black Horse Cav.	Templeman	1/25/1833	1/24/1896
TRUSSELL, Howard	not stated	Ivy Hill	8/3/1833	10/24/1903
TULLOSS, Joseph D.	SGT Brooke's Battery	Grove Presbyterian	3/8/1824	8/23/1909
TURNER, Bradshaw B.	Black Horse Cav.	Church of Our Savior	10/12/1841	2/14/1910
TURNER, John R.	Black Horse Cav.	Warrenton	4/30/1838	4/7/1918
TURNER, Thomas B.	43rd Bn. Va. Cav.	Turner (Kinloch)		4/29/1863
UNKNOWN	Union & Confed.	near Woods Cem.		
UNKNOWN		Cedar Grove		
UNKNOWN	Union	near Smith Cem.		
UNKNOWN (2)		Ivy Hill		
UTTERBACK, Addison W.	CPT Brooke's Battery	Warrenton		2/23/1893
VAUGH, Franklin T.	Co. F 43rd Bn. Va. Cav.	Church of Our Savior	1845	3/6/1916
WALDEN, Gabe	Union Army	Green		
WALDEN, Richard E.	Warrenton Rifles	Warrenton	1841	1905
WALDEN, Thomas	not stated	Cedar Grove		
WALKER, James Mason	Co. C 43rd Va. Cav.	Marshall	1837	1873
WALKER, John T.	not stated	Warrenton	9/5/1845	3/14/1863
WALKER, Lewis Franklin	Co. E 43rd Va. Cav.	Lawler - Walker	1847	1928
WALTON, J.B.	not stated	Walton		
WARD, Henry C.	LT Fauquier Guards	Warrenton	5/10/1819	7/21/1861
WARD, John Dr.	unit not stated	Warrenton	6/26/1826	4/17/1885
WEAVER, John A.	not stated	Warrenton	5/8/1839	2/17/1914
WEAVER, Mason A.	CPL Warrenton Rifles	Orlean		
WEAVER, Richard A.	Warrenton Rifles	Warrenton		5/15/1862
WEEDON, Robert	not stated	Warrenton	3/28/1820	4/9/1906
WEEKS, William H.	Black Horse Cav.	Warrenton	3/9/1833	4/29/1902
WELCH, W.R.	SGT Wise's Dragoons	Marshall Community	5/10/1831	10/7/1915
WELLS, James H.	not stated	Warrenton	5/13/1833	10/21/1905
WHITE, Hugh W.	8th Va. Inf./Co. B 43rd Bn. Va. Cav.	Church of Our Savior	1839	after 1909
WHITE, John W.	CPL Brooke's Battery	Warrenton	9/30/1835	10/9/1902
WILLINGHAM, Alexander	Co. I 11th Va. Inf.	Cedar Grove	1823	1/22/1894
WINE, James	Brooke's Battery	Warrenton		
WINGFIELD, Thomas S.	not stated	Warrenton	1813	1897
WITHERS, S. Melville	Black Horse Cav.	Warrenton	1844	1936
WITHERSPOON, John C.	CPT unit not stated	Mt Holly Baptist		11/8/1863
WOODWARD, Luke	CPT Co. F 43rd Bn. Va. Cav.	Woodward	3/6/1845	12/10/1934
WOODZEL, George	Black Horse Cav.	Warrenton	1842	1933
YATES, Benjamin B.	not stated	Warrenton	3/13/1843	3/5/1929
YATES, Henry C.	not stated	Warrenton	9/11/1844	5/8/1895
YEATMAN, William H.	Co. C 47th Va. Regt	Peake	1841	1913

* moved to family estate in St. Louis, Missouri

Confederate Soldiers Buried at the Memorial Wall in Warrenton Cemetery

ALABAMA

ALLISON, Wm B. Co. E. (F), 4 Rgt. Died: Oct 1 (15), 1862
CHAMBERS, Robert T. Co. D, 4 Rgt. Died: Sept 18, 1862
DAVENPORT, Edward H. Co. H, 4 Rgt. Died: Sept 4, 1862
FENNELL, W. Henry Co.B, 15 Rgt. Died: Dec 3, 1861
FRANKLIN, Gillis Co. I (F), 11 Rgt. Died: Sept 24, 1862
FRANKLIN, J. F. Co. A. 11 Rgt. Died: Sept 13, 1862
GILL, T. A. Co. H., 15 Rgt. Died: Dec 8, 1861 (GILL William, Jr. CSR's only listing found)
GRIMES, J. Co. E, 15 Rgt. Died: Dec 23, 1861
HARRISON, Hartwell Btry Died: Nov 1, 1861
HOOPER, M. W. Co. A, 15 Rgt. Died: Dec 27, 1861
JAMES, W. A. Co. K, 14 Rgt. Died: Sept 8, 1862
JONES, Felix Co. G, 12 Rgt. Died: Nov 30, 1861
MASON, T. S. Co. G, 5 Rgt. Died: Dec 14, 1861
McGILVRAY, W. A. Co. D, 15 Rgt. Died: Nov. 29, 1861
MIZELL, J. W. Co. E. 15 Rgt. Died: Dec 8, 1861
NEWMAN, Thomas Co. B, 4 Rgt. Died: Sept 29, 1862
PEOPLES, Thomas Co. I, 6 Rgt. Died: Dec 18, 1861
PETERMAN, Wm. S. Co. K, 6 Rgt. Died: Nov 1, 1861
PURIFOY, William D. Co. C, 44 Rgt. Died: Oct 25, 1862
RAMEY, Wm. H. Co. C, 14 Rgt. Died: Sept 20, 1862
ROBERTS, A. J. Co. I, 48 Rgt. Died: Sept 11, 1862
ROBBINSON, Thomas J. Co. D, 4 Rgt. Died: Sept 6, 1862
ROLIN, Zacharia A. Co. A, 44 Rgt. Died: Oct 22, 1862
SINGLETON, John T. Btry Died: Sept 7, 1861
TARVAR, Wm. H. Co. B, 15 Rgt. Died: Nov 3, 1861
TERRY, James Co. K, 12 Rgt. Died: Nov 20, 1861
THOMAS, James H. Co. E, 4 Rgt. Died: Sept 8, 1862
TRAWEEK, Israel C. Co. A, 44 Rgt. Died: Sept 5, 1862
TURNER, Daniel M Co. C, 4 Rgt. Died: Sept 4 (7), 1862
WALTERS, William E. Co. I, 15 Rgt. Died: Feb 6, 1862
WATSON, Samuel Co. IL 4 Rgt. Died: Sept 20, 1862
WEST, J. J. (Jacob) Co. E, 15 Rgt. Died: Dec 1, 1861
WHITLOW, J. J. Co. C, 9 Rgt. Died: Dec 13, 1861
WILLIAMS, Wm. J. Co. H, 11 Rgt. Died: Dec 12, 1861

FLORIDA

CRIBBS, Austen S. Co. G, 5 Rgt. Died: Sept 28, 1862
GOODMAN, R. Co. A, 8 Rgt. Died: Sept 13-15, 1862
LEE, Charles Co. H, 8 Rgt. Discharged Oct 10, 1862
MANSON, J. W. (J. M.) Co. A, 5 Rgt. Died: Sept 3, 1862
MOORE, C. (Simeon) Co. K, 5 Rgt. Died: Sept 9, 1862
STARLING, Thomas Co. K (I), 8 Rgt. Died: Sept 11, 1862

GEORGIA

ADAMS, J. L. Co. G, 7 Rgt. Discharged: Nov 20, 1861
AKINS, (AIKENS), L.S. Co. I, 9 Rgt. Died: Oct 24, 1862
ARRINGTON, James T. Co. E, 9 Rgt. Died: Sept 12, 1862
AUSTIN, Joseph A. Co. H, 7 Rgt. Died: Oct 11, 1862
BAGGETT, James M. Co. D, 7 Rgt. Died: Nov 19, 1861
BALDY, Samuel Hamilton Co. I, 8 Rgt. Died: Sept. 2, 1862
BALLEW, George E. Co. K, 14 Rgt. Died: Oct 3, 1862
BARNETT, Thomas A. Co. C, 11 Rgt. Died: Sept 14, 1862
BOICE (BOYCE), James R. Co. F, 18 Rgt. Died: Sept 18, 1862
BRAMBLETT, Nathan Co. C, 11 Rgt. Died: Sept 7, 1862
BRASWELL, Aldred T. Co. A, 20 Rgt. Discharged: Oct 21, 1862
BREEDLOVE, Hiram Co. D, 20 Rgt. Died: Sept 2, 1861
BROOKS, W. J. Co. I, 7 Rgt. Died: Nov 22, 1861
BROOME, Asgill Co. D, 18 Rgt. Died: Nov 8, 1862
BROWN, R. A. Co. G, 7 Rgt. Died: Sept 28, 1862
BROWN, J. B. E. Co. G, 7 Rgt. Died: Aug 31, 1861
BROWN, Wm. D. Co. I, 9 Rgt. Died: Dec 29, 1861

Confederate Soldiers Buried at the Memorial Wall in Warrenton Cemetery

BROWN, W. J. Co. G, 19 Rgt. Died: Dec 10, 1861
BURCH, Thomas Co. C 1, 48 Rgt. Died: Sept 16, 1862
CALLAGHAN, Thomas Co. I, 9 Rgt. Died: Oct 12, 1862
CANNON, Nathaniel W. Co. 4, 49 Rgt. Died: Sep 30, 1862
CHAMPION, George M. Co. A., 17 Rgt. Died: Sept 22, 1862
CHISHOLM, W. P. Co. A, 19 Rgt. Died: Oct 15, 1862
CLARK, Joseph J. A. Co. H, 9 Rgt. Died: Sept 19, 1861
CLEVELAND, John H. Co. D,- 7 Rgt. Died: Oct 6, 1862
COBB, Wm. Daniel Co. A, 11 Rgt. Died: Oct 19, 1862
COKER, O. N. Co. I, 3 Rgt. Died: on/or after Sept. 30, 1862
COLLINS, M. S. Co. E, 18 Rgt. Died: Sep 5, 1862
COLEMAN, James K. Co. E. 18 (48) Rgt. Died: Sept 15, 1862
COLMAN, John Co. E, 18 Rgt. Died: (not given)
CONN, George W. Co. F, 18 Rgt. Died: July 15, 1862
CONNELLY, James A. Co. G. 9 Rgt. Died: Sep 4, 1862
CRISLER, T. J. Co. E, 22 Rgt. Discharged: Oct 8, 1862
DAVIS, Benjamin F. Co. B, 20 Rgt. Died: Sept. 12, 1862
DAVIS, William F. Co. A, 48 Rgt. Died: Oct 6, 1862
DEAN, Thomas Co. D, 20 Rgt. Died: Dec 31, 1861
DENSON, John M. Co. E, 9 Rgt. Died: Sept 22, 1862
DENTON, James Co. A, 48 Rgt. Died: Sept 8, 1862
DOZIER, L. P. Co. B, 48 Rgt. Died: Sept 4, 1862
DYE, Wm. H. Co. K, 2 Rgt. Died: Nov. 18, 1861
ESLEY, (ESPEY) James A. Co. C, 18 Rgt. Died: Sept. 11, 1862
ESTIS, T.C. Co. E, 8 Rgt. Discharged Oct 12, 1862
FAULKNER, Wm. Co. G, 9 Rgt. Discharged Oct 12, 1862
FERAN-TERAN Co. I, 1st Rgt. Died: Sept 2 (7), 1862 (illegible name)
FIELD, A. F. Co. I, 19 Rgt. Discharged Feb 16, 1862
FIELDS, Allen Co. A, 17 Rgt. Died: Oct 23, 1862
FREEMAN, John W. Co. C, 1st Rgt. Died: Nov 22, 1861
FRITH, Joseph Co. I, 11 Rgt. Died: Oct 5, 1861
FUSSELL, James P. Co. F, 1st Rgt. Died: Sept 11, 1862
GAREY, (Gary) Micajah A. Co. B, 7 Rgt. Died: Nov 24, 1861
GILLEY, Wm. J. Co. F, 7 Rgt. Died: Sept 14, 1862
GOWER, James C. Co. A, 11 Rgt. Died: Sept 21, 1862
GREESON, Joseph A. Co. K, 21 Rgt. Died: Nov 1862
GREY, J. M. Co. C, 27 Rgt. Died: Sept 23, 1862
HANDLEBERRY, J. Co. K., 28 Rgt. Died: Jan 27, 1862 (Hanberry, Hezekiah (cannot confirm match))
HARRIS, J. M. Co. H, 9 Rgt. Died: Sept 20, 1862
HARRIS, N. L. Co. G, 11 Rgt. Died: Sept 15, 1862
HARVILLE, John T. Co. B, 45 Rgt. Discharged: Oct 17, 1862
HAYS, R. W. (Robert) Co. G, 17 Rgt. Died: Oct 13, 1862
HENRY, Andrew J. Co. B, 18 Rgt. Died: July 15, 1862
HERRING, Robert A. Co. H, 9 Rgt. Died: Sept 14(17), 1861
HICKS, T. A. Co. A, 18 Rgt. Died: Sept 27, 1862
HIGHTOWER, Joseph Co. B, 2 Rgt. Died: Oct. 14, 1862
HIGHTOWER, William E. Co. B, 20 Rgt. Died: Sept 22, 1862
HILL, Hilliard J. Transferred to 7 Rgt. Discharged: Aug 3,'63
HINDMAN, David I. (J) Co. A, 7 Rgt. Discharged Oct 10, 1862
HOOD, John T. Co. F, 20 Rgt. Died: Sept 9, 1862
HOWARD, John R. Co. C, 18 Rgt. Died: Sept 11, 1862
HOWELL, Joseph M. Co. D, 15 Rgt. Died: Dec 19, 1862
HUMPHRIES, Shadrach H. Co. B, 35 Rgt. Died: Sept. 25, 1862
JAMESON, William T. Co. B, 38 Rgt. Died: Sept 21, 1862
JARRETT, D. L. Co. C, 18 Rgt. Died: Sept 6, 1862
JEFFRIES, Frederich Co. K, 17 Rgt. Died: No date
JENKINS, Frank (George F.) Co. K, 17 Rgt. Died: No date
JOHNSON, B. D. Co. C, 1st Rgt. Died: Sept 1862
JOHNSON, Frank Co. B, 9 Rgt. Discharged Oct 8, 1862
JOHNSON, Wm. T. Co. E, 20 Rgt. Discharged Oct 10, 1862
JONES, James H. Co. K, 18 Rgt. Died: Oct 11, 1862
JONES, Nathan David Co. H, 9 Rgt. Died: Aug 20, 1861
KEITH, Nathaniel S. Co. A, 11 Rgt. Died: Sept 30, 1862
KEYS (KAYS), J. Co. E, 1st Rgt. Discharged Oct 10, 1862

Confederate Soldiers Buried at the Memorial Wall in Warrenton Cemetery

KILGO, W. L. (Wade Co. B, 9 Rgt. Died: Sept 3, 1862
KING, Wm. J. Co. A, 17 Rgt. Died: Sept 30, 1862
LAMAR, L. (Lafayette) Co. G, 15 Rgt. Died: Nov 16, 1861
LANE, J. D. Co. K, 11 Rgt. Discharged Dec 1, 1861
LANE, Marcus A. Co. O Died: Nov 5, 1862
LANE, Thomas Co. K, 9 Rgt. Died: Jan 1863
LEWIS, R. S. (Robert) Co. K 48 Rgt. Died: Oct 25, 1862
LIVELY, Henry H. Co. E, 7 Rgt. Died: Feb1862
LOWE, J. F. Co. A, 17 Rgt. Died: Sept 19, 1862
LOYD (LLOYD), B. F. Co. G, 22 Rgt. Died: Sept 1, 1862
MARTIN, George W. Co. I, 9 Rgt. Died: Dec 24, 1861
MASON, J Co. K, 18 Rgt. Died: Sept 18, 1862
MATTHEWS, James R. Co. I, 48 Rgt. Died: Sept 4 or Sept 17, 1862 (CSR)
McCONNELL, J. W. (Wiley J.) Co. I, 7 Rgt. Died: Nov. 19, 1861
McDANIEL, Daniel R. Co. F, 35 Rgt. Discharged Oct 12, 1862
McELVIE (McELWEE), John Co. B, 7 Rgt. Died: Sept 23, 1862
McNAIR, John T. Co. D, 17 Rgt. Died: Sept 23, 1862
McNEIL (McNEAL) Lucius Co. H, 9 Rgt. Died: Oct 12, 1861
McPHERSON, Angus Campbell Co. K, 7 Rgt. Died: Oct 12, 1862
McVICKERS, James A. Co. I, 19 Rgt. Died: Sept 20/23, 1862
MERCER, Harmon S. Co. D, 9 Rgt. Died: Sept 30, 1862
MERRILL, Thomas J. Co. F, 19 Rgt. Died: Sept 25, 1861
MESSER, B. H. Co. D, 17 Rgt. Died: Sept 26, 62
MILES, J. E. (James) Co. H, 18 Rgt. Died: Sept 18, 1862
MOAT, W. W. Co. A, 48 Rgt. Died: Oct 13, 1862
MONTGOMERY, W. G. Co. G, 17 Rgt. Discharged: Sept 29, 1862
MORRIS, Isham Co. I, 19 Rgt. Died: Dec 11, 1861
MORROW, John Co. K, 18 Rgt. Died: Sept 17, 1862
NEWTON, Isaac T. A. Co. K 9 Rgt. Died: Oct 15, 1861
ODEMES (ODOMS)S. Co. B, 20 Rgt. Died: Dec 31, 1861
OGLETREE, R. L. Co. D, 49 Rgt. Died: Nov 15, 1862
PATILLO, Benjamin F. Co. K, 22 Rgt. Died: Sept 1, 1862
PEAK, William S. Co. A, 7 Rgt. Died: Sept 26, 1862
PEARCE, John Co. B, 7 Rgt. Died: Oct 20, 1862
PEELING (PILING) F. S. Co. I, 20 Rgt. Discharged Oct 10, 1862
PENLAND, G. W. Co. D, 11 Rgt. Died: Oct 16, 1862
PHILLIPS, John A. Co. A, 19 Rgt. Died: Dec 25, 1861
PITTMAN, John G. D. Co. I, 11 Rgt. Died: Sept 20, 1861
POWELL, W. B. (Wm) Co. E, 9 Rgt. Died: Sept 25, 1862
PRICE, B. F. Co. E, 8 Rgt. Died: Sept 14, 1861
RAMEY, (RAINEY), Wm. Co. H, 9 Rgt. Died: Sept 15, 1862
RICHARDSON, Wm. C. Co. K, 2 Rgt. Died: Oct 23, 1861
RIDLEY, W. J. (Joseph W.) Co. I, 18 Rgt. Died: Oct 17, 1862
ROBERTSON, James B. Co. H, 1st Rgt. Died: Sept 20, 1862
RODGERS, James M. Co. C, 48 Rgt. Died: Sept 15, 1862
ROGERS, A. G. (Alex) Co. K, 19 Rgt. Died: Dec 10, 1861
RUTH, W. A. "Dock" Co. B, 11 Rgt. Died: Sept 26, 1862
SANDULLIN, Griffon S. Co. I, 11 Rgt. Died: Nov 23 , 1861
SANFORD, J. Co. I, 9 Rgt. Died: Sept 7, 1862
SCOTT, William W. Co. C, 48 Rgt. Died: Oct 12, 1862
SIBLEY, Clement C. Co. H, 9 Rgt. Died: Sept 25, 1861
SINGLETON, Janus Co. I, 51 Rgt. Died: Oct 15, 1862 (SINGLETARY, J. Thomas left sick at Manassas Oct 6, 1862)
SKINNER, William H. Co. E, 8 Rgt. Died: Sept 16, 1861
SMITH, Osborn R. Co. I, 11 Rgt. Died: Sept 14, 1862
SPINKS, R. Thomas Co. B, 18 Rgt. Died: Sept 23, 1862
STARR, J. T. (Joseph) Co. I, 11 Rgt. Died: Oct 21, 1862
STRICKLAND, Peter Co. I, 9 Rgt. Died: Sept 28, 1862
TALLEY, J. S. Co. K, 11 Rgt. Died: Sept 30, 1862 (CSR's list Sept 17 1862)
TANKERSLEY, R. A. B. Co. K, 48 Rgt. Died: Sept 4, 1862
TARVER, John Co. D, 51 Rgt. Died: Oct 12, 1862
TARVER, L. B. Co. E, 48 Rgt. Died: Nov 15, 1862
THORNTON, John Co. G, Ist Rgt. Died: Sept 1862
TYNER, G. S. Co. D, 9 Rgt. Died: Sept 20, 1862
VAUGN, Edgar J. H. Co. B, Ist, Rgt. Died: Sep 1862

Confederate Soldiers Buried at the Memorial Wall in Warrenton Cemetery

VICKERS, H. T. Co. G, 7 Rgt. Died: Sept 11, 1862
WALLACE, J. M. Co. G, 20 Rgt. Died: Sept 3, 1862
WASDEN, Alexander Co. C, 20 Rgt. Died: Nov 5, 1862
WEAVER, A. T. Co. B, 51 Rgt. Died: Nov 15, 1862
WHEELER, Charles M. Co. G, (K), 11 Rgt. Died: Oct 6 (15), 1862
WHITNIR, J. R. Co. A, 18 Rgt. Died: Sept 6, 1862
WILEY, John T. Co. A, 20 Rgt. Died: Sept 15, 1862
WILLIAMS, Wm. Jasper Co. B, 38 Rgt. Discharged Oct 17, 1862
WILLIAMS, William W. Co. C, 48 Rgt. Died: Oct 12, 1862
WILLIS, William B. Co. A, 7 Rgt. Died: Nov 6, 1861
WILSON, W. O. (Wm.) Co. C., 18 Rgt. Died: Oct 10, 1862
WINFREY, J.L. Co. I, 11 Rgt. Died: Sept 22 (23), 1862
WITHERSPOON, George Wash. Co. G, 11 Rgt. Died: Sept 7, 1862
WISE, Henry L. Co. E, 51 Rgt. Died: Oct 5, 1862
WOODS, George Co. I, 19 Rgt. Died: Nov 27, 1862

LOUISIANA

BARNES, B. E. Co. K 9 Rgt. Died: Aug 2, 1861
BUTTERWORTH, Jerome R. Co. F, 9 Rgt. Dicd: Aug 7, 1861
BUDD, R. Co. I, 2 Rgt. Died: Sept 14, 1862 (illegible name not found on LA CSR's)
DONAHOE, Phillip Co. K, 15 Rgt. Died: Sept 20, 1862
FUSSELL, James P. Co. I, 9 Rgt. Died: Sept 11, 1862
GALLOWAY, J. R. Co. H, 8 Rgt. Died: Nov 15, 1862
HATCHER, Henry Co. C, 9 Rgt. Died: Nov 30, 1861
JOHNSON, Pinckney Co. H, 9 Rgt. Died: Oct 25, 1861
JONES, J. L. (Sr.) Co. F, 9 Rgt. Died: Oct 11, 1861
LEE, John F. Co. F, 9 Rgt. Died: Aug 3, 1861
MARSHALL, William H. Co. B, 9 Rgt. Died: Oct 10, 1861
MATTHEWS, Moses Co. F, 9 Rgt. Discharged May 30, 1862
McCANNEY, Hugh Co. K, 8 Rgt. Died: Nov 1, 1862
PERRY, Griffin Co. I, 9 Rgt. Died: Aug 9, 1861
PITTMAN, D. S. Co. D, 6 Rgt. Discharged: Oct 1, 1861
SAUNDERS, J. Co. K, 9 Rgt. Discharged Dec 5, 1861
SAUNDERS, Orrin Co. I, 9 Rgt. Died: July 31, 1861
SCARBOROUGH, A. J. Co. A, 2 LA Rgt. Died: Sept 8, 1862
SHIELDS, James Y. Co. C, 9 Rgt. Died: Sept 18, 1861
WALSH, Joseph Co. G, 15 Rgt. Died: Sept 12, 1862
WORDLEY, Hiram Co. A, 9 Rgt. Died: 1861

MISSISSIPPI

ADAMS, James A. Co. H, 19 Rgt. Died: Oct 22, 1862
AIKEN, Robert S. Co. I, 19 Rgt. Died: Dec 27, 1861
ALEXANDER, W. H. Co. G, 21 Rgt. Discharged Dec 17, 1861
ALEXANDER, W. T. Co. E, 21 Rgt. Discharged Dec 14, 1861 (2 listings may be the same man)
ALLEN, G. W. (George) Co. E, 16 Rgt. Died: Jan 6, 1862
ALSIP, F. Co. G, 16 Rgt. Discharged: Feb. 10, 1862
BAGBY, William R. Co. H, 19 Rgt. Died: Jan 3, 1862
BARR, William Co. G, 2 Rgt. Dishcarged Nov 1, 1861
BARRY, John B. Co. G, 11 Rgt. Discharged: Nov 20, 1861
BASS, Jasper W. Co. B, 16 Rgt. Died: Nov 18, 1861
BATES, James T. Co. C (E), 2 Rgt. Died: Oct 24, 1862
BATY, J. Co. I, 2Bn Died: Oct 24, 1862
BAUGH, H. H. Co. H, 16 Rgt. Died: Nov 18, 1861
BELL, L. R. Co. B, 2 Rgt. Died: Sept 12, 1862
BOBO, D. P. Co. D, 11 Rgt. Discharged Oct 20, 1862
BOGGAN, Charles A. Co. I, 19 (11 Rgt.) Died: Sept 2, 1861
BOOKOUT, W. G. Co. B, 2 Rgt. Died: Sept 16, 1862
BOONE, James J. Co. C, 16 Rgt. Died: Jan 7, 1862
BOST, R. M. Co. E, 19 Rgt. Discharged: Jan 11, 1861
BOSTWICK, Mark R. Co. B, 2 Rgt. Died: Sept 6, 1862
BOWEN, Daniel W. Co. H 2 Rgt. Died: Sept 22, 1862
BRADY, Edmond Co. I, 19 (16) Rgt. Died: Nov 18, 1861
BRIGHAM, (BINGRAM) C. S. Co. F, 16 Rgt. Died: Nov 23, 1861

Confederate Soldiers Buried at the Memorial Wall in Warrenton Cemetery

BROWN, Daniel F. Co. D Died: Feb 11, 1862
BUFORD, Walter S. Co. G, 11 Rgt. Died: Sept 16,24, 1862 (Oct 1, 1862)
CALTHIZ, I. C. Co. B, 12 Rgt. Discharged Jan 2, 1862
CARTER, Jasper L. Co. G, 19 Rgt. Died: Dec 10, 1861
CARTER, John B. Co. F, 16 Rgt. Died: Nov 13, 1861
CHRISTMAN, John C. Co. A, 2 Rgt. Died: Sept 21, 1862
COLTHORP, Brantley H. Co. B, 2 Rgt. Died: Sept 17, 1862
COLTRAIN, John Co. G, 12 Rgt. Died: Sep 24, 1862
CONN, Michael Co. C, 19 Rgt. Discharged: Dec 15, 1861
CRUM, G. (James G.) Co. B, 2 Rgt. Died: Sept 8, 1862
DANIELS, L. J. (Lumpkin) Co. D, 12 Rgt. Died: Nov 11, 1861
DENTON, Benjamin A. Co. A, 9 (16) Rgt. Died: Oct 3, 1861
DRURY, C. G. Co. F, 19 Rgt. Died: Dec 7, 1861
DUNN, Martin Co. D, 16 Rgt. Died: Sept 21, 1862
EARLOE, C. J. Co. E, 21 Rgt. Discharged Jan 20, 1862
EARLOE, G. W. Co. E, 21 Rgt. Discharged Jan 20, 1862
EVANS, J. H. Co. H, 19 Rgt. Discharged Jan 22, 1862
FAHY, Patrick Co. C, 19 Rgt. NFR believed he died
FALTREE, C. P. Co. K 16 Rgt. Discharged Jan 13, 1862
FRALY, (FRAILY) J. A. Co. C Died: Jan 28, 1862
GARDNER, Benjamin F. Co. G, 11 Rgt. Died: Sept 7, 1861
GARNER, R. Co. E, 16 Rgt. Discharged Feb 8, 1862
GOLDING, Wilson S. Co. I, 2 Rgt. Died: Sept 24, 1862
GOODMAN, W. M. Co. C, 16 Rgt. Discharged Dec 16, 1861
GOSSETT, L. J. Co. B, 2 Rgt. Died: Nov 25, 1861
GRACE, (GROCE), Asa N. Co. E, 19 Rgt. Died: Nov 24, 1861
GREEN, J. N. Co. G, 16 Rgt. Died: Oct 14 (18)1861
HALE, J. T. Co. H, 16 Rgt. Died: Feb 22, 1862 (not found in 16 Miss CSRs)
HAMILTON, Francis M. Co. E, 19 Rgt. Died: Nov 26, 1861
HAMPTON, Wade Co. H, 16 Rgt. Discharged Jan 12, 1862
HARRIS, Lansdell Co. H, 19 Rgt. Died: Jan 6, 1862
HARRIS, N. L. Co. G, 19 Rgt. Discharged Dec 19, 1861
HASSELL, Noah's Ark Co. H, 19 (16 Rgt.) Died: Oct 16, 1861
HENDERSON, Robert M. Co. K, 16 Rgt. Discharged Dec 17, 1861
HERRING, Isaac Co. G, 19 Rgt. Discharged Dec. 26, 1861
HINES, Wm. P. Co. K, 7 Rgt. Died: Sept 16, 1862
HUGHS, George W. Co. C, 16 Rgt. Died: Oct 30, 1862
HUGHS, W. P., Co. A, 19 Rgt. Discharged Dec 3 1, 1861
HUMPHRIES, Hugh B. Co. D, 19 Rgt. Died: Dec 29, 1861
JARRETT, Absalom Co. D, 6 Rgt. Died: Oct 1, 1862
JEFFRIES, Edward W. Co. G, 16 Rgt. Died: Sept 3, 1862
JENNINGS, R. N. Co. E, 12 Rgt. Discharged Dec 5, 1861
KIRKLAND, C. R. Co. C, 18 Rgt. Discharged Jan 19, 1862
LACORTE, J. L. Co. I, 16 Rgt. Died: Nov 22, 1861
LANCASTER, C. B. Co. K 16 Rgt. Died: Nov 6, 1861
LENORE (LENORR), N. B. Co' A, 16 Rgt. Died: Oct 8, 1861
LEWIS, Benjamin F. Co. D, 16 Rgt. Died: Oct 30, 1862
MATTBEWS, T. F. Co. G, (F) 19 Rgt. Died: Jan 17, 1862
McDONALD, D. E. Co. D, 16 Rgt. Discharged: Jan 22, 1862
McFALLS, C. A. Co. B Died: Jan 28, 1862
McGALTK A. J. Co. B Died: Dec 9, 1861
McNABB, James Co. E, 16 Rgt. Died: Jan 1, 1862
MEARS, Thomas L. Co. G, 2 Rgt. Died: Oct 15, 1862
MEARZ, (MEARS) John Co. F. 16 Rgt. Died: Jan 20, 1862
MONTGOMERY, Wm. H. Co. A, 16 Rgt. Discharged Dec 1, 1861
MOORE, Spright Co. K, 2 Bn Died: Sept 10, 1862
MURKLE, James H. Co. D, 11 Rgt. Died: Nov 6, 1861
MURPHY, Enoch F. Co. A, 16 Rgt. Died: Nov 2, 1862
MYERS, William W. Co. B. Died: Feb 19, 1862
NEWSOM, John R. Co. B, 19 Rgt. Died: Oct 6, 1861
NORWOOD, P. (Theophills) Co. B 19 Rgt. Died: Jan 21, 1862
ORR, Samuel Co. I, 16 Rgt. Died: Jan 22, 1862
ORR, Wm. David Co. E, 19 Rgt. Died: Dec 19, 1861
OWENS, J. W. Co. I, 17 Rgt. Died: Dec 15, 1861

Confederate Soldiers Buried at the Memorial Wall in Warrenton Cemetery

PARKER, J. F. Co. F, 16 Rgt. Discharged Dec 18, 1861
PEARL, Seth W. Co. E, 16 Rgt. Discharged Dec 3, 1861
PEARSAL, E. J. Co. B Died: Feb 28, 1862
PIERCE, J. C. Co. G, 21 Rgt. Discharged Jan 30, 1862
PITTS, Isaac T. Co. I, 2 Rgt. Died: Oct 3, 1861
PRATER, Jesse E. Co. F, 19 Rgt. Died:Dec 18, 1861
RAGLAND, Andrew J. Co. G, 11 Rgt. Died: Sept 5, 1862
REED, James D. Co. F, 12 Rgt. Died: Nov 18, 1861
REYNOLDS, Thomas G. Co. A, 2 Rgt. Died: Oct 11, 1861
RIGGS, Cole J. Co. D, 16 Rgt. Died: Jan 1, 1862
ROYALS, W. D. Co. H, 16 Rgt. Died: Jan 1, 1862
ROYALS, Z. Co. H, 19 (16) Rgt. Died: Nov 29, 1861
SANDIFER, E. Cobb Co. B, 16 Rgt. Died: Nov 18, 1861
SINGLETON, Wm. L. Co. C, 11 Rgt. Died: Sept 30, 1861
STEWART, John Co. H, 16 Rgt. Died: Jan 23, 1862
STROUD, William A. Co. F, 12 Rgt. Died: Dec 18, 1861
STITT, E. J. Co. E, 12 Rgt. Died: Dec 5, 1861
THORNTON, George W. Co. K, 16 Rgt. Died: Sept 18, 1862
TISDALE, J. W. Co. E, 16 Rgt. Discharged: Jan 22, 1862
TOWLES, T. Co. E (F), 12 Rgt. Died: Nov 9, 1861
WELLS, John P. Co. C, 2 Bn Died: Sept 2, 1862
WELSH, Thomas J. Co. E, 19 Rgt. Died: Dec 30, 1861
WESTMORLAND, Jerome Co. H, 2 Rgt. Discharged Oct 17, 1862
WHITTEN, John C. Co. B, 2 Rgt. Died: Sept 24, 1862
WIGGLE, (WEGUL) Alfred R. Co. C, 2 Rgt. Died: Oct 10, 1862
WILKERSON, Ancus (Angus) M. Co. C, 16 Rgt. Died: Oct 30, 1861
WILLIAMS, Robert F. Co. L, 2 Bn Died: Sept 28, 1862
WRIGHT, W. A. (William H.) Co. F(L) 21 Rgt. Died: Dec 3, 1861

NORTH CAROLINA

BOONE, James J. Co. C, 16 Rgt. Discharged Jan 7, 1862
BURDETT, Reuben W. Co. H, 25 Rgt. Died: Sept 28, 1862
CALLOWAY, John Wesley Co. B, 16 Rgt. Discharged Oct 12, 1862
COATES, W. Co. C, 7 Rgt. Discharged Oct 17, 1862
CONLEY, Jesse F. Co. A, 16 Rgt. Died: Oct 14, 1862
FRANKLIN, William A. Co. E, 16 Rgt. Died: Dec 23, 1861
GILBERT, Simon P. Co. D, 28 (38) Rgt. Died: Sept 13, 1862
HILL, F. (David F.) Co. G, 4 Rgt. Died: Dec 17, 1861
HINES, W. P. (Wm.) Co. K, 7 Rgt. Died: Sept 16, 1862
JARRETT, Absalom Co. D, 6 Rgt. Died: Oct 1, 1862
LACKEY, James Wm. Co. G, 38 Rgt. Discharged: Oct 10, 1862
LANIER, John M. Co. A, 38 Rgt. Died: Oct 1, 1862
MANNING, A. A. Co. E, 3 Rgt. Died: Sept 23, 1862
MITCHELL, G. Co. D, 4 Rgt. Discharged Jan 21, 1862
SPERLIN, John E. Co. D, 16 Rgt. Died: Dec 23, 1861
TUSSEY, David Co. H, 48 Rgt. Died: Oct 3, 1862
TUSSEY, R. A. Co. A (H), 48 Rgt. Died: Sept 12, 1862
SPERLIN, John E. Co. D, 16 Rgt. Died: Dec 23, 1861
WALKER, James Thomas Co. I, 34 Rgt. Died: Oct 1, 1862
WEBB, Bryant Co. D, 15 Rgt. Died: Feb 27, 1862
WILLIAMS, F. H. (Fielding) Co. A, 34 Rgt. Died: Oct 12, 1862
WILLIAMS, F. H. Co. C, 35 Rgt. Died: Nov 1, 1862
WILLIAMS, H (Hugh) Co. K 34 Rgt. Died: Nov 9, 1862

SOUTH CAROLINA

AKIN, G. W. Co. K, 17 Rgt. Died: Sept 27, 1862
ALLISON, William Terry Co. A, 3 Rgt. Died: Dec 22, 1861
ALTMAN, S. Co. F Died: no date given
ARMSTRONG, E. C. Co. H(C), 5 Rgt. Died: Sept1862
ARNOLD, J. Co. C, 22 Rgt. Died: Sept 18, 1862
ASHBY (ASHLEY), J. Co. F. Died: Sept 12, 1862
AUTREY (AUTRY), James Co. E, 7 Rgt. Died: Jan 5, 1862
BAILES, John Co. B, 6 Rgt. Died: Nov 13, 1862

Confederate Soldiers Buried at the Memorial Wall in Warrenton Cemetery

BAKER, Thomas Co. E. Died: Sept 30, 1862
BENSON, Joseph F. Co. H Died: Nov 6, 1862
BIGHAM, J. H. Co. B, 12 Rgt. Died: Sept 29 (30), 1862
BLACKWOOD, Thomas Wm. Co. C Died: Sept 6, 1862
BOAG, (POAG), D. K. Co. F. (1), 6 Rgt. Died: Sept 12, 1862
BOLIN, John Co. C. 17 Rgt. Died: Nov 10, 1862
BOULEWARE, R. D. Co. B, 17 Rgt. Died: Sept 17, 1862
BOWERS, Malcom K. Co. C. Died: Sept 11, 1862
BRANSEN, J. W. Co. G Discharged Oct 10, 1862
BRINSON, T. W. Co. G, 10 Rgt. Discharged Oct 10, 1862
BRITTON, Henry Co. E, 6 Rgt. Died: Sept 6, 1862
BROACH, S. S. Co. E, 23 Rgt. Died: Sept 2 1, 1862
BROOM, A. (Able) Co. E, 12 Rgt. Died: Sept 18, 1862
BROWN, E. T. Co. L. Died: Sept 22, 1862
BRUNSON, Wm. L. Co. I, 23 Rgt. Died: no date given
CALHOUN, W. (Warren R. D.) Co. E. Died: Oct 1, 1862
CALVERT, W. J. Co. G. Died: Sept 23, 1862
CAMPBELL, Ancel Hutchins Co. E, 4 Rgt. Died: Jan 13, 1862
CLINTON, E. B. Co. I, 5 Rgt. Died: Dec 24, 1861
COX, A. E. (A. Elijah) Co. D, 18 Rgt. Died: Sep 13, 1862
CROCKER, Anthony C. Co. B, 13 Rgt. Died: Sept 16, 1862
DOVE, H. G. Co. I, 18 Rgt. Died: Aug 9, 1861
DUTART, James E. Co. I, 4 Rgt. Believe died
ELGIN, Thomas Co. K. Died: Sept 1, 1862
ENTRICAN, William Co. G, 4 Rgt. Died: Nov 28, 1861
ESTERLING, Enos Co. H. Died: Oct 31, 1862
FANT, Ephraim H. Co. B, 17 Rgt. Died: Sept 16, 1862
FEASTER, A. C. Co. D, 6 Rgt. Died: Sept 30, 1862
FEASTER, A. C. (Andrew C.) Co. B, 17 Rgt. Died: Oct 25, 1862
FLEMMING, Gaston Co. B Died: Sept 30, 1862
FOWLER, H Co. E Died: Sept 30, 1862
FOWLER, J. W. Co. B, 18 Rgt. Died: Sept 23, 1862 (FOWLER, J. J. filed in J. J.'s CSR)
GARDNER, J. H. Co. E, 12 Rgt. Discharged Oct 8, 1862
GARNER, William Co. H, 15 Rgt. Died: Sept 19, 1862
GASTON, W. H. Co. B, 13 Rgt. Died: Sept 5, 1862
GODLEY, Henry D. Co. H, Died: Sept 17, 1862
GORE, Edward James Co. F. Died: Sept 30, 1862
GRANT, Neely Co. H Died: no date given
GRUBBS, R. W. (Richard W.) Co. D. Died: Sept 20, 1862
HALL, Francis M. Co. E, Died: Sept 19, 1862
HALLEY (HOLLY), Wm. Co. H, 5 Rgt. Died: Sept 28, 1862
HAMBY, Joseph H. Co. K, 3 Rgt. Died: Dec 11, 1861
HARTZOG, J. B. Co. A. -.Died: Sept 6, 1862
HARTZOG, W. W. Co. A. Died: Sept 23, 1862
HARVEY, Morgan Co. B Died: Sept 14, 1862
HEARST, J. L. (James L-) Co. B. Discharged Oct 10, 1862
HENDRICK, Bailus Co. H Died: Sept 15, 1862
HOGG, Thomas D. Co. G Died: Sept 30, 1862
HOWARD, George McDuffie Co. C, 4 Rgt. Died: Dec 25, 1861
HUGHS, Timothy H. Co. K, 12 Rgt. Died: Sept 29, 1862
HUGHS, William F. Co. K. Died: Oct 25, 1862
HUNGERPELER, J. S. Co. H Died: Sept 19, 1862
HUNTEIR, J. B. Co. G. Discharged: Oct 14, 1862
JOHNSON, S. B. (S. S. Burdett) Co. B Died: Oct 5, 1862
JOHNSON, Wm. D. Co. G, 23 Rgt. Died: No date given
JOHNSTON, Robert D. Co. E. Died: Sept 16, 1862
JONES, John Co. I, 6 Rgt. Died: Sept 10, 1862
JONES, Madison J. Co. F. Died: Dec 19, 1861
JONES, Wm. Clayton Co. C, 4 Rgt. Died: Dec 25, 1861
JORDON, J. Co. H. Died: Sept 5, 1862
KEASLER, John B. Co. L. Died: Sept 26, 1862
KEE, John F. Co. I, 17 Rgt. Died: Sept 18, 1862
KELLY, W. D. Co. B, 23 Rgt. Died: Sept 28, 1862
KENDRICK, W. Robert Co. B, 13 Rgt. Died: Sept 23, 1862

Confederate Soldiers Buried at the Memorial Wall in Warrenton Cemetery

KENNEDY, G. (H. G.) Co. K 17 Rgt. Died: Sept 19, 1862
LAWSON, J. M. Co. F Died: Oct 1, 1862
LOCKWOOD, H. A. Co. H Died: Oct 7, 1862
LOMINACK, Wm. T. Co. G Died: Sept 15, 1862
LOWERY, William Co. B Died: Sept 30, 1862
LYLES, Erskine Co. B. Died: Oct 4, 1862
LYNES, George W. Co. C. Died: Sept 25, 1862
McCORMICK, James Co. A, 18 Rgt. Died: Sept 30, 1862
McGUIRE, G. W. Co. K IS Rgt. Died: Sept 14, 1862
McMANUS, Albert Co. I, 17 Rgt. Died: Sept 24, 1862
MILLER, Paul G. Co. I Died: Dec 19, 1861
MOORE, Daniel W. Co. A, 12 Rgt. Died: Oct 1, 1862
MORRIS, W. Co. E Died: Sept 12, 1862
MULLINEAU, W. W. Co. H (B), 12 Rgt. Died: no date given
NANCE, Thomas C. Co. H, 5 Rgt. Discharged Sept 30, 1861
NICHOLS, Benjamin N. Co. H, 23 Rgt. Died: Oct 2, 1862
NICHOLS, John C. Co. E Died: Oct 2, 1862
NISBET, John C. Co. I, 17 Rgt. Died: Sept 6, 1862
PACK, Benjamin J. Co. C Died: Sept 18, 1862
PALMER, Francis G. Lt. Col. Died: Dec 5, 1862
PINCKNEY, Hopson Co. I, 4 Rgt. Died: unknown
PLOWDEN, J. Belton Co. CDied: Sept 19, 1862
POAT, Charles John Co. C Died: Sept 17, 1862
POOL, D. J. Co. E, 18 Rgt. Died: Oct 18, 1862
RANKIN, John M. Co. E. Died: Dec 1, 1862
REYNOLDS, Ransom Co. I, 6 Rgt. Died: Oct 18, 1861
RICKENBACKER, F. M. Co. B Died: Sept 23, 1862
ROBINSON, E. S. D. Co. B Discharged Oct 24, 1862
ROBINSON, Robert Co. F, 5 Rgt. Discharged Oct 17, 1862
ROEBUCK, J. H. Co. E. Died: Oct 2, 1862
ROGERS, A. H. Co. E Died: Nov 7, 1862
RUFFIN, Charles L. Co. I, 4 Rgt. Died: unknown
SANFORD, J. W. Co. E Died: Oct 9, 1862
SANFORD, W. L. Co. C (H) Died: Sept 18, 1862
SHEPPARD, Thomas G. Co. L. Died: Sept 17, 1862
SHIPLEY, J. Co. C, 5 Rgt. Discharged Oct 12, 1862
SISTAR (SISTARE), A. J. Co. D Died: Sept 17, 1862
SIMS, William Co. I, 18 Rgt. Died: Oct 10, 1862
SLICE, J. F. Co. A (H), 13 Rgt. Died: Sept 27, 1862
SMITH, James W. Co. B Died: Sept 22, 1862
SMITH, Josiah M. Co. H. Died: Sept 22, 1862
STANTON, R. E. Co. B, 17 Rgt. Died: Oct 28, 1862
STEVENS, Enoch Co. A Discharged Oct 12, 1862
STEWART, Daniel Co. B Died: Sept 25, 1862
STONE, Reuben J. Co. G Died: No date given
TARRANT, Sumter W. Co. K, 15 Rgt. Died: Nov 17, 1861
TAYLOR, James S. Co. G, 23 Rgt. Died: Sept 28, 1862
THOMASON, Churchwell Co. F Died: Nov 12, 1862
TOLLESON, J. Belton Co. C Died: Sept 13, 1862
TURNER, B. Co. K, 6 Rgt. Died: Sept 25, 1862
TURNER, H. A. Co. K, 5 Rgt. Died: Sept 13, 1862
TURNER, J. P. Co. E, 13 Rgt. Died: before Sept 30, 1862
VICKERY, G. B. Co. B (1), 12 Rgt. Died: Sept 3, 1862
WADDELL, J. J. Co. E. Died: Oct 8, 1862
WALKER, Henry A. Co. F Died: Feb 3, '63
WALKER, J. Felix Co. F, 18 Rgt. Died: Sept 10, 1862
WARREN, W. D. Co. D, 15 Rgt. Died: Sept 25, 1862?
WEED, W. W. Co. H, 3 Rgt. Died: Nov 20, 1861
WHITE, O. H. Co. I, 23 Rgt. Died: Oct 1, 1862
WILLIAMS, Theodore F. Co. C (G) Died: Sept 25, 1862
WILLIAMS, W. W. Co. I, 17 Rgt. Died: Sept 26, 1862
WILLIS, R. S. Co. A Died: Oct 2, 1862
WILSON, D. A. Co. A Died: Oct 8, 1862
WINEBRENNER, George Co. D, 3rd Bn Died: Nov 11, 1862

Confederate Soldiers Buried at the Memorial Wall in Warrenton Cemetery

WISE, John A. Co. IFL (no date listed)
WISE, A. J. Co. B Died: Sept 29, 1862
WOOD, W. J. Co. A Died: Oct 4, 1862

TENNESSEE

ANDERSON, Joseph F. Co. C, 7 Rgt. Died: Sept 18, 1862
CUNNINGHAM, James W. Co. K, 1st Rgt. Died: Oct 12, 1862
DENTON, Jefferson H. Co. D, 3 Rgt. Died: Nov 20, 1861
DOAK, Rufus P. Co. H, 7 Rgt. Died: Sept 16, 1862
GASKINS, Thomas M. Co. I, 1st Rgt. Died: Oct 9, 1862
HEARN, Edward A. W. Co. D, 7 Rgt. Died: Sept 16, 1862
JACKSON, Robert N. Co. H, 7 Rgt. Died: Oct 8, 1862
LUTTRELL, J. Co. H, 1st Rgt. Died: Oct 2, 1862
MATTHEWS, Robert H. Co. C, 14 Rgt. Died: Oct 5, 1862
NORVELL, Nathan G. Co. D, Ist Rgt. Died: Oct 26, 1862
WALKER, William W. Co. C, 7 Rgt. Died: June 13, 1862

TEXAS

ANGEL, Albert Co. A, 5 Rgt. Died: Sept 5, 1862
ALLEN, J. W. Co. G, 5 Rgt. Discharged Oct 16, 1862
BURRAM, Stephen B. Co. B, 4 Rgt. Died: Spet 22, 1862
BUSTER, J. C. Co. E, 5 Rgt. Discharged Oct 21, 1862
CARRIGAN, John Co. B, 5 Rgt. Died: Oct 23, 1862
CHURCH, J. F. Co. F, 5 Rgt. Died: Oct 22, 1862
CLARK, B. C. Co. K, 5 Rgt. Discharged Oct 16, 1862
DEAN, Sam H. Co. E, 5 Rgt. Died: Sept 21, 1862
DELESDENIER, John W. Co. A, 5 Rgt. Died: Sept 23, 1862
DEYOUNG, John Co. A, 5 Rgt. Died: Sept 18, 1862
DUNKIN, G. W. Co. B, 4 Rgt. Died: Sept 19, 1862
DUNN, H. B. Co. C, 5 Rgt. Died: Sept 10, 1862
EASTERLING, H. A. Co. H (K), 5 Rgt. Died: Oct 3, 1862
ESTILL, Ben P. Co. D, 5 Rgt. Died: Oct 5, 1862
FREEMAN, Benjamin Co. H, 5 Rgt. Died: Sept 7, 1862
GALLOWAY, J. J. Co. G (C), 4 Rgt. Discharged Oct 9, 1862
HARRIS, James K. P. Co. D, 5 Rgt. Died: Sept 16, 1862
HEFFERAN, John Co. A, 5 Rgt. Died: Sept 7, 1862
HEPPERLA, J. C. Co. G, 2 (Ist) Rgt. Died: Oct 3, 1861
HUTCHINSON, James Co. E, 5 Rgt. Died: Sept 23, 1862
JONES, R. M. Co. E, 4 Rgt. Discharged Oct 21, 1862
KING, Samuel P. Co. K 4 Rgt. Died: Oct 4, 1862
KIRK, Winchell S. Co. C, 4 Rgt. Died: Oct 5, 1862
LONG, G. T. Co. G, 5 Rgt. Discharged Oct 17, 1862
MCANELLY, C. W. Co. B, 4 Rgt. Died: Sept 22, 1862
McDONALD, Elisha, Jr. Co. G, 5 Rgt. Died: Nov 2l, 1862
McMURTY, J. M. Co. A, 5 Rgt. Died: Nov 7, 1862
MORRIS, T. R. Co. I, 4 Rgt. Died: Oct 3, 1862
NELMS, W. M. Co. D, 5 Rgt. Died: Sept 7, 1862
NETHERLY, James R. Co. A, 5 Rgt. Died: Oct 4, 1862
NORMAN, P. W. Co. G, 5 Rgt. Died: Sept 24, 1862
POOLE, J. W. Co. F, 1st Rgt. Died: Oct 14, 1862
PRATER, Virgil S. Co. L. 2 (Ist) Rgt. Died: Sept 21, (22) 1861
ROGERS, J. L. Co. E, 4 Rgt. Died: Oct 5, 1862
ROYSTON, W. B. Co. K. 5 Rgt. Died: Sept 15, 1862
SCHULTZ, William Co. F. 5 Rgt. Died: Sept 10, 1862
SENSEBAUGH William Co. E, 5 Rgt. Died: July 21, '63
SPIVY, B. J. Co. D, 5 Rgt. Died: Sept 12, 1862
STARNES, G. W. Co. F, 5 Rgt. Died: Dec 12, 1862
UMBARGER, J. P. Co. B, 5 Rgt. Died: Sept 23, 1862
WALKER, D. W. Co. A, 5 Rgt. Died: Sept 18, 1862
WARD, D. W. Co. A, 5 Rgt. Died: Sept 18, 1862
WARD, W. J. Co. K,5 Rgt. Died: Sept 14, 1862

Confederate Soldiers Buried at the Memorial Wall in Warrenton Cemetery

VIRGINIA

AINSKO, Joseph Co. I, 1st Reg Died: Sept 3, 1862
BARKER, William D. Co. A, 38 Rgt. Died: Feb 26, 1862
BATEMAN, J. M. Co. E, 24 Rgt. Discharged Oct 21, 1862
CARTER, Charles A. Co. K, 24 Rgt. Died: Oct 20, 1862
CLEEK, Jacob K. Co. K, 52 Rgt. Died: Sept 21, 1862
CRAIG, J. D. Co. I, 11 Rgt. Died: Nov 8, 1862
DAMRON, Lindsey C. Co. C, 19 Rgt. Died: Jan 13, 1862
DAVIS, Thomas H. Co. H, 12 Rgt. Died: Oct 30, 1862
DELANEY, George Co. E, 47 Rgt. Died: Aug 24, 1862
DICKERSON, Thomas Henry Co. D, 24 Rgt. Died: Sept 25, 1862
EANES, John H. Co. D, 24 Rgt. Died: Sept 29, 1862
EDMONDS, A. B. Co. H, 49 Rgt. Discharged Oct 20, 1862
FLANAGAN, William H. Co. G, 16 Rgt. Died: Sept 25, 1862
FLETCHER, Robert H. Co. K, 17 Rgt. Died: no date given
FORD, Norval E. Co. A, 17 Rgt. Discharged Jan 21, 1862
GARNETT, David C. Co. H, 18 Rgt. Died: Nov 5, 1861
GRAHAM, A. W. Co. E, 6 Rgt. Died: Jan 5, 1862
GRANVILLE, George A. W. Co. G, 2 (22) Bn Died: Sept 26, 1862
HATCHER, Virinius Co. A, 12 Rgt. Died: Sept 25, 1862
HAMMON, E. H. Discharged Jan 10, 1862
HARMON, Henry T. Co. D, 17 Rgt. Died: Sept 5, 1862
HILTON, Enos B. Co. H, 48 Rgt. Died: Sept 24, 1862
HOPE, James W. Co. K, 17 Rgt. Died: Sept 15, 1861
HORNER, G. B. Co. H, 49 Rgt. Discharged Oct 20, 1862
HUDGINS, James L. Co. E, 11 Rgt. Died: Sept 5, 1862
HUDSON, James D. Co. I, 19 Rgt. Died: Sept 18, 1862
JEFFRIES, Fredrich Co. K, 17 Rgt. Died: No date given
JENKINS, Frank (George F.) Co. K, 17 Rgt. Died: no date given
KELLY, James T. Co. K, 47 Rgt. Died: Oct 29, 1862
LEFFELL, W. H. Co. C, 28 Rgt. Died: Oct 24, 1862
LONG, Benjamin R. Co. F, 11 Rgt. Died: Sept 5, 1862
LYNCH, John C. 27 Rgt. Died: Oct 15, 1861
MARKHAM, Virgil A. Co. H, 28 Rgt. Died: Jan 4, 1862
McCARTNEY, A. J. Co. B, 28 Rgt. Died: Oct 2, '63
MEERITT, John B. Co. B, 6 Rgt. Died: Sept 20, 1862
NORFLEET, Augustus B. Co. E, 6 Rgt. Died: Jan. '64
NYE, J. J. (James) Co. D, 7 Rgt. Died: Sept 8, 1862
PATRUM, William A. Co. E, 11 Rgt. Died: Sept 4, 1862
PERKINS, Thomas M. Co. F, 38 Rgt. Died: Feb 27, 1862
PERRY, William H. Co. I, 6 Rgt. Died: Sept 21, 1862
PIGG, Hezikiah H. Co. D, 18 Rgt. Died: Sept 25, 1862
PRESTON, Alfred L. Co, D, 28 Rgt. Died: Sept 1862
RAMSEY, William H. Co. H, 12 Rgt. Died: Nov 20, 1862
RANSOM, John Francis Co. E, 9 Rgt. Died: Sept 4, 1862
RICHARDS, Samuel M. Co. B, 42 Rgt. Died: Sept 20, 1862
RIDDLE, John Co. E, 47 Rgt. Died: Oct 1862
SANGSTER, J. H. L. Co. A, 17 Rgt. Died: Sept 8, 1862
SEMONES, Samuel M. Co. D, 24 Rgt. Died: Sept 6, 1862
SHELER, B. F. Co. F, 7 Rgt. Died: Sept 18, 1862
SMITH, Jacob H. Co. I, lst Rgt. Died: Sept 6, 1862
SMITH, Jonathan J. Co. K, 17 Rgt. Died: Jan 26, 1862
STAUNTON, J. C. Asst/Surgeon Died: Nov 12, 1862
STONE, William Co. H, 12 Rgt. Died: Sept 16, 1862
SWAIN, Pleasant P. Co. G, 28 Rgt. Died: Sept 16, 1862
THEWATT, James E. Co. A, 12 Rgt. Died: Nov 15, 1862
THOROUGHGOOD, George Co. D, 6 Rgt. Died: Sept 28, 1862
THRIFT, Charles Wm. Co. K, 6 Va Cav. Died: Aug 23, 1862
WATKINS, W. J. Co. I, 6 Rgt. Died: Sept 27, 1862
WELLS, Daniel L. Co. H, 24 Rgt. Died: Sept 26, 1862

Warrenton's possible deaths; but cannot be confirmed:

Confederate Soldiers Buried at the Memorial Wall in Warrenton Cemetery

BARKLER, R. Co. K, 1st SC Rgt.
BECKWORTHY, James Co. D, 9 Ga/Rgt.
SAUNDERS, R. T. Co. C, 47 VA Rgt.
SMIKE, E. S. Co. A, Gregg's 1st SC/Rgt.
YEATMAN, W. H. Co. C, 47 VA/Rgt.

Revolutionary War Soldiers Buried in Fauquier County Cemeteries

Name	Military Unit	Cemetery	Date of Birth	Date of Death
ADAMS, Littleton	Pvt. James Scott's Co. Pvt. Valentine Peyton's Co.,3rd Va. Rgt. CL		1753	1834
ASH, Francis	Pvt. Benj. Harrison's Co. Fauq. Mil. 2nd Lt. Fauquier Militia	Ash - Blackmore (unmarked grave)		1800/03
ASHBY, John	Capt. 3rd Va. Rgt. CL Maj. Fauquier Militia		1740	1815
AUSTIN, John	Pvt. John Porterfield's Co. Morgan's Rifle Rgt. Pvt. Gabriel Long's Co. 11 Va. Rgt.			
BAILEY, Carr	Pvt. Wm. Triplett's Cav. Co.			1781
BALLARD, William	Lt. Fauquier Militia		1732	1799
BARBEE, John	QM Sgt. Wm. Payne's Co. 1st Va. Rgt.		1753	1835
BARNETT, Ambrose	Ens. Fauquier Militia			
BLACKWELL, John	Lt. Col. 2nd Bn Fauquier Militia Lt. Col. 1st Bn Fauquier Militia		1755	after 1795
BLACKWELL, Joseph	2nd Lt. John Chilton's Co. 3rd Va. Rgt.	Joseph Blackwell	1752	1826
BLACKWELL, Joseph	Pvt. Capt. Wm. Blackwell's Co. Culp. Min. Bn. Cadet John Ashby's Co. 3rd Va. Regt. 2nd Lt. Thomas Blackwell's Co. 10th Va. Rgt. 1st Lt. Capt.		1755	1823/26
BLACKWELL, Samuel	Maj. 1st bn Fauquier Militia Lt. Col. Fauquier Militia Capt. Col. Thomas Marshall's 1st Va. Regt. of Artillery		1745	1782/83
BLACKWELL, William	Capt. Culpeper Minute Men Bn. Capt. 11th Regt. Capt. Co. No. 6 Morgan's Rifle Rgt. Capt. Fauquier Militia		1738	1782
BLAKE, Richard E.				
BOYD, Samuel	Pvt. John Chilton's Co. 3rd Va. Rgt. CL			
BRADFORD, Alexander	1st Lt. Fauquier Militia			
BRADFORD, John	Ens. Fauquier Militia			
BRAY, Jr. Timothy	Fauquier Militia			3/4/1830
BRONAUGH, Samuel	Ens. Fauquier Militia			
BRONAUGH, Thomas	Capt. Fauquier Militia		1741	1794
BROWN, Jonathan	Pvt. Wm. Pickett's Co. Culpeper Minute Men			5/1799
BURK, William	Pvt. Wallace's Co. King Geo. Co.		1750	1803/5
CHILTON, Charles	1st Lt. James Bell's Co. Fauquier Mil. Capt. Fauquier Mil.		1741	1793
CHUNN, John Thomas	Pvt. James Scott's Fauquier Indep. Co. Maj. Fauquier Militia			
CLAGGETT, Samuel MD	Surgeon CL. from Charles Co. Md.	Buried in Fauquier Co.		1820
COCKRAN, Stephen		Cockran	1758	1835
COMBS, Robert	Simon Trplett's Co. Loudoun Co. Mil.		1753	1843
COURTNEY, Samuel	Pvt. in Marines under Capt. Alexander Dick Pvt. John Gillison's Co. Col. John Green's 10th Va. Regt. Alexander Parker's Co. Va. Vols.	Buried on family farm near Hartwood Airfield	1755	after 1837
COURTNEY, William		Buried on family farm near Hartwood Airfield		
DEARING, John	2nd Lt. Wm. Ball's Co. Fauquier Militia 1st Lt. under Maj. Francis Triplett at Cowpens			
DIGGES, Edward	Maj. 2nd Bn. Fauquier Militia			before 11/29/1844
DONAPHAN, Joseph	QM. Sgt. Wm. Triplett's Cav. Co. Fauquier Militia			before 7/1/1818
DRUMMON, William	Sgt. Fauquier Militia		1750	1794
DUNCAN, Charles	Wm. Blackwell's Co. 11th Va. Rgt. CL		1761	1838
DUNCAN, James	Pvt. Benj. Harrison's Co. Fauq. Mil.		1757	after 1833

Revolutionary War Soldiers Buried in Fauquier County Cemeteries

Name	Military Unit	Cemetery	Date of Birth	Date of Death
DUNCAN, Joseph	Armorer Clark's Illinois Rgt.			1820

Revolutionary War Soldiers Buried in Fauquier County Cemeteries

Name	Military Unit	Cemetery	Date of Birth	Date of Death
EDMONDS, Daniel	Pvt. John Triplett's Co. Culpeper Regt. Transferred to CL		1757	after 1833
EDMONDS, Elias	Capt. Fauquier Militia Lt. Col. 1st Va. State Regt of Artillery Col. Fauquier Militia	"Ivy Hill"	1754	1800
EDMONDS, William	Col. 1st Bn. Fauquier Militia	Oak Springs/Warrenton	1734	1816
EDWARDS, John	Pvt. Fauquier Militia			
EDWARDS, Thomas	Ens. Fauquier Militia 2nd Lt. Francis Atwell's Co. 2nd Lt. Daniel Floweree's Co.			
ELLIOTT, John	Pvt. Wm. Triplett's Cav. Co.			before 10/25/1790
ELLIS, Nathan	Pvt. John Ball's Co. Fauquier Militia			
EMMONS, James	Pvt. James Winn's Co. Va. Mil. Regt. Thomas Helm's Co. Fauquier Militia		1761	1839
ENGLISH, Robert	Pvt. John Hilton's Co. 3rd Va. Regt. CL			
ETHERINGTON, Jr. John	Pvt. John F. Mercer's Co. 3rd Va. Regt. CL			
EUSTACE, William	Pvt. Benj. Harrison's Co. Fauq. Mil. 1st Lt. Fauquier Militia			
EVANS, Thomas	Sgt. Benj. Harrison's Co. Fauq. Mil.			
FISHBACK, Jacob	Pvt. Wagoneer Fauquier Militia		1749	1821
FLETCHER, John	2nd Lt. Fauquier Militia Lt. Fauquier Militia			
FLORENCE, William	Lt. Fauquier Militia			
FOLEY, Enoch	Pvt. Elias Edmonds' Co. 1st Va. State Regt. of Artillery			1801
FOLEY, Jr. James	Lt. Fauquier Militia Capt. Fauquier Militia			3 or 4/1797
FORD, Henry	Pvt. Col. Elias Edmonds' Regt. Fauquier Militia			
FORD, William	Pvt. Wm. Kincheloe's Co. Pvt. Wm. Jennings' Co. Francis Triplett's Co. Wm. Frost's Co. Col. Elias Edmonds' Regt. Wm. Bayliss' Co. Fauquier Militia		1762	after 1833
FORESTER, John	Pvt. John Ashby's Co. 3rd Va. Regt. CL Wm. Triplett's Co. Morgan's Rifles		1739	after 1820
FRENCH, Jr. John	2nd Lt. Fauquier Militia		1760	1806
FRENCH, Mason	Pvt. Benj. Harrison's Co. Fauq. Mil. Ensign Peter Grant's Co. Grayson's Additional Cont. Regt. 2nd Lt.		1757	1819
GIBSON, John	Pvt. John Ball's Co. Fauquier Militia			
GIBSON, Thomas	Cornet Wm. Triplett's Cav. Capt. Fauquier Militia			1833
GLASCOCK, Thomas	Soldier Fauquier Militia			1793
GRAHAM, Duncan	Capt. Fauquier Militia			1798
GRANT, William	Pvt. Charles Gallahue's Co. No. 2 11th Va. Regt.			
GREEN, William	Pvt. James Pendleton's Co. Culpeper Militia		1755	1835
GRIGSBY, William	Capt. Fauquier Militia			5/1782
HARRIS, John	Pvt. 4th Va. Light Dragoons			
HARRIS, Thomas	2nd Lt. Fauquier Militia			10/1826
HARRISON, Burr	Capt. Fauquier Militia 1st Lt. Wm. Grigsby's Co. Fauq. Mil.			1820
HARRISON, William	Soldier Fauquier Militia			1790
HATHAWAY, James	2nd Lt. James Bell's Co. Fauq. Mil. 2nd Lt. James Scott's Co. Fauq. Indep. Co. 1st Lt. John Ball's Co. Fauquier Militia			1799

Revolutionary War Soldiers Buried in Fauquier County Cemeteries

Name	Military Unit	Cemetery	Date of Birth	Date of Death

Capt. John Ball's Co. Fauquier Militia

Revolutionary War Soldiers Buried in Fauquier County Cemeteries

Name	Military Unit	Cemetery	Date of Birth	Date of Death
HATHAWAY, John	1st Lt. James Scott's Co. Fauq. Indep. Co. Capt. Fauquier Militia		1733	1786
HAWKINS, William	Soldier Fauquier Militia			
HEALE, William	Ens. Wm. Kincheloe's Co. 2nd Lt. Fauquier Militia			
HELM, Thomas	2nd Lt. 3rd Va. Regt. CL 1st Lt Fauquier Militia Capt. Fauquier Militia		1750	1816
HELM, William	Capt.			1832 or 33
HENSON, Robert	Soldier Fauquier Militia			
HITT, Peter	Pvt. Elias Edmonds' Co. 1st Va. State Regt. of Artillery Fauquier Militia	Hitt		
HOGAIN, John	2nd Lt. Fauquier Militia			
HOPPER, John	Pvt. John Chilton's Co. 3rd Va. Regt. CL Pvt. 1st Va. State Regt. of Artillery			
HUBBARD, Epaphroditus	Pvt. 4th Va. Light Dragoons			
HUDNALL (HUDNELL), Joseph	Pvt. Benj. Harrison's Co. Fauq. Mil.			
HUME, William	Soldier Fauquier Militia			1796
HUNTON, William	Pvt. Fauquier Militia		1730	1809
HUNTON, William	Pvt. Fauquier Militia		1730	1796
JAMES, John	Pvt. Benj. Harrison's Co. Fauq. Mil. Ens. Fauquier Militia			
JAMES, Joseph	Capt. Fauquier Militia			
JAMES, Thomas	2nd Lt. Fauquier Militia			8/1804
JEFFRIES, Alexander			1764	1841
JEFFRIES, Joseph	Fauquier Militia			
JENNINGS, Augustine	2nd Lt. Fauquier Militia 1st Lt. Fauquier Militia			
JENNINGS, Baylor	Ens. Fauquier Militia			
JENNINGS, George	Ens. Fauquier Militia			1789
JENNINGS, William	Capt. Fauquier Militia			
JETT, Anthony	Pvt. John Ball's Co. Fauquier Militia			
JETT, Thomas	Pvt. Wm. Pickett's Co. Culpeper Min. Bn. Pvt. Elias Edmonds Co. 1st Va. Regt. of Artillery			
JOHNSON, George	Pvt. 4th Va. Light Dragoons			1828
JOHNSTON, Gideon	Pvt. R. K. Meade's Co. 2nd Va. Regt. Lt. Arundell's Co. Va. Artillery Capt. & Brigade QM Col. Thomas Marshall's 1st Va. Regt. of Artillery		1749	1825
JONES, Charles	Pvt. Wm. Pickett's Co. Culpeper Minute Men Bn.			1790
JONES, John	Pvt. Wm. Pickett's Co. Culpeper Minute Men Bn. Sgt. Corps of Guards			Oct. 1793
JONES, John Warner	Pvt. Wm. Triplett's Cav. Co. Fauquier Militia			
JONES, Thomas	Fauquier Militia			Sep 1858
JONES, William	Pvt. Wm. Pickett's Co. Culpeper Minute Men Bn. Sgt. Wm. Triplett's Cav. Co. of Col. Francis Triplett's Regt.		1759	1834
JORDAN, Thomas	Pvt. 3rd Va. Regt. CL			1817
KEARNS, William	7th Va. Regt. CL			1802
KEITH, Alexander	Pvt. Co. No. 2 Col. Alexander Spotswood's 2nd Va. Regt. CL Lt. Col. John Green's 6th Va. Regt. Capt. Maj. Francis Triplett's Regt.		1748	1822
KEITH, Isham	Ensign Wm. Pickett's Co. Culpeper Minute Men Bn. 2nd Lt. 3rd Va. Regt. CL		1735	1787

Revolutionary War Soldiers Buried in Fauquier County Cemeteries

Name	Military Unit	Cemetery	Date of Birth	Date of Death
KEITH, Thomas	1st Lt. 3rd Va. Regt. CL 2nd Lt. Capt. Turner Morehead's Co. Fauquier Militia Capt.			1802
KEMPER, Charles	Pvt. Hezekiah Turner's Co. Fauquier Militia Pvt. & Gunner Elias Edmond's Co. 1st Va. State Regt. of Artillery Orderly Sgt. Wm. Jenning's Co. Col. Elias Edmonds Regt. Fauquier Militia Ens. Col. Elias Edmond's Regt.		1756	1841
KEMPER, John	Neville's Co. Col. Richard Campbell's Regt. Jacob Wrinker's Co. Gen. Edward Steven's Regt.		1749	after 1833
KEMPER, John	Cpl. Benj. Harrison's Co. Fauquier Militia Sgt. John Ball's Co. Fauquier Militia			before 2/1799
KEMPER, Jr. Peter	Ens. Fauquier Militia			
KEMPER, Tilman	Pvt. Leonard Helm's Co. Clark's Ill. Regt. Tilman Weaver's Co. Col. Armistead Churchill's Bn. Fauquier Militia Cpl. John Ball's Co. Fauquier Militia		1759	1836
KENEARD, Joshua	Pvt. Elias Edmonds Co. 1st Va. Regt. of Artillery			
KENTON, Mark	Cpl. Henry Lee's Co. Col. Theodorick Bland's 1st Regt. of Light Dragoons Sgt. Lee' Legion			
KENTON, William	2nd Lt. Fauquier Militia			
LAWLER, Nicholas	Pvt. James Winn's Co. Col. Elias Edmond's Regt. Pvt. Leonard Sharp's Co. Col. Armistead Churchill's Regt. Fauquier Militia Pvt. James Winn's Co. Fauquier Militia		1743	after 1831
LEACH, Jr. George	Pvt. Elias Edmond's Co. 1st Va. State Regt. of Artillery		1756	1838
LEACH, Sr. George	Pvt. Elias Edmond's Co. 1st Va. State Regt. of Artillery			
LEACH, Thomas	Pvt. Fauquier Militia			
LEE, William	Pvt. Wm. Pickett's Co. Culp. Min. Bn.			
LEWIS, James	Pvt. Benj. Harrison's Co. Fauq. Mil.		1752	1/1802
LEWIS, William	Pvt. Benj. Harrison's Co. Fauq. Mil. Pvt. Lee's Legion	Lewis	1750	1832
LINOR, Philip	Pvt.			
LUTTRELL, John	Pvt. John Ball's Co. Fauquier Militia			
LUTTRELL, Joshua	Pvt. John Ball's Co. Fauquier Militia			1790
LUTTRELL, Richard	Pvt. Benj. Harrison's Co. Fauq. Mil.			
LUTTRELL, Robert	Pvt. John Ball's Co. Fauquier Militia			
MADDOX, John	Pvt. Wm. Pickett's Co. Culp. Min. Bn.			
MARKHAM, James	Capt. Va. Navy *(Dragon & Tempest)*		1752	1816
MARTIN, Benjamin	Pvt. Wm. Pickett's Co. Culp. Min. Bn. Enl. James Winn's Co. Fauquier Militia Cpl. Benj. Harrison's Co. Fauq. Mil. Cpl. John Combs' Co.		1758	after 1833
MARTIN, John	Pvt. Benj. Harrison's Co. Fauq. Mil. 2nd Lt. Tilman Weaver's Co. Fauquier Militia			1/1823
MASSIE, Thomas	Capt. 6th Va. Regt. CL Maj. 11th Va. Regt. CL 2nd Va. Regt. CL		1745	1801
MAUZY, John	2nd Lt. Fauq. Mil.			
MAY, James	Pvt. Elias Edmond's Co. 1st Va. State Regt. of Artillery			
McCLANAHAN, James	Pvt. Elias Edmond's Co. 1st Va. State Regt. of Artillery			1/23/1802

Fauquier County, Tombstone Inscriptions Volume 2

Revolutionary War Soldiers Buried in Fauquier County Cemeteries

Name	Military Unit	Cemetery	Date of Birth	Date of Death
METCALF, John	Ens. Fauq. Mil.			

Revolutionary War Soldiers Buried in Fauquier County Cemeteries

Name	Military Unit	Cemetery	Date of Birth	Date of Death
METCALF, Wm.	Sgt. John Ball's Co. Fauq. Mil. (promoted to Ensign)			3/1802
MOFFETT, Henry	Pvt. Wm. Pickett's Co. Culp. Min. Bn. Sgt. 3rd Va. Regt. CL John Ashby's Co.			
MOFFETT, Jesse	Pvt. Benj. Harrison's Co. Fauq. Mil. Ens. Wm. Grigsby's Co. Col. Elias Edmond's Regt.			
MOFFETT, John	Maj. 2nd Bn. Fauq. Mil.			5/1810
MONROE, Alexander				1786
MONROE, George	Pvt. John T. Chunn's Co. Fauq. Mil.		1762	1839
MOREHEAD, Turner	Sgt. James Scott's Fauq. Indep. Co. Capt. Fauq. Mil.			
MORGAN, Benjamin	Pvt. Fauq. Mil.		1762	1814
MORGAN, Charles	Pvt. Wm. Blackwell's Co. 11th Va. Regt. Morgan's Rifles			11/1854
MORGAN, John	Sgt. Wm. Blackwell's Co. Morgan's Rifles Regt.			7/1821
MORGAN, Simon	Capt.		1755	1810
MORRISON, Edward	Fauquier Militia			after 1833
MURPHEY, John	Pvt. John Chilton's Co. 3rd Va. Regt. CL Pvt. 4th Regt. Light Dragoons Pvt. Wm. Triplett's Cav. Co.			1836
O'BANNON, John	Capt. Fauquier Militia Maj. Fauquier Militia		1735	1797
O'BANNON, William	Pvt. Fauquier Militia		1730?	1807
PATTIE, William			1763	after 1841
PATTON, Alexander	Pvt. John Ashby's Co. 3rd Va. Regt. CL Valentine Peyton's Co. 3rd Va. Regt. CL		1745	1820
PAYNE, William	Capt. Va. Militia	Payne (Clifton)	1755	1817
PAYNE, Winter	Capt.		1755	1837
PETERS, John	Pvt. Tilman Weaver's Co. Fauquier Militia 2nd Lt. Wm. Pope's Co. Fauquier Mil.		1762	1833
PEYTON, Henry	1st Lt. Fauquier Militia	Gordonsdale	1744	1812
PICKETT, Martin	Lt. Col. 1st Bn Fauquier Militia Col. 2nd Bn. Fauquier Militia		1740	1809
PICKETT, William	Capt. Culpeper Minute Men Lt. Col. 2nd Bn. Fauquier Militia Maj. Fauquier Militia		1742	1814
PICKETT, William Sanford	Capt. Fauquier Militia		1735	1798
POWELL, John	Pvt.			
PURCELL, George	Pvt.		1751	1841
RECTOR, Henry	Soldier			1799
RIDDLE, William	Soldier		1757	1833
ROBINSON, William			1758	1833
ROWLES, William	Pvt. Capt. Norrard's Co. Col. Josias Carvill Hall's 4th Md. Regt. CL.	Buried on his farm, now Moss Hollow Rd.	1759	1840
RUST, John	Lt. Turner Morehead's Co. Fauquier Militia			1797
SEATON, William	Ens. Francis Triplett's Co. Fauquier Militia			10/1782
SETTLE, Edward	Pvt. Wm. Triplett's Cav. Co. Fauquier Militia		1764	1839
SETTLE, William	Capt. Fauquier Militia			1781
SHUMATE, Daniel	Ensign Nicholas George's Co. Fauquier Militia 2nd Lt. Fauquier Militia		1749	1826
SMITH, James E.	Pvt. Fauquier Militia			
SMITH, John D.				6/1796
SMITH, Thomas	2nd Lt. Fauquier Militia		1747	1796

Revolutionary War Soldiers Buried in Fauquier County Cemeteries

Name	Military Unit	Cemetery	Date of Birth	Date of Death
SMITH, William	Pvt. Benj. Harrison's Co. Fauquier Militia Pvt. 1st Va. State Regt.			2/1798
TOMLIN, John	Pvt. Charles Porterfield's Co. Morgan's Rifle Regt. 11th Va. Regt. CL			before 11/1796
TRIPLETT, Francis	Adj. Fauquier Militia Capt. Fauquier Militia Maj. Fauquier Militia Col. Morgan's Va. State Regt.		1728	1794(w)
TULLOSS, Benjamin	Ens. Fauquier Militia			
TULLOSS, Joshua	Lt. Nicholas George's Co. Fauquier Militia Capt. Fauquier Militia			2/1818
TULLOSS, Rodham	Ens. Fauquier Militia	Tulloss		12/1815
TURNER, Hezekiah	Capt. 3rd Va. Regt. CL.	Turner (Delaplane)		
WEAVER, Tilman	Capt. Fauquier Militia	Germantown	1747/8	1809
WELCH, Sr. Sylvester	Pvt. Samuel Denny's Co. 1st Va. Regt. of Artillery	Marshall	1762	1832
WINN, Jr. Minor	1st Lt. Fauquier Militia	Winn (Halfway)(vanished)		1812

C

H

MITCHEM, 73
MITTIER, 111, 220
MIZELL, 224
MOAT, 226
MOATEN, 112
MOFFATT, 166
MOFFETT, 4, 86, 145, 150, 220, 242
MOLCHANOFF, 177
MONEYMAKER, 118
MONROE, 1, 17, 79, 242
MONTGOMERY, 42, 137, 226, 228
MOORE, 9, 22, 26, 38, 39, 41, 53, 69, 71, 85, 100, 116,
    126, 128, 145, 146, 172, 212, 220, 224, 228, 231
MORAN, 31, 162
MOREHEAD, 4, 90, 146, 157, 242
MORGAN, 150, 185, 242
MORRIS, 112, 118, 137, 153, 226, 231, 232
MORRISEY, 17
MORRISON, 71, 242
MORROW, 226
MORSON, 157
MORTON, 83, 84
MOSBY, 151, 220
MOSELEY, 193
MOSELY, 186
MOSS, 73, 91, 103, 143
MOUNTJOY, 72, 220
MOXLEY, 22, 78
MOYER, 125
MUDD, 185
MULLINEAU, 231
MULLINS, 38, 39, 193
MURKLE, 228
MURPHEY, 242
MURPHY, 228
MURRAY, 34, 88, 152
MURRY, 179
MUSE, 9, 77
MUSSELMAN, 171
MYERS, 32, 168, 177, 228
MYLES, 49, 152
MYRTLE, 177

N

NALLE, 89
NALLEY, 152
NALLS, 97, 109, 110, 126, 127, 220
NANCE, 231
NAPIOR, 112
NASH, 58, 176
NEAL, 55
NEALE, 20, 31, 33, 39, 175
NEER, 57, 58
NEESE, 36, 37
NEFF, 108, 119, 129, 130
NEITZEW, 197

NELMS, 232
NELSON, 42, 140, 142, 160, 170, 190, 200, 201, 211, 220
NESSELRODT, 198
NETHERLY, 232
NEVERDON, 51
NEVILLE, 43, 96
NEWBY, 178
NEWHOUSE, 153
NEWMAN, 31, 151, 198, 201, 202, 224
NEWSOM, 228
NEWTON, 119, 226
NEYHOUS, 192
NICHOLS, 36, 38, 96, 231
NICKENS, 140, 163, 164
NICKLAS, 127
NICOLSON, 70
NISBET, 231
NISSIBRODT, 172
NOBLE, 79
NOEH, 65, 66
NOLAND, 191
NORFLEET, 233
NORMAN, 232
NORRIS, 3
NORTH, 220
NORVELL, 232
NORWOOD, 228
NOURSE, 71, 153
NUICK, 147
NYE, 233

O

O'BANNON, 114, 154, 159, 191
O'MALLEY, 73
O'REAR, 214
O'ROARK, 29
OAKIE, 64
ODELL, 84
ODEMES, 226
ODER, 137
ODOMS, 226
OGDEN, 36, 113
OGLETREE, 226
OLIFF, 130
OLINGER, 3, 4, 21, 22, 24, 25, 28, 33, 38, 167, 169, 170,
    172, 173, 178, 220
OLIVER, 32, 45, 53, 77, 85, 107, 118, 150, 153, 154, 165,
    166, 192, 220
OREBAUGH, 32
ORICK, 199
ORNDOFF, 195, 196
ORR, 228
OTT, 129, 177
OTTERBACH, 65, 66
OVERBY, 2, 220
OVERTON, 20

OWENS, 41, 111, 113, 155, 164, 220, 228

P

PACE, 196
PACK, 220, 231
PACKARD, 69
PADGETT, 155, 198
PAGE, 43, 44, 63, 106, 153, 187
PALMER, 23, 33, 220, 231
PANNELL, 16
PARK, 170
PARKER, 51, 53, 146, 157, 229
PARKINSON, 220
PARKS, 168
PARSONS, 193
PATILLO, 226
PATRUM, 233
PATTERSON, 19, 51, 52
PATTIE, 134, 220, 221, 242
PATTON, 73, 242
PAYNE, 1, 18, 23, 25, 41, 54, 60, 85, 96, 110, 118, 123,
    126, 141, 144, 154, 155, 156, 157, 158, 160, 163, 168,
    169, 171, 172, 176, 184, 188, 208, 212, 221, 242
PAYTON, 200
PEACH, 94
PEAK, 93, 226
PEAKE, 159
PEARCE, 226
PEARL, 229
PEARSAL, 229
PEARSON, 41, 76, 92, 96, 97, 111, 113, 122, 124, 125,
    127, 128, 129, 130, 171, 180, 191, 221
PECK, 116
PEELING, 226
PEER, 107
PENCE, 191
PENDELETON, 161
PENDELTEN, 161
PENDELTON, 160
PENDLETON, 161
PENLAND, 226
PENN, 161, 162, 164
PENNINGTON, 151, 175
PEOPLES, 224
PERCELL, 160
PEREZ, 37
PERKINS, 233
PERROW, 173, 179
PERRY, 16, 19, 20, 33, 39, 163, 227, 233
PETERMAN, 224
PETERRSON, 52
PETERS, 9, 10, 39, 59, 148, 159, 194, 242
PETTIT, 204
PETTITT, 159
PETTY, 148
PEYTON, 68, 69, 242

PHELPS, 129
PHILLIPS, 62, 96, 119, 138, 147, 175, 192, 226
PHIPPS, 114
PICKETT, 181, 242
PICKRELL, 179
PIERCE, 102, 104, 110, 120, 204, 221, 229
PIGG, 233
PILCHER, 24, 52, 160, 221
PILING, 226
PILKERTON, 128
PILLION, 112
PINCKNEY, 231
PINKETT, 209
PIQUET, 22
PIRIE, 39
PITTMAN, 226, 227
PITTS, 85, 229
PLASKITT, 121, 122
PLATT, 64
PLOWDEN, 231
POAT, 231
POE, 147
POLLARD, 53, 183
POLLOCK, 221
POOL, 231
POOLE, 16, 232
POPKINS, 129
PORTER, 17, 189, 211
PORTIS, 173
POSEY, 73
POSTEN, 124
POSTON, 129, 204
POWELL, 113, 226, 242
POWERS, 112, 113, 194
PRATER, 229, 232
PRESTON, 233
PRICE, 20, 22, 34, 85, 147, 201, 226
PRIEST, 21, 44, 221
PRIMM, 164
PROCTOR, 41, 208, 209
PULLEN, 43, 118
PULLER, 40
PULLIAM, 168
PURCELL, 186, 242
PURIFOY, 224
PUTNAM, 165
PYNE, 122

Q

QUACKENBUSH, 176
QUINN, 141, 142

R

RABER, 198
RAGLAND, 229